The Economy of Renaissance Florence

The Economy of Renaissance Florence

RICHARD A. GOLDTHWAITE

The Johns Hopkins University Press

Baltimore

© 2009 The Johns Hopkins University Press
All rights reserved. Published 2009
Printed in the United States of America on acid-free paper

Johns Hopkins Paperback edition, 2011
2 4 6 8 9 7 5 3

The Johns Hopkins University Press
2715 North Charles Street
Baltimore, Maryland 21218-4363
www.press.jhu.edu

The Library of Congress has catalogued the hardcover edition of this book as follows:
Goldthwaite, Richard A.
The economy of Renaissance Florence / Richard A. Goldthwaite.
p. cm.
Includes bibliographical references and index.
ISBN-13: 978-0-8018-8982-0 (hardcover : alk. paper)
ISBN-10: 0-8018-8982-0 (hardcover : alk. paper)
1. Florence (Italy)—Economic conditions. 2. Renaissance—Italy—Florence.
I. Title.
HC308.F6G64 2008
330.945'51105—dc22   2007052602

A catalog record for this book is available from the British Library.

ISBN 13: 978-1-4214-0059-4
ISBN 10: 1-4214-0059-6

Title page illustration: This florin, in the collection of the Museo Nazionale del Bargello at Florence (Dep. no. 3206, on deposit from the Museo Archeologico), is one of the second series, minted sometime between 1252 and 1303. The obverse bears the lily, the symbol of the city, with the inscription + FLOR ENTIA; the reverse bears the image of Saint John the Baptist, the patron saint of the city, with the inscription S IOHA NNES • B •. The coin has a diameter of 20.8 mm (about two-thirds that of the illustration) and contains 3.48 grams of gold. Florins of the first series are very rare, none being in public collections; they differ in the halo of the saint, which is undecorated, whereas here the halo is beaded along the border. Florins in these early series do not bear the coat-of-arms of the men who were Masters of the Mint at the time the coin was issued and therefore cannot be precisely dated.

Special discounts are available for bulk purchases of this book. For more information, please contact Special Sales at 410-516-6936 or specialsales@press.jhu.edu.

The Johns Hopkins University Press uses environmentally friendly book materials, including recycled text paper that is composed of at least 30 percent post-consumer waste, whenever possible. All of our book papers are acid-free, and our jackets and covers are printed on paper with recycled content.

CONTENTS

TABLES

FIGURES

MAPS

An economic history of medieval and Renaissance Florence at once focuses on a single city and opens a perspective on all of Europe. At home, the city had a textile industry that was as strong as any in Europe yet completely dependent on the importation of raw materials from faraway places and on the exportation of its finished products to altogether different faraway places, while the success of its artisan sector was celebrated throughout Italy and Europe for all that the city's very name still conjures up for art lovers today. Abroad, its entrepreneurs built up the most extensive international network of commerce and banking in western Europe, in the process establishing their florin as a universal monetary standard. They also moved into the courts of some of Europe's most prominent rulers to serve as government financiers.

Much of the early history of capitalism is written around the activities of these men. They effected the transition from the individual merchant-adventurer to the sedentary firm, the evolution of the partnership form of business organization, and the refinement of many business practices, such as double-entry accounting, maritime insurance, and all those instruments designed to facilitate monetary transfers and the extension of credit, from the check to the bill of exchange and the certificate of deposit. To do all this, Florentines built the protective structure of a judicial system that guaranteed the sanctity of contracts for everyone, be they merchant-bankers or artisans, thereby allowing them all to dispense with the notary for business transactions. And along the way they challenged some of the strongest norms, both social and religious, of European culture at the time.

It is the objective of this book to tell the remarkable story of how all this happened in the course of the economic growth and development of one of the world's most famous cities.

It is surprising that no one has attempted to do this before. Surprising because so much of the fame of Florence is built on entrepreneurial activity. On the one hand, we have projected on the city's past the business icons of our own time, calling its bankers the Rothschilds of the Middle Ages and its florin the dollar of the Middle Ages; on the other hand, we have appropriated the name of the city's most prominent family, the Medici, as an icon encapsulating the symbiosis of enlightened patron and entrepreneur that is so central to our own culture. Surprising, too, because the documentation is so rich. Florence enjoys preeminence in the history of early capitalism, more so even than Venice and Genoa, not because capitalism found its earliest manifestations there (it certainly did not) or because it reached a higher stage of development there (this can be argued), but because, quite simply, the story is so much better documented for this city than for any other. The private account books surviving from the early thirteenth century to 1500 number about 2,500, more than exist for all the other Italian cities put together; and that number increases to close to 10,000 by the time we get to 1600, most of them business accounts of one kind or another. This enormous patrimony establishes a documentary preeminence of Florence in the history of early capitalism that could be extended to all of Europe and well beyond the chronological confines of this book. Moreover, these documents, in this city as nowhere else, testify to the extraordinarily wide diffusion of the practices and instruments of capitalism throughout the society, far beyond the counting houses of merchants, bankers, and industrialists.

Surprising, finally, because the historiographical tradition is so rich. This tradition goes back to the very origins of the discipline of economic history—to the German scholars who, beginning in the last quarter of the nineteenth century and culminating in Werner Sombart's 1902 book, began right off to explore the origins of capitalism, for some of them (including Max Weber) focused on Florence.[1] At the very end of the century Robert Davidsohn began his lifelong search in the archives for the mass of material, including anything he could find about the economy, that he eventually incorporated into his classic history of the city down through the time of Dante, published in the 1920s. Historians then went to work on the history of business in the following period—first Armando Sapori (who was

---

[1] Robert von Pöhlmann, *Die Wirtschaftspolitik der florentiner Renaissance und das Princip der Verkehrsfreiheit*, Preisschriften der Fürstlich Jablonowski'schen Gesellschaft, Historisch-Nationalökonomischen Sektion, 13 (Leipzig, 1878); Gustav Lastig, *Florentiner Handelsregister des Mittelalters* (Halle, 1879); Max Weber, *Zur Geschichte der Handelsgesellschaften in Mittelalter, nach südeuropäischen Quellen* (Stuttgart, 1889), esp. ch. 5; Richard Ehrenberg, *Das Zeitalter der Fugger: Geldkapital und Creditverkehr im 16. Jahrhundert* (Jena, 1896), with a chapter on the Florentines; Alfred Doren, *Entwicklung und Organisation der Florentiner Zünfte im 13. und 14. Jahrhundert* (Leipzig, 1897); idem, *Studien aus der Florentiner Wirtschaftsgeschichte*, 2 vols. (Stuttgart, 1901–8); Werner Sombart, *Der moderne Kapitalismus* (Leipzig, 1902); Heinrich Sieveking, "Die Handlungsbücher der Medici," in *Sitzungsberichte der Philosophisch-Historischen Klasse der Kaiserlichen Akademie der Wissenschaften* 151 (1905): fasc. 5, 1–65; Otto Meltzing, *Das Bankaus der Medici und seine Vorläufer* (Jena, 1906).

the first to explore the vast archive of accounting materials), then Florence Edler de Roover (who matured as a scholar in the ambiance of the Harvard School of Business) and Raymond de Roover (who started out as a businessman), and finally Federigo Melis (who started out as an accountant). We, the epigoni, have continued digging around in the documents, throwing light on this and that aspect of the economy and adding to the ever-growing accumulation of particular studies. At the moment, in fact, the field is prospering as never before, reinvigorated by a crop of some half-dozen younger economic historians dedicated to archival research. Yet, for all the considerable bravura of many of the scholars who constitute this venerable tradition, no one has yet looked up to see what it is all about.[2]

Several intellectual barriers block the view of the larger picture. One is chronological. We generally have focused on a narrow period, with the result that we rarely confront change or instead, and perhaps more significantly for economic history, explain its absence. Another barrier is geographic. Parochialism—what the Italians call *campanilismo*—is a malaise throughout most subdivisions within the discipline of Italian history, no less so for economic history than for any other kind. We all recognize the preeminence of Florence, Venice, Genoa, and Milan in the economic history of medieval and Renaissance Italy, but notwithstanding the very different economies of these cities, economic historians studying this or that activity in any one of these places rarely put their subject in perspective by looking abroad to see how things were done elsewhere, let alone do a broader comparative study. The failure to compare either over time (change) or across space points to a third barrier in the historiography: the dominance of the descriptive over the analytical mode of doing history. In this sense economics, a discipline of analysis, has had little impact on the study of the economic history of Florence. The result is an economic history without much sense of what an economy, as distinct from the particular economic activity being studied, is. Moreover, this intellectual myopia is compounded by disciplinary isolation, yet another barrier to a larger vision of what it is we are doing. Thus we study the businessmen of Florence forgetting that these men spent much of their time and energy deliberating on the innumerable councils that constituted their republican government

---

[2] For a guide to the bibliography of particular periods in the economic history of the city, see Richard A. Goldthwaite, *The Building of Renaissance Florence: An Economic and Social History* (Baltimore, 1980), ch. 1. Since then, the notable studies are, for the fifteenth century, Bruno Dini, "L'economia fiorentina dal 1450 al 1530," reprinted in *Saggi su una economia-mondo: Firenze e l'Italia fra Mediterraneo ed Europa (secc. XIII–XVI)* (Pisa, 1995), 187–214; and, for the later period, Paolo Malanima, *La decadenza di un'economia cittadina: L'industria di Firenze nei secoli XVI–XVIII* (Bologna, 1982), to which should be appended his later view on the subject, "L'economia toscana dalla peste nera alla fine del Seicento," in *Storia della Toscana*, vol. 1, *Dalle origini al Settecento*, ed. E. Fasano Guarini, G. Petralia, and P. Pezzino (Bari, 2004), 183–97. Also useful is Rita Mazzei, "Continuità e crisi nella Toscana di Ferdinando II (1621–1670)," *Archivio storico italiano* 145 (1987): 61–79.

and contending with others in the often vicious factionalism that so character-ized the political realities behind the façade of that government, or we study artisans ignoring their contribution to the extraordinary fame the city enjoys for the objects they made. Political history, social history, and art history have not figured into our story. And since we have thus not communicated with our col-leagues in these other branches of the discipline, who currently dominate the study of Florence, we can hardly blame them for having so little sense of how the economy bears on their subject. It will therefore be a long time before we get a truly integrated history of this remarkable city, so rich in political action and thought, so famous for its art and so successful in its economic enterprise.

In this book I make no pretense about having crossed any of these barriers. No one could write a history that goes from the beginning to 1600, however, without encountering them—that, in fact, has been the joy of engaging in the enterprise—and on those occasions I have attempted to raise some of the problems that will need to be examined in order to widen our vision beyond the current historio-graphical confines. Although this book is a survey of the entire period directed to orient the reader to the economic history of the city, unlike so many surveys it is not presented as a conclusive summing up of the current state of research with-out exposing the gaps or problems in the historiography. The holes in the story told here are in fact numerous and are duly noted, for I want to alert the reader to the limitations of our knowledge in the hope not only of stimulating new re-search but also of thinking differently about the subject so that someday a much more comprehensive and profound history than this one can be written.

And so much archival work remains to be done. Indeed, the most important collections of documents for the economic history of the city have hardly been explored. The catasto records, especially those for 1427, the most thorough eco-nomic survey of any European city before the nineteenth century, have been mined for this and that particular piece of information, but they have been studied com-prehensively only for their demographic content. In addition, an astounding number of volumes—almost five thousand from the years 1314 to 1600—survive recording the proceedings of cases involving debt claims brought before the court of the Mercanzia, but only now is someone, Luca Boschetto, finally undertaking a systematic study of this vast material, so essentially economic in its nature. And then there are all those account books. Many have been studied, but even more remain to be studied. The personal memoranda *(ricordi)* that appear at the end of many of these ledgers have been gone over time and time again by social his-torians, but too often the accounts themselves have been completely ignored.

No Italian city, in fact, has so much unexplored material of a specifically eco-nomic nature, and that makes the venture undertaken herein particularly precarious. But maybe debate—not polemics, which is as characteristic of the historiography of this city as it is of the spirit of the people who live there today—is what is needed to get things started.

The chronology of this book ranges from the beginning to 1600, but the concentration is on the fourteenth and fifteenth centuries. These are constraints imposed by the historiography. Not much can be said about the earlier growth of the Florentine economy. For Florence, the notarial record, which tells us so much about Lucca, Genoa, and other cities from as early as the eleventh century, does not begin much before 1300; and by this time Florentines, both entrepreneur and artisan, had abandoned the notary for almost all business transactions. After 1500 the problem is hardly the lack of documentation, given the overpowering immensity of the accounting record as one goes forward in the sixteenth century; it is, instead, the historians' lack of interest. Indeed, the paucity of studies of the economy in the sixteenth century is symptomatic of the historiographical situation indicated above. No economic historian could venture into this period of relatively rapid change without having to explain the change from what had gone before, or absence of it, for change itself is such a central theme in the economic history of all of Europe in that century. My venture into this relative unknown, however, only goes as far as 1600. I am well aware that in the early decades of the seventeenth century the economy is thought to have taken a turn for the worse and even undergone a serious crisis. In some respects this turn is explained by what went before; but if I had moved ahead to confront this problem, I would have found myself writing in a teleological mode to explain how it all came out in the end, which would have required a rather different frame of mind and much more research. It is to be expected, of course, that when the history of that crisis is written, we shall have a different perspective on the immediate past as described here. The present book recounts a story that is, therefore, open ended and, in the final analysis, designed to arouse curiosity and even incite criticism, not to present a finished picture.[3]

This book starts with a brief introduction to provide the reader with a general knowledge of the role of the Tuscan towns in the so-called commercial revolution of the eleventh to thirteenth centuries, which marked the first chapter in the

---

[3] For the sixteenth century and later we have only Malanima, *La decadenza*, which deals exclusively with the wool and silk industries. The paucity of subsequent studies is apparent in the recent comments of Jean Boutier, "Les formes et l'exercise du pouvoir: Rémarques sur l'historiographie récente de la Toscane à l'époque des Médicis (XVIe–XVIIIe siècles)," in *La Toscana in Età Moderna (secoli XVI–XVIII): Politica, istituzioni, società; Studi recenti e prospettive di ricerca*, ed. Mario Ascheri and Alessandra Contini (Florence, 2005), 14–16, the only pages in this historiographical survey dedicated to economic history.

growth and development of the European economy in the Middle Ages. It then places Florence in this context, surveying the development of its economy to about 1300, when the story told in the rest of the book begins. By 1300 Florence, with its strong textile industries, was one of the most industrialized cities in medieval Europe, and the city's economy grew on this foundation. This industrial activity, however, was completely dependent on the importation of raw materials and the exportation of finished cloth; and it was the city's merchants, not foreigners, who made this trade abroad possible. Part I, therefore, is dedicated to the history of the international commercial and banking network through which these merchants operated. Chapter 1 offers an overall view of their operations. It traces the changing geography of their business interests abroad and the general course of their success over the entire period of this book and describes the underpinning business structure of their enterprise. The final section of the chapter looks at Florence as the center of this international network. Chapters 2 and 3 break down the business activity of the network into two distinct kinds, commerce and banking, for purpose of analysis. Part II focuses on the local economy. Chapters 4, 5, and 6 survey the main sectors: the textile industries producing for foreign markets, workers in other activities oriented to the local market, and, finally, local banking and credit. Chapter 7 reaches out to wider contexts for all this market activity by examining the role of government in the economy, the ties between the urban and regional economies, and the function of the economy to distribute wealth throughout the society. The conclusion presents some ideas about the economic culture of Florentines and offers an assessment of the performance of the economy over the entire period. This last section might serve the reader as an introduction to the book, a general survey of the subject as I see it, before he or she plunges into the details.

A fundamental problem in surveying the economic activity of this city over such a long period is the changing value of the gold florin. Its price as stated in lire, the money of account used for most local transaction, rose steadily, and the value of the lira changed with respect to its purchase power in the local market. Moreover, several florins of account came into use during the period, each with its own price history. In view of the complexity of this situation, a study such as this one would do well to convert all values stated in florins into lire, since the lira is the best measure of value over the long run for the cost of goods and services—the cost of living—in the local market. The reader would thereby gain a more immediate sense of comparison over time. To convert florins into lire, however, would be to go so much against the force of tradition within the discipline as to be a laughing matter, and I have not had the courage to do this. My ambitions for this book, although directed to arousing debate and stimulating further research, are not so high. Yet we historians would do well to learn to "think" in lire, as did

Florentines, because the distortions that arise from the blind attachment to the florin are considerable, since the florin can mean several moneys, all of which were subject to either deflation or inflation with respect to value in the local market, even in the short run. In any event, I can only call the reader's attention to the problems of comparing values in florins over a long period of time. In the attempt to offer some assistance, on occasion in the text I establish one criterion for comparison by translating monetary values into what they meant in terms of the daily wage of an unskilled laborer, presumably a minimum wage. I also use 1427 as a base year for comparisons, since the catasto documents of that year—justifiably famous for their extraordinary detail—are so familiar to historians of this city. The appendix offers some explanation of the monetary system, and table A.1 provides a basis for comparing values quoted in florins that are encountered in the text. In accordance with the standard system for organizing monetary units throughout medieval Europe, both the florin and the lira were divided into 20 soldi, each of which, in turn, was divided into 12 denari; these are moneys of account, not coins. In the text they are abbreviated as, respectively, *fl.*, *£*, *s.*, and *d.*; soldi and denari of the lira are identified as *di piccioli*.

The book does not include a comprehensive bibliography on the subject, nor will one find references to all the scholarship on particular subjects in the notes. Instead, I use the notes to cite the most recent and most relevant literature on the subject at hand, and these references can be used as guides into the further bibliography. With respect to the many unstudied subjects referred to in the text, however, references to these have been collected as "categories of open problems" under the entry "historiography" in the index, the intention being to point the way for research that will extend our knowledge of the economic history of Florence beyond the parameters of this book. Terms for which there is no exact or concise translation in English have been kept in the original Italian. On their first appearance in the text they are defined, and entries for them in the index direct the reader to those places. In the Florentine identification of a firm, the phrase *e compagni* is rendered as "& Partners," the symbol indicating the formality of the organization and the literal translation "partners" being preferred to the cognate "company" to avoid the implication in our use today of this latter term for a different kind of business organization. All passages in Italian quoted in the text have been translated, with the original given in a note only if it does not appear in a cited published source. For reference to documents cited from the Florentine State Archives I use the standard abbreviation ASF.

My thanks to Graziella Coi for the graphics in this book and to Joanne Allen for her careful editing of the text. I am especially grateful to Henry Tom, who for many years now has made it a pleasure to work with the press, and to those colleagues who have commented, helpfully and critically, on parts or all of the text—Luca Boschetto, Alison Brown, Judith Brown, Shannon Brown, Humfrey Butters, Gian Mario Cao, Enrico Faini, Franco Franceschi, Francesco Guidi Bruscoli, F. W. Kent, Marco Spallanzani and Sergio Tognetti.

The Economy of Renaissance Florence

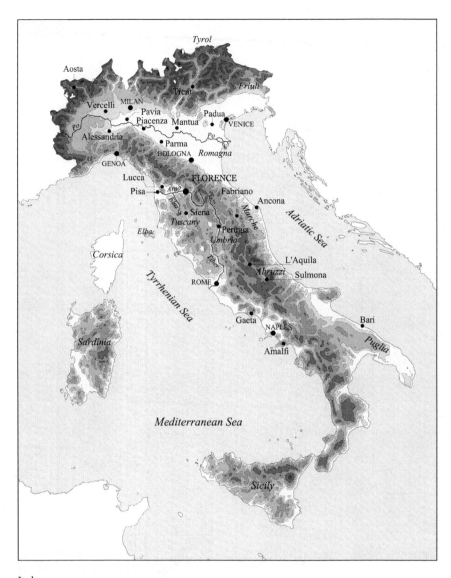

Italy

Introduction

The Commercial Revolution

Economic Growth and Development in Italy to 1300: *Trade with the Levant, Links to the North.*
The Tuscan Towns.
Florence: *Rise to Predominance, The Dynamics of Growth.*

Economic Growth and Development in Italy to 1300
Trade with the Levant

The intensification and expansion of Italian trading activity throughout the Mediterranean and western Europe has given rise to the rubric "commercial revolution" to cover the period of early trade-led growth of the European economy, from the tenth to the fourteenth century.[1] For some, however, this expansion of trade did not really reach a revolutionary stage but was simply the acceleration of a process already under way, a consequence partly of the emergence of the new barbarian kingdoms, which generated demand for luxury goods, and partly of the slow improvement of agricultural technology, which, by increasing food surpluses, gave rise to local markets and their expansion into regional markets. As early as the eighth and ninth centuries Italian merchants ventured out to cross the boundaries separating three major areas: the new Carolingian Empire, in economically backward Europe; the Byzantine heir of the old Roman Empire, extending from southern Italy to Constantinople; and the Arab world, rapidly

---

[1] The use of this term in this general sense was popularized by Robert S. Lopez in *The Commercial Revolution of the Middle Ages, 950–1350* (Englewood Cliffs, NJ, 1971). For an earlier and much more precise use of the term by Raymond de Roover, see chapter 1. The best detailed description of the role of Italy in this expansion down to the fourteenth century is Marco Tangheroni, *Commercio e navigazione nel Medioevo* (Bari, 1996), which has an extensive and recent bibliography. For the activity of Italians throughout the western Mediterranean, see the various studies of David Abulafia, now collected in *Italy, Sicily and the Mediterranean, 1100–1400* (London, 1987), *Commerce and Conquest in the Mediterranean, 1100–1500* (Aldershot, 1993), and *Mediterranean Encounters: Economic, Religious, Political, 1100–1550* (Aldershot, 2000).

expanding along the southern and eastern Mediterranean. This incipient trading activity, barely perceptible today in extant documents and much debated in the historiography, was uncertain, cautious, and limited, but its general direction is clear enough. It was not to be suppressed by the violence accompanying the disintegration of the Carolingian Empire within western Europe and the raids from without by Vikings, Saracens, and Magyars from the ninth into the eleventh century. Merchants from the semiautonomous cities in the Byzantine south were in the vanguard: from Bari they ventured into the eastern empire and to Syria and Egypt, while from Amalfi they ranged throughout the western Mediterranean. From their newly founded city, dating to the settlement by fugitives from the mainland in the late sixth century, Venetians ventured down the Adriatic to trade in the eastern Mediterranean and soon gained commercial privileges in the Byzantine Empire that made Venice a major port in the eastern Mediterranean and a center for trade on the mainland extending into the Po valley and northward across the Alps. The emergence of Venice represented a shift in long-distance trade away from the traditional Roman routes and a reorientation of commerce toward northern Europe. Merchants from the south, from Gaeta and Naples to Otranto, ventured into the region, attracted to the fairs that sprung up at Pavia and other towns in the Po valley.

On the western coast, Genoa and Pisa grew as major ports serving the growing hinterland towns. From the tenth century on, these cities reacted aggressively to raids by Saracen pirates, and they went on to pursue commercial interests throughout the western Mediterranean. Merchants from both cities moved along the coast of southern France to Moorish Spain and out to the Balearics and North Africa, and they eventually entered into the eastern Mediterranean, where they competed for markets with the Venetians. Pisans and Genoese sought grain and other raw materials in Sardinia, and they, along with merchants from other Italian cities, settled in Messina, where they succeeded in pushing out the Jewish and Islamic merchants established there. Both islands thus came into the Italian commercial orbit as places of transit for wider Mediterranean trade. Merchants ventured out from other port cities too, especially Marseilles and Barcelona in the northern Mediterranean, Amalfi in southern Italy, and ports along the eastern coast of southern Italy. By 1100 trade had transcontinental and trans-Mediterranean dimensions, clearly signaling the significant presence of new sectors within the predominantly agricultural economy of Europe. The three great maritime powers of Genoa, Pisa, and Venice, all of which now had merchants in the Levant, from Constantinople to Egypt, had come to enjoy the leading role in this commercial revolution.

In contrast to what was taking place in northern Europe, the most striking characteristic of the recovery in Italy—perhaps, indeed, a necessary precondition for it—was the urban nature of its growth. The Roman towns had never altogether disappeared, and once a more favorable political environment emerged, they attracted immigrants from the countryside in enormous numbers, especially in the north, where rising agricultural productivity lay behind both the emigration to the city of surplus rural population and the wherewithal to support this growing urban population. During the twelfth and thirteenth centuries towns enlarged their walls more than once to accommodate an expansion that increased the area they enclosed by a factor of two or three, in some instances even more. The walls of Florence begun at the end of the thirteenth century, in expectation of a continuing high rate of growth, enclosed an area almost fifteen times the area enclosed two centuries earlier. This rapid urbanization gave rise to steadily increasing industrial production and intensive regional trade, the essential components of the commercial revolution.

The major dynamic driving this enterprise arose out of the imbalance in the relative development of two vast economic areas, Europe and the Near East. On the one hand, there was the slowly evolving rural economy of Europe, with its rich resources in raw materials; on the other, the developed imperial economy of Byzantium and the rapidly expanding economy of the Muslim world, along the southern and eastern shores of the Mediterranean. With the political stabilization of Europe, demand arose for the luxury products to be found in the markets of Byzantine and Muslim cities. Some of these products, such as silks, paper, metalwork, ceramics, and rugs, were manufactured in the many cities of the region, while natural products such as spices, perfumes, incense, medicines, sugar, and precious and semiprecious stones were imported through the vast commercial network the Arabs built up from sub-Saharan Africa to the Far East. Both the Byzantine and Muslim economies had large urban markets and administrative and juridical systems in place, assuring political stability for the conduct of trade. Moreover, they were well integrated in a trading system, and the Italians had only to plug into it. Italy was the fulcrum between the two economic areas, and Italian merchants had the geographical advantage of ready access to the sea that separated them. In exchange for what they bought in the Levant, western merchants had to sell what they could obtain from the relatively backward economy of Europe, mostly raw materials such as furs, timber, metals, and slaves but also agricultural products and, increasingly, some manufactured goods made from these raw materials, such as arms and, especially, wool cloth. The quantity of these bulky, low-priced goods needed to balance the luxury imports from the East, however, was immense, and the considerable labor and organizational input required to produce them and get them to distant markets was a major stimulus to economic growth and development in all the major sectors, from agriculture in Italy to the textile industry in the Low Countries, from maritime shipping and commerce in Venice, Genoa, and Pisa to international banking in Lucca, Siena, and Florence. The initiatives for this trade came from the undeveloped West, not from the Near East; thus, during the later Middle Ages, from the twelfth to the fifteenth century, the European economy expanded, while the economies in the Levant stagnated and declined.

Essential to this enterprise was the growth of an industrial sector in Europe, which is often overlooked in discussions of the commercial revolution. Initially, Europeans had an unfavorable balance of payments, if we can talk about the phenomenon in modern monetary terms; and initially they made up the difference through piracy and plundering but above all through the export of silver and gold. Silver could be obtained in significant quantities from mining, but gold very much less so, although by the twelfth century trade to North Africa brought gold into the area from south of the Sahara. With the growth and development of the European economy, the Italians steadily improved their situation.[2] They began to produce for themselves the manufactured goods they had been importing, and by the fifteenth century they had gone beyond import substitution (if one can lift that term out of the contemporary context in which it has been formulated, leaving behind many of its current political implications) and were exporting these very goods to the Muslim world. The growth of the silk industry in Italy, which was of considerable importance because of the luxury quality of the finished product, encapsulates this development. The first stage consisted in the transfer of technology and imitation of designs from Byzantium and the Muslim world. Lucca was producing silk fabrics by the twelfth century, and in the following century production also got under way in Sicily and Venice. Subsequently the industry became a major activity in other Italian cities, including Florence. Initially these Italian producers imported raw silk from the Levant, where, in fact, sericulture expanded as a result of growing Italian demand for the raw material. The diffusion of sericulture in Italy and Spain marked a second stage in the history of this industry—the forging of backward linkages to the supply of raw materials in Italy itself. By the sixteenth century most of the raw silk for the industry came from the western Mediterranean. Meanwhile, in what we might call a third

---

[2] On the thorny question of the balance of payments, see Michel Balard, "Les relations économiques entre l'Occident et le monde islamique à la fin du Moyen Âge: Quelques remarques," in *Europe's Economic Relations with the Islamic World, 13th–18th Centuries*, ed. Simonetta Cavaciocchi (Florence, 2007), 193–218, which reviews the general situation by reference to the latest literature.

stage of this development, under way by the end of the fourteenth century, Italians began to export their silks, designed according to their own taste, to Muslim markets in the Levant. The tables had turned completely.

The same general pattern—import substitution and even reversal of market positions—characterizes the history of many other industries that developed in Italy in the Middle Ages. For example, originally Italians imported high-quality paper from the Levant. In the thirteenth century production got under way at Fabriano, in the Marche, whence the industry spread to other places in Italy and Europe, and by the later Middle Ages paper was being exported to the Levant, virtually destroying the industry there. Italians also began to make tin-glazed ceramics for their own consumption, with the eventual result that demand for imports from the Levant dried up completely, and by the end of the Middle Ages some of these Italian products showed up in Levantine markets. Likewise, by the fifteenth century soap, another early import, was being exported to the Levant from Venice and Puglia. Venetians improved the technology of glassmaking and succeeded in manufacturing the superior products for which the industry there is famed, much better in quality than anything produced in the Levant. After the conquest of Cyprus in 1191 Europeans introduced sugar production there; in the next century production got under way in Sicily, and subsequently imports from the Levant steadily declined. The West built up a cotton industry based on importation of the raw material from the Levant, and while the output of cotton in the Muslim world expanded to meet this growing demand, some of this European cloth found markets back in the Levant, where the raw materials were coming from. With respect to other natural products originally imported from the Levant, the Italians eventually found new sources closer at hand in the western Mediterranean, thanks to the growth and development of their commercial system. Skins, for example, had been a major import, but by the second half of the fourteenth century they were coming from North Africa, Spain, and northern Europe. Alum, a necessary fixative for dyeing cloth, was an important import for the European cloth industries, and the Genoese, who gained control of the output of the major mines at Phocaea, on the western coast of Anatolia, were able to establish a virtual monopoly over its distribution in the West. The conquest of the centers of production by the Ottomans in the later fifteenth century, however, sent Italians scurrying to find new sources in Italy itself, and their discovery of a significant supply at Tolfa, near Rome, in 1460 shifted the center of production to Italy. All these products—silk, paper, ceramics, soap, glass, sugar, skins, alum—which had been the staples of the Italian import trade from the Levant at the beginning of the commercial revolution, by the fifteenth century were being produced by the Italians themselves or imported from elsewhere. The Levant remained a source for some natural products, such as spices, medicines, dye-stuffs, and ash, but about the only manufactured items among Italian imports were rugs, a typical product of underdeveloped and command economies, and camlets, made from a raw material native to the region.

Commercial activity put the Italians at the forefront in the growth and development of the European economy, especially in the evolution of what has come to be called the transaction sector. The commercial revolution was not just a matter of merchants venturing out to find and develop what markets they could; it was a matter of doing this in a way that continually strengthened their position by reducing risks and improving efficiency. If the revolution began with merchant adventurers, it culminated in the business organization that allowed the merchant to stay at home and manage his affairs from an office. In their effort to reduce the costs of transactions in international commerce, merchants improved the efficiency of the exchange of goods and services, from the enforcement of contracts and defense of property rights to the refinement of information systems, monetary exchange, shipping, insurance, and marketing. Moreover, their entrepreneurial adventures generated a distinct subculture—call it bourgeois or what you will—within European feudal society, at least within some of the more important cities where they resided. Their involvement in communal government slowly conditioned them to a moral sense of citizenship, and operating in markets with international horizons, they developed an economic sense of investment as the calculated employment of money for the purpose of making a profit. Here, in short, was the nascent spirit of European capitalism. Florence was one of the places where this new economy took shape, and it is the place where the phenomenon is best documented.

Links to the North

The story of the so-called commercial revolution hardly centers on Italy alone. Italy was a pole in the trade between West and East, but Italian merchants were also the intermediaries in the growing trade between Europe as a whole and the Byzantine and Muslim East. Much of the demand for Eastern goods they sought to satisfy arose in northern Europe, and many of the goods needed to balance their trade with the Levant came from the area. Northern Europe, however, was not a passive area waiting to be exploited by Italian merchants. Once the political situation stabilized with the emergence of feudal states out of the dissolution of the Carolingian Empire, local and regional markets developed independently of what was happening in the Mediterranean, although one stimulus for the growth of this traffic in the north came with the links that were forged to Italian merchants. The famed Champagne fairs had their origin in local agricultural trade probably as early as the tenth century, and by the later twelfth century the area had become a central place for the exchange of other products, especially cloth produced by the growing wool industry in the Low Countries and luxury goods from the eastern Mediterranean. These fairs, held six times a year and in four different places in this region of northeastern France, thus became a major structural link between the north and Italy. They represented an important stage in the growth of trade in northern Europe: the convergence of regional trading systems and hence their integration into a wider, international system extending into northern France, the Low Countries, the Rhineland, and the North Sea system of the Hanseatic towns. Originally merchants from this area ventured further afield to sell their products in northern Italian towns. However, Italian merchants—from Asti, Chieri, Alba, Milan, Piacenza, Parma, and Bologna in the north and from Pisa, Lucca, Siena, Pistoia, San Gimignano, and Florence in Tuscany—also showed up at the fairs, and by the mid-thirteenth century they controlled the bulk of this trade to the Mediterranean.

Toward the end of the thirteenth century the northern pole in this trading system shifted from Champagne northwestward to the Flemish towns. The shift is usually explained as a result of various developments, including military disturbances, harmful local tax policies, the tendency of merchants to travel less and to organize their trade as a sedentary operation, and the opening of the maritime route from the Mediterranean to the Atlantic ports of Flanders and England. More fundamental to this shift, however, were the exigencies of commercial growth in and of itself. First, the intensity and volume of trade eventually outpaced the capabilities of the periodic, scattered fairs of rural Champagne; and second, trade could be better managed in the Low Countries, the center of production of the main item of trade, wool cloth. Moreover, by this time Flanders and Brabant had become the most densely urbanized area in Europe and hence offered much stronger markets than did rural Champagne. From these towns overland routes stretched eastward to central Germany, down the Rhine to Basel, and over the Saint Gotthard pass to Italy, a route that took in a larger urban area and was easier to travel than the older one from the fairs down the Saône and through the Saint Bernard pass. Another route went southward to Paris, then into a major regional market extending on to Avignon and the Mediterranean. Furthermore, the opening of the route by canal and the Zwin River from Bruges to the sea attracted maritime trade with England, a major source for wool, and with the Hanseatic cities in the North Sea. The Low Countries, in short, had their own internal dynamics of growth, having undergone something like a commercial, even industrial, revolution parallel to that in the Mediterranean.

Working within this extensive northern European commercial system, Italians set up sedentary operations in various cities over an area that extended from Flanders and Brabant into Picardy, Normandy, and the Île de France. Their primary interest was the export of wool cloth produced in the region, and to balance this trade they moved into the business of importing raw wool from England. Bruges was the largest of the international emporia in northwestern Europe, while Paris, the capital of the region's most powerful monarch, was the only city north of the Alps that already by 1200 was as large as the great Italian cities, if not much larger. The position of the Italians was further strengthened after the Genoese first sailed beyond the Mediterranean in 1277, leading the way to regular voyages by Venetian and Catalan as well as Genoese ships from the mid-fourteenth century on. The Italians thus dominated the trade southward, both overland and by sea, but they did not push their trade network eastward beyond the region overland into Germany or by sea into the Baltic. The staples in this trade were wool cloth headed for markets in Italy and the Near East and, in the other direction, supplies for the local cloth industry, namely, alum, woad, and other dyes, as well as spices and the traditional luxury products from the Near East and increasingly from Italy, especially with the growth of the silk industry in the fifteenth century. All kinds of other items were traded, of course, wherever profits were to be made, but the total volume and value were lower. These ranged from cheaper agricultural products such as wine and dried fruits from the Mediterranean area to luxurious tapestries made in Flanders and Brabant.

Three other developments in the relations between northern Europe and Italy also contributed to the growth and development of the Italian economy from the twelfth to the sixteenth century: the Crusades, the assertion of papal authority over the European church, and the military and political adventures of northern European rulers in Italy. All brought wealth into Italy.

The Crusades by their very nature impinged directly on the business interests of Italian merchants in the Levant, but they also opened up opportunities for merchants to offer services that led them into government finance and banking. When the First Crusade was called in 1095, Genoa, Pisa, and Venice launched major naval forces in support of the Europeans. They took advantage of military campaigns in the Levant to strengthen their commercial position in the region, and in fact the evolving political situation in the area found them pitted more aggressively against one another in pursuing their separate interests. Moreover, with their extensive trade networks, Italians were in a position to advance funds to crusading nobles and to transfer credits to them in the East. Perhaps the first

Italian merchants to visit England went not for commercial reasons but to recoup credits put up in the form of guarantees for advances they had made to English knights and clerics in need of funds in Italy and the Holy Land during the first crusades. Moreover, the creation of the crusader states in the Levant, which existed, with varying territorial adjustments and gradual erosion, until the seizure of Acre by the Mamelukes in 1291, expanded the opportunities of the maritime enterprise of the Genoese, the Pisans, and the Venetians. The existence of these states made it easier for these merchants to move into the preexisting local trade networks linking Constantinople and Egypt, which they eventually came to dominate. Investment by the conquerors in their newly established states, especially in the agricultural sector, also stimulated commercial activity in the region.[3]

A second development creating an enormous investment potential for Italians back in Europe was the assertion of papal authority over the European church. The pope thereby strengthened his hand in the extraction of revenues, both ecclesiastical and spiritual, from local bishops and abbots, but at the beginning he needed the Italians—especially the Sienese, whose home base was near Rome—to effect the international transfer of funds for him. Moreover, ecclesiastics everywhere had recourse to merchants, and especially Italians, to get advances so they could pay their assessments. In exchange for this extension of credit, they granted merchants local tax-collecting and commercial privileges. Thus merchants entered into another service sector that eventually took them, above all the Florentines, as we shall see, to the highest level of international finance and banking following the growth of the papal bureaucracy at Avignon in the fourteenth century, during the so-called Babylonian Captivity, and then at Rome in the later fifteenth century, when the popes were carving out their own territorial state.

A third dynamic in the history of northern Europe that had important implications for the Italian economy arose from the political ambitions of feudal rulers directed toward Italy. Their invasions and conquests are central themes in the history of medieval Italy, the major players being the Germans from Otto I, crowned emperor in 972, to Frederick II (1211–50), who sought to establish their new "Holy" empire on a Roman foundation; Charles of Anjou, who conquered the Kingdom of Naples in 1268; the kings of Aragon, who took over Sicily in 1282 and went on to wrest the mainland kingdom from the Angevins in 1435; Charles VIII of France, whose invasion in 1494 set off the competition among the French,

---

[3] David Jacoby, "The Economic Function of the Crusader States of the Levant: A New Approach," in Cavaciocchi, *Europe's Economic Relations with the Islamic World*, 159–91.

Spanish, and Hapsburg rulers for a foothold in Italy; and the emperor Charles V, whose successful domination of Lombardy and southern Italy brought this long saga to an end. The resources these rulers poured into these efforts brought a certain amount of wealth into Italy. The Hohenstaufen emperors resided in Italy, living partly off income from their German homeland. Alfonso of Aragon made Naples the capital of his western Mediterranean empire, bringing with him the resources of the Catalan commercial and maritime system. And Charles V and his Spanish successor, Philip II, spent some of their vast wealth from the New World to secure their Italian possessions and to build up a base for military operations against the expansion of the Turks in the Mediterranean and against threats to their empire and the church in northern Europe. This Spanish presence in Italy, however exploitative it may have been in fiscal terms in those areas Spain controlled directly, had some positive effects on the Italian economy in general, for it froze the rest of Italy into a political stability it had never known. As a result the independent states could drastically reduce expenditures for defense, thereby easing the tax burden on their subjects and leaving them with more disposable income for investment and consumption. In addition, Italian merchant-bankers, especially the Genoese, found extraordinary business opportunities open to them in Spain, where they could tap the enormous treasure that was flowing in from the New World.

These ecclesiastical, political, and military developments brought wealth into Italy in the form of both direct transfers and new business opportunities, supplementing the wealth generated in Italy during this period of economic expansion and that coming in from abroad in the form of business profits.

The Tuscan Towns

Because of the political division of Italy into a multiplicity of states and the existence of a prominent class of merchants and bankers, wealth was widely distributed, both geographically and socially. And it was continually redistributed as a result of both the political instability inherent in the Italian state system before Spain came to dominate the political scene in the sixteenth century and the social fluidity characteristic of a business class. This process of redistribution, inherent in the economic, political, and social lives of Italians, was one of the ongoing dynamics that drove the Italian economy.

Economic growth proceeded at very different paces throughout the peninsula. The initial stimulus came from the maritime trade of port towns. These were to be found all along Italy's exceptionally long coastline, but it was the hinterland that determined which ones would develop into major commercial and maritime

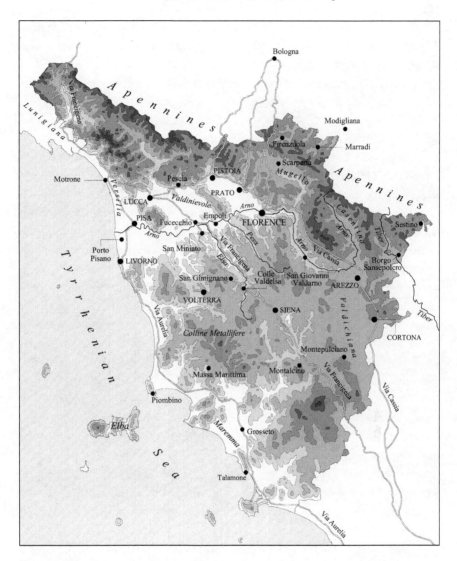

Tuscany

centers. Tuscany was one of the four general hinterland areas that emerged as distinct economic identities in response to the opening up of overseas trade. The ports in the south of Italy, from Amalfi to Bari, were among the first to take commercial initiatives, having a geographical advantage and a political base in the remnants of the Byzantine Empire in the West, but the hinterland they served, eventually incorporated into the Kingdom of Naples, saw the least economic development, which was largely limited to the agricultural sector. As a hinterland area it was defined by its political unity, not by geographical cohesion around river systems or inland transportation routes. The area had no major urban markets in the interior and little potential for forging trade links to the north. A second economic area was that in central Italy opening onto the small ports on the Adriatic. It took in the Marche, the Abruzzi, and Umbria and reached into the Tiber valley, whence there were links to the major capital cities of Rome and Naples to the southwest and, through the Valdichiana, to Tuscany, with its ports on the Tyrrhenian Sea. The many small cities in this hinterland, including Perugia, L'Aquila, and Ascoli, developed as market centers in response to the commercial possibilities in the Adriatic and the eastern Mediterranean. The third of these hinterland areas, and by far the most important, was the vast Po valley, extending triangularly southwestward from Venice to Bologna, northwestward along the Apennines to Milan and the Piedmont, and back eastward along the Alps. The economy of this area had a solid foundation in its rich agricultural resources and in the markets of its many towns of Roman foundation, some of which had access to resources that eventually gave rise to local industries—rope at Bologna, wool cloth at Verona, metalwork at Milan. Moreover, the topography of the area permitted easy overland, fluvial, and canal transportation and communication throughout. Finally, however formidable the Apennines, to the southwest, and especially the Alps, to the north, were as barriers to travel, they were not insurmountable, and the region had access across them to the rest of Italy and to both France and Germany in northern Europe. When Venice and Genoa, on opposite sides of the peninsula, opened the gates to international trade, they had behind them a hinterland unlike that of any other port in the western Mediterranean. Venice, moreover, given its location in lagoons and the lack of other ports in the vicinity, grew without political threats from the mainland and without serious competition from other nearby ports, both of which are continuing themes in the history of Genoa and Pisa on the other side of the peninsula.

Tuscany, opening to the west on the Tyrrhenian Sea, was the fourth hinterland area. The Tuscan towns were at the forefront in the expansion of Italian trade abroad. The port of Pisa led the way, becoming one of the three great Italian maritime powers, and merchants from the inland towns followed behind, venturing above all to northern Europe. Moreover, two of these towns, Lucca and Siena, soon became dominant among Italian towns in other sectors. Lucca became a great industrial center as early as the twelfth century, being the first in Europe to manufacture silk cloth for international luxury markets. The merchants of Siena, who led in exploiting the possibilities of financial service to the papacy nearby, became Europe's first great international bankers. Florence emerged a latecomer among the towns of the region, but by the end of the thirteenth century it had surpassed the others to become an international capital in all three sectors—commerce, banking, and industry—and one of the four or five largest cities in all of Europe.[4]

Tuscany is largely defined by the Apennines on the north and east and the Tyrrhenian Sea on the west. Within these natural borders the landscape is dominated by hills, but a basic river system further defines much of the northern part of the region as a geographical entity oriented to the sea at a single point. The Arno was navigable eastward from the sea all the way to within a few miles of Florence, and it continued on, following the mountain range southeastward to facilitate relatively easy access to central Italy. The valley of its main tributary, the Elsa, left it not far from its mouth to penetrate the hills southward almost as far as Siena, whence a route proceeded on to Rome. Almost all of the major towns of the region were located along the valleys of these two rivers, which gave them access to the sea at Pisa.

With the growth of the Roman Empire, this region, lying between the capital and northern Europe, increased in importance, but the full economic advantage of its position came only after the demise of the empire. The principal Roman road to northern Italy, the Via Flaminia, crossed Umbria and came out on the Adriatic coast at Fano, bypassing Tuscany altogether, while the two roads that led out of ancient Rome northward to Tuscany skirted much of the region. The Via Aurelia followed the coast, and the Via Cassia passed through the Valdichiana and the Valdarno to join the Via Aurelia in Versilia. Lying in potentially unhealthy lowland areas that required heavy maintenance, both of these roads fell into disuse for long-distance travel after the disappearance of the imperial government. Travel, such as it was, took to highland routes along valley walls, and the principal road linking Rome and northern Europe that eventually most people took was the Via Francigena. It went north to Siena, entered the Valdelsa, crossed the Arno valley, going through Fucecchio to Lucca, proceeded along the coast through Versilia at Pietrasanta and Sarzana and on to Aulla, crossed the Apennines at the Cisa pass and entered the Po valley. From there it went on to Piacenza, Pavia, Vercelli, and Aosta and over the Alps through the Great Saint

---

[4] The best general introductions, with recent bibliography, to the early history of these Tuscan towns are the essays of Giovanni Cherubini collected in *Città comunali di Toscana* (Bologna, 2003) and those of Giuliano Pinto collected in *Toscana medievale: Paesaggi e realtà sociali* (Florence, 1993) and in *Città e spazi economici nell'Italia comunale* (Bologna, 1996). For Pisa, see Marco Tangheroni, *Medioevo tirrenico: Sardegna, Toscana e Pisa* (Pisa, 1992); and idem, *Politica, commercio, agricoltura a Pisa nel Trecento* (Pisa, 1973). There are also some excellent essays in *Pisa e il Mediterraneo: Uomini, merci, idee dagli Etruschi ai Medici*, ed. Marco Tangheroni, exhibition catalog (Milan, 2003). A comprehensive view of Lucca emerges from the various essays of Thomas Blomquist, now collected in *Merchant Families: Banking and Money in Medieval Lucca* (Aldershot, 2005), which can be supplemented with the much more narrowly focused study of Ignazio Del Punta, *Mercanti e banchieri lucchesi nel Duecento* (Pisa, 2004).

Bernard pass. Unlike the Roman roads, the Via Francigena passed through the very center of Tuscany, where there were many small towns of Etruscan origin. Travel along this route increased with the movement of pilgrims, crusaders, and merchants beginning in the eleventh century, much to the profit of towns along it. It is no coincidence that the first Italian merchants from inland towns who went north came from places along the way—Chieri, Asti, Piacenza, and, in Tuscany, Lucca, San Gimignano, and Siena. The Via Francigena thus constituted one of the overland infrastructures from which the commercial revolution took off, complementing the maritime systems that the port cities began to build in the eleventh century.

Pisa was one of these port cities, along with Venice and Genoa. Its hinterland was smaller than the other three, and its topography rendered its agricultural base insufficient to support the extraordinary population growth the area underwent down to the mid-fourteenth century. Yet Tuscany is a region endowed with a great variety of natural resources, more perhaps than any other region of comparable size in Italy, if not, indeed, in Europe. The quantity of many of these resources is not significant by modern standards, but in early medieval Europe the particularly strong concentration of so many resources in the region gave Tuscans considerable potential for growth.

The wool industry provided one of the dynamics of that growth. The maremme around Pisa and Grosseto, even before the extensive reclamation of these unhealthy marshes, offered the possibility of the transhumant herding of flocks from upland zones for pasturage along the Apennines. The region was also suitable for the cultivation of some of the principal plants from which vegetable dyestuffs were derived—saffron around San Gimignano, woad around Borgo Sansepolcro, saffron, woad, and madder around Arezzo. Production of these dyes was sufficiently strong to be directed to international markets, providing a major economic activity for these towns. Alum, needed both as a cleanser and as a fixative for dyeing, was found at Piombino, not far away to the south, in at least sufficient quantity to supply the needs of local industries before the Genoese began importing this product toward the end of the thirteenth century from the mines over which they had a monopoly at Phocaea, on the coast of Asia Minor. With these natural resources at hand, it is hardly surprising that a cloth industry grew up in most of the major towns of Tuscany and in some of the minor ones. Although the quality of cloth was mediocre at best, by the thirteenth century the production level in some of these places was sufficiently high to give rise to an export trade beyond the region. By the early fourteenth century, when the Florentine industry comes to light in surviving documents, production there had expanded beyond the region's capacity to produce the necessary quality and quantity of wool. Eventually it was taking just about everything else—alum, saffron, even woad, along with other dyestuffs not native to the region—from beyond Tuscany and beyond Italy. Yet all the raw materials necessary to get the industry started were at hand, and if it outgrew the confines of its origins and pulled up most of its roots in the resources of the region, it was thanks to the city's merchants and to the Arno, which provided more waterpower and easier access to the sea than most of the other towns had.

Tuscany also had all the resources it required to be self-sufficient in iron. The largest mines in the entire Mediterranean area, worked since Etruscan times, were on Elba. Some ore was also mined in the Apuane Alps, on the mainland above Pisa. The ore mined on Elba was transported to the mainland for processing, since the island did not have sources for fuel. During its heyday Pisa controlled this traffic, having assumed rights over mining on the island from the twelfth century. Difficulties in the relations between Pisa and the mining community in the fourteenth century, however, led eventually to the intervention of the Appiani lords of Piombino, who controlled the distribution of the ore to the several ports in the area. There, the ore was delivered to contractors who had exclusive rights for selling it in specified areas that changed from time to time—Siena, Pisa, Lucca, Pistoia, and, beyond Tuscany, Bologna and Urbino. The operations, called *magone,* consisted in subcontracting the ore out for processing and then selling the semifinished iron in the markets where the contractor had monopoly privileges. The Tuscan subcontractors delivered ore to blast furnaces all along the wooded mountainsides of the Apennines to the north and east, from Monte Pisano and the Garfagnana to the Pistoiese mountains, the Mugello, and the Casentino. The area around Monte Amiata also had ironworks supplied by ore from Elba. The vast forests supplied fuel for the furnaces used to remove impurities and reduce the metal to a malleable substance, while mountain streams provided hydraulic power to mills for the hammering process and for the operation of bellows. What the subcontractors did not reclaim in semi-worked iron to be returned to the magona was sold to local ironworkers. Artisans working iron and steel were to be found all along the Apennine slopes, and notwithstanding their isolation in the mountains, they had expensive and sophisticated machinery for the production of tools, utensils, and arms, which they supplied to local peasants and artisans as well as to nearby urban markets. Among the earliest documented exports from Pisa to the eastern Mediterranean, in fact, were timber and basic iron products, especially arms. Villa Basilica, above Pescia, was noted for its arms, and the fame of the arms makers in the mountains above Pistoia has survived in the word *pistola.* Later we shall note the success of armament production in Florence itself, after the textile industries perhaps the sector of the urban economy most oriented to production for export.[5]

The hills of Tuscany are rich in other mineral resources. None had the industrial potential of the iron from Elba, and most are found in relatively insignificant quantities, but some had at least temporary historical importance in the initial growth and development of the medieval economy of the region. One of the earliest codifications of laws regarding mining in medieval Europe was issued to regulate operations in the Sienese maremma in 1310. It distinguished between ownership of land and rights to the subsoil, and it presumed that mines might be worked by a partnership organization. The largest concentration of mineral resources, including gold, silver, copper, lead, mercury, and sulfur, is found in an area known as the metalliferous hills *(colline metallifere),* south of Volterra between Siena and the sea. Copper and silver provided the materials for the early coinage of some of the towns in the region, and possession of the mines was a source of conflict among these towns. The richest of these mines was at Montieri, and Florentines were among the men contracted by the bishop of Volterra for their operation, the earliest instance being in 1218. The mines gave out in the later fourteenth century, however, and were abandoned.

At this early stage of commercial expansion, then, Tuscan merchants had something to peddle in markets throughout the western Mediterranean. The natural resources of the region were modest by the standards of the expanding European economy in the early modern period; in fact, Tuscany eventually got left behind in that growth. In this earliest stage of growth, however, these raw materials, together with the human resources of its many towns of Etruscan and Roman origin, gave Tuscany the potential of a hinterland with a solid industrial base to support commercial expansion. By the time of Dante and Giotto, at the end of the thirteenth century, the region was one of the most highly urbanized—according to some the most urbanized—in Europe, with perhaps a third of its population living in some dozen towns.

Pisa, located on a natural lagoon at the mouth of the Arno and near the point where the Via Aurelia and the Via Cassia met, emerged in the late Roman republican period as the major regional port, with maritime contacts throughout the Mediterranean. However much it suffered as a result of the collapse of the empire, trade seems to have picked up after its conquest by the Lombards in the seventh

---

[5] Ivan Tognarini, "La via del ferro: Un patrimonio dell'umanità?" *Ricerche storiche* 31 (2001): 5–39; Mario Borracelli, "Sidururgia e imprenditori senesi nel '400 fino all'epoca di Lorenzo il Magnifico," in *La Toscana al tempo di Lorenzo il Magnifico: Politica, economia, cultura, arte* (Pisa, 1996), 3:1197–1223. The accounts of two ironworkers active in the Casentino in the second half of the fifteenth century have been studied by John Muendel; see "The Mountain Men of the Casentino during the Late Middle Ages," *Annals of the New York Academy of Sciences* 441 (1985): 29–70.

century. Recent archaeological excavations have revealed the existence of a local ceramics industry dating from this time, and the presence of Islamic ceramics in the following centuries is evidence of overseas trade. By the tenth century Pisa clearly had become an active port and a competitor against Genoa for commercial profits in the western Mediterranean. In the following two centuries Pisan merchants were active throughout the area. They built up a strong position on the islands of Corsica, Sardinia, and Sicily and in North Africa, all important sources for grain and metals, including silver, and from ports in southern France they penetrated inland as far as Montpellier. As early as the end of the eleventh century Pisan merchants also had a foothold in the East, with a warehouse in Cairo and a large community in Constantinople. Early in the next century they won trading privileges in the Byzantine Empire and in the new crusader states and extended their base in Egypt to Alexandria. In 1155 Pisa gained minting privileges from the emperor and began minting its first silver denari in imitation of the Lucchese denaro. These were the two major coins in regional markets, and both also circulated widely abroad. At the beginning of the thirteenth century Pisa minted its first silver *grosso,* valued at twelve times the value of the denaro, an event that is another indicator of economic growth.

Pisa did not, however, have a commanding position over its hinterland. The other two cities in the vanguard of the commercial revolution, Lucca and Siena, emerged largely on their own. Since they lay on the Via Francigena, their growth was not altogether dependent on the extension of commercial tributaries leading out of Pisa. Moreover, each built up an economic base in other sectors, Lucca in industry and banking, Siena in banking.

Lucca, a valley city of Roman origin, became an important stop on the pilgrimage route because its cathedral housed the Volto Santo, a relic at the center of a cult that spread throughout Europe in the second half of the eleventh century. In the earliest stage of the commercial revolution the city was one of several places in Tuscany that developed a modest wool industry oriented to exports, but it built its fame on its silk industry. High-grade Byzantine fabrics were one of the major luxury imports in the growing European markets, and the Lucchese industry somehow got its start imitating these products. Lucca thus became the first major center in Europe for the production of silk, the industry being already well established by the mid-twelfth century. Real competition did not appear elsewhere in Italy until the fourteenth century, and the history of the diffusion of the industry throughout Italy at that time is centered largely around the emigration of silk workers from Lucca. Even then the Lucchese industry remained strong despite the consequent growth of competition from other cities. From this industrial foundation, Lucchesi merchants were soon traveling throughout Europe selling silks. They were among the first Italians to appear at the Champagne fairs, and as early as the end of the twelfth century some were conducting this trade through agents from a sedentary base in their native city. Following a trajectory to be described later, in tracing the rise of Florentine banking, these merchants moved into moneychanging, the lending of money, and deposit-and-transfer banking. At the end of the thirteenth century some twenty international merchant-banking firms were operating out of the city. Lucchesi were to be found at the highest level of international finance, doing business in England and at Paris, Venice, and Genoa and dealing with monarchs and popes. They retained their prominence in banking as well as in the industrial sector until the end of the sixteenth century, a longer span than that of Sienese and even Florentine banking.

The Lucchese economy thus had a solid foundation in its commercial, industrial, and banking sectors. Already in the tenth century it was minting its own silver denaro, the first Tuscan town to do so, and through to the thirteenth century this coin would dominate a monetary area that extended beyond Tuscany to all of central Italy. The strength of the city's economy is attested most by its relative independence from the port of Pisa. Lucchesi merchants sometimes used Pisa, but they also had independent routes to maritime traffic. The valuable raw materials and finished products of its silk industry were neither heavy nor bulky; hence, the import-export merchants could use small ports in Versilia or the Lunigiana, which were served by cabotage out of Genoa, and the overland route via the Cisa pass into the Po valley and on to Milan and Venice. Lucca had its own small port at Motrone (just south of present-day Forte dei Marmi) and hence direct access to Genoese shipping. As a result of its strong commercial and hence political ties to Genoa, in fact, the city found itself repeatedly pitted against Pisa in the power struggle among the city-states of the region.

The third city at the forefront in the take-off of the Tuscan economy was Siena. Its Spedale di Santa Maria della Scala was a major hospice for pilgrims traveling the Via Francigena. The city's position on this route was particularly favorable for the growth of trade, being within the orbit of Pisa but to the south, toward Rome, so that it had access to both a major port and urban markets in central Italy and, above all, to the papacy. Its position atop a hill without a stream precluded much growth of a local wool or iron industry, and therefore, unlike Lucca and other Tuscan towns, it did not have a major industrial base with production oriented to export. However, it did have direct access to some important natural resources in the vicinity. The metalliferous hills were to the west, and to the south and in the maremma of Grosseto was some of the best cultivable land in Tuscany. Siena's initial economic growth probably came primarily from the activity of merchants working the trade routes leading to the north. Documents do not reveal anything about commercial companies until the end of the twelfth century, much later than the earliest evidence for the activity of Lucchesi merchants abroad. However, the thirteenth century saw both the rise and the fall of the Sienese as Europe's leading bankers. They showed up at the Champagne fairs and all across Europe, from England and France to Germany and Friuli. Although in 1248–49 Sienese merchant-bankers accompanied the French king, Louis IX, on his crusade, their commercial contacts with the Levant were, with rare exception, limited to the ports of Pisa and Genoa, where they had resident communities.

It was their activity as papal bankers that gained them the greatest wealth and fame. Beginning with Innocent III (1198–1216), the popes sought to strengthen their revenue flow by imposing taxes on dioceses and religious houses throughout Europe, and Italian merchants were in a position to serve local bishops and abbots both in the collection of taxes and in the transfer of funds to Rome. Because of Siena's close association with the papacy—wherever it was located, be it Rome, Perugia, Viterbo, or elsewhere in the vicinity—its merchants took the lead in moving into this new sphere of banking activity, and they served as the principal papal bankers, with official status as merchants and bankers of the Apostolic Chamber, through the second and third quarters of the thirteenth century.

Pisa, Lucca, Siena—these were three of the great cities that were in the forefront of the commercial revolution down through the thirteenth century. It was only during the thirteenth century that Florence joined them, to become, by the end of the century, by far the largest of them all. But many smaller towns in Tuscany had the resources, however modest, to enter into regional and extraregional trade networks during this early stage of the commercial revolution. Staples in this trade were locally manufactured products, chiefly wool cloth and metalwork, or natural resources found in the vicinity. Merchants from these places ventured far afield to make their fortunes in this expanding world of international commerce and banking, and in the thirteenth century they can be documented just about everywhere. Merchants from Pistoia were at Acre, in the Levant, in 1245; they had a consul at the Champagne fairs in the second half of the century; and they have been found also in England, at Paris, and at various places in Provence and in the Po valley. Merchants from San Gimignano conducted a major trade in saffron, a product used as a dye, a medicine, and a spice that was produced in their home region. They exported it to the Levant, where they are documented at Acre in 1224 and at Aleppo, as well as to other places around the Mediterranean. Merchants from other small towns too were to be found at many places along the international trade routes. Of the 345 Tuscans found in Sicily between 1286 and 1320, 23 were San Gimignanesi, the third most numerous group after the Pisans and the Florentines and ahead of the Lucchesi and the Sienese. Others came from Empoli, Vinci, Signa, San Miniato, Poggibonsi, Castelfiorentino, and Volterra, all in the general vicinity of the Valdelsa. Aretines, much farther inland, exported woad from their area out of Genoa, some also going to Sicily and the Levant. Merchants from Volterra have been found in Marseilles.

Merchants from these towns, including Florence, traveled to Sicily, North Africa, Egypt, and the Byzantine Empire, taking advantage of Pisa's trading privileges in these places. Although they had no formal agreement, they often presented themselves under the Pisan flag (the Lucchesi alone often associating themselves instead with the Genoese). In many of the relevant documents they tend to be categorized more generally as Pisans or Tuscans, hence losing their specific identity. Presumably the Pisans accepted this situation because these merchants used Pisan ships and also because, as a collectivity, they together represented a stronger trading group, some of them, like those from San Gimignano, having their own expertise in the trade of certain products. Sometimes they joined together in particular markets as a foreign resident community for local legal and political reasons. In 1278 twelve Tuscan and Lombard cities formed such a union at the Champagne fairs, and at about the same time there was a similarly constituted organization *(universitas)* at Nîmes that included merchants from Lucca, Siena, Florence, and Pistoia. Moreover, these towns, although politically independent at the time, used the same money for purposes of foreign trade: the silver coins of Lucca and Pisa and eventually, after 1252, the gold florin of Florence. In short, the Pisan hinterland had a relatively strong economic identity centered on its principal port city.[6]

By the time of Giotto and Dante, Tuscany was the most urbanized area in Europe, second, if that, only to the Low Countries. About 1200 the populations of both Florence and Pisa were estimated at 15,000–20,000, Siena's was 10,000–15,000, and those of Lucca and Pistoia were closer to 10,000. A century later Florence had become one of the four or five largest cities in Europe, with a population that is variously estimated as somewhere between 90,000 and 130,000, while Pisa and Siena had populations approaching 50,000; Lucca, 20,000–30,000; Arezzo, 17,000–18,000; Pistoia and Prato, 11,000–15,000; and Volterra, Cortona, and Massa Marittima, about 10,000.[7]

[6] This identity under the flag of Pisa is discussed by David Abulafia in "Crocuses and Crusaders: San Gimignano, Pisa and the Kingdom of Jerusalem," *Italy, Sicily and the Mediterranean*, no. 14; and Thomas W. Blomquist discusses the monetary union in *Merchant Families*, no. 14.

[7] Josiah Cox Russell, *Medieval Regions and Their Cities* (Bloomington, IN, 1972), 43; and Maria Ginatempo and Lucia Sandri, *L'Italia delle città: Il popolamento urbano tra Medioevo e Rinascimento (secoli XIII–XVI)* (Florence, 1990), 148.

Perhaps as much as 30 percent of the region's population lived in towns with more than 5,000 inhabitants. In 1300 the region of Ghent had eleven cities—two more than Tuscany—with populations over 10,000, but only Ghent had as many as 40,000 inhabitants. At that time, in fact, only five cities in all of northern Europe had more than 40,000 inhabitants, as compared with three in Tuscany. However, the underlying economic structure of these two most populated areas in Europe differed. The basis of the growth of the Flemish towns was primarily a single industry, the manufacture of wool cloth, and the international trade that the demand for these products generated was largely in the hands of merchants from outside the region who crowded into these numerous local markets. The situation was very different in the Tuscan towns, the industrial base for whose growth was much more modest than that of the Flemish towns. The notable exceptions were Lucca, with its silk industry, and eventually Florence, with its wool industry, but the growing trade in their products was the result of local merchants' initiative to sell these products abroad wherever they could. Moreover, Mediterranean trade attracted merchant adventurers from even the smallest hinterland towns. It was thus that they built up their international networks dealing in whatever products they found a market for, and it was both the geographic and the economic scale of their operations that allowed some of them to enter also into international banking. Foreign merchants were not to be found in any number in the Tuscan towns beyond the port of Pisa; Lucca and Siena, unlike Bruges in the north, were not international emporia, nor did Florence ever become one.

Florence

Rise to Predominance

Florence was a latecomer to the commercial revolution, or so some argue, mostly on the basis of silence in the documents.[8] Indeed, at first sight it would seem that the city's location hardly favored commercial growth. Huddled against the foothills of the Apennines, far inland from the port of Pisa, it did not lie on any major trade routes to other large Italian cities, not even on those linking other

---

[8] The survey of the evidence for economic activity down to the early fourteenth century by Robert Davidsohn, *Storia di Firenze* (Florence, 1956), esp. vol. 4, pt. 2, is still fundamental. For the earliest period, however, much important new evidence has emerged in Enrico Faini, "Firenze nell'età romanica (1000–1211)" (in preparation), which exhaustively analyzes all the relevant notarial documents. William R. Day Jr., "The Early Development of the Florentine Economy, c. 1100–1275" (PhD diss., London School of Economics and Political Science, 2000), has also studied this early period; his view is summarized in "Population Growth and Productivity: Rural-Urban Migration and the Expansion of the Manufacturing Sector in Thirteenth-Century Florence," in *Labour and Labour Markets between Town and Countryside (Middle Ages–19th Century)*, ed. Bruno Blondé, Eric Vanhaute, and Michèle Galand (Turnhout, 2001), 82–110.

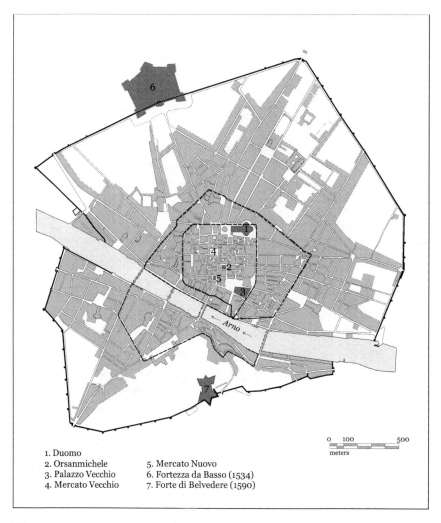

Florence
The map shows the walls of 1070, 1173–75, and 1284–1333. The shading indicates the part of the city built up at the time of the Bonsignori view of 1584.

1. Duomo
2. Orsanmichele
3. Palazzo Vecchio
4. Mercato Vecchio
5. Mercato Nuovo
6. Fortezza da Basso (1534)
7. Forte di Belvedere (1590)

major Tuscan cities—Lucca, Siena, Pistoia—to the several Tyrrhenian ports. Moreover, there were no natural resources in the immediate countryside to give it more potential for commercial growth than the other Tuscan towns had, except for the Arno, and a very notable exception it was, given the difference the river made. The wide flood plain at the point where the Arno emerges out of the hills provided an agricultural base for population growth, and the river itself presented the city with a way out of its geographical isolation. Downstream, it gave

Florentines access to the sea, and because the flow in this direction is not rapid, fluvial transport from the sea to the city was relatively easy, it being possible at times to use sails to power river-going vessels. Upstream, the river valley provided an easily traveled route into central Italy, and although it was not navigable, the river could be used to float timber, needed for fuel, construction, and furnishings, from the heavily wooded Apennine slopes of the Casentino, where it rises, downstream to the city. In the city the river provided Florentines the wherewithal they needed to build a major wool industry: water for the washing and dyeing of wool and power for driving fulling mills, both on a scale that none of the other Tuscan towns, and very few Italian towns, had. In many other ways, too, the river made life in the city much easier: it was used for the cleaning and working of leather, probably the most important product after food and drink in the daily life of everyone at the time; its banks supplied the building industry with sand and gravel; it powered flour mills; it yielded fish of high quality; and it carried away the waste from the city's butcher shops, on the Ponte Vecchio. In short, the importance of the Arno to the growth and development of the Florentine economy can hardly be overemphasized; and it is a fitting tribute to its historical role that it has, even today, a majestic presence in the lives of Florentines, right at the bustling center of the urban scene, such as no river has in any other European city.

According to some, the political situation in which the city emerged retarded its economic development. It was an urban island in a feudal sea. The low-lying hills surrounding the city provided a strong economic as well as a geographically secure foundation for the growth of feudal lordships, and in the early Middle Ages these men had dug in deep roots, especially in the hills of the Chianti to the south and in the upper reaches of the Arno to the north and west—in the Mugello, the Casentino, and the foothills of the Apennines. The web of different jurisdictions in the immediate vicinity complicated the conduct of trade in and out of the city. It also bred conflict both outside the walls, where the city sought to seize control over its countryside, and inside, where the presence of the feudal magnates who took up residence there exacerbated the conflict for political power during this formative period in the history of the commune. That history centers on two complementary themes, on the one hand the extension of the city's jurisdiction over its countryside and on the other hand, the slow social and economic fusion within the city of magnate and merchant families to form the dominant political class. And violence riddles the history of both developments. Political factionalism within was particularly vicious, since the emerging ruling class, although increasingly homogeneous in its involvement in commerce and finance, was not yet weaned away from a strong corporate sense of the fiercely autonomous family clan, often reinforced by a feudal heritage.

Despite the turbulent political history of the city down to the time of Dante and Giotto, at the end of the thirteenth century, Florentine merchants went abroad, laying the foundation for their great international commercial and financial network. However, less is known about these early adventurers than about merchants from the other centers of commercial expansion in Tuscany and elsewhere in Italy. Notarial acts of the kind that tell us much about business activities in Lucca, Genoa, and even Marseilles from the eleventh century on do not survive for Florence. Robert Davidsohn argued that Florentine merchants must have been trading in the Po valley by 1081, for they are specifically excluded from the privileges Henry IV granted to Lucchesi merchants there. It is not until the second half of the next century, however, that we begin to get bits and pieces of information about Florentines, by which time we have a fairly clear outline of the economic development of Pisa and Lucca. In 1158 Florence made a trade agreement with Lucca to allow Florentine merchants free passage there; in 1171 a treaty with Pisa gave Florentine merchants certain port privileges; in 1176 a treaty with Siena had to do with trade at Poggibonsi in the Valdelsa; and a few other documents attest to Florentines' commercial interest in nearby towns during these last years of the century. Outside of Tuscany, a certain Ugolino Fiorentino is documented in Venice in 1169 as contracting for a maritime loan for trade to Constantinople;[9] in 1178 Florentine and Sienese merchants made a pact with the Marchese of Monferrato for goods passing through that town on their way to and from France; Pierre Toubert thinks Florentines were active as merchant-bankers in Rome doing business with the papacy from at least 1177;[10] and Davidsohn considered the Florentine Rainucinus Tedaldini, documented at Rome in 1193, a merchant. About 1193 Florentines are documented in Messina, and since a street took its name from their presence, they must have been there in some number and for some time. Little more can be said about Florentine merchants abroad, and nothing about them outside of Italy, before 1200. Yet by this date we are confronted with the startling demographic evidence of the new walls the city built in 1172. They enclosed more than three times the space enclosed by the walls built a century earlier (80 hectares as compared with 25 hectares) and must have accommodated fifteen thousand to twenty thousand inhabitants, making Florence one of the two largest cities in Tuscany (the other being Pisa), somewhat larger than Siena and perhaps twice the size of Lucca and Pistoia. We can only assume that the Florentine economy had been expanding as its entrepreneurs too followed the great maritime powers of

---

[9] R. Morozzo della Rocca and A. Lombardo, *Documenti del commercio veneziano nei secoli XI–XIII* (Turin, 1940), 1:212.

[10] Pierre Toubert, *Les structures du Latium médiéval: Le Latium méridional et la Sabine du IXe siècle à la fin du XIIe siècle* (Rome, 1973), 1:618.

Pisa, Genoa, and Venice to the Near East and throughout the Mediterranean and went on to blaze their own overland tributaries branching out from these principal maritime routes of international commerce, the most important of which led to the great Champagne fairs deep in the hinterland of northwestern Europe.

The evidence for Florentines abroad dating from the first quarter of the thirteenth century, unlike the bits and pieces mentioned above, indicates that Florentine merchants had by then established the basis for an extensive international trade network.[11] The oldest extant fragment of an entrepreneur's ledger, dated 1211, was kept by a banker active in Bologna. It reveals that already by this time Florentines were using a fully professional accounting jargon.[12] In the second decade of the century they are documented in Milan and other places in the Po valley and in Friuli;[13] and, together with the Lucchesi, they had consuls in Genoa. By midcentury Florence had made commercial treaties with Bologna, Imola, Faenza, and Forlì across the Apennines, with Città di Castello and Perugia to the southeast, and with Siena to the south. In Rome merchants made loans to the papacy, the bishop of Chartres, the archbishop of Cologne, and English clerics, and they were involved in the transfer of revenues to the papacy. Outside of Italy Florentines first appear at the Champagne fairs in 1211, conducting an exchange operation; in 1215 they negotiated an insurance policy at fairs in Provence for a shipment of wool cloth; and in 1248 they are documented in Montpellier and Marseilles.[14] The first clear evidence from the British Isles dates from 1223, when two Florentines are documented as serving Henry III; and the next year the king granted licenses to Florentine, along with Sienese and Bolognesi, merchants. Documents from the 1220s on attest to the activity of Florentine companies in England and Ireland handling papal revenues and serving the king.[15] In Paris the first documented Florentine moneychanger dates from 1230. In the western Mediterranean a Florentine moneychanger at Cagliari, in Sardinia, is documented in 1220 as having been there for some time; and by midcentury others were present in Corsica, Majorca, Catalonia, and Tunis.[16] Florentines are first documented at

---

[11] Unless otherwise indicated, references here and below to Florentines abroad are from Davidsohn, *Storia di Firenze.*

[12] The ledger is published by Arrigo Castellani in *Testi toscani di carattere pratico* (Bologna, 1982), 21–40.

[13] For Milan, see Paolo Grillo, *Milano in età comunale (1183–1276): Istituzioni, società, economia* (Spoleto, 2001), 213.

[14] For Montpellier, see Kathryn L. Reyerson, *Business, Banking and Finance in Medieval Montpellier* (Toronto, 1985), 12.

[15] Elisabeth von Roon-Bassermann, "Die ersten Florentiner Handelsgesellschaften in England," *Vierteljahrschrift für Sozial- und Wirtschaftsgeschichte* 39 (1952): 97–128; M. D. O'Sullivan, *Italian Merchant Bankers in Ireland in the Thirteenth Century* (Dublin, 1962), 37–38.

[16] David Abulafia, *A Mediterranean Emporium: The Catalan Kingdom of Majorca* (Cambridge, 1994), 113, 125–26; Maria-Teresa Ferrer i Mallol, "Els italians a terres catalanes (segles XII–XV),"

Constantinople and in Egypt in 1248 and 1249, respectively.[17] The earliest documentation for the international activity of Florentine merchants and bankers, in short, dates only from the thirteenth century, as it does for merchants and bankers from most of the other Tuscan towns; and only from this time on can we chart the trajectory they followed over the century, bringing them to the fore with the most extensive commercial and banking network in the West.

The best evidence for the success of this economy, however, is its physical manifestations at the time, and these are as dramatic as such things can be. In 1252 Florence struck its first gold florin, and by the end of the century the florin was the universal money in international commercial and financial markets throughout western Europe. In 1284 the city began a new (third) set of walls; when they were finished about fifty years later, they enclosed almost eight times the space incorporated in the walls of 1172—about 630 hectares (counting the river) as compared with about 80 hectares (or 1,575 acres as compared with 200 acres)—making them one of the largest sets of walls built by any medieval city. The population had grown to somewhere between 90,000 and 130,000, depending on the estimates one accepts—a five- to sixfold increase in the course of a century, leaving the other Tuscan cities far behind to become one of the five largest cities in Europe (the others being Paris, Venice, Milan, and Genoa).[18] The new walls, moreover, extended well beyond the populated area, presumably in anticipation of even further growth. (Instead, later outbreaks of the plague in the fourteenth century reduced the population to about half, and only in the late nineteenth century did the city's population overflow this third circle of walls.) In 1296 a new cathedral was projected, and when, after two subsequent decisions to increase its size, it was dedicated on the completion of its great cupola in 1436, it was the largest cathedral, and perhaps the largest church of any kind, in Europe. In 1299 work began on the city's great public hall, which has been called one of the most original buildings in medieval Italy. The standard international money of the time, one of the largest sets of walls of any European city, what was to become the largest cathedral in Christendom, and a massive and original seat of government were not insignificant indicators of the success of the Florentine economy at the time when both Dante and Giotto were on the scene.

Anuario de estudios medievales 10 (1980): 453–54; Morozzo della Rocca and Lombardo, *Documenti del commercio veneziano*, 2:301–4.

[17] David Jacoby, "Italian Migration and Settlement in Latin Greece: The Impact on the Economy," in *Die Kreuz Fahrerstaaten also multikulturelle Gesellschaft: Einwandern und Minderkeiten in 12. und 13. Jahrhundert*, ed. H. E. Meyer (Munich, 1997), 97–127, reprinted in Jacoby, *Byzantium, Latin Romania and the Mediterranean* (Aldershot, 2001).

[18] William R. Day Jr., "The Population of Florence before the Black Death: Survey and Synthesis," *Journal of Medieval History* 28 (2002): 93–129.

Florence's commanding position in Tuscany by 1300, when it was much larger than any of the other cities in the region, was complemented by the decline of Siena and Pisa. The prominence of the Sienese on the international business scene had, in fact, lasted hardly longer than the two middle quarters of the thirteenth century. Whereas Lucca maintained its position as a major center for the production of silks and as the home of some of Europe's principal merchant-bankers throughout the entire period covered in this book, Siena began to fade away toward the end of the thirteenth century. Some of its leading companies went bankrupt—the Bonsignori, the largest of them all, in 1298 and the Tolomei in 1313—and most of the great banking families withdrew from business and invested instead in land. In 1303 Siena purchased the port of Talamone and began making improvements to its facilities, but this was done more to attract foreign merchants, above all Florentines, than to strengthen the position of its own merchants. Apart from the occasional appearance of a major figure, the Sienese had little presence in the banking community at Avignon, where banking moved into a new phase following innovations in the papal bureaucracy beginning in the second quarter of the fourteenth century. And they had little presence in contemporary Bruges, then emerging as the major emporium of northwestern Europe.

Several interlocking explanations for this decline have been proposed: internal divisions among partners within family companies, the increasing competition of bankers from Florence, the lack of a strong industrial sector, the decline of the Champagne fairs, the slight interest of the Sienese in maritime commerce, disinterest in trade to the Levant and even in the western Mediterranean, the move of the papacy to faraway Avignon, the city's Ghibelline and hence antipapal policy in the regional political arena. But both Giovanni Cherubini and Giuliano Pinto, the leading historians of late medieval Tuscany, emphasize, too, the lack of a true entrepreneurial ethos among these merchant-bankers. Members of the second generation began buying land complete with feudal rights, attracted by the model of the feudal nobility, which had remained deeply entrenched in the Sienese countryside and never, unlike in Florence, absorbed and subjected by the city. In other words, these merchants fell into a classic European pattern of the upward, three-generational social mobility from merchant to noble, from city to countryside, perhaps, in fact, offering the first concrete historical instance of such behavior, and certainly a very notable one. In Siena, however, no new men moved in to renew the cycle.

It was at the end of the thirteenth century that Pisa too went into decline as a maritime power. Its longtime rivalry with Genoa in the Mediterranean culminated with its disastrous 1284 defeat by the Genoese at the naval battle at

Meloria, a rocky island just off the coast of Livorno, where Pisa lost many ships and an enormous number of men, between those killed and the great many captured. In 1290 the Genoese followed up this victory by destroying Porto Pisano, the port Pisa used. However, Meloria marked the end, not the beginning, of Pisa's decline as a great maritime power, for Genoa had long been rising to dominance in western Mediterranean trade at the expense of Pisa. With the growth of the cloth trade between the Mediterranean and northern Europe, Genoa had a clear geographical advantage over Pisa as the maritime link. The ports in southern France were closer at hand, as was the Po valley, with its urban markets and overland routes to the north, and that position was strengthened in 1277 when Genoa established a direct sea route to Flanders. Moreover, the Genoese, who controlled the alum mines at Phocaea in Asia Minor, were the principal suppliers of this essential resource to northern cloth producers. During the thirteenth century Pisa also faced growing competition from Catalan merchants, who penetrated into Sicily and the Maghreb and had behind them the crown of Aragon, which began its expansion across the western Mediterranean at this time. The king conquered Sicily after the revolt of the Sicilian Vespers in 1282, and in 1297 Boniface VIII granted him the overlordship of Sardinia and Corsica (which, however, were not conquered until 1324), all strongholds of Pisan mercantile interest.

Thus during the later thirteenth century Pisa lost markets to significant competition throughout the western Mediterranean. It found some compensation in the growing wool exports from Florence, but here its position was compromised by political rivalries between the two cities and the alternatives Florentines had in the port of Lucca at Motrone and the port the Sienese began developing at Talamone in 1303 for the precise purpose of attracting Florentine merchants. Yet despite its decline as a maritime power, Pisa remained the principal Tuscan port, and the port of preference for Florentines. Its geographical advantage at the mouth of the Arno guaranteed this status, especially given the bulky nature of many of the products that constituted the import-export trade of the region— wheat, raw wool, finished wool cloth, skins, leather, metalwork. Many of the great Florentine firms—including the big three, Bardi, Peruzzi, and Acciaiuoli—had factors there, and Pisan merchants themselves continued to be active as importer-exporters throughout the western Mediterranean. By the end of the fourteenth century, in fact, many Catalan merchants were also operating out of the city.

The Dynamics of Growth

The economic and social origins of the first Florentine entrepreneurs and the initial process of capital accumulation that provided the investment stimulus for growth can hardly be known from the documentary record. As traditional views have it, a nascent capitalist class may have sprung from profits on usurious loans made to large landowners who needed liquidity, especially ecclesiastical institutions, or landowners themselves may have looked for investment outlets for the capital accumulated from the earnings the land, in fact, produced. In the most recent study of the problem, based on the closest inspection of the earliest documents, down to 1211, so far, Enrico Faini emphasizes a sharp division between the city and rural landowners and hence the pressure on city dwellers to find sources of income independent of the land.[19] The precondition for whatever dynamic drove expansion was an increasingly monetized market of a growing urban population. And the very magnitude of this growth, far outpacing that of all the other hinterland cities, suggests where to look to uncover two further dynamics that generated the commercial activity the city depended on: the provisioning and the employment of so many people.

The basic search for food was essential to sustain such an enormous urban population. Because Florence was located in an area of limited agricultural potential, in contrast to the smaller cities in the fertile Po valley, its very size generated intense efforts to supply its growing population with the staff of life. By the late twelfth century, if not earlier, merchants were venturing out in search of wheat wherever they could find it in the islands of the western Mediterranean, especially Sicily, and they eventually established a major base in Puglia for a supply line to the city. This trade brought the Kingdom of Naples into the Florentine network as a major hub, a position the area retained long after the demographic disasters of the mid-fourteenth century reduced the city's need to go abroad in search of grain.

The second major dynamic for trade that can be linked to population growth arose from the chief industry that provided the employment of so many people, the production of textiles, both wool and, later, silk. Each required both the importation of raw materials and the export of finished products for sale abroad. Demographic growth in itself can be taken as evidence that the rise of a vigorous wool industry long predates its earliest direct documentation at the end of the thirteenth century. In any event, from the fourteenth century on, throughout the period covered here, the textile industries, first wool and then silk, provided the major dynamics that extended and strengthened the commercial network. The changing geography of the network, and of the hubs within, followed both shifts in the supply of raw materials and shifts in markets—on the one hand, shifts in the source of wool from the western Mediterranean area to England,

---

[19] See Faini, "Firenze nell'età romanica."

then to central Italy, and finally, in the sixteenth century, to Spain, and shifts in the source of raw silk first from the Near East and Spain to Italy, including Tuscany itself; on the other hand, shifts in markets for finished products from the Near East to Italy itself and finally, in the sixteenth century, to northern Europe. The kaleidoscopic changes in the geography of the Florentine network over the four centuries covered in this book take on some perceptible patterns if seen through the filter of the import-export exigencies of the city's principal industries.

The size of the city explains what may have been another dynamic behind the growth of medieval Europe's largest and most integrated trade and banking network: the larger number of merchants who went abroad. Most merchants from all over central and northern Italy who ventured out to take advantage of the growing opportunities in regional and international trade following the commercial revolution came from much smaller towns, some no larger than Asti, Chieri, and Pistoia, whose population reached a maximum of ten thousand to fifteen thousand inhabitants before the disastrous plagues of the early fourteenth century, and some came from even smaller places, such as San Gimignano and Volterra in Tuscany. In short, many more Florentines must have taken their chances in foreign trade, and numbers alone can explain greater geographical diffusion and growth of a more extensive, denser trade network abroad than merchants from small places could possibly have formed among themselves. In contrast to Genoa and Venice, both of which reached comparable, if not higher, population levels during the early period of Italian commercial expansion, Florence was not a port city, and therefore its merchants, not being tied into a maritime system, were possibly more aggressive in extending their network into hinterland trading areas. By their sheer numbers, not to mention the density of the network they built up among themselves, Florentines eventually shoved the other Tuscans out of the markets where they did business. For instance, during the Avignon papacy, from 1309 to 1376, 100 Florentines have been documented active there as compared with 50 from Lucca, 9 from Siena, 6 from Pistoia, 5 from Pisa, and 2 from Arezzo.[20]

Beside these principal dynamics arising from the very size of the city, its further growth was generated by the network in and of itself. Since markets where raw materials for the textile industry were purchased hardly ever coincided with those in which finished products were sold, merchants had to find ways to balance purchases with sales, and this involved them in secondary trade in virtually

---

[20] These figures are from Giovanni Cherubini, "Sintesi finale," in *Storia di Pistoia*, vol. 2, *L'età del libero comune: Dall'inizio del XII alla metà del XIV secolo* (Florence, 1998), 438.

any item that entered the markets where they operated. Like the merchants of other hinterland towns, Florentine merchants engaged in the transit trade, taking any opportunity they could to plug into the increasingly intricate web of trade routes, whether it be distributing spices, medicines, and luxury goods taken from the central supply lines coming out of the Near East or, more modestly, shipping almonds from Valencia to Bruges, sweet wines from southern Italy to England, or pewterware from England to Italy. In this way the main currents of trade set off eddies of secondary trade systems that could take on a life of their own, thereby significantly extending the geographic reach of the main network. Finally, the network also enabled these merchants to shift credits and debits among themselves throughout western Europe, and the traffic in international transfer and exchange took on its own life, independent, even, of commercial activity. The geography of the Florentine network and the location of major areas within it shifted continually according to changes in all these dynamics.

The role of Florence in the commercial revolution, for all the city's fame in the economic growth of the West, had nothing of the romance that characterizes the parts played by Pisa, Genoa, and Venice in this story. The merchants of these great port cities ventured out across the Mediterranean to open trade relations with the Byzantine Empire and with the lands of the infidel. They set up shop in the great cities of the Levant and plugged into the vast commercial networks extending to the Far East, trading in the luxury products produced in the Middle East and the exotic spices and jewels from the Far East. They established zones of exclusive influence and even colonies and ended up fighting one another, in the case of Pisa to a fatal end. Florence was too land locked; at home Florentines knew nothing of the excitement of a port city like Venice, with the coming and going of merchants from all over Europe and the Mediterranean, the sailing and return of galleys, news reports from distant colonial outposts, and a bustling market of everything from bullion and exotic goods to slaves. Florentines, instead, ventured individually into the heartland of Europe, establishing trade networks among themselves and developing the techniques of international banking, for the most part leaving maritime shipping to others. The romance of their story was that of emergent capitalism: the Bardi and Peruzzi were the Rothschilds of the Middle Ages, Francesco Datini the personification of the medieval sedentary merchant directing far-flung commercial operations from a home office in Prato, the Medici the great international financiers as princes in disguise and art patrons. We do not know for certain that the Florentines were the first to mint a gold coin, that they invented double entry, that they were the only Italians to use the check, or that they kept better accounts, but there is no question that they left behind by far the most impressive archives of the business documents on which a good part of the early history of capitalist institutions and practices is based.

What, then, was this "capitalism"?

INTERNATIONAL MERCHANT BANKING

CHAPTER ONE

The Network

Performance: *Dynamics of Change, Periodization, The Era of
the Florin, Balance of Payments.*
Structures: *The Firm, The Conduct of Business, Interfirm
Relations.*
The Center: *Florence and Regional Trade, Florence as
International Emporium.*

The strength of Florence in international commerce and finance was in its network abroad. Firms were scattered all about the western Mediterranean and northern Europe, in hinterland towns as well as the major ports of trade, and although they were autonomous businesses, these firms worked through one another and thus tied themselves into a comprehensive international network that was more extensive than that of merchants of any other city down to the sixteenth century. Throughout their network Florentines operated in three spheres: commerce, banking, and, to isolate one aspect of banking that took its own distinct course, government finance. These spheres were interdependent, with commerce being the principal dynamic that drove the system, since activity in the other spheres arose from efforts to utilize favorable balances and to direct payments through the network. Banking was largely an extension of commerce, given the merchant's involvement in international exchange and transfer. Some men, like Francesco Datini, engaged primarily in commercial activity, and others, like the Medici, in banking. Relatively few merchant-bankers moved into government finance, since this possibility depended on local circumstances and usually required considerable resources.

This chapter presents an overall view of the network from various perspectives and attempts to overlay the geographic kaleidoscope of commerce, banking, and finance with some general observations about the network as a whole through the four centuries covered in this volume. Also discussed are the business organization through which the movers and doers built up the network and, in conclusion, Florence itself as the center of the network. The different activities of the network—commerce, banking and finance—are taken up separately and in greater detail in chapters 2 and 3. Presented here are generalizations largely derived from the material treated therein.

Unless otherwise indicated, all merchants and bankers mentioned are Florentine.

Performance
Dynamics of Change

The network was not exactly coterminous with the major patterns of Mediterranean and European trade. Florentines followed the well-beaten paths blazed by the maritime powers to the Levant and by the other towns of northern Italy across the Alps, and they superimposed their network on these commercial systems. Yet, while being subject to changes in these patterns of trade, the network underwent shifts that arose also from its own internal dynamics. These were primarily two: for the early period, the need for provisioning the city's rapidly growing population, and for the entire period, the exigencies of the local cloth industries, which employed much of this population.

The search for grain to feed a population that, judging from the enlargement of the city's walls, grew more than threefold from 1078 to 1172 and then from five- to sixfold over the following century was the primary dynamic that drove commercial expansion in the twelfth and thirteenth centuries. The merchants who ventured abroad looking for grain in the islands of the western Mediterranean and, above all, in southern Italy laid the foundations of a commercial network that extended throughout the entire area. The demographic crises of the mid-fourteenth century considerably reduced the pressure for provisioning, and this dynamic ceased to be of major importance in the commercial sector. Pressures grew again with the population growth in the later sixteenth century, but this time the solution lay not with Florentine merchants who went abroad in search of grain throughout a trade network but with a state policy to have it brought in by foreign suppliers from northern Europe, now organized in their own networks based on major supply lines originating in the Baltic.

The dynamics that drove the trade related to the textile industries were more complex. Both the wool and silk industries were entirely dependent on the importation of raw materials and on the export of finished products, and for each there was virtually no overlap between the markets where they took their supplies and those that were sales outlets. Furthermore, these markets were continually shifting, without there ever being much of an overlap between the two industries.

The wool industry initially depended on the importation of both raw wool from all around the western Mediterranean, including the islands and North Africa, and semifinished cloth from the Low Countries for refinishing. When in the fourteenth century the industry retooled, so to speak, discontinuing its refinishing of northern cloths and concentrating its own production on higher-quality cloths made from English wool, the northern supply line remained important, although it shifted from the Low Countries to England. In the fifteenth century, however, wool imports from England declined, and the industry turned to sources within Italy itself, in the Abruzzi. Finally, toward the end of the century, it shifted to Castilian wool and redirected production yet once again to a new kind of cloth called rascia. By the sixteenth century northern Europe no longer was part of the main supply line for the city's chief industry; moreover, with the shift to Spanish wool Florentine merchants for the first time lost much of this import trade to foreigners, both Castilian and Genoese merchants. Meanwhile, the area that supplied raw materials for the silk industry underwent a similar contraction. The industry first used raw silk imported primarily from the Levant and to a lesser extent from Spain and southern Italy, but by the sixteenth century virtually all of it came from Italy alone, a significant amount of it from Tuscany itself. In short, by the end of the sixteenth century the market area that supplied the raw materials for Florence's two principal industries, which had extended from the Levant to northwestern Europe, had shrunk to Italy itself, with only one major supply line from beyond, from Castile, along which, however, the traffic was largely in the hands of foreigners.

The network for marketing the products of the textile industries underwent shifts in altogether different directions. The Levant was a chief foreign market for wool cloth over much of the period covered in this book, down to the early sixteenth century, when Florentine products began to lose out to competition from Venice and other places. In the fifteenth century two important new markets opened up in Italy, in Rome and Naples, both rapidly growing capital cities with strong demand for luxury products. Meanwhile, with the development of the silk industry in the fifteenth century, Florentines for the first time produced goods that found major outlets in Europe—at the Geneva and then the Lyons fairs, in Spain, at London, Bruges, and Antwerp, and eventually in central and eastern Europe as well. This expanding European market was targeted also as a principal outlet for rascia, the new cloth the wool industry began producing toward the end of the fifteenth century.

It is difficult to perceive overall trends in the kaleidoscopic shifting of the geography of the supply and sales networks tied to these two Florentine industries until we get to the sixteenth century, when four trends emerge, all leading to the shrinkage of the network: weakening control over the supply line for raw wool from abroad, withdrawal from non-Italian markets for the supply of raw silk, declining trade with the Levant, and greater concentration of sales of both silk and wool cloth in markets within Italy. All these trends mark a convergence of commercial activity on Italy itself and less recourse to the network abroad. A fifth trend, however, points in a different direction: increasing sales in the north resulting from the rise of the silk industry in the fifteenth century and the shift in the wool industry to rascia at the beginning of the sixteenth century.

The convergence on northern European market outlets for both industries in the course of the sixteenth century, however, marked the final chapter in this geographic history. At least in theory the sales orientation to northern Europe had enormous potential, given the expansion the northwestern European economy was undergoing at the time, but the Florentines, finding themselves for the first time pushing their textiles in the highly competitive markets of a dynamically growing economy, failed to meet the challenge. In the market for wool cloth they very soon, by the beginning of the seventeenth century, lost out completely, perhaps inevitably inasmuch as they were trying to sell their products on the home turf of what had always been northwestern Europe's strongest export industry. The "new draperies" from the north invaded Mediterranean markets, and the Florentine wool industry virtually shut down its production for export. In the market for silks, Florentines had to face competition from the numerous other Italian towns that developed their own industries, but in the end they survived by adjusting production to a niche at the low end of the market.

These shifts of markets for the supply of raw materials and for sales of finished products cannot be read as indices of the performance of the textile industries, as we shall see; they mark only the major geographic parameters of the commercial network abroad. The needs of the textile industries, however, were not the only dynamics that shaped the geography of the network. Many merchants had other interests, ranging from the luxury goods from the Near East to products in regional markets, that arose from the necessity of balancing payments across the network; merchant-bankers focused much of their activity on international money markets, the principal ones, in chronological order from the fourteenth to the sixteenth century, being Venice, Geneva, Lyons, Antwerp, and the so-called Besançon fairs; and some of the largest of these entrepreneurs moved into government finances in various places.

The network reached its fullest extent by the early fourteenth century, and thereafter it hardly penetrated into new territory. At the time of Dante, when the walls of the city were being enlarged and a new cathedral erected, Florentine merchants were to be found throughout Italy, in the Levant, around the western Mediterranean from Provence and Spain to North Africa and across northwestern Europe from France and the Low Countries to England. Outside this relatively dense area of activity a few ventured into northern Germany and eastern Europe. The three largest and most prominent companies—Bardi, Peruzzi, Acciaiuoli—had agents at places throughout this network: Genoa, Venice, Naples, Barletta, and Sicily in Italy; Rhodes, Cyprus, and Constantinople in the East; Avignon, Spain, Tunis, and the islands in the western Mediterranean; and Paris, Bruges, and London in northwestern Europe. Over the following three centuries the internal geographic configuration of the network changed constantly as some areas grew in importance and others receded, but the trend was toward contraction, to the point that by 1600 the network had become largely coterminous with Italy itself.

Within this larger framework of three centuries, shifts can be localized in two general areas: northwestern Europe and the Mediterranean. In northern Europe the original pole was at the Champagne fairs, and then toward the end of the thirteenth century it shifted to two centers, London and Bruges. From England Florentines exported wool to the Low Countries and in time to their home industry, and they also became heavily involved in ecclesiastical transfers and royal finances. The crown reduced its dependence on Florentine bankers after the failures of the 1340s, and although the wool trade continued, eventually the rise of the industry in England cut into that country's export of wool, forcing the Florentine industry to adjust its production to wool from Italy itself. By the end of the fifteenth century England had receded as a major pole in the commercial and banking activities of the network. On the Continent, the Low Countries maintained their centrality to Florentine commerce and banking in the northwestern sector of the network, and the Florentine presence in the area was never imperiled by overentanglement in government finance. Florentines followed the shifts from Bruges to Antwerp at the beginning of the sixteenth century and then to Amsterdam at the end of the century, but these shifts were just one aspect of a larger phenomenon—the geographic expansion of trade and the entrance of many more large players on the stage of international commerce and finance—that in the course of the century much reduced the relative importance of Florentines in these sectors and eventually pushed them very much to the sidelines.

In the Mediterranean, Venice was a key node in the network, as it was indeed in the entire commercial system that linked western Europe to the Levant. For the Florentines in particular Venice was central not just to their commercial interests as a point of exchange between East and West but to their banking activities as well, since it was by far the most important bullion market to be found anywhere. With respect to trade, however, Florence was able to forge other links to the Levant and to northern Europe; to this extent Venice, albeit always important, never was a dominant node in the network. Through Tyrrhenian ports Florentines had access to other maritime systems, above all those of Genoa and Barcelona, and overland they could reach Ancona and plug into yet other systems, including those of Ancona itself and especially Ragusa. And of course Florence eventually got its own port, at Pisa, and at least for about a half-century its own galley system. All these contacts meant that most Florentine trade circumvented Venice. By the sixteenth century hardly any raw materials for the Florentine textile industries came by way of Venice, and relatively few of their products reached markets by way of Venice. Instead, the western Mediterranean, enlivened by the expansion of its regional economies beginning in the second half of the fourteenth century, became the most important area of commercial activity within the network, with its inland routes to Avignon and then Lyons and its major ports at Naples, Barcelona, Valencia, and other places along the Iberian littoral to Lisbon. In Spain, however, the Genoese from the beginning established larger resident communities than did the Florentines, many of them in the hinterland, and on this foundation they eventually built strong ties to the Hapsburg monarchy that assured their rise to dominance in both the commercial and financial sectors. Then came the invasion of the Mediterranean by the English, the Dutch, the French, and all the others from outside the region. The building of Livorno as the area's great free port was Florence's last effort to profit from this expanding commercial activity, but its passive role as a free port signaled the retrenchment, if not the withdrawal and resignation, of the city's merchants.

Periodization

If we shift the perspective from the geography of the network to the chronology of the general course of the economy across these centuries as reflected in the activities abroad that drove the network, developments can be seen as falling, roughly and with much overlap, into four phases, each as distinct as this way of organizing historical phenomena allows. The earliest period, barely documented, extended into the thirteenth century. It was marked by the expansion of the economy outside the immediate region, when the objective was to find wheat and to accommodate the need of its nascent cloth industry for both raw materials and sales outlets. Trade was directed to the immediate environs, to central and north-

ern Italy and to the western Mediterranean. In northern Italy the great emporium at Venice opened the network to the eastern Mediterranean trading system,
and the city long remained a major node in the network, though not one from
which the network itself expanded.

The second phase, from roughly the mid-thirteenth to the mid-fourteenth
century, saw the full affirmation of entrepreneurial efforts to build up the network, the expansion of the network abroad to its widest geographic extent, and
the underpinning of the network at home with the growth of the wool industry.
Florentines moved into the trading system that bound the Mediterranean to
northwestern Europe, where they bought cloth both for resale and for finishing
and resale in the south and in the Levant and then, somewhat later, English wool
for their home industry. At the same time the network also expanded in the
opposite direction, into southern Italy, to meet the provisioning needs of the
population back home in Florence. The banking crisis in the 1340s and the demographic disaster brought on by the Black Death mark the end of this phase of
expansion. The bankruptcies reduced, at least momentarily, merchant-bankers'
entrance into government finance abroad on a large scale, and the population loss
in 1348 cut deeply into their traffic in the grain trade. These events, therefore,
signaled the relative decline of both southern Italy and England from their prominence in the Florentine international network.

After the Black Death the network entered into its third, perhaps most vigorous phase, which extended through the fifteenth century. In the second half of
the fourteenth century trade intensified all along the western Mediterranean
littoral in the north and extended into the Atlantic as far as Lisbon. The penetra-
tion of this trade into the hinterland of southern France and the Iberian Peninsula stimulated the growth of regional economies. The new opportunities that
opened up for Florentine merchants are personified in the career of the well-
known merchant of Prato, Francesco di Marco Datini (d. 1410). At home in Tuscany the conquest of Pisa in 1406 and the acquisition of the ports of Porto Pisano
and Livorno in 1421 gave Florence major port facilities from which the city
launched its own galley system to northwestern Europe and the Levant. In the
second half of the century Florentines also established a trade route to the East
that went overland to Ancona and thence across the Adriatic to Ragusa, two major ports for the Levantine trade that saw increased activity during this period.
Merchants turned to central Italy for raw wool once the supply channel from
England became more difficult and to both central and southern Italy, as well
as the Levant, for raw silk to supply the city's growing silk industry. At the same
time they found major new sales outlets for both wool and silk fabrics in the
booming metropolises of Rome, Naples, and Constantinople and, toward the

end of the century, at Nuremberg, a central market in the growing trade network that extended across Germany and into eastern Europe. In the financial sector, Florentine bankers brought centrality to the network with the founding of the first great international exchange markets, at Geneva in the first half of the fifteenth century and then at Lyons, both in northern Europe, thereby consolidating their position as Europe's leading bankers. Meanwhile in Italy they emerged as major bankers in the expanding, increasingly sophisticated financial apparatus that the Apostolic Chamber developed to tighten its control over the universal church and to pursue the formation of a territorial base as a major state in central Italy. All this far-flung activity in both commerce and banking marks the century and a half following the Black Death as the period of the network's greatest vitality.

The geography of the network changed profoundly enough during the sixteenth century to justify talking of a fourth phase, one that has more coherence than might be expected, given that it is by far the least studied, notwithstanding the abundance of the documentary record. In all sectors—industry, commerce, banking, and government finance—Florentines failed to meet two challenges: how to face significant competition and how to find a place in a rapidly expanding European economy. In the north the market for silks saw increased competition from the growing industry in other Italian cities, while the market for rascia, the innovative product developed from Castilian wool, after steadily expanding throughout the century, rapidly closed down after 1600. The western Mediterranean segment of the network, in an area now largely under the control of the Spanish crown, underwent, if not shrinkage, at least a thinning-out process in both the commercial and financial sectors. The Genoese, being maritime shippers as well as merchants, had been more successful than the Florentines in colonizing Spain in the fourteenth and fifteenth centuries, and hence they were in a better position to take advantage of the extraordinary business opportunities of all kinds that opened up with the unification of Spanish territories under the Castilian monarchy, the Atlantic expansion to the New World, and the aggressive orientation of Spanish policy under the Hapsburgs toward both Italy and northern Europe. In 1503 a Genoese became the first factor of the Casa de Contratación, instituted to control the new transatlantic trade. And as bankers to the throne, the Genoese controlled the largest international movement of bullion and credit that Europe had ever seen. The Genoese presence in both commercial and financial circles in sixteenth-century Spain, in short, far overshadowed that of the Florentines. Few Florentine merchants participated in the Atlantic expansion, and few Florentine bankers took part in the new exchange fairs in Castile. Also coming to the fore in this reinvigorated economy of Spain was a new generation of Castilian merchants who were able to take over the supplying of wool to the Florentine industry to the extent that some of them set up branches in Florence itself to handle the traffic.

In Italy too the Genoese challenged the Florentines in their two largest markets. They colonized Spanish Naples as bankers and as merchants, pushing the Florentines out of government finance and taking over much of the trade in raw silk, including some of that directed to Florence. They also put down roots in the local landed nobility as the Florentines never had. In Rome, where they moved to the top rung of papal bankers under the Genoese popes at the end of the fifteenth century, they invested heavily in the various schemes devised in the early sixteenth century for handling the papal debt, often cooperating with the Florentines but eventually gaining clear predominance. Meanwhile, their own international exchange fairs at Besançon and then Piacenza, originally established under Hapsburg auspices in competition with the Lyons fairs, sponsored by the French king, grew in importance as a principal mechanism for Spanish financing of Hapsburg military initiatives in the north. Florentine bankers themselves gradually moved into the Genoese orbit, by the end of the sixteenth century abandoning Lyons altogether. In the second quarter of the seventeenth century they set up their own fairs within Italy, but eventually they had to return to those of Genoa. In any event, by this time the Florentines were probably using fairs more for their own credit operations at home rather than for international transfers. In short, the Genoese, from their foundation in Spain as bankers to a government that had vast supplies of bullion and heavy financial commitments abroad, operated at a level of international finance much beyond the reach of Florentines. "The century of the Genoese," the phrase that encapsulates these developments, found what was perhaps its most telling manifestation, at least in the context of this book, in the establishment of resident Genoese firms in Florence itself, where they both supplied raw materials to the textile industries and exported finished products.

The southern German merchant-bankers presented another challenge to the Florentines in the early sixteenth century. The Germans, having access to the rich deposits of silver in the mines of the Tyrol and eastern Europe, like the Genoese had the power of bullion behind them, and they arrived on the scene in western Europe under the umbrella of the expanding Hapsburg empire, which under Charles V stretched from Germany to the Low Countries in the north and to Spain and Italy in the south. Moreover, these German firms had strong organizational structures: they were based in large, centralized family associations, sometimes explicitly so called, and they worked through cartel arrangements with one another. The Fuggers had a foundation in imperial privileges for the exploitation of copper and silver mines in the Tyrol, which required a much higher long-term investment than did the Florentine commercial firms; and they amassed capital far beyond the capability of any Florentine merchant-banker. The Florentines encountered the Fuggers, the Welsers, and the other German firms most directly in Rome, at least down to the sack of 1527, and in Antwerp, where German silver paid for Portuguese spice imports. It was the Genoese, however, not the Florentines, who put up the competition against the Germans. With a more solid foundation in a long-established commercial and shipping system, a strong presence in Spain, and an international exchange network extending across Europe to Antwerp, the Genoese were in a better position than the Germans to serve the needs of the Spanish monarchy, with its more direct access to even greater bullion resources, in the pursuit of its international military policy. The Germans, in short, lacked the solid foundation in the Mediterranean and in the international exchange market that the Genoese had. "The age of the Fugger" (the title of Richard Ehrenberg's classic study, still valid after more than a century) got cut short as it gave way to the much longer "century of the Genoese."

The Florentine network begins to look even smaller in the context of the rapid changes that took place in the European economy after powerful new players such as the Genoese and the Fuggers appeared on the scene in the sixteenth century. Geographic horizons expanded to seemingly infinite distances, a strong injection of bullion shook up markets everywhere, war-driven governments intensified the dynamics of fiscal borrowing, and international commerce and finance gravitated to Antwerp and the northwest. On this international scene Florentines had their most notable presence in Lyons, where they had built up a solid foundation in commerce and international exchange in the preceding century. But it was their last stand abroad. The trade fairs declined as links between north and south, and the expanding international exchange market moved south to Piacenza and north to Antwerp. The Grand Parti in the 1550s marked the last major venture of the Florentines into government finance outside of Italy, and it was a far cry from their involvement in fiscal affairs of the Neapolitan and English kings two and a half centuries earlier. They lost out completely in the vast international financial operations of the Hapsburgs that made the Genoese rich. Despite the base they had established on the Iberian Peninsula, Florentine merchants did not participate significantly in the overseas expansion of Spain and Portugal, and in the north they almost got lost in the crowd of merchants from virtually everywhere who poured into the great new emporium at Antwerp. In this expanding economy Florence did not enjoy the advantages that Genoa did as a result of its strategic geographic position in the western Mediterranean, namely, a solid maritime tradition complete with port and ships and, above all, close financial ties to a great European power.[1] Florentines had no way to keep up with the rapid growth of the European economy in general, which left them behind in its expansion overseas and outnumbered in the ever-growing community of international merchants and bankers in the great capitals of trade and finance.

In the second half of the sixteenth century the network contracted, and its ranks of merchants and bankers thinned out. Still, it is difficult to assess the overall situation. Florentines continue to show up in most of the major centers. In the following chapters we shall encounter some of these businessmen abroad who had a high profile in the sixteenth century—Filippo di Bernardo Corsini and his sons at London, Gaspar Ducci at Antwerp, Albizzo Del Bene and Antonio di Antonio Gondi at Lyons, Francesco and Piero Capponi at the Besançon fairs, Sebastiano Montelupi at Cracow. Old families such as the Capponi, the Gondi, and Guicciardini made large fortunes, as did some new families, such as the Riccardi.[2] At the end of the century merchants bearing old family names—Bardi, Capponi, Corsini, Ricasoli, Rinuccini—were still conducting trade from Livorno, among other things handling grain shipments from the North Sea to Marseilles, Bologna, and Sicily.[3] Moreover, the scale of operations of some of these later businesses exceeded that of earlier businesses significantly. In 1582 Simone and Heirs of Giovanni Corsi & Partners, a merchant bank in Florence with no branches abroad, had a capital of *sc*.50,000, and its assets under management amounted to 50 percent more, in real value, than those of the Medici firm in Rome in 1427 and twice those of Filippo Strozzi's firm in 1484.[4] In the 1590s the Riccardi had *sc*.115,000 invested in their agglomerate of firms in Florence, Pisa, Venice, and Messina.[5] The registers of *accomandite,* or limited liability partnership contracts, drawn up from 1602 to 1604 document investments of *sc*.63,000 by the Capponi, *sc*.40,000 by the Guicciardini, *sc*.38,000 by the Corsini, and *sc*.33,000 by the Bartoli. The firms they invested in were in Rome, Naples, Messina, Palermo, Seville, and Hamburg;[6] however, two-thirds of the capital channeled through all accomandite at this time went to Rome and Naples. Thereafter, total investments declined, first in France and the Low Countries and then, by

[1] See Thomas Allison Kirk's analysis in *Genoa and the Sea: Policy and Power in an Early Modern Maritime Republic, 1559–1684* (Baltimore, 2005), 186–202.

[2] Richard A. Goldthwaite, *Private Wealth in Renaissance Florence: A Study of Four Families* (Princeton, NJ, 1968); Paolo Malanima, *I Riccardi di Firenze: Una famiglia e un patrimonio nella Toscana dei Medici* (Florence, 1977).

[3] Anna Maria Pult Quaglia, *"Per provvedere ai popoli": Il sistema annonario nella Toscana dei Medici* (Florence, 1990), 120–21.

[4] Richard A. Goldthwaite, "Banking in Florence at the End of the Sixteenth Century," *Journal of European Economic History* 27 (1998): 485 (table 3).

[5] Malanima, *I Riccardi*, 74–75.

[6] R. Burr Litchfield, *Emergence of a Bureaucracy: The Florentine Patricians, 1530–1790* (Princeton, NJ, 1986), 207.

midcentury, in Germany, Spain, and even Venice, as well as in the south of Italy.[7]

How accurately this type of contract reflects trends remains to be seen. At present we have no other way of taking the measure of the involvement of Florentine entrepreneurs abroad at the end of the sixteenth century. We cannot balance out the contraction of the commercial and banking network in a literal geographic sense with any judgment about the intensity of traffic throughout it or estimates of the number of firms and the volume of business they transacted, especially outside of Italy. This terra incognita in the historiography is worth exploring, judging from how the Venetian officials of commercial affairs, the Cinque Savi alla Mercanzia, viewed the local Florentine community in 1606:

> It has the best links to every country, because not only in every province but almost in every city they have firms [*case*] open for major trading; [and they are] very intelligent in this profession of circulating money throughout the world, which they do with considerable knowledge and facility, much to their profit; and they never lose whatever occasion presents itself, inserting themselves in every kind of traffic not only in exchange but in every kind of merchandise.[8]

And surely the Venetians, if anyone, were reliable observers in these matters.

The Era of the Florin

AN INTERNATIONAL MONEY   A history of the Florentine network could be entitled "The Era of the Florin," for the international fame of this one city's money followed on the success of the city's merchant-bankers abroad. Whether the florin or the *genovino,* of Genoa, was the first gold coin issued by a mercantile state is a matter of only a few months in the year 1252, but there is no question which found instant success abroad both as a circulating gold coin representing a stable intrinsic value and as a money of account serving as a referent for an international monetary standard. Both the genovino in its eventual form (we know nothing about the original coin) and the Venetian gold ducat, first minted in 1285, took the florin as their model for size, weight, and fineness. The Venetian gold ducat, however, was the only rival to the florin, but its area of dominance was

[7] Maurice Carmona, "Aspects du capitalisme toscan aux XVIe et XVIIe siècles: Les sociétés en commandite à Florence et à Lucques," *Revue d'histoire moderne et contemporaine* 11 (1964): 98–99; José-Gentil Da Silva, *Banque et crédit en Italie au XVIIe siècle* (Paris, 1969), 97–100; Paolo Malanima, "Florentine Nobility and Finance in the Age of Decline," in *Cities of Finance,* ed. H. A Diederiks and D. Reeder (Amsterdam, 1996), 207–21; Litchfield, *Emergence of a Bureaucracy,* 208–10 (table).

[8] Quoted in Isabella Cecchini, "Piacenza a Venezia: La ricezione delle fiere di cambio di Bisenzone a fine Cinquecento nel mercato del credito lagunare," *Note di Lavoro* (Dipartimento di Scienze Economiche, Università Ca' Foscari di Venezia), no. 18 (2006): 14.

Venice's great maritime empire in the eastern Mediterranean. The minting of the florin, the genovino, and the ducat by Italy's great commercial cities at this moment marked the return to a gold standard, and the need for coins with an intrinsic value some dozen times greater than the same weight of silver was in part the result of the intensification of international trade. The largest silver-based coin then being used by merchants was the grosso, and its replacement by the florin, whose value was originally twenty times greater, is a benchmark in the advance of the commercial revolution, just as the replacement of the denaro by the grosso, worth twelve denari, had been a century earlier. Not irrelevant to the situation was the greater availability of gold as a result of the trans-Sahara trade and more intense mining efforts in eastern Europe. Moreover, the Italians were accumulating the profits of trade and, through import substitution, reducing their trade deficit with the Levant. It has also been observed that inasmuch as Florence, Genoa, and Lucca, the cities that minted gold coins in the 1250s, were Guelf in their political sentiments, the coincidence in the timing may be explained by their readiness to challenge imperial authority, which included the legitimization of mints, in the wake of the death in 1250 of Emperor Frederick II, who himself had been minting a smaller gold coin of his own, the *augustalis*.[9]

"Il maladetto fiore," which Florence "produced and scattered" around Europe (*Paradiso* 9.130), first took root abroad with its immediate recognition by the other great international business centers in Tuscany—Lucca, Siena, and Pisa. These cities, albeit rivals, shared certain economic interests, and it seems that they formed a kind of monetary union among themselves for the acceptance of one another's money, especially the silver denari and grossi of Lucca and Pisa. Thus Pistoia, for all the prominence of some of its merchants abroad, had no mint whatsoever, and Florence did not start to mint its own silver grosso until 1237, by which time it was well on its way to becoming the dominant city in Tuscany. If Florence waited so long, it was presumably because the city's merchants were content to use Pisan and Lucchesi coins. As early as the 1171 commercial treaty with Pisa, one of the first documents we have for Florentine commerce abroad, Florentines were supplying at least half of the silver that arrived at the Pisan mint,[10] and they presumably continued to do so for another half-century before finally minting their own grosso. Once in operation, the city's mint must have produced coins in relatively large quantities, for they gained immediate acceptance. By the late 1250s the grosso was already replacing the local Pisan moneys

[9] Monica Baldassarri, "La città e il commercio internazionale: La monetazione a Pisa tra XII e XVII secolo," in *Pisa e il Mediterraneo: Uomini, merci, idee dagli Etruschi ai Medici*, ed. Marco Tangheroni, exhibition catalog (Milan, 2003), 267.
[10] Enrico Faini, "Firenze nell'età romanica (1000–1211)" (in preparation), ch. 2.

in remittance from Cremona of proceeds from cloth sales.[11] And none of Florence's neighboring rivals in the commercial and banking sector attempted to challenge the florin. Lucca, in fact, may have made agreements with Florence about the first minting of the florin and the minting of a limited quantity of its own smaller gold coin, a grosso, in 1256.[12]

The circulation of the florin abroad took place extraordinarily rapidly.[13] A hoard of 229 gold coins uncovered in Pisa dating from the late 1250s included 91 florins. In 1273, just twenty years after the minting of the first florin, the coin was being used in Rome for the purchase of real estate.[14] About this time the papacy established the florin as the preferred money of account for its revenues. The florin predominated among the gold coins used for payments by the Tuscan bishoprics to the papacy in 1296, the other coins being mostly silver grossi and denari, the largest number being the *gros tournois.* By this time, at the end of the century, the florin was beginning to circulate throughout western Europe, especially in the region of the Champagne fairs, and even in the Levant (to judge from a hoard discovered near Aleppo of more than 600 gold coins, almost all florins, dating from 1291–92).[15] In 1314 a Genoese merchant brought 50,000 florins into England. The revenues of the papal see in Avignon from 1316 to 1334 included more than 3 million florins, as compared with 3,000 Venetian ducats and only 350 genovini. In 1339 the collector of papal revenues in Lombardy, knowing that 2,500 ducats he had received would not be accepted by the Curia, had to change them into florins.[16] Florins are the only foreign coins to appear in the records of the bishopric of Troyes for the 1340s, and they appear in significant quantities. In 1340 and again in 1343 the king of France tried without success to ban their circulation, and in 1346 he assigned them an official value for use in ordinary transactions.[17]

---

[11] Hidetoshi Hoshino, "I Chiarenti di Pistoia a Cremona, 1256–1261," in Hoshino, *Industria tessile e commercio internazionale nella Firenze del tardo Medioevo,* ed. Franco Franceschi and Sergio Tognetti (Florence, 2001), 154.

[12] Thomas W. Blomquist, "The Second Issuance of a Tuscan Gold Coin: The Gold Groat of Lucca, 1256," *Journal of Medieval History* 13 (1987): 317–25, reprinted in Blomquist, *Merchant Families: Banking and Money in Medieval Lucca* (Aldershot, 2005); Lucia Travaini, "Aree monetarie e organizzazione delle zecche nella Toscana dei secoli XII e XIII," in *L'attività creditizia nella Toscana comunale,* ed. A. Duccini and G. Francesconi (Pistoia, 2000), 25–42.

[13] Peter Spufford, "The First Century of the Florentine Florin," *Rivista italiana di numismatica* 107 (2006): 421–36.

[14] Ivana Ait, "Roma: Una città in crescita tra struttura feudale e dinamiche di mercato," in *La città del Mediterraneo all'apogeo dello sviluppo medievale: Aspetti economici e sociali* (Pistoia, 2003), 318–19.

[15] Philip Grierson, "The Coin List of Pegolotti," in *Studi in onore di Armando Sapori* (Milan, 1957), 1:488–89.

[16] Alan F. Stahl, *Zecca: The Mint of Venice in the Middle Ages* (Baltimore, 2000), 213.

[17] Carola Small, "Coinage and Accounting in the Fourteenth Century: The Record of the Bishop's Receiver in Troyes," *Proceedings of the Western Society for French History: Selected Papers of the Annual Meeting* 24 (1997): 420–21.

When governments elsewhere began minting their own gold coins, many of these were imitations of the florin, whereas the genovino had no imitations, and the Venetian ducat was imitated mostly in the eastern Mediterranean. As early as 1259 Perugia minted a gold coin that, while not an imitation, had the same weight and purity as the florin, although the city turned to Lucchesi for technical help. Perhaps the earliest imitation was a coin minted in Rome about 1270, which, however, also bore the symbol of the city's popular government.[18] In the 1270s the counts Guidi in the Casentino tried to issue fraudulent imitations, and toward the end of the century Philip the Fair minted a coin known as the *florin d'or,* which had the same size, weight, and fineness as the florin but a different design. In 1322 Pope John XXII in Avignon began the minting of a cameral florin that was almost an exact reproduction. An imitation minted in the Dauphiné in 1327 was lighter. In France the very word *florin* came to be used for any gold coin. The Duke of Aquitaine, later Edward III of England, gave the name to the gold coin he issued in 1344 (under the direction of a mint master of Florentine origin), worth one-third of the pound sterling. At about the same time the Marquis of Montferrat began striking florins. In 1346 the king of Aragon, Pedro IV, followed suit with his own imitation, which, however, soon underwent debasement. The florin penetrated into western Germany too even though the area fell outside the Florentine network. In the early 1340s Lübeck, having appointed a Tuscan to head its new mint, began producing florins, and the name was used for the *rheingulden,* first minted in 1348 with the same weight and purity (this changed in time). Imitations were attempted in Poland in the 1320s, and at about the same time, following a sharp increase in the output of the gold mines at Kremnica, the Hungarian king issued a florin that differed only in the substitution of his name for that of Florence. In short, the geography of these mints includes heavy concentrations extending from Catalonia across southern France and into the Piedmont in Italy and from the Low Countries into the Rhineland, as well as scatterings across eastern Europe, and it is probably no coincidence that Florentine mint masters, with the expertise learned at home, showed up at many of these mints. Many imitations bore the figure of John the Baptist, the Florentine lily, and sometimes even the inscription of the original; in addition, there were numerous hybrids, similar but with certain modifications. "Even today," observed Gregorio Dati in the early fifteenth century, "many gold florins are found among those of the pope, the emperor and other kings and rulers that are florins with the lily and St. John, although they may have some other small sign of theirs."[19]

[18] Ait, "Roma," 318–19.
[19] *L'istoria di Firenze di Gregorio Dati dal 1380 al 1405,* ed. Luigi Pratesi (Norcia, 1904), 135–36. Mario Bernocchi, *Le monete della Repubblica fiorentina,* vol. 5, *Zecche di imitazione e ibridi di monete*

The solidity of the florin's reputation lay in the city's guarantee of its fixed value, both its weight of approximately 3.5 grams and its purity at as close to 24 carats as was technically possible at the time (except for the minting of a few "light" florins in 1408). The one adjustment made to the coin's form came in 1422 with the minting of the slightly wider (by 1–2 mm) but thinner *fiorino largo* (sometimes deceptively translated as "large florin"). With this new coin, designed to resemble the Venetian ducat, the commune aspired, without much success, to extend the network ever farther afield by challenging the ducat within its own realm in the Levant, this being the moment when the city was setting up a galley system to facilitate trade in that region. The florin also infringed on the identity of the gold coin of Genoa. The Genoese referred to their coin as a ducat, its original distinctive name having never caught on even in its native city, but they sometimes called it the "gold florin of Genoa" and commonly used *ducat* and *florin* interchangeably with reference to the money of account.[20] The florin's success abroad, in fact, arose also from its utility as a money of account. As such it was an essential instrument for the functioning of the network, and its fame is a mark of the international presence of that network.

THE FLORIN IN FLORENCE   One reason that Florence could mint gold coins in the first place was the plentiful supply of gold in the local market, and what records we have for the history of mint production of florins indicate that down to the mid-fourteenth century the market was fairly flooded with these coins: output exceeded *fl.*100,000 every semester from 1344 to 1351, then never approached this level again. A surviving balance of mint operations for six months in 1347 shows that the mint was paying out about *fl.*1,432 annually in salaries and other labor charges for the minting of both gold and silver coins, making it possibly the largest workshop in the city.[21] Florence, like Genoa, occasionally minted gold coins of other sizes, from the quarter to the double florin, but these were insignificant issues.

The only other gold money of importance issued by the government was the *fiorino di suggello* (sealed florin). These were leather purses into which were put

---

fiorentine (Florence, 1985), is a catalog of 421 imitative coins from 62 mints, most dating from the first half of the fourteenth century; maps on 34–36 show the distribution of these mints. Bernocchi's dating of the earliest coins, however, has been called into doubt by William R. Day Jr., "Early Imitations of the Gold Florin of Florence and the Imitation Florin of Chivasso in the Name of Theodore I Paleologus, Marquis of Montferrat (1306–1338)," *Numismatic Chronicle* 164 (2004): 183–99. See also the index to Peter Spufford, *Handbook of Medieval Exchange* (London, 1986).

[20] Jacques Heers, *Le livre de comptes de Giovanni Piccamiglio hommes d'affaires génois, 1456–1459* (Aix-en-Provence, 1959), 11–12; Adela Fábergas García, *La familia Spinola en el reino nazarí de Granada: Contabilidad privada de Francesco Spinola (1451–1457)* (Granada, 2004), 175.

[21] Bernocchi, *Le monete della Repubblica fiorentina* (Florence, 1976), 3:41–43.

gold florins reduced in value as a result of wear or clipping and foreign gold coins of varying values; the purses were then sealed with red wax and stamped with an official value. Florentines could request such purses to be made up with more than one florin, and hence a purse could contain any number of florins, sometimes as many as a thousand. The government offered this service through the Saggio, or public assayer's office, set up in the Mercato Nuovo, the city's banking center. The sealed florins circulated as specie at a price slightly lower, by 1–3 percent, than that of the gold coin, the difference representing what could be tolerated by the market. This practice of sealing coins in purses can be documented from the late Roman Empire on into the Byzantine and Islamic worlds; it arose in Florence toward the end of the thirteenth century, the first legislation directed to regularizing the practice being in 1294, just over a generation after the minting of the first gold florin.

Besides serving to utilize valuable coins that had lost their original purity (as the historiographical tradition has it), fiorini di suggello must also have simplified large cash transactions in the local market by obviating the need to count out a large number of coins. The practice of sealing florins in purses may in fact have arisen primarily as a practical solution to a problem in a marketplace where these highly valuable coins were circulating in great abundance and being used in large numbers for major transactions. Evidence for the use of gold coins for sizable transactions in the periods preceding and immediately following the institution of the fiorino di suggello can be found in two late thirteenth-century documents, one showing the deposits made for the Riccomanni estate in 1273–75, which ranged from *fl.*100 to *fl.*800, and one showing the activity in the current account of Filippo Cavalcanti, which includes many deposits and withdrawals of more than *fl.*100.[22] The practical use of bagged and sealed florins that did not have to be counted out can be appreciated in an entry of 1350 in the accounts of Caroccio di Lapo Alberti & Partners that records a payment of *fl.*6,840 in seven purses, three containing *fl.*1,000, one containing *fl.*1,132, and one, *fl.*2,000.[23] Yet there was always the danger that the coins in the purses did not in fact correspond to the official value, as the sons of Caroccio Alberti discovered on several occasions.[24] Over the course of the fourteenth century the greater recourse to bank transfers for effecting transactions of high value (which we shall see in chapter 6) precluded

---

[22] In both documents a distinction is made between the gold florins handled by the principal and the *lira a fiorini*, a money of account, in which the florins were registered in the accounts of the other party.

[23] Richard A. Goldthwaite and Giulio Mandich, *Studi sulla moneta fiorentina (secoli XIII–XVI)* (Florence, 1994), 151–52.

[24] Richard A. Goldthwaite, "Contabilità e monete," *Due libri mastri degli Alberti: Una grande compagnia di Calimala, 1348–1358,* ed. Richard A. Goldthwaite, Enzo Settesoldi, and Marco Spallanzani (Florence, 1995), 1:cxx.

handling of large quantities of cash, thereby reducing the usefulness of sealing coins in purses, and the government stopped doing this in the very early fifteenth century. The history of the fiorino di suggello as specie, however, remains murky. It survived as an official money of account of considerable importance for the government's fiscal policy, and we shall continue with that history in chapter 7.

The gold florin, being worth so much more than the lira, became the money used for quoting relatively high salaries, such as those of company and communal administrators, and for pricing more expensive things, from jewelry to real estate and capital investment of a company in any of the leading sectors of the economy. Moreover, despite its great value, much evidence from the fifteenth century indicates that at that time it circulated in the marketplace even among working people. In an economy where the working man had no place to put the little savings he might be able to accumulate, the gold florin, having a guaranteed intrinsic value and a steadily rising price, served a unique function as a store of value, one of the basic definitions of money. Having approximately the diameter of the five-cent piece of the euro and slightly thinner, florins were all the more useful for their miniscule size, which made it possible to carry one's savings around on his own person, whether it be the *fl.*5 found on the body of the laborer Niccolò di Luca after he fell to his death from a crane at the building site of Santo Spirito in 1496 or the *fl.*300 in a sealed bag stolen from the wool manufacturer Niccolò di Buono Busini while he was sleeping on a bench outside a house of the Peruzzi in 1407.[25] In case of need there was no problem cashing florins in at a local moneychanger for more convenient silver-based and billon coins. If the need for ready cash was only temporary, the florin could be pawned; the balances of Cerchi's local bank (discussed in chapter 6) included pawned florins among its assets, and tradesmen in nearby Prato also accepted them as pawns.[26]

Given these functions of the florin, and notwithstanding the inconvenience of its relatively high value, laborers, whose wages were quoted in soldi di piccioli, not infrequently wanted to be paid in gold. In order to have florins they were willing to wait to be paid, sometimes for several weeks, until they had built up sufficient credit on their employer's payroll account, and they were also willing to pay a fee in the form of a slightly higher exchange rate between the florin and the lira. On the huge project for the building of the Strozzi palace in the early 1490s, the paymaster regularly handed out florins on Saturday paydays even to unskilled labor-

---

[25] Richard A. Goldthwaite, *The Building of Renaissance Florence: An Economic and Social History* (Baltimore, 1980), 294; ASF, Carte strozziane, ser. 4, 564 (record book of Niccolò di Buono Busini, 1400–1411).

[26] Richard K. Marshall, *The Local Merchants of Prato: Small Entrepreneurs in the Late Medieval Economy* (Baltimore, 1999), 94.

ers. At the site of the modest construction work done on the Della Scala palace in the mid-1470s enough workers wanted to be paid in florins that the accountant found it useful to open a separate account just to record the relatively insignificant profits of about 2 percent made from the unfavorable exchange rates workers were prepared to accept in order to receive florins. Artisans were not infrequently paid in gold, sometimes in amounts equivalent to several months' earnings, and they too paid their employees in gold. In short, there is abundant evidence that in the fifteenth century the gold florin circulated widely throughout the population; notwithstanding its relatively high value with respect to the daily needs of ordinary people, it served a real function in their lives.[27]

THE DECLINE   The florin declined, however, even on its home ground, in a sense heralding the change the network underwent in the sixteenth century. In fact, the erosion and demise of the florin encapsulates a major transition from "the era of the florin" to "the age of the Fugger" and "the century of the Genoese." That transition, however, hardly marked as dramatic a change in the history of money as its inception had in 1252. Indeed, the florin simply faded away, almost imperceptibly, yielding its place to both the ducat and the scudo; it was the victim, in a sense, of its own success. The many imitations it had generated that had less gold content eventually undermined confidence in the original. Moreover, from the end of the fourteenth century governments began to mint their own gold coins of very different weights and with their own distinctive iconography and names; and as these gained circulation, the florin as a coin showed up less and less in northern Europe.

In any event, for reasons that are not altogether clear, the terms *ducat* and *scudo* came to be used as generic terms for the florin and other gold coins of equal value, even though the Florentine original never underwent debasement. The success of the former term is not easily explained, since the Venetian coin hardly circulated in the West.[28] The term *scudo*, on the other hand, rose to a competing prominence thanks to Florentine bankers themselves. At the international exchange market they

---

[27] Examples in works by me of the use of the gold florin by ordinary people, even unskilled laborers, include the following: *Building of Renaissance Florence*, 304–5; "Il sistema monetario," in Goldthwaite and Mandich, *Studi sulla moneta fiorentina*, 39–40; "Un nuovo libro di conti e la storia economica, sociale e artistica di un palazzo fiorentino del Rinascimento," *Archivio storico italiano* (hereafter *ASI*) 157 (1999): 786–87; and "An Entrepreneurial Silk Weaver in Renaissance Florence," *I Tatti Studies* 10 (2005): 94–95.

[28] According to Philip Grierson, "La moneta veneziana nell'economia mediterranea del Trecento e Quattrocento," in *La civiltà veneziana del Quattrocento* (Florence, 1957), 93–94, the many imitations of the florin that had less gold content raised doubts about the value of them all, with the result that increasingly over the fifteenth century the ducat came to be used as a model for new gold coins. But in view of the lack of imitations of the Venetian ducat, it is difficult to accept this thesis, which Grierson presented without documentation.

set up, first in Geneva and then in Lyons, they established the local écu (*scudo* in Italian), a coin of slightly less gold content than the florin, as the standard foreign money of account for exchange transactions. The other great Italian commercial cities soon fell into the orbit of Lyons and eventually began minting their own scudi—Genoa in 1508, Milan about 1520, Venice in 1528. At this point Florence could hardly hold out, and it minted its first gold scudo in 1530. The next year the new ducal government returned to minting a coin of traditional gold content but tended to call it a ducat. In 1533, however, a reform at the fairs of Lyons established the final victory of the *écu au soleil* as the international monetary standard. The reform fixed the weight of the écu at 3.08 grams of gold, about 14 percent less than that of the classic florin, and established it as the gold standard for international exchange.

Florentines themselves, rather suddenly toward the end of the fifteenth century, began to refer to their own florin of account and the coin itself as a scudo or ducat. These terms—*florin, ducat, scudo*—are often used interchangeably in Florentine documents from the early sixteenth century, and in the resulting confusion (creating no small problem also for modern researchers) the florin lost its distinct identity. Foreign influence penetrated even more deeply into the Florentine monetary system to determine the names of two new silver-based coins used in the local market that came out of monetary reforms in 1504: the *crazia,* as the new *quattrino grosso* came to be called, which took its name from the German kreutzer, and the *carlino,* so called in the mint documents, which took its name from a Neapolitan coin dating from the time of Charles of Anjou (the Florentine carlino itself underwent a name change to become the *giulio,* originally a Roman coin named after Pope Julius II). These small coins were the media of exchange essential for the functioning of the local market, and their lack of a specifically Florentine identity can perhaps be read as evidence of the contracting vision Florentines themselves had of their role as an international economic power.

During the sixteenth century gold coins came to be used less and less in international commerce. The government of the Medici dukes ceased to mint florins, or ducats, although the terms remained in use for moneys of account. It minted scudi, which had a higher price than the florin-ducat (150 as compared with 140 soldi di piccioli), and other gold coins of various denominations, but this production was directed more toward boosting the prestige of the court than toward satisfying any monetary function in the marketplace. By the 1560s and 1570s legislation recognizing the scarcity of gold permitted the payment of bills of exchange in silver money.[29] Moreover, the policy of Grand Duke Francesco (1574–87)

---

[29] *Legislazione toscana raccolta e illustrata dal dottore Lorenzo Cantini socio di varie accademie,* 32 vols. (Florence, 1802–8), 5:43–45 (1583), 7:153–54 (1574).

to fix the legal price of the gold scudo so as to countervail its upward market trend meant that these coins were undervalued locally, and as a result they tended to migrate to other markets, above all to Genoa and Spain. By the end of the century the gold output of the mint had fallen off considerably, leaving the monetary system based on a single metallic standard. The new equivalent of the gold florin was the silver *piastra,* or silver ducat, a comparatively bulky coin twice as wide as the old florin and much thicker, since, given the silver-gold ratio at the time, it weighed about ten times more.

This last, brief chapter in the history of the gold florin, often called the dollar of the Middle Ages, is one of its sad fall in prestige abroad, its loss of clear identity even at home, the compromise of standards, and finally its replacement by less precious silver. The florin lived on in its native land, but only as a ghost money, surviving, mostly thanks to nostalgia alone, as just one, and not even the most valuable, of four moneys of account (along with the scudo, the ducat, and the lira). It eventually gave up even the ghost, and today it is nothing more than a token loaded with memory that the mayor of Florence every so often presents to someone the city wants to honor. Abroad the florin was succeeded by the many progeny it had generated in those moneys given its distinguished name by other medieval governments in northern Europe, but those moneys too have died out, even in our own time, and its descendants survive today only in the Hungarian florint, probably also destined to die as a victim of the euro. The full story of these adventures of the florin—traveling abroad at the highest levels of international business and finance and inspiring imitations everywhere, while back at home in Florence being enclosed in bags, clutched as savings in the hands of working people, disembodied to become a ghost, and eventually abandoned altogether, to survive, however, another half-millennium in the progeny it spawned abroad —would make a worthy companion study to Carlo Cipolla's famous book on the lira.

Balance of Payments

The network contracted, the era of the florin came to an end, and Florence got left behind in the worldwide expansion of the European economy. However, to go on to talk about a consequent decline of the economy in general, or even of international merchant banking in particular, is to put all this into just one perspective. Unfortunately, we have no precise way of tracing the performance of the sector over time or measuring its overall place in the economy. The best we can do is to dredge through the secondary literature for some figures and to put them into a pattern for constructing an argument. And although the process is a bit like projecting cantilevers on cantilevers, when we get to the end, however precarious the position, the vision that appears is not altogether a mirage. The figures used here to play this statistical game will be of two kinds—the profits of those few firms that are well documented and what figures we have for the wool industry—and the objective is to get some idea of the relative importance of these two leading sectors of the economy.

Studies of some twenty-five firms provide data about profits for virtually every year from 1398 to 1526, usually from more than one firm, and the sample represents a fair cross section of the sector through the fifteenth century.[30] The geographic scope of these firms reaches beyond Florence and Pisa to include Naples, Rome, Venice, Milan, Avignon, Geneva, Lyons, Catalonia, and Bruges; and they range in size from the relatively modest firms of the Cambini in Rome and Florence and the Della Casa, Guadagni in Geneva, which earned somewhat more than *fl*.1,000 per year in the 1460s, to the great Medici agglomerate, which paid an average of *fl*.12,000 to *fl*.15,000 a year for more than thirty years, from 1420 to 1450, when it

---

[30] The sample consists of the following firms, listed in chronological order:

— Medici companies (all references are from Raymond de Roover, *The Rise and Decline of the Medici Bank, 1397–1494* [Cambridge, MA, 1963]). Florence, Rome, and Venice, 1398–1451; Naples, 1398–1435; Geneva, 1421–51: 47, 55, 69 (annual averages calculated). Bruges, 1439–43, 1447–50: 322–23. Milan, 1457–59: 265. Geneva, 1461–65: 289. Avignon, 1462–72: 313. Lyons, 1467–68, 1471–72: 299.

— Datini companies in Catalonia, 1400–1407, and in Florence, 1405–10: Federigo Melis, *Aspetti della vita economica medievale: Studi nell'Archivio Datini di Prato* (Siena, 1962), 203, 247–53 (annual averages calculated).

— Spinelli company in Rome, 1437–42: William Caferro, "L'attività bancaria papale e la Firenze del Rinascimento: Il caso di Tommaso Spinelli," *Società e storia*, no. 70 (1995): 728.

— Della Casa–Guadagni company in Geneva, 1451–54, 1460–64: *Il libro giallo di Ginevra della compagnia fiorentina di Antonio Della Casa e Simone Guadagni, 1453–1454*, ed. Michele Cassandro (Prato, 1976), 38.

— Cambini companies in Rome, 1452–59, 1462–65, and in Florence, 1456, 1460–68, 1470, 1473–77: Sergio Tognetti, *Il banco Cambini: Affari e mercati di una compagnia mercantile-bancaria nella Firenze del XV secolo* (Florence, 1999), 147, 150, 152 (for Rome, profits are quoted in the *fiorino di camera*, which was somewhat less in value than the Florentine florin).

— Serristori company in Florence, 1471–92, 1496–1501: Sergio Tognetti, *Da Figline a Firenze: Ascesa economica e politica della famiglia Serristori (secoli XIV–XVI)* (Florence, 2003), 129–30 (annual averages calculated).

— Strozzi companies in Naples, 1472–83, and Florence, 1472–83, 1487–89: Goldthwaite, *Private Wealth*, 61 (only Strozzi's share of profits reported); idem, "Banking in Florence," 534.

— Bartolini companies in Florence and in Lyons. Archivio Bartolini Salimbeni, Vicchio di Mugello (villa di Collina), 106 (*libro segreto*, Lyons, 1482–87), fol. 24; 225 (*libro segreto*, Lyons, 1490–92), fol. 7; 108 (*libro segreto*, Lyons, 1505–6), fol. 7; 221 (*libro segreto*, Lyons, 1535–41), fol. 4; 224 (*libro segreto*, Florence, 1482–87), fol. 27 (profits made locally from government finance are not included).

— Capponi company in Florence, 1495–1521: Goldthwaite, *Private Wealth*, 209.

— Gondi company in Florence, 1497–1503, 1511–16: ibid., 172.

— Guicciardini company in Florence, 1507–9, 1515–17: ibid., 127.

— Bartolini and Lanfredini company in Florence, 1518–26: Pierpont Morgan Library, New York, ms. 78802 (*libro segreto* of the bank at Florence of Lanfredino Lanfredini), fol. 15.

— Corsi company in Florence, 1583–87: Goldthwaite, "Banking in Florence," 485.

— Riccardi company in Pisa, 1588–93: Malanima, *I Riccardi*, 72.

consisted of from five to nine firms. In the 1460s the profits of the Medici branch in Geneva alone exceeded *fl.*10,000. At the beginning of the century the Datini companies in Florence and Catalonia together paid the partners an annual average of from *fl.*3,000 to *fl.*4,000 in profits. The annual average Tommaso Spinelli received from his company in Rome in the early 1440s amounted to almost *fl.*2,000. In the 1480s the Serristori firm in Florence and the Bartolini firm in Florence and Lyons averaged about *fl.*2,500 each, and the Strozzi firm in Naples exceeded *fl.*6,000. In the second decade of the sixteenth century the Capponi earned *fl.*2,600 and the Gondi, *fl.*4,500.

From these data one could force the conclusion that the nominal average annual earnings of a firm in the sample amounted to *fl.*2,200 (the median is *fl.*2,400). But this figure by itself means little inasmuch as the real value of the florin, as measured by its power to buy labor in the local market, increased by 87 percent over the fifteenth century (see the appendix). Thus the *fl.*1,667 the Gondi firm was earning in 1500 was equivalent to twice that in 1400, close to the profits of *fl.*3,443 of the Medici branch in Rome. And, to throw yet another figure into the equation, at any one time in the fifteenth century there were probably about a hundred firms doing business. When these odds and ends of figures are viewed, from our cantilevered position, in the context of the figures we have for the performance of the wool industry, what we see is astounding: annual *gross* sales of wool cloth ranged somewhere between *fl.*450,000 and *fl.*600,000 from the end of the fourteenth to the early sixteenth century, and of this only about 10–15 percent at the very most ended up as profits returned to the manufacturers in Florence (based on what we know from specific studies), with the average firm probably earning several hundred florins a year.[31] There is no need to force the argument with statistical rhetoric by going on to play arithmetic games with the figures, for the conclusion is startling: while we might well expect that the really big profits were to be made in international merchant banking, the total profits from the sector were probably greater than those earned by the textile industries. What we do not know is how much of those profits came from the sale of

[31] For estimates of total output of the wool industry, see table 4.1. Figures for profits of wool companies can be found in Federigo Melis, "La formazione dei costi nell'industria laniera alla fine del Trecento," in *Industria e commercio nella Toscana medievale*, ed. Bruno Dini (Florence, 1989), 253, 256, 261 (1390s); Goldthwaite, *Private Wealth*, 41 (1398–1406); de Roover, *Medici Bank*, 173, 175 (1402–29, 1435–50); Florence Edler, *Glossary of Medieval Terms of Business: Italian Series, 1200–1600* (Cambridge, MA, 1934), 340, 341 (1440–67); Raymond de Roover, "A Florentine Firm of Cloth Manufacturers: Management and Organization of a Sixteenth-Century Business," in *Business, Banking, and Economic Thought in Late Medieval and Early Modern Europe: Selected Studies of Raymond de Roover*, ed. Julius Kirshner (Chicago, 1974), 91 (1531–34), reprinted from *Speculum* 16 (1941); and Richard A. Goldthwaite, "The Florentine Wool Industry in the Late Sixteenth Century: A Case Study," *Journal of European Economic History* 32 (2003): 529, 553 (1580s).

the products of the local textile industry, from trade in other goods, and from financial operations.

Hardly any comparable figures can be found, on the basis of current research, for the later sixteenth century, hence we cannot project yet another cantilever to see what happened in this period of contraction. Those firms we know something about, however, had very high annual earnings: the Bartolini company in Lyons earned *fl.*2,690 from 1535 to 1541, the Corsi company in Florence earned *fl.*3,149 from 1583 to 1587, and the Riccardi company in Pisa, *fl.*2,881 from 1588 to 1593. All three were as profitable as many in our sample from a century earlier. Moreover, the profits of the Corsi bank amounted to eight times what the Corsi were earning (*fl.*391) from their wool company, which had as big an output as any, over the same years.

Looking back over the history of the network in an attempt to assess its overall performance, the most significant index we can use in the final analysis is the balance of payments. The principal strength of the network derived from its function as a mechanism for shifting funds from places with positive trade balances to places with trade imbalances, but at the end of the day something got skimmed off to be sent home to Florence in the form of specie or bullion, for there was little that Florentines wanted to buy abroad, even in their consumption of luxury goods. Already by the mid-thirteenth century the city had enough gold to mint the florin in such quantities that within a decade the coin was circulating over a wide territory well beyond Tuscany. The expansion of industry, commerce, and banking over the following century resulted in the accumulation of enormous profits, much of which must have come home in the form of gold and silver. In a four-year period in the middle of the fourteenth century, from 1347 to 1351, notwithstanding the famed bankruptcies a few years earlier, the mint issued 865,000 gold florins.

How gold flowed back into the city is not well documented. Unfortunately, shipments of money to the city got recorded only in the accounts of the merchants who brought their profits home in this material form, and it is not until the fifteenth century that these documents exist in such quantity as to yield up impressive evidence of the silver and gold that poured into the city. At this time the chief nodes for the balancing of international accounts through shipment of specie for the Italians in general and the Florentines in particular were the Low Countries, Catalonia, and the Levant. The Low Countries had an unfavorable balance with Italy but a favorable balance with Catalonia, so the Florentines could draw on credits in Catalonia to remit directly to Florence, but since these were not sufficient to balance accounts in the Low Countries, they remitted from the north in cash. The balance with the Levant also grew increasingly favorable as a result of, on the one hand, import substitution in the Italian economy and reduced demand for products from the region and, on the other, increased demand for European cloth, especially after the establishment of the Ottoman Empire in Constantinople. Florentines brought a large portion of these profits home in specie or bullion. Finally, the expansion of the market for silks into Germany and eastern Europe in the sixteenth century further increased the city's favorable balance of payments.

Money came into Florence from throughout the network. A letter sent by the Signoria to its ambassadors in Rome in 1406 emphasizes the importance of Florentine merchants in Ragusa for the importation of silver to Florence.[32] In 1428–30 the Avignon firm of Raimondo Mannelli and Lorenzo Tacchini shipped gold to Florence as well as to Milan and Venice.[33] In the late 1430s the Geneva agent of the silk producer Andrea Banchi sent home as much as two-thirds of the proceeds from sales in specie.[34] In one year, 1453–54, Antonio Della Casa, Simone Guadagni & Partners, also in Geneva, shipped *sc.*5,414 in various gold coins to Florence.[35] In an accomandita contract made in 1462 for the sale of wool cloth in Constantinople, Battista di Taccino Bizzini strictly limited the goods his agent was to buy with the proceeds, specifying a preference for cash (see chapter 2). In another accomandita contract made the following year for trade in Constantinople, Bernardo Banchi and Piero Segni similarly restricted their agent, who in fact sent back *fl.*1,500 in cash, almost the full amount realized from sales.[36] The galley fleet returning from England and Spain in 1466 carried *du.*40,000 in gold; and at least twice galleys returning from the Levant arrived with money taken on in Sicily, *du.*12,000 in 1467 and *du.*40,000 in 1469.[37] From 1473 to 1477 the firm of Filippo Strozzi in Naples sent about one shipment of cash a month, averaging about *fl.*4,000 a year.[38] In 1484 the king of France directed a decree against Italian bankers in Lyons who allegedly carried specie out of the realm.[39]

---

[32] The letter is quoted in Filippo Naitana, "I beni dei Pazzi all'indomani della congiura: Un 'passaporto' per la storia delle relazioni fra Firenze e Ragusa nel tardo Medioevo," *Quaderni medievali* 47 (1999): 53.

[33] Mario Del Treppo, *I mercanti catalani e l'espansione della corona aragonese nel secolo XV* (Naples, 1968), 197–98, 206–7, 300–301.

[34] Florence Edler de Roover, "Andrea Banchi, Florentine Silk Manufacturer and Merchant in the Fifteenth Century," *Studies in Medieval and Renaissance History* 3 (1966): 267.

[35] Cassandro, *Libro giallo di Ginevra*, fols. 266, 282, 380, 660.

[36] Goldthwaite, *Building of Renaissance Florence*, 55. See also Hidetoshi Hoshino and Maureen Fennell Mazzaoui, "Ottoman Markets for Florentine Woolen Cloth in the Late Fifteenth Century," *International Journal of Turkish Studies* 3 (1985–86): 21.

[37] Michael E. Mallet, *The Florentine Galleys in the Fifteenth Century* (Oxford, 1967), 119–20, 141.

[38] Goldthwaite, *Building of Renaissance Florence*, 54.

[39] De Roover, *Medici Bank*, 307.

The accounts and correspondence of the Medici company alone document many shipments of gold specie and bullion spanning the entire period from the 1430s to the 1480s, most of them coming from Bruges and Geneva but also one from North Africa.[40] From 1483 to 1486 Andrea di Leonardo Bartolini in Milan, formerly an agent of the Medici bank there and probably still acting on the Medici's behalf to clear up matters after the bank closed in 1478, sent home twenty-eight shipments of coins, mostly gold ducats, for a total of *fl.*11,143, about half going to the Medici bank and half to his brother's bank, and the cash account in his ledger would indicate that most of the specie he received in those years came from Lorenzo Spinelli & Partners in Lyons and from Mauro Arrighetti in Venice.[41]

A favorable balance was virtually a structural feature of the silk trade Florentines promoted in central Europe in the early sixteenth century, and many brought their profits back in the form of bullion, as we shall see. Imports from the Levant were particularly notable from the end of the fifteenth century through the first few decades of the next. Benedetto Dei, writing about 1470, boasted about the gold coins of Genoa, Venice, and Hungary that Florentines imported from the "Gran Turcho." Numerous accounts from the 1520s document the importation of gold and silver for the settlement of favorable balances in the Ottoman Empire.[42] In 1527 at least one shipment of thousands of gold coins the government sent to the Papal States to pay troops in the field consisted of Turkish ducats, undoubtedly turned into the mint by merchants returning from the Levant.[43] When Süleyman the Magnificent threatened to block the export of gold, the Florentines feared that such a move would end their export trade in silk and wool cloth to the East.

The proposition that Florence had a favorable balance of payments resulting in the inflow of large quantities of specie and bullion does not depend solely on

[40] Ibid., 123, 237, 271, 284–85, 287, 288–89, 320, 459n82, 461n5.

[41] Archivio Bartolini Salimbeni, Vicchio di Mugello (villa di Collina), 208 (ledger of Andrea Bartolini in Milan, 1483–86).

[42] To the references in Goldthwaite, *Building of Renaissance Florence*, 55, can be added Hidestoshi Hoshino, "Alcuni aspetti del commercio dei panni fiorentini nell'impero ottomano ai primi del '500," reprinted in Hoshino, *Industria tessile e commercio internazionale*, 131; and two articles by Angela Orlandi: "Vestire l'Islam alla fiorentina e importare oro: Luigi di Carlo da Castelfiorentino in Oriente," in *La storia e l'economia: Miscellanea di studi in onore di Giorgio Mori* (Varese, 2003), 1:541–50, and "Oro e monete da Costantinopoli a Firenze in alcuni documenti toscani (secoli XV–XVI)," in *Europe's Economic Relations with the Islamic World, 13th–18th Centuries,* ed. Simonetta Cavaciocchi (Florence, 2007), 981–1004. See also, for silver from Germany, Hermann Kellenbenz, "Mercanti tedeschi in Toscana nel Cinquecento," in *Studi di storia economica toscana nel Medioevo e nel Rinascimento in memoria di Federigo Melis* (Pisa, 1987), 203–29; for gold and other monetary metals from Hungary, Bruno Dini, "L'economia fiorentina e l'Europa centro-orientale nelle fonti toscane," in his *Saggi su una economia-mondo: Firenze e l'Italia fra Mediterraneo ed Europa (secc. XIII–XVI)* (Pisa, 1995), 279, 285–86; for gold from Poland, Henryk Samsonwicz, "Relations commerciales Polono-Italiennes dans le bas Moyen Âge," in *Studi in memoria di Federigo Melis* (Naples, 1978), 2:299–301.

[43] Maurizio Arfaioli, *The Black Bands of Giovanni: Infantry and Diplomacy during the Italian Wars (1526–1528)* (Pisa, 2005), 80.

this scattered evidence. The presence of gold in the local market in the form of a coin—the florin—that circulated widely throughout the society, even in the hands of ordinary working people, has already been remarked. In addition to the documentary evidence for the presence of gold in the local market, there is, finally, the argument of the logic of the Florentine economic system itself. The economy was largely self-sufficient for ordinary necessities, and its growth and development sprung from an industrial foundation with two major sectors whose performance impinged directly on the trade balance: first, cloth industries geared to export that brought profits home, and second, an artisan sector capable of meeting the demand for luxury goods generated by those profits in such a way as to preclude recourse to imports.

The contraction of the network abroad, therefore, is not the whole story of what happened to the economy in the sixteenth century. As we shall see, the cloth industries were still going strong, probably producing at an even higher level than ever, and private wealth, and not just at the upper rungs, rose to by far its highest level. The international banking sector, especially the involvement of banks in government finance, also assured the city a favorable balance of payments inasmuch as this activity cost the home economy nothing beyond partners' equity but yielded enormous profits. Judging from the correspondence of the Castilian merchant Simon Ruiz from 1577 to 1585, at the end of the sixteenth century Florence still had a favorable balance: although the city had an unfavorable balance with Spain as a result of wool imports, Ruiz's agent in Florence comments on the importation of silver and the endemic abundance of money *(larghezza)* in the local exchange market.[44] This market at Florence, in fact, was one of the principal places in Italy where the Genoese, seeking to make payments in the north for the Spanish king, sought bills to draw on the credits Italians in general were still accumulating in places such as Lyons, Antwerp, and various German cities, an operation that depended on the favorable balance that Italians in general, and Florentines in particular, had in the north.[45]

Structures: Business Organization

Raymond de Roover coined the phrase *commercial revolution* some thirty years before Roberto Lopez appropriated the term as a general rubric to cover the

[44] Felipe Ruiz Martín, *Lettres marchandes échangées entre Florence et Medina del Campo* (Paris, 1965), cxxxi–cxxxii. Cf. Carlo M. Cipolla, "Argento spagnolo e monetazione fiorentina nel Cinquecento," in *Aspetti della vita economica medievale* (Florence, 1985), 482.

[45] Fernand Braudel saw this as a sign of the continuing prosperity of Italy. See "L'Italia fuori d'Italia: Due secoli e tre Italie," in the Einaudi *Storia d'Italia*, ed. Ruggiero Romano and Corrado Vivanti, vol. 2, *Dalla caduta dell'Impero romano al secolo XVIII*, pt. 2 (Turin, 1974), 2164.

initial, medieval period in the economic growth of the West, a usage that has gained wide acceptance among historians. For de Roover, however, the term did not have such a broad application; he had in mind only the specific development of a new way of doing business that evolved during the thirteenth century with the emergence of the sedentary mercantile firm. As he wrote:

> By a commercial revolution I understand a complete or drastic change in the meth-
> ods of doing business or in the organization of business enterprise just as an indus-
> trial revolution means a complete change in the methods of production, for ex-
> ample, the introduction of power-driven machinery. The commercial revolution
> marks the beginning of mercantile or commercial capitalism, while the industrial
> revolution marks the end of it.[46]

The history of business leading up to this revolution is written on the basis of no-tarial documents in Genoa, Lucca, Venice, and a few other places. For lack of such documents, Florence does not have a prominent role in the story. Beginning in the fourteenth century, however, the growth of the documentary record for Florence far outpaces that for any other place, eventually, but still in the period examined here, reaching an overwhelming, even unmanageable abundance; and most of this material was generated by sedentary firms. At this point, precisely at the moment of the full affirmation of the sedentary firm, the story takes a definite Florentine turn. If Florentines did not initiate the revolution, they carried it forward, and the documentary trail they left behind has assured them a dominant role in discus-sions of the refinement of business organization and practices that came with the further growth and development of commercial capitalism in late medieval Italy.

The Firm

PARTNERSHIPS   Florentines conducted their business activities as a social enterprise organized by *compagni* and called a *compagnia,* here translated as "partners" and "partnership" to avoid any confusion with the modern term *com-pany.* The partnership represented the final stage in the evolution of the business organization of Florentine enterprise abroad. We have no specific information about the historical process by which it emerged. The earliest notarial formulary, dating from the mid-thirteenth century, contains nothing about company con-tracts (and little about business activity in general). In the early years of the com-mercial revolution Florentines, like other merchants, probably engaged in

---

[46] Raymond de Roover, "The Commercial Revolution of the Thirteenth Century," in *Enterprise and Secular Change: Readings in Economic History,* ed. Frederic Lane and Jelle Riemersma (Home-wood, IL, 1953), 80, reprinted from *Bulletin of the Business Historical Society* 16 (1942).

single-venture enterprises, going off on their own or on a *commenda* contract with a sleeping partner who provided some capital but remained at home. In the course of time they advanced to a sedentary organization that had a fixed base at home and operated through partners, employees, or agents abroad.

By the early fourteenth century, when we have information about the internal organization of firms derived from either surviving contracts or accounts, the partnership was a fully evolved institution. Men joining together as compagni drew up articles of association according to which they agreed to contribute capital toward a business venture that was to last usually from three to five years. Many of these agreements survive from the later fourteenth century on, and they resemble one another in their content, although they do not follow a standard model. They specify each partner's contribution to the capital and how his share of the profits was to be determined; they indicate the name of the firm, its duration, its place of business, and its activity in generic terms; they designate the partner who has management authority; they obligate the partners not to engage in any other business during the period of the partnership; and they forbid withdrawal of capital before the termination of the partnership. The partnership agreement might specify that a small portion of the profits, perhaps 1–2 percent, go to charity *(i poveri di Dio)*, and where such a provision was not written into the contract, firms almost always made such a donation before profits were distributed. Given the legal tradition, it was taken for granted that partners were subject to unlimited liability with respect to the affairs of the firm, and this generally went unstated in the articles of association. The partnership contract, however, was a private instrument, not a notarized document. The abandonment of the notary and the consequent confidence in such a private contract indicate that certain legal principles and institutions were in place by the early fourteenth century; they are significant benchmarks in the evolution of business practice.[47] Each firm had its own merchant's mark, a distinctive logo used to mark account books, correspondence, and shipments of merchandise, but these are not always indicated in the articles of association. Contracts might, of course, vary slightly in all of these respects, but all of the contracts were limited to formal organizational matters. It is rare to find one that goes into any detail about the specific business activity of the firm.

---

[47] On the variety of arrangements set out in partnership contracts, see the following by Armand Sapori: *Una compagnia di Calimala ai primi del Trecento* (Florence, 1932), 34–40; "La banca Medici," in Sapori, *Studi di storia economica: Secoli XIII, XIV, XV,* 3 vols. (Florence, 1955–67), 2:1023ff.; "Una compagnia di prestatori fiorentini ad Avignone nella prima metà del Trecento," ibid., 3:103–6, 121–33. And see de Roover, *Medici Bank,* 77–86; and idem, "The Story of the Alberti Company of Florence, 1308–1348, as Revealed in Its Account Books," in Kirshner, *Business, Banking, and Economic Thought,* 59–64, reprinted from *Business History Review* 32 (1958).

The capital that partners needed to go into business was primarily start-up capital to make initial investments of a commercial or financial nature and to provide liquidity during the ensuing operations, which could last for months. They had no need for fixed capital, neither property nor equipment. The head office of the firm was presumably located in the residence of the principal investor (but we have hardly any precise information on this subject), and branch offices and warehouses were rented. Once up and going, the firm had several ways to increase its stock of capital beyond the primary capital invested by the partners, the distinction being between, respectively, the *sopraccorpo* and the *corpo*, in the terminology of the time. Partners could commit further capital on specific terms, and they often left some of the profits in the firm on the renewal of the articles of association. Moreover, firms accepted time deposits from outsiders. As we shall see, deposits from foreigners were more significant than those from fellow citizens at home in Florence and could easily amount to much more than partners' equity. Finally, once in operation, the firm had trade credit on its books from its numerous transactions, and given the Florentines' mastery of accounting and their ability to shift credits and debits, this too could increase the firm's assets under management. In short, a firm had disposable capital that went well beyond partners' equity. The size of a firm's primary capital, or corpo, as specified in its articles of association, was determined by the liquidity needed to get it up and running and hence could be more an indicator of the partners' ambitions from the beginning than an index to the eventual scale of its operations.

With the capital of its corpo, a long duration, and only a general mandate about its enterprise, the firm could engage in a variety of activities and count on a sustained commitment. Furthermore, the possibility of both extending the contract by renewal and increasing its stock of capital greatly enlarged the parameters for planning and organizing activities as well as for raising the scale of operations. The firm, in short, had the maximum latitude for taking advantage of any business opportunity that arose in the market where it did business, whether a commercial deal or a financial service, whether a short- or long-term trading venture involving a bulky, inexpensive item or a luxury good, whether a small individual loan, an international transfer, or a major service for the local government. The firm thus offered the entrepreneur infinitely greater flexibility than the kind of single-venture arrangements typically used by merchants of port cities who engaged in maritime commerce tied to specific sailing enterprises; it represented a step forward from speculation to planning, from a venture to a sedentary enterprise. The partnership was the basic business unit within the organizational structure of the Florentine commercial and banking network abroad.

For the most part, articles of association undergo little change in substance over the entire period covered by this book. The only formal innovation of any consequence was the accomandita, a contract enabled by legislation promulgated by the commune in 1408 that allowed outsiders to invest in a partnership and share profits on the same terms as the other partners, without, however, risking anything beyond their investment. In other words, these investors were not subject to the personal unlimited liability characteristic of the classic partnership contract. Recognizing the innovative nature of this arrangement, the legislation called for the keeping of books—still extant—just for the registration of these investments (which, as we shall see, could be made in any partnership, not just those of merchant-banking firms). These investors were silent partners in the sense that their investments were really deposits fixed for the duration of the partnership and paying a rate of return determined by their share in the capital. After the mid-fifteenth century, however, entrepreneurs themselves began using this instrument to set up enterprises in which their liability was limited. This use of the instrument grew to the point that in the later sixteenth century new statutes of the Mercanzia, the merchant court, recognized the distinction between deposits and partnerships *in accomandita*. Some of the firms organized to sell cloth abroad were of the kind in which the investor, a wool or silk producer, consigned cloth to a traveling partner, who managed sales, but only the former had limited liability in the operation.

The instrument, however, was not used to amass capital beyond that of one investor, and it was not used very frequently. From the late fifteenth century to the 1530s fewer than six such contracts, on the average, were registered annually, and the annual total investment was less then *fl.*8,000. Toward the end of the sixteenth century, however, the capital channeled through this investment instrument approached an annual average of *fl.*100,000, and during the seventeenth century it amounted to between *fl.*200,000 and *fl.*300,000. Whether this increase represented economic expansion or the emergence of a *rentier* mentality on the part of investors seeking protection against risks in a time of contraction remains a moot point inasmuch as the registers of contracts have never been exhaustively studied. Much of this investment, however, was directed to activities within Florence, not to international commerce and banking. In any event, Florence seems to have been far ahead of the other Italian centers in devising this kind of limited-liability contract, although the instrument never realized its potential for evolving into something like a joint-stock company, at least not during the period surveyed here.[48]

[48] On the evolution of the accomandita see Federigo Melis, "Le società commerciali a Firenze dalla seconda metà del XIV al XVI secolo," in *L'azienda nel Medioevo*, ed. Marco Spallanzani (Florence, 1991), 170–78. Some data from the registers of contracts have been published by Dini, in "L'economia fiorentina e l'Europa centro-orientale," 207–12 (for the late fifteenth and early sixteenth

MORPHOLOGY OF THE FIRM   The partnership organization emerged as a way for sedentary merchants to amass working capital, and since liability of partners was unlimited, it is hardly surprising that the first documented firms, dating from the later thirteenth century, were largely family affairs, representing a pooling of capital by close relatives (not, however, a part of an undivided family patrimony). This was a period, after all, when the commune lacked a strong central authority and leading families organized themselves as a large corporate group, or *consorteria*, that assumed certain political, juridical, and policing authority for their own protection. Judging from the surnames of partners, most of these early firms eventually opened up to outsiders, although it may be that, as in contemporary Lucca, these other men were in fact relatives by marriage.[49] In any event, the configuration of partners changed with each renewal, usually every three to five years. In 1263 the Bardi firm consisted only of family members, in the sense that it was a single cognate group, but in 1299, 6 out of 11 partners are identified as Bardi, and in 1310, 10 out of 15 are so identified. For the Acciaiuoli firm the numbers were 4 out of 10 in 1289 and 7 out of 19 in 1312. The number of partners in the Peruzzi firm fluctuated from 17 to 22 over the years 1300 to 1343, but usually only 8 or 9 of these were members of the family, rarely constituting a majority. The Macci firm, however, still had 11 family members out of its 13 partners in 1321, and the Alberti del Giudice firm seems never to have taken in outsiders. One is struck by how many partners belonged to these early firms. Some were larger than those just mentioned: the Scali had 25 partners at the time of its failure in 1326, and the Spini, with 37 partners about 1300, was the largest on record.[50]

Apart from the capital partners contributed, firms needed reliable representatives in the many places where they operated abroad in addition to the salaried staff at home. The larger firms had branches throughout the entire network, ex-

---

centuries); by Carmona, in "Aspects du capitalisme toscan," 81–108 (for the later sixteenth century); and by Da Silva, in *Banque et crédit*, 97–109 (for the seventeenth century). Paolo Malanima, *La decadenza di un'economia cittadina: L'industria di Firenze nei secoli XVI–XVIII* (Bologna, 1982), 130–35, interprets the seventeenth-century data as a sign of conservative investment habits. For a comment on the instrument elsewhere, see Renato Ago, "Politica economica e credito nella Roma del Seicento," in *La Corte di Roma tra Cinque e Seicento: "Teatro" della politica europea*, ed. Gianvittorio Signorotto and Maria Antonietta Visceglia (Rome, 1998), 244. Tognetti, *Il banco Cambini*, 238, cites a 1460 accomandita through which two firms acting jointly, one in Barcelona and the other in Rome, made an investment with an individual merchant for an enterprise in Valencia.

[49] Thomas W. Blomquist, "La famiglia e gli affari: Le compagnie internazionali lucchesi al tempo di Castruccio Castracani," *Actum Luce* 13–14 (1984–85): 145–55, reprinted in Blomquist, *Merchant Families*.

[50] Much of the data on these early firms, here and in what follows, comes from Robert Davidsohn, *Forschungen zur Geschichte von Florenz*, vol. 3 (Berlin, 1901); Armando Sapori, "Il commercio internazionale nel Medioevo," in *Studi*, 1:495–533; and idem, "Storia interna della compagnia mercantile dei Peruzzi," ibid., 2:653–94.

tending from Bruges, London, and Paris in northern Europe to the eastern Mediterranean. At its height the Peruzzi had sixteen branches, and the Bardi, over a period of thirty-five years, from 1310 to 1345, had branches in twenty-five places and paid a total of 346 salaried employees. Federigo Melis, putting together all the evidence for the total time worked by all the employees and partners of these two firms, came up with what he called an "intensity index," a measure for the average size of the employment roster of these firms. On the basis of this index he estimated that, between employees and partners, the Bardi firm employed 96 men annually over thirty-five years and the Peruzzi, 85 men over eight years.[51] In the proceedings following its bankruptcy in 1343 the Acciaiuoli firm produced an inventory of no fewer than 1,501 account books kept in twenty different places, where it employed a total of 92 people.[52]

Presumably the slow infusion of outsiders affected the family nature of the partnership as the renewal process extended into several generations, but the reduced presence of family members may instead have resulted from a weakening of family ties over successive generations during a period that saw the strengthening of communal government and the consequent disintegration of the consorteria. The Peruzzi firm extended for five generations, during which time it went through seven documented renewals. In the 1335 renewal, the twelve partners who were Peruzzi represented the third, fourth, and fifth generations, all stemming from two sons of a common ancestor. However, one of these men from the third generation, Giotto di Arnoldo d'Amideo, had been a partner for the preceding thirty-five years, since 1300, and his continuing presence as a senior family member may have served as a cohesive force. The test would have come with his death in 1336, but at this point the firm was headed into bankruptcy and so on to its demise. The five partners of the Covoni firm in 1336 were all first cousins, sons of three brothers; in 1367, six of the nine partners were Covoni—four sons of three of the original cousins and two brothers whose grandfather was a brother of the others' great grandfather—and three were outsiders. The last documented firm of this kind, that of Carlo di Strozza Strozzi, had sixteen partners in 1369, eleven of whom were Strozzi representing only two generations but including cousins to the second and third degree—Carlo's three sons, one brother, two cousins, four sons of two cousins, and one son of a cousin of Carlo's father's.[53]

[51] Melis, *Aspetti*, 302.

[52] Hidetoshi Hoshino, "Nuovi documenti sulla compagnia degli Acciaiuoli nel Trecento," in *Industria tessile e commercio internazionale*, 83–97, reprinted from the *Annuario* of the Istituto Giapponese di Cultura in Roma 18 (1982–83).

[53] Armando Sapori, "La compagnia dei Covoni e il suo libro giallo: Per la storia delle compagnie mercantili bancarie medievali; Ragioni di una scelta," in *Libro giallo della compagnia dei Covoni*, ed. Sapori (Milan, 1970), xiii–xviii; Marco Spallanzani, "Una grande azienda fiorentina del Trecento: Carlo Strozzi e compagni," *Ricerche storiche* 8 (1978): 417–36.

One must be cautious about transferring to these corporate firms the familial rivalries that characterized the consorteria in the political life of the commune. Their cooperation with one another in conducting business abroad was at the foundation of the network, and often the large firms, such as those of the Bardi, the Peruzzi, and the Acciaiuoli, worked together in handling financial arrangements with the governments they had to deal with, whatever their politics were back home in Florence. And who knows what personal ties may have bound together men working in different firms. For example, the chronicler Giovanni Villani was a partner and one brother was both a partner and a factor in the Buonaccorsi firm, while another brother was a partner and a fourth brother a factor in the Peruzzi firm.

The historiographical tradition has emphasized the disappearance, about the mid-fourteenth century, of these large, what we might call corporate familial, partnerships. Firms we know about from this time on had fewer partners, often only two or three, and a more circumscribed scope, many limiting their operation to one place abroad. If an investor in one firm wanted to expand his business interest to other places, he set up a new firm with different partners, complete with its own articles of association, its own name, and its own set of books. Thus a major merchant-banker worked through a business structure that consisted of several autonomous partnerships held together only by his investment in them all. We might call such a structure, in contrast to the early corporate partnership, a partnership agglomerate.[54] In the earlier period many men operating on a smaller scale than the extensive range of the famous companies may in fact have organized their business in this way, but the documentary evidence for them does not appear until about the mid-fourteenth century. In the later 1330s the aforementioned Covoni company in Florence, a family partnership of cousins (five sons of three brothers) that engaged primarily in export-import trade with Padua, sent partners to Padua, where, however, they worked through a second company, set up there with native Paduans.[55] In the 1360s Giovacchino di Gucciarello Pinciardi worked through three separate partnerships organized around the traffic in woad from his native city, Borgo Sansepolcro: a dye shop in Florence, a carrier service to transport woad to Florence and wool cloth to Sansepolcro, and an enterprise in Sansepolcro that included both a local wool-producing shop and a ware-

[54] Throughout his work Federigo Melis called this new structural type a "system of businesses" (*sistema d'aziende*).

[55] Giulio Mandich, "Per una ricostruzione delle operazioni mercantili e bancarie della compagnia Covoni," in Sapori, *Libro giallo della compagnia dei Covoni*, cxiv–cxvii. Mandich has also uncovered another contemporary company, Duccio di Banchello, Banco Bencivenni & Partners, which may have had separate but interlocking companies in Venice, Mantua, and Bruges. See idem, "Una compagnia fiorentina a Venezia nel quarto decennio del secolo XIV (un libro di conti)," *Rivista storica italiana* 96 (1984): 131.

house in Urbino for the regional distribution of cloth.[56] Many such partnership agglomerates have been documented in Florence as well as in Pisa and Lucca at the end of the fourteenth century, the best known of these being that of Francesco Datini. In 1398, when he was at his most extended, his portfolio of partnership investments consisted of a wool shop and a dye house in Prato, a company in Avignon, a local bank in Florence, and a commercial company in Florence, his principal investment, which in turn invested in separate companies in Pisa, Genoa, and Catalonia, the latter in turn having branches in Barcelona, Valencia, and Majorca.[57]

For the fifteenth century it is not difficult to find instances of a partnership that, like Datini's company in Florence, itself became a partner in another company, an arrangement that Raymond de Roover called a "holding operation." Two notable examples of an extensive partnership agglomerate constructed through this investment mechanism are the Medici and Capponi companies. In 1451 Cosimo de' Medici, his brother, a cousin, and Giovanni d'Amerigo Benci had a partnership set up as a local bank that invested most of its capital with other individual investors in no fewer than nine separate partnerships—a silk shop, two wool shops, and six companies abroad, at Pisa, Venice, Geneva, Avignon, Bruges, and London.[58] In 1485 five sons of Gino di Neri Capponi worked through a more complex three-tier structure. The five brothers invested *fl.*42,000 in a parent company, each with a different quota, that operated an alum mine at Campiglia, engaged in banking in Florence, and invested in two separate companies with an outsider, Bartolomeo Buondelmonti. One of these latter companies, along with two other partners, operated in Lyons but invested some of its capital in three companies with yet other partners—a silk company, a firm at the court of the king of France, and a firm at Avignon. The second subsidiary company operated in Florence and invested some of its capital in a wool company, a firm at Pisa, and another in Rome. The Capponi, in short, personally invested only in the parent company, but through it they extended their interest through two subsidiary firms to six other firms, eight firms in all located in five places abroad.[59] In 1455 the silk manufacturer Andrea Banchi organized a firm for operations at

[56] Giuliano Pinto, "Giovacchino Pinciardi da Borgo San Sepolcro, mercante e tintore di guado nella Firenze del Trecento," in *La Toscane et les Toscans autour de la Renaissance: Cadres de vie, société, croyances; Mélanges offerts à Charles-M. de La Roncière* (Aix-en-Provence, 1999), 99–100.

[57] Federigo Melis, *Note di storia della banca pisana nel Trecento* (Pisa, 1955), reprinted in *La banca pisana e le origini della banca moderna,* ed. Marco Spallanzani (Florence, 1987), 212–22; idem, *Aspetti,* pt. 3 (for Datini's system).

[58] De Roover, *Medici Bank,* 66–67 (tables with all the details). On 367–68 de Roover notes a project of about 1482 for reorganizing the Medici company in a three-tier holding structure, which, however, was not realized.

[59] Biblioteca Nazionale di Firenze, Capponi, Libri di commercio 2, fols. 126v–129r.

L'Aquila in which both he personally and his silk company were separate partners along with the agent on the scene.[60]

By using one partnership to invest in another, the original investors clearly increased the capital they controlled, but they hardly exploited this possibility. The Medici thereby extended their *fl.*54,000 share of the capital in their parent company to control *fl.*90,687, the total capital invested by the sixteen other investors in the agglomerate of ten partnerships, but this represented only *fl.*18,687 beyond the *fl.*72,000 capital of the parent company. Likewise, Datini's principal commercial company, to which he contributed half of the capital of *fl.*12,000, drew in no more than *fl.*3,000 at the most from the partners in the three other companies it set up. In short, the holding company, if we can use the anachronistic term found in so much of the secondary literature, was of the mixed, not the pure, kind, serving more as an instrument of flexibility than as a device to enlarge the stock of capital it controlled. Moreover, the parent firm was never merely an investment mechanism; it functioned as a commercial or banking firm in its own right.

Ties of the extended family counted for much less in these later companies. The early fourteenth-century firms mentioned above—Acciaiuoli, Alberti, Bardi, Covoni, Peruzzi, Strozzi—lasted through several generations, first among brothers, then among cousins as partners, but by the fifteenth century it is difficult to come up with a company of this nature. The practice of partible inheritance among sons assured the individual rather than familial ownership of private wealth, and after the death of a father, brothers showed little inclination to share investments. "We separate ourselves," as the four sons of Francesco Cambini agreed in 1413, "each from the others, and the others from each."[61] These later Florentine firms, organized as a partnership that underwent periodic reorganization, were hence subject to fluid economic ties among relatives. Most consisted of only several partners, often not relatives, and after the death of a principal partner, his sons tended to go their own ways, if they had not already done so on entering their maturity. Those companies whose family nature we know something about—Cambini, Capponi, Corsi, Della Casa, Gondi, Guicciardini, Martelli, Medici, Riccardi, Salviati, Serristori, Strozzi—continued through successive reorganizations from father to sons and perhaps to the next generation as long as the principal was alive, but few of them reached a third generation with cousins included among the partners without a grandfather holding them together. As a social institution the family partnership at its most expansive thus

---

[60] Edler de Roover, "Andrea Banchi," 232–33.
[61] Tognetti, *Il banco Cambini,* 28.

follows the cycle of what F. W. Kent calls the household of "the grand family." The Venetian *fraterna,* an agreement by which brothers kept their patrimonies intact for business purposes without a formal partnership organization, was almost unknown in Florence, as was the similar family business system of Genoa consisting of what Edoardo Grendi called "non-closed" *(non chiuse)* companies inasmuch as they had no defined duration and their capital was not clearly distinct from family patrimonies.[62]

There also appear to have been what we might call clusters of family firms, that is, different firms carrying the same surname but not bound together into a single agglomerate. The most notable example by far is that involving various members of the so-called *antichi* branch of the Alberti family. At the end of the fourteenth century Alberti firms were to be found throughout the Florentine network, at London, Bruges, Paris, Montpellier, Avignon, Barcelona, Valencia, Venice, Bologna, Pisa, Rome, Palermo, and Rhodes, and in some places there appear to have been two Alberti companies active at the same time. Twenty-one different Alberti active in these firms, some as agents in yet many other places, show up in Datini's correspondence, and they include cousins to the second and third degree. No one, however, has sorted out the ownership of these numerous firms and the relationships between partners; hence the composite picture remains confused. They were certainly not organized in anything like the corporate structure of the earlier firms, and they seem to have lacked the centrality of a partnership agglomerate. The cluster had thinned out considerable by the 1430s, when it consisted of two firms in both Bruges and London, one in Rome, and one at the papal court in Basel, and relationships between partners did not extend beyond cousins. Although nominally these firms had distinct identities, ownership overlapped; and the fact that they all came down together in bankruptcy in 1439 indicates that the cluster had some kind of underlying family structure. Nevertheless, the litigation among family members in the years preceding formal bankruptcy proceedings would indicate that by this time kinship bonds were strained to the breaking point.[63]

The Ricci constitute another family cluster of firms in the second half of the fourteenth century, but even less is known about them.[64] At midcentury they were

[62] Edoardo Grendi, "Associazioni familiari e associazioni d'affari: I Balbi a Genoa tra Cinquecento e Seicento," *Quaderni storici* 31 (1996): 23–39. The Venetian fraterna is described by Frederic C. Lane in "Family Partnerships and Joint Ventures," in *Venice and History: The Collected Papers of Frederic C. Lane* (Baltimore, 1966), 36–55, reprinted from *Journal of Economic History* 4 (1944).

[63] Kurt Weissen has presented the most comprehensive view of the Alberti in his "Florentiner Bankiers und Deutschland (1275 bis 1475): Kontinuität und Diskontinuität wirtschaftlicher Strukturen" (Habilitationsschrift, Basel, 2000), 28–35; and Luca Boschetto, *Leon Battista Alberti e Firenze: Biografia, storia, letteratura* (Florence, 2000), 20–31, clarifies the situation in the 1430s and includes a complete bibliography on the history of the Alberti companies.

[64] A preliminary survey based on archival materials can be found in Antonia Borlandi, *Il manuale di mercatura di Saminato de' Ricci* (Genoa, 1963), 17–35.

prominent at Avignon and also in Umbria, where the papacy was directing efforts to reestablish a territorial base in Italy, and by the 1380s several Ricci had established major firms in Genoa. Both the Ricci and the Alberti were also deeply involved in the divisive factional politics in Florence in the aftermath of the Ciompi revolt and during the years of the Visconti threat to the city's independence. This led to the occasional exile of a member of the family—and for the Ricci to the public beheading in 1400 of one of their more prominent businessmen, Saminiato di Gucciozzo, known today for his merchant manual.

For the fifteenth century only two other notable clusters of family firms have been identified—the Pazzi and the Salviati. An inquest into the Pazzi firms following the conspiracy of 1478 against the Medici revealed a cluster of five separate firms—in Florence, Rome, Valencia, Lyons, and Bruges—that deliberately disguised the fact that their corpo came from the undivided patrimony of three brothers, two of whom were dead, dating back to the death of their father, Andrea, in 1445. This family group, however, was limited to the one surviving brother, Iacopo, and the five sons of his two brothers (Guglielmo di Antonio di Andrea, whose wife was the sister of Lorenzo de' Medici, being the only one to escape punishment in 1478 by death or life imprisonment). A year after the conspiracy, in 1479, a group of seven surviving Pazzi and the heirs of two others representing a cluster of seven companies—four abroad (in Rome, Valencia, Lyons, and Avignon) and three in Florence, including a wool firm—made a joint settlement of outstanding debts with a similar group of two Salviati representing a cluster of eight companies—five abroad (one each in Lyons, Bruges, and London and two in Pisa) and three in Florence, also including a wool firm. The men in each of these groups were closely related, all the Pazzi being grandsons of Andrea and the Salviati being sons and grandsons of Alamanno di Iacopo (d. 1456). The Pazzi seem not to have survived in any force after the disaster of the conspiracy.

The Salviati, in contrast, shared their investments through two additional generations extending well into the next century. Alamanno and his descendants built up a cluster of major firms in Florence, Pisa (where they also had the contract for marketing iron ore), Lyons (where they had a tax farm and a receivership for ecclesiastical revenues), and Rome (where they became one of the principal bankers to the Medici popes). The family group of partners, however, remained very small, usually consisting of no more than four adults. When the division finally came in 1540, following a decade of tensions, only two sets of brothers were involved, sons of first cousins who had only a great-grandfather in common, and the rupture was accompanied by litigation. Neither the Pazzi nor the Salviati cluster of firms has been studied, but the slight evidence we have for them points to something like a family policy behind individually organized enterprises; as a business family, however, neither approached the Alberti in its genealogical spread.[65]

In the second decade of the sixteenth century four Olivieri brothers and a cousin built up a family agglomerate of firms that looks like another cluster, but their enterprises do not seem to have continued beyond one generation. The dynamo in this family was the banker Benvenuto di Paolo Olivieri, whose rise to prominence in Rome in the second quarter of the sixteenth century is charted in chapter 3. Benvenuto was one of ten brothers, and their father is not known to have had a manufacturing or commercial business. In 1516 Benvenuto went to Rome to make his fortune, and he was eventually joined by four younger brothers. About 1520 Iacopo went to Valencia, Alessandro to Naples, and a cousin, Giovanni di Piero, to Nuremberg, while Michele, the oldest brother, stayed in Florence. All of these, like Benvenuto and Giovanni, the only two whose early careers are documented, probably started out at the bottom rung as junior employees of a firm, and four of them went on to set up their own firms. Michele in Florence, not Benvenuto in Rome, was the common link in a family agglomerate that reached its greatest extension in the 1540s: he and Alessandro were partners in a Neapolitan firm, and they set up subsidiary firms in the name of Michele's sons, still children, in Cosenza, L'Aquila, and Bari. Michele and Giovanni were partners in a firm in Florence, and this firm went into partnership with the firm in Naples to set up a third firm in Nuremberg. As we shall see, the firms in this family agglomerate came together in at least one common commercial enterprise, the silk trade. The firms in the provinces in the south supplied raw silk to Naples, which was then forwarded to Florence; the firm in Florence sold the silk to *setaioli* and bought finished fabrics, which, along with some raw silk, it then sent to the firm in Nuremberg for marketing.[66]

In contrast to a family cluster of firms is what we might call the dynastic, or patrilineal, firm, a sequence of firms that carried the same family name through several generations by partners who, if traced on a genealogical tree, fall into just one line, to the exclusion of other derivative branches at each generational

---

[65] The Pazzi cluster was brought to light by Marco Spallanzani in "Le aziende Pazzi al tempo della congiura del 1478," in *Studi di storia economica toscana*, 305–20. Reinforcing the documentation for this cluster is a 1490 copy of the 1479 agreement with the Salviati in the Archivio Salviati at the Scuola Normale of Pisa, ser. 3, no. 1, fols. 10v–11v. The Salviati cluster can be recreated from Pierre Hurtubise, *Une famille-témoin: Les Salviati* (Vatican City, 1985), 87–88, 145–47, 206–12.

[66] Francesco Guidi Bruscoli, *Benvenuto Olivieri: I "mercatores" fiorentini e la Camera Apostolica nella Roma di Paolo III Farnese (1534–1549)* (Florence, 2000), esp. 34–46, now translated as *Papal Banking in Renaissance Rome: Benvenuto Olivieri and Paul III, 1534–1549* (Abingdon, England, 2007).

juncture. The familial nature of these firms, in other words, extended vertically through time without expanding horizontally to take in cadet lines. In the notable instances of the Medici and Riccardi "family" companies, however, there were no cadet branches. The sense some men had of the continuity, if not the family tradition, of their business manifests itself in the habit of identifying the sequence of ledgers according to a single system that continued through more than one generation. Firms used the alphabetical sequence of letters, starting with *A,* to identify the series of company ledgers resulting from periodic renewal of the partnership. The dynastic firm continued the series, notwithstanding the passage from one generation to another, sometimes, as with the Salviati, which continued on for more than a century, reaching the point of having to start the lettering all over again with *AA.* Some of these men expressed the dynastic sensibility of a businessman in their testaments, exhorting their sons to maintain the family business. For example, in 1468 Tommaso Spinelli instructed his heirs to continue his silk company, and in 1501 Giuliano Gondi encouraged his sons not to close down the business but instead to continue the seventy-three-year family tradition.[67] Indeed, the chronicler Giuliano de' Ricci, writing in the second half of the sixteenth century, refers to a bank as a "house" (*casa*).[68]

Dynasty, in any event, is a linear, not a corporate, concept. In view of the strong kinship ties that historians of Florence have noted in spheres of activity outside the business world, it is more precise to talk of business partnerships of relatives as specifically patriarchal or fraternal or avuncular or dynastic rather than as more generally familial in any extensive corporate sense.

It is not altogether clear what accounts for the transformation of the business organization of international merchant banks from the larger corporate partnership characteristic of the earlier period to the smaller, more individualistic firms and the partnership agglomerate of the later fourteenth century on. It would seem to have been a logical step following the slow dilution of the family component of the early partnerships and hence the loss of internal social cohesion, which may not have been unrelated to the disintegration of the family consorteria as a cohesive economic body. Moreover, in the aftermath of the great bankruptcies of the 1340s, investors were perhaps more cautious about entering

---

[67] William Caferro, "The Silk Business of Tommaso Spinelli, Fifteenth-Century Florentine Merchant and Papal Banker," *Renaissance Studies* 10 (1996): 433; Andreas Tönnesmann, *Der Palazzo Gondi in Florenz* (Worms, 1983), 128.

[68] I have found *casa* used also in the 1621 contract for a company in Ancona and Ragusa. See Maurice Carmona, "La Toscane face à la crise de l'industrie lainière: Techniques et mentalités économiques aux XVIe et XVIIe siècles," in *Produzione, commercio e consumo dei panni di lana (nei secoli XII–XVIII),* ed. Marco Spallanzani (Florence, 1976), 164ff. Note also the Venetian use of the term above, in the text before n. 8, with reference to Florentine companies.

into a contract that by its very nature exposed them to the unlimited liability of a single company managed by a large and unwieldy body of partners without strong corporate ties and operating on a vast international scale through many branches far removed, in both time and place, from central control. Under these changed circumstances, without access to the resources of a consorteria and confronted with more cautious investors, an ambitious entrepreneur anxious to expand his business stood a better chance of attracting partners and outside capital by organizing separate partnerships for different operations, since this kind of arrangement protected the secondary investors from any liability beyond the one company within the agglomerate they invested in. The principal investor himself, however, found no protection by thus distributing his investment over several companies rather than putting it all in one large company, for if any one company in an agglomerate went bankrupt, he was personally liable to the full extent of his patrimony, which included his investments in all the companies.

The recourse to separate companies, however, was a protective device for secondary investors who were interested only in specific operations and wanted to avoid the comprehensive liability characteristic of the corporate partnership. And in fact new dynamics came into play within the economy in the second half of the fourteenth century that called for a looser, more flexible business structure for entrepreneurial energies. On the one hand, after the Black Death many new men with no family backing moved onto the scene, anxious to take advantage of the situation to make their fortunes. Moreover, at precisely this time, as a result of both the expanding trade of the western Mediterranean and the return of the papacy to Rome, new opportunities opened up close to home for new men with less wealth to invest. On the other hand, at home in Florence the shift in the wool industry toward higher-quality cloth also had its impact. Most of the great companies of the early fourteenth century were run by Calimala merchants, who brought semifinished cloth to Florence for finishing and reexport, but with the upgrading of the wool industry, local manufactures themselves took the initiative to get their new products to foreign markets. And with the growth of the silk industry toward the end of the century, these producers too extended their businesses from production into international commerce. In other words, with the transition in the textile industries from finishing imported cloth to the full-scale production of quality cloth, both wool and silk, the commercial initiative shifted from the Calimala importer-exporters to local producers, and many of these men took initiatives to get their products to markets abroad. In the consequent outburst of individual entrepreneurial energy a business organization with less expansive ambitions and greater flexibility was more appropriate for both finding capital and attracting entrepreneurial talent.[69]

SIZE OF FIRMS   It is difficult to say much about the size of these later partnership agglomerates as compared with earlier corporate partnerships. They certainly were less geographically extensive, having far fewer branches abroad scattered over a much more restricted area, mostly confined to Italy and western Europe; and accordingly they employed fewer people. The Medici had the most extensive network, with seven branches at its maximum (these changed from time to time), but only four outside of Italy—London, Bruges, Avignon, Geneva (then Lyons)—and in 1470 it had fifty-seven employees on its staff. Datini confined his system to the European rim of the western Mediterranean, from Pisa around to Majorca, going inland only to Avignon. The Capponi limited its branches to Rome, Venice, and Lyons; and some major figures, like Filippo Strozzi and Giuliano Gondi, made the fortunes that paid for their great palaces without operating outside of Italy. Likewise, the large Riccardi agglomerate at the end of the sixteenth century consisted of firms in Italy alone, at Florence, Pisa, Venice, and Messina. Only a handful of firms have been identified as operating by this time in either Lyons or Antwerp, the major European centers of commerce and finance.

The smaller number of partners of these later agglomerates limited the size of the corpo, the norm being no more than three or four, if indeed that many, and often the capital came predominantly from just one of these. Datini, for instance, provided 88 percent of the total capital invested in his agglomerate in 1398. Entrepreneurs themselves imposed limitations on the growth of the firm. They might increase the stock of capital by not withdrawing all their profits and by investing additional funds as interest-bearing deposits. They were reluctant, however, to use devices internal to the firm itself, such as the holding mechanism and the limited-liability accomandita, to enlarge the corpo much beyond their personal resources. The total capital invested by all partners in the Medici agglomerate in 1451 (*fl.*90,687) amounted to less than half the capital, in real

[69] The only study dedicated to an explanation for this transformation of the business organization of Florentine international merchant-banking firms is John Padgett and Paul D. McLean, "Organizational Invention and Elite Transformation: The Birth of Partnership Systems in Renaissance Florence," *American Journal of Sociology* 111 (2006): 1463–1568. Padgett and McLean see this change as an "invention" that occurred at a precise moment, in 1382, the agents being Cambio bankers who expanded their operations at the time of the reaffirmation of oligarchical government following the Ciompi revolt. They buttress their argument with a mass of data gathered from wide-ranging research in archival sources as well as the secondary literature, which they analyze to uncover social, political, and economic relations; and their interpretation of this material, built on the techniques of their discipline as political scientists, awaits a critical response from political and social historians. This structural analysis, however, does not include a consideration of the dynamics of economic change.

value, of the Peruzzi company at its highest level, in 1310 (£149,000 *a fiorini*, or *fl.*102,758), and no other fifteenth-century agglomerate we know about reached the level of the Medici. In 1398 Datini, at the height of his career, was working with a total invested capital of *fl.*45,500; the Capponi agglomerate came closer to the Medici when in 1485 its total invested capital amounted to *fl.*61,000. On his death in 1491 Filippo di Matteo Strozzi had *fl.*35,000 invested in firms in Florence, Rome, and Naples. The largest company on record for this later period is the Medici's parent firm in 1451, with *fl.*72,000, and this is followed by the firm of Carlo Strozzi in 1367, with *fl.*53,600. A major international merchant-banking firm in Rome in the early sixteenth century had about *fl.*20,000–25,000 in capital—the capital, respectively, of Filippo di Filippo Strozzi & Partners in 1515 and of Benvenuto Olivieri & Partners in 1543. Even if we factor in the index of the rising real value of the florin over this period (for which see the appendix), these figures for the corpo of the largest firms fall within a limited range, the relatively modest level of which can be appreciated by noting that the estates of the richest Florentines in the fifteenth century, such as Palla Strozzi at the beginning of the century and Filippo Strozzi at the end, reached *fl.*100,000 and that the latter spent no less than *fl.*35,000 for his private residence.[70] In the later sixteenth century, as already observed, the level of investment rose significantly.

The corpo of an international merchant-banking firm, however, is hardly an index to the scale of its operations, especially for a large firm that engaged heavily in banking and finance as opposed to purely commercial activities. To increase the stock of capital beyond partners' equity, it could attract deposits from outsiders, and both time and demand deposits might constitute a significant liability on a firm's balance sheet. As we shall see, a large firm could raise significant sums from depositors abroad, much more than it could attract in the home market at Florence. Moreover, in the later fifteenth and sixteenth centuries the continuing growth of the international exchange market and the escalation of government debt increased exponentially the traffic in credit handled by banks. In 1543 the assets under management of the Olivieri company in Rome exceeded partners' equity by fifteen times. Nevertheless, the scale of operations of the Genoese and the Germans left Florentines far behind in the expanding international financial markets of the sixteenth century.

---

[70] For the data mentioned here, see de Roover, *Medici Bank*, 66–67; Melis, *Aspetti*, 328 (Datini); Spallanzani, "Una grande azienda fiorentina," 424 (Strozzi); Goldthwaite, *Private Wealth*, 60, 92, 200 (Strozzi, Capponi); and Guidi Bruscoli, *Benvenuto Olivieri*, 340.

The Conduct of Business

The organization of business operations of an international merchant-banking firm can be broken down into two general areas: management and long-distance transmission. The former is a problem of agency and involves policymaking and directing office activities; the latter is a problem of communication, transfer of credit, and transport of goods over long distances.

MANAGEMENT   We know little about policy behind the operation of these firms—how merchants judged markets, estimated profits, set prices, considered product development, dealt with competition, projected expansion, and planned for the long term. Their correspondence does not reveal much about this level of decision making; or rather the few collections of business letters, above all those of Datini, have not been analyzed with this objective in mind. Advice about running a business can be found in the personal documents of these men, but it is directed to matters of character and behavior rather than to what we might call professional business education: the merchant must guard his reputation, seek not to arouse envy, conduct his affairs with reason and honor, know how to deal with others, and judge everything not by absolute standards but by the circumstances of the moment. At its most practical, advice emphasizes the importance of doing things secretly, attending to correspondence and accounts, being able to dictate and use language effectively, watching expenditures, and knowing how to handle merchandise.[71] Raymond de Roover was the first scholar to wring from company accounts something about internal management problems, but accounts record activity that, at the most, constituted the basis for making decisions, not the policy that went into those decisions. More helpful are letters regarding political negotiations in which a firm engaged in order to win a contract in the sphere of government finance.[72] De Roover used the Medici correspondence of this kind to learn much about the management of the family company, especially during the period of Lorenzo the Magnificent, but his judgments about the policies and ability of Lorenzo's managers as they emerge from these documents are highly impressionistic.[73]

---

[71] This is a summary of the "Consiglio sulla mercatura di un anonimo trecentista," published by Gino Corti, *ASI* 110 (1952): 114–19.

[72] Raymond de Roover contrasts his approach with that of Sapori in de Roover, "Story of the Alberti Company of Florence," 39–84.

[73] For a revision of de Roover's judgment of two of the Medici partners, see Marc Boone, "Apologie d'un banquier médiéval: Tommaso Portinari et l'État bourguignon," *Le Moyen Âge* 15 (1999): 31–54; and Elisabetta Scarton, *Giovanni Lanfredini: Uomo d'affari e diplomatico nell'Italia del Quattrocento* (Florence, 2007), chs. 3–4. Melissa Bullard has studied the management style of two bank directors in Rome, one representing Lorenzo de' Medici and the other representing Filippo di Fi-

The principal investor obviously dominated the management of a firm, but it is not clear what role the other partners played in the decision-making process. The 1472 articles of association renewing the partnership of Tommaso Spinelli, Iacopo Spini & Partners at Rome state that the *governo* of the firm was to be with Spini and, alongside him, the administrator, Simone di Mariano di Vanni Filipepi (a brother of the painter Botticelli), and "that for everything of importance the said Iacopo must consult with the said Simone and Simone with him, and that nothing can be done without the consent of one with the other as equals, always reserving the overall direction to the above-mentioned Tommaso [Spinelli] as the senior partner, who can manage [the firm] and delegate management to both or to either one of them as may please him."[74] Spinelli and Spini each contributed *fl.*2,000 *di camera* to the corpo of the firm, but Spinelli was more established as a major merchant-banker, having been depositary of the Apostolic Chamber (he died immediately after this renewal of the firm). The extent of the senior partner's involvement in the day-to-day management of the firm obviously depended on individual circumstances, which, in any event, are difficult to measure on the basis of surviving materials, even business letters. Francesco di Marco Datini emerges from his correspondence as an indefatigable, heavily hands-on partner, whereas Lorenzo de' Medici, who had vastly more extensive commitments outside the bank, left just about everything to his partners (often to the misfortune of the family business, if we are to accept de Roover's reading of their correspondence).

The articles of association setting up a partnership generally specify who was to have direct, on-the-job administrative responsibility. If the administrator was not explicitly named, the designation was implicit in the assignment of a share in the partnership to one of the partners on the basis, not of his investment, but of his service to the firm. In other words, the value of his service to the firm, apart from whatever capital he might have invested in the corpo, would be established as a nominal share in the corpo or as an otherwise stated share in the

---

lippo Strozzi a generation later, through their correspondence. See "Middle Managers and Middlemen in Renaissance Banking," in *Travail et travailleurs en Europe au Moyen Âge et au début des temps modernes,* ed. Claire Dolan (Toronto, 1991), 271–90, reprinted in Bullard, *Lorenzo il Magnifico: Image and Anxiety, Politics and Finance* (Florence, 1994). The correspondence reveals something about the diplomatic relations these men had with the papacy in order to obtain advantages for their businesses but nothing about the internal management of their firms.

[74] "E siamo d'accordo che 'l governo di detta compagnia sia Jachopo Spini per il principale e sSimone di Mariano co llui, e che d'ogni chosa d'inportanza il detto Jachopo debba chomferire chol detto Simone, e sSimone cho llui, e che non si possa fare alcuna cosa sanza comsentimento l'uno dell'altro anzi d'un pari volontà, tuttavolta conservando lo ministero a Tonmaso sopradetto chome maggiore, che llui possa ghovernare e fare ghovernare a tutti e due e uno di loro a cchi gli parrà e piacerà." Yale University, Beinecke Library, Spinelli Papers, box 85a, no. 1597. On this company see Philip Jacks and William Caferro, *The Spinelli of Florence: Fortunes of a Renaissance Merchant Family* (University Park, PA, 2001), 254–55.

profits. For example, the abovementioned Simone Filipepi, who contributed nothing to the capital of the Spinelli-Spini firm, was to have a share of the profits calculated as 2*s*. 4*d*. per lira (11.67 percent) in return for his services. In the contract for the silk firm set up in 1429 by three sons of Domenico Corsi and Bernardo di Bartolomeo Gherardi, the manager, Orlando di Bartolomeo Gherardi, added *fl*.200 to the *fl*.9,800 invested by the partners but was to receive 10 percent of the profits.[75] An administrator was thus given a share in the profits, usually in lieu of a salary. In the fourteenth century his service to the firm is sometimes referred to as the *petto* ("chest"—in the sense of confronting reality?) or *industria,* but by the fifteenth century *persona* had become the standard term. The position of administrator is sometimes called *governatore* in the fifteenth century, but in the later sixteenth century *ministro* or *primo ministro* was more common.

All the complexities of international trade—extensive geography, innumerable commodities, various monetary and measurement systems, exchange rates, various customs tolls and practices, transport costs, commercial practices peculiar to different places—necessitated the recording of all this information for quick reference. The surviving merchant manuals are compilations of these records that seem to contain all the information a merchant might need to conduct business throughout the system. Since the situation was constantly changing, however, they probably had little practical function as reference tools in daily operations and served more as guides to introduce the novice to the kinds of problems he was likely to encounter. The best known of the extant manuals is that put together by Francesco di Balducci Pegolotti. In the course of his career with the Bardi company from 1310 to its failure in the 1340s, he was stationed for long periods in London and Cyprus, giving him experience and knowledge that extended across the span of the network. The manual attributed to Giorgio di Lorenzo Chiarini was printed in Florence in 1481, the first to circulate in that form, and its reprinting in 1490 and 1498, along with its inclusion in Luca Pacioli's *Summa di arithmetica, geometria, proportioni et proportionalità,* printed at Venice in 1494 and 1523, indicates something of the market for this kind of educational tool.[76]

---

[75] ASF, Archivio Guicciardini Corsi Salviati, filza 1, no. 1.

[76] Ugo Tucci, "Manuali di mercatura e pratica degli affari nel Medioevo," in *Fatti e idee di storia economica nei secoli XII–XX: Studi dedicati a Franco Borlandi* (Bologna, 1977), 215–31. Peter Spufford, "Late Medieval Merchants' Notebooks: A Project; Their Potential for the History of Banking," in *Kaufmannsbücher und Handelspraktiken vom Spätmittelalter bis zum beginnenden 20. Jahrhundert,* ed. M. A Denzel, J. C. Hocquet, and H. Witthöft (Stuttgart, 2002), 47–62, lists all these manuals, published and unpublished, and lays out his project to study them. Chiarini's manual is published by Franco Borlandi in *El libro di mercatantie et usanze de' paesi* (Turin, 1936).

STAFF   The number of people on a company's staff at any one place obviously varied according to the size of the company.[77] From the 1450s to the 1470s the Cambini, a medium-sized bank, had three to five clerks in the home office at any one time, and a large firm such as the Medici, might have as many as ten at its headquarters and usually somewhat fewer in its branch offices. The tasks of staff clerks consisted primarily in keeping accounts and handling correspondence. Invariably the staff included one or more youths who were learning the trade on the job. They all had attended an abacus school *(scuola d'abaco)*, where the basic training program, well known from the numerous practical treatises on the subject that survive, had taught them above all how to deal in different moneys and to make the four basic arithmetic calculations, using what for them was the standard mensural system based on vigesimals and duodecimals. "Without this, one cannot do anything," wrote Francesco di Giuliano de' Medici, somewhat desperately, in 1433, when, now a married adult who had not frequented such a school, he suddenly found himself in exile in Padua and, much against his natural interests, faced with the task of having to learn something about the subject so he could help run the family business.[78]

The typical career began at about age eleven to thirteen, immediately after finishing the course in commercial arithmetic at an abacus school (having already learned to read and write in an elementary grammar school). It was assumed that this was the age at which a boy, even one from the highest ranks of the entrepreneurial class, went to work, although he was not formally emancipated, that is, given full legal autonomy, until he was eighteen or older. According to his biographer, Vespasiano da Bisticci, the humanist Giannozzo di Bernardo Manetti (1396–1459), son of one of the richest men in the city, was only ten when he finished the abacus school and went to work in a bank. Most boys were probably twelve to fourteen when they left the abacus school and took a job. Lapo di Iacopo Alberti (d. 1319) set up a trust fund for his children and grandchildren to provide them with money when they reached the age of thirteen or fourteen. Likewise his son Caroccio provided for a cash payment to his son Duccio when he reached fourteen, and his other sons entered into the family business at about the same

---

[77] By far the most comprehensive description of the career of company clerks is to be found in Rita Mazzei, *Itinera mercatorum: Circolazione di uomini e beni nell'Europa centro-orientale, 1550–1650* (Lucca, 1999), ch. 3. It is focused on firms in Germany and Poland in the later sixteenth and early seventeenth centuries, but all the literature on the earlier period is cited (see esp. 119n), and there is no reason to think that things had changed. For the earlier period, useful data have been assembled in Melis, *Aspetti*, 295–312 (on Datini and earlier companies), and Tognetti, *Il banco Cambini*, 347–54.

[78] Dale Kent, "I Medici in esilio: Una vittoria di famiglia e una disfatta personale," *ASI* 132 (1974): 24.

age.[79] Francesco Sassetti, writing from India in 1585, sent his sister in Florence advice for her son "who was leaving childhood to enter into the years of discretion" as a beginning office clerk: he was to put aside "all the thoughts of a boy and a child" and "to give himself up to [his employers'] every desire and pleasure, above all not soiling his hands with their money but always accounting to them for every penny."[80] "In short," wrote Matteo Botti in 1525 to a youth *(garzone)* in Cadiz, "conduct yourself so [your employer] may love you, and that's sufficient; tie up your wishes and throw them into the sea, and seek to get ahead."[81]

A boy, usually called *fanciullo* or *garzone*, started out his employment keeping the accounts of activity in the cashbox, a simple enough task that entailed recording income and expenditures, the easiest introduction to the basic techniques of accounting. One might think that boys would have learned this skill in the abacus school, but the dozens upon dozens of surviving manuals used in these schools dating from the fourteenth to the sixteenth century yield not the slightest evidence for this. Instead, it seems that they learned the skill on the job. The career path of Francesco di Stoldo degli Strozzi, which is summarized in the claim he filed in 1345 for payment of back salary from his bankrupt employer, Taddeo dell'Antella & Partners, was probably typical. He joined the firm as a small boy *(piccolo garzone)*, and after eight months he was assigned the key to the cashbox for local banking operations. A year later he was assigned the key to the chest where the firm's documents were kept; nine months later he was sent to Pisa, where he kept accounts; then it was back to Florence, where he kept the ledger for eight months before being sent off again, this time to Siena and Grosseto to handle the firm's affairs *(a fare loro fatti)*, presumably now, after four and a half years, on his own.[82]

Besides accounting, the chief task of the youth on a firm's staff was to write. In 1446 Lorenzo di Matteo Strozzi, then fourteen and working in Valencia, wrote to his mother in Florence that he got only three hours of sleep at night and went on to say, "I want to let you know that I don't mind writing. I spend the whole day in the writing room, and I copy twelve letters a day. I write so fast that you would be amazed at me, faster than anyone else in the house: it is best to do things in this way."[83] Giovanni di Francesco Morelli, newly arrived on the job at Lisbon in 1509,

[79] Armando Sapori, "La famiglia e le compagnie degli Alberti del Giudice," in *Studi,* 2:1006; idem, ed., *I libri degli Alberti del Giudice* (Milan, 1952), 207, 232, 276.

[80] Quoted in Mazzei, *Itinera mercatorum,* 146.

[81] Quoted in Angela Orlandi, "Mercanti toscani nell'Andalusia del Cinquecento," in *Historia. Instituciones. Documentos* 26 (1999): 377.

[82] Armando Sapori, "Il quaderno dei creditori di Taddeo dell'Antella e compagni," *Rivista delle biblioteche e degli archivi,* n.s., 3 (1925): 171–72.

[83] Alessandra Macinghi negli Strozzi, *Lettere di una gentildonna fiorentina del secolo XV ai figliuoli esuli,* ed. Cesare Guasti (Florence, 1877), 30.

wrote home about how "one spends all day and half the night writing in the writing room, so much work is required. . . . I am buried in work [*in gran travaglio*], yet I shall go on doing the best I can."[84] And for the merchant this travail lasted a lifetime: "We can no longer take this burden of writing, because we are over sixty-one years old and it is past midnight," wrote one of Datini's correspondents in 1395, "and we have to write until daylight, and writing keeps us busy all night."[85] Indeed, the contemporary term for a firm's office, whether outside or inside the senior partner's house, was *scrittoio* (writing room). "Paper costs little," was one anonymous merchant's advice, "and often it returns a good profit." "Don't ever spare the pen," advised Giovanni di Paolo Morelli; and indeed Alberti explained that one of his relatives "did so well in business having his hands always stained with ink."[86]

The point of a boy's education was thus to become, as Benedetto Dei described himself, "a good writer and a good arithmetician [*abachisto*] and a good accountant." And along the way came travel: "See with your own eyes," advised Giovanni Morelli, "the countries and the lands where you are thinking about conducting trade."[87] A young clerk was likely to be sent abroad to one of the firm's branches, where, as a member of a smaller staff, he assumed more responsibilities as an accountant and gained experience from direct engagement in commerce and finance. Guido di Filippo dell'Antella, whose career is one of the earliest that can be traced, moved all across the Mediterranean from 1278 to 1290, working in Genoa, Florence, the kingdom of France, Provence, Pisa, Rome, Naples, and Acre. Likewise Francesco Balducci Pegolotti, author of the well-known merchant manual, traveled for the Bardi to Antwerp, London, Cyprus, Avignon, and Bruges in the early fourteenth century. Some continued to travel as adults as they were transferred from place to place. "Whoever is not a merchant and hasn't investigated the world and seen foreign nations and returned with possessions to his native home is considered nothing," wrote Gregorio Dati.[88] And he had to learn the language of the place where he worked. In early 1379 the merchant Simone di Rinieri Peruzzi, on a diplomatic mission to Barnabò Visconti at Milan to deal

---

[84] Quoted in Marco Spallanzani, *Mercanti fiorentini nell'Asia portoghese (1500–1525)* (Florence, 1997), 42–43.

[85] Maria Giagnacovo, *Mercanti toscani a Genova: Traffici, merci e prezzi nel XIV secolo* (Naples, 2005), 36.

[86] Corti, "Consiglio sulla mercatura," 118; Giovanni di Pagolo Morelli, *Ricordi*, ed. Vittore Branca (Florence, 1956), 228–29; Leon Battista Alberti, *I primi tre libri della famiglia*, ed. F. C. Pellegrini (Florence, 1946), 321.

[87] Benedetto Dei, *La cronica dall'anno 1400 all'anno 1500*, ed. Roberto Barducci (Florence, 1984), 125; Morelli, *Ricordi*, 226.

[88] Quoted by Alison Brown, "Insiders and Outsiders: The Changing Boundaries of Exile," in *Society and Individual in Renaissance Florence*, ed. William J. Connell (Berkeley and Los Angeles, 2002), 359.

with matters regarding two condottieri, the German Lutz von Landau and the Englishman John Hawkwood, thought he could help in dealing with them since "I am at home and skilled in the one language and the other," both of which he must have picked up on his travels as a youth learning the business.[89] Some of the work Giovanni Morelli in Lisbon wrote about being buried in was learning Portuguese, and another clerk just arrived in Cracow in 1584 borrowed money to buy a book to learn Polish.[90]

At some point a clerk came to be called a *giovane,* which it is better to translate as "junior staff member" rather than, literally, "youth" inasmuch as older men were also thus identified. If things went well, he would then, in his early twenties, become a branch manager or the chief administrator in the home office and perhaps, finally, go on to become a partner. Along the way he might change firms and in the end go into business on his own. Mobility in the ranks of a firm's staff was, in fact, high. Of the 61 youths traced in the documents of the Del Bene wool firm in the third quarter of the fourteenth century, 42 worked fewer than two years. Of the 150 employees who worked at one time or another in the various firms of Francesco Datini over a half-century, 42 worked for a year or less and 39 for between one and two years. Some who went away returned.[91] In the course of their movement from one firm to another learning the trade, these youths widened the circle of their personal acquaintances within the business community, which must have heightened the sense of professional camaraderie they felt once they were businessmen on their own.

Salaries were always quoted in florins. From the mid-fourteenth to the mid-sixteenth century they ranged from *fl.*12–15 to *fl.*100–200. Given the predominance of young boys on the staff and the high turnover, it is hardly surprising that most salaries fell into the lower end of this range. Of all the salaries paid out by Datini over his long career, 72 percent were under *fl.*35; the highest was *fl.*100. Those who remained on the job, however, saw their salaries rise rapidly at a certain point. Giuliano di Giovanni di ser Matteo, who was on the staff of the local bank of the Medici, saw his salary quadrupled in six years: he was paid *fl.*48 in 1401, *fl.*65 in 1402, *fl.*80 in 1403, *fl.*100 in 1406, and *fl.*200 in 1407, when he was treated as a partner, and the next year as partner and manager he

---

[89] *I libri di commercio dei Peruzzi,* ed. Armando Sapori (Milan, 1934), 523 (from Peruzzi's *libro segreto*).

[90] Rita Mazzei, "I mercanti e la scrittura: Alcune considerazioni a proposito degli Italiani in Polonia tra Cinque e Seicento," in *La cultura latina, italiana, francese nell'Europa centro-orientale,* ed. Gaetano Platania (Viterbo, 2004), 102.

[91] Bruno Dini, "I lavoratori dell'arte della lana a Firenze nel XIV e XV secolo," reprinted from *Artigiani e salariati: Il mondo del lavoro nell'Italia dei secoli XII–XV* (Pistoia, 1984) in his *Manifattura, commercio e banca nella Firenze medievale* (Florence, 2001), 141–71; Melis, *Aspetti,* 296.

went from a salary to a one-seventh share of the profits.[92] Most staff salaries of firms in the second half of the century, such as those paid by the Cambini and Strozzi firms, ranged from *fl*.12 to *fl*.50; relatively few men saw their salaries go higher.

It is not possible to compare these nominal values in florins across time, however, without factoring in, first, the increasing price of the florin in lire, the money most used in the local market, and, second, an index to the changing real value of the lira. Using the criteria laid out in the appendix, we can compare these salaries with the earnings of construction workers. A boy who started out on his first job earned somewhat less than what an unskilled laborer might earn in a year of full-time work; the *fl*.35 maximum Datini paid to most of his clerks was equivalent to only slightly more than the annual earnings of such a worker. The first recorded salary of the abovementioned Medici clerk, Giuliano di Giovanni, was what a middle-level skilled construction worker might earn, and his raise to *fl*.65 the next year put him at the level of the highest-paid skilled construction workers. In these terms, the Cambini and Strozzi salaries at the end of the century fall into line with those throughout the entire period for which we have documentation, from the beginning of the fourteenth century to the end of the sixteenth century.

It is impossible to generalize about the social origins of company clerks. Some were sons or relatives of the partners, but others were not. Some came from prominent business families, while others were sons of artisans. Filippo di Matteo Strozzi employed his son, along with several distantly related Strozzi, in his firm, but the Medici, whose companies span several generations, had hardly anyone from the several collateral lines of the family on the staffs of their various companies. Boys with upper-class names—Adimari, Albizzi, Biliotti, Canigiani, Cavalcanti, de' Neri, Gherardi, Ginori—passed through the rosters of the Cambini company in the third quarter of the fifteenth century, and all received low salaries, apparently as beginners, and remained on the job for only several years at the most. Some of these boys resurface later with their own companies. Baldassarre di Gualtieri Biliotti, who worked as a cashier from 1450 to 1455 at a salary that went from *fl*.24 to *fl*.36, shows up in 1461–62 as a correspondent of the Cambini in Pera. In 1462 he was contracted by Lorenzo di Ilarione Ilarioni, one of the city's most prominent merchants, to conduct trade throughout the Levant, and ten years later he was a partner of a company in Valencia. Giovanni di Francesco Ginori, whose brother Tommaso had a prosperous business in Naples, did two stints with the Cambini, from 1458 to 1462 at a salary of *fl*.18–20 and from 1466 to 1468 at a salary of *fl*.24–25, and some twenty years later, in 1485, he

---

[92] De Roover, *Medici Bank*, 44–45, 231.

was one of the syndics administering the bankruptcy proceedings of his former employers.

In contrast to these men, another clerk, Bartolomeo di Domenico Marchionni, came from a family of shopkeepers and got his start in business with the Cambini. From 1466 to 1468, in his later teens, he worked for a salary of *fl.*15–20, and then in 1470 the firm sent him on business to Portugal, where he launched himself on the successful career recounted in chapter 2.[93] The clerks and partners who trained in the Medici firms in the early fifteenth century and then left to become prominent merchant-bankers in their own right included Alessandro Bardi, Niccolò di Francesco Cambini, Antonio di ser Lodovico Della Casa, Antonio di Messer Francesco Salutati, and Leonardo di Cipriano Spinelli. Of these, it is to be noted, Cambini's father was a linen draper, Della Casa's a notary, and Spinelli's a furrier. Unfortunately, no one has yet collected the available data to construct some kind of statistical description of the social origins and early careers of Florentine merchant-bankers, which might reveal patterns of relations, relationships, and origins.

The office staff busied itself primarily with correspondence and keeping accounts (the latter survive in infinitely greater quantity than the former). The Datini archive in Prato is a famous monument to the extent of the paperwork generated during just one man's career at the end of the fourteenth century—573 account books, 497 files of correspondence containing 125,549 business letters and 27,099 other letters and papers. The Salviati archive at the Scuola Normale at Pisa, probably the largest extant collection of a Florentine family's business papers, has vastly more account books documenting many generations of the family's business activity from the fifteenth century on but little correspondence. The 1353 inventory of the papers of the bankrupt Acciaiuoli company, mentioned above, made on the occasion of their transfer by the court to a new storage place, lists no fewer than 1,501 account books, 125 large and small bags of correspondence, and 5 chests of several sizes (2 *cassette*, 1 *cassa*, 1 *cassone*, 1 *forziere*) filled with miscellaneous papers and account books; it is an archive against which the extraordinary archive of Francesco Datini of Prato appears almost insignificant.[94]

Abroad, firms needed a representative on the local scene to conduct their affairs, including looking after such practical matters as payment, storage, shipping, and insurance. The large corporate partnerships in the age of the Bardi, the

---

[93] On these men, consult the index to Tognetti, *Il banco Cambini.*

[94] Hoshino, "Nuovi documenti sulla compagnia degli Acciaiuoli." For an idea of the formation and organization of such a vast amount of material, see the study of Datini's habits by Jérôme Hayez, "L'Archivio Datini: De l'invention de 1870 à l'exploration d'un système d'écrits privés," *Mélanges de l'École française de Rome: Moyen Âge* 117 (2005): 121–91.

Peruzzi, and the Acciaiuoli were so geographically extensive that they could probably transact much of their business through partners within the firm, even that going in different directions across great distances. Still, they also used agents in places where they did not have branches, and some of these agents were more or less permanently located abroad and could shift from one company to another. For instance, Duccio Pucci in Ragusa represented the Bardi in 1323–24 but was with the Acciaiuoli in 1330; later that year he joined the Peruzzi, and three years later he was back with the Bardi.[95] The later firms, with fewer branches, were more dependent on one another or on commission agents. Datini could work within his agglomerate as long as he did not have business outside of the places where his firms were located, but the geographic analysis of his massive correspondence documents the extent to which he had to work with other firms and with independent agents, not all of them by any means Florentine, located in places where he had no branch firm or employee.[96]

The commission agent, the independent resident merchant abroad who worked as a broker for those firms not present on the local scene, came into his own in the later period of smaller and less geographically extensive firms. English documents record the work on the local scene of one Florentine agent, Paolo Morelli, for thirty years, until his death in 1448. Morelli arranged for payment of port dues, for the sale of goods in the local market, for transport of goods overland within England, and for export abroad by ship. The goods he handled belonged mostly, but not exclusively, to Florentines, and only occasionally was he himself the owner.[97] Commission agents were not dependents of a single firm but worked for any number of merchants. The surviving records of two agents in Constantinople after the Turkish conquest—Giovanni di Marco Salviati, who died there in 1493, and Girolamo di Carlo Strozzi, who also died there, in 1525—reveal that they operated, not independently, but on behalf of a partnership organization, in effect a brokerage firm. The firm Strozzi worked for had two partners: one, his father, remained in Florence to solicit clients, while the other, along with Girolamo, went to the Ottoman capital to execute these commissions.[98] Some of these agents abroad were veritable entrepreneurs who served

[95] Bariša Krekić, "Four Florentine Commercial Companies in Dubrovnik (Ragusa) in the First Half of the Fourteenth Century," in *Dubrovnik, Italy and the Balkans in the Late Middle Ages* (London, 1980), 36–37, reprinted from *The Medieval City*, ed. H. A. Miskimin, D. Herlihy, and A. L. Udovitch (New Haven, CT, 1977).

[96] Melis, *Aspetti*, 17–24.

[97] Alwin A. Ruddock, *Italian Merchants and Shipping in Southampton, 1270–1600* (Southampton, 1951), 98–102.

[98] Bruno Dini, "Aspetti del commercio di esportazione dei panni di lana e dei drappi di seta fiorentini in Costantinopoli, negli anni 1522–1531," in *Saggi*, 246–59, reprinted from *Studi in memoria di Federigo Melis*.

men back in Florence as both local correspondents and partners in ventures undertaken through accomandita contracts. One of these, Giovanni Guidetti, who went to Lisbon as a young man sometime before 1453, took initiatives to organize joint ventures along with other companies and individual merchants, not all of them Florentine, involving trade in coral, fish, and leather.[99] Like Guidetti, Bartolomeo Marchionni (who got his start with Guidetti and the Cambini company), also in Lisbon, and Giannotto Berardi in Seville, seem to have been independent entrepreneurs of this kind, working on their own as commission agents who also represented men back home in local joint ventures that they too invested in and directed.[100]

ACCOUNTING   Accounting was the principal technical tool to be mastered by any staff clerk, and it is the one for which Italian merchant-bankers are most famed in the historiography of medieval business practice. Their accounts, the official record of debts and credits, constituted one of the most concrete ties that bound firms together in the network. In the minutes of the tribunal of the Mercanzia recording the proceedings of cases brought before it by disputants with credit claims, possibly the largest single collection of documents from the republican period to survive in the Florentine state archives today, nothing is more striking than the many account books parties were forever hauling before the judges to substantiate their position. Already by the end of the thirteenth century, even before the Mercanzia was established, Florentines had taken one big step toward defining the bonds that held the network together by abandoning the notarized act in favor of the accounting record as the legal documentation for exchange transactions.[101] Since, in fact, the notarized act had given way to the accounting record, this kind of document in Florence, in contrast to many other places at the time, does not, as a rule, include information about business loans, insurance contracts, articles of association, and, in short, business activity in general. Accounting provided an instrument for more efficient operations by cutting transaction costs in time and money, and it generated bonds of trust between Florentines throughout the network. Thus the Corbizzi bank in Avignon, active in the 1330s, could seal a contract for loans to Florentines by simply making a record on the company books, whereas for loans to non-Florentines it usually had

---

[99] Something of Guidetti's career can be pieced together from information collected in Tognetti, *Il banco Cambini*, 184, 223–24, 241–42, 247–48, 295, 297.

[100] Unfortunately, no surviving business correspondence from Florence, not even Datini's, has been explored to define the role of the commission agent in the way Frederic C. Lane used the letters of the Venetian Andrea Barbarigo to expose the problems as well as the advantages of working through an agent. See *Andrea Barbarigo, Merchant of Venice, 1418–1449* (Baltimore, 1944), 94–131.

[101] Introduction to *Ser Matteo di Biliotto notaio: imbreviature*, vol. 1, *Registro (anni 1294–1296)*, ed. Manila Soffici and Franek Sznura (Florence, 2002), lxii–lxxviii.

to have recourse to the outside authority of a notary.[102] As the head of the Scali company had to explain in 1324 before an English court, where he found himself as a result of a dispute over debts, "it was usual amongst the alien merchants of the realm [by which he meant Florentines], in the case of loans and other financial transactions between them, for memoranda thereof to be made in their papers on both sides, stating the amount, the cause and the term of payment without any bond being made between them."[103] The centuries-old, almost sacred bond of the private accounting record between these men was threatened in 1605 by a proposal of the grand duke, who was concerned about tampering of accounts in cases of bankruptcy, to establish some government control over these documents by requiring public registration of all current business ledgers and the attachment of official seals to all closed ledgers going back twenty years. The grand duke, however, had to back down in face of the outcry from the city's merchants: reacting to his proposal, these "masters [*padroni*] of the money of other countries," as they styled themselves (somewhat nostalgically, by that time), argued that such a requirement went against the age-old traditions of their profession and that, if enacted, it would discourage youths of the "noble and well-born" from entering business.[104]

Accounting, as stated above, was not taught in the abacus school, to judge from the complete absence of the subject in the many surviving abacus treatises. It was the first thing a youth just arrived in a business office learned on the job. And yet a high degree of standardization of accounting practices had evolved by the second half of the fourteenth century. Debits were separated from credits in bilateral form on the two folio sides facing each other when the account book was open (a format called *alla veneziana*), values were entered in columns at the right of the entries, Arabic numerals were in general use by the fifteenth century, entries followed highly formulaic procedures and were written out using a fully developed jargon. Double entry—the entering of the same transaction in two different accounts, one on the debit side, the other on the credit side—was used extensively, complete with cross references, although a perfected double-entry system, with all entries so entered, is not widely found until the fifteenth century.

As important as the practice of double entry were, first, the fine-tuning in the articulation of accounts to separate different activities from one another in different accounts and, second, the emergence of a hierarchy of account books

---

[102] Sapori, "Una compagnia di prestatori," 112.

[103] Edmund Fryde, "The Bankruptcy of the Scali of Florence in England, 1326–1328," in *Progress and Problems in Medieval England: Essays in Honour of Edward Miller*, ed. R. Britnell and J. Hatcher (Cambridge, 1996), 116.

[104] Armando Sapori, "La registrazione dei libri di commercio in Toscana nell'anno 1605," in *Studi*, 1:35–51.

separating journals of first entry and other waste books—cashbooks, income-and-expenditures journals, merchandise journals, record books—from books of general synthesis or ledgers. This procedure of articulating activities and synthesizing the multiplicity of transactions facilitated an overview of all activities. Double entry, once it was rigidly observed and hence had evolved into a system, provided the supreme tool of analysis, the periodic balance that made it possible to see operating results. Also impressive in all this, and already manifest in the few accounts that survive from the thirteenth century, is the discipline with which accounts were kept: in books that span years and even decades the practice is uniform throughout, and corrections and erasures are rare.

There was progress in bookkeeping over the course of the fifteenth and sixteenth centuries in the sense that these features became more diffused and the practice was perfected, so that it is not at all unusual to find a set of books belonging to a firm from the second half of the sixteenth century that would meet the highest standards of modern practice. Put in this later perspective, the famed business records of Datini two centuries earlier seem primitive. Yet, all the essential features of accounting practice were in place, to a greater or lesser degree, by Datini's time, when the surviving patrimony of account books—unique to Florence—reaches impressive proportions.

It is not difficult to understand why Florentines, and perhaps Italians in general, although there is little evidence from elsewhere, came to surpass merchants in northern Europe in their mastery of accounting techniques. First was simply the volume of transactions they had to keep track of. A quantitative analysis of one journal of Filippo Strozzi's firm in Naples shows that in just seven months in 1472–73 there were seventy-three hundred operations, an average of thirty-four each day. The money that came into the cashbox over the period totaled *du*.171,625, and the total value of all the transfers effected from one account to another amounted to *du*.1,247,992. And all this traffic recorded day by day in the journal had to be cross-referenced to the more articulated organization of other books higher up in the hierarchy, capped by the ledger.[105] Contributing to the volume of transactions was the extraordinary variety of goods merchants handled. Although the bulk of Datini's trade could be categorized under the general rubrics of leather, metalwork, and, above all, raw wool and wool cloth, he dealt also in dozens and dozens of other items as well, from dried fruit to ostrich feathers and from arms to devotional art. The index to the commodities mentioned in the

---

[105] Mario Del Treppo, "Aspetti dell'attività bancaria a Napoli nel '400," in *Aspetti della vita economica medievale*, tables on 592–93 (see the text for analysis of the quantitative data). This journal has been published in Alfonso Leone, *Il giornale del banco Strozzi di Napoli (1473)* (Naples, 1981).

modern edition of the Pegolotti merchant manual, compiled in the first half of the fourteenth century, is twenty-four pages long.

Finally, the geographic extent of their operations required a sophisticated accounting system. The account books listed in the abovementioned Acciaiuoli inventory were kept in twenty-five different cities scattered across Europe and the Mediterranean from London to North Africa and the Byzantine Empire; the vast collection of business correspondence of the Datini archive has letters sent from 267 places. Moreover, the geography of a single operation could be quite complex. Take, for example, the arrangements the Datini company had to make in 1398–99 to fulfill a commission from a client in Florence to obtain ceramics in Valencia for sale in Genoa: the order in Florence, its transmission to the branch in Valencia, negotiations with the potter, shipment to the branch in Barcelona, shipment to the agent in Genoa, sale of the ceramics in Genoa on order of the client in Florence, and the report back to Florence. This operation, which we shall return to in the next chapter, involved keeping a record of payments for packing, handling, shipping, and customs in different ports, effecting transfers of charges in different moneys from one branch to another, and seeing to the related correspondence—all this for a few pieces of ceramics worth only *fl.*2½. Yet, a detailed record was kept of everything, and since the operation took place within one business agglomerate, all of whose accounts from the several branches are now assembled in the Datini archives, it is no problem whatsoever to trace this petty transaction every step of the way through the vast and diverse paperwork and to reconstruct a cost analysis. Accounting techniques had been perfected to this end.

Accounting is the technique that is always mentioned in any comment, even at the textbook level, about the modernity of business practice at the time. In view of the fact that entrepreneurs in the rest of Europe, even down to the industrial revolution, managed their affairs quite satisfactorily without recourse to double entry, doubt has been raised about the merits of the system as an index to the emergence of a capitalistic mentality. Double-entry accounting, even in its non-systemic form, served the specific needs of the Florentine entrepreneur confronted with the geographic and mercantile complexity of the network. What is often overlooked in discussions of the technique, however, is its utter simplicity: the rules could hardly be simpler and clearer, and they do not rest on difficult intellectual premises. Practice, however—and this is the point—required the most demanding discipline. Florentines acquired this discipline as children in their long apprenticeship, and the hundreds upon hundreds of account books still extant are proof enough, in their conformity to the rules and in the absence of mistakes, corrections, and erasures, of how disciplined these men were.

LONG-DISTANCE COMMUNICATION   Communication over long distances was a primary concern of the firm. Merchants needed to notify one another about book transfers, and they had to send bills back and forth. And in addition they wanted to be kept informed about what was going on in the various markets where they did business. "Keep me informed about spices," Datini wrote to his contact in Genoa in 1392, "and about everything related to our trade, especially all the rumors and all the news that you hear about the sea and other things. . . . When you see anything that involves importing or exporting merchandise, let us know."[106] In the thirteenth century the Calimala guild ran a mail service that had one courier going to the Champagne fairs and one returning every day, and there was also a service to other places in France. Each firm had its own packet of letters, which was sealed before it was put in the courier's bag along with packets of other merchants. In the mid-fourteenth century the Mercanzia organized some communication services, and merchants themselves made arrangements through consortiums for shared mailing service *(scarsella)* to specific places. In 1357, for example, nineteen firms joined in a contractual agreement to establish a service to Avignon. In addition, merchants used their own private couriers. A firm's set of records usually included a letter book containing copies of letters sent out and a separate courier journal recording departures. To assure arrival, it might send another copy in a second shipment or by a different route. Couriers were generally held to a certain schedule for arrivals, and depending on how the delivery went, they were subject to a penalty or enjoyed a bonus *(vantaggio)*. The overall cost of this service did not figure prominently in a firm's operating expenses, however extensive its operations. Iacopo and Bartolomeo di Caroccio degli Alberti & Partners averaged a little more than *fl.*30 annually from 1348 to 1350; the Datini firm in Avignon spent *fl.*20–40 a year from 1386 to 1402; and the Datini firm in Florence, a more limited operation, spent only about *fl.*13 annually from 1396 to 1398—costs that were more or less equivalent to the annual salary of a junior clerk on the firm's staff.[107]

Getting information before the other firms could be important. "If you engage in trade and your letters arrive together with others," advised Paolo da Certaldo in the middle of the fourteenth century, "always keep in mind to read yours first before passing on the others. And if your letters advise you to buy or sell some merchandise at a profit, call a broker immediately and do what the letters advise, and then consign the other letters that arrived with yours. But don't consign them

---

[106] Quoted in Louis Stouff, "Une famille florentine à Arles: Les Benini vers 1360–vers 1440," in *La Toscane et les Toscans autour de la Renaissance,* 274.

[107] Marco Spallanzani, "Spedizioni e tempi di percorrenza," in Goldthwaite, Settesoldi, and Spallanzani, *Due libri mastri degli Alberti,* 1:lxxxv–xci.

before having finished your own business."[108] The merchant might, in fact, pay a bonus to a shared courier of a *scarsella* for collusion in such an intervention. In a letter from a firm in Avignon to the Datini agent in Genoa in 1393, the writer informs his correspondent that

> we are agreed with this courier, whose name is Cola da Bisso, that he have a bonus of *fl*.3½; and there [in Genoa] it should be Sunday the 9th at vespers. Less time was not desirable because these are bad times to travel and also because we did not want to increase expenses. If he is there on time, give him two florins. And we have an agreement with him that he must not deliver any letter before delivering the packet for you and the one for Marchionne de' Marini, and all the other letters he must hold back until the next day at vespers. If he does good service, reward him well. We have paid this bonus only so that you have time to talk to Marchionne and to do what is said herein below before the others there know anything about it. Go to see Marchionne as soon as the courier arrives, even if he arrives at night.[109]

We get occasional glimpses of these *maestri dei corrieri,* as they were called, in the accounts of their client firms, and enough of these scattered references survive for one of these, Antonio di Bartolomeo Del Vantaggio, that we can put together a sketch of his career. He appears to have been something of an entrepreneur (his success perhaps giving rise to his surname).[110] Operating out of Florence from at least 1457 to his death in 1480, he offered a service that took in almost the entire network: it covered all of Italy, from Milan and Venice to Rome and Naples, and extended beyond, throughout all of western Europe, to Geneva, Lyons, Catalonia, Lisbon, Bruges, and London. He carried about four hundred letters a year for the Cambini company alone, and in one eighteen-month period in 1473–74 he sent eighty-one couriers to Venice for the wool firm of Benedetto di Antonio Salutati and Ristoro di Antonio Serristori. He offered a kind of subscription, contracting his service for set periods of time; thus one of his clients, the firm of Filippo and Lorenzo di Matteo Strozzi, paid him £40 on 1 January 1473 to handle all their correspondence to and from Rome for a year. Del Vantaggio, along with who knows how many others, marks one step toward the regular and rapid postal service on a European scale organized by the Tasso family of Bergamo in the early sixteenth century. At the very end of the sixteenth century the grand duke established a

---

[108] Paolo da Certaldo, *Libro di buoni costumi,* ed. Alfredo Schiaffini (Florence, 1946), 149–50.

[109] Quoted in Giagnacovo, *Mercanti toscani a Genova,* 34.

[110] Federigo Melis, "Intensità e regolarità nella diffusione dell'informazione economica generale nel Mediterraneo e in Occidente alla fine del Medioevo," reprinted in Melis, *I trasporti e le comunicazioni nel Medioevo,* ed. Luciana Frangioni (Florence, 1984), 190; this volume of Melis's collected essays includes statistical data about mail service especially at the time of Datini. The Strozzi recorded their arrangement with Del Vantaggio in their record book, ASF, Carte strozziane, ser. 5, 26, fol. 60.

mail service to Venice, but how Florence figures into the refinement of official postal systems and the evolution of business newsletters on a European scale in the sixteenth century is yet another untold story.

TRANSPORT   Merchants, of course, also had to ship goods, and Florentines could never have built up their network without both long-distance maritime and terrestrial transport services. They themselves, however, did not operate a subsidiary transport sector. Merchants contracted with others for shipment of goods. For maritime transport they had access to any number of well-organized shipping services, ranging from the great international systems of the Venetians and Genoese down to those of the Catalans, Basques, Anconetani, and a host of others whose sailings were more geographically limited, including the local cabotage service that was to be found in any port. Datini, over a period extending from 1383 to 1411, used almost three thousand ships belonging to twenty-five different "national" groups, the most important being Ligurians and Catalans, followed far behind by Venetians. Datini himself never participated in the ownership of a ship; like most merchants, he contracted with ship owners for transport of merchandise. Some merchants, acting either singly or jointly with others, bought their own ships (or shares in them), which were then consigned to the charge of foreign captains. For a time, through the second and third quarters of the fifteenth century, Florence had its own galley system, but it closed down largely because its policy, directed primarily to serving the needs of the local wool industry, overlooked the interregional traffic so important to the Florentine network, which was already well served by private arrangements. Florentines, in short, were able to build up their network because a solid foundation of maritime shipping systems had been put into place by others, albeit, at least in part, in response to the network's demands.[111]

Indeed, we know of no Florentine entrepreneur who went beyond the purchase of a single ship to build up any kind of larger shipping service. There were those, however, who made their fortune in this sector, serving as the agents of contractors and traveling with goods from port to port, taking advantage of any market opportunity. Bongianni di Bongianni Gianfigliazzi, an orphan from a branch of a prominent family that had fallen on hard times, seems to have been one of these. In his record book he notes the traveling abroad he did at the beginning of his career, all to port cities. In 1432, at the age of fourteen, he went off to Naples and Gaeta with only £3 *di piccioli* his mother had given him. In 1434 he

---

[111] Melis's articles on transport of merchandise, especially useful for the statistical data derived from the Datini materials, have been collected in his *I trasporti*.

went to Valencia, and the next year, he went on to Barcelona, where he had good contacts with established firms. In 1436 his employers, Giovanni Ventura and Riccardo Davanzati in Barcelona, bought a ship and made Gianfigliazzi, then only eighteen, its *padrone,* the agent who had full responsibility for handling the cargo, for a voyage to Venice and then another to Nice. After moving around to other places on the sea—Almeria, Malaga, and Majorca—he returned to Florence in 1446 without much money, having spent too much and suffered losses, but apparently with some experience, for he immediately found a position as *padrone* of a state galley in a fleet going to North Africa and Catalonia and then in another going to Alexandria. In 1451, at the age of thirty-three, he went into business as a minor partner with his brother Gherardo to set up a company in Valencia but continued his links to the state galleys, now as occasional contractor as well as captain of the fleet on voyages to Catalonia, North Africa, Flanders, and England. In 1463 he estimated that he had accumulated *fl.*11,000, although his total net worth was *fl.*37,000, thanks to his inheritance from Gherardo. Bongianni lived on for some twenty more years, to 1484.[112]

Merchants also dealt with independent contractors for overland transport. In port cities the local market probably functioned in such a way as to preclude their involvement in the traffic of merchandise into and from the hinterland. In inland cities, where merchants had to get goods to a port, the largest shipments they themselves had to arrange were probably those for raw wool and finished cloth, about the only merchandise Florentines handled in large quantities. In England they went inland to contract for raw wool and to arrange for getting it to a port, and much of the cloth they purchased in the Low Countries went overland to a Mediterranean port. In the period from 1352 to 1357 the agent in Bruges of Bartolomeo di Caroccio degli Alberti & Partners, for example, sent two or three shipments of cloth every month from several cities in the region to Avignon, about half consisting of fewer than fifty bolts and few over one hundred bolts.[113] Unfortunately, merchants' accounts give few hints about how such shipments were arranged. In any event, it is not likely that shipments in western Europe approached the size of the pack train of 114 beasts of burden that Giovanni Maringhi conducted over the difficult and probably dangerous route across the Balkans, from Ragusa to Pera, in 1497 (see chapter 2).

[112] ASF, Istituti esterni, 1 (Gianfigliazzi's record book), fol. 3 (microfilm of the original in the Archivio della Congregazione dei Buonomini di San Martino). Biographical information can be found in V. Arrighi and F. Klein, "Da *mercante avventuriero* a *confidente dello stato:* Profile di Bongianni Gianfigliazzi attraverso le sue *ricordanze,*" *ASI* 161 (2003): 53–79; and Brenda Preyer, "Around and in the Gianfigliazzi Palace in Florence: Developments on Lungarno Corsini in the 15th and 16th Centuries," *Mitteilungen des kunsthistorischen Institutes in Florenz* 48 (2004): 55–104.

[113] Marco Spallanzani, "Spedizioni e tempi," lx–lxiv.

Arrangements made abroad for transport probably did not differ from those made in Florence itself, for which we have better documentation. There, local carriers handled everything as independent entrepreneurs working on contract. One of these, Battista di Taccino di Bizzino (or Bizzini), left behind six account books documenting his business—a sequence of four journals recording shipments from 1445 to 1478, along with two accompanying record books—not to mention a book kept for the administration of his estate.[114] Battista identifies himself as a hosteller, like his father, and his inn, which probably had accommodation for pack animals and storage, was the base for his operations. His transport service may have been something he arranged on the side, for his records contain no evidence that he himself did any traveling. He worked through partnerships with muleteers, he being the silent partner who probably drummed up business. According to an agreement made in 1446, he contributed one mule, the muleteer contributed the other, and the two were to share the profits equally. In June 1448, when Florence was engaged in military operations around Piombino against the invading forces of Alfonso, king of Naples, Battista had four contracts from the city government for a one-month service, during which time he sent out five carriers with a total of twenty-four mules. Battista's commercial shipments, in contrast, apparently did not require more than several mules at a time. His muleteers carried principally wool cloth but also any number of other goods, and they traveled to Milan, Rome, Naples, and many other cities and towns throughout the Po valley, Tuscany, and central Italy, and, outside Italy, to Geneva and Lyons. Ledgers of the Cambini firm record payments to Battista for shipments to Rome in 1451–53. From 1452 to 1467 he transported an average of 680 bolts of wool cloth every year (of which 340 went to Rome), a scale of operations at the level of that of the Alberti mentioned above and equivalent to the yearly output of about six wool firms. In chapter 2 we shall encounter Battista again, when in 1461 he invested in an accomandita for shipments to Constantinople. It remains to be seen how many other men worked in this sector of the local economy and what scale of operations any of them reached.

INSURANCE   To reduce the risks of transport, Florentines perfected the insurance contract. Among the earliest documentation for Florentines operating abroad is insurance they took out for shipment of merchandise—cotton from

---

[114] Archive of the Ospedale degli Innocenti, Florence, ser. 144 (Estranei), 199–205 (including a ledger of his estate). In addition, three of his father's books and three of his son Giovanni's survive. Hidetoshi Hoshino used some of this material for his study of the wool industry; see *L'arte della lana in Firenze nel Basso Medioevo: Il commercio della lana e il mercato dei panni fiorentini nei secoli XIII–XV* (Florence, 1980), 244–45, 248–49, 285.

Genoa to Arezzo in 1214 and cloth from the Champagne fairs to Vercelli in 1215. The earliest insurance contracts, however, date from the first half of the fourteenth century and, as one might expect, are found mostly in port cities. They were notarized documents, usually following the model of a maritime loan or a purchase-sale contract to preclude any charge of usury. By the end of the century, however, Florentines alone among the great international merchant nations had eliminated the notary and cut through the convoluted ways of a notarized document to transform the insurance contract into an entirely private agreement that involved no more than writing out the particulars—the voyage, coverage, the commitment of the insurer to pay the claim should the goods insured not arrive safe and sound at their destination—and payment of a premium up front.[115] The basic structure of this business in premium insurance was small in scale: merchants took out contracts for specific shipments, and the insurer was anyone willing to take the risks for the advantage of being paid the premium, the latter generally wanting to limit the risk to between *fl.*50 and *fl.*200. In other words, there was no blanket coverage for multiple shipments or for set periods beyond the duration of a single voyage, and the business was highly fragmented among many individual insurers. The only increase in scale came with the recourse to more than one underwriter for a single policy and the association of several individuals into a syndicate acting as a single underwriter, both being instruments devised to increase coverage beyond what any one person was willing to risk.

The nature of this structure emerges from statistical surveys of insurance contracts from two different but complementary sources: the 128 contracts made by one merchant, Francesco Datini, over the eleven years from 1390 to 1401 and the 908 contracts arranged through a single broker, Raggio di Nofero Raggi, over twenty-nine months from 1524 to 1526.[116] The underwriters for Datini's 128 policies numbered 490, but since many of these were the same parties, the actual number of different underwriters, both individuals and syndicates, was 88, and the total number of persons, acting individually and in syndicates, was 124. The data from Raggi's journal recording 908 contracts can be ordered in a different way to illustrate the same features: Raggi dealt with 119 persons, who took out policies with 326 underwriters. Insurers on the average underwrote 27 policies

---

[115] The classic article surveying the evolution of premium insurance is Florence Edler de Roover, "Early Examples of Marine Insurance," *Journal of Economic History* 5 (1945): 172–200. The evidence for insurance contracts in the thirteenth and early fourteenth centuries is surveyed in Robert Davidsohn, *Storia di Firenze* (Florence, 1956), 4, pt. 2:429–37.

[116] Giovanni Ceccarelli, "Tra solvibilità economica e status politico: Il mercato delle assicurazioni marittime a Firenze (sec. XIV–XV)," in *Politiche del credito: Investimento consumo solidarietà* (Asti, 2004), 191–221 (on Datini); Bruno Dini, introduction to Federigo Melis, *Origini e sviluppi delle assicurazioni in Italia (secoli XIV–XVI)*, vol. 1, *Le fonti* (Rome, 1975), xxxv–xlii (on Raggi) and 282–307 (data collected by Melis).

each, with each policy having an average of about 10 underwriters. For one policy Raggi put together a group of 51 underwriters. The vast majority of these individual insurers from both samples committed themselves to no more than *fl.*50–200, the average being *fl.*134 for the Datini sample and *fl.*78 for the Raggi sample (about the same in lire: £509 and £546, respectively). Through multiple and syndicate subscription, however, a policy could have a high value. The policies taken out by Datini averaged *fl.*515; those brokered by Raggi averaged *fl.*755 but ranged from *fl.*40 to *fl.*6,500.

There do not appear to have been specialized underwriters. The largest number of Datini's 128 policies underwritten by the same person was only 49 over eleven years, the next highest was 32, and then the number falls to 16 and below. Raggi's best client, Averardo di Alamanno Salviati, acting for himself and also for his company, participated as an underwriter in 439 policies in just twenty-nine months, almost half of the contracts Raggi brokered and an average of about one every other day; but at the same time he paid out premiums for coverage for his own shipments that amounted to much more than the value he underwrote. Most underwriters, however, participated only occasionally and acted singly, not through organized syndicates. In fact, judging from evidence scattered among the many private account books of the period, most people with means, whether they were merchants or not, were from time to time willing to take the risk, within limits, of underwriting a policy. They presumably worked through brokers like Raggi, whose business it was to bring the two parties together.

The practice of underwriting remained unchanged across this century and a quarter, from the end of the fourteenth to the early sixteenth century: single underwriters, not professionals, worked through brokers, limiting their risks and offering the possibility of increased coverage through multiple subscriptions. The study of rates, still in its infancy, has revealed a certain coherence, suggesting that they were structured around the obvious variables—length of the voyage, the season, the degree of a ship's defense, the presence of pirates, the state of war or peace.[117] In other words, the sector came to thrive less on man's instinct to gamble and more on rational calculation of risks based on shared knowledge. Moreover, by Datini's time the language of the insurance contract had become standardized in a way that became formulaic for the next century. Nevertheless, if we compare averages for the policies arranged by a single broker, Raggi, with those taken out a century earlier by a single merchant, Datini, we can conclude that the insurance sector grew: there were more underwriters per policy (9.68

[117] Alberto Tenenti, "Sui tassi assicurativi mediterranei del Quattrocento e della prima metà del Cinquecento," in *Studi di storia economica toscana,* 347–63 (using published rates for Barcelona, Florence, and Ragusa).

compared with 3.82), more policies per underwriter (26.95 compared with 3.95), and, if we look at values in terms of the local purchasing power of the florin (see table A.1), much higher coverage per policy (*fl.*755 compared with *fl.*515) without any change in the maximum value the single underwriter was willing to commit himself to.

During the same period there were also major structural refinements to the sector. Legislation, directed not to the codification of the insurance contract but to the regulation of its use, gradually liberalized practice. A 1393 provision prohibited insurance of merchandise belonging to foreigners; in 1405 such insurance was permitted if the merchandise was purchased in Florentine territory; in 1441 prohibitions were relaxed for insurance taken out for voyages on the state galley system; and finally, in 1464, by which time inadequacies of the galley system were apparent, the sector became completely liberalized with respect to foreigners and private ships. Legislation in 1523 created the Ufficiali di sicurtà, a commission set up within the Mercanzia to license brokers on an annual basis. These brokers alone were authorized to write policies, they were to keep accounts of their activity and report regularly to the commission, and the fixed fee they charged was to be shared with the Mercanzia. Raggi, whose ledger was open in this year, was therefore the very first of these official professional brokers. The Ufficiali, moreover, acted as a claims court. A volume of the commission's proceedings for the years 1591–92 records the meetings, averaging about six times a month, during which the commissioners settled claims, assessing the actual damage to goods and fixing the compensation to be paid by the insurer. To judge from these claims, most syndicates of individual insurers by this time were acting through the agency of a merchant-banking firm, perhaps by this time a firm organized specifically for this purpose, such as the "compagni degli otto assicuratori" set up by some Genoese at Venice in 1594. By this time, too, policies were being printed. The oldest form to survive, dated 1593, leaves blank spaces to be filled in for the names of the insured and the insurers, the amount insured, the goods insured, the specific voyage, and the signatures of all the subscribers. The regularization of insurance by the state at this late date is yet another index of Florentines' continuing involvement in foreign trade.[118]

It should be noted that almost all the underwriters in the two samples used above were Florentines in Florence, and although most policies covered shipments out of the local ports of Pisa and Livorno, these men were also underwriting shipments between just about any two points in the network, whatever the

---

[118] Bruno Dini, in Melis, *Origini e sviluppi delle assicurazioni*, publishes the legislation (234–35) and the printed form (237–38). The volume of the deliberations of the Ufficiali in 1591–92 is ASF, Mercanzia, 14155; an earlier volume for 1524, perhaps the first, but only a fragment, is ibid., 14154.

distance between them. Florentines abroad were also active as insurers serving foreign merchants wherever they were located, although they had to adapt the contracts to local legal demands, which usually required a notarial act. In the second quarter of the fifteenth century they and the Genoese were the major insurers in Barcelona, and they were more active than the Genoese. Likewise in contemporary Valencia, then beginning its rise as a major commercial port, Florentines were the most numerous insurers, and they insured almost half of the contracts made there that have been studied. In fact, influenced by the simplicity and directness of the Florentine contract, the notaries of Barcelona abandoned the standard model that they had adopted for insurance contracts in order to avoid the usury restriction and developed in its place a distinct model for this kind of risk contract that was explicit about the premium. When the same development took place in Genoa, a major center of insurers, the model was described as following Florentine custom (with respect to its sense, not its form).[119] We shall see that in Venice too marine insurance was an important activity of Florentines there at the end of the sixteenth century.

Florentine merchants had as sophisticated a system of marine insurance as was to be found anywhere in Europe. The contract was simple and straightforward, not requiring a notary; a fairly coherent system of rates facilitated a rational decision on the part of the insurer; many people in the population could be found who had the financial security and the willingness to underwrite policies; brokers existed to bring these potential insurers together with those who sought insurance; the merchant could insure his goods at about any value he wished by recourse to multiple subscription (although individuals limited the value they were willing to underwrite); and finally, the state allowed for the complete liberalization of the sector. Thus Florentine merchants had all the protection they needed to operate their international network even though they, in general, did not directly control a transport system, except in the years when the state offered the limited services of its galleys.

The above discussion is confined to marine insurance. Evidence for terrestrial insurance is rare, and little is known about it, although the very first documentation we have for insurance taken out by Florentine merchants, mentioned above, was for overland shipments across France into the Piedmont and across Tuscany to Arezzo in the early thirteenth century. A century and a half later, however, the

---

[119] For Florentines as insurers in Barcelona, see Del Treppo, *I mercanti catalani,* 460–61, 470–76. For their activity in Valencia, see Enrique Cruselles, *Los mercaderes de Valencia en la edad media (1380–1450)* (Lleida, 2001), 211; and idem, "Los mercados aseguradores del Mediterráneo catalano-aragonés," in *Ricchezza del mare, ricchezza dal mare, sec. XIII–XVIII,* ed. Simonetta Cavaciocchi (Florence, 2006), 611–39.

Alberti company insured only two overland shipments during the decade documented by two of its ledgers, 1348–58, one of *fl.*12,800 in specie from Florence to Pisa (for which it paid a premium of only *fl.*15) and one of wool cloth sent through Germany to Italy. The firm did not take out insurance for any of its numerous shipments of cloth sent out of the Low Countries overland across France to Avignon and ports further south, notwithstanding the raging of the Hundred Years' War at the time. Federigo Melis found hardly any evidence that Datini ever insured overland shipments, and he observed that misfortunes during such trips are rarely mentioned in Datini's vast correspondence. Florence Edler de Roover cites several Florentine contracts from the mid-fifteenth century for shipments from Bologna to Geneva and one from Lille to Geneva; their low rates—3 percent for the former and 2.5 percent for the latter, both at the lowest level of the schedule of rates for marine insurance—are an index to the relative security of these routes. At the end of the sixteenth century carters assumed the financial responsibility for shipments overland from Antwerp to Italy, and they did not take out insurance to protect themselves against claims from their clients.[120]

SUMMARY   Florentine merchant-bankers worked within a highly sophisticated business structure. The partnership organization of the firm provided them with the means to raise working capital and assured them the use of that capital over the duration of several years. Since partnerships tended to be dominated by one or two investors, they were limited in the number of partners they took on and therefore in their potential for amassing a corpo, but this made it easier to determine policy and make decisions. Moreover, by taking on banking functions, they were able to raise the stock of capital they commanded well beyond what the partners invested in the business. In short, these merchant-bankers worked within a business organization that gave them the flexibility they needed with respect to capital, time, and management to meet the challenges of doing business in the fluid economy of Europe at the time.

The firm had a management team in place that coordinated commercial and financial operations throughout the network by getting information from one place to another to ensure equilibrium of supply and demand of goods and capital. Staff members had had formal technical education in commercial arithmetic, which gave them the ability to deal with complex monetary systems, and once on

---

[120] Marco Spallanzani, "Assicurazioni," in Goldthwaite, Settesoldi, and Spallanzani, *Due libri mastri degli Alberti*, 1:xcviii–cc; Federigo Melis, "Da un bacino all'altro del Mediterraneo attraverso la peninsola italiana," in *I trasporti*, 172–73; Edler de Roover, "Early Examples of Marine Insurance," 195–96; Florence Edler, "The van der Molen, Commission Merchants of Antwerp: Trade with Italy, 1538–44," in *Medieval and Historiographical Essays in Honor of James Westfall Thompson,* ed. James Lea Cate and Eugene N. Anderson (Chicago, 1938), 138.

the job, they received expert training in accounting and business correspondence and acquired the discipline of keeping records. Through years of apprenticeship in the office, they learned how to run a business, and travel abroad extended their experience to the farthest reach of the network, just as their frequent change of jobs enlarged their knowledge of how things were done and widened their circle of acquaintances within their profession. Moreover, these men started on their careers as mere children, many even before adolescence. They literally grew into a business frame of mind, just as artisans grew into their skills.

Finally, the firm developed techniques for dealing over long distances and handling a great variety of merchandise. They used barter or, better, trade exchanges to reduce the problem of money transfers; accounting enabled them to keep precise track of far-flung and complex operations and to shift credits here and there throughout the network; and with the bill of exchange they effected payments abroad in different moneys. They collectively and individually organized a postal service to expedite communication; and although the network did not incorporate a permanent and comprehensive transport system, it could depend on an efficient insurance sector at home for securing shipments of merchandise anywhere within it.

Interfirm Relations

We know much about the geographic extent of the network abroad, but hardly any precise figures exist for the number of firms or merchants that constituted it. A 1322 census of Florentines engaged in trade outside of the city that was drawn up by the tribunal of the Mercanzia for tax purposes lists 262 names of firms and individuals operating on their own (for a total, including partners who are identified, of 338 names), but no distinction is made between those who engaged in international commerce and local shopkeepers and artisans who traded in the immediate countryside.[121] Of the men who served on the governing council of the Mercanzia over a forty-year period from 1308 to 1348, all, in theory at least (according to the enabling legislation), involved in some way in foreign trade, 228 can be identified, but they constituted only 42 percent of those who held this office.[122] According to Villani, writing about the same time, some 300 merchants operated outside of Florence. A list of Florentine firms with interest in the port of Pisa drawn up in 1369, after the demographic disasters at midcentury, has 108

---

[121] Antonella Astorri, "Gli spazi politici dei mercanti a Firenze nel primo Trecento," *ASI* 159 (2001): 291–92; the list is published in an appendix.

[122] Antonella Astorri, *La Mercanzia a Firenze nella prima metà del Trecento* (Florence, 1998), 90.

names on it.[123] John Padgett and Paul McLean, using archival sources and searching through secondary work, have put together a list of some 42 partnership agglomerates working through 81 firms outside of Florence in the years 1385 to 1399.[124] They found 103 firms operating outside of the Florentine state in the catasto of 1427 (in addition to 15 at Pisa and 11 in Florentine territory), and this before Lyons emerged as a major center in the network.[125] Some rough estimates for specific places are mentioned in chapter 2: 50 merchants in the Levant in 1469, 25–30 bankers in the Rome of the Medici popes, about 40–45 residents in Lyons across the sixteenth century. The problem with these and other numbers that turn up in the literature is to distinguish firms from individuals and, among the latter, to distinguish resident employees of firms from the commission agents who worked independently for nonresident firms. It is probably safe to say that at any one time from the later fourteenth to the sixteenth century 100–150 firms and several hundred men were working outside the Florentine state. The number probably reached its height in the second half of the fifteenth century, when Naples, Rome, Lyons, and Constantinople were all growing as markets for Florentine cloth and financial services.

COMPANY AUTONOMY   The firms in the network were bound together by their mutual dependence on commercial contacts with one another to get goods from one place to another and on an exchange system to get money from one place to another. The process by which they built up the bonds of trust among themselves as they were laying the foundation of their network across the twelfth and thirteenth centuries evades us today, given the nature of the documents. Especially significant were the social implications of the two principal instruments through which these men tied themselves into the system: accounting, which served as an efficient tool to keep a record of their complex relations, and the bill of exchange, which allowed them to circulate money—the sinews of their business—freely throughout the system. Accounting required trusting the written record, and the bill of exchange required reliance on a financial relation with a merchant in a different place and on a collective agreement for the fixing of

[123] Simone Luigi Peruzzi, *Storia del commercio e dei banchieri di Firenze in tutto il mondo conosciuto dal 1200 al 1345* (Florence, 1868), 219–22.

[124] Padgett and McLean, "Organizational Invention and Elite Transformation," app. A.

[125] The complete list, including those in the Florentine state but outside Florence, comprised agglomerates in the western Mediterranean, northern Europe, and Italy. Those in the western Mediterranean were in Catalonia (17), Avignon and Montpelier (9), southern Spain (3), and Barbary (1). Those in northern Europe were in London and Bruges (7), Buda (3), and Paris (2). And those in Italy were in Pisa (15), Venice (13), Rome (13), Naples (12), Genoa (2), central Italy (5), Bologna and Mantua (7), Siena (2), Lucca (1), the Florentine state (11), and other places (2). These data are from John Padgett's "Census of firms in 1427 catasto," which is accessible on the Internet through his home page: http://home.uchicago.edu/~jpadgett/.

exchange rates at each of the various international centers. Firms worked through one another and used the same agents abroad to handle their business. These horizontal ties that bound these businessmen together were strengthened by their Florentine origins and the shared business culture in which they had been trained, not to mention an apprenticeship that widened the circle of their professional acquaintances beyond the office of one firm.

Sometimes these firms entered into joint ventures in the commercial sphere with one another, and sometimes with non-Florentines, usually to share expenses and risks or to gain monopoly privileges for the supply, distribution, and sale of a particular item of trade in a limited market. For instance, the Cambini company, active in the third quarter of the fifteenth century, participated in syndicates with other merchants to rent and arm galleys and to find and market coral. Bankers also worked with one another in the area of government finance, where risks were often great and the scale of operations beyond the reach of any one firm. In the early fourteenth century the Bardi, the Peruzzi, and the Acciaiuoli— the big three—seem to have had agreements among themselves for dealing with the king in Naples; they shared the same geographic areas of operations and had deep financial interests in the same governments; and they all went bankrupt at the same time. By the sixteenth century the scale of government borrowing was such that arrangements for sharing in it were institutionalized—in the tax farms at Rome, the *asientos* in Spain, the Grand Parti in France—in a way that opened investment to bankers everywhere and allowed them to reduce risks.

Beyond specific ventures undertaken jointly for a limited period, these firms did not form associations committing them to a common policy in overall operations to which modern terms invented to describe industrial capitalism can be applied: they did not form trusts, subjecting themselves to a single policy and direction, and they were not multinationals in the contemporary sense since they did not establish industrial operations abroad, as did, for instance, the English Muscovy Company with its rope factory in Russia or the Dutch East India Company with its refining plant for saltpeter and a printworks for textiles in Bengal. The tendency, so prevalent among economic historians, to use terms implying analogies with modern business practices—*trusts, multinationals, holding companies*—can lead to profound misunderstanding about the mentality and practice of entrepreneurs in the past.

Moreover, at the level of day-to-day transactions with one another, these firms do not appear to have been dependent on any other single firm or group of firms. None could have existed without working with others in the network, but no one firm emerges as having a commanding leverage over others, let alone a dominant position in the network or at any of its nodes. A hierarchy of firms organized by size does not translate into a power structure. Fluidity is a notable feature of the business relations among them. Take, for instance, two ledgers of the firm of Filippo di Matteo Strozzi, one of the largest firms in the last quarter of the fifteenth century. Of the 21 accounts open in the name of other merchant-banking firms in ledger F (1480–83), only 2 were open for the entire duration of the ledger, only 10 had accounts in ledger I (1487–89), open for five years, and only 1 of the accounts in the latter ledger was open for the entire duration of the ledger. Taking the accounts of these firms in both ledgers together, 17 were open for less than a year, while only 5 were open for more than two years. Two ledgers from the Corsi firm a century later, M (1576–78) and P (1582–88), reveal the same fluidity. Of the 22 companies in Florence and the 87 companies abroad on the books in ledger M, only 5 of the former and 15 of the latter show up on the books of ledger P, opened four years later.[126]

Not even the Medici bank had a commanding position over other firms, notwithstanding its great size—it was larger and more geographically extensive than any of its contemporaries—and the political power of the family. Although it had branches in the major banking centers of Europe—Venice, Milan, Rome, Naples, London, Bruges, Avignon, Geneva, then Lyons—it did not dominate business in any one of these places. Moreover, judging from the numerous business accounts that survive from the period, many Florentine merchant-bankers operated abroad without doing any business at all with the Medici. The two aforementioned ledgers of Filippo Strozzi's firm have only three accounts open to a Medici firm during three years of activity, from 1487 to 1489: one with Lorenzo de' Medici, Francesco Sassetti & Partners of Lyons for two large transactions in international exchange in 1487 totaling *fl.*11,656, another with Lorenzo de' Medici & Partners of Florence for exchange transactions in late 1488 and 1489 totaling *fl.*10,501, and one with Piero di Lorenzo de' Medici & Partners, silk manufacturers, for one bill of exchange for *fl.*484.[127] In fact, neither the near bankruptcy of the Medici agglomerate in the years 1478–80 nor the exile of the family in 1494 sent serious repercussions throughout the business world, a situation that contrasts sharply with that of the bankruptcy of the Bardi and the Peruzzi a century and a half earlier. One could write a history of Florentine banking in the fifteenth century without so much as mentioning the Medici, and if, as here, their bank is to be mentioned at all, it is primarily because its size, the largest on record at the time, offers a yardstick for measuring the others. Nor did the Medici, in its business activities on the local scene back home in Florence, have a notable influence in other sectors

[126] Goldthwaite, "Banking in Florence," 486.
[127] ASF, Carte strozziane, ser. 5, 44, fols. 73, 123, 235, 280.

of the economy. As we shall see in chapter 4, wool and silk firms dealt with any number of importer-exporters both for the supply of raw materials and for the marketing of finished products, and ties between merchants and these industrial firms were as fluid as the ties between merchants themselves. Likewise, no one firm, not even the Medici, had a dominant interest in the state's finances, and nothing like a financial oligarchy of firms emerged to control the floating debt. The only coagulants in all this fluidity in the relations among firms, whether in the commercial, the banking, or the industrial sector, are the few central clearance banks that emerge on the local scene in the second half of the sixteenth century (see chapter 6).

THE NAZIONE   The network did not have a formal institutional structure. At the local level wherever they found themselves Florentines did not organize politically in a way that imposed much of an institutional cohesion on them. They did not establish colonies abroad that became bases for political and military control of a local area as well as centers of trade, such as those of the Venetians and Genoese in the Near East. At the most, resident communities of Florentines in some places organized themselves into a corporation known as a *nazione,* or "nation." The nazione was an association set up to handle commercial and juridical disputes among its members and to deal collectively with a local government to try to gain legal status and privileges. Statutes established the parameters of its authority, and elected officials, usually a consul and two councilors, directed its affairs, perhaps aided by a notary and a treasurer.

Florentines had a nazione at one time or another in many centers throughout the network where their numbers merited one. In many instances, however, they set up a formal nazione long after establishing a resident community; for instance, they did not establish one at Bruges until 1427, at Rome until 1515, and at Antwerp until 1546. They never had one in Barcelona. The initiative for forming a nazione may have depended on the exigencies of the local political situation, but some, like the one in Rome, grew out of a confraternity organized around mutual assistance and religious activities and provided with its own chapel, invariably dedicated to John the Baptist, in a prominent local church, usually Franciscan. The political and religious functions were not, of course, mutually exclusive; in fact, the nazione in Venice strongly resembled a confraternity. For the most part the nazioni were autonomous, subject to little regulation from the government in Florence other than the appellate authority of the city's courts.[128]

---

[128] For generalizations about the *nazioni* and the publication of their statutes, see Gino Masi, ed., *Statuti delle colonie fiorentine all'estero (secc. XV–XVI)* (Milan, 1941).

The nazione in no way defined Florentines as a specific ethnic group, set off from others in the places where they did business by religious or strong cultural differences of much consequence, of the kind that have recently interested scholars studying foreign merchant communities in the Mediterranean, from the Maghrebi traders in the eleventh century to the Sephardic Jews in the early modern period. At the most, Florentines came in for their share of the prejudice that sporadically took a nasty turn against Italians in general for their usurious practices, for their financial power, and for the special favoritism they enjoyed from the local government—in the France of Philip the Fair, at Barcelona at the end of the fourteenth century, at London in the mid-fifteenth century, at Protestant Lyons in the later sixteenth century. On the whole, however, most Florentines, whether in fourteenth-century Southampton or sixteenth-century Lyons, managed to merge into the local population at least temporarily during their residency, some becoming local citizens. There were always a few, especially among the great bankers closely associated with a local court, who went on to marry a native, enter into local politics, and set down permanent roots, perhaps nowhere more so than in Lisbon, where many of the Florentine merchants who went out on overseas voyages have been described as becoming ever more Portuguese and ever less Florentine.[129] Most of these merchants living abroad, however, never became expatriates who pulled up their Florentine roots. Zanobi di Taddeo Gaddi (d. 1400), whom we shall encounter again in chapter 7, made his fortune in Venice, where he lived as a citizen most of his life and where he died, but he married a woman from an exiled Florentine family there, bought property back in Florence, returned to his native city often, occasionally assumed official responsibilities for the government of Florence, and left a testament that documents his complete commitment to his native city.[130]

THE MERCANZIA   Nor did merchants have any kind of formal collective organization back in Florence. Unlike merchants in many other cities throughout medieval Europe, Florentine merchants had no single guild through which they exercised political influence. Sometime in the second half of the twelfth century merchants operating abroad organized themselves into the Arte di Calimala, the oldest of the Florentine guilds; and in the period before the foundation of the guild republic they became one of the major forces in local politics, along with the associations of knights. In the early thirteenth century other guilds appeared—the Cambio (moneychangers) in 1202, followed in the next decade by

[129] Spallanzani, *Mercanti fiorentini*, 35.
[130] Paula Clarke, "The Identity of the Expatriate: Florentines in Venice in the Late Fourteenth and Early Fifteenth Centuries," in Connell, *Society and Individual in Renaissance Florence*, 384–408.

the Lana (wool manufacturers), the Por Santa Maria (retail cloth merchants), and the Giudici e Notai (judges and notaries)—and some members of these guilds, and of others as they emerged, also engaged in foreign trade. The entrepreneur who wanted to venture abroad, in other words, did not have to belong to a guild, and even minor guildsmen appear on the aforementioned list of foreign merchants drawn up by the Mercanzia in 1322 (although their trade may not have extended much beyond the confines of the territorial state). A major economic activity in the city itself, by contrast, required membership in the appropriate guild, but trade abroad was open to members of virtually any of the major guilds and was not subject to guild regulations. Even the guild of local bankers (the Cambio) required membership only of those who opened a local business; an international banker who, like Filippo Strozzi, did not have a local bank was not required to take out guild membership. In the kind of guild government that emerged in Florence by the fourteenth century, especially after the creation of the great guild conglomerates that absorbed diverse activities, guilds lost much of their traditional economic function and served instead as vehicles for participation in the political life of the city. One could become a member of a guild without having any economic interest whatsoever in the activities incorporated in the guild, and membership in more than one guild was not unusual. In short, the relations between merchant-bankers abroad were not conditioned by guild membership at home.

The foundation of the Mercanzia in 1308, however, looks very much like a tentative step toward the formation of a merchant guild. As John Hicks observed in elaborating his theory of economic history, any developing mercantile economy requires above all the political and legal institutions to assure the protection of private property and the sanctity of contracts to merchants operating in the "inside" market, that is, the market involving people in credit-debit relations (a notion that has since become an essential component of what is called "the transactional sector," which includes all those instruments and practices designed to reduce risks for investors).[131] As merchants and investors became an increasingly major force in the local politics in Florence, as in most Italian cities, there emerged a political environment that favored the development of a market economy and engendered trust in men's economic relations with one another. One result was the elaboration of a body of mercantile law and related institutions, a process that culminated in the organization of the Mercanzia in 1308. The model may have been the college of merchants in Lucca, which had its own statutes and tribunal for the settlement of disputes arising in the three principal sectors of the economy

---

[131] John Hicks, *A Theory of Economic History* (Oxford, 1969), esp. ch. 5.

oriented to international markets—banking, commerce, and the cloth industry. Florentine merchants took the initiative to set up the Mercanzia, allegedly, according to some modern scholars, motivated by the immediate concern over the status of credit claims arising, on the one hand, from a contemporary run of bankruptcies and, on the other, from heightened tensions in their class relations at home following the institution of a more popular government with the Ordinances of Justice in 1292–93. At a moment in the evolution of the republic when factionalism was still rife and no clear ruling class had yet emerged, these men wanted a magistracy to serve them both as a political organ to give them a distinct voice within the government and as a tribunal for handling disputes.

The management of the Mercanzia lay in a foreign (and therefore presumably impartial) rector and a council of five representatives, one from each of the five principal guilds, the Calimala, the Lana, the Por Santa Maria, the Cambio, and the Medici e Speziali. According to the enabling legislation, the five councilors were to be merchants engaged in trade outside the city. The Mercanzia was thus conceived as a principal institution, indeed the only one, giving a single corporate structure to entrepreneurs who belonged to different guilds: it institutionalized their influence as a pressure group within the government, and it established a court of law controlled by them for the settlement of all disputes among themselves involving credit and debit claims. It seems to have been a reasonably open institution. The lists of men it drew up for assessments included not only members of the founding guilds but also any merchant from a minor guild who engaged in trade outside the city (these numbered 38 out of the 264 firms and individual operators on the aforementioned list of 1322). Moreover, there was considerable fluidity in the ranks of the councilors, the men who served three-month terms on the executive committee. No fewer than 228 family names appear on the list of the 324 tenures that can be documented from 1308 to 1348 (42 percent of the total); only 7 families held more than 5 offices, and the most any family held was 12. Taken together, the partners and employees of the Bardi, Peruzzi, and Acciaiuoli firms held only 11 percent of these tenures.

The early history of the Mercanzia reveals an emerging function as an instrument of a specific constituency and not just a communal magistracy. Set up to handle disputes among merchants abroad that might lead to reprisals and hence interruption of the smooth conduct of trade, it also negotiated trade treaties with foreign governments, supervised security on overland and fluvial trade routes, especially those leading to the sea, and administered contracts for the collection of gate gabelles imposed on imports and exports. The council of five increasingly worked in conjunction with informal groups of merchants that it called in for consultation, in effect acting as a direct representative of the community of merchants and thereby bypassing the guilds that the councilors formally represented. It assured its financial independence from the government by meeting operating expenses through fees charged for the services it rendered as a court and assessments levied on all merchants who conducted trade outside Florentine territory. The Mercanzia never evolved into anything resembling a merchant guild, however; in fact, its move in that direction was cut short by the mid-fourteenth century, the victim of the widening of the popular basis of government in the 1340s. Subsequently, its political autonomy was further curtailed by the increasing concentration of power in the central organs of communal government. It survived, but as a major magistracy brought fully into the orbit of the state, as a tribunal and as a central organ in the state's complex process of election to public office. By the fifteenth century it had ceased to be the instrument of an economic pressure group within the government, having lost its direct influence on economic policy; and its six councilors (which since 1387 had included a representative of the lesser guilds) were no longer necessarily men who engaged in international trade.[132]

The course of the subsequent evolution of the Mercanzia as a central political organ of the state, becoming the controlling body over the guilds in the complex electoral process, has been well studied, but its function in the administration of justice has not. The tribunal of the Mercanzia represented the one institutional structure merchants erected for their common benefit to guarantee the legal context for doing business with one another. Hence, very soon after its foundation it extended its jurisdiction to the handling of disputes arising from business activity within the local market at home in Florence. As a tribunal adjudicating cases brought by creditors against debtors, the Mercanzia evolved as a court of appeal from the guild courts, handling everything from the bankruptcy of major international firms—the best studied is that of the Cambini in 1481–82—to minor disputes involving the most modest of workingmen. "All the major problems and major cases throughout the whole world show up before this office," commented the chronicler Goro Dati at the end of the fourteenth century, "litigation over things done at sea or on land, over bankrupt firms, over acts of reprisal, over an infinity of cases; and it makes extraordinarily admirable judgments and the most remarkable settlements." And at least by the fifteenth century all the evidence points to the court's objectivity, freed from the class interest of the men who

---

[132] Antonella Astorri has studied the Mercanzia as a political and economic magistracy but not as a tribunal. See the following by Astorri: "Note sulla Mercanzia fiorentina sotto Lorenzo dei Medici: Aspetti istituzionali e politici," *ASI* 150 (1992): 965–93; *La Mercanzia a Firenze;* "Gli spazi politici dei mercanti a Firenze"; and with David Friedman, "The Florentine Mercanzia and Its Palace," *I Tatti Studies* 10 (2005): 11–68.

controlled it, as we shall have occasion to note in reporting some cases involving workingmen versus capitalists in chapter 5.[133] Florentine merchants are not known to have had recourse for the settlement of disputes to informal private arrangements such as arbitration, which merchants in early modern England preferred over equity proceedings.[134]

If the early history of the Mercanzia is indeed to be read as an aborted effort by international merchants to create something like a strong and independent merchant guild within communal government, one might think their time eventually came with the affirmation of the oligarchic government in 1382, after the Ciompi fiasco, when capitalist entrepreneurs of all kinds, not just merchants, closed ranks against the minor guilds and asserted their domination of the state, without, however, eliminating its guild structure. By this time the political elite was more homogeneous than it had been at the beginning of the century, and merchants now constituted a core group within it. None of the many studies of the ruling class, however, has isolated them within the elite for specific attention, let alone analyzed the economic policies of the state as an expression of their interests. Yet, despite their influence in political affairs, merchants do not seem to have coalesced around a policy directed to controlling the state as an instrument for the promotion of their specific business interests in foreign markets. The state's economic policy—of which more in chapter 7—included maintaining the purity of the gold florin, establishing standards for weights and measurements, regulating road and river trade routes throughout its territory, administering a court of mercantile law, negotiating trade treaties with foreign governments. In short, it did all those things most city-states at the time did to assure favorable conditions for a flourishing sector of foreign trade. International merchants, however, did not generally use their political influence to gain direct intervention by the government in their affairs. The creation of the Sea Consuls in 1421 to set up and operate a galley system is a notable exception to this generalization, but the state eventually closed down this enterprise largely because many merchants were not using it. If in the republican period the state can be said to have had any policy at all toward the commercial and banking sectors of the economy, it was one of laissez faire.

---

[133] The enormous archive of the court records of the Mercanzia is finally being studied by Luca Boschetto. The Cambini bankruptcy is discussed in Tognetti, *Il banco Cambini,* ch. 12. The Dati quote comes from Astorri, "Note sulla Mercanzia fiorentina," 972; in that study Astorri refers to dissatisfaction with the administration of justice by the tribunal at the time of Lorenzo but does not examine court records.

[134] Jacob M. Price, "Transaction Costs: A Note on Merchant Credit and the Organization of Private Trade," in *The Political Economy of Merchant Empires: State Power and World Trade, 1350–1750,* ed. James D. Tracy (Cambridge, 1991), 296.

The lack of any institutionalized corporate organization among the merchant-bankers of Florence at the company or government level sets them off sharply from some of their most prominent contemporaries in international markets, such as the Venetians, who worked through the institutions of a state that (following Frederic Lane's analogy) they ran through the Senate as a board of directors runs a company, or the north Germans, who operated under the umbrella of the supraurban commercial federation of the Hanseatic League, or the south Germans, who joined together in cartel-like arrangements, or the Londoners, who directed their regulated companies as a common enterprise complete with its own charter, statutes, monopoly privileges, and government backing. It remains to be seen whether these Florentines had any change of heart as the network contracted in the sixteenth century and whether as a pressure group they had any input in the vigorous protomercantilist program formulated by the first Medici dukes to stimulate the economy, including the development of Livorno as a free port.

The Center

Florence and Regional Trade

Florence was the home base for its great international commercial and banking network. Control of many of the companies operating abroad emanated from central headquarters in the city, and even those merchant-bankers working out of autonomous companies organized abroad seldom broke the familial and patrimonial ties that kept their ultimate economic objective focused on their homeland. Florence as a cultural and legal foundation was, in any case, what they all had in common as each pursued his own interests through the vast interlocking web of business relations that constituted the network. In what sense, however, was Florence the central node of its network?

The city's dependency on its network was complete. In its early history it needed wheat to feed its growing population, it eventually needed all the raw materials for the industry that gave much of the population its livelihood, and it needed to find markets abroad where it could sell the finished products of that industry to pay for these imports. The fall in population following the plagues of the fourteenth century reduced the city's dependency on grain imports, although in the recurring moments of bad local harvests it always had to have emergency recourse to supplies from farther afield. The growth of the population during the sixteenth century increased pressure to open more regular supply channels abroad once again, but eventually the government had recourse to the international emporium at Livorno, with its maritime links to the vast sources available through the Baltic trade. For the wool industry the only raw materials at hand in the immediate region were dyestuffs, mostly woad *(guado)* from the upper Tiber valley but also archil *(oricello)*, madder *(robbia)*, and saffron *(zafferano)* from the Romagna and the Marche. The wool itself and the alum used in the dyeing process came from abroad, as did other dyestuffs—kermes (a red dyestuff made from insects) and saffron from Spain, kermes and madder from southern France, and indigo, brazilwood, lapis lazuli, and others from the Levant. With the rise of the silk industry at the end of the fourteenth century, the city took measures to promote sericulture throughout the countryside, an important development given the high percentage of overall production costs for raw silk as compared with wool, but local supply never reached the point of rendering the industry self-sufficient.

A first glance at a map might lead one to think that Florence was well located for interregional trade within Italy and therefore well positioned to launch ventures into international trade. The Arno valley provided routes downstream to Tyrrhenian ports and upstream to the towns of central Italy and on to Rome and to the Adriatic ports, while directly across the Apennines to the north lay Bologna and all the cities of the Po valley, including the great emporia of Milan and Venice. No other Tuscan town would seem to have had such a central position from which to plug into the different hinterland trading systems of Italy and even serve as a node linking them together.

This geographic centrality, however, did not make Florence an emporium linking these other systems. On the contrary, on a map of the trade routes of medieval Italy the city appears off to the side, almost in isolation. The Apennine barrier separated it from the great triangular urbanized area of the Po valley marked by Milan, Venice, and Bologna. Within this region the main southward axis of trade followed the Via Emilia from Milan to Bologna and further on to Rimini and other ports on the sea. At Fano it linked with the ancient Via Flaminia, crossed the mountains to enter Umbria, far to the south of Florence, to proceed on to central Italy and Rome. A certain amount of overland shipping from Venice and other Po valley towns crossed the Apennines directly into Tuscany, but much of this traffic followed the Porrettana road to come out at Pistoia or the valleys of the Reno and the Bisenzio to come out at Prato. Transit trade passing through these nearby towns linking the Po valley and Pisa thus circumvented Florence altogether. And there was the route to Lucca by way of the Via Francigena over the Cisa pass and through Versilia. In short, there were several routes linking Tuscany with the extensive Po valley, and only one, and not the most important one, went through Florence.

The long-distance maritime commerce involving the towns downstream on the Arno in the Valdinievole and the Valdelsa also circumvented Florence. Prato, today virtually a remote suburb of Florence, was within easy reach of the last port on the Arno, at Ponte a Signa, several miles downstream from Florence. The route from Pistoia went by way of either the Via Cassia, passing through Serravalle and into the Valdinievole, or the road going to the south of Monte Albano into the lower Valdarno. Lucca directed its silks to its own port at Motrone, to Pisa, or overland to Ligurian ports with cabotage service to Genoa or across the Cisa pass into the Po valley. Merchants from the towns in the Valdelsa operated out of Pisa. Siena had access to ports in southern Tuscany as well as to Pisa. Moreover, all these towns in the Valdinievole and the Valdelsa lay in the path of the principal route leading out of Tuscany to the south. In short, extraregional trade out of these inland towns to the west of Florence that linked them to the Mediterranean, to northern Italy, and to Rome and the south did not converge on Florence. The trading system within this most urbanized area in Europe, far from being centered on Florence, was highly skewed toward Pisa (or the other Tyrrhenian ports, depending on the political situation), leaving the city off on the periphery to the extreme east, huddled against the Apennines, beyond most of the region's cities and about as far away from Pisa and the other Mediterranean ports as it could be.

Florence had stronger commercial ties through the upper Valdarno, the Valdichiana, and the Valtiberina to central Italy and the towns of Umbria, the Marche, and the Abruzzi. It lay on the easiest route these towns had to the port of Pisa, although the towns farther away were also oriented to Adriatic ports. Moreover, this region was much less urbanized than either the Po valley or Tuscany before the Black Death. The upper Valdarno was a principal source for woad, one of the very few raw materials of the Florentine industry that was to be found close at hand in Tuscany. Florentine merchants penetrated further into this region to obtain a variety of local products, especially cotton and linen cloth, for export to Pisa. This trade intensified in the fifteenth century as a result of the region's increasing importance for the city's textile industries. Following the decline in imports of English wool, the wool industry turned to the Abruzzi as its major supplier of raw wool, and the growing silk industry took raw silk from the region. At the same time the new markets for finished cloth opening up in the growing capital cities of Rome, Naples, and Constantinople were reached through the area, the route to the former two going to the south and the route to the latter going to Ancona on the Adriatic. In this trading system, however, Florence was more a polar terminus than a redistribution hub. Moreover, apart from the transit trade through towns lying on the route linking Florence to central Italy and the Adriatic ports, this part of central Italy constituted a separate hinterland with its own trading system well beyond the orbit of Florence. Only 29 percent of the gate duties paid at Arezzo in 1401–2 came from trade with Florence, whereas 60 percent came from trade in the other direction.[135] The cotton industry, which was widely diffused throughout the area, was supplied with raw cotton by way of Adriatic ports, and local merchants controlled much of the export trade.

Merchants in Arezzo had their own contacts in Perugia, Ancona, and other places in central Italy, and some had companies in Pisa. Giubileo di Niccolò Carsidoni, a cloth producer there whose activity is documented from 1348 to 1360, bought wool, along with the tools and equipment he needed for his work (as well as his account book and inkwell), in Florence, but he also had wool sent to him directly from Pisa. Likewise a merchant of the next generation, Simo d'Ubertino, in business at Arezzo from 1362 to 1390 with a cloth-producing firm and a warehouse, in 1382 moved his family to Pisa for several years, setting up a partnership engaged in the trade generated by the sale of cotton products from his native region. An Aretine merchant from yet the next generation, Lazzaro Bracci, working in the first quarter of the fifteenth century, also had a base in Pisa, to which he sent woad, cotton veiling, and paper that he imported from the Valtiberina, Umbria, and the Marche. From Pisa he shipped all those things that came into the port—skins, leather, wool cloth, wax, spices, foodstuffs—throughout Tuscany, to Siena, Montevarchi, San Giovanni Valdarno, Cortona, and Arezzo, as well as back to the markets in central Italy where he had purchased the goods he exported.[136] This trade out of Pisa to these towns on the far side of Florence perhaps passed through the city, but in transit, not through its market. And there were routes that avoided Florence altogether.

Thus in a literal geographic sense Florence was on the periphery of trade in its own region. Florence's geographic centrality was not a centrality relative to a major interregional trading system. The trade routes that radiated out from Florence to the Po valley, to the Tyrrhenian ports, and to central Italy were not major arteries of trade that passed through Florence on their way between these areas, thereby connecting them. In fact, much of the trade involving the region's most important secondary urban centers bypassed Florence altogether. Hence regional trade involving the city, although never comprehensively studied, does not appear to have been a major activity in its local market except for the basic goods that came in from the countryside. The merchandise books of Florentines in

---

[135] Bruno Dini, "Le vie di comunicazione del territorio fiorentino alla metà del Quattrocento," in *Mercati e consumi: Organizzazione e qualificazione del commercio in Italia dal XII al XX secolo* (Bologna, 1986), 286.

[136] Amintore Fanfani, *Un mercante del Trecento* (Milan, 1935), 28–29, 38–39, 49–51, 66, 71 (on Carsidoni); Giovanni Cherubini, "La proprietà fondiaria di un mercante toscano del Trecento (Simo d'Ubertino di Arezzo)," in *Signori, contadini, borghesi: Ricerche sulla società italiana del Basso Medioevo* (Florence, 1974), 326–36; Federigo Melis, "Lazzaro Bracci (la funzione di Arezzo nell'economia dei secoli XIV–XV)," reprinted in *Industria e commercio*, 175–91. Further details on both Simo and Bracci are to be found in Bruno Dini, *Arezzo intorno al 1400: Produzioni e mercato* (Arezzo, 1984).

Pisa—the fullest collections are those of Datini, dating from about 1400, and of the Salviati, dating from the second half of the fifteenth century—record much traffic in a variety of goods to provincial places within Tuscany, whereas the business records kept in Florence register trade to Pisa, to Bologna, and to Umbria and central Italy but hardly any direct trade to towns lying closer at hand in the territorial state. The goods from Lucca, Siena, and the other towns in western Tuscany that Datini sold in his shop in Avignon did not pass through Florence. Florence was not even of great importance to most of these towns as a market for the local exchange of goods, let alone as a hub in an extraregional trading system.

Florence's importance as a market center was limited to the trade generated by the city itself, through exports and imports. Apart from what was driven by the city's textile industry, the city's import-export trade amounted to little more than what was commensurate with the needs of its population for food, fuel, and raw materials. Of course, many of these basic necessities came from close by, within the city's immediate territory and the region. It also imported a great variety of items from farther afield, some quite bulky and of low value, some essential to the city's well being, and a few satisfying demand from the high end of the local market. The staples in this import trade over the long period included foodstuffs (salt, wine, dried fruits, meat, conserved fish, spices), leather, skins, furs, tin, wax, coral, and these things came from all over, from northern Europe to North Africa and the Levant. In addition, Datini on occasion imported a wide variety of other objects in insignificant quantities, such as ostrich feathers from North Africa, ceramics from Valencia, pewterware from England, and the occasional oriental carpet from the Levant. And the odds and ends of luxury imports that show up on merchants' accounts in the fifteenth century also include tapestries from the Low Countries and antique sculpture from Rome. Over the period covered in this book the list of imports changes somewhat, but the scattered evidence from merchants' ledgers does not give us a very good picture of these shifts. In any event, this material, including the extensive collection of Datini's specialized merchandise records (*libri di mercanzia, memoriali*) and similar records from later firms, has not been studied to document the trade in and out of the city unrelated to the textile industry. In chapter 5 we shall see how little this import trade was balanced by exports, which, other than textiles, consisted of those few things the city could produce utilizing the natural and human resources at hand, namely, ironwork and what we might lump together as artwork.

We have no way of measuring the quantity or value of trade in any of these categories since not even significant fragments of customs and toll records of any kind survive from the entire period under examination here. Business accounts show that individual merchants like Datini traded in a wide variety of goods to a greater or lesser extent, but there can be little doubt that the commerce in items not subsumed under the category of the textile and leather industries constituted a minor part of the global value of the city's traffic in imports and exports. In assessing the significance of this trade for the Florentine economy, it is important to note also that almost everything Florence exported was manufactured in the city and that almost everything it imported was a raw material or an agricultural product. In fact, a notable characteristic of the city's economy, as we shall see, was its ability to produce virtually all the luxury items demanded by the rich as they became richer from the profits they brought in from abroad.

In conclusion, Florence, unlike the port cities of Genoa, Venice, and Antwerp or the inland centers of transcontinental trade such as Milan and Lyons, was not a major emporium for the international redistribution of goods. Although the Florentine commercial and banking network extended throughout Europe, it did not include a major international transport system. It was something the Florentines built up themselves operating within the major maritime systems centering on the great emporia of Venice, Genoa, Bruges, and Antwerp, as well as within a host of secondary systems. Most merchandise coming into the city found its ultimate market there, and what left had been produced there. What transit trade there was, for example, between Venice or Arezzo and Pisa, passed through the city to its destination only because the route went that way, and in transit it was not subject to any dynamic generated by the local market. Moreover, much of the business conducted by Florentine merchants abroad had nothing to do with their native city. Wherever merchants were located, their engagement in local trade often constituted subnetworks that appear as eddies and currents at the periphery of the larger structure, leaving the home market untouched, and it would not be surprising if at least some merchants made major profits at this lower level within the network.

Nor did international banking center on Florence itself, for all the power and influence of Florentine bankers. The international exchange market that they largely dominated for so long never had its center in the city. Technically, of course, it needed to be located in a different monetary area so that exchange could be legitimately effected, for the very reason that later the Genoese could never bring their fairs all the way home to Genoa (and when they did eventually bring them into Genoese territory, at Novi, special legislation was required). But for practical reasons too the exchange fairs, with the exception of those at Besançon, had to be held in concurrence with trade fairs since so much activity in the money market took place in conjunction with commercial exchange; hence the centrality of Venice, then Geneva, Lyons, and Antwerp, but never Florence. The city was the home of Europe's major bankers, but it was no more a banking capital than it was an international emporium.

Florence as International Emporium

In the period before the Black Death, merchants from other Italian towns traveled to Florence to purchase wool cloth, and they may, in fact, have exported much of the production of the Calimala industry. Instead of going to a central market, however, they had to make the rounds of the manufactories accompanied by an official guild broker, who oversaw sales to assure observance of guild regulations regarding measurement and prices. Moreover, companies from Milan, Genoa, and Venice were also present in the city selling wool. For a while in the early fourteenth century the Genoese had a warehouse for selling imported English wool, but we hear little about them. After the mid-fourteenth century, however, Florentine firms came to dominate this traffic, and guild statutes no longer mentioned the brokers who served merchants coming from outside the city. Some foreign merchants continued to show up in Florence to buy cloth or sell raw wool, but their numbers were small, and their nationality changed with shifts in the international markets that served the local industry. Only occasionally do ledgers of Florentine firms record local transactions involving foreign merchants in the city, from the Abruzzi to sell *matricina* wool or from Ragusa to buy cloth, and none of the great international commercial capitals—for instance, Venice—ever had a significant resident community of merchants in Florence. In the fifteenth century foreigners in general never numbered very many, and almost all were immigrant artisans or soldiers stationed there temporarily, not merchants.[137] And hardly any foreign entrepreneurs are known to have invested in the local economy. We shall later encounter Jacques Coeur as a partner in one of the city's silk-producing firms, but his singularity as a foreign investor in Florence is about as notable as his prominence in the business world abroad.[138]

It is not surprising, therefore, that the city had nothing of the commercial life of an international emporium. It was not a major center for the market exchange of goods coming in and going out, and what transit trade came through the city on international routes did not pass through a market nexus. Not even the in-

---

[137] On foreigners documented in the 1427 catasto, see David Herlihy and Christiane Klapisch-Zuber, *Les toscans et leurs familles: Une étude du catasto florentin de 1427* (Paris, 1978), 140–50.

[138] In the 1480s two prominent Catalan international merchant-bankers, the brothers Francesco and Raffaele da Besalú, transferred their business to Florence after fleeing Naples for political reasons, but they disappear from the scene after the exile of the Medici in 1494, and nothing is known about their business activity. Lorenz Böninger, "Politics, Trade and Toleration in Renaissance Florence: Lorenzo de' Medici and the Besalú Brothers," *I Tatti Studies* 9 (2001): 139–71.

tense trade generated by the textile industries manifested itself as a bustling activity in a central place such as the prominent market halls of the wool-producing towns in northern Europe, where raw materials and finished textiles were stored and traded. In Florence the import-export traffic was through brokers, who moved through the city to bring individual merchants and producers together to make their deals. In fact, we hear nothing about periodic fairs of any importance. Nor did the city's hotels serve a major economic function as did the commercial hostels in fourteenth-century Bruges: these places of imposing architectural presence, complete with warehouse facilities, were run by men, themselves often merchants, who served as guarantors, bankers, and brokers to the foreign merchants they put up during the city's fairs.[139] Florence had nothing comparable to the large market halls concentrated on the Groote Markt in Bruges dominated by the Belfry, the symbol of the city, where foreign merchants assembled on their buying trips; nor was there any space like the Bruges Bourse, on which opened the impressive lodges of resident foreign merchants, including that of the Florentines. The need never arose in Florence to print bulletins on prices and moneys of the kind that appeared in the markets at Antwerp in 1540, at Frankfurt in 1581, at Amsterdam and Venice in 1585, and at Hamburg and Augsburg shortly thereafter. Unlike Antwerp, where, according to Lodovico Guicciardini, there were schools where boys and girls could learn French, Italian, and Spanish, Florence had no need to teach its children the languages of foreign merchants.

Emblematic of the strictly local parameters of Florence as a market center is a comparison of the art market there with that of the great emporia in the north, Bruges and Antwerp, the only places outside of Italy that could rival Florence for the presence of artists in this period. Although the production of art hardly counted for much in the overall performance of either economy, trade in art objects is probably the most visible market activity in these three places, at least in the light of the current historiography, and the one involving artisans that has been the most studied in all three places. The markets in which artists in the two areas worked could hardly have differed more. By the second half of the fifteenth century Bruges had become a year-round fair attracting merchants from England, France, central Germany, and the Hanseatic cities, as well as Italy and Spain. Probably about a thousand foreign merchants resided there during the year, and their numbers doubled during the annual May fair—this in a city that was about the size of Florence. With an outlet to such a wide market area, local artists were stimulated to increase production of the kind of popular religious artwork that, serving liturgical and devotional functions, merchants could export

---

[139] James M. Murray, *Bruges, Cradle of Capitalism, 1280–1390* (Cambridge, 2005), ch. 5.

to markets abroad. Not surprisingly, their numbers increased: the painters' guild took in no fewer than 242 apprentices from 1456 to 1490, and perhaps a third of the new masters who appear during the last third of the century were immigrants. In 1482 the city constructed a permanent exhibition gallery for the sale of luxury products, which included paintings, and painters (and perhaps also dealers) had a notable presence there as renters of stalls.

Antwerp had not been a center for the production of art, but once it grew into a principal international entrepôt, very much in competition with Bruges, local production of paintings got under way and expanded rapidly. The painters' guild joined with other artisans who produced luxury objects to establish an exclusive exhibition place for its members in the vicinity of the cathedral. In 1540 permanent exhibition galleries were open in the city's recently built Bourse, a kind of centralized merchandise mart originally administered by the city government along with the guild but eventually taken over by the painters themselves. This market in Antwerp was large, with dozens of stalls and a large inventory of wares. Middlemen, or dealers, emerged to play a major role in it, commissioning work directly from artists for resale, much of it in the export market. By the end of the century some dealers themselves took paintings to fairs in Holland, France, and Spain, from where they were exported to the New World. The presence of a permanent centralized place for display of artists' wares in a great international emporium explains why so many paintings and carved altarpieces, some of them by prominent artists, were produced in numerous replications following standard formulas for design and content and directed to an anonymous, impersonal market—a notable characteristic of the Flemish school well into the seventeenth century. Moreover, a significant percentage of commissions for even prominent painters, such as Hans Memling, came from abroad.[140]

The art market in Florence was quite a different place. At the end of the fifteenth century the city, for all the fame of its artists, had perhaps only one-third as many painters as did Bruges, a city of the same size. And production in Florence never approached the annual output of ten to twenty thousand paintings that has been estimated for Antwerp in the second half of the sixteenth century. Florentine painters, like most of the city's artisans, worked in a local market where routine was not broken by the occasional fair, where they had no need of a central place for the display of their wares, and where there was not enough business to give rise to either dealers or specialized producers. They too produced devotional pieces in series for direct sale across the counter. But for the most part

---

[140] The Bruges and Antwerp art markets are analyzed, with full bibliographical references, in Neil De Marchi and Hans J. van Miegroet, "The History of Art Markets," in *Handbook of the Economics of Art and Culture,* ed. V. Ginsburgh and D. Throsby (Amsterdam, 2006).

demand for these products from the low end of the market arose from within the city walls; it was in no way export driven. Their major clients were local, and their principal relation to them was in fact based on a commission, not a market, exchange. Many Florentine artists went abroad, but on summons by a patron: at home and abroad they depended almost entirely on the traditional personal-commission nexus, not on a larger anonymous market. In contrast to the Flemish and Brabantine emporia, the Florentine market for art, and for most artisan production, was both parochial in its geographic reach and primitive in its infrastructure.

The situation in the Florentine marketplace changed somewhat toward the end of the fifteenth century as merchants from many different places, from Portugal to southern Germany, moved more aggressively into western Mediterranean markets in general, including Florence. Foreign merchants begin to have a certain presence, as they never had before, in the ledgers of Florentine merchants recording local transactions, almost all of these foreigners coming to buy cloth and sell what they could. In the 1490s the Salviati company dealt with no fewer than twenty-nine Spanish merchants, most from Castile, and subsequent records of Salviati wool-producing firms in the second quarter of the sixteenth century reveal local sales to merchants from Genoa, Naples, Sicily, and the Marche within Italy, as well as from Ragusa, Albania, and Greece. Spaniards came in especially large numbers, having taken the initiative as importers of the Castilian wool that the local industry came increasingly to depend on for the production of rascia. The Genoese, with their base in southern Italy, came to sell raw silk, and a few Portuguese also show up selling spices. In 1548 Cosimo I granted Portuguese Jews full rights to engage in trade, including protection against the Inquisition, and in 1551 a similar license was granted to a Levantine Jew. How many Sephardic Jews arrived in Florence is unknown, but they were not required to move into the ghetto when it was opened in 1571.[141]

The Florentine wool firm Cristofano di Tommaso Brandolini & Partners, operating from 1580 to 1597, purchased 75 percent of its raw wool from seven Spanish and three Genoese firms, and it sold 30 percent of its production to foreigners—to some dozen and a half Spanish firms, half as many Genoese firms, four Germans, two Frenchmen, two Sicilians, and one each from Bologna and Cremona. The contemporaneous silk-producing firm of Baccio Martelli, Pierfrancesco Del Giocondo & Partners bought little silk from foreigners during the first six years of its operation, from 1584 to 1591, but sold fabrics to twenty

---

[141] Renata Segre, "Sephardic Settlements in Sixteenth-Century Italy: A Historical and Geographical Survey," in *Jews, Christians and Muslims in the Mediterranean World after 1492*, ed. Alisa Meyuhas Ginio (London, 2002), 127–28.

foreign firms—ten Spanish, seven German plus a German firm from Lucca, and one each from Paris and Flanders (not to mention eight firms from elsewhere in Italy). The business correspondence of the Florentine agent of the Spanish merchant Simón Ruiz, spanning the years 1577–85, refers to weekly meetings of a "università" of international bankers in the city to vote on exchange rates and clear their books, but this seems to have been an informal organization, completely dominated by the Florentines, for the only foreigners mentioned are Spanish. Some of these foreign firms were major businesses, operating at the level of the Florentines. Baltasar Suárez, Ruiz's agent, who dealt in wool, sugar, and leather from Spain, as well as cochineal from New Spain, opened a branch in Venice in partnership with the Bonvisi, the great merchant-banking family from Lucca, and Teramo Brignole & Partners, which shows up in the ledgers of both the aforementioned wool and silk companies, belonged to one of the most prominent Genoese merchant-banking families.[142]

Florentines had never seen such large foreign firms on the local scene. In fact, the city had never had much of a resident community of foreign merchants, but now, at the end of the sixteenth century, the Castilians and Genoese were there handling a significant amount of the import-export traffic that was the lifeblood of the city's major industrial sector. By the last quarter of the century Livorno was growing into a major international port, attracting foreign merchants from virtually everywhere, many organized into formal resident communities, and it is not surprising that some showed up in Florence, in greater numbers than before. When they came to Florence, however, it was for specific business linked to the textile industries, not for the attraction of an international emporium.

By this time, however, Florence was no longer one of Europe's great cities. In 1300 it ranked at the very top, high above the others, one of the cities, along with Venice, Milan, and Paris, that had a population of more than a hundred thousand. In 1600, between the growth of other cities in the meantime and its own failure to recuperate from the losses of population it had suffered in the fourteenth century, its population of about seventy thousand put it well below the eight or so cities, five of them in Italy, whose populations numbered a hundred thousand or more. Notwithstanding the vast commercial and banking network

---

[142] The only study of any of these foreign merchants in Florence is Bruno Dini, "Mercanti spagnoli a Firenze (1480–1530)," in *Saggi,* 289–310. Additional information on this community can be found in Böninger, "Politics, Trade and Toleration." Dini has also noted the presence of other foreigners in the Salviati accounts from the early sixteenth century in his "Aspetti del commercio di esportazione," 233–37, 242–43. See also de Roover, "Florentine Firm of Cloth Manufacturers," 101, for references to Greek and Ragusan merchants at midcentury. On the Brandolini firm see Goldthwaite, "Florentine Wool Industry," 527–54. The reference for the Martelli firm is ASF, Archivio Martelli, 165 (utilized in my unpublished study of this firm); and for the Ruiz correspondence, Ruiz Martín, *Lettres marchandes,* c–ciii.

operated by its business elite out of their urban palaces, and notwithstanding its fame in the world of learning and the arts, which knew no geographic frontiers, Florence remained what it had been for centuries: probably the most provincial of the great European capitals of international business. Therein lay its greatness as a center of early capitalism.

CHAPTER TWO

The Shifting Geography of Commerce

Northwestern Europe.
Naples and Southern Italy.
The Western Mediterranean: *A Transport Revolution, The Iberian Peninsula, Southern France, The Later Sixteenth Century.*
Central Italy and Rome.
Venice, the Adriatic, and the Levant.
Central Europe.

Northwestern Europe

The dynamic that drove the commercial revolution was trade between Europe and the Levant, and in Europe the principal pole of this trade was in the northwest. By the third quarter of the twelfth century much of the trade in this area had converged on the great fairs of Champagne, in northeastern France. Then, toward the end of the next century, this northern node shifted northwestward toward the Channel and to the Flemish towns. The documentation does not tell us much about Florentine participation in the early growth of this northern trading system. Florentine merchants are documented in 1178 as being involved in the trade going through Monferrato on the way to France and in 1211 as active in exchange operations at the Champagne fairs. In the last quarter of the thirteenth century the Cerchi operated at Liège, the Bardi at Ghent and Brussels, the Mozzi at St. Omer, the Pulci at Cambrai, Douai, and St. Quentin, all of these at Ypres, and some, along with yet others, at Antwerp, Caen, and above all Bruges and Paris.

By the early fourteenth century Florentines are well documented as having a major role in the commerce of the Low Countries alongside the Venetians and the Genoese. Besides the general traffic in Flemish cloth headed to Mediterranean markets, the Florentine merchants of the Calimala guild had a particular inter-

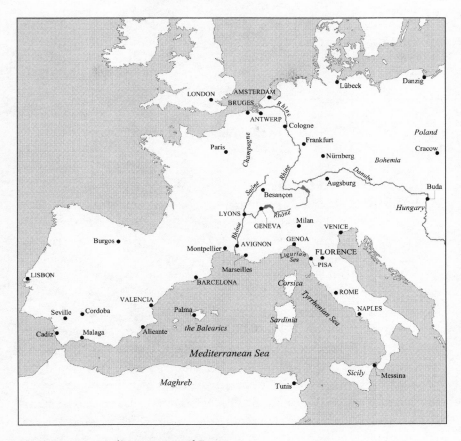

Italy, the western Mediterranean, and Europe

est, at least down to the mid-fourteenth century, in buying semifinished cloth for refinishing in their home industry and then reexport. Bruges was the central emporium out of which they conducted their business. The chronicler Giovanni Villani was a factor in the Peruzzi bank there from 1306 to 1308. The city was also a major center for international monetary exchange, perhaps the largest outside of Italy before the rise of Lyons in the second half of the fifteenth century. Rates were posted daily in Bruges for Venice, Genoa, Barcelona, Paris, and London, and Florentines enjoyed preeminence in this traffic, thanks to their more extensive business network. The ledger of Bartolomeo di Caroccio degli Alberti & Partners, open from 1352 to 1358, documents frequent transfers made by the Bruges branch to its branch at the papal court at Avignon for the archbishop of Riga, for the Teutonic Knights, and for merchants from Lübeck, and Bruges remained a major center for the transfer of ecclesiastical revenues from northern Europe to Rome through the fifteenth century.[1] Most of the large Florentine firms, from the Bardi, the Peruzzi, the Acciaiuoli, and the Alberti in the fourteenth century to the Medici and the Pazzi in the fifteenth, had agents in Bruges and its vicinity. The Florentines were not the largest group of Italian merchants in Bruges, being outnumbered by the Genoese, the Venetians, the Milanese, and perhaps at times even the Lucchesi. Nor do they appear at the very top of the list of the foreign communities who paid taxes and made loans to the local government, although they made major loans to the city in 1379–80 and again in 1422. Evidence for their corporate organization in a nazione there dates only from 1427.[2] The nazione had a lodge, the grandest the Florentines built anywhere, on the Bourse, the city's principal market square for foreign merchants; the building figures prominently in early urban views. And in Bruges, as in no other city where Florentines were located, their commercial interests extended also to the traffic in local artwork.[3]

To get to the Champagne fairs, Italians originally used overland routes going north through eastern France, but after about 1250, when Louis IX developed the port of Aigues-Mortes as his kingdom's outlet to the Mediterranean, the Genoese and the Tuscans used this port and then traveled overland through the valleys of the Loire and the Seine. This brought them to Paris, and the city grew in commercial importance when their trade shifted to Bruges and the other Flemish cities. Although Paris did not emerge as a great international emporium, its size alone—it was perhaps the largest city in Europe as early as the late twelfth century and the seat of a strong monarchy—made it a major urban and regional market that attracted foreign merchants, including Florentines. There is no comprehensive survey of their presence in the city, however, and most of what we know about them is limited to two moments. At the end of the thirteenth century between three hundred and four hundred "Lombards" were organized in a "universitas mercatorum lombardorum et toscanorum," but of the sixty-three Italian companies listed in an inquest of 1309–11 to free the city of foreign moneylenders, only eight were Florentines, compared with twenty-four from Genoa and ten each from Lucca and Piacenza.[4] However, no one had more prominence as lenders to the

[1] See *Due libri mastri degli Alberti: Una grande compagnia di Calimala, 1348–1358,* ed. Richard A. Goldthwaite, Enzo Settesoldi, and Marco Spallanzani (Florence, 1995), index; and Arnold Esch, "Brügge als Umschlagplatz im Zahlungsverkehr Nordeuropas mit der romischen Kurie im 15. Jahrhundert: Die vatikanischen Quellen," in *Hansekaufleute in Brügge,* ed. Werner Paravicini, vol. 4, *Beiträge der internationalen Tagung in Brügge, April 1996* (Frankfurt am Main, 2000), 109–37.

[2] André Vandewalle and Nöel Giernaert, "Bruges and Italy," in *Bruges and Europe,* ed. V. Vermeersch (Antwerp, 1992), 183–204, summarizes the recent literature on Italians in Bruges; it has sections on the Venetians, the Genoese, and the Lucchesi but only a few observations about the Florentines.

[3] See Paula Nuttall, *From Flanders to Florence: The Impact of Netherlandish Painting, 1400–1500* (New Haven, CT, 2004), esp. chs. 3–4.

[4] Pierre Racine, "Les marchands italiens dans le royaume de France (XIIe–XIVe siècles)," in

crown at this time, during the reign of Philip the Fair (1285–1314), than the legendary Miche and Bouche, whose careers are recounted in chapter 3. A century later we glimpse Florentines through the letters of the Prato merchant Francesco di Marco Datini to his agent there, dating from 1384 to 1410.[5] A list of Florentines in Paris compiled in 1419 has some three dozen names, including four Pazzi and an Alberti, both prominent merchant-banking families. The political scene in this part of France throughout much of the later Middle Ages was racked by the turbulence of the Hundred Years' War, and conditions were far from favorable for the market at Paris or for transient trade across the area. When the authority of the crown finally reasserted itself in the person of Louis XI (1461–83), it was Lyons, in the south, not Paris, that emerged as the great commercial and financial center of the kingdom, and Florentines were in the forefront of that development.

In this early period Florentines built up a much stronger commercial base in England than in Paris. In fact, they are better documented there in the thirteenth century than in any other place in the northwest. It is thought that the first Italians showed up in England as traders to utilize credits that they had accumulated in Italy in the form of loans to English nobles passing through Italy on a crusade. When in the mid-thirteenth century the Italians, and above all the Tuscans, got the contracts for the transfer of English and Irish ecclesiastical revenues to the popes in Italy, they gained access to funds that gave them a clear advantage over Flemish and other foreigners for financing the export trade. The earliest documentation for Florentine merchants in England dates from the second quarter of the century. They, together with Sienese and Bolognese merchants, received a license to trade from Henry III in 1224 and a safe-conduct for trade in 1234.[6] Florentine merchants are also documented as handling papal revenues in Ireland about midcentury, and under Edward I the Donati were among the Italians who had major tax farms there.[7] Rucco di Cambio de' Mozzi, representing one of the great family companies at the time, was active in England from 1253 to 1263.[8] The Pulci Rimbertini, Bardi, Cerchi, and Frescobaldi firms

---

Spazio urbano e organizzazione economica nell'Europa medievale, ed. Alberto Grohmann (Naples, 1994), 99–126; idem, "Paris, rue des Lombards (1280–1340)," in *Comunità forestiere e "nationes" nell'Europa dei secoli XIII–XVI,* ed. G. Petti Balbi (Naples, 2001), 95–111.

[5] Mathieu Arnoux, Caroline Bourlet, and Jérôme Hayez, "Les lettres parisiennes du carteggio Datini: Première approche du dossier," *Mélanges de l'École française de Rome: Moyen Âge* 117 (2005): 193–222.

[6] Alwin A. Ruddock, *Italian Merchants and Shipping in Southampton, 1270–1600* (Southampton, 1951), 16; Edward Miller and John Hatcher, *Medieval England: Towns, Commerce and Crafts, 1086–1348* (London, 1995), 187.

[7] M. D. O'Sullivan, *Italian Merchant Bankers in Ireland in the Thirteenth Century* (Dublin, 1962), 44–45, 49, 62–66.

[8] Richard Kay, "Rucco di Cambio de' Mozzi in France and England," *Studi danteschi* 47 (1970): 49–57.

first appear in the documents in the 1260s and early 1270s. In a 1283 document recording deposits with Italian firms of papal revenues directed to the Holy Land, eight of the sixteen firms are Florentine, and they account for almost 40 percent of total deposits.[9] By the last quarter of the thirteenth century Florentines were major exporters of wool to the Low Countries, and subsequently their position in the wool market was further strengthened by demand from the growing cloth industry at home in Florence.

The Florentines, along with other Italians, were able to expand their share of the market through arrangements made in return for loans to the crown. After the failure of the Lucchese firm of the Ricciardi in 1301, Florentines followed one another in sequence as the king's principal bankers down to the crises of the 1330s and 1340s. In no other place, and at no other time, were the Florentines so drawn into the finances of a secular ruler. Through the reigns of Edward I (1272–1307) to Edward III (1327–77) the crown was constantly in need of funds to finance wars in Wales, Scotland, and above all on the Continent. England being an island kingdom with more concentrated customs controls, the king had relatively easy access to substantial and fairly regular income in return for advances in the form of loans from merchant-bankers. For their part, the merchants needed cash to buy wool for export and some way to balance their international payments in a country with a limited market for imports. In addition, close relations to the court improved the chances of finding buyers for the luxury products they could provide. They also stood to profit from exchange transactions resulting from arrangements with the crown for financing wars on the Continent. This foundation in government finance gave them a commanding position in the lucrative export trade of wool to the Low Countries as well as to Florence itself. However, the series of bankruptcies culminating in the enormous losses of the Bardi, the Peruzzi, and the others exposed the weakness of this foundation. These firms were not able to attract significant funds in long-term deposits;[10] moreover, London, unlike Bruges, was not a major international emporium with an extensive exchange network. As a result, Florentines lacked the instruments that would have given them much more flexibility in dealing with liquidity crises.

After the bankruptcies of so many of these firms in the 1340s, the Florentines lost their special relation to the crown, never to regain it, although they probably maintained their role in the transfer of ecclesiastical funds to the papacy. They remained active as merchants, however, making the necessary adjustments to ma-

[9] Ignazio Del Punta, *Mercanti e banchieri lucchesi nel Duecento* (Pisa, 2004), 154 (table).

[10] Michael Prestwich, "Italian Merchants in Late Thirteenth- and Early Fourteenth-Century England," in *The Dawn of Modern Banking* (New Haven, CT, 1979), 77–104, observes that at this time most deposits by nobles and ecclesiastics were for temporary placement of funds.

jor developments in the later fourteenth century that affected the local market in which they operated: the rapid rise of an English cloth industry, an increasingly vigorous government policy to promote and protect English interests in this sector, and the shift of the main port from London to Southampton. For the Italians the market in London was tied into that of Bruges. Throughout the fourteenth and fifteenth centuries the two together constituted the major pole in northern Europe for the trade with the Mediterranean that followed the opening of the maritime route by the Genoese in 1277–78. Most Florentine firms had branches, or at least agents, in both places. Wool and cloth were always their primary interest. They exported raw wool both to the Low Countries and to their home industry, and they took the initiative to go to the sources in the countryside to commission deliveries. They also shipped low-priced English wool cloth to Pisa and its hinterland markets and to Venice for reexport to the Near East. In the long run this trade in cloth probably compensated for the slow decline in wool exports in the fifteenth century as the home industry shifted to other sources. Florentines in England imported mostly spices from the Near East, kermes from Spain, and, in the fifteenth century, silks from Florence, and they also brought wine, dried fruit, and other agricultural products from the western Mediterranean area, where by this time they had extensive commercial interests. Datini at the end of the century, for instance, imported from England both wool and cloth, along with small quantities of other native products such as lead, tin, and pewterware, and he sent back almost exclusively pepper, ginger, and kermes. As merchants, however, the Florentines trailed behind the Genoese and the Venetians, who had their own shipping service and dominated the trade in expensive products from the Near East.

Florentine trade with England was in clear decline by the last third of the fifteenth century. The last Florentine galley sailed in 1477, and although the collapse of the galley system at this time resulted primarily from problems unrelated to commercial activity, the end of direct maritime trade with England was symptomatic of the decline in the wool trade as a result of export restrictions designed to protect the local cloth industry. For a short time the Florentines profited from the sale of alum in England. In 1455 the lucrative alum monopoly, for centuries in the hands of the Genoese, collapsed as a result of the loss of its source following Turkish conquests in the eastern Mediterranean, and the discovery of alum at Tolfa, in the Papal States, gave the papacy the impetus to establish its own monopoly in the production of a product that had its largest markets in England and the Low Countries, both centers of major cloth industries. This opened marketing opportunities to Florentine merchants with strong ties to the papacy. Major contracts with certain monopoly privileges went to the Medici in 1466 and to the Pazzi in 1476, but after the Pazzi conspiracy two years later, the contract went to non-Florentines, including the Chigi firm of Siena and a series of Genoese merchants. The closing of the Medici branches in London in 1477 and in Bruges in 1481, though the result of the company's own internal problems, as we shall see, can nevertheless be taken as a sign of the withdrawal of the Florentine international network from England. Maritime trade in general between the Mediterranean and England fell off in the early sixteenth century, and the Italians shifted their trade from London to the rising emporium of Antwerp, whence the routes to Italy by that time went overland rather than by sea.

Florentine merchants continued to turn up in London to buy wool, cloth, and the usual variety of other items of the English export trade, such as lead, tin, hides, and beeswax, and they supplied the market in luxury goods, especially strong for their own silks, that grew with the establishment of the Tudor court. Antonio Corsi, active in England from 1486, supplied Henry VII with luxurious liturgical vestments in cloth of gold, some of which still survive.[11] Giuliano Serristori & Partners, like other such silk firms that went on to become trading companies to market their own products, opened a branch in London in 1496 and within four years was earning 14 percent on its investment.[12] The extensive business records of the partnership between Giovanni Cavalcanti and Pierfranceso de' Bardi in the early sixteenth century document sales of everything from eyeglasses to highly luxurious silks and arms, as well as financial dealings with the court. In return the firm gained certain privileges, including a license to import all kinds of luxury cloths with gold and silver threads, for which the king was to have first choice. Cavalcanti had personal ties to Henry VIII, whom he accompanied to the Field of Cloth of Gold in 1519, and he was involved in the commission for two royal tombs, one in 1511 for Henry VII's mother by Torrigiano, for whom he stood guarantor, and the other in 1519 for Henry VIII and Catherine of Aragon.[13] In 1559 Filippo di Bernardo Corsini went to London and together with his brothers accumulated the enormous fortune, estimated at sc.800,000, that was the foundation of the family's wealth in Florence.[14] A few of these merchants achieved a high profile on the local scene, usually for diplomatic service to the throne, but they did not play a major role in royal finance. The most infamous was Roberto Ridolfi, who engineered the plot to overthrow Elisabeth in 1570–71. No Florentine

[11] Lisa Monnas, "New Documents for the Vestments of Henry VII at Stonyhurst College," *Burlington Magazine* 131 (1989): 345–49.
[12] Sergio Tognetti, *Da Figline a Firenze: Ascesa economica e politica della famiglia Serristori (secoli XIV–XVI)* (Florence, 2003), 161.
[13] Cinzia M. Sicca, "Consumption and Trade of Art between Italy and England in the First Half of the 16th Century: The London House of the Bardi and Cavalcanti Company," *Renaissance Studies* 16 (2002): 162–201; idem, "Pawns of International Finance and Politics: Florentine Sculptors at the Court of Henry VIII," ibid. 20 (2006): 1–34.
[14] *Archivi dell'aristocrazia fiorentina* (Florence, 1989), 87.

reached the heights of the Genoese merchant Horatio Pallavicino, who became one of the most powerful men at court in the 1580s. In general the Italians got left behind in the expanding business world of sixteenth-century London, and their resident colony all but disappeared after midcentury.[15]

By this time Antwerp had replaced Bruges as the northwestern European pole of Italian international commerce. The decline of Bruges can be attributed partly to local political problems, partly to the silting of the Zwin, and partly to the protection of the local Flemish cloth industry from imports from England, an increasingly important item of commerce in the area. Antwerp, in contrast, encouraged the importation of English cloth since it had no cloth industry to protect, and the Hapsburgs actively promoted its growth. The cloth trade grew as an outlet for the international distribution of products from the growing English industry, as well as for cloth from the Low Countries in general. English commission agents moved in to handle orders for English cloth, hence supplanting foreigners, including Italians, in the exportation of cloth from that country. More general economic forces, however, played a major role in the rise of Antwerp. The intensification of overland trade routes along the Rhine into central Germany and to Italy and the new commercial system arising from the fairs of Frankfurt integrated much of Germany into international routes, thus expanding the orbit of trade out of Antwerp. Overland transport along these routes also improved considerably in efficiency as a result of both new technology in the use of horse-drawn wagons and the improved business organization of shippers. Moreover, in 1508 the Portuguese crown decided to make Antwerp the distribution center in Europe for the spices it was importing from the Far East, and this triggered a shift in the silver market controlled by the southern German merchants from Venice to Antwerp. The Portuguese spice trade, in fact, destroyed the balance of the older polarity of the traditional Italian commercial system between the Near East and the Low Countries, and even the Italian market came to be supplied with spices now also coming out of Antwerp. In short, the principal dynamics driving the rise of Antwerp as the major international emporium in northwestern Europe were cloth from England, silver, copper, metal products and fustians from Germany, and spices from Portugal.

Antwerp surpassed all earlier commercial cities in the geographic scope of its market with respect to both the extent of its hinterland and the reach of its maritime traffic. It attracted merchants from Italy, England, and the Hanseatic towns away from Bruges and became the center of a vigorous transcontinental trade extending into Germany and southward to Lyons and the Mediterranean. All this

---

[15] G. D. Ramsey, "The Undoing of the Italian Mercantile Colony in Sixteenth Century London," in *Textile History and Economic History: Essays in Honour of Miss Julia de Lacy Mann*, ed. N. B. Harte and K. G. Pontin (Manchester, 1973), 22–49.

commercial activity soon took its own course, so that it carried on even after the Portuguese, once they found their monopoly weakened owing to the revival of Venetian trade through Alexandria, closed down operations in 1548 and shifted their distribution center to Lisbon. Moreover, as the financial center of the empire of Charles V, enriched by bullion from the Americas, Antwerp became a major emporium also for Spanish merchants, and in the second half of the century Philip II poured even greater wealth into the Low Countries in pursuit of his military policy in the region. In 1557 the Venetian ambassador estimated that 40 million ducats passed through Antwerp in the course of a year.[16] All this trade, moreover, took place year-round and did not center on periodic fairs. In 1531 the Exchange, or Bourse, was set up in its own building, a single central place to facilitate transactions. From the end of the fifteenth century to 1565 the city's population rose from 30,000 to about 100,000 (to level off to around 60,000 by the seventeenth century, following the rise of Amsterdam).

The Milanese left Bruges for Antwerp sometime before 1494, the Venetian colony was gone by 1515, the last Florentine consul left sometime between 1518 and 1521, and the Genoese left shortly after 1522. In Antwerp, however, the Italians found themselves in a situation quite different from that in Bruges. They lost ground in transport to the Dutch and the English at sea and to the Flemish and the Germans on the overland routes going south. They also lost their relative importance in the city's resident community of international merchants. Already at the beginning of the sixteenth century Germans far outnumbered other foreigners, and among them were the great merchant-banking families from southern Germany who had strong connections to the emperor. Of the thirteen hundred to fourteen hundred foreign merchants there at midcentury, the Italian community numbered only two hundred, well behind the English, German, and Spanish communities and not far ahead of the Portuguese, and the Florentines did not have a dominant presence among the Italians. Of the four Italian "nations" they ranked third, after the Genoese and the Lucchesi and ahead of only the Lombards, and among the Italians active in the second half of the century, 47 percent were Genoese, 17 percent Lucchesi, and only 10 percent Florentines. Florentines do not show up at all in the study of the business correspondence of the Flemish company of the van der Molen, which conducted an extensive overland trade to many cities all across Italy (but not to Florence), some relatively minor, working through Italian correspondents in all these places. A study of the customs records for goods shipped out of Antwerp to Italy over terrestrial routes

[16] Richard Ehrenberg, *Capital and Finance in the Age of the Renaissance: A Study of the Fuggers and Their Connections* (London, 1928), 280.

from 1543 to 1545 reveals that only eight of the forty-eight Italians among the seventy-seven largest exporters were Florentines. And of the 63 percent of the total value of goods exported by Italians, Florentines account for 20 percent (after the Lombards and the Lucchesi). Of these exports, most went on to the ports of Venice and Ancona, and only 1 percent was directed to Florence itself. Neverthe-less, Florentines, like the Italians in general, succeeded in maintaining a favorable balance of trade through the sixteenth century, thanks to the importation of the products of a vigorous silk industry at home.[17]

Some of the Florentines in Antwerp, however, had a high profile. For instance, the Gualterotti in association with the Affaitati of Cremona held monopoly rights from the Portuguese for the distribution of spices from 1508 to 1525, and they contributed to the loan Charles V needed to win the imperial election in 1519. Another Tuscan on the scene, Gaspar Ducci (ca. 1495–ca. 1585), about whom more later, has gained considerable fame in the historiography as the new kind of entrepreneurial intermediary that the credit market at Antwerp brought into ex-istence. In the 1590s the Giunti family network of printers and booksellers, with its major branches in Florence, Venice, and Spain, expanded to Antwerp as well as to Lyons and to Germany. In general, however, little is known about the Flo-rentine community among the merchants and bankers from all over Europe who operated in the city. Even among the Italians it does not appear that any Floren-tine company achieved the international status of the Affaitati of Cremona, the Spinola of Genoa, or the Bonvisi of Lucca.

The military situation following the revolt of the Netherlands in 1568, which reached a climax in the long siege of Antwerp in 1584–85, took its toll, at least temporarily, on the economic life of the city, and some Italians shifted their op-erations to Cologne during these years. But it was the take-off of the Dutch econ-omy in the 1580s that led to the slow eclipse of Antwerp as an international em-porium and as a financial market by Amsterdam, a city much more oriented to the sea and one run by merchants themselves. Some Florentines—we do not know how many—followed the move. In 1604 the Riccardi company in Florence turned down an offer from Amsterdam to participate in a major venture involv-ing shiploads of skins, salmon, sturgeon, and caviar to be sent from Russia to Hamburg and then on to Italy. Many Florentines made the move to Amsterdam,

---

[17] Florence Edler, "The van der Molen, Commission Merchants of Antwerp: Trade with Italy, 1538–44," in *Medieval and Historiographical Essays in Honor of James Westfall Thompson*, ed. James Lea Cate and Eugene N. Anderson (Chicago, 1938), 78–145; Wilfred Brulez, "L'exportation des Pays-Bas vers l'Italie per voie de terre au milieu du XVIe siècle," *Annales: Économies, sociétés, civilisa-tions* 14 (1959): 461–91. Paola Subacchi, "Italians in Antwerp in the Second Half of the Sixteenth Century," in *Minorities in Western European Cities (Sixteenth–Twentieth Centuries)*, ed. Hugo Soly and Alfonz K. L. Thijs (Brussels, 1995), 73–90, mentions Genoese and Lucchesi but hardly any Florentines.

but they got lost in the ever-growing crowd of international merchants and bankers in a new kind of world emporium where an identity was no longer to be found in the corporate organization of a "nation."[18]

Naples and Southern Italy

A second pole in the Florentine network was southern Italy.[19] Sicily and the ports around the southern half of the peninsula, from Gaeta to Bari, lay along the central maritime routes Italians in the western Mediterranean used for their trade with North Africa and the Near East. In addition, the area had intrinsic importance as a source of grain and other foodstuffs for northern Italians, and the dynamic that drove this trade intensified with the rapid population increase in the northern towns. Venice and Genoa, with virtually no hinterland possessions, were completely dependent on provisioning from abroad, and in the course of the thirteenth century Florence too far outgrew the capacity of its countryside to supply the population with the basic staff of life. There were so many Florentines in Messina by the 1190s—probably there to buy grain—that a street took its name from their presence in the city. They found markets in southern France, Sardinia, and the other western Mediterranean islands as well but eventually concentrated their efforts on tapping the larger resources in Puglia, where they confronted stiff competition from the Pisans, the Sienese, the Genoese, and the Venetians, all of whom had arrived earlier.

The absolute necessity of gaining access to this market to assure a reliable source for the provisioning of a city growing so rapidly that in the 1280s it projected an enormous extension of its walls in anticipation of continuing growth, was a major consideration in the commune's Guelf policy to support the invasion of the Kingdom of Naples by Charles of Anjou that culminated in his victory over the heirs of the emperor Frederick II in 1268. That support took the concrete form

---

[18] Violet Barbour, *Capitalism in Amsterdam in the 17th Century* (Ann Arbor, MI, 1966), 57; Antonella Bicci, "Italiani ad Amsterdam nel Seicento," *Rivista storica italiana* 102 (1990): 922. Cinzia Cesari, *Mercanti lucchesi ad Amsterdam nel '600: Girolamo e Pompeo Parensi* (Lucca, 1989), lists only two or three Florentines in its index, but Rita Mazzei makes a brief comment on their presence in Amsterdam in "Continuità e crisi nella Toscana di Ferdinando II (1621–1670)," *Archivio storico italiano* (hereafter *ASI*) 145 (1987): 68–69. For the Riccardi, see Paolo Malanima, *I Riccardi di Firenze: Una famiglia e un patrimonio nella Toscana dei Medici* (Florence, 1977), 69.

[19] For Florentines in Naples through the fourteenth century, see David Abulafia, "Southern Italy and the Florentine Economy, 1265–1370," *Economic History Review* 33 (1981): 377–88, reprinted in his *Italy, Sicily and the Mediterranean, 1100–1400* (London, 1987), as well as the collections of his various articles cited in n. 1 to the introduction, above; and Giuseppe Petralia, "I toscani nel Mezzogiorno medievale: Genesi ed evoluzione trecentesca di una relazione di lungo periodo," in *La Toscana nel secolo XIV: Caratteri di una civiltà regionale*, ed. Sergio Gensini (Pisa, 1988), 287–336.

of major loans to the new king by Florentine firms such as the Frescobaldi, the Bardi, the Peruzzi, the Acciaiuoli, the Scali, and the Mozzi.

These firms found themselves in a situation much like that of their contemporaries in England, and the larger ones were active in both places. They wanted a larger share in the area's commercial activity, especially the trade in wheat, which Florence needed to feed its growing population as much as it needed the wool from England to supply its local industry. Grain was the Florentines' major export item, but they dealt also in oil, wine, vegetables, almonds, and other agricultural products. Exports were mostly bulky, low-cost goods of this kind, and most came from Puglia, after Sicily the most important grain-producing area in the Mediterranean. Under the German emperors Venice had dominated trade in the area, but with the Angevin conquest Florentines moved in and established themselves in all the ports along the heel of the peninsula, from Manfredonia southward to Barletta, Trani, Bari, and Brindisi. From this base in Puglia they succeeded in managing the export trade not only to Florence but to northern Italy and throughout the Adriatic as well. Business in the area also included the considerable traffic in the transit trade of spices, medicines, and sugar imported from the Near East and cotton and wool from North Africa for reexport to northern Europe, as well as furs and cloth going the other way. Moreover, with the incorporation of this area into the Florentine network, firms expanded their business in international transfer and exchange from Venice and Ragusa in the Adriatic to Avignon. In the south, as in England, Florentines had to confront the problem of balancing payments inasmuch as this predominantly agricultural economy did not generate much demand for manufactured goods from abroad. They were able to sell some northern cloth and luxury goods to the court, but in general they sent much less to the area than they exported from it. In contrast to their situation in England, they also engaged in shipping and exchange, since the area lay on the path of the central trade routes that bound North Africa and the Levant to Europe. They thus enlarged their share of international trade centering on the kingdom, although in this sphere they could hardly rival the great maritime powers of Venice and Genoa.

Yet even profits from these additional sources probably did not balance payments, and merchants made up that difference, as in England, by dipping their hands in the till of a monarchy whose pressure on them for loans to finance costly military policy did not let up. Like their contemporaries in England, the first three Edwards, the Angevin kings continued to pursue an aggressive military policy. In the 1270s Charles I occupied Albania and Morea, and an Angevin line was established in Hungary in 1308 (and in both places, as we shall see, they were followed by Florentine merchants). Meanwhile, ruling a kingdom that had a base in southern France and another in southern Italy, they directly confronted the Aragonese, who, after the conquest of Sicily in 1282, also had a trans-Mediterranean empire to the west, and they could hardly resist ambitions to move onto the fluid political scene in northern Italy as well. The firms that helped finance Angevin military policy used profits from both the lucrative grain market and their financial role in the newly established kingdom to provide them with the liquidity they needed to do business. In fact, the victory of Charles of Anjou in 1268 opened the way for the "conquest" of the area by Florentines as bankers and financiers.[20] The considerable financial privileges they received in return for loans to the crown to support the invasion (see chapter 3) included major export and tax powers over the grain trade in Puglia, a major economic plum in a period of rapid population growth before the Black Death. The complex ties of economic dependence binding together the Angevin monarchy and Florentine merchant-bankers made the Neapolitan south one of the most important areas of operations abroad in the period of early growth of the Florentine economy.

The dramatic banking crises of the 1340s took their toll on this special relation, as did the Black Death. Following immediately on the bankruptcies, this demographic disaster dealt a blow to the centrality of southern Italy in the Florentine commercial system. The decline in the population of Florence, by perhaps more than one-half, and elsewhere in urbanized northern Italy radically reduced the demand for grain in international markets. Tuscany, where land was now freed for more efficiently agricultural uses, became, except for the not infrequent moments of famine, largely self-sufficient in the supply of basic foodstuffs until its population began to grow again in the later sixteenth century. The firms that survived the bankruptcies of the 1340s reduced or closed down their commercial operations in the south, and many of the new firms that appeared on the scene worked through agents rather than setting up separate branches. Iacopo and Bartolomeo di Caroccio degli Alberti & Partners, for instance, closed its branch in Puglia in 1348 and the one in Naples the next year, and the firm turned to agents for the conduct of its business in the area. Later in the century Francesco Datini (d. 1410) built up an extensive network of companies in the major ports on the northern shores of the western Mediterranean but used only agents for business in the Kingdom of Naples. Giovanni di Bicci de' Medici opened a branch in Naples about 1400—his second branch after that in Venice—but it did not prosper and was closed down in 1426.

---

[20] Georges Yver uses the term in *Le commerce e les marchands dans l'Italie méridionale au XIIIe et au XIVe siècles* (Paris, 1903), ch. 5.

The situation of the Florentines in the kingdom took a decided turn for the worse in 1435, when the conquest of the realm by Alfonso V of Aragon threatened the political foundations of their commerce and banking interests. Alfonso took over his new kingdom in Italy with a strong prejudice against Florentine businessmen in general, fed in large part by the discontent among his subjects, the merchants of Barcelona and Valencia, who resented the Florentine dominance of banking and commerce in their region. The king had an ambitious project to promote the interest of these Catalan merchants by creating a kind of economic unity throughout his expanded trans–western Mediterranean kingdom, which by this time also included Naples and southern Italy. Obviously this policy was aimed against the Florentines, and in 1447 he committed himself to what was to be almost continual warfare against Florence directed to "the total military and economic destruction" of the city. In 1447 Alfonso expelled Florentines from Barcelona and even outlawed the wearing of cloth made from Florentine wool and silk, and he took measures against them also in Naples. The war came to an end only with the general peace arranged by the principal Italian states at Lodi in 1454. That treaty restored all the rights and privileges that the Florentines had enjoyed previously as foreign merchants, but in the meantime they had been at least temporarily uprooted, and the Catalans had gained a strong presence in the regional trade.[21]

Business prospects in the kingdom improved under Alfonso's successor, Ferrante, or Ferdinando, I (1458–94). The state he inherited spanned the western Mediterranean to take in Catalonia and the whole of southern Italy, and Naples itself was transformed into a capital city of an economy that now included the Catalan commercial empire. The influx of wealth and an explosive growth in population, going from no more than forty thousand under the last Angevins to more than two hundred thousand a century later, made the capital a major luxury market. Ferrante had an aggressive policy directed to stimulating the economy and putting the monarchy on a more solid administrative foundation, and except for some brief interruptions, especially in the aftermath of the Pazzi conspiracy, he was favorably disposed toward Florentines. He recognized the economic importance of the greater scale of their operations over that of the Catalans, and he enjoyed good relations with Lorenzo de' Medici. He confirmed the commercial privileges of the Florentines and established close financial ties to bankers, in

---

[21] See Mario Del Treppo, *I mercanti catalani e l'espansione della corona d'Aragona nel secolo XV* (Naples, 1972), 310–37; the quotation is from this discussion. Despite the title, Maria Elisa Soldani, "Alfonso il Magnanimo in Italia: Pacificatore o *crudel tiranno?* Dinamiche politico-economiche e organizzazione del consenso nella prima fase della guerra con Firenze (1447–1448)," *ASI* 166 (2007): 267–324, adds little about the economic aspect of Alfonso's campaign against Florence.

effect elevating them to the most favored status among all foreigners. His capital became a principal luxury market for Florentine textiles, particularly silks; at the same time, as a result of the diffusion of sericulture in Calabria and Sicily, the kingdom gradually replaced the Near East as the primary source for raw silk for what was becoming Florence's major industry. The Kingdom of Naples thus reentered the Florentine network as a major center: its agricultural economy became again a major resource for Florence, now for supplying its growing silk industry rather than for provisioning its population, while its capital, the most rapidly growing city in Europe, provided one of the most important outlets for the products of its textile industries.

Florentines, in short, found many possibilities for profits. Although they were outnumbered by the Catalans, their network enabled them to conduct trade in greater volume and over a wider geographic area. Even the Catalans used Florentine banks to balance credits and debits in the trade between Naples and southern France. A document from one of the major fairs at Salerno in 1478 reflects the status of the Florentines. Along with the Catalans, they appear as one of the most numerous groups of foreign merchants, far outnumbering the Genoese; one-third of total sales taken in by foreigners went to them, amounting to seven times what they paid out in purchases; and of the cloths traded at the fair, three-fourths of the silks came from Florence, as did the most expensive wool cloth.[22] Florentines were still active in the export of grain, oil, almonds, saffron, and other agricultural products from Puglia, although they faced competition from Venetians and Lombards. Many firms, like the Medici, sent agents to the area, while the Venetians, who controlled much of this trade, and German buyers, who utilized Venetian shipping, negotiated payments through Florentines in Venice, Florence, and Naples. One of these firms active in Puglia in the 1480s, Carlo Borromei, Agnolo Serragli & Partners, exported grain, oil, almonds, and saffron from Puglia, wool from the Abruzzi, and iron from the Basilicata, sending some of these things to Venice, and it imported silks from Florence and wool cloths from the Veneto. In the local market the firm functioned as a bank, accepting deposits, making small loans, and trafficking in bills of exchange, and through the usual arrangements with the government, it had contracts for collecting customs tolls in Barletta, Trani, and other smaller ports, for a salt farm and hearth taxes in the region of Bari, and for privileges in the iron market in the region of Otranto.[23]

---

[22] Armando Sapori, "Una fiera in Italia alla fine del Quattrocento: La fiera di Salerno del 1478," in his *Studi di storia economica: Secoli XIII, XIV, XV,* 3 vols. (Florence, 1955–67), 1:443–74.

[23] Michele Cassandro, "La Puglia e i mercanti fiorentini nel Basso Medioevo," *Atti e relazioni dell'Accademia Pugliese delle Scienze: Classe di Scienze Morali,* n.s., 2 (1974): 37.

The business records of the firm Tommaso di Leonardo Ginori opened in Naples in 1475, probably the most complete to survive for any Florentine active in the kingdom, document how impressive profits could be. The firm engaged in local banking and trade, exporting agricultural products and raw materials, especially silk, and importing finished cloth and other luxury items. From 1491 to 1494 it executed 680 exchange operations for a total amount of *du.*230,000. In seventeen years of documented activity to 1495, earnings averaged about *fl.*2,000 a year on an original investment of *fl.*6,000. The extraordinary wealth accumulated at Naples by Giuliano di Leonardo Gondi and Filippo di Matteo Strozzi, the latter the son of a man exiled there by Cosimo de' Medici in 1434, manifested itself back in Florence in two of the most magnificent palaces built in the Renaissance, both under construction in the 1490s. Gondi, like Ginori, seems to have been primarily a merchant. The company in Florence of his nephew Alessandro di Antonio imported much linen from the family company in Naples. Strozzi also had significant business with the crown as banker. Two of his journals, dating from 1472–73 and 1475–76, record a turnover that amounted to more than 2 million ducats annually. Strozzi did not, however, hold an official position as collector of taxes or fiscal administrator in the traditional manner of banker-financiers; rather, his bank served as a depository for royal funds. In 1471 the Medici opened an office in Naples as a subsidiary of the branch in Rome, and it had extensive operations in the Pugliese fairs. It did not have notable success, however, until it became, along with other branches of the firm, more involved in loans to the king and the luxury trade with the court.[24]

During the sixteenth century, the Florentine presence in the kingdom declined along with that of the Catalans, the Lucchesi, and the Lombards. The inheritance of the Spanish crown by Charles V in 1516 favored the special interests of the Fuggers and the Genoese, but by midcentury the Genoese, whose banking and commercial interest extended throughout the western Hapsburg territories from Spain to the Low Countries, had gained a hegemony in Spanish royal finance even over the Fuggers. Their loans to the government in Naples amounted

[24] For Ginori, see Michele Cassandro, "Affari e uomini d'affari fiorentini a Napoli sotto Ferrante I d'Aragona (1472–1495)," in *Studi di storia economica toscana nel Medioevo e nel Rinascimento in memoria di Federigo Melis* (Pisa 1987), 103–23; for Gondi, Alfonso Leone, "Rapporti commerciali fra Napoli e Firenze alla fine del secolo XV," in *Studi in memoria di Giovanni Cassandro* (Rome, 1991), 2:490–501; and for Strozzi, Mario Del Treppo, "Aspetti dell'attività bancaria a Napoli nel '400," in *Aspetti della vita economica medievale* (Florence, 1985), 557–601, and idem, "Il re e il banchiere: Strumenti e processi di razionalizzazione dello stato aragonese di Napoli," in *Spazio, società, potere nell'Italia dei Comuni*, ed. Gabriella Rossetti (Naples, 1986), 229–304. Michele Cassandro, "L'irradiazione economica fiorentina nell'Italia meridionale tra Medioevo e Rinascimento," in *Fra spazio e tempo: Studi in onore di Luigi De Rosa*, ed. Ilaria Zilli (Naples, 1995), 1:191–221, offers a general survey, with bibliography, of Florentines active in Naples in the second half of the fifteenth century.

to six times those of the Florentines and the Fuggers, and they gained a major share of the trade in grain and raw silk. Moreover, they strengthened their base in the kingdom by entering into the possession of feudal estates and holding state offices, moves made by few Florentines. Merchants from Antwerp and Spain also appeared on the scene, and at the end of the century the English too were enlarging their role in Mediterranean commerce. Florentine firms, in short, confronted more competition and had a decreasing share of the market.

They can still be found in the region, however, and fortunes were still to be made there. Guglielmo and Giuliano Del Tovaglia, for instance, won a major contract for managing iron mines throughout the kingdom in 1546, and Angelo Biffoli was a major lender to the court in the third quarter of the century. Nevertheless, commerce was the main attraction. A ledger of the company of Bardo di Iacopo Corsi, open from 1537 to 1541, documents the richly varied and busy Mediterranean traffic in goods conducted by the company agent at the port of Messina. From Florence he imported wool cloth, silks, and gold threads and sent back raw silk and some cotton imported from Malta. In addition to handling these staples in the trade between the south and Florence, he dealt on the side in numerous other commercial operations throughout the Mediterranean as importer-exporter. He sent raw silk to Lyons and London, linen to Valencia, spices from Alexandria to Lyons, brazilwood from the Americas to Alexandria, grain from Sicily to Genoa and Lisbon, wine from Crete to Antwerp and London; and for the local market in Messina he imported wool cloth from Flanders and England, tin from England, hats and scissors from Naples, almonds from Puglia, pitch from Cadiz, and skins from England, Valencia, Naples, and the Near East. Most of Corsi's trade, however, was in cloth of one kind or another and related raw materials, and he had to balance his trade with the Near East with shipments of gold coins. One has the impression that as the century wore on, Florentine commercial firms like the Corsi increasingly confined their activity to the immediate needs of the Florentine textile industries, namely, the purchase of raw silk and the sale of both wool and silk cloth.[25]

[25] On foreign merchants in sixteenth-century Naples, see two contributions to *Sistema di rapporti ed élites economiche in Europa (secoli XII–XVII)*, ed. Mario Del Treppo (Naples, 1994): Aurelio Musi, "Le élites internazionali a Napoli dal primo Cinquecento alla guerra dei Trent'anni," 138–39, 150; and Giovanni Muto, "Cittadini e 'forestieri' nel regno di Napoli: Note sulla presenza genovese nella capitale tra Cinque e Seicento," 168. On the Genoese, see Aurelio Musi, *Mercanti genovesi nel Regno di Napoli* (Naples, 1996), esp. 34–38. The Corsi is the only Florentine firm that has been studied. See Hidetoshi Hoshino, "Messina e l'arte della lana fiorentina nei secoli XVI–XVII," in *Studi dedicati a Carmelo Trasselli*, ed. Giovanna Motta (Soveria Mannelli, CZ, 1983), 427–46; and Lorenzo Lombardi, "Commercio e banca di fiorentini a Messina nel XVI secolo: L'azienda di Bardo di Iacopo Corsi dal 1537 al 1541," *ASI* 156 (1998): 637–69. These two studies, however, have only scratched the surface of the rich archives of this family (ASF, Archivio Guicciardini Corsi Salviati), which includes some one hundred account books for their business activity in Sicily alone through the sixteenth century.

The Western Mediterranean

One of the first scenes of the commercial revolution was set in the western Mediterranean, where Genoa and Pisa took aggressive initiatives to promote the maritime trade that extended throughout the entire area, bringing in other players, especially Barcelona, along with Marseilles and Palma in the Balearic Islands. The first evidence of Florentine participation in this trade, at Messina in 1193 and at Genoa in 1213, has already been remarked. They probably ventured out primarily motivated, as observed above, to find both grain, in the islands and in southern Italy, to support the growing population, and raw wool, also in the islands as well as in North Africa, to supply the budding textile industry. In addition, they traded in any other marketable item to be found in these places, and they ventured farther afield to the Near East. By the end of the thirteenth century, with their solid base in the Kingdom of Naples and close financial ties to the papacy, Florentines—the Bardi, the Peruzzi, the Acciaiuoli, and others—had a presence in all the major commercial centers.

From its beginning, therefore, the commercial revolution was marked by steadily growing trade throughout the western Mediterranean. In the second half of the fourteenth century, however, its intensity increased, and the area emerged as a central place in the Florentine commercial and financial network.

A Transport Revolution

Although the Genoese opened the maritime route from the Mediterranean to England and the Low Countries in the 1270s, it was not until about the mid-fourteenth century that Genoese and Venetian galleys made the trip more or less regularly, thereby not only expanding the range of commerce in the western Mediterranean but also opening up new possibilities for some regional economies to plug into this enlarged Mediterranean–North Atlantic commercial system. The Iberian Peninsula especially saw the growth of a number of port cities that provided outlets for resources in the hinterland, from Valencia and Malaga in the Mediterranean to Cadiz and Lisbon on the Atlantic, and the Genoese extended their colonization inland beyond these ports to Seville, Granada, and Cordova, laying the foundations for their prominence in Spanish trade and finance for the next three centuries. The Balearics, important in the island traffic passing through the western Mediterranean for reasons of winds and currents, became a major node for commercial traffic linking Barcelona, Valencia, and southern Spain to Italy. This trade also brought into its orbit North Africa, important for skins, pelts, raw wool, kermes, wax, and ostrich feathers, which were exchanged primarily for copper arriving from Venice.[26] The Balearics also underwent considerable economic development as an important source of wool and a producer of wool textiles. Venice too began to have a larger presence in the West, and ships in great numbers from Portugal, the Bay of Biscay, England, and Germany began to move into the Mediterranean from the Atlantic. Trade also increased between the western and eastern Mediterranean with the opening of Alexandria as a major port for the redirection of the Far Eastern trade from the northern overland route to one using the Red Sea. By the end of the fourteenth century Barcelona was sending more ships than ever to the Levant.

The political scene is not irrelevant to these economic developments. As we have seen, in the second half of the thirteenth century two kingdoms expanded their power in the area: the Angevins moved across the Ligurian and Tyrrhenian seas from Provence to take over the Kingdom of Naples (1268) from the last of the imperial heirs, and then the Aragonese crown, which already had an island base in Majorca, extended its rule from Catalonia, with its great commercial center at Barcelona, out to the islands of Sicily (1282), Minorca (1287), and Sardinia (1297). These two states incorporated much of the trading area in the western Mediterranean, and indeed, when Alfonso the Magnificent united these two kingdoms in 1435, he had, as already noted, grandiose ambitions, unusual for his time, to promote a commercial empire centered on the Barcelona-Naples axis.

The southern regions of France also fell into the western Mediterranean commercial system. Marseilles developed as a major port on the Mediterranean following on the growth of Genoa and Barcelona, and by the last quarter of the thirteenth century Florentine merchants were to be found throughout its hinterland—the Bardi at Lyons, the Altoviti and the Valori at Valence, the Gianfigliazzi at Orange, and most of the major firms (the Bardi, the Peruzzi, the Spini, the Mozzi, the Frescobaldi, the Franzesi, the Canigiani) at Nîmes, while the big three in the Angevin kingdom (the Bardi, the Peruzzi, and the Acciaiuoli) were in Aix, the capital of Provence. Trade throughout this area intensified from the early fourteenth century on, following the growth of Avignon as a major market once it had become the capital of the papacy (in 1305). At the end of the century, merchants from towns in southwestern Germany also penetrated into the region. Organized into a trade consortium known as the Ravensburger Handelsgesellschaft, taking its name from the Swabian town where they had their headquarters, these merchants built up a vast network extending from Bruges to southern France and

---

[26] Martin Malcolm Elbl, "From Venice to the Tuat: Trans-Saharan Copper Trade and Francesco di Marco Datini of Prato," in *Money, Markets and Trade in Late Medieval Europe: Essays in Honour of John H. A. Munro,* ed. Lawrin Armstrong, Ivana Elbl, and Martin Malcolm Elbl (Leiden, 2007), 411–59.

into the Aragonese kingdom as well as to Genoa and Milan. The role of these merchants in bringing Germany, with its many towns, into the orbit of western Mediterranean trade at this time is often overlooked in the evaluation of the renewed vitality of the economy of western continental Europe at the end of the Middle Ages. Theirs was strictly a trade, not a banking, consortium, however, and they had no reason to extend their network to Florence, nor do they have much of a presence in Florentine merchants' business records.[27]

Avignon became a major node in the Florentine network. Finding themselves for the first time settled in a reasonably secure capital, the popes began building up a large bureaucracy and transforming their court into the most cosmopolitan and splendid in Europe. The population of the city grew to about thirty thousand, about the size of Rome at the time. The demand all this growth generated gave rise to a lively market for goods and services. Moreover, the city had a key position on trade routes extending northward along the Rhône valley to central France and the Low Countries, westward to Montpellier and Spain, and southward into the western Mediterranean commercial system. The company of Bartolomeo di Caroccio degli Alberti sold more than half of the cloth it exported from Flanders from 1352 to 1358 in the Avignon market (the rest went on to Florence, probably for finishing and reexport). The many abbots, bishops, and cardinals from all over whose names appear in the accounts of this firm testify to the wider service Florentines performed for churchmen in the new papal capital. They did everything from lending money to selling goods in the retail market— the former activity well documented by the firm of Iacopo Girolami and Tommaso Corbizzi, active in the 1330s, and the latter by the career of the merchant of Prato Francesco Datini at the end of the century.

Much of the dynamic behind this intensification and extension of trade in the western Mediterranean came from commerce in cheaper and bulkier goods. For Florentine merchants the staples were still raw wool and finished cloth, which supplemented imports of both from northwestern Europe, followed probably by hides, skins, and leather. Myriad other items of trade, most of them relatively inexpensive and bulky agricultural products, arrived in markets from North Africa, Spain, and the islands for redistribution throughout the area: principally wheat, sugar, rice, dried fruit, raw silk, kermes, and dried and salted fish but including also wine, oil, almonds, wax, ostrich feathers, coral, saffron, ceramics, and slaves. In all this traffic spices were still present and very valuable, but most of them got lost in the abundance of other goods. The profusion of these products

[27] Aloys Schulte, *Geschichte der grossen Ravensburger Handelgesellschaft, 1380–1530* (Stuttgart and Berlin, 1923).

being sent all around the Mediterranean and to the north testifies to the growth of regional economies to the point that they were producing surpluses for this international trade. On the one hand, cabotage intensified, and more local merchants expanded the geographic range of their activity; on the other hand, great international merchants like Datini engaged in local traffic and the trade in secondary goods on the side, some becoming more involved in regional markets than in business directly connected to their native city. Genoese merchants, well supported by their own shipping service, had a particularly strong presence in this interregional trade all around the western Mediterranean and out into the Atlantic, much of it completely bypassing Genoa. A complex infrastructure thus developed within this segment of the network, but this was not a closed system, for it linked North Africa to western Europe and extended both to the Levant and out to the Atlantic and northern Europe.[28] This regionalization of the western Mediterranean economy was a development not considered in the older views of economic decline at the end of the Middle Ages.

If this intensification of local trade, now plugged into a wider commercial network, was a major stimulus to regional economic development around the northern rim of the western Mediterranean, it also led to important innovations in the way it was handled. Many shippers, including the Genoese, abandoned the galley for slower moving and less defensible but larger round ships and carracks to carry more bulky cargo. And to accommodate merchants dealing in a greater variety of goods that ranged more widely in value, they calculated shipping charges more finely. Federigo Melis contended that these developments in shipping added up to a "transport revolution," yet another step in the development of the European economy after the "commercial revolution" of the eleventh century and the "nautical revolution" of the thirteenth century (which marked an improvement in sailing and navigational techniques). Melis estimated that from the second to the fourth quarter of the fourteenth century the overall range of shipping rates in the Mediterranean for the same products was reduced from 11:1 to 2.3:1 and that within this range the calibration of rates for the different products increased from 2:1 to 10:1. The contemporaneous refinement of maritime insurance to reduce risk and attract investors, as we have seen, also testifies to these new conditions of trade. It is very likely that the rapid diffusion among Florentines of the habit of keeping accounts in bipartite form, with debits and credits opposite each other, as we keep them today—the oldest example dates from 1382—resulted

---

[28] Recent statements about these developments are Marco Tangheroni, *Commercio e navigazione nel Medioevo* (Bari, 1996), ch. 9; and David Abulafia, "L'economia italiana e le economie mediterranee ed atlantiche," in *L'Italia alla fine del Medioevo: I caratteri originali nel quadro europeo*, ed. Francesco Salvestrini (Florence, 2006), esp. pp. 358–65 and 375–80.

from the convenience this practice offered for keeping track of the much greater number and frequency of transactions that characterized this trade.[29]

The career of Francesco Datini, spanning the second half of the fourteenth century and documented by the extraordinarily complete archive he left behind, recapitulates the commercial opportunities that opened up as a result of these developments. In 1350, still in his teens, he moved to Avignon, where he eventually was able to go into business on his own, and his firm there continued in business after his return, in 1382, to Italy, where he died in 1410. Datini was attracted to Avignon because, falling into the orbit of the expanding western Mediterranean commercial system and with links to the north, it had become a major commercial center for Florentine merchants. No fewer than 126 surviving ledgers, as well as letters and other papers, cover almost a half-century of his commercial activity in the city and, through agents, in its trade area, which included Nice, Arles, Marseilles, Montpellier, and Milan. He stocked his shop with an incredible variety of items imported from virtually everywhere, from ostrich feathers from North Africa, leather falcon hoods from Paris, and devotional panel paintings from Florence to the full range of hunting and military gear, including suits of armor (possibly assembled in his shop from imported parts). He also opened a moneychanging business there. Datini thus made his start in the bustling urban market that grew up around the papal court in Avignon, not in financial service to the papacy itself.

Having established a solid basis in a regional business during his thirty-two years at Avignon, Datini returned to Italy in 1382 to expand his operations. He immediately set up additional companies at Prato, Florence, and Pisa; in 1392 he opened another in Genoa, and in the following year yet another in Barcelona. He thus ended up with a network of firms located at all the strategic centers of the region except Naples, incorporating the major ports and the key hinterland market center at Avignon as well as the financial capital at Florence itself. From each of these his agents and correspondents extended the tentacles of trade contacts throughout the entire region. The firm in Genoa did business in the hinterland along the upper Po valley from Piacenza to Turin and along the coast from Portovenere to Ventimiglia. The firm at Barcelona operated throughout that city's trading region, extending to Perpignan and into Languedoc, and it had major branches in Valencia and Palma in Majorca, each with its own regional network. From Valencia the web of contacts reached into the city's vast hinterland as far as Castile and extended southward along the coast to Malaga, Cadiz, Seville, and

---

[29] The studies by Melis on ships, shipping rates, and insurance are collected in *I trasporti e le comunicazioni nel Medioevo*, ed. Luciana Frangioni (Florence, 1984).

Lisbon and outward to Las Palmas in the Canary Islands and West Africa. The voluminous correspondence and accounting materials that survive for Datini's operations constitute the best documentation we have for this vast trading region extending along the entire northern rim of the western Mediterranean, just as the great fortune he accumulated, making this man of modest origins one of the wealthiest men in Florence, testifies to the opportunities that came with the economic growth of the region at this time. Of the forty-two firms that can be identified as operating outside of Italy in the 1427 catasto, just a few years after Datini's death, twenty-nine were located in an area extending from southern France to the south of Spain.[30]

Datini's career can be taken as emblematic of Florentine business enterprise in exploiting the new opportunities that opened up with the regionalization of Mediterranean international commerce. The evidence of his story can be complemented at a more general level by the contemporaneous revival of the port of Pisa. After the victory of the Genoese at the battle of Meloria in 1284, Pisa lost its maritime power, but it remained an important center of trade, where the Bardi, Peruzzi, Acciaiuoli, Buonaccorsi, and many other Florentine firms at various times had branches, depending on the political relations between the two cities. In the second half of the fourteenth century, after the crisis of the 1340s removed the Florentine firms from the scene, Pisa came into its own again as a major port for the growing commercial activity in the western Mediterranean, now as an emporium attracting ships from elsewhere, no longer as a maritime power with its own merchant marine. The Genoese and the Venetians made it a port of call for their ships, and the Catalans had a large colony among the foreign merchants who took up residence in the city. Its trading region extended throughout the western Mediterranean—to Marseilles and the Rhône valley, to Aigues-Mortes and Languedoc, to Gaeta and Naples, to Malaga and southern Spain, and to North Africa. Political relations permitting, Florentines set up businesses in Pisa, utilizing the vast shipping services offered by foreigners. Datini's widespread commercial interests virtually overlay the entire

---

[30] Federigo Melis has done the most thorough work in the Datini archives but did not live to present a grand synthesis. He summarized the business history of Datini's firms abroad in *Aspetti della vita economica medievale: Studi nell'Archivio Datini di Prato* (Siena, 1962), but his work by no means invalidates the more general biography of Iris Origo, *The Merchant of Prato: Francesco di Marco Datini* (London, 1967). In the essays collected in his *I mercanti italiani nell'Europa medievale e rinascimentale*, ed. Luciana Frangioni (Florence, 1990), Melis cites much material from the Datini archives that richly illustrates the extent, variety, and intensity of trade throughout the western Mediterranean at the end of the fourteenth century. Datini's local trade in Avignon is described in Luciana Frangioni, *Chiedere e ottenere: L'approvvigionamento di prodotti di successo della bottega Datini di Avignone nel XIV secolo* (Florence, 2002). The first volume of the project to publish a new inventory of the vast Datini archive is dedicated to Avignon: *L'archivio di Francesco di Marco Datini: Fondaco di Avignone*, ed. Elena Cecchi (Rome, 2004). For the data on firms in the 1427 catasto, see n. 125 in chapter 1, above.

geography of the trade coming in and out of the port. Entrepreneurs from Pisa itself and nearby towns played a major role in this revival during the second half of the fourteenth century; these included forebears of the Borromei and the Quaratesi, both from nearby San Miniato al Tedesco, whose descendants became major merchant-bankers in Florence, Milan, Venice, Bruges, and London. The business records of these Pisans, even more than those of contemporary Florentines, have been used to illustrate the refinement of some major commercial and banking practices, including especially credit instruments and written orders of payment, in the second half of the fourteenth century.[31]

Not surprisingly, this renewed activity of Pisa as a major Mediterranean emporium aroused the economic as well as the political ambitions of Florence. It occurred at the time when Florence was pushing its territorial borders toward the coast. The growing state absorbed the Valdinievole as far as Pescia and the lower Valdarno as far as Fucecchio in the second quarter of the fourteenth century and then moved into the hills south of this area as far as San Miniato al Tedesco and Volterra in the third quarter, and the logic of geography and economic interests combined to target Pisa as well for conquest. Moreover, rocky political relations between the two cities and the external interference of Genoa, which had the maritime power to exercise authority over Porto Pisano and Livorno, the ports of Pisa, called for a definitive solution. Florentine merchants were able to use other Tuscan ports—Motrone, the port of Lucca just north of Pisa in Versilia; Piombino to the south; and Talamone, the port of Siena, further south—but the advantages of Pisa at the mouth of the Arno were patent. The problem of access to a port came to a head during the Visconti invasion of Tuscany in the 1390s, when Florence found itself momentarily surrounded and cut off from virtually all the routes leading out to the Tyrrhenian ports, as well as to Bologna in the north and to Perugia in the southeast. No sooner had the impending threat of isolation and even conquest evaporated, on the sudden death of the duke, Giangaleazzo, in 1402, than Florence moved against Pisa, conquering it in 1406, although it still had to deal with Genoa, which controlled the port of Pisa at Porto Pisano. Florentine merchants took over virtually all international commercial business in the city, forcing many of the city's merchants to transfer their operations to other ports, such as Piombino and Valencia. In the following two decades Pisa lost almost half of its population, much owing to emigration, and the local economy declined to that of a provincial town. Florence completed its takeover of port activity in 1421 with the purchase of Porto Pisano and Livorno from the Genoese.

---

[31] Federigo Melis, *Note di storia della banca pisana nel Trecento* (Pisa, 1955), reprinted in his *La banca pisana e le origini della banca moderna*, ed. Marco Spallanzani (Florence, 1987), 55–293.

By this time most shipping was being directed to Livorno, but it was little more than a port facility subject to customs and administrative control from Pisa, where the arsenal was located. Thus Florence entered into this growing western Mediterranean trading area with its own port city, now fully dominated by Florentine merchants.

The absorption of Pisa into the network as a central place must have led Florentines to abandon Genoa. Genoa was among the places abroad where Florentines were first documented, in the early thirteenth century, and most of the large firms in the age of the Bardi, the Peruzzi, and the Acciaiuoli had branches there. In the second half of the fourteenth century, when trade intensified throughout the western Mediterranean, Genoa was almost as important as a center for Florentine operations as Venice, Rome, and Naples.[32] The Ricci and the Alberti, both among the largest merchant-banking houses, had branches in Genoa. Datini set up a business there in 1392, and it was from Genoa that he extended his commercial activity into Catalonia. In the fifteenth century, however, Genoa loses its presence in Florentine business records. Only two firms located there appear in the 1427 catasto, as compared with fifteen in Pisa and thirteen in Venice. Not one ledger survives of a Florentine doing business in the city, and in the hundreds of extant account books of Florentine businesses, an account in the name of anyone connected with Genoa is hardly to be found. Moreover, the records of accomandita contracts dating from the latter half of the century do not reveal investments with firms doing business there. In fact, the monographic studies of such fifteenth-century companies as the Medici, which had its own network throughout Europe, the Cambini, which concentrated on western Mediterranean markets, and the Della Casa, which operated out of the international exchange market in Geneva, mention Genoa only in passing. These firms did not have any significant commercial ties to the city, and for the relatively few exchange transactions made through Genoa, they used Genoese correspondents there, not agents of other Florentine firms. The ledger of Giovanni Piccamiglio, the only one to survive for any fifteenth-century Genoese merchant, confirms this impression from the Genoese perspective: although he engaged in much exchange activity, hardly any Florentines are named in his accounts. In short, the conquest of Pisa seems to have entailed a major shift within the network—yet another unstudied subject.

---

[32] In the list of 42 Florentine companies operating abroad from 1385 to 1399 drawn up by John F. Padgett and Paul D. McLean, 9 had branches in Genoa, as compared with 11 in Rome, 12 in Venice, and only 5 in Naples. See the appendix to their article "Organizational Invention and Elite Transformation: The Birth of Partnership Systems in Renaissance Florence," *American Journal of Sociology* 111 (2006): 1463–1568. The Florentine presence in Genoa as documented by the Datini materials is discussed in Maria Giagnacovo, *Mercanti toscani a Genova: Traffici, merci e prezzi nel 14. secolo* (Naples, 2005), 52–58.

If anything, the conquest led to a major new initiative that saw Florence challenge Genoa on its own grounds. In 1421, the same year as the purchase of Livorno, Florentines revealed their full economic ambitions to become a maritime as well as a commercial power by setting up an agency, the Sea Consuls, to direct a state maritime trade enterprise. An arsenal was built that eventually covered an area of some forty thousand square meters, complete with a chapel, houses, and shops. The gold florin, the very hallmark of the city's international network, was changed in shape to resemble more closely the Venetian ducat, which it was meant to challenge in Levantine markets. The first galley departed for Alexandria in 1422, and a fleet of three inaugurated the route to the Low Countries in 1425. A third route in the Florentine system made the rounds in the western Mediterranean, to Barcelona, Sicily, and the Barbary Coast. The galley system was driven, not by the general commercial interests of merchants, but by a government policy directed to supporting the city's wool industry at a time when it was undergoing a depression and the silk industry was taking off. Rather than plugging into the vigorous trading activity in the western Mediterranean, the galley system had the limited economic objective of supporting local industries by importing raw wool above all from England and raw silk from Spain and southern Italy and exporting finished products, especially to markets in the Levant. Guided by this policy, the consuls built only galleys that had limited capacity, and they planned voyages with little interest in coastal traffic. The system had some modest, intermittent success in the beginning, but it faced serious problems. The state failed to give it wholehearted financial support, and merchants found that the rigidity of its policy precluded the flexibility they needed in organizing the kind of short-distance trade in the myriad goods that by this time characterized commerce in the western Mediterranean. In the long run the enterprise failed since its original function became outdated with the shift in the market orientation of the industry it was designed to support. By the second half of the fifteenth century the industry was taking less and less wool from England and more from central Italy and less silk from the Levant and more from southern Italy, while at the same time major new markets for its products opened up in Italy itself, in the growing metropolises of Rome and Naples. What might be called the Italianization of the textile industries, in short, rendered the galley system as originally conceived obsolete within a half-century of its inception. Moreover, when the Florentines lost the contract for the alum trade from Tolfa after the Pazzi conspiracy, the galleys lost one of the most important items they carried to the north. The last galleys sailed in 1478, headed for Catalonia and the Barbary Coast.[33]

[33] Michael E. Mallett, *The Florentine Galleys in the Fifteenth Century* (Oxford, 1967).

The Iberian Peninsula

The galley system became outmoded in part because it failed to build on the dense commercial interest of Florentine merchants like Datini, who were exploiting the new opportunities that opened up with the regionalization of trade in the western Mediterranean. Beginning with the generation of Datini, many Italians sent agents and partners, or went themselves, to the Aragonese cities of Barcelona, Valencia, and Palma di Majorca, and some went beyond as far as Lisbon, penetrating into the interior along the way. This grand invasion of the Iberian Peninsula by Italian merchants has been commented on extensively by historians, but with almost all the emphasis on the Genoese, who rose to clear dominance by the later sixteenth century. There is some literature on the Lombards but hardly anything specifically about Florentines besides that building on the rich Datini materials. The story of the Florentines' role in the commercial growth of the area is yet another that waits to be told.

During the commercial revolution of the eleventh century Barcelona took the initiative in the transit trade between a constellation of cities in Languedoc and Provence, including Narbonne, Carcassonne, and Montpellier, and Florentines could be found in all these places at the end of the thirteenth century. Barcelona became a major port with its own fleet, the most important maritime power in the Mediterranean after Genoa and Pisa, but it was not a center of major production and did not have a vast hinterland. The Bardi, Peruzzi, and Acciaiuoli firms had interests in the general area tied to their trade in raw wool and grain. Florentines, however, had difficulty maintaining a base in Barcelona because of local merchants' resistance to competition, and they had to face repeated royal legislation against foreign merchants in general throughout the kingdom. Down through the 1350s they had a slight presence in the city.

The reorientation of western Mediterranean trade in the later fourteenth century boosted the importance of the port of Barcelona, which became a veritable international emporium handling the increased transit trade in goods from northern Europe as well as those moving along the Mediterranean rim—"the large lungs through which Aragon, and not only Aragon, breathed," in the words of Mario Del Treppo.[34] Florentines began to arrive in large numbers, their inter-

---

[34] Del Treppo, *I mercanti catalani*, 284. There is a vast literature on Italians in Catalonia, most of it concentrating on the Genoese. For the region in general and specifically for Barcelona, with further bibliographical references, see Maria-Teresa Ferrer i Mallol, "Els italians a terres catalanes (segles XII–XV)," *Anuario de estudios medievales* 10 (1980): 393–466; Patrizia Mainoni, "Mercanti italiani a Barcellona e a Valenza nel tardo Medioevo," in Del Treppo, *Sistema di rapporti ed élites economiche*, 199–209; and Manuel J. Paláez, "Notas sobre las relaciones económicas entre Cataluña e Italia desde 1472 a 1516," in *Oriente e Occidente tra Medioevo ed Età Moderna: Studi in onore di Geo*

est no longer confined to the limited trade of the earlier period but now directed to the numerous products available from the hinterland, especially in the vast region of Valencia. Of particular importance, however, were markets that opened up in Spain for both wool cloth and silks from Florence. In his record book Goro Dati, who had a silk-producing shop, not an international merchant bank, notes at least five business trips he made to Valencia in the years 1390–1408; on the last trip he stayed three years. Merchant-bankers used Barcelona as a control center for organizing trade and shipping. Datini, for instance, had his branch in Barcelona, although much of his trade was organized through agents in Valencia and Palma. Among the numerous companies in the complex and far-flung agglomerate of the Alberti family, two had branches in Barcelona in 1400, by which time the Florentines ranked with the Genoese as the city's most important foreign merchants. According to fragmentary customs records for 1437, Italian products accounted for 21 percent of all imports, and the bulk of these were luxury silks from Florence.[35] The Florentines had their own niche in the banking sector as well, making loans at all levels of society, buying tax farms, facilitating international exchange, speculating in the local money market, and selling marine insurance, an essential service in a port city. Since Florentines used Barcelona as an outlet for channeling their surplus trade balances in the north, the city also became a major center for international monetary exchange, one whose rates were quoted at the fairs of Geneva in the mid-fifteenth century.

The monarchy often displayed considerable ambiguity in its efforts to balance the interests of these foreigners against the continuing hostility of the merchants of Barcelona toward them. The natives resented the city's dependence on outsiders for some imports, especially grain, and for the monopoly they had in certain banking services. The Florentines, however, enjoyed much favor at court as purveyors of silks and other luxury objects. Moreover, like the Genoese and the Lombards, they had the advantage of a more developed international trade network for the supply and redistribution of many foreign products, and in addition they could offer banking services not otherwise readily available. Catalan merchants provided many of the shipping services, but they found it difficult to rise to the higher levels of operations dominated by the Italians. As we have seen, after the conquest of Naples by Alfonso the Magnificent, Catalan merchants moved into southern Italy in large numbers, thereby gaining easier access to Italian markets

---

Pistarino, ed. Laura Balletto (Genoa, 1997), 977–1003. On Florentines in Barcelona, see Maria-Teresa Ferrer i Mallol, "Intorno all'assicurazione sulla persona di Filippozzo Soldani, nel 1399, e alle attività dei Soldani, mercanti fiorentini, a Barcellona," in *Studi in memoria di Federigo Melis* (Naples, 1978), 2:441–95.

[35] Del Treppo, *I mercanti catalani,* 179.

than they ever had before. But even though they soon outnumbered all other foreigners and had the support of the king, very few of them ever made it into the highest ranks of international merchants and bankers.

Symptomatic of a difference between the economic cultures of the Catalans and the Florentines was the malaise induced in the former by the sophisticated business practices of the latter. Florentines came in for considerable blame in a treatise on monetary problems written by Arnau de Capdevila in 1437. He proposed that they should be denied residence since, like thieves, they emptied the kingdom of its capital: they operated out of various places, took control of mints to coin weak moneys, and then, through their system of exchange and trade, paid debts in weak money and collected credits in strong money, taking away the good money. The result was that "all the treasure of this Realm, or the better part of it, that goes or falls into the hands of the said Florentines is seized to be sent out of this Realm and transported to Florence." De Capdevila went on to recount an incident involving a Florentine who allegedly exported eighteen barrels of anchovies from Barcelona to Livorno, where it was discovered that the barrels were filled with Valencian gold coins. Early in the century, in fact, Florentines—including Domenico Mannelli, Andrea de' Pazzi, and Primerano de' Girolami—were by far the largest suppliers of silver to the mint in Barcelona. Given the local political atmosphere, however, Florentines were notably reluctant to get involved in government finance and take on political roles as they did in so many other places.[36]

Florentines turned up in Valencia in even larger numbers.[37] The city emerged as a major emporium in the second half of the fourteenth century, and a century later its population had grown to about forty thousand, about the size of Florence itself. Valencia's hinterland, far vaster than that of Barcelona, supplied its market with a wide range of products for export, from wine, rice, and dried fruit to skins and raw wool, to which the city itself added the products of its growing textile industry. In

[36] Ibid., 306–7.

[37] David Igual Luis, *Valencia e Italia en el siglo XV: Rutas, mercados y hombres de negocios en el espacio economico del Mediterráneo occidental* (Vila-real, 1998), is far more comprehensive than anything written on Italians in Barcelona. For Florentines in particular, see also José Hinojosa Montalvo, "Cesaro Barchi y otros mercaderes florentinos en la ciudad de Valencia en el transito del Medievo a la Modernidad," in *Sardegna, Mediterraneo e Atlantico tra Medioevo ed Età Moderna: Studi storici in memoria di Alberto Boscolo*, ed. Luisa D'Arienzo (Rome, 1993), 3:231–49 (and also on Barchi, Paulino Iradiel Murugarren and David Igual Luis, "Del Mediterráneo al Atlántico: Mercaderes, productos y empresas italianas entre Valencia y Portugal [1450–1520]," in *Portogallo mediterraneo*, ed. Luis Adão da Fonseca and Maria Eugenia Cadeddu [Cagliari, 2001], 178–89); Davis Igual Luis, "La ciudad de Valencia y los toscanos en el Mediterráneo del siglo XV," *Revista d'història medieval* 6 (1995): 79–110; Enrique Cruselles Gómez, "Un corredor aretino en la Valencia del Cuatrocientos," *Estudis històrics i documents dels arxius de protocols* 16 (1998): 237–58; idem, "Las relaciones comerciales entre Valencia y Florencia (1450–1550)," in *Logge e/y lonjas: I luoghi del commercio nella storia della città* (Florence, 2002), 39–48; and Giampiero Nigro, "Relazioni commerciali tra Firenze e Valenza (metà XIV–metà XV secolo)," ibid., 33–38 (on a Datini employee).

addition, its port was more advantageously located than Barcelona for trade all along the coast and out to the islands and on to the Atlantic routes. The city thus inserted itself into the Mediterranean commercial system as a major center, attracting one of the largest resident communities of foreign merchants in the Mediterranean, including Italians from Genoa, Milan, and Florence. Research in the registers of four notaries dating from 1452 to 1482 has revealed 228 Italian moneylenders, while one lawyer alone had 557 Italian clients over the last twenty-five years of the century.[38] Florentines had preeminence among these Italians down to the second half of the fifteenth century, when the Genoese became more numerous, by which time merchants from Marseilles and even Germany were also arriving in the city.

The extraordinary growth of Valencia strengthened the presence of the Aragonese kingdom in the Florentine network. Like Datini earlier, many companies opened branches or worked through agents in both Barcelona and Valencia. For instance, the Roman bank of Averardo di Francesco de' Medici opened a branch in both places in 1420, tying them to a branch in Pisa; the brothers Filippo, Giacomo, and Niccolò di Leonardo Strozzi brought the two cities into their operations in Bruges and Naples in the 1440s; and the company of Bartolomeo Marchionni in Lisbon had a factor in Valencia whose activities there have been documented for the years 1488 to 1492. The vast majority of Florentines were merchants, whereas the Genoese colony also included many artisans, especially silk workers. They did not, however, follow the lead of the merchants of the Ravensburger Handelsgesellschaft in extending their commercial interest in the local sugar trade to the purchase of land in the countryside for the cultivation and refinement of sugar.[39] So far as we know, in fact, Florentine merchants, who for the most part operated individually, rarely invested in such backward linkages to the production of any of the goods they traded in.

Florentines moved along the coast of the Iberian Peninsula as far as Lisbon. They turned up in Malaga, Seville, and Cadiz, and some traveled inland into Andalusia and Castile to exploit the opportunities opening up with the orientation of the hinterland economy to the growth of trade in the Mediterranean ports. The port cities were important markets for raw silk, sugar, and dried fruit, and they figured in the maritime trade between northwestern Europe and the Mediterranean. Datini had an agent in Malaga who dealt with Genoese merchants in Granada.[40] Giovanni de' Bardi is recorded in Seville in the early 1420s

---

[38] Igual Luis, "La ciudad de Valencia y los toscanos," 89–90.

[39] David Abulafia, "La produzione dello zucchero nei domini della Corona d'Aragona," in *Medioevo, Mezzogiorno, Mediterraneo,* ed. Gabriella Rossetti and Giovanni Vitolo (Naples, 2000), 112–16.

[40] Adela Fábregas García, "Estrategías de los mercaderes toscanos y genovesos en el reino de Granada a través de la correspondencia Datini," *Serta antiqua et mediaevalia* 5 (2001): 259–304.

loaning money and sending merchandise to both Pisa and Southampton.[41] Opportunities greatly expanded with the extension of trade routes to the Far East and the Americas. Giannotto di Lorenzo Berardi, one of the more prominent merchants in Seville, had links to the king and participated in the financing of the 1492 conquest of La Palma, the last island of the Canaries to be seized by the Spanish. Berardi was a friend of Columbus's and helped finance his second voyage; and at the time of his premature death in 1495, at the age of thirty-eight, he had taken on as a partner Amerigo Vespucci, who had arrived in Seville only three years earlier as an agent of Lorenzo di Pierfrancesco de' Medici. At least two other Florentines, Giovanni Alberto Giraldini and Bernardo Scarlatti, had interests in the economic development of the Canaries and took up residence there. Operating out of Seville and Cadiz, Florentines dealt in sugar, skins and leather, grain, preserved fish, wool and cloth found in local markets, as well as black West African slaves sent to them by contacts in Lisbon and goods coming in from the growing trade with the New World. Francesco di Giovanni Lapi, working from 1532 to 1536 as a partner of Filippo di Filippo Strozzi and Giuliano and Piero Capponi back in Italy, exported slaves, wine, and manufactured cloth to Mexico in exchange for silver. The firm of Iacopo Botti, operating out of Florence through branches in Seville, Cadiz, and Valladolid in the second and third quarters of the sixteenth century, handled more than 150 different kinds of products from literally around the world and maintained regular contacts with Antwerp, Paris, and London in addition to Rome and Venice in Italy. The Florentines in the south of Spain, however, were relatively few; the extensive Botti documents, both accounts and correspondence, covering about a half-century of activity, have yielded the names of fewer than a dozen firms and only about seventy individual merchants active in Cadiz and Seville. In general, Florentines were far outnumbered by the Genoese, although at Seville at the end of the century they were still, after the Genoese, the most important bankers dealing in bills of exchange as credit instruments through the Besançon fairs.[42]

---

[41] Consuelo Varela, *Colón y los florentinos* (Madrid, 1988), 22–23.

[42] Federigo Melis, "Il commercio transatlantico di una compagnia fiorentina stabilita a Siviglia a pochi anni dalle imprese di Cortes e Pizarro," reprinted in his *I mercanti italiani*, 45–134 (on Lapi); Enrique Otte, "Los Botti y los Lugo," *III Colloquio de historia canario-americana* 1 (1980): 49–85; Luisa D'Arienzo, "La società Marchionni-Berardi tra Portogallo e Spagna nell'età di Cristoforo Colombo," in *Actas das II Jornadas Luso-Espanholas de História Medieval* (Porto, 1990), 4:3–19; Angela Orlandi, "Mercanti toscani nell'Andalusia del Cinquecento," in *Historia. Instituciones. Documentos* 26 (1999): 365–82 (summarizing her doctoral thesis, "La compagnia dei Botti in terra di Spagna al tempo delle scoperte [1524–1566]" [Università di Bari, VIII ciclo, 1996]).

Other studies specifically on Florentines in this area of Spain are Varela, *Colón y los florentinos* (which has chapters on Giannotto Berardi, Amerigo Vespucci, Simone Verde, Francesco de' Bardi, and Piero Rondinelli, all merchants in Seville), and the contributions of Alberto Boscolo, Consuelo Varela, and Francisco Núñez Roldán in *Presencia italiana en Andalucia, siglos XIV–XVII: Actas del III cologuio hispano-italiano* (Seville, 1989). Germán Navarro Espinach et al., "Italianos en Zaragoza

Florentines, however, dominated in Lisbon, where their presence is well documented. In 1338 Alfonso IV granted commercial privileges to the Bardi, and subsequently other Florentines turn up in the kingdom along with the Genoese and other Italians.[43] In 1429 the Signoria of Florence, promoting its newly founded galley system, obtained privileges from the king for the communal galleys on their northward trip, and subsequently a local merchant colony grew up. One of the earliest firms to show an interest in Lisbon was that of the Cambini. In the 1420s, Andrea di Francesco Cambini, who had been in Lisbon since as early as 1414, and his brother Niccolò had a partnership in Florence with Adovardo di Cipriano Giachinotti that dealt with an agent in Lisbon. The firm of Niccolò's sons Francesco and Carlo, active in the 1460s and 1470s, has left extensive records documenting business activity of a Florentine firm in Lisbon.[44] The Cambini worked through agents in Barcelona and Valencia as well as Lisbon. They imported Florentine silks and wool cloth along with odds and ends of other things, such as books and eyeglasses, and exported kermes, raw silk, slaves, coral, and especially cloth, leather, and skins imported from Ireland, England, and Flanders. In 1459 the firm, working through its principal agent, Giovanni Guidetti, and another Florentine resident of Lisbon, organized a syndicate with the Pierozzi firm in Barcelona for the trade in coral. In 1460 the two Cambini brothers in Florence, Francesco and Carlo, personally entered into a five-year accomandita contract with Guidetti for a joint venture with two other Florentines and a Venetian in the fishing and marketing of mullet. In 1467 they contracted again with Guidetti for trade in leather and skins. The Cambini also handled transfer of funds for royal officials and ecclesiastics traveling to and from Italy. In 1459 Jaime di Lusitania, cardinal of Lisbon and nephew of Alfonso V, died in the Cambini residence, where he was staying on a stopover in Florence, and since the firm served as local banker to the executor of the cardinal's estate, its surviving accounts document all the expenses for the building of his famous burial chapel in San Miniato al Monte.

(siglos XV–XVI)," *Historia. Instituciones. Documentos* 30 (2003): 301–98, refers to work in progress on the presence of Florentines in this city.

In contrast, there are numerous studies of the Genoese, and their presence far overshadows that of the Florentines in the many surveys of Italians in the region. For bibliography, see Anna Unali, *Mercanti e artigiani italiani a Cordova nella seconda metà del Quattrocento* (Bologna, 1984), 15n1. Cf. Charles Verlinden, "Les influences italiennes sur le développement économique de la Péninsule Ibérique," and Henri Lapeyre, "L'influence italienne dans le développement économique de l'Espagne dans la seconde moitié du XVI siècle," both in *Aspetti della vita economica medievale*.

[43] Five letters written from Lisbon to Datini are published by Virginia Rau in *Estudos de história* (Lisbon, 1968), 59–74.

[44] Sergio Tognetti, *Il banco Cambini: Affari e mercati di una compagnia mercantile-bancaria nella Firenze del XV secolo* (Florence, 1999), chs. 9–11 passim.

In 1466 the Cambini firm in Florence hired as an office assistant Bartolomeo di Domenico di Marchionne dei Marchionni, about sixteen years old, the son of a spice and drug dealer *(speziale);* four years later, in 1470, the firm sent him to Lisbon. In 1476 Marchionni was associated with the Cambini as a partner in an accomandita contract; after the Cambini firm failed in 1481–82, he ventured out on his own to become the wealthiest and most prominent Florentine in Portugal. His business interests extended into the hinterland to Castile and Aragon and out to the Atlantic islands and Africa, and he also invested in voyages to the Indies and the spice trade. Besides the usual items of trade in Portugal—Irish leather and skins, kermes from Sintra, Spanish silk, Madeira sugar—Marchionni trafficked in slaves from Guinea. From 1486 to 1495 he had a lease on the Niger delta that included privileges for trade extending throughout West Africa, primarily in slaves, whom he marketed through Giannotto di Lorenzo Berardi in Seville and his agent in Valencia. Marchionni had close ties to King Ferdinando, and it was presumably through him that the king learned about the work of Paolo dal Pozzo Toscanelli in Florence. One of the largest Florentine firms, that of Averardo di Alamanno Salviati, working out of Pisa, was also represented in Lisbon by an agent who sold silks and wool cloth from Florence and paper from Colle Valdelsa and sent back principally leather, some of it from Ireland, and also salt and kermes.[45]

Once the Portuguese had rounded the Cape and reached the Indies in 1498 and began to bring back spices from the region, the many well-entrenched Florentine merchants in Lisbon had a golden opportunity to profit from the European distribution of these precious products. Their high expectations for the new traffic that would result from the shift of the spice trade from the Red Sea route to the Portuguese route are evident in a letter one of Marchionni's clerks wrote home to Florence in 1508:

> If things in Italy work out to make Porto Pisano the backbone for all the spice dealers of Italy, then with time Pisa is apt to become a new Venice. . . . We can then tell the Sultan and the Venetians to go sun themselves [*a stare al sole*]. And if these things happen, then with time Pisa—that is, Porto Pisano—will become a new Venice to the convenience of all Italy. . . . Thus with time everything will happen [here] in Portugal and there at Porto Pisano.[46]

---

[45] Ivana Elbl, "The King's Business in Africa: Decisions and Strategies of the Portuguese Crown," in Armstrong, Elbl, and Elbl, *Money, Markets and Trade in Late Medieval Europe*, 107–8 (on Marchionni); Marcello Berti, "Le aziende da Colle: Una finestra sulle relazioni commerciali tra la Toscana ed il Portogallo a metà del Quattrocento," in *Toscana e Portogallo: Miscellanea storica nel 650° anniversario dello Studio Generale di Pisa* (Pisa, 1994), 57–106.

[46] Quoted in Virginia Rau, "Un florentin au service de l'expansion portugaise en outre-mer: Francesco Corbinelli," in *Fatti e idee di storia economica nei secoli XII–XX: Studi dedicati a Franco Borlandi* (Bologna, 1977), 278.

It did not quite happen that way, of course, because in that very year the Portuguese crown opened its distribution center in Antwerp, consigning monopoly privileges to the firms of the Affaitati from Cremona and the Gualterotti from Florence, and spices were soon arriving in the Mediterranean overland by way of Lyons.

Some Florentine resident merchants in Lisbon participated in the financing of voyages overseas, and a few went off on these ventures. Those voyages Marchionni financed included Vespucci's in 1501–2 and Vasco da Gama's in 1502–3 (which had financing also from the Fuggers and the Welsers and included the Florentine Giovanni Buonagrazia as one of the captains), and later, in 1518, one of his sons went to the Indies.[47] Girolamo Sernigi, perhaps the most successful Florentine merchant in Lisbon after Marchionni, financed several voyages to the East beginning in 1499, the most notable one being the first to Malacca in 1510, for which he owned all four ships. Luca Giraldi (d. 1565), one of the richest merchant-bankers of the generation after Marchionni and Sernigi, started his career working for the Affaitati, licensee of the spice monopoly, and later financed a number of voyages to the Indies, at least once going there himself. Giraldi received lands and jurisdictional rights in Brazil in 1547 and eventually entered the Portuguese nobility. The Portuguese voyages also attracted Florentines from other places in the network. Giovanni da Empoli, for example, made his initial voyage in 1503–4 for his employer, Antonio and Filippo Gualterotti, Girolamo Frescobaldi & Partners in Bruges, and on his second voyage, in 1510–14, he went as a partner of the firm, now bearing the names of the Gualterotti alone. Moreover, financial supporters of both voyages included, besides Florentines in Lisbon (among whom were Marchionni for the first and Sernigi for both), Florentines in Lyons. Many of the Florentines who went on these voyages, however, were not wealthy merchants but men of modest means in search of fortunes in this vast new market of luxury products. For some the adventure included also the commanding of ships and engagement in military action. Piero di Andrea Strozzi was one of these who met with notable success. In 1510, at the age of twenty-six and with only several hundred florins, he sailed from Lisbon, never to return. On his death in the East twelve years later, in 1522, he bequeathed to his brother back in Florence a patrimony of *fl.*8,301, an estate that would have ranked in the upper 1 percent of the 1427 catasto. In short, many Florentine merchants financed and joined the Portuguese on the earliest ventures to the Indies during the first quarter of the sixteenth century, and the letters they wrote about the voyages and the places where

---

[47] D'Arienzo, "La società Marchionni-Berardi." The business activities of both the Cambini and Marchionni firms in Portugal are reviewed in the larger Iberian commercial context, with full bibliography and archival references, in Iradiel Murugarren and Igual Luis, "Del Mediterráneo al Atlántico," esp. 169–89.

they went are a major source for the history of this episode in the overseas expansion of Europe.[48]

The busy traffic in the western Mediterranean obviously underwent changes from the later fourteenth through the sixteenth century. Fluctuations in the dynamics that drove it, changes in the many directions it took, shifts among the major centers around which it was oriented, and renewal within the ranks of merchants who dominated it slowly transformed the overall picture in a way that by 1600 left the Florentines with a much reduced presence. One change that had a major impact on Florentine business interests was the unification of Spain as a consequence of the marriage of Ferdinand of Aragon and Isabella of Castile in 1469. This political development, which also eventually pulled Naples into the orbit of their united crowns, opened up opportunities for two groups of merchants in markets where Florentines had been most active, the Genoese and the Castilians. The Genoese had been increasing their presence throughout Spain, including the hinterland, in the fifteenth century, and they consolidated their dominant position throughout the kingdom under the Hapsburgs. They helped finance the sugar plantations in the Atlantic islands, the voyages overseas, the colonization of the Americas, and the exploitation of the major silver mines in Mexico and Peru. Genoese bankers came to play the key role at the highest level of royal finance, loaning heavily to the crown and facilitating the transfer of funds in the service of Hapsburg international military policy. At the same time, the expanding Spanish economy brought local Castilian merchants to the fore, and they took initiatives in all sectors. The fairs they organized at Medina del Campo, near Burgos, at the center of the wool trade, grew considerably in the course of the fifteenth century, and when these fairs gained official status for the execution of inland and international payments in 1500, the place rose to become a major center in the European exchange market alongside Lyons and Antwerp, at least until the mid-sixteenth century, when it went into decline. Here too the Genoese, with Hapsburg backing, moved in to play a dominant role, although they had some competition from the great southern German bankers for a while, during the reign of Charles V. In the 1580s one Florentine firm, that of the Capponi, held the contract for the cochineal (a superior red dyestuff) imported at Seville from the Americas, giving it a virtual monopoly in European markets for a product that found one of its principal

---

[48] On Giraldi, see Virginia Rau, "Um grande mercador-banqueiro italiano em Portugal: Lucas Giraldi," in her *Estudos de história*, 75–129. Marco Spallanzani, *Mercanti fiorentini nell'Asia portoghese (1500–1525)* (Florence, 1997), documents the Florentines who went to the East and publishes much of the Florentine material related to the Portuguese voyages. See also his *Giovanni da Empoli: Un mercante fiorentino nell'Asia portoghese,* 2nd ed. (Florence, 1999). Nunziatella Alessandrini, "La presenza italiana a Lisbona nella prima metà del Cinquecento," *ASI* 164 (2006): 37–54, has little information about merchants from Florence.

outlets in Florence itself.[49] Otherwise, in all this commercial and financial activity generated by the boom of the Spanish economy in the early sixteenth century, we hear little about the Florentines, notwithstanding the presence they had established everywhere over the preceding century and a half. Here is yet another chapter still to be written in the history of the Florentine network.

The rise of Castilian merchants that followed on the unification of Spain impinged directly on the internal economy of Florence in at least two ways. First, they were prominent in the expansion of the international trade of woad from southwestern France at the end of the fifteenth century, supplying it to the growing wool industry in both Spain and northern Europe and thereby cutting into a market that had traditionally been supplied largely by Italy. The Tuscan economy in particular must have felt the impact of reduced exports, since woad was the only raw material produced in the region for which there had been significant demand from abroad. Second, Castilian merchants moved into the Mediterranean commercial world to sell the high-quality raw wool that was being developed in their home region. Working out of the ports of Cadiz and Alicante, they supplied the wool that allowed the Florentine industry to shift its production to rascia (see chapter 4). A significant portion of the insurance contracts taken out by merchants in Burgos from 1481 to 1507 covered shipments of wool and alum to Italian Tyrrhenian ports, especially Pisa.[50]

The Castilians aggressively pursued their interests to the point of setting up sales operations in Florence itself, as we saw in chapter 1. Much of what is known about their activity in the western Mediterranean, in fact, comes from the extensive correspondence, dating from 1577 to 1585, between one of these merchants, Simón Ruiz, and his agent in Florence.[51] Among all the foreign merchants, the Castilians were particularly welcome toward the end of the sixteenth century because of Cosimo I's policy to cultivate relations with the Spanish king in order to boost his prestige among his fellow Italian princes. Symbolic of the Spanish presence in the city was the gesture the duke made in 1566 in turning over the prominent space of the chapter room of the Dominican house at Santa Maria Novella, one of the city's most prestigious churches, to serve as the chapel for the Spanish community (now known as the Spanish Chapel). Many Spaniards belonged to the new ducal Order of Santo Stefano, and there were many Spanish students and faculty at the university in Pisa.[52]

---

[49] Felipe Ruiz Martín, *Lettres marchandes échangées entre Florence et Medina del Campo* (Paris, 1965), cxxv–cxxviii.

[50] Hilario Casado Alonso, "Comercio internacional y seguros marítimos en Burgos en la época de los Reyes Católicos," in *Bartolomeu Dias e a sua época: Actas* (Porto, 1989), 3:599.

[51] Ruiz Martín, *Lettres marchandes.*

[52] Recent work on the activity of Castilian merchants abroad is represented in the collection of

Southern France

The intensification of maritime trade in the western Mediterranean in the second half of the fourteenth century had an impact on the regional economy of southern France, as we have seen, and toward the end of the century the shift from maritime to terrestrial trade routes between northern Europe and the Mediterranean brought much traffic into southern France. The hereditary unification of much of the Low Countries with the Duchy of Burgundy in 1384 resulted in the creation of a single political entity with a strong economic foundation in the region's widely diffused cloth industry and its many large urban markets, and this rearrangement of the political geography of the region favored the opening of overland trade to the south. Hence, merchants could travel from northwestern Europe on a route that, avoiding central France, then in the throes of the Hundred Years' War, led to Basel and Geneva and then either to the Po valley in Italy or to the Mediterranean down the Rhône valley. This new route also attracted traffic from a growing trade with Germany, resulting especially from the rise of Europe's strongest fustian industry toward the end of the fourteenth century. Along this overland route to and from Italy, Geneva had a particularly strategic location where trade with the Low Countries, central Germany, and Italy converged. The city had been little more than a stopping-off place on the route south from the Champagne fairs, but by the end of the fourteenth century it was emerging as a major international commercial and financial market. Its population doubled in the second half of the century, and it doubled yet again over the first half of the fifteenth century. The Italian merchants who attended the Geneva fairs came from Florence, Lucca, Milan, Genoa, and the Piedmont, but only the Florentines organized themselves into a formal nazione with statutes and officials. Six firms, including the Medici, are known to have been resident in Geneva about 1440. For the Florentines, the market in Geneva assumed considerable importance especially as a major outlet for their nascent silk industry, which provided their city, for the first time, with products that could be marketed in northern Europe. Nevertheless, as we shall see in chapter 3, it was banking more than commerce that attracted the Florentines.[53]

The intensification of overland trade from the north allowed Avignon to maintain its importance as a major regional market with an outlet southward to the sea during the schism and even after the departure of the last, schismatic

---

studies published in *Castile y Europa: Comercio y mercaderes en los siglos XIV, XV y XVI*, ed. Hilario Casado Alonso (Burgos, 1995). There is no discussion, however, of the Castilian community of merchants in late sixteenth-century Florence.

[53] Michele Cassandro summarizes his earlier work on Geneva, citing the standard bibliography, in "Le élites internazionali a Ginevra e Lione nei secoli XV–XVI," in Del Treppo, *Sistema di rapporti ed élites economiche*, 231–47.

pope. For the Florentines Avignon was still an important exchange center and bullion market, and on the list of firms extracted from the 1427 catasto nine were in the region.[54] Lorenzo Tacchini, Raimondo Mannelli & Partners conducted commercial and exchange operations there on a grand scale, radiating out to Palermo, Barcelona, Paris, Bruges, Geneva, Milan, and Venice. In 1428–29 the firm sent large amounts of silver by mule to Barcelona and Valencia, apparently for speculation rather than for balancing trade deficits, and in 1430 it exported gold to Florence, Milan, and Venice. From Avignon Florentine merchants penetrated into the hinterland. Matteo Benini, resident in Arles from at least 1360 until his death in 1402 and working through Barcelona, Valencia, Genoa, and Pisa, dealt in skins, wool, cloth, salt, and grain from the region and spices from the Levant. He also engaged in financial operations, loaning money and buying annuities *(rentes),* and at one point he joined with others in financing the construction of a cargo ship.[55] Florentine firms in Avignon opened subsidiaries also in Montpellier, Aix, and the port of Marseilles; the Medici had a branch in Montpellier, and the Pazzi had one in Marseilles. Rinaldo Altoviti, who moved to Marseilles in 1471, entered into the service of King René in 1477 and became vicar of the city in 1503.[56]

Once the political situation in France stabilized, this traffic in the south attracted the attention of the king. In the early 1460s Louis XI took initiatives to promote Lyons as a rival center to Geneva for international trade fairs. He offered merchants freedom from restrictions on importing and exporting and on exchange activity and granted them exemptions from tolls and duties, certain legal privileges, and other advantages. Lyons was within easy reach of the Mediterranean by way of the Rhône River, and this meant more direct access through what has been called the French isthmus connecting the valleys of the Rhône and the Saône to markets in central and northern France, the Low Countries, and Germany. Hence Lyons replaced Geneva and Avignon both as the principal international exchange market in the south and the principal entrepôt for trade flowing from all over western Europe into the Mediterranean commercial system. The staples in this trade were wool cloth from England, the Low Countries, and France, fustians, metals, and metal products from Germany, silks from Italy, and spices from the Levant, along with other luxury objects from both these latter

---

[54] See chapter 1, n. 125.

[55] Louis Stouff, "Une famille florentine à Arles: Les Benini vers 1360–vers 1440," in *La Toscane et les Toscans autour de la Renaissance: Cadres de vie, société, croyances; Mélanges offerts à Charles-M. de La Roncière* (Aix-en-Provence, 1999), 274. In the same volume there is a study of a Florentine merchant who lived in Aix, also based on local materials: Noël Coulet, "Une famille aixoise d'origine florentine au bas Moyen Âge: Chiaro di Bernardo et ses descendants," 257–69.

[56] Gérard Giordanengo, "Le élites internazionali in area provenzale: Artisti, mercanti, uomini di legge (secoli XI–XV)," in Del Treppo, *Sistema di rapporti ed élites economiche,* 188.

areas. Over the latter half of the fifteenth century and the first quarter of the sixteenth the population of the city tripled, going from about twenty thousand to between sixty and seventy thousand, becoming the second city of the realm after Paris and as large as Florence.

It took time to attract business from Geneva and to overcome resistance from French merchants with interests in other cities to the north that had a growing trade with Germany. Lyons, however, had a place in the policy of an emerging kingdom that was directed to building a veritable "national" economy by suppressing local seigniorial power, encouraging interregional trade, and authorizing fairs. With royal support the Lyons fairs became the principal link between the northern and southern commercial worlds and the central exchange market for southern Europe. Moreover, the crown made Lyons a center for its financial activities, and in the early sixteenth century the king and his court were often in residence there. All this opened opportunities for bankers to offer their financial services to the fiscal administration of a monarchy that, after the Hundred Years' War, was rapidly asserting itself on the European stage and badly in need of funds.

Immediately on the opening of the fairs under royal auspices, the city attracted merchants from Florence, Lucca, Milan, Genoa, and the Piedmont. For the Florentines in particular this new market opened just as they were looking for outlets for their growing silk industry, and the market expanded considerably at the end of the century with the shift of their wool industry to the production of a new wool cloth, rascia, the first wool product they were able to direct primarily to northern European markets. The Medici company and fourteen others were resident in Lyons by 1466. The Florentines strengthened their position in the city when, in 1494, they were able to negotiate more favorable conditions with Charles VIII on the occasion of his invasion of Italy. They alone had a formal corporate organization as a nazione with a permanent consul and councilors, and their loggia was used for foreign exchange by the other international bankers.[57] Forty-six resident Florentines attended a meeting in 1502, and about the same number signed a document in 1522 affirming their loyalty to Francis I in a moment when he was taking measures against their native city because of its alliance with Charles V. In the sixteenth century the principal companies were those of the Capponi, the Del Bene, the Guadagni, the Gondi, the Martelli, the Rucellai, and the Salviati. In 1523 a consortium consisting of Tommaso Guadagni, Guglielmo Nasi, Roberto degli Albizzi, Antonio Gondi, and Giuliano Buonaccorsi,

---

[57] On the Florentine nazione, see Michele Cassandro, "I forestieri a Lione nel '400 e '500: La nazione fiorentina," in *Dentro la città: Stranieri e realtà urbane nell'Europa dei secoli XII–XVI,* ed. Gabriella Rossetti (Naples, 1989), 151–62.

along with three French merchants related to Guadagni, joined together with Giovanni da Verrazzano, himself in business with the company of Zanobi Rucellai, to finance his first voyage "to a place called the Indies in Cathay."[58] Some of these Florentine have left behind rich archives, but only the Lucchese firm of the Bonvisi has been the subject of a monographic study.[59] Outside the sphere of economics, the extraordinary concentration in Lyons of Italian merchants and bankers, and of Florentines in particular, transformed the city into the principal conduit for the diffusion of Renaissance culture to France. The Florentines, however, did not put the stamp of their physical presence on the city by building anything of significance, and today it is difficult to identify the residences of the great merchant families or even to know where the loggia of their nazione was located.[60]

The French also took major initiatives in Mediterranean trade after the inheritance of Provence by Louis XI in 1481 brought the port of Marseilles into the orbit of royal authority and aroused ambitions to promote trade with the Levant. Almost immediately foreign merchants, including the great firms of the Bonvisi of Lucca and the Welser of Augsburg, took up residence in the city, while the customs authority of Lyons opened an office there, and the crown transferred its arsenal from Aigues-Mortes to this growing port. Moreover, traffic through the port and at the fairs at Lyons increased considerably following the rapid growth of Antwerp as Europe's major entrepôt linking the Atlantic with central Europe. The population of Marseilles doubled from 1520 to the mid-1550s, growing from fifteen thousand to thirty thousand, and over the second half of the century it grew by another 50 percent. After the battle of Lepanto in 1571 it emerged as the chief port for trade with the Levant. By this time Marseilles' own merchants, operating with privileges from the sultan, were taking a commanding position over foreigners. Its rise as a port for the international redistribution of goods, including now even spices from the Far East arriving by way of Antwerp and headed to places like Florence, can be taken as the measure of how much the commercial system in the western Mediterranean had changed over the course of the century.

The decline of Lyons in the last quarter of the sixteenth century has not been well studied, but it is generally thought that the commercial fairs declined more rapidly than the exchange fairs (of which more in chapter 3).[61] The Florentines

[58] Michel Mollat and Jacques Habert, *Giovanni et Girolamo Verrazano, navigateurs de François Ier* (Paris, 1982), 62–71.

[59] Françoise Bayard, "Les Bonvisi, marchands banquiers à Lyon, 1575–1629," *Annales: Économies, sociétés, civilisations* 26 (1971): 1234–69.

[60] Giuseppe Iacono, *Les marchands banquiers florentins et l'architecture à Lyon au XVIe siècle* (Paris, 1999), 101.

[61] Richard Gascon, *Grand commerce et vie urbaine au XVIe siècle: Lyon et ses marchands (environs de 1520–environs de 1580)* (Paris, 1971), 1:357–62. For a general view, with further bibliography, see Cassandro, "I forestieri a Lione." The crisis of the early 1580s at Lyons is analyzed in Ruiz Martín,

lost their relative importance in the market for silks as a result of competition from other Italians following the rapid diffusion of the silk industry throughout northern Italy. In 1569 Italian silks accounted for perhaps two-thirds of the value of all imports as compared with about 10 percent for pepper, but no Florentine appeared in the top 10 of 532 importers, the value of whose imports accounted for 36.6 percent of the total. Seven of these ten were from Lucca and Milan; the top Florentine ranked twentieth on the list.[62] For all Italians, however, the conduct of trade in the city became increasingly difficult, especially in the charged religious and political atmosphere of the Wars of Religion. Anti-Italian sentiment began to mount, directed against the Italians' usurious practices and their association with the morally suspect taste for luxurious silk clothes, not to mention their tax privileges, monopolies, and favor at court. The fairs too felt the full effects of the religious wars when the city itself became a focus of hostilities. Meanwhile, a growing antipathy of French merchants toward the Italians, who had begun to infringe on the trade within France radiating out from Lyons, led to the rise of competing fairs in other major cities, while the government initiated a protectionist tax policy that penalized foreign operations. After the turn of the century, by which time Henry IV had reestablished the central authority of the monarchy at Paris, the Lyons market revived, but it never reached its earlier levels of activity, mainly because other important commercial centers had emerged in the meantime, above all at Paris. Moreover, as a result of the growth of the royal bureaucracy in Paris, the Italian bankers at Lyons ceased to have a role in royal finances. The decline of the commercial fairs was a principal cause for the eventual collapse of Lyons in the Florentine system, but there were other forces at work as well, namely, competition in the international money market from Antwerp in the north and Besançon in the south and the loss of financial business with the royal government (both subjects to be discussed in chapter 3).

The departure of the Italians began as early as the 1570s. Of the 183 foreigners on the tax rosters of 1571, 154 were Italians, 132 of whom were from Florence, Milan, Lucca, and Genoa in that order of importance, although Florentines accounted for 31.2 percent of the taxes collected from the entire group. The majority of the 42 Florentines, however, were registered as bankers, not merchants. In 1580 they numbered only about 20, and by 1600 there were hardly any left.

Lettres marchandes, xciii–c. Jacques Bottin offers a revision to the traditional view in "Les foires de Lyon et les italiens autour de 1600: Décline ou reconfiguration?" in *La pratica dello scambio: Sistemi di fiere, mercanti e città in Europa (1400–1700),* ed. Paola Lanaro (Venice, 2003), 201–18. He suggests that the decline cannot be measured just in terms of the number of firms, since firms may have increased in size and these larger firms may have changed their strategy. An excellent summary of the problems leading to the decline of Lyons is found in Bayard, "Les Bonvisi." For anti-Italianism, see Henry Heller, *Anti-Italianism in Sixteenth-Century France* (Toronto, 2003).

[62] Gascon, *Grand commerce et vie urbaine,* 1:203–5.

However, when the Bonvisi, who remained in Lyons, went bankrupt in 1629, leaving debts amounting to somewhere between 30,000–40,000 and 100,000 écus, 7 of the 19 major creditors were Florentine (although we are not told whether these were on the scene at Lyons).

The Later Sixteenth Century

The general reconfiguration of Mediterranean trade over the first three quarters of the sixteenth century came about, in part at least, as a result of "the rise of the modern state," to refer to one of the central themes in the historiography of late medieval and early modern Europe. In France, royal policy promoted Lyons as an international emporium and exchange market and Marseilles as a port. In Spain the unified monarchy opened opportunities for both Castilian merchants and Genoese merchant-bankers, as well as Germans tied to the Hapsburgs, while the Portuguese and, later, the Spanish monarchy sponsored the Atlantic expansion that brought many new products and an immense amount of bullion into the Mediterranean system. Another factor in the transformation of the trade system during the last quarter of the sixteenth century was the incorporation of the Mediterranean, now with peripheral status, into the growing economy of northwestern Europe. Two forces that brought about this reversal of the traditional relation between the two economic areas hit the Italians particularly hard. First was the replacement of Italian shipping by northern shipping. Sailings to the north by the Genoese, the Venetians, and the Ragusans gradually decreased: the last Genoese ship sailed in 1522, although the Venetians continued to 1569–70. Meanwhile the Mediterranean was invaded by northern ships, especially those of the English and Dutch, and the commercial world became more international and diverse than ever, crowded with merchants from Portugal, Castile, France, and Germany, as well as Italians. The real loss to Italy came at the end of the century with the establishment of trading posts in the Levant by the English as well as the French working out of Marseilles. A much more direct blow to the Florentines in particular was the eclipse of Lyons as an international exchange market by Antwerp and then Amsterdam in the north and by the Besançon fairs in the south, controlled by the Genoese.

Slowly but surely the Florentines were being crowded out of their central place in this system. They could still be found everywhere, but not in the same numbers and not with the same presence. Florence, however, had one last card to play in this losing game, the port of Livorno. It was played, however, not by her merchants and bankers but by the Medici princes, whose policy was directed to attracting foreign merchants, not to launching merchants from their own state. They completely transformed the place. The policy that evolved over the years of the first three grand dukes—Cosimo I (1537–74), Francesco (1574–87), and Ferdinando I (1587–1609)—was halting and sometimes inconsistent, but the ultimate objective was clear from the beginning. Cosimo I set the direction early in his reign. In the 1540s he began work aimed at modernizing the port at Livorno, and at Florence, as if to send a signal, he initiated the planning of a grand loggia, still a prominent monument on the urban scene, to incorporate the entire Mercato Nuovo, the international business center of the city. In 1551 he issued a proclamation inviting all merchants from "the Levantine nations," specifying Greeks, Jews, Armenians, Turks, Moors, Persians, and other non-Arab Muslims (Aggiani) to take up residence in any city in the state, and in 1561 he announced semiannual duty-free fairs at Pisa linked to the port at Livorno.[63]

Building up the port of Livorno was a major enterprise. It had been a mere village of several hundred inhabitants, used (as Porto Pisano, nearby, had been) for little more than its docking facilities to serve Pisa once silting of the Arno began to complicate direct access to and from the sea. Work begun in the 1540s and continuing over the next twenty years included new docks, a customs house, an arsenal, and a canal linking Livorno to Pisa and the Arno. In 1575 the architect Bernardo Buontalenti was commissioned to draw up plans for a completely new city, with walls extensive enough to enclose twelve thousand inhabitants, half again as large as Pisa at the time. Since the place was not on the Arno, canal works were undertaken to improve the link to river traffic and to build commercial facilities as well as the necessary civic amenities—aqueducts for the supply of water, a cathedral, a governor's palace. A Greek Orthodox church and a synagogue, to accommodate two specific communities of merchants of growing importance in Mediterranean commerce, were finished in 1606. It took time to accomplish all this: Livorno achieved city status in 1606, but the population did not reach the anticipated twelve thousand until about midcentury. Meanwhile, the expectations that rode with the city's growth found their symbolic manifestations, first, in the great fountain dominating the port, with Ferdinando I standing high above Pietro Tacca's four bound Moors (1626), representing the four corners of the earth served by the port's trade, and, second, in the names Nuova Venezia and San Marco, given to the new quarters of the city, laid out complete with canals in 1629 to accommodate the ever-growing population. But—to expose the conceit behind these analogies—the grand duke hardly enslaved the trade passing in and out

---

[63] *La legislazione medicea sull'ambiente,* ed. Giovanni Cascio Pratilli and Luigi Zangheri (Florence, 1994–98), 1:82–83, 113–16.

under his view from high on the fountain, for what was new as compared with the old Venice was the state's passivity in the vital activity that made Livorno one of the busiest ports in the Mediterranean. How active Florentine merchants themselves were in this great new Mediterranean emporium on their home turf has yet to be assessed.

In making Livorno a free port, a place where goods in transit could be exchanged without customs charges, the Medici hoped to exploit fully the intricate trading system that had grown up in the western Mediterranean from the mid-fourteenth century on. The success of this policy was evident already in the last quarter of the sixteenth century: "the key to my lands" is how Ferdinando I referred to Livorno in a letter to the emperor. The port was the center for short-distance coastal trade in the Tyrrhenian Sea, from Naples and Sicily to Marseilles and other Provencal ports; a major route linked it to Spain, now at Alicante, no longer at Barcelona; it attracted business from the other maritime powers, especially from Marseilles, which was growing into a major commercial port in the western Mediterranean; and with the arrival in 1573 of the first English ships, sailing out of London and Southampton, it became the destination of merchants from England, Amsterdam, Hamburg, and Danzig, who began invading the Mediterranean at this time. The French established a consul in Livorno in 1579, followed by the Venetians in 1585, the Ragusans in 1588, and the Genoese in 1596. From beyond Gibraltar, consuls were set up by the Portuguese, the Dutch, and the Swedish in the 1590s and, finally, by the English in 1634. Raw wool from Spain and raw silk from southern Italy were the single most important imports for the Florentines. When in 1590 Grand Duke Ferdinando took the initiative to have agents of the Torrigiani firm in Nuremberg arrange for shipments of badly needed grain from northern Germany and Poland, the port took on an essential function in the provisioning of a rapidly growing population in Italy. The bulk of the trade, however, came from ships that were virtually "floating bazaars," carrying that great variety of goods that had long characterized commerce in the western Mediterranean, with its diverse regions and links to the Levant and now also to the wider Atlantic world. If the arrival in Livorno of pepper from Alexandria by way of Marseilles signaled one stage in that revolution already in the last quarter of the century, its arrival from Amsterdam in 1605 marked another. The rise of this new free port without any fleet of its own was clearly a threat to the Genoese, who were forced to reconsider the very foundations of the maritime power they had enjoyed for so long, and the spectacular success of Livorno as a free port over the following decades justified their concern. In view of the invasion of the Mediterranean by the new maritime powers of northern Europe, the opening of a free port may have been the most intelligent

response made by any of the formerly great commercial states of Italy to a rapidly changing economic situation.[64]

Central Italy and Rome

In comparison with trade out of the Tuscan maritime ports to the west of Florence, the traffic on overland routes leading out of the city southeastward to central Italy and the Adriatic was small, although the historiography provides no
evidence to assess its extent. In the first half of the thirteenth century Florence
had commercial treaties with Faenza (1204), Perugia (1218), Città di Castello
(1232), and Imola (1238), and in the course of the century the overland routes out
of the city into central Italy—the upper Tiber valley, Umbria, the Abruzzi, the
Marche—became heavily traveled. Before the Black Death, grain and salt from
the Romagna to feed the growing population were major objectives, and the importance of maintaining these trade routes led to the construction of the new
towns of Scarperia and Firenzuola along the way. The cloth trade, however, was
the major dynamic driving merchants deep into central Italy. As early as the late
thirteenth century merchants ventured into central Italy to sell wool cloth, both
that imported from Milan and northern Europe and the products of the city's
own growing industry, some of which was sent to the smaller Adriatic ports in
the Romagna, the Marche, and further south for export to the Levant. Balancing
this, at least in the early period, was raw wool from central Italy and whatever
local products merchants found abroad for shipment back to Florence for the
home market or for reexport into the network, chiefly woad from Borgo Sansepolcro, fustians and cotton veiling from Perugia and Foligno, paper from Fabriano, and saffron from the Abruzzi. Florentines are documented in Ascoli as early
as 1297 as by far the city's most active moneylenders.[65] This central Italian network reached eastward to the small ports along the Adriatic coast, from the Romagna to northern Puglia, and southward along the "via degli Abruzzi" to Peru-

[64] The economic development of Livorno is the subject of Fernand Braudel and Ruggiero Romano, *Navires et marchandises à l'entrée du Port de Livourne (1547–1611)* (Paris, 1951); the term *bazar
flottant* is theirs. For the place of Livorno in the opening of free ports in early modern Europe, see
Thomas Allison Kirk, *Genoa and the Sea: Policy and Power in an Early Modern Maritime Republic,
1559–1684* (Baltimore, 2005), esp. 181–85; for the "menace" Livorno presented to Genoa, see 155–67.
See also idem, "A Little Country in a World of Empires: Genoese Attempts to Penetrate the Maritime
Empires of the Seventeenth Century," *European Economic History Review* 25 (1996): 407–21. R. Burr
Litchfield has studied a merchant working out of Livorno, Roberto Pepi: "Un mercante fiorentino
alla corte dei Medici: Le 'memorie' di Roberto Pepi (1572–1634)," *ASI* 157 (1999): 727–81. Pepi made
four trips to Alexandria in the 1590s, two to Spain in 1604–5, and one to Danzig in 1606–7. Lucia
Frattarelli Fischer, "Livorno città nuova, 1574–1609," *Società e storia*, no. 46 (1989): 873–93, discusses
the urban growth of the city.
[65] Giuliano Pinto, "Ascoli: Una città manifatturiera ai confini col Regno," in *Città e spazi economici nell'Italia comunale* (Bologna, 1996), 197–98.

gia, L'Aquila, and into the Kingdom of Naples, thereby extending the commercial opportunities in the area. Florentine merchants took up residence in L'Aquila as early as the 1290s, and some of the largest firms—the Scali, the Bardi, and others operating out of Naples—had active interests in the area. Likewise merchants from places such as Sulmona turned up in Florence to buy cloth.[66] The direction and intensity of trade along these routes varied, being conditioned primarily by the changing needs of the domestic textile industry both for the supply of raw materials and for market outlets. Florentines imported both raw and spun cotton and distributed it to towns throughout southeastern Tuscany and Umbria, which became major areas for the production of cotton veiling for export to international markets. They managed much of this trade headed toward both Ancona and Pisa, on opposite sides of the peninsula. Unfortunately, we have only bits and pieces of information about all this overland traffic between Florence and central Italy in this early period.

This trading activity may have lost some of its vigor in the course of the fourteenth century as a result of a decline in the cloth trade that came with the shift of the home industry to production of higher-quality cloth made with English wool. However, it picked up considerably in the fifteenth century, when the area again became important for the supply of raw materials to the city's textile industries, now the silk as well as the wool industry. With the growth of the silk industry in the early fifteenth century, firms set up operations in L'Aquila for the purchase of raw silk from the area around Sulmona. The region became even more important as the Florentine wool industry made yet another shift, well under way by midcentury, this time from English to *matricina* wool from the Abruzzi, following the increased herding of sheep that came with the transhumance sponsored by the new Aragonese rulers in Naples. In addition to supplying raw materials to the Florentine textile industries, the region also replaced San Gimignano as a major source for saffron, another local product that attracted Florentine (as well as other) merchants from abroad. Thus once again L'Aquila became for a time the center of a large regional commercial network built up by resident Florentines, who were by far the major buyers of both wool and silk. Another major development leading to the increased economic importance of central Italy

[66] This central Italian trade system is described by Alberto Grohmann, "Aperture e inclinazioni verso l'esterno: Le direttrici di transito e di commercio," in *Orientamenti di una regione attraverso i secoli* (Perugia, 1978), 55–95. For the history of Florentine interest in the region, see Hidetoshi Hoshino, *I rapporti economici tra l'Abruzzo aquilano e Firenze nel Basso Medioevo* (L'Aquila, 1988). The diary kept by a factor of Datini on a commercial trip into Umbria, from 16 December 1384 to 30 January 1385, has been studied by both Bruno Dini, in "Il viaggio di un mercante fiorentino in Umbria alla fine del Trecento," *Miscellanea storica della Valdelsa* 96 (1990): 81–103, and Luciana Frangioni, in "Mercanti viaggiatori nel Basso Medioevo: Un nuovo contributo dell'archivio Datini di Prato," *Seges: Quaderni di studi storici* 1 (1992): 3–28.

toward the mid-fifteenth century was the growing traffic through it to the booming consumer markets for wool cloth, silks, and other luxury-craft products that
opened up to the south, both at Naples, after it became the capital of the trans–
western Mediterranean kingdom of Aragon, and at Rome, after the papacy returned to its capital city.

Florentines, of course, had been going to Rome since the end of the twelfth
century in pursuit of their interest in papal finances. Before the end of the fourteenth century, however, they had had no major commercial interest in the Holy
City itself. Rome did not even lie on a major interregional trade route, let alone
an international one, and it had no export industries of any importance. The city,
with a population of perhaps thirty thousand, was little more than the capital
of a relatively isolated region. Moreover, the tumultuous political life of the city,
largely in the hands of feudal families with a base in the countryside, induced
the popes themselves to settle instead in nearby towns for long periods. Eventually, Clement V, on his election in France in 1305, made the decision to abandon the region altogether and to take up a more secure residence in Avignon.
There the papacy was able to build up a stable bureaucracy, complete with a refined fiscal machine, and to surround itself with a more elaborate court. The
papacy that Urban VI reestablished in Rome some three-quarters of a century
later, on his election in 1378, was a somewhat different one, even though he had to
leave much of the bureaucracy back in Avignon with his schismatic rival. The
move had an immediate impact on the local market: the presence of the papal
bureaucracy, albeit reduced by the schism, and the bankers who served it marked
a new beginning for the ancient city. Some sixteen hundred of Datini's business
letters sent to agents in Rome from 1383 to 1404 testify to his interest in the new
opportunities that opened up there.[67] However, Datini, whose business was more
commercial than financial, did not close down his Avignon branch, nor did he
open a new one in the Holy City. In contrast to the situation in Avignon, Rome's
potential for economic growth rested entirely with the newly established papacy,
not with the regional economy. That growth was assured, however, when in 1420,
after the settlement at Constance among the contending popes, the new pope,
Martin V, took up residence there as head of a united church. Over the following
century Rome emerged as one of Europe's great monumental cities, the seat of
an ever more splendid cosmopolitan court and the capital of a growing territorial state in central Italy. The population more than doubled, from about thirty

---

[67] These letters have been examined by Arnold Esch, in "La fine del libero comune di Roma nel
giudizio dei mercanti fiorentini: Lettere romane degli anni 1395–1398," *Bullettino dell'Istituto Storico
Italiano per il Medio Evo e Archivio Muratoriano* 76 (1976–77): 235–77; and Luciano Palermo, in *Il
porto di Roma nel XIV e XV secolo: Strutture socio-economiche e statuti* (Rome, 1979), 103–37.

thousand to from fifty-five to sixty thousand, by the time of the sack in 1527, and it reached almost a hundred thousand by the end of the sixteenth century. Hence Rome, even more than Avignon before it, and like contemporary Aragonese Naples, exploded into an enormous market for luxury goods and for financial services to both ecclesiastics and the papal government.

What remains of the city's customs records, the kind of source material lacking for most other Italian cities, documents the prominence of Florentines as importers. More than a quarter of all goods taxed from 1452 to 1462 arrived in the hands of the ten largest Florentine importers, and half of the cloth came from Florence.[68] The city became a major outlet for the Florentine industry, and some producers directed all their output to it. Merchants also supplied the market with a host of other high-quality products of Florentine artisans. The intensity of trade was such that independent carriers set up a regular overland transport service from Florence to the papal capital. Florentine painters and sculptors traveled to Rome, where they virtually monopolized the lively art market until the early sixteenth century. Rome, however, was a city that consumed but did not produce; in contrast to Avignon, it was not a regional export market of any importance. Most of the great Florentine firms were primarily interested in banking activity linked to the Apostolic Chamber, but most also had side interests in commercial activities, above all the local grain market, the state salt monopoly, the export of alum from the mines at Tolfa, and the importation of luxury cloth from Florence. Some must have invested also in the local rural economy, as did Carlo di Ugolino Martelli, who, besides maintaining a warehouse and operating a bank in the city, made agricultural improvements on his land at Montefiascone, operated a water mill there, and invested in the mining and processing of iron from a mine at Corneto.[69] Moreover, as in no other city where they took up residence, Florentine merchant-bankers marked their presence individually with impressive palaces and collectively with the grandest church they built anywhere, San Giovanni dei Fiorentini, initiated by the Medici pope Leo X (but not finished until much later).

In short, behind the emerging economic importance of central Italy were the exigencies of the city's textile industries: the need for raw materials, both wool

[68] Arnold Esch, "Le importazioni nella Roma del primo Rinascimento (il loro volume secondo i registri doganali romani degli anni 1452–1462)," in *Aspetti della vita economica e culturale a Roma nel Quattrocento,* by Arnold Esch et al. (Rome, 1981), esp. 30–50 (on Fiorentine merchants). See also two contributions to *Forestieri e stranieri nelle città basso-medievali* (Florence, 1988): Ivana Ait, "La dogana di terra come fonte per lo studio della presenza di mercanti stranieri a Roma nel XV secolo," 29–43, and Luciano Palermo, "Un aspetto della presenza dei fiorentini a Roma nel '400: Le tecniche economiche," 81–96.

[69] Ivana Ait, "Credito e iniziativa commerciale: Aspetti dell'attività economica a Roma nella seconda metà del XV secolo," in *Credito e sviluppo economico in Italia dal Medio Evo all'Età Contemporanea,* ed. R. Allio (Verona, 1988), 81–95.

and silk, and the complementary need for markets, which opened up in Rome and Naples as well as in central Italy itself. We know of at least four firms that were resident in Perugia and three in L'Aquila in 1427,[70] and records survive for others who went into business in the region. One was Paliano di Falco Falcucci (or da Paliano), who, having started out about 1370 as a local banker in Florence, was by 1382—with the papacy just back in residence—in partnership with Giovanni Portinari and Ardingo de' Ricci in a firm with a capital of *fl*.16,000 that did business in Florence, Rome, and Perugia. Falcucci himself spent a number of years in Perugia, where he exported one of the local products, cotton veils. In his personal record books, noting the subsequent reorganizations of the company, he mentions the increase in his share of the capital from *fl*.1,500 in 1382 to *fl*.9,000 in 1405 and annual profits averaging about 10 percent. Another documented firm is Matteo di Simone Gondi & Partners, which operated in L'Aquila through an agent in the early 1480s. The agent, Giovan Francesco di Antonio Peruzzi, purchased mostly wool but also silk, both for the home industry, and saffron, which was sent on to the fairs at Geneva and Lyons. To balance payments, Peruzzi imported wool and silk cloth from Florence and wool cloth from northern Italy, southern France, Bruges, and London, which he sold in the region or sent on to Naples and to Adriatic ports. From L'Aquila the firm also had dealings with Florentines in Naples.[71]

The overland trade routes in and out of Florence used by the Cambini firm in the third quarter of the century for all of its commercial activity (the only firm studied from this point of view) fell into what was probably the overall pattern at the time: the route to Pisa dominated, followed by those going to Rome and to the Abruzzi and southward, while the one headed to Bologna and the north trailed well behind. Of the firm's shipments of Florentine wool cloth alone from 1453 to 1480, 46 percent went to Naples and southern Italy, 22 percent went to Rome and central Italy, and almost all the rest went overseas to the Levant, most through central Italy

[70] See chapter 1, n. 125.

[71] Falcucci's accounts survive in ASF, Carte strozziane, ser. 2, 7, and ser. 4, 364–66. On legal problems related to the execution of Falcucci's testament, see Thomas Kuehn, "Inheritance and Identity in Early Renaissance Florence: The Estate of Paliano di Falco," in *Society and Individual in Renaissance Florence,* ed. William J. Connell (Berkeley and Los Angeles, 2002), 137–54. On the Gondi firm, see Paola Pierucci, "Lo zafferano e le altre materie prime," in *Abruzzo: Economia e territorio in una prospettiva storica,* ed. M. Costantini and C. Felice (Vasto, 1998), esp. 168–95 (with reference to her two earlier articles on the firm) and, with a narrower focus, two articles by Benigno Casale, who does not cite Pierucci's articles: "Alcune notizie sulla fiera di Lanciano nella seconda metà del XV secolo" and "Il commercio della lana a L'Aquila durante la seconda metà del Quattrocento," both in *Il commercio a Napoli e nell'Italia meridionale nel XV secolo: Fonti e problemi,* by Benigno Casale, Amededo Feniello, and Alfonso Leone (Naples, 2003), 127–40, 141–55; the latter article has also been published in English as "The Wool Trade in L'Aquila during the Second Half of the Fifteenth Century," in *Wool Products and Markets (13th–20th Century)* (Padua, 2004), 149–62.

to the ports of Ancona and Pesaro.[72] Being structurally dependent primarily on the wool trade, the Florentine presence in L'Aquila declined at the end of the century, when the home industry turned to the better-quality Castilian wool from Spain. The heaviest overland traffic out of Florence was probably still directed through the region, but mainly to carry exports to Rome and Naples, both major consumer markets where profits could be invested in government obligations rather than plowed back into trade heading the other way, back to Florence. However, the route out of Florence into central Italy still carried fairly heavy traffic destined for the Adriatic port of Ancona, at least until the second quarter of the sixteenth century.

Venice, the Adriatic, and the Levant

The major players who drove Mediterranean trade with the Levant came from the port cities of Venice, Genoa, and Pisa. Florentine merchants operated in the wake of these maritime powers and did not take any direct initiatives of major importance in the eastern Mediterranean. They ventured into the area on crusades in the later eleventh and twelfth centuries, and there is every reason to think that they, like other Italians, engaged in business both as bankers handling transfers for crusaders and as merchants dealing in Eastern markets. Florentines, however, have little presence in these early documents, since merchants from the region are identified as Pisans, with whom they traveled, or, more generally, as Tuscans. In 1248 the banker Buondelmonte Ugolini is documented as having made a loan to the Empress, and so one could presume that he had a certain status at the imperial court in Constantinople. In 1249 the Scali firm appears at Damietta in Egypt, and later it had an agent in Acre, where the Peruzzi also had a warehouse. By the second half of the thirteenth century Florentines can be documented as both merchants and bankers throughout the Near East along with merchants from Barcelona, Marseilles, Ancona, and Sicily, as well as Pisa, Venice, and Genoa. Florentine merchants were active in the Genoese colony in Constantinople, some venturing into the Black Sea area, and after 1290 they obtained certain trading privileges in the empire for themselves. In the early fourteenth century the Bardi, the Peruzzi, and the Alberti were among those operating in the imperial capital. Florentine merchants and bankers also established a base in the Angevin principalities in Albania and the Peloponnesus after the conquest by Charles I in the 1270s. The large Florentine companies were in a

---

[72] Tognetti, *Il banco Cambini*, 170–79, 225–35, 283–93; Hidetoshi Hoshino, *L'arte della lana in Firenze nel Basso Medioevo: Il commercio della lana e il mercato dei panni fiorentini nei secoli XIII–XV* (Florence, 1980), 284–85 (tables of the firm's wool shipments).

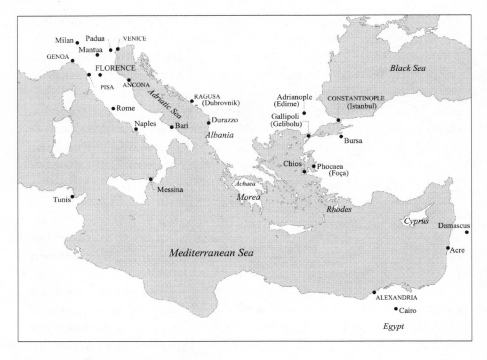

Italy and the eastern Mediterranean

particularly favorable position to supply demand in the East for two products
from the West, quality wool cloth, which they obtained through their network to
northern Europe, and grain from southern Italy, where they dominated the market. In exchange, they bought raw silk, cotton, skins, spices, and all the other
goods to be found in Near Eastern markets. They were, of course, dependent on
the shipping services of one of the maritime cities. As bankers, Florentines along
with other Italians served Western rulers by providing loans for their military
operations, facilitating monetary transfers, and effecting exchange into local
moneys.

Villani reported how much Florentine merchants suffered from the fall, in
1291, of Acre, the citadel of the last European crusader state, since they thereby
lost direct access to markets on the mainland. Christian merchants, however,
shifted their base to Cyprus, which became a major node for the intersection of
trade routes crisscrossing the eastern Mediterranean. The Bardi were at Fama-
gusta in 1290, and Pegolotti was in Cyprus working for them from 1324 to 1329
and again in 1335. In 1324 the Florentine companies on the island—including the
Buonaccorsi, Mozzi, and Peruzzi firms—gained certain trading privileges. Meanwhile, Florentine companies assisted in the financing of the conquest of Rhodes

by the Knights Hospitalers of St. John in 1309, after their expulsion from Jerusalem, and the Bardi, the Peruzzi, and the Acciaiuoli had a major role in the finances of the new state. In 1335 the Peruzzi company there had no fewer than 164 debtors on its books. It was in the islands under Christian domination that the great Florentine firms gained a particularly notable presence in the early fourteenth century. In addition to their commercial interests, they performed the same important banking functions as in the West that provided the liquidity they needed locally to engage in trade. Once they had thus extended their network into the area, the Florentines could offer better banking services than could the Genoese and the Venetians, who otherwise dominated the economic and often the political scene. Above all, Florentines served ecclesiastics in the acceptance of deposits, extension of credit, collection of taxes, and transfer of funds to the papacy. Cyprus, particularly important as a meeting place for merchants from all around the eastern Mediterranean, was in fact one of the most distant centers in the Florentine network for drawing bills of exchange.

Florentines, along with Genoese and Venetian merchants, also moved into Greece once it came under French control in the fourteenth century, some of them entering the aristocracy. The Bardi, the Peruzzi, and the Acciaiuoli had permanent agents in Chiarenza, in the Peloponnesus, where they conducted financial operations for local rulers and the papacy and imported grain from southern Italy. In those areas ruled by the Angevins—Durazzo and the Morea—some administered feudal estates for the nobility and entered into military service, and a few became owners of fiefs. The Acciaiuoli managed to predominate in the Morea. In 1325–26 their company was awarded a fief, which was later transferred to Niccolò Acciaiuoli personally, and the family remained there as major feudal landlords for almost a century, active in military and political affairs as well as in the area's economic life. Thanks to them, Florentines gained concessions for conducting trade in Greek ports.[73]

After the disappearance of the major merchant-banking houses as a result of the bankruptcies of the 1340s, firms seem to have operated less through resident branches in the East and instead engaged in specific ventures, buying or renting a ship, sending out a factor or an agent on contract, or using a resident commission agent, who might also work for other merchants and firms. Beginning in the 1360s, wool producers took initiatives to get their products to the Levantine

---

[73] For this early period, see Robert Davidsohn, *Storia di Firenze* (Florence, 1956), 4, pt. 2: ch. 7; Silvano Borsari, "L'espansione economica fiorentina nell'Oriente cristiano fino alla metà del Trecento," *Rivista storica italiana* 70 (1958): 477–507; and Sandra Origone, "I toscani nel Mediterraneo: L'area bizantina, il Mar Nero," in *La Toscana nel secolo XIV: Caratteri di una civiltà regionale*, ed. Sergio Gensini (Pisa, 1988), 271–85.

markets, and some operators ventured out on their own. In 1382 the merchant Bonifazio di Maso di Neri accepted Florentine wool cloth along with some silver bullion and tin in consignment from other merchants and went to Alexandria on a Pisan ship, where these goods were exchanged, mostly through barter (or, better, countertrade), for indigo, linen, sugar, pearls, rubies, and, above all, pepper and other spices. In 1397 the Alberti company in Bruges sent one of its employees to Alexandria to procure spices for the Bruges market. In the same year two Florentines left Alexandria on a ship belonging to one of them loaded with sapan (a red dye), ginger, cinnamon, and cloves; they took on sponges at Rhodes and alum, camlets, and gall (an insect dye) at Chios and then headed for Barcelona and Bruges.[74]

Notwithstanding these ventures into the eastern Mediterranean, the main focus of Florentine commercial interest in Levantine markets was on the western maritime cities that had extensive shipping networks throughout the East. Genoa and Venice, and to a lesser extent Barcelona and Marseilles, were the Western emporia where Florentines like Datini traded in the goods coming from or going to the Levant. Of these, the principal pole in the Florentine network for maritime transport to the east was Venice, and the route between Florence and Venice over the Apennines and crossing the Po valley became a major artery of trade. A principal node for this traffic was Bologna, a major regional market center where Florentines sold cloth and bought local products such as cotton veiling, rope, and foodstuffs. Already in 1203 Florence made a commercial treaty with Bologna, and the oldest extant fragment of a Florentine account book, dated 1211, belonged to a moneychanger working there. Statutes of the resident Florentine community survive for the years 1279–89. Besides the route out of Bologna to Venice, trade networks also led to Mantua, Cremona, Milan, and other cities in the Po valley where Florentines also were to be found in this early period.

Yet it does not seem that in the fourteenth and fifteenth centuries many Florentine firms had a presence in the cities along the route carrying traffic out of Bologna and northwest across the Po valley, then over the Alps to northern Europe. Very little of the Flemish cloth the Calimala firm of Bartolomeo di Caroccio degli Alberti & Partners imported in the 1350s for finishing and reexporting came all the way overland, altogether skipping any of the ports on the Tyrrhenian Sea.[75] Datini's correspondence with his agents in Milan does not re-

---

[74] These examples come from Hidetoshi Hoshino, "I mercanti fiorentini ad Alessandria d'Egitto nella seconda metà del Trecento," reprinted in Hoshino, *Industria tessile e commercio internazionale nella Firenze del tardo Medioevo*, ed. Franco Franceschi and Sergio Tognetti (Florence, 2001). See also idem, *L'arte della lana*, 173–74.

[75] Marco Spallanzani, "Mercatura," in Goldthwaite, Settesoldi, and Spallanzani, *Due libri mastri degli Alberti*, 1:lxxv.

veal the presence of any other Florentines in the city.[76] Nor do the many more letters written while he was in exile at Bologna in 1401–2 to escape the plague report activity of any importance in that city.[77] On the list of firms extracted from the 1427 catasto, six were in Bologna, thirteen were in Venice, and only one was located in between, at Mantua, but none were located elsewhere in the entire Po valley.[78] With the rise of the silk industry in the early fifteenth century, Florence had, for the first time, products it could export to northern European markets, and a carrier system existed for getting them to the Geneva fairs.[79] But the eclipse of Geneva by Lyons in the second half of the century, while not leading to the abandonment of overland routes, probably resulted in the shift of much of this trade to Mediterranean ports.[80] Not much of the heavy wagon traffic between Antwerp and Italy that got under way in the early sixteenth century seems to have involved Florence. The Medici had a bank in Milan, but it seems to have served primarily the ducal court. The ledger Andrea Bartolini kept in Milan in the 1480s, probably to take care of winding down the operations of the Medici bank after its closing in 1478, has accounts open in the name of Milanese and other merchants and bankers but none in the name of a Florentine located in the city.[81]

Venice, in contrast to both Genoa and Milan, was a major focus for Florentine business abroad. Although Venice, compared with Genoa, was geographically remote from the western Mediterranean and Atlantic trade networks, it had a much vaster hinterland, and the easy access to the many urban markets scattered throughout the Po valley extending across all of northern Italy offered more opportunities for trade out of the city than did Genoa. Moreover, the influx of silver bullion from southern Germany provided the wherewithal to balance payments with the Levant and made the city a major international money market. Venice also offered a much more stable political environment for the conduct of trade. Florentine merchants are documented at Venice by the second half of the thirteenth century as importing cloth from their native city and dealing in the Eastern trade. In 1274 they obtained certain exemptions from tax charges on traffic through

---

[76] Luciana Frangioni, *Milano fine Trecento: Il carteggio milanese dell'Archivio Datini di Prato* (Florence, 1994), ch. 2.

[77] Melis, *Aspetti,* 17–24; Roberto Greci, *Mercanti, politica e cultura nella società bolognese del Basso Medioevo* (Bologna, 2004), ch. 4 (on Datini).

[78] See chapter 1, n. 125.

[79] Brief references to these carriers are found in Jean-François Bergier, "Lettres genevoises des Medici, 1425–1475," in *Studi in memoria di Federigo Melis,* 3:296 (with reference to the carrier Battista di Taccino, discussed in chapter 1); and Michel Mollat, *Jacques Coeur, ou l'esprit d'entreprise au XVe siècle* (Paris, 1988), 97.

[80] Pierucci, "Lo zafferano," 181–83, refers to a carrier who transported saffron from L'Aquila to both Geneva and Lyons in 1470.

[81] Archivio Bartolini Salimbeni, Vicchio di Mugello (villa di Collina), 208 (ledger of Andrea di Leonardo Bartolini in Milan, 1483–86).

Venice to outlying towns, and by 1290 they had organized themselves locally into what soon became a "nation," with statutes and officials. At the beginning of the next century many Florentines—merchants, tradespeople, and artisans—were also emigrating in large numbers to Friuli and Venezia Giulia (see chapter 3). In Venice itself Florentines became one of the most prominent groups of foreigners. They and the Germans collectively were the most important clients of the Rialto bankers, and they outnumbered all other foreigners in seeking citizenship privileges.

Much of the business Florentines conducted in Venice was related to their home textile industry. An account book of Piero Del Buono & Partners in Venice, open from 1336 to 1339, documents the importation of wool cloth from its parent company in Florence and the export back of raw wool. A ledger of the Covoni company in Padua, open in the same years, documents shipments along the route from Florence by way of Bologna and Mantua to Padua, with Florentine wool cloth going north and linen and raw wool from Verona going south to both Bologna and Florence.[82] Even raw wool coming from England reached Florence by way of Venice in those moments when, before the conquest of Pisa, access to Tyrrhenian ports was blocked for political reasons. As import-export merchants Florentines also engaged in the redistribution of the great variety of goods going in and out of this, the greatest emporium in the Mediterranean, although rigid Venetian regulations severely limited the direct involvement of foreigners in maritime trade. The aforementioned ledger of Del Buono & Partners, the only surviving record of this kind for a Florentine firm in Venice during the fourteenth century, shows that the firm had its own regional network of agents and contacts throughout northern Italy—at Faenza, Bologna, Mantua, Ferrara, Brescia, and Cremona—who supplied it with a large variety of consumer goods, from fruit, flour, and capons to nails, clothing, and cloth. In the early fifteenth century the Medici branch in Venice accepted on consignment saffron from a correspondent in L'Aquila, furs, amber, linen, and tin vessels from a German merchant in Lübeck, cloth from an Italian in Bruges, cloth from a Florentine firm in London, wool from Valencia, and cloth from Florence, and it bought spices and cotton from Venetian importers for resale. Firms without a branch or their own factor in Venice used resident consignment agents, who worked on commission. One of these, Girolamo di Francesco Corboli, frequently served the Cambini company

---

[82] Reinhold C. Mueller, *The Venetian Money Market: Banks, Panics, and the Public Debt, 1200–1500*, vol. 2 of *Money and Banking in Medieval and Renaissance Venice*, by Frederic C. Lane and Reinhold C. Mueller (Baltimore, 1997), 264 (for del Buono); Giulio Mandich, "Per una ricostruzione delle operazioni mercantili e bancarie della compagnia Covoni," in *Libro giallo della compagnia dei Covoni*, ed. Armando Sapori (Milano, 1970), clv–clx.

over the third quarter of the fifteenth century, sending to Florence kermes from Greece, Syrian cotton, Tartar slaves, German leather, as well as lead, glass, silver, sugar, capers, alum, and insignificant amounts of spices. Transport from Venice to Florence was probably by sea and river to Ferrara, then overland or by canal and river to Bologna, and from there by pack animals over the Apennines.[83]

Although the Venetian government occasionally disrupted Florentines' activities as a result of tensions with Florence arising from conflicting interests in the fluid world of Italian politics, it generally recognized their importance in the economic life of the city. Probably no other city attracted as many Florentine merchants and bankers. The ledger of the Covoni company in Florence reveals operations with some sixty Florentine firms in Venice in the years 1336 to 1340. As bankers who could transfer funds anywhere throughout their network, Florentines performed an essential function in the life of what was Europe's major international emporium. As we shall see in chapter 3, Venice emerged in the fourteenth century as the principal center in their international network for the traffic in bills of exchange. Venetians themselves relied on Florentines for international transfer and exchange. When Cosimo de' Medici went into exile in 1433–34, first to Padua and then to Venice, the central direction of his bank moved with him, and he probably found it just as easy to manage international operations there as in Florence, perhaps even easier.

Venice was also a place where someone could make a fortune. For example, Zanobi Gaddi, whose father and brother were painters, went to Venice sometime before 1369 and somehow set himself up in business. "Opportunities do exist here," he wrote to Datini's factor in Pisa in 1384 on establishing relations with that firm, "may God preserve them and make them grow." And indeed for him they did grow, for he laid the foundation for one of the most prominent dynasties of Florentine international merchant-bankers over the next century.[84] Another Florentine from an old magnate family, Baldassarre di Simone degli Ubriachi (sometimes Embriachi), already a well-established international merchant-banker who had had close relations with Richard II in England and had been made a count palatine by Emperor Charles IV, moved to Venice following problems in Florence and became a citizen there in 1395. He brought a Florentine carver of ivory to Venice and set up a workshop in his house for the manufacture of luxury objects

---

[83] For the firms mentioned, see Giulio Mandich, "Una compagnia fiorentina a Venezia nel quarto decennio del secolo XIV (un libro di conti)," *Rivista storica italiana* 96 (1984): 129–49; Raymond de Roover, *The Rise and Decline of the Medici Bank, 1397–1494* (Cambridge, MA, 1963), 240–53; and Tognetti, *Il banco Cambini*, 175–76, 229, 287–88.

[84] Reinhold Mueller, "Mercanti e imprenditori fiorentini a Venezia nel tardo Medioevo," *Società e storia*, no. 55 (1992): 29–60; idem, *Venetian Money Market*, ch. 7, quotation from 268. For the early period, see also Davidsohn, *Storia di Firenze*, 4, pt. 2:860–67.

in ivory, some executed on commission, some consisting of standardized parts put together according to the desire of clients, and yet others produced for sale in the market. Ubriachi traveled throughout southern Europe to market these highly prestigious products and take orders for them, and his illegitimate son became a major ivory artist. Production included the famous triptych at the Certosa of Pavia and many other pieces that survive in museums.[85]

In addition to merchant-bankers, Venice, being Europe's major port city, attracted entrepreneurs and artisans from everywhere, including Florence, in the pursuit of their own business interests. Prominent among Florentines who immigrated to Venice were manufacturers of wool and silk cloth, who thereby located themselves closer to the export market for their products. In the course of the fourteenth century, in fact, Florentine producers of wool cloth came to represent a significant portion of the Venetian industry and may have contributed to the rise of a native industry that in the sixteenth century became a major competitor in the Levant. Finally, as one would expect, there was always a large floating population of Florentines, coming and going on business for one reason or another. Given the large Florentine community and the political importance of the city in Italian affairs, exiles too often headed for Venice, where they could plot their return and possibly make a living in their own line of work as merchants and bankers in the meantime.

At the beginning of the fifteenth century Florentines took a new, aggressive interest in trade in the Levant that largely bypassed Venice. The purchase of Porto Pisano and Livorno in 1421, following the conquest of Pisa in 1406, gave Florence direct control over major port facilities for the first time and led to the immediate establishment of an official galley system. The first galleys departed the very next year for Alexandria, and that same year Florence received permission to have consuls in both Alexandria and Damascus. Subsequent sailings were sporadic, but after 1445 they became more regular. In the 1430s the first sailings were made to Constantinople, and in 1437 Florentine merchants there entered into an agreement with the Genoese for the supply of alum. Contemporaneous with the formulation and active promotion of an Eastern commercial policy by the government was the private activity of Florentine merchants operating on their own now out of Pisa, where they had quickly established their hegemony over the other resident merchant communities, especially the Pisans themselves, many of whom went into exile. The commune also opened negotiations with the Eastern em-

[85] Richard C. Trexler, "The Magi Enter Florence: The Ubriachi of Florence and Venice," *Studies in Medieval and Renaissance History* 1 (1978): 129–218; Michele Tomasi, "Gli Embriachi: l'avorio per il mercato," in *Artifex bonus: Il mondo dell'artista medievale*, ed. Enrico Castelnuovo (Bari, 2004), 207–14.

peror to gain trade agreements, and these produced concrete results in 1439, when it dealt directly with Emperor John VIII while he was in Florence for the church council, which had moved from Basel. The emperor conceded to the Florentines the privileges previously enjoyed by the merchants of Pisa. Driving this intensified interest in Eastern markets were, as usual, pressures from the local textile industries. The wool industry was able to move into these Eastern markets as a result of both the crisis in the Flemish industry, which had earlier provided much of the cloth the Florentines and others had directed to the Levant, and what seems to have been the decadence of the industry in the Near East. This was also a time when the silk industry was beginning its impressive growth, and the need for raw silk sharpened commercial interest in supply lines from the East. In short, local pressures from both textile industries generated new supply-and-demand forces that converged on Eastern markets, bringing the area more sharply into focus for Florentine commercial interests than ever before.[86]

We do not know how much the military situation in the Levant impinged on the growth of this trade. Investments in two major accomandita ventures in Rhodes and the surrounding area, each for four years, made in 1452, just a year before the Turkish conquest of Constantinople, suggest that the merchant-banking community was not overly concerned: in separate contracts but both with the same agent, Bernardo di Marco Salviati, Cosimo de' Medici's son Giovanni and his nephew Pierfrancesco invested *fl.*5,000 and Niccolò and Bartolomeo di Piero Capponi invested *fl.*1,000.[87] In any event, no sooner had the Ottoman Turks seized Constantinople than Florentines quickly sought to take advantage of the market opportunities that opened up in the capital of this new powerful and rich state. The pursuit of this policy came at a high diplomatic cost, however, since they antagonized the Venetians by moving into the commercial void resulting from hostilities between Venice and the Turks, and at the same time they

[86] On this later phase of relations with the East, see, in addition to the items cited in the following notes, Giuseppe Müller, *Documenti sulle relazioni delle città toscane coll'Oriente cristiano e coi Turchi fino all'anno MDXXXI* (1879; repr., Rome, 1966); Guglielmo Heyd, *Storia del commercio del Levante nel Medio Evo* (Turin, 1913 [trans. from the French ed. of 1885, which in turn was translated, with additions by the author, from the original German ed. of 1879]), 863–69, 902–11, 1044–46; Sergio Camerani, "Contributo alla storia dei trattati commerciali fra la Toscana e i Turchi," *ASI* 47 (1939): 83–101; Mallett, *Florentine Galleys*, 63–72 (on sailings), 113–23 (on nature of trade); Franz Babinger, "Lorenzo de' Medici e la corte ottomana," *ASI* 121 (1963): 305–61; Hidetoshi Hoshino, "Il commercio fiorentino nell'impero ottomano: Costi e profitti negli anni 1484–1488," in *Aspetti della vita economica medievale*, 81–90; and idem, "Alcuni aspetti del commercio dei panni fiorentini nell'impero ottomano ai primi del '500," reprinted in Hoshino, *Industria tessile e commercio internazionale*, 113–23.

[87] Bruno Dini, "Aspetti del commercio di esportazione dei panni di lana e dei drappi di seta fiorentini in Costantinopoli, negli anni 1522–1531," reprinted from *Studi in memoria di Federigo Melis* in *Saggi su una economia-mondo: Firenze e l'Italia fra Mediterraneo ed Europa (secc. XIII–XVI)* (Pisa, 1995), 247n85.

had to maintain a delicate balance between their commercial interests and the vigorous efforts by the papacy to arouse Christians to respond to Turkish expansion with crusades and prohibitions on trade. As early as December 1455 the commune sent thanks to Mehmed II for his favorable treatment of Florentine merchants, and the very next year sailings of the state galleys resumed. Three accomandita contracts survive from 1459 for investments in partnership ventures in Turkish lands, one for *fl.*2,000 for four years and another for *fl.*1,000 for three years.[88] In 1461 a consul was appointed to Constantinople, and an official accord was arranged between the two states. In that year Benedetto Dei went off to Turkey, where he remained until 1466, presumably to serve as a kind of unofficial representative, even spy, to keep an eye on Florentine interests and especially any competition from Venice (hence the infamous, almost pathological diatribes against the Venetians in his chronicle).[89] Florentines had resident communities at Pera, on the Golden Horn, and at other market centers near Constantinople—Adrianople in the European hinterland, Gallipoli on the Dardanelles, Bursa in Asia Minor, Rhodes in the southern Aegean. Dei named fifty merchants residing in this general area in 1469.[90] In 1507 the Florentine resident community at Constantinople numbered from sixty to seventy, perhaps the largest in the Florentine network outside of Italy at that time.[91] By then the Florentines had their own nazione in Pera, complete with statutes and a consul. Florentines also gained renewal of consular privileges in Alexandria and Damascus in 1489 and again in 1496 and 1497, but these markets were less important for the sale of cloth.

For Florentines, in contrast to merchants from the great maritime cities, the staples in this trade—in fact, about the only items they handled—were wool and silk cloth produced by the home industry (or imported from the north) and raw silk needed for the home industry. They brought back from the East anything they thought they could sell in the West, from rugs to precious stones, but they often came home with cash or bullion, usually gold. There were occasional ups and downs in their trade relations with the Turks, but over the long run, at least well into the sixteenth century, Florentines prospered from them, the balance being almost always in their favor. Although the relative importance of an activity in the past can never be read into the chance survival of pertinent documents, it is worth noting that of all the extant business accounts kept outside of Italy at

[88] Dini, "Aspetti del commercio di esportazione," 247n85.

[89] Benedetto Dei, *La cronica dall'anno 1400 all'anno 1500*, ed. Roberto Barducci (Florence, 1984).

[90] The published version of Dei's *Cronica* does not list the fifty merchants individually, but they are identified in the manuscript consulted by Giovanni Francesco Pagnini del Ventura, who published them in his *Della Decima e delle altre gravezze . . .* (1765; repr., Bologna, 1967), 1, bk. 2:303.

[91] Heyd, *Storia del commercio del Levante*, 909.

any time before the end of the last republic in 1530, those of merchants in Pera dating from the last quarter of the fifteenth century through the first quarter of the sixteenth are probably more numerous than for any other place after London and Lyons (excepting the Datini materials).

A truer measure of the importance of these cloth exports for the home wool industry can be taken in the accord of 1482, arranged with an ambassador sent to Florence by the new sultan, Bayezid II. It reconfirmed trade relations and granted permission to import five thousand bolts of cloth each year, close to one-third of the industry's estimated total production at the time, a percentage confirmed a half-century later by the study of three wool firms operating at different times from 1518 to 1532 that directed output to Eastern markets.[92] A 1487 document of the wool guild refers to the new Levantine market as "the stomach for our Garbo cloth"; and Hidetoshi Hoshino, the historian of the Florentine wool industry, believed that it was the opening up of this Eastern market that led to the rapid shift of the industry to the new kind of cloth made from matricina wool. One initiative taken already in 1462 by the hosteller and operator of a commercial transport service we encountered in chapter 1, Battista di Taccino di Bizzino (Bizzini), gives us some sense of the excitement even modest entrepreneurs must have felt about the new market prospects opening up at Constantinople almost as soon as trade relations had been established after the fall of Constantinople, notwithstanding the concurrent efforts of Pius II to incite Christians to action in a crusade against the Turks. Battista sent the son of his cousin to Constantinople with forty-six bolts of wool cloth to be sold, the proceeds to be used to buy silk and pepper and little else, it being better, according to his instructions, to bring back "above all money in cash rather than other merchandise."[93] Wool producers themselves often took direct action to get their products to these Eastern markets. In the same year as Battista's venture, one of the industry's richest producers, Lorenzo di Ilarione Ilarioni, made a three-year contract with a commission agent at Pera, Baldassarre di Gualtieri Biliotti, committing *fl.*6,000 for trade throughout the area centering on the sale of wool cloth and the purchase of raw silk.[94] In 1483 the Guanti wool firm sent one of the its partners, Bartolomeo di Piero Guanti, to Bursa to handle sales, and over the next fifteen years, to 1498, it made thirty-two shipments, for an annual average of about one hundred bolts per year, almost equivalent to one firm's production (some of the cloth sent by the

[92] Dini, "Aspetti del commercio di esportazione," 232–37.

[93] Archive of the Ospedale degli Innocenti, Florence, ser. 144 (Estranei), 201 (record book of shipments, 1461–78), fols. 141v–142r.

[94] Tognetti, *Il banco Cambini*, 235–37.

Guanti firm, however, had been purchased from other firms).[95] In 1507 the commune, recognizing the importance of these cloth exports, set up an agency, the Procurators of Eastern Empire Affairs (Procuratori delle cose di Romania), to oversee trade relations with the Turks, a charge it was to share, significantly, with the wool guild.

Cloth exports followed three major routes to the East. The galleys went from Pisa directly to Pera, making stops along the way, coming and going, especially in Sicily, southern Italy, and the Greek islands. They carried wool and some silk cloth and certain natural products (almonds, tin, lead, coral, saffron) and manufactured goods (paper, soap) picked up along the way, and they brought back raw silk, linen, hides, dyestuffs, and a variety of other products but few spices (the most important being pepper and ginger), much of which they dropped off along the way. The last sailings were in 1477–78, but the galley system had never had a trade monopoly, and after its demise merchants continued commercial activity on their own on two other routes that had been blazed while the galley system still operated. One of these went overland to one of the Adriatic ports in central Italy and from there to Pera by sea using local shippers as well as those from Ragusa, a route that largely replaced the earlier one by way of Venice. A third route that became increasingly important after the Turkish conquest of Albania in 1478 also went overland to an Adriatic port, then across the Adriatic to Ragusa (or overland to Lecce and then to Valona), and then overland to Constantinople. Despite the presumed increased cost of overland travel, this route had the advantage of avoiding the risks at sea, especially at a time of hostilities between the Turks and Venice, the latter hardly well disposed to increased Florentine commercial activity in its traditional area of operations. This overland route is well documented in the business correspondence of Giovanni di Francesco Maringhi, a commission agent in Pera from at least 1495 to his death in 1507. On a business trip in 1497 from Ancona to Ragusa and then on to Adrianople and Pera conducting a team of no fewer than 114 pack animals, he was accompanied by Bernardo Michelozzi, the son of the architect, and Bonsignore Bonsignori. These two men, who were on a mission to find manuscripts, wrote letters back to Florence all along the way, from Florence to Pera, that in effect provide a diary of a trip over this heavily traveled and difficult route.[96] Not all exports of cloth were handled

[95] Hidetoshi Hoshino and Maureen Fennell Mazzaoui, "Ottoman Markets for Florentine Woolen Cloth in the Late Fifteenth Century," *International Journal of Turkish Studies* 3 (1985–86): 17–31.

[96] Gertrude Richards, ed., *Florentine Merchants in the Age of the Medici: Letters and Documents from the Selfridge Collection of Medici Manuscripts* (Cambridge, MA, 1932); Eve Borsook, "The Travels of Bernardo Michelozzi and Bonsignore Bonsignori in the Levant (1497–98)," *Journal of the Warburg and Courtauld Institutes* 36 (1973): 145–97. Bartoldo di Lodovico Tedaldi, who traveled to Constantinople over the same route in 1489 with goods belonging to several men in Florence, kept a complete accounting of his expenses in an unpublished ledger and record book now in the private

by Florentines, however, for one inauspicious consequence of this market activity was the appearance in Florence itself of merchants from Ragusa, Albania, and Greece who made significant purchases directly from local producers.[97]

The preference for this overland route brought two Adriatic ports, Ragusa and Ancona, into focus for Florentine commercial interests. The former was by far the more important, having long been the leading Adriatic port after Venice. Already in the twelfth century Ragusa (Dubrovnik) was an important player in the commercial revolution, with ties to Pisa, although it was long under Venetian influence. A 1272 statute documents the importation of cloth from Florence as well as from Milan and northern Europe. The earliest notice of a Florentine firm in the city regards the ownership of a house by an agent of the Peruzzi company in 1318, and documents over the next quarter-century testify to the presence of agents of the Bardi, Acciaiuoli, and Buonaccorsi firms. These merchants engaged primarily in the importation of grain from southern Italy and had only a small role in the local credit market. One merchant who emerges from the documents as having a certain presence on the local scene in Ragusa from 1318 to 1341 was Benci di Uguccione "il Buono" Sacchetti, the father of the writer Franco Sacchetti (who, in fact, may have been born in Ragusa). Sacchetti dealt in the silver trade between Ragusa and Venice, but he also had trade contacts throughout the eastern Mediterranean—in the Balkans, Greece, and Constantinople, as well as southern Italy and Florence—and he was a major lender to both local patricians and the government.[98] The Venetians, however, were far more important players in the Ragusan economy in this early period. In any event, the Florentines disappeared from the scene at the time of the great crisis of the 1340s.

In 1378 Ragusa, together with Dalmatia, passed from Venetian dominance to the kingdom of Hungary, but this gave it the opportunity to assert greater autonomy, and when Dalmatia returned to Venice in 1409, the city remained for all practical purposes an independent state. Ragusans, in fact, became rivals to the Venetians in the Levantine trade with Europe, largely owing to their ability to remain neutral in the face of the rising threat from the expanding Ottoman Empire, and after the conquest of the Balkans by the Turks Ragusa managed to assert itself as a port of entry to a major overland route to Constantinople. All this transformed Ragusa into a preferred port for trade between Europe and the Balkans, and Florentines now came in greater numbers.

Frescobaldi archives (at Villa di Poggio a Remole, Le Sieci, near Florence), no. 18. A brief diary, including travel expenses, kept by Daniele Strozzi on his trip in 1523 is referred to by Bruno Dini in "Aspetti del commercio di esportazione," 260–61.

[97] Dini, "Aspetti del commercio di esportazione," 232–42.

[98] Susan Mosher Stuard, *Gilding the Market: Luxury and Fashion in Fourteenth-Century Italy* (Philadelphia, 2006), 186–96.

Ragusa was more than just a port of transit, however. It served as a market for the products from its hinterland, which included wax, salt, skins, and above all silver from Serbian mines. The mines saw a jump in output beginning in the 1370s. In a letter sent in 1406 by the Signoria of Florence to its ambassador in Rome, it was noted that "Ragusan merchants have filled up our commune with silver" and that "in large part we made the acquisition of the city of Pisa with the said silver that they have brought here."[99] The letters written from 1419 to 1434 by Giuliano di Marco Marcovaldi, of Prato, an agent in Ragusa working for Florentine merchants, further document shipments of silver to Florence and elsewhere.[100] In this emporium Florentine merchants could therefore exchange the cloth that was always at the center of their commercial interests for goods that had markets in the western Mediterranean. Merchants came to sell cloth from Florence and elsewhere, and wool producers from both Florence and Prato also arrived, attracted by the city's encouragement of local production to supply the hinterland markets. In addition, Florentines built up a trade axis between Barcelona and Ragusa on the exchange of raw wool for silver. Florentines and other Tuscans also became important players in the credit market, financing both local industry and hinterland trade.

During the fifteenth century major firms—the Medici, the Pazzi, the Pitti, the Strozzi—had resident agents at Ragusa, and the first official consul was appointed in 1495. The activities of Martino Chiarini, who was at Ragusa from 1448 to at least 1486, reflect the busy and varied traffic that involved a merchant in this port city. Besides serving Iacopo Pazzi as an agent for the importation of wool from Barcelona and the exportation of Ragusan cloth, he imported wax, eels, and fish from Valona, on the Albanian coast, sold a Russian slave to a Ragusan, assisted in the construction of the breech of a large cannon for the city's defenses, transferred funds from Adrianople to Florence for the banker Dono Doni, insured maritime shipments, and engaged in credit operations that in the years 1459–60 alone exceeded *du.*17,000. It was in a house rented by Chiarini in the name of the Barcelona company of the Pazzi that Giorgio di Lorenzo Chiarini in 1458 compiled the earliest manuscript of the merchant manual mentioned in chapter 1. Chiarini very likely knew the most notable of the local Ragusan merchants who did much business with Florentines in the 1440s, Benedetto Cotrugli, author of the treatise *Il libro dell'arte di mercatura,* which he wrote after leaving for Naples in 1451. Cotrugli, along with his brothers, served as an agent, or perhaps partner, of Francesco di Nerone Neroni in Barcelona, importing wool from Spain and cloth from

---

[99] Quoted in Gino Guarnieri, "Intorno alle relazioni commerciali marittime nel Medio Evo fra la Toscana e gli scali adriatici dalmati," *ASI* 125 (1967): 352–64.
[100] Paola Pinelli, "L'argento di Ragusa," *Storia economica* 8 (2005): 484–573.

Florence and exporting silver and dyestuffs, and on his business travels to southern Italy and Barcelona he went at least once to Florence.[101] The ties between
Florence and Ragusa remained strong well into the sixteenth century. In 1461 the
city attracted the architect Michelozzo to be its chief consultant for new fortifications, paying him an annual salary of *du.*240, far more than he could ever have
earned in his native city or perhaps anywhere in Italy.[102] In 1512 Ragusa offered
asylum to Piero Soderini, *gonfaloniere* for life, when he was driven from Florence
on the return of the Medici.

On the Italian side of the Adriatic Florentine merchants used several ports,
including Rimini, Pesaro, Ancona, Pescara, and others further south. These ports
were tied into two regional trading areas within Italy, mentioned above, where
Florentine merchants had long been active. Those to the south served the markets
for grain and other foodstuffs from the Kingdom of Naples, where Florentines
had major commercial interests. The ports to the north were tied into the regional commercial system in central Italy extending through the Romagna, Umbria, and the Marche, which was thoroughly penetrated by Florentines working
the overland routes out of the city in their efforts to sell wool cloth, both that
imported from northern Europe and that produced in Florence. Florentines were
also active in the import-export trade extending from these ports to Venice, the
Balkans, and the Levant and to the western Mediterranean system. Again, their
primary interest was in the marketing of cloth.

Of these Italian cities on the Adriatic, Ancona alone emerged as a major port
in the fifteenth century. At the end of the fourteenth century the city made a
deliberate effort to attract foreigners. It specifically targeted Florentine merchants
by offering them lower customs charges and permitting them to invest directly
in maritime trade by renting ships and traveling with their merchandise on

---

[101] For Florentines in Ragusa, see the following articles by Bariša Krekić, all reprinted in his
Dubrovnik, Italy and the Balkans in the Late Middle Ages (London, 1980): "I mercanti produttori
toscani di panni di lana a Dubrovnik (Ragusa) nella prima metà del Quattrocento," in *Produzione,
commercio e consumo dei panni di lana (nei secoli XII–XVIII)*, ed. Marco Spallanzani (Florence,
1976), 707–14; "Four Florentine Commercial Companies in Dubrovnik (Ragusa) in the First Half of
the Fourteenth Century," in *The Medieval City*, ed. H. A. Miskimin, D. Herlihy, and A. L. Udovitch
(New Haven, CT, 1977), 25–41; and "Italian Creditors in Dubrovnik (Ragusa) and the Balkan Trade,
Thirteenth through Fifteenth Centuries," in *Dawn of Modern Banking*, esp. 246–49, with the reference to Sacchetti on 247. Filippo Naitana, "I beni dei Pazzi all'indomani della congiura: Un 'passaporto' per la storia delle relazioni fra Firenze e Ragusa nel tardo Medioevo," *Quaderni medievali* 47
(1999), esp. 49–58, cites much original material on the Florentines in Ragusa, including the 1406
letter of the Signoria and the information about Sacchetti. Giorgio Chiarini's life is surveyed by F.
Cristofani Innocenzi in the *Dizionario biographico degli italiani*. Cotrugli's career in business, based
on new documents, is surveyed by Luca Boschetto in "Tra Firenze e Napoli: Nuove testimonianze
sul mercante-umanista Benedetto Cotrugli e sul suo *Libro dell'arte di mercatura*," *ASI* 163 (2005):
687–715.

[102] Harriet McNeal Caplow, "Michelozzo at Ragusa: New Documents and Revaluations," *Journal
of the Society of Architectural Historians* 31 (1972): 108–19.

locally owned ships, an inducement to investment in trade that foreign merchants did not have in the more rigidly closed system of Venice. Florentines, artisans as well as merchants, made up one of the largest foreign colonies in the city. Although their primary interest was in marketing wool cloth, merchants dealt in the usual variety of goods one found in a port opening to the Levant. Datini's agents in Barcelona, Valencia, and Palma dealt with agents in Ancona, and at least twice Cosimo de' Medici set up a company in the city to engage in the Levantine trade. The increased presence of Florentines in Ancona coincided both with their intensified commercial interests in central Italy resulting from the shift the domestic industry made to matricina wool from the Abruzzi and with the increased demand for cloth in the Ottoman Empire. Moreover, Ancona offered Florentines an alternative to the flagging galley system, which finally closed down after the last sailing in 1478, and it became even more important during the long period of Pisa's rebellion, from 1494 to 1509. In a treaty between the two cities in 1499 Florentines gained the privilege of leasing any ship they wished, of whatever nationality, and the recognition that any ship they leased belonging to someone from Ancona would be considered a Florentine ship. Whereas earlier it had been primarily a port of transit, Ancona now became a veritable market where merchants from Ragusa and the East exchanged goods with merchants from Italy, among whom the Florentines dominated into the second half of the century. Ancona, however, lacked the underpinning of an expansive economic structure at the local and regional level, and following changes in the pattern of trade between Europe and the Ottoman Empire in the course of the sixteenth century, its port went into decline.[103]

Florentine trade of all kinds must have fallen off sharply during the desperate struggle for survival of the Last Republic, from 1527 to 1530, and exports to the Turkish market never really revived. The reasons for the decline, however, are to be found, not in a particular crisis, but in larger economic and political forces that took their own inexorable course. Most importantly, the dynamics of the textile industries changed. The wool industry slowly shifted its production from Garbo cloths to the lighter, more expensive rascia, made from superior Castilian wool, and these cloths sold better in the luxury markets of Europe than in the Near East. We cannot assess the extent to which this shift represented an effort

[103] Peter Earle, "The Commercial Development of Ancona, 1479–1551," *Economic History Review* 22 (1969): 28–44; Jean Delumeau, "Ancône, trait d'union entre l'Occident et l'Orient à l'époque de la Renaissance," in *Sociétés et compagnies de commerce en Orient et dans l'Océan Indien* (Paris, 1970), 419–32; E. Ashtor, "Il commercio anconetano con il Mediterraneo occidentale nel Basso Medioevo," *Atti e memorie della Deputazione di storia patria per le Marche* (papers of the conference "Mercati, mercanti, denaro nelle Marche [secoli XIV–XIX]") 87 (1982): 9–71; Giovanni Cherubini, "I Toscani ad Ancona nel Basso Medioevo," in *Atti del XXX Convegno di Studi Maceratesi, 1994* (Pollenza, MC, 1996), 165–74.

to target new markets at the expense of holding on to the older one in the East or whether instead the shift followed the failure on the latter front as a result of greater competition from other Italian producers, especially from the rapidly rising Venetian industry, which found a major outlet in Levantine markets. As to the silk industry, over the fifteenth century it took more and more of its raw material from Italy itself, and increasingly even from Tuscany, and by the second quarter of the sixteenth century the supply line from the Levant had all but collapsed. In other words, the Middle Eastern market, where manufactured products had been exchanged for raw materials (leaving a favorable trade balance), lost its central importance for the textile industries and hence its only real function in the Florentine network.

Political forces too impinged on trade. On the one hand, French merchants came to have a dominant presence among westerners in trade with the Turks. Rapidly increasing their trade from the 1530s on, they eventually entered into a special relation with the empire that gave them precedence over other Western merchants and also a certain influence in the official authorization for these other merchants even to conduct trade in the empire. On the other hand, the pro-Spanish sympathies of the Medici dukes prejudiced commercial relations with both the French and the sultan, and the foundation of the military order of the Knights of Santo Stefano in 1561, whose activity was centered on galley warfare for the cause of Christianity in the Mediterranean, only worsened the situation. This political policy obviously contradicted ducal efforts to promote commercial interests in the East. Emissaries sent to Constantinople in 1574 met with no success, in part because of the sultan's suspicions about the Knights of Santo Stefano and in part because of opposition by the French. A report requested by the duke in 1577 for the purpose of evaluating the prospect of trade between the two states reflects how the tables had turned in their commercial relations over the preceding half-century. The writer, Filippo Sassetti, a man with some business experience (but little proclivity for it), gives priority to the problem of how to attract Levantine merchants, both Turks and Jews, to Livorno. Only at the end of his report does he add, almost parenthetically, that one advantage of this would be to oblige the Turks to open their markets in turn to Florentine merchants, the implication being that they had little access to them at the time. He concludes, perhaps in resignation, that "in the final analysis it would not be impossible for us to live without any goods that come from the Levant."[104] Even pepper, he observes, presumably the item most in demand, could be imported instead from

[104] "Sul commercio tra la Toscana e le nazioni levantine: Ragionamento di Filippo Sassetti (1577)," in *ASI*, app. 9 (1853), 169–88.

Lisbon. And he could have added that with respect to the other principal goods exported from the Levant, silk and cotton, Florentines had a source for the former closer at hand in Italy itself, and they had no need for the latter. The next year, 1578, Francesco I sent Bongianni Gianfigliazzi to Constantinople to work out some kind of arrangement for merchants, but without notable success. The merchants we know about who still engaged in the Eastern trade, now working out of Livorno—the Riccardi firm made at least twenty trips from 1582 to 1598, and Roberto Pepi, working for the Ricasoli firm, made four trips between 1592 and 1598, serving other firms as well—seem to have focused entirely on Alexandria, not Constantinople, primarily selling silks and buying cotton and spices, paying the difference in gold to settle what had become an unfavorable balance.[105] In 1598, with Livorno now a growing port, Ferdinando I sent a representative to Constantinople to negotiate privileges for Florentine merchants, but this attempt also failed.

One comment Sassetti made in his report indicates how much the situation had changed in the Adriatic as well: he observed that if Levantine merchants were to be attracted to Livorno, they would have to be lured away from Venice, Ragusa, and Ancona. In fact, trade in this area was by this time largely in the hands of merchants from the Ottoman Empire. Official policy of the sultans promoted the interests of native merchants over foreigners, and slowly Turkish, Greek, Albanian, and above all Jewish merchants replaced westerners within the empire and took over much of the foreign trade with Italy. They moved into the major Adriatic ports, especially Ancona, and already in the early sixteenth century, as we have seen, they turned up in Florence as major buyers of cloth, taking the initiative against Florentine exporters on the latter's home turf. In the course of the later sixteenth century Florentine merchants had much less of a presence in both Ancona and Ragusa, in part as a result of this influx of merchants from the Ottoman Empire into Florence itself but also as a result of the increased activity at the port of Livorno.

How much of a presence Florentines continued to have in Venice is another unknown. In the previous century it had lost its centrality both to the Florentine textile industry and to the banking system. It was no longer on the route for the supply of raw wool, and the channel to the source of raw silk in the Levant slowly closed down with the shift of the supply line to southern Italy. Venice also lost its relative importance for the export of both wool and silk cloth to the Levant as a result of the opening of the great urban markets in Rome and Naples and the expanding market in northern Europe for silks and eventually, in the sixteenth

---

[105] Malanima, *I Riccardi,* 68; Litchfield, "Un mercante fiorentino alla corte dei Medici," 730–31.

century, for rascia, the new wool cloth the industry began to produce. The rise of a wool industry in Venice at that time, in fact, was a major force in pushing Florentine products out of Near Eastern markets. Venice was less affected than Genoa by the direct access to shipping facilities Florence gained after the conquest of Pisa and the purchase of Livorno, since it was, after all, not just a port but Europe's major emporium on the Mediterranean, with its own vast hinterland. The development of the overland route from Florence to the Adriatic ports in central Italy, however, circumvented Venice, and already in the course of the fifteenth century the city seems to have become less a commercial than a financial market for the Florentines. Yet that market too lost its centrality in the Florentine banking network with the rise of the exchange fairs in Geneva and then Lyons. Nevertheless, Venice remained a key node in the network as an international bullion market, essential for the balancing of payments with Germany resulting from ecclesiastical transfers in the fifteenth century and, increasingly after the turn of the century, from the expanding markets for silks in central and eastern Europe. Moreover, Florentine merchants still had a role to play in the economic life of this international port city as merchant-bankers who could transfer funds just about anywhere, and they were also major insurers of maritime shipments.

How long Florentines held on to their hegemony in financial services in Venice is unknown. It will be suggested in the next chapter that toward the end of the sixteenth century they were more important than the Genoese in serving the Venetians as bankers dealing in bills drawn on the fairs at Piacenza, controlled by the Genoese. Accounts—still unstudied—survive for Florentines operating in Venice at the end of the century as both merchants and bankers, and at least one company, the Riccardi, represented a major investment there. The nazione was sufficiently large to merit the maintenance of a postal agent on the scene: the new agent, who took up his position there in 1599 and charged the Strozzi, Capponi, Guadagni, and other firms with finding a suitable residence for him, reported back to the grand duke that they wanted him to have a house all to himself so that no one else would know about their business affairs.[106]

[106] Besides account books Florentines kept in Venice that survive in Fiorentine archives, there are unexplored sixteenth-century materials in Venice, referred to by Renzo Pecchioli in "Uomini d'affari fiorentini a Venezia nella seconda metà del Cinquecento: Prime ricerche," in his *Dal "mito" di Venezia all' "ideologia americana": Itinerari e modelli della storiografia sul repubblicanesimo dell'Età Moderna* (Venice, 1983), 74–90. The hint about the Genoese comes from Luciano Pezzolo's review of Mueller's book, "Note sul mercato finanziario a Venezia fra Tre e Cinquecento," *ASI* 157 (1999): 346. On the Riccardi, see Malanima, *I Riccardi*, 62–63, 74. The postal agent's letter is reported in Rita Mazzei, "Il mercante italiano nella città europea fra Cinque e Seicento," in *Le ideologie della città europea dall'Umanesimo al Romanticismo,* ed. Vittorio Conti (Florence, 1993), 281. On the importance of Florentines in the bill market, see Isabella Cecchini, "Piacenza a Venezia: La ricezione delle fiere di cambio di Bisenzone a fine Cinquecento nel mercato del credito lagunare," *Note di Lavoro* (Dipartimento di Scienze Economiche, Università Ca' Foscari di Venezia), no. 18 (2006).

Central Europe

Italian merchants in general, and Florentines in particular, did not penetrate into Germany in large numbers. In the thirteenth century they served the German emperors as their bankers in Italy, and they were also collectors of ecclesiastical revenues in Germany working out of the Champagne fairs and then Bruges. From the later thirteenth through the fourteenth century one can find scattered references to individual Florentines as merchants, local moneylenders, and collectors of customs in various places all across central Europe, from the Rhineland to Vienna, but hardly any firms had branches or even agents in the area. Among the Italians, Florentines seem to have been outnumbered by merchants from Lucca and the upper Po valley, although even these were not very numerous. More than any of the other Italians, however, Florentines went to Germany to administer government mining operations and mints, especially in the metal-rich area extending from the Tyrol in a northeastward arc through Hungary and Bohemia to Poland, but few of them moved from this base into moneylending, banking, and government finance, subjects discussed in chapter 3. In the later thirteenth century Florentine merchants operating out of Venice and Padua, including most notably men from the Frescobaldi and Pegolotti families, moved up the valley of the Adige into the bishopric of Trent and the territory of the counts of the Tyrol, where many became active also as moneylenders, but when the Tyrol passed to the Hapsburgs in the later fourteenth century, German merchants largely replaced Italians in these areas. Germany as a whole, however, was never fully incorporated into the international exchange system, and there were no German cities among the commercial and banking centers for which rates were quoted on the international exchange market dominated by Florentines. Moreover, nothing about conducting trade in the area is to be found in Florentine merchant manuals, the practical handbooks kept for consultation in a firm's offices that provide all kinds of useful information about international commerce anywhere that Florentines did business, from England to the Levant.[107]

It is not difficult to understand why the Florentines did not extend their commercial network into Germany in the early period of expansion. In the first place, the area lay outside the routes of the principal traffic in wool and cloth that drove Florentine ventures abroad. In the second place, the Florentines did not play as important a role in the transfer of ecclesiastical revenues from Germany to Rome as they did elsewhere. They handled a large part of those revenues that were chan-

---

[107] Davidsohn, *Storia di Firenze,* 4, pt. 2:594–616, presents the scattered evidence for the earlier period, to which should be added the later research of Anna Maria Nada Patrone, "Uomini d'affari fiorentini in Tirolo nei secoli XIII e XIV," *ASI* 121 (1963): 166–236.

neled from northern Germany to Bruges, but another important channel passed from the north to Cologne, where the Lucchesi were important bankers, and yet a third passed through Bavaria, completely outside the Florentine network, to Venice. Finally, and above all, the Germans built up their own trading systems, and it was enough for Italians to plug into these at key places of contact along the periphery. In the north the Hanseatic cities, though working through a loose structure, shared a strong common interest in their cartel-like arrangements. Their system extended across the Baltic and North Sea area, and their base in the west, at Bruges, was a major point of exchange with Italian and other merchants. Likewise, German merchants in the southeast, albeit without the same unifying policy, handled the much more valuable trade that grew up around silver shipments to Venice, and there they dealt directly with other Italians. Already in the thirteenth century Nuremberg was at the center of a regional money market that extended northward to the Hanseatic cities, eastward to Prague, and southward to Venice and Milan. It was in this area that the great German banking houses of the Fugger and the Welser of Augsburg emerged to move to center stage on the European banking scene in the sixteenth century. Some German merchants also crossed the Alps to enter Italian markets in both Genoa and Milan, and by the fifteenth century they show up elsewhere in Italy, for example, in the Abruzzi, where they were major purchasers of saffron, used as a dye for their growing fustian industry. Florentines, therefore, had access to well-developed trade networks in Germany through contacts especially at Bruges and Venice, the principal poles in their own network, and, as we know from the Datini materials, at Milan and Genoa. Within Germany there were also points of contact along the major trade artery of the Rhine, above all at Cologne. At the very beginning of the fourteenth century, the Peruzzi had a warehouse in Cologne, and the Macci and Agli operated in the Hapsburg territory of Swabia. From the later fourteenth century on the fairs at Geneva and subsequently at Lyons also served as trade links to central Germany. Although the network did not extend into Germany, the luxury trade with the area was not unimportant. Florentines sold spices and other products from the Near East and their own silks, as well as such items as saffron from the Abruzzi, and they bought nonferrous metals, furs, pelts, and manufactured products, especially linen and metalwork.

With these points of contact in place, therefore, commercial interests rarely led Florentines eastward from the Rhine into central Germany. Before the end of the fifteenth century no German city had a significant Florentine merchant colony, nor does it appear that any firm had a permanent branch in the country for any length of time. In the fifteenth century some big firms took the initiative to make direct contact with Germans at Lübeck, the Hanseatic capital in the north, and at Nuremberg in the southeast, but their primary interest was to facilitate international transfers to their main place of business in either Bruges or Venice and then on to Italy. The nature of this activity, being more financial than commercial, required only a correspondent on the local scene. Thus the Alberti, from a base in Bruges, and the Medici and the Spinelli, from bases in Venice, had agents at one time or another in Cologne, Nuremberg, and Lübeck. In Lübeck both the Medici and Spinelli used the same correspondent. One of these, Gherardo di Niccolò Bueri, was in business there on his own during the first half of the fifteenth century, working sometimes in partnership with Germans and perhaps serving other Italian bankers from abroad as well. The last resident Florentine, Francesco di Filippo Rucellai, left the city no later than 1470. Very few such agents have been documented anywhere in Germany in the fifteenth century, however, and the ones that have, like Bueri and Rucellai, appear isolated from any larger community of fellow Florentines.[108]

A significant community of resident Florentines grew up in Hungary, at Buda, in the last quarter of the fourteenth century. The area came into closer relations with Italy, and with the Florentines in particular, following the establishment of Charles I, a grandson of the Angevin king of Naples, on the throne of Hungary in 1308. Florentines were the first masters of the mint that was established in the 1320s following the opening of the gold mines at Kremnica, in Slovakia, then in the kingdom of Hungary, which became the largest-scale operation of its kind in northern Europe.[109] This newly found wealth stimulated market activity in the kingdom, and during the reign of Louis I (1342–82), who undertook two ventures to Naples to claim the throne, Florentine merchants began to arrive in significant numbers. Their trade consisted principally in the importation of Florentine cloth and the exportation of copper. A few came to serve the king as tax collectors, as administrators of the salt monopoly, and as director of the royal mint with responsibility also for the commercial operation of the area's mines. The first-documented company doing business there was set up in 1373 by Giovanni di Sandro Portinari, a future partner of the Medici, together with Ardingo di Corso Ricci and Cristiano di Migliore Albizzi, both members of major business families. This firm, organized to deal primarily in the cloth trade, worked out of

---

[108] Esch, "Brügge als Umschlagplatz im Zahlungsverkehr Nordeuropas," 125–30, comments on the Florentines in Lübeck. The definitive work on Florentine bankers in Germany down to the end of the fifteenth century is Kurt Weissen, "Florentiner Bankiers und Deutschland (1275 bis 1475): Kontinuität und Diskontinuität wirtschaftlicher Strukturen" (Habilitationsschrift, Basel, 2000), which includes much new research, especially for the fifteenth century. For the fourteenth century, see his "Florentiner Kaufleute in Deutschland bis zum Ende des 14. Jahrhunderts," *Beziehungen, Begegnungen und Konflikte in einem europäischen Kernraum von der Spätantike bis zum 19. Jahrhundert,* ed. Franz Irsigler (Trier, 2006), 363–401.

[109] Peter Spufford, *Power and Profit: The Merchant in Medieval Europe* (London, 2002), 358, 371.

Florence, Perugia, and Venice but soon extended its business to Buda, and it reported extraordinary profits three years later. In his diary Buonaccorso Pitti recounts a trip he made to Buda in 1376, taking with him saffron worth *fl.*1,000; with what he had left of the profits after heavy gambling losses, he bought horses to take back to Italy. In the same year, the government of Florence gained official privileges from the king for its merchants in the country. In 1382 Vieri di Cambio de' Medici opened a branch in Venice to engage in trade with Hungary, especially for the importation of copper to Venice. Filippo Scolari (known as Pippo Spano) arrived sometime in the early 1380s as a factor of a merchant, beginning a career that led to a powerful position at the royal court as a military commander complete with a title of nobility.

When Sigismund of Luxemburg was elected emperor in 1411, Buda became an imperial capital with a court that attracted many Italians, including, from Florence, the architect Manetto Ammanatini, the painter Masolino da Panicale, and the humanist Ambrogio Traversari. The names of twenty-eight persons or companies with residence in Buda have been found in the 1427 catasto. During the reign of Matthias Corvinus (d. 1490), who had an Italian wife, Beatrice of Aragon, the court took on a distinctly Italian flavor, and cultural ties to Florence in particular were strengthened through his commissions to Florentine artists and scribes for the production of manuscripts for his famous library. After the turn of the century there were still many Florentines in the city, to judge from those mentioned in the ledgers the merchant Antonio di Piero Bini kept in Buda from 1501 to 1503. All Italian business there came to an end, however, after the battle of Mohács in 1526 and the subsequent occupation of much of Hungary by the Turks.[110]

In the meantime, beginning in the last quarter of the fifteenth century German markets became more accessible as a result of the development of an integrated system of fairs across Germany in the fifteenth century based on strong regional trade networks centering on the area's many towns. In contrast to the Hanseatic system's greater dependence on basic raw materials, the strong trade in cloth and metals to the south was behind the developments leading to the consolidation of a commercial system within central and eastern Europe, and thereby the greater integration of the area into a wider European system. Toward the end of the fourteenth century southern Germany emerged as a major center of a fustian industry supplying markets all over Europe, including Italy, and in the second half of

[110] Susanna Teke, "Operatori economici fiorentini in Ungheria nel tardo Trecento e primo Quattrocento," *ASI* 153 (1995): 697–707; Bruno Dini, "L'economia fiorentina e l'Europa centro-orientale nelle fonti toscane," in *Saggi,* 271–88 (mostly about Fiorentines in Hungary from 1480 through the early sixteenth century). For the Medici interests in the copper trade, see Wolfgang von Stromer, "Medici-Unternehmen in den Karpatenländern: Versuche zur Beherrschung des Weltmarkts für Buntmetalle," in *Aspetti della vita economica medievale,* 370–97.

the fifteenth century improved technology led to a resurgence of the mining of copper and silver in the Tyrol and central Europe. The commercial system also drew strength from the increased use of overland routes that we have already remarked in explaining the shift from maritime to terrestrial transport from the Low Countries to Italy that saw the rise of Geneva and then Lyons as centers of major trade fairs. In fact, the emergence of cartage firms that organized convoys and utilized improved wagons for this overland trade marked something of another transport revolution. In Germany the most important fairs took place at Frankfurt, the center of trade routes in all directions—westward to the north-south Rhineland axis centering on Cologne and then on to Antwerp, northward to the Hanseatic cities, and eastward to Nuremberg. Nuremberg, with major routes leading to Venice in the south and to Leipzig in the northeast, emerged at this time as a major center of extraregional fairs that extended the system onward to Cracow and eastern Europe. One of the dynamics behind this eastward expansion was the attraction to markets in the East that had been cut off from trade to the Mediterranean through the Black Sea as a result of the Turkish conquests. The measure of this economic vitality can be taken in the rise of the great international merchants and bankers in southern Germany, led by the Fuggers and the Welsers of Augsburg. This new generation of bankers in southeastern Germany, tied to Hapsburg imperial ambitions, largely replaced Florentines in the transfer of ecclesiastical revenues to Rome. Under their auspices Augsburg grew into an international exchange market in the sixteenth century. It remained a secondary market on the periphery of the European system, however, and hardly any foreign merchants, and certainly no Florentines, did business through it.[111]

Greater wealth and a more integrated and active system of fairs attracted Florentines, Lucchesi, Genoese, and other Italians to Germany in search of new outlets for the luxurious products of their growing silk industries. The fairs at Frankfurt, at the center of the German commercial system, became, along with Lyons, one of the biggest markets in northern Europe for silks, largely supplied by Genoese and Lombard merchants crossing the Alps through the Saint Gotthard pass. The Florentines concentrated in Nuremberg, which had direct links to Italy through Venice, to Frankfurt, and to Leipzig and the East. Commercial exchanges between Florence and Nuremberg, mostly metal- and silverwork from Germany and silks from Florence, have been documented in the 1460s. The first Florentine on record to show up in the city, in 1471, was Benvenuto di Daddo

[111] Pierre Jeannin, *Change, crédit et circulation monétaire à Augsbourg au milieu du 16e siècle* (Paris, 2001).

Aldobrandi, sent by Guasparre di Niccodemo Spinelli, nephew of the great banker Tommaso Spinelli. Others followed almost immediately, and it would seem that many of the firms that became active there grew out of ventures by new men, not members of established merchant-banking families. They operated on a large scale and dealt almost exclusively in silks.[112]

The two firms for which business records survive, the Saliti and the Olivieri, were both newcomers to the higher ranks in Florentine business circles. Zanobi di Francesco Saliti seems to have had a commercial firm of indeterminate nature in the 1490s. In 1512 he invested *fl.*400 in an accomandita contract for trade in Germany, and in the following years his sons Bernardo and Piero were active in Nuremberg. In 1515 Bernardo was associated with Bernardo Acciaiuoli & Partners, and three years later this firm, with a capital of *fl.*6,500, carried his name as a partner. In 1519 this new firm had an inventory of silk worth about *fl.*17,000. At some point in the following years the Saliti organized their own company, and when Zanobi died in 1526, Piero Saliti & Partners, as the company was then called, had a capital of *fl.*14,000, all of which was in Zanobi's name. Ten years later, in 1536, Piero Saliti was still in Nuremberg, but now as a partner in Gherardo Bartolini & Partners of Florence in charge of sales of silks sent from Florence. With a capital of *fl.*24,000, this was a major firm, and it belonged to a well-established international banking family.[113]

Giovanni di Piero Olivieri, a slightly later contemporary of the Saliti, was another newcomer who made his career in Nuremberg. He started out in Florence working for Paolo and Amadio Del Giocondo & Partners, probably setaioli, but he must still have been very young in 1521, when he is first documented in Nuremberg as an employee with a salary of only 25 Rhenish florins (a money worth about three-fourths of a Florentine florin) in Raffaello and Ridolfo Torrigiani & Partners. Over the next three years his salary rose to 70 Rhenish florins, and in 1526 he became a partner. In 1541 Giovanni returned to Florence, where he and a cousin organized their own company. This company, along with the Neapolitan company of another cousin, went into partnership with two others to set up a

---

[112] Kurt Weissen, "I mercanti italiani e le fiere in Europa centrale alla fine del Medioevo e agli inizi dell'Età Moderna," in *La pratica dello scambio: Sistemi di fiere, mercanti e città in Europa (1400–1700)*, ed. Paola Lanaro (Venice, 2003), 161–76, offers an overview of the arrival of Italians, and above all Florentines, in Germany at this time and of their activity in the numerous fairs of the region; and Lorenz Böninger, *Die deutsche Einwanderung nach Florenz im Spätmittelalter* (Leiden, 2006), 266–71, provides the earliest evidence of the involvement of Nuremberg merchants in commercial exchange between the two cities.

[113] Marco Spallanzani, "Le compagnie Saliti a Norimberga nella prima metà del Cinquecento (un primo contributo dagli archivi fiorentini)," in *Wirtschaftskräfte und Wirtschaftswege: Festschrift für Hermann Kellenbenz*, ed. Jürgen Schneider (Nuremberg, 1978), 1:603–20; idem, "Tessuti di seta fiorentini per il mercato di Norimberga intorno al 1520," in *Studi in memoria di Giovanni Cassandro*, 3:995–1016.

third company in Nuremberg that had a capital of 10,500 Rhenish florins. This interlocking company structure, a part of the Olivieri cluster of firms mentioned in chapter 1, was in large part organized around the silk trade: the Neapolitan firm supplied raw silk to the Florentine firm, which sold most of the silk to local setaioli and then bought finished silks, which it sent, along with some raw silk, to the firm in Nuremberg for sale. The firm in Florence engaged only in trade, not in production.[114]

Neither the Saliti nor the Olivieri remained in business at Nuremberg beyond one generation. The family most prominent for longevity in the city was the Torrigiani, another family that emerged from modest origins, although not altogether unknown in the fifteenth century. In 1515 Raffaello di Luca Torrigiani had a company in Florence with his brother Ridolfo and was also a partner in Alessandro Antinori, Iacopo Bettoni & Partners in Nuremberg; by 1521 he and his brother were operating on their own there. Their descendants carried on the business for four more generations, into the seventeenth century. Meanwhile, back in Tuscany they set up silk shops in Florence, Lucca, and Pisa, presumably to supply their German outlet. They also had a bank in Florence.[115]

The opening of markets in Germany presented opportunities to a new generation of entrepreneurs who came from outside the traditional business class. The Torrigiani, the Saliti, the Olivieri, and most of the other merchants who rode this wave of commercial expansion into Germany and eastern Europe in the sixteenth century—the Chiaro, the Leri, the Montelupi, the Sini, the Talducci, the Viviani—emerge out of economic and social anonymity. Their names do not appear in the lists of the city's ruling class during the fifteenth century as defined by officeholding and tax status.[116] Firms of established business families, such as the aforementioned Acciaiuoli, Antinori, and Bartolini firms, were also present, but they by no means dominated the scene in either size or number. For their part, German merchants were not unaware of the profits to be made in these markets, and by the last quarter of the sixteenth century they were going to Florence to buy. The ledger of Baccio Martelli, Pierfrancesco Del Giocondo & Partners, setaioli, open from 1584 to 1591, records sales to seven German firms in the city.[117]

Florentines in Nuremberg dealt almost exclusively in silk; given the size of their firms, this new market must have become a major outlet for the home in-

[114] Francesco Guidi Bruscoli, "Drappi di seta e tele di lino tra Firenze e Norimberga nella prima metà del Cinquecento," *ASI* 159 (2001): 359–94.

[115] Rita Mazzei, *Itinera mercatorum: Circolazione di uomini e beni nell'Europa centro-orientale, 1550–1650* (Lucca, 1999), 59–72.

[116] Compare the many names that appear in the text of Mazzei, *Itinera mercatorum*, with those on the list of the "Florentine ruling class" in Anthony Molho, *Marriage Alliance in Late Medieval Florence* (Cambridge, MA, 1994), app. 3.

[117] ASF, Archivio Martelli, 165 (utilized in my unpublished study of this firm).

dustry. The 1519 inventory of Acciaiuoli, Saliti & Partners shows that the firm had 5,544 meters of silk textiles in stock, eight times the average annual production of the weaver with the largest shop in Florence in these very years, Iacopo di Tedesco (of whom more later), who at times had as many as twenty-five looms working. Since silks came in an infinitely greater variety than wool cloth and cost much more, merchants had to be especially attentive to a highly variable demand. A design, along with a description, survives that a merchant in Frankfurt sent back to Florence in 1555 to indicate the kind of fabric that sold well in that market.[118] In exchange for silks there was little that Florentines wanted, certainly nothing of comparable value. They sent back inexpensive cotton, linen, and hemp cloth, skins and pelts, metalwork, and even horses, but at the end of the day they balanced their accounts with bullion—copper, silver, and even gold.[119] Firms in Nuremberg worked through a network that extended to all the major fairs in Germany and eastern Europe. A balance of the Saliti firm lists debtors from Augsburg, Frankfurt, Cologne, Lübeck, Deventer, Breslau, and Bratislava; and the Torrigiani had clients also in Basel, Halle, Hamburg, Leipzig, and Prague. Firms outside of Germany did business with the same cities: in the later sixteenth century the Riccardi, in Florence, had correspondents in Cologne, Frankfurt, Augsburg, and Nuremberg, and Francesco Cambi & Partners, in Antwerp, worked through agents in Hamburg as well as these other cities.[120] Nuremberg remained the major residential base in Germany, and although firms might send out agents to these other places, this secondary network was, for the most part, in German hands.

In the second half of the sixteenth century Italians established another base for the sale of silks in Cracow, and of the ninety-six merchants who became citizens there from 1550 to 1650 twenty-six were Florentines. A leading figure was Bernardo Soderini, one of the relatively few merchants who came from an old business family. Being able to guarantee large loans through his banking contacts at Lyons, Soderini played a decisive role in the election of Henry of Valois, the son of Catherine de' Medici, to his brief occupation of the Polish throne in 1573. The richest and most influential of these Florentines in Poland was Sebastiano Montelupi, another new man. Montelupi started out as a partner of Soderini's but eventually struck out on his own, having established lucrative personal relations with the king. On his death in 1600 he left an estate worth *fl.*150,000, including

---

[118] Spallanzani, "Le compagnie Saliti."

[119] Guidi Bruscoli, "Drappi di seta," 375–76, 386, cites shipment of gold by the Olivieri company in the 1540s.

[120] Malanima, *I Riccardi*, 69, 97–98; Valentin Vasquez de Prada, *Lettres marchandes d'Anvers* (Paris, 1960), 1:196 (Cambi).

property in Poland worth *sc.*70,000.[121] It would seem that at the end of the sixteenth century Florentine merchants were doing as lively a commercial business in Germany, northeastern Europe, and the Baltic as anywhere else. The increasing number of initiatives for business in the area taken through accomandita contracts from 1591 to 1615 confirms this impression.[122] Subsequently, however, the number of these contracts fell off. The Florentine colony in Cracow, once the largest in the city, began to shrink, and by the 1630s merchants from both Lucca and the Veneto far outnumbered the Florentines.

Much of the demand in Poland for silks and other luxury goods came from landlords whose incomes rose in the course of the later sixteenth century as a result of the growing market in western Europe for grain from their vast estates. Some of this grain went also to the Mediterranean, and this new supply line became increasingly important for Italian states confronted with an ever-growing population, especially in moments of bad local harvests. Feeling such pressures in the later 1580s, the grand-ducal government of Tuscany made a major initiative in 1590 to procure grain from the Baltic to be delivered to Livorno, and over the following years it sent agents to Danzig and Hamburg to make the arrangements. Hence this new market attracted yet other merchants to Poland, including Venetians and Genoese as well as Florentines.[123] By the second quarter of the seventeenth century, however, Amsterdam had moved into position as the central intermediate market for the grain trade between the Baltic and the Mediterranean. Yet, if this Dutch system usurped the role of Florentine merchants in Poland, it also regularized the grain trade to the advantage of the Tuscan port of Livorno.[124]

---

[121] Mazzei, *Itinera mercatorum*, esp. ch. 3, offers a full account of the Tuscan merchants in Poland.

[122] Maurice Carmona, "Aspects du capitalisme toscan aux XVIe et XVIIe siècles: Les sociétés en commandite à Florence et à Lucques," *Revue d'histoire moderne et contemporaine* 11 (1964): 98–99.

[123] Mazzei, *Itinera mercatorum*, 348–63. Litchfield, "Un mercante fiorentino alla corte dei Medici," 727–81, publishes the diary of one merchant who made the trip to Poland in 1606–7.

[124] For the subsequent history of Florentines in Poland, see Rita Mazzei, *Traffici e uomini d'affari italiani in Polonia nel Seicento* (Milan, 1983); and idem, *La trama nascosta: Storie di mercanti e altro (secoli XVI–XVII)* (Viterbo, 2006).

CHAPTER THREE

Banking and Finance

Banking: *Deposits and Loans, International Transfer and
Exchange, The Bill of Exchange as Credit Instrument.*
The International Exchange Market.
Government Finance: *Loans to Rulers, Risks, The Papacy,
Competition and Innovation in the Sixteenth Century.*

The first impulse for going abroad may have been trade, but Florentine merchants also engaged in activities that mark the emergence of international banking and finance. Given the extent of their network ties with fellow citizens all over Europe, they were in a better position than anyone else to transfer funds as well as goods from one place to another and thereby effect exchange from one money to another. The network thus served as a channel through which the merchant could extend trade beyond the confines of commerce in goods to include also the traffic in money, that is, transfer, exchange, and arbitrage in the international money market. Moreover, given the imperfect balance of trade in regional and local markets throughout the system, merchants often found themselves momentarily either with surplus funds or without enough cash on hand; these monetary exigencies in the local market induced them to find ways to put available capital to work or to search for additional capital. On the one hand, they were ready to loan out any surplus funds at interest to borrowers of all kinds, especially to feudal nobles and ecclesiastical institutions, whose landed wealth limited liquidity, and to governments, both urban and princely, whose tax-collecting mechanisms were slow and inefficient and whose financial administration was often makeshift at best. On the other hand, to supplement working capital, they attracted interest-bearing deposits from these same people, who had few alternative investment outlets for any surplus funds they happened to have. This trafficking in both the international money market and the local credit market transformed the merchant into a banker. Moreover, offering their services to governments, some moved into the political sphere to become financiers. Commerce, banking, and government finance were thus complementary activities, often involving the same entrepreneurs and overlapping in many ways.

The early history of banking is written around the activity of the Genoese, the Sienese, the Lucchesi, and men from other towns in Tuscany and in the upper Po valley, from Piacenza to Asti. Surviving documents from Florence do not allow us to introduce Florentines into this history until later. The Florentine international merchant-banker operating on a grand scale who first emerges most clearly from this shadowy past is Clarissimo Falconieri, who had a company with his sons.[1] A document of 1243 records an exchange transaction he effected between Bologna and the fair at Troyes, in northern France, and a papal document of 1264 identifies him as having been active for some sixty years as a major importer of wool cloth from northern Europe, probably for finishing in Florence. He also had an agent in Rome. English documents from the late 1270s record loans made to the king by the Frescobaldi, Cerchi, Bardi, and Falconieri firms and deposits of papal taxes with a number of Italian firms, including the Cerchi, the Mozzi, the Pucci, and the Rimbertini from Florence.[2] In fact, since private business papers before 1300 survive only in fragments, our earliest glimpses of Florentine entrepreneurs abroad in the later thirteenth century come not from Florentine sources but from government records of the places abroad where they operated that document their international transfer of funds, loans, and fiscal services.

Banking

Florence enjoys a preeminent role in the history of late medieval banking. The frequent appearance of Florentine bankers outside their sphere of business and in more visible arenas of human affairs, notably as financial advisers to princes and as patrons of art, has added a certain luster to the subject. For all their fame as politicians and patrons, the Medici are always remembered as bankers too, and their rise from bankers to popes and princes has given a special aura to the history of Florentine banking. Yet the internal history of late medieval banking in general, which has necessarily been written chiefly on the evidence of Florentine materials, is not without its own aura, created by the business historian, who, largely focusing on business techniques and anxious to find the earliest examples

---

[1] Elisabetta Gigli, "Operatori economici fiorentini a cavallo del primo popolo: Intorno alla *societas filiorum Falconerii*," in *Studi sulla società e le culture del Medioevo per Girolamo Araldi*, ed. L. Gatti (Rome, 2002), 1:229–43.

[2] Armando Sapori, "La compagnia dei Frescobaldi," in *Studi di storia economica: Secoli XIII, XIV, XV*, 3 vols. (Florence, 1955–67), 2:860–61.

of modern practice, has more often than not been inspired by the technologist's confidence in progress.

Commerce and banking went hand and hand. Merchants in the very nature of their activity with one another performed several banking functions, and the instrument fundamental to their business through which they did this was accounting. They needed an accounting system to gain some central control over operations that were geographically far-flung and long protracted. In the normal course of keeping track of their activities, they opened current accounts in the names of their clients and transferred debits and credits by simple book entry; given the temporal and spatial dimensions of international commerce, these accounting practices facilitated credit and exchange operations. Merchants extended short-term credit on their clients' current accounts by allowing overdrafts, and through mere book transfer they effected payments abroad in different centers of trade and shifted debits and credits from one place to another in various monetary areas. They also extended and received credit through agreements concerning delayed payment for goods consigned. Thus they allowed time to pay for the raw materials consigned to producers of wool and silk cloth in Florence, just as they, in turn, were given time to pay for finished cloth consigned to them by these producers. The period allowed for payment could be as long as a year, and the interest charged was disguised in a discount granted for payment in advance of the due date. Federigo Melis, who more than any other scholar studied this subject of business credit—which he called *credito di esercizio*—has shown how important this kind of credit was in the day-to-day operations of merchants at the end of the fourteenth century.[3] Nevertheless, as important as they were in thus facilitating liquidity for the conduct of business, these credit and exchange operations did not make a merchant a banker. He came closer to that function when he advanced beyond these business arrangements with clients to offer his services to people outside the commercial sector, a trajectory he followed almost from the beginning.

Deposits and Loans

In theory a primary function of a bank is to channel savings, or surplus funds in the hands of private persons, into investment. It has various devices for attracting capital and then loaning it out, but it does this in such a way that it can extend credit beyond the cash reserves it has on hand at any one time, thereby increasing

[3] Federigo Melis, "La grande conquista trecentesca del 'credito di esercizio' e la tipologia dei suoi strumenti fino al XVI secolo," in Melis, *La banca pisana e le origini della banca moderna,* ed. Marco Spallanzani (Florence, 1987), 307–24.

the supply of money. At the point where the merchant begins to make direct loans beyond his commercial operations and needs to attract additional capital to be able to do this, he is entering into banking. This banking function becomes significant when he goes beyond the original capital invested in a firm—what at the time was called the *corpo* of the firm—and its undistributed profits, representing investors' savings, to seek the unutilized funds of other people. In theory the principal, defining source of a bank's capital is not its corpo but the deposits made by people outside the partnership, and indeed deposits are so essential to the business of a bank that founders of a bank do not necessarily have to put up any capital at all. Attracting deposits from some and extending credit to others, the merchant performed the economic function of an intermediary, channeling passive wealth into active use and increasing the money supply in the process, thereby becoming a banker in the essential sense of that activity. The route to offering these banking services was well charted by the thirteenth century, and some entrepreneurs became full-time financiers and moneylenders—in other words, bankers in the full sense of the term.

The principal instrument used by the banker to attract other people's savings, so that he could make them available to yet other people, was the interest-bearing, short-term time deposit, something like a modern certificate of deposit. He raised some funds from depositors in the home market at Florence, but he had much greater opportunities in his branches at places abroad where rich nobles and clerics were attracted by the possibility of having a secure place for liquid funds as well as a central treasury for temporary deposits out of which they could make payments without risk. In the last quarter of the thirteenth century princely depositors with Florentine banks included the Marchese d'Este, the Marchese Malaspina, the Duke and Count of Carinthia and the Tyrol, the Count Palatinate of Modigliano, the prior of the Knights Hospitalers of Corsica and Sardinia, and the sons of Guido Della Torre, lord of Milan.[4] In England one man alone, Hugh Despenser the Younger, a close adviser to Edward II and possibly the most powerful man in the country, deposited no less than £9,930 sterling with the Bardi and the Peruzzi over the last years of his life, from 1321 to 1326. Although these apparently were not long-term deposits, they provided the firms at least temporarily with the equivalent of more than *fl.*30,000, about a third of the corpo of the Peruzzi company at the time and more than what it received from the collection of papal revenues.[5]

[4] Robert Davidsohn, *Storia di Firenze* (Florence, 1956), 4, pt. 2:398–401.
[5] Edmund Fryde, "The Deposits of Hugh Despenser the Younger with Italian Bankers," *Economic History Review* 70 (1955): 344–62, reprinted in his *Studies in Medieval Trade and Finance* (London, 1983). According to Fryde, there is no evidence of interest payments on these deposits.

The most detailed information about deposits from outside Florence comes from the Medici company a century later. In 1427 the branch in Rome had twelve depositors with a total of *fl.*55,480 *di camera,* and the Venetian branch had *du.*9,300 in deposits, some of which came from people far from Venice, for example, *du.*4,000 from a woman in Bologna and *du.*1,050 from a German. In 1459–60 deposits in the Milan branch included more than *fl.*15,000 from just two men, the duke's chancellor and another favorite. In 1467 the Medici branch in Lyons had *sc.*42,000 from only nineteen depositors. When the family went into exile in 1494, one of the bank's most famous depositors, Philippe de Commines, had nearly 25,000 écus on deposit—of which he lost about 8,000 écus—an amount that exceeded the corpo of all but a very few Florentine international banks. The bank's various branches raised more from deposits than it had in partners' equity—twice as much in Milan, three times as much in Lyons, more than four times the corpo of all branches combined in Rome. In fact, in 1427 the Roman branch, with deposits amounting to almost *fl.*100,000 *di camera* (including nearly *fl.*25,000 from the papal treasury), had no need of investment capital from its partners, so easy was it to attract savings from the rich in one of the most rapidly growing cities in Italy at the time.[6] Florentine bankers could hardly have raised capital of this magnitude at home.

Complementing the merchant's acceptance of deposits was his lending of money. From the very beginning of their venture abroad beyond the Alps, Italian merchants everywhere advanced loans to what at the time might be considered the general public, and some made this their major activity. One of the earliest indications of the presence of Florentines in northern Europe is the appearance of an unnamed but "esteemed citizen of Florence" as a creditor on a 1244 inventory of the debts of the Flemish countess Jeanne de Constantinople, where his credit of £2,100 *parisis* ranks the highest after that of the Knights Templar of Paris.[7] The earliest ledger documenting loans of this kind is that of the Sienese firm of Ugolino and Gentile di Ugolino Ugolini, open from 1255 to 1262, recording the firm's activity at the Champagne fairs. The company made 312 loans, most ranging from several to fifty *livres provinois* and a few reaching as high as several hundred *livres;* the borrowers included everyone from artisans to local nobles and clerics (loans to the latter were shared with other operators).[8] Rates of interest

---

[6] Raymond de Roover, *The Rise and Decline of the Medici Bank, 1397–1494* (Cambridge, MA, 1963), 102–7, 208, 267, 295. The Cambini bank had deposits from, and made loans to, ecclesiastics and other persons of high rank at the papal court. Sergio Tognetti, *Il banco Cambini: Affari e mercati di una compagnia mercantile-bancaria nella Firenze del XV secolo* (Florence, 1999), 199.

[7] Wim Blockmans, "Financiers italiens et flamands aux XIIIe–XIVe siècles," in *Aspetti della vita economica medievale* (Florence, 1985), 196.

[8] Michele Cassandro, "La banca senese nei secoli XIII e XIV," in *Banchieri e mercanti di Siena,* by Franco Cardini et al. (Siena, 1987), 134–42.

reached as high as 40–50 percent, but whether such rates are an index to profits or to the risks involved, especially from default, is not clear. Robert Davidsohn, who examined the few surviving lists of debtors of the Bardi company from the second decade of the fourteenth century, was impressed by how many people of all ranks and from every country he found thereon, from the kings of England, Naples, and Cyprus, the Grand Master of the Knights of Rhodes, cardinals, prelates, monasteries, and the landed nobility down to a Jew, a broker, a hosteller, and a *buffone*.[9]

The Champagne fairs were a central place that originally attracted Italian merchants who also engaged in moneylending. From there they spread throughout France and into the Low Countries and England, where they replaced the Jews. Many of these men, especially those who were from Lombardy or the Piedmont, operated primarily as petty pawnbrokers, alternating travel abroad with long stays at home. Locally called Lombards, because many of them came from the upper Po valley, many were in fact Genoese and Tuscans, including Florentines, such as "Zino the Lombard from Florence," who resided in Mainz in the early fourteenth century.[10] Some, especially the Tuscans, increased the scale of their operations by organizing partnerships, accumulating capital, and establishing a base abroad. Some Florentines organized firms that, in fact, engaged principally in lending money, not in commercial activity. A ledger documenting exclusively this kind of activity survives for the Avignon firm of Iacopo Girolami and Tommaso Corbizzi: from 1332 to 1337 they extended loans of from a few florins to several thousand, at rates ranging from 18 percent to 60 percent, to other Florentines in the city, as well as to a clientele comprising the complete array of local nobles, knights, clerics, ecclesiastical institutions, and court officials to be found in the papal capital.[11] Florentines, however, by no means dominated this activity. In a census of Italian companies made for the French king in 1303–4 they numbered only eight out of the sixty-four on the list, falling well behind the Genoese, with twenty-five, and the Lucchesi and the Piacentini, with ten each.[12] The term *Lombard*, in short, no more implied a distinction between petty moneylenders

[9] Quoted, with the publication of a new document, in Marco Spallanzani, "Una carta inedita della compagnia Bardi (ca. 1316–1320)," in *La storia e l'economia: Miscellanea di studi in onore di Giorgio Mori* (Varese, 2003), 1:695.

[10] Davidsohn, *Storia di Firenze*, 4, pt. 2:598.

[11] *Il libro vermiglio di corte di Roma e di Avignone del segnale del C, della compagnia di Iacopo Girolami e Tommaso Corbizzi, 1332–1337*, ed. Mario Chiaudano (Florence, 1963); Armando Sapori, "Una compagnia di prestatori fiorentini ad Avignone nella prima metà del Trecento," in his *Studi*, 3:101–19.

[12] Robert-Henry Bautier, "I lombardi e i problemi del credito nel regno di Francia nei secoli XIII e XIV," in *L'uomo del banco dei pegni: "Lombardi" e mercato del denaro nell'Europa medievale*, ed. Renato Bordone (Turin, 1994), 44–45; Antonio Battistella, *I toscani in Friuli e un episodio della guerra degli Otto Santi* (Bologna, 1898), 55–56.

and merchant-bankers than it designated the specific part of Italy these men came from.

Lombard became a term of deprecation with the widespread increase in strong antiusury sentiment directed against them, fired by social and economic resentment as well as religious zeal. One Florentine moneylender, Castello Gianfigliazzi (d. ca. 1300), whose family firm operated in Provence and the Dauphiné, ended up in the seventh circle of Dante's hell, where he was spotted amidst the flames along with other usurers, their tear-filled eyes destined to feed forever on the personally marked moneybags hanging around their necks (*Inferno* 17).[13] Over the decades from the 1240s to the 1260s Italians were repeatedly expelled from England for their usurious practices. Likewise the French kings, especially Philip the Fair (1285–1314), issued ordinances to limit their practice and impose fines on them, and in 1291 he had all Italian merchants arrested on the charge of usury, and their goods sequestered. In Friuli, the patriarch Raimondo Della Torre, wanting to rid his state of usurers, issued a decree in 1298 ordering all Tuscans to leave Gemona within a week, but it never took effect, probably because they were indispensable both to the general public and to the patriarch himself.

In fact, for these rulers, as indeed in Florence itself, as we shall see, the usury restriction was a useful excuse for imposing fines on moneylenders, and in the end these occasional but continuing extortions amounted to little more than a fee for a license to practice. In the late thirteenth century the Count of Tyrol licensed Italian moneylenders as, in effect, public officials who operated pawn banks for the population in general. In return for annual payment *(census)* to the count, the moneylender received a contract that, on the one hand, gave him monopoly privileges and certain immunities within a defined area and, on the other hand, laid down the rules for his sale of pawns, his right to sequester goods of debtors, procedures arising from claims of heirs and the right of appeal, but rarely set the rate of interest. Contracts could run for one to six years, and Florentines held many of the earliest ones, dating from before 1300, for Trent, Bolzano, Merano, Gries, Innsbruck, and other places. A public pawn bank of this kind, taking its name from the contract, was called a "money house" (*casana,* a fusion of words meaning "house" and "pile of money"). A similar institution in Friuli, where Florentines were also active as pawnbrokers, was called a "mountain of pawns" (*monte di pegni*).[14] Florentines, many of them political exiles, were also active as merchants and above all as moneylenders in Trieste and Istrian towns to the south beginning in the late thirteenth century. As moneylenders some had public

[13] Armando Sapori, "Le compagnie bancarie dei Gianfigliazzi," in his *Studi,* II, 927–73.

[14] Anna Maria Nada Patrone, "Uomini d'affari fiorentini in Tirolo nei secoli XIII e XIV," *Archivio storico italiano* (hereafter ASI) 121 (1963): 166–236.

contracts, and others worked on their own. Beginning in 1338 Trieste took legislative action against them, and by midcentury almost all of them were gone, replaced by Jews, but when the city set up a public lending bank in 1359, its first director was a longtime Florentine resident.[15]

International Transfer and Exchange

Given the risks of travel and the problem of different moneys in different markets, the merchant preferred not to handle specie for buying and selling goods abroad. A basic device, used especially in markets where he was trading one principal product for another, was counterexchange. The merchant exchanged goods for others in countertrade—so much wool cloth for so much raw silk—on the basis of monetary values assigned to each kind of good, a stage of exchange that removes this practice from mere barter, with which it is often confused. To the extent that he found himself with a favorable balance, in either cash or credit, he often preferred to use it to buy anything else in the market that he might be able to export. Hence a merchant who dealt in the staples of Florentine trade, buying raw wool and silk and selling finished cloth, found himself dealing on the side in the myriad products that are found in any merchant manual. The development of the techniques of transferring credit from one place to another to avoid cash shipments, however, freed Italians merchants from these narrow confines of a relatively undeveloped trading system. They did this primarily through two instruments, accounting and the bill of exchange.

With an accounting system that allowed them to transfer debits and credits through book entry on clients' accounts, regardless of the place of business and the moneys involved, merchants could send orders of payment to their agents in different places and effect the exchange on their books. The most complete merchant's archive to survive from the fourteenth and fifteenth centuries, that of Francesco Datini (d. 1410), has ledgers from all his many branches abroad that document how this was done at every step in an international transaction, even of the most petty kind. For example, in 1399 the Florentine merchant Inghilese di Inghilese placed an order with the Datini firm in Barcelona for ceramics from Valencia (which cost only *fl.*2½) that he wanted to sell in Genoa. The Datini agent in Valencia handled the order with the potter and the shipment of the ceramics to the company branch in Barcelona, where Inghilese's account was debited for all the relevant expenses, including charges for shipment to the Datini

---

[15] Camillo De Franceschi, *Esuli fiorentini della compagnia di Dante: Mercanti e prestatori a Trieste e in Istria* (Venice, 1939), reprinted from *Archivio veneto*.

agent in Genoa. The Datini agent in Genoa, in turn, debited Inghilese's account on his books but then credited the account for the sale of the ceramics there, which the company effected for him. The Datini books in Spain were kept in *lire di Barcelona*, those in Genoa in *lire genovine*, and any accounts Inghilese kept in Florence would have been in florins.[16] The exchange between these two foreign moneys for a transaction was thus handled as a bookkeeping operation requiring only orders of payments within one business organization; sometimes the rates of exchange are included in the entry, but often not.

Accounting worked only within the limited circle of a merchant's personal network of business relations with other merchants, Florentine or not. If transactions required going beyond the network of a single firm, a merchant could use bills of exchange to transfer funds from one place to another through his contacts with other Florentine firms. The bill of exchange was more complex than the simple order of payment. Whereas the latter was an internal instrument, directed by a merchant to his correspondent abroad to make a payment on his behalf, the bill of exchange evolved from a notarized letter to a party outside his firm in which he recognized receipt of funds and promised to pay them back elsewhere in the money of that place where he had a credit balance. By the fourteenth century the instrument had freed itself from the notarial encumbrance and shed the form of a letter to become a formulaic bill issued by a merchant on receipt of funds in one money that the purchaser of the bill could send to someone abroad for collection in the money of that place from the agent of the issuer. Thus, merchant A in Florence wanting to make a payment in sterling to B in London could pay florins to merchant C in Florence to have a bill payable in sterling that he could then send to B in London for collection from C′, C's correspondent there. C issues the bill, drawing on C′ to make the payment, gives it to A, who sends it to B, who in turn takes it to C′ for payment (see fig. 3.1). In the language of the instrument, A (the buyer of the bill) is the *remitter* in Florence, who wants to remit to London; C (the seller of the bill) is the *drawer* in Florence, who drafts the bill, drawing on his credit with C′ in London; C′ is the *drawee* in London; and B is the *beneficiary*. With reference to the actual transmission of money, the terms are, respectively, *deliverer, taker, payer,* and *payee*.

A ledger of the firm of Filippo Strozzi (d. 1491) in Naples provides examples of transfers by both orders of payment and bills of exchange outside of a single business organization: the Strozzi firm in Florence instructs its office in Naples to make a payment to a party in Palermo with a credit it has with a party in Avignon;

---

[16] Marco Spallanzani, *Maioliche ispano-moresche a Firenze nel Rinascimento* (Florence, 2006), 365–67.

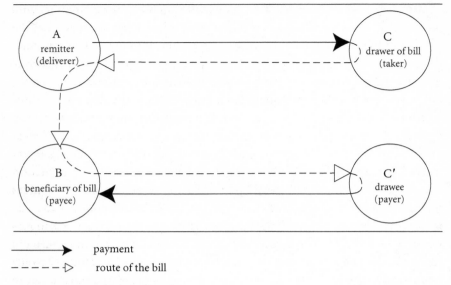

Figure 3.1 The bill of exchange

the Strozzi firm in Naples receives instructions from a party in Valencia to make a payment to a party in Rome and does so by going through the Medici bank in Naples and Rome; wanting to make a payment to a party in Valencia, the Strozzi firm in Naples orders the office in Rome to order a party in Palermo with whom it has a credit to transfer that credit to Valencia for payment; a party in L'Aquila loans money to a German there, who, by agreement, pays it back by ordering a party in Florence to pay the Strozzi office in Florence, but then the party in L'Aquila requests the firm in Naples to transfer the credit there.[17] All these payments involve book transfers and payments in different moneys requiring simple orders of payment or bills of exchange (although in these instances, as is usually the case—and in contrast to the Datini documentation—we have only the evidence from the Strozzi ledger in just one place). Both instruments served to minimize the physical transfer of money for international commercial transactions, an expensive and risky operation. With them, merchants could shift debits and credits between different firms throughout the entire European theater of operations, thereby balancing profits in one place against losses in others in the ongoing effort to avoid shipment of specie.

[17] The examples are from Alfonso Leone, "Some Preliminary Remarks on the Study of Foreign Currency Exchange in the Medieval Period," *Journal of European Economic History* 12 (1983): 619–30.

The bill of exchange, in short, was the device with which the Florentines built the unique commercial and banking system that bound them together. They did not have a monopoly, however, contrary to what one finds in much of the literature. The early history of exchange instruments, in fact, is written on the basis of Genoese, not Florentine, materials dating from the thirteenth century, and the bill first emerged in the practice of Italian merchants at the Champagne fairs, where there is little documentation of a Florentine presence. Merchants from other Italian cities, especially the Genoese and the Lucchesi, engaged in international exchange, and they and the Florentines all sent bills through one another when it was convenient. For example, the ledgers of the Alberti of the "nuovi" branch in the 1350s record many exchange transactions effected by Florentines through Genoese colleagues. Moreover, merchants from these other places had their own networks, through which they could operate without recourse to Florentines. According to two surviving ledgers of the Spinola kept in Granada in the 1440s and 1450s, this great Genoese merchant family had recourse to only two Florentines—Francesco di Nerone in Pisa and Clemente degli Albizzi in Venice—for its traffic in wool cloth, raw silk, sugar, dried fruit, and other merchandise over routes that extended to England and Bruges in the north and to Genoa and other ports in the western Mediterranean.[18] Likewise, the Venetian merchant Andrea Barbarigo, documented by accounts for the second quarter of the fifteenth century, conducted his commercial and exchange operations with London, Bruges, and Valencia, all within the Florentine system, through other Venetians.[19] Since the Florentines had by far the most far-flung and densest network in Europe, they were predominant in the international money market through the fourteenth and fifteenth centuries, but they did not control it.

The formal nature of the bill contrasts with another instrument merchants used to transfer money from one place to another: letters of credit to travelers and pilgrims. In the early period of the Crusades the military order of the Knights Templar played an important role in international transfer in the service of pilgrims and crusaders. The order had houses along the principal routes of these travelers, and it was prepared both to transfer and to store funds for them. By the thirteenth century, however, Italian merchant-bankers were performing this function for society in general. The merchant issued a letter of credit, addressed to an agent abroad, to travelers who on departure consigned money to him; they

[18] Adela Fábergas García, *La familia Spinola en el reino nazarí de Granada: Contabilidad privada de Francesco Spinola (1451–1457)* (Granada, 2004), 48. Cf. idem, *Un mercader genovés en el reino de Granada: El libro de cuentas de Agostino Spinola (1441–1447)* (Granada, 2002).

[19] Frederic C. Lane, *Andrea Barbarigo, Merchant of Venice, 1418–1449* (Baltimore, 1944), 25, 113–14, 127, 129–30. Notwithstanding the large resident community of Florentines in Venice, virtually none except the Medici surface in Lane's text.

could then collect the money along the way during their journey or at their destination by presenting the letter to the agent. One such general letter, valid in three different places, was purchased by a member of the pope's household staff, Diego Diaz, before leaving Rome for a trip home to Lisbon. On 19 January 1454 he ordered the bank of Tommaso Spinelli to pay the Cambini bank for the "lettera ginerale" of credit that could be honored in any of three places along his route back—Genoa, Avignon, Lisbon—where designated bankers would pay him any part, or all, of the money he might want. After he returned to Lisbon, not having used all of his credit, he ordered the Cambini to pay the balance to his legal representative back in Rome (and the entry in the banker's book notes that in the meantime Diaz had lost the letter).[20] These letters of credit were informal, written generally on behalf of people outside the merchant's circle and often outside his economic and social class. The merchant might therefore include, for the benefit of his agent, an identifying characteristic of the traveler—a broken tooth, a thick beard, a scar, a birthmark, a wart—and a more precise indication of his age than the result of merely rounding off an estimate to the nearest fifth or tenth year.[21] The bill of exchange mentioned none of these personal characteristics; it was not a letter but a formulaic document, and its validity lay in bankers' recognition of one another's writing, something they were careful to attend to. When in 1384 Manetto Davanzati & Partners in Venice entered into a business relation with the Datini company in Pisa, its factor wrote to Pisa, "We are taking note of your handwriting, and you take note of ours."[22]

Through the instruments of accounting and the bill of exchange merchants could largely avoid moving specie or bullion from one place to another. In fact, business records rarely document such shipments. The Cambini firm, for instance, one of the best-documented firms from the fifteenth century, managed its extensive operations across the western Mediterranean from Rome to Lisbon in such a way as to keep its traffic in money in and out of Florence, and to and from several cities within Italy, at a relatively modest level.[23] Trading activity in the market rarely balanced perfectly, however, and at the end of the day the merchant might well find himself either needing specie or having to handle a surplus of it. Hence merchants occasionally transported money from one place to another just as they moved goods. The accounts of the firm of the Alberti "nuovi"—first that

[20] Tognetti, *Il banco Cambini*, 185–88.

[21] Marco Spallanzani, "Alcune lettere di credito con 'segnali' dell'inizio del Cinquecento," in *Studi in memoria di Mario Abrate* (Turin, 1986), 757–64.

[22] Quoted in Reinhold C. Mueller, *The Venetian Money Market: Banks, Panics, and the Public Debt, 1200–1500,* vol. 2 of *Money and Banking in Medieval and Renaissance Venice,* by Frederic C. Lane and Reinhold C. Mueller (Baltimore, 1997), 271; for another example in the Datini correspondence, see 268.

[23] Tognetti, *Il banco Cambini*, 188.

of Iacopo and Bartolomeo di Caroccio, then that of Bartolomeo alone—over the decade from 1348 to 1358 record shipments of funds from Barletta to Naples and Venice, from Naples to Capua, from Ascoli to Perugia, from Volterra to Florence, from Florence to Pisa, Siena, and Avignon, from Paris to Bruges, and from Avignon to Perugia. The firm made some of these shipments as a service for others. At least two were made for the Acciaiuoli, who probably needed to pay troops: *fl.*2,100 from Florence to Pisa in November 1348 and *fl.*6,000 from Barletta to Naples in February 1349. For the pope, in Avignon, the firm sent *fl.*5,600 to Perugia in six shipments over the period from March to November 1355.[24] Leonardo di Tommaso Spinelli, whose father had been depositary of the Apostolic Chamber, made a trip to Venice in 1464–65 principally to oversee the transport of a large quantity of gold florins; he kept a pocket-size ledger during the journey, from his departure at the beginning of November to his return to Florence on 3 April, that documents primarily this activity.[25] At Venice he arranged for seven shipments of gold coins, mostly florins and Venetian ducats, totaling *fl.*4,497 *di suggello* to Florence and another of *fl.*464 to Rome. On his return trip to Florence he himself carried the extraordinary number of 5,613 gold coins of differing value, and once back in Florence he sent *fl.*1,976 on to Rome. Spinelli, like many merchants, may have undertaken this operation simply to shift assets from one place to another for the internal needs of his business or, especially when all other outlets were closed, to get profits back to Florence, the shipment of specie or bullion being the only way, in the final analysis, of solving the perennial problem of Florence's overall favorable balance of payments. Some merchants also shipped bullion as they might any other marketable item or shipped coins for speculation in different money markets. Barcelona, high on the rising tide of commercial activity in the western Mediterranean in the later fourteenth and early fifteenth centuries, was a major bullion and money market of this kind, where Florentines imported gold from North Africa, silver from Ragusa, and silver coins from Avignon and other places in southern France.[26]

Shipments of such valuable goods obviously required very special attention. For transport over the short distance from Florence to Pisa the Alberti firm charged Acciaiuoli a fee of 1 percent to cover the cost of three men on horseback and insurance; and for the shipment from Barletta to Naples, the money was carried by the firm's factor himself, accompanied by four armed men. Spinelli's

---

[24] Marco Spallanzani, "Spedizioni e tempi di percorrenza," in *Due libri mastri degli Alberti: Una grande compagnia di Calimala, 1348–1358,* ed. Richard A. Goldthwaite, Enzo Settesoldi, and Marco Spallanzani (Florence, 1995), 1:xcii–xciv, xcix.

[25] Yale University, Beinecke Library, Spinelli Papers, box 93, no. 1779.

[26] Mario Del Treppo, *I mercanti catalani e l'espansione della corona aragonese nel secolo XV* (Naples, 1968), 203–6, 291–310.

ledger records the names of the carriers, most of them employees of an associate, but nothing about provisions for security. Generally shipments consisted of somewhere between *fl.*300 and *fl.*500 and therefore involved a weight of only 1–1.75 kilograms and a bulk of no more than what today would consist of a half-dozen to nine rolls of fifty modern coins the size of the five-cent piece of the euro. The money was put in bags, sealed, and usually hidden away in bales of cloth to be transported in caravans of pack animals carrying commercial goods; if there were a number of bags, they might be distributed among several carriers to reduce the risk. The 1439 articles of association for the Medici branch in Geneva enjoined the firm's factor there to consider the risk involved in shipping specie and to use his best judgment concerning the quantity to be sent in any one shipment and the safest way to send it.[27] It was possible to insure such shipments, as Lorenzo Acciaiuoli did in 1348. In fact, in a record book in which the broker Raggio di Nofero Raggi registered the insurance contracts he arranged over the years 1524–26, gold and silver, probably specie, are the items most frequently mentioned among the imported goods insured, although most entries do not specify what was being insured.[28] Much of this traffic in specie involved a large variety of coins from different mints, but once it reached its destination, the importer took bullion and foreign coins to the local mint for coining or recoining.

Florentines came to dominate the growing traffic in international transfer because they had the most geographically diffuse network of firms, through which they could easily effect transfers either within their own widespread business organization or by recourse to other Florentines. Even the Venetians, themselves major players in the rise of medieval capitalism, had little choice but to use Florentines to get to Avignon the *fl.*100,000 that they had to pay the papacy in 1312 as the enormous indemnity for removal of the interdict imposed on the city during the War of Ferrara.[29] Once they were operating in various places and faced with the practical problem of what to do with accumulating profits, short of the risky shipment of cash, merchants were in a position to move into yet other places to offer services of exchange and transfer of money. Indeed, it is likely that already by the mid-twelfth century firms located themselves in some towns, not for purposes of trade, but to offer this kind of service to non-Florentine merchants. This gave them locally the capital to engage in commerce of goods without having to ship specie. Hence, exchange and transfer service could lead to commerce, rather

[27] De Roover, *Medici Bank*, 284–85.

[28] Bruno Dini, "Aspetti del commercio di esportazione dei panni di lana e dei drappi di seta fiorentini in Costantinopoli, negli anni 1522–1531," in *Studi in memoria di Federigo Melis* (Florence, 1978), 4:13 (table), reprinted in his *Saggi su una economia-mondo: Firenze e l'Italia fra Mediterraneo ed Europa (secc. XIII–XVI)* (Pisa, 1995). On Raggi, see chapter 1.

[29] Mueller, *Venetian Money Market*, 258–59.

than the other way around. Florentines have been documented in Cremona from 1256 to 1261 as dominating the traffic in foreign exchange for remittance from local sales of northern European cloth even when they themselves did not enter the market for these goods.[30] If commerce led to the traffic in money and therefore to banking, exchange banking, and not just trade in the first instance, could be a primary dynamic that further extended the international network.

To sum up, the merchant had the instruments for moving credits from one place to another, shifting them around according to his need either to dispose of surpluses in one place or to find funds in another. He could thus avoid the risk of transporting specie or bullion and at the same time gain greater flexibility in the markets where he operated. The ability to shift funds across Europe and the Mediterranean from England to the Near East at a time when bullion shipments were slow and risky served an essential function for everyone from simple travelers who went on pilgrimages to feudal princes who fought wars abroad and popes who needed to get church revenues from throughout Christendom to Rome. Demand for bills came from anyone, from non-Florentine merchants to the papacy, who had to get funds from one place to another. In the thirteenth century merchants charged what they sometimes called "portagium" for transfer service, when, in fact, physical transport was not involved. They made profits on these transactions from favorable exchange rates and from commission fees charged for the service; the miniscule rate of the latter, usually several per thousand, testifies to the commonness of the practice. In short, merchants also trafficked in money as well as goods, and in this activity too they performed a banking function.

The Bill of Exchange as Credit Instrument

The bill of exchange had an inherent credit function inasmuch as it usually involved an advance of credit for the time that elapsed between the receipt of funds in one place and payment in another. By the fourteenth century merchants had learned to manipulate the bill to exploit this function, transforming it into a principal instrument through which they could make money on the credit they extended.[31] This refinement of the bill gave them a device to circumvent the

---

[30] Hidetoshi Hoshino, "I Chiarenti di Pistoia a Cremona, 1256–1261," reprinted in *Industria tessile e commercio internazionale nella Firenze del tardo Medioevo,* ed. Franco Franceschi and Sergio Tognetti (Florence, 2001), 154–55.

[31] A general introduction to the complexities of the bill of exchange as a credit instrument can be found in de Roover, *Medici Bank,* ch. 6 (with further references to that author's extensive investigation of the subject); useful also is Mueller, *Venetian Money Market,* ch. 8. For a definitive analysis of the various forms of the bill as seen through the banker's accounts, see Giulio Mandich, "Per una ricostruzione delle operazioni mercantili e bancarie della compagnia Covoni," in *Libro giallo della compagnia dei Covoni,* ed. Armando Sapori (Milan, 1970), cxli–clv, clxxiv–cxciii.

church's condemnation of direct interest-bearing loans as manifest usury.[32] The credit function arose from the time that elapsed between the issuance of the bill in one place and the presentation of it for payment in another place. How it worked can be explained with reference again to figure 3.1: A, the remitter, who paid C, the drawer, to have a bill to make a payment abroad in effect did not see the benefit of the bill until B, the beneficiary, presented it to C′, the drawee, for payment. Thus the bill inherently had the elements of a loan. Florentines, with their expert knowledge of exchange and money markets and their far-flung network of contacts abroad, learned how to manipulate the instrument in various ways to exploit this possibility. Some interesting examples come from the accounts of Bartolomeo di Caroccio degli Alberti & Partners, active in the 1350s. Once, the firm, as remitter, took a pawn from the drawer in exchange for a bill it purchased. A number of times it sold a bill as drawer but in fact accepted payment after the bill had arrived at its destination and been paid, in effect selling the bill on credit: the remitter's correspondent abroad, the beneficiary, had his money from the Alberti agent before the firm in Florence was paid by the remitter. In this instance the credit was extended not by the remitter but by the drawer.[33]

Certain practices of this kind eventually became standardized, so that the bill became refined as a credit instrument. The normal procedure, to refer again to figure 3.1, was to have the payer abroad, C′, on agreement with C, protest the validity of the bill, a formal procedure that gave the beneficiary, B, the right to draw another bill on the original drawer, C, to be paid to the original remitter, A. In other words, A now received his money back from B, but meanwhile time had elapsed and exchange rates had changed to the advantage, usually, of A. This operation was in effect a loan by A to C, the duration being the usance allowed for the round trip and the interest being determined by the difference in exchange rates. Or the beneficiary of the original bill, B, on agreement with A, could purchase a new bill from someone else made payable to A, the original remitter. In this way A speculated on the international money market.

A further refinement was the standardization of the travel time, that is, usance, by convention as a precise period no longer determined by the duration of the actual journey, thereby fixing the term of a loan, for example, two months each way between Florence and Bruges, one month from Florence to Avignon but

---

[32] For what has become the classic explanation of the bill of exchange and its historical development, see two articles by Raymond de Roover in his *Business, Banking, and Economic Thought in Late Medieval and Early Modern Europe: Selected Studies of Raymond de Roover,* ed. Julius Kirshner (Chicago, 1974): "What Is Dry Exchange? A Contribution to the Study of English Mercantilism," 183–99, and "Cambium ad Venetias: Contribution to the History of Foreign Exchange," 239–59.

[33] Richard A. Goldthwaite, "Banca," in Goldthwaite, Settesoldi, and Spallanzani, *Due libri mastri degli Alberti,* 1:cix–cxiii.

forty-five days from Avignon to Florence, five days from Florence to Venice but three weeks from Venice to Florence. Already by the 1330s Florentines had worked out these conventions for usance, to judge from Pegolotti's observation that bills taken out with them, unlike those taken out with others, did not need to have the time specified. A further refinement was what is known as dry exchange, which made a fiction of remittance, and thereby of the exchange function of the bill, by collapsing the two parties abroad into one. In this usage the remitter paid the drawer for a bill but wanted it repaid directly to him, not to a beneficiary abroad, so the agent of the drawer abroad served as both drawee and beneficiary, with the understanding that he would simply send another bill back ordering the original drawer in Florence to pay (back) the remitter. This arrangement of exchange and reexchange (or rechange) involving only one party abroad and no payment of money abroad, known as dry exchange, became formalized into a straight credit instrument in the course of the first half of the fourteenth century. The duration of the loan was the time, fixed by convention, for the bill to travel to and from the place abroad (usance), and the interest was the probable profit the lender, the fictional remitter, would make on the play of exchange rates between two moneys in two places at two different times. A final step in this direction, following the fictionalization of the exchange operation abroad, was to fictionalize also the journeys of the two bills: the drawer's bill was never sent, and the entire operation, known in fact as fictitious exchange, was reduced to accounting entries. The bill, in a sense, never became completely fictionalized, because what remained from the original operation was the necessary correspondence between the banker and his contact abroad, where rates were established and clearance among bankers effected. The bill thus became a formal credit instrument for short-term loans specific to international merchant banking alone. None of this, of course, precluded the continuing use of the bill in its original form as an instrument for the simple international transfer and exchange of funds.[34]

A major breakthrough in the diffusion of the bill of exchange as a credit instrument occurred when merchants began using it to make loans not just to one another but also to people outside the commercial system, who could not engage in exchange for lack of commercial contacts abroad. They did this by yet another fiction: they assumed the position of drawer for the borrower, thus reversing the positions of drawer-borrower and remitter-lender. To judge from an instance that will be cited in chapter 6, the merchant could apparently take this practice yet one step further by preparing a bill for a loan contract between two parties in which he himself did not enter as either lender or borrower. In any event, with

---

[34] For more detailed illustrations based on specific bills, see de Roover, *Medici Bank,* 114, 133.

this possibility the merchant, now banker, had the perfect instrument to engage in moneylending. He could extend his potential market for loaning money well beyond his business circle; moreover, he could do so by evading the church's restriction on manifest usury. The bill gave him the means to disguise its real function, since no one could doubt the legitimacy of an exchange operation. Despite all the fictitious uses of the bill, the quotation of exchange rates in a foreign place remained essential to the contract, and the unpredictable fluctuation of rates added a certain risk to the operation—an important element in the defense of the instrument against charges of usury, since the operation precluded a fixed rate of interest. Normally, however, exchange and rechange of this kind favored the buyer of the original bill, or the remitter, that is, the lender, inasmuch as differences in rates of exchange worked to his advantage. Theologians, of course, knew that there might be deceit behind certain uses of the bill, but they could not detect it from entries in the banker's books. Nor, in many instances, can modern scholars, who, in fact, debate the extent to which the bill was used for legitimate exchange or for disguising a loan. In any event, whatever course the rates took, bankers earned profits from small commission fees charged on these operations, even the fictitious ones involving no more than accounting entries.

When the merchant extended his traffic in the exchange market to enter also the credit market, he became a banker in the modern sense. Since the bill in its credit function, as in its exchange function, became available to anyone as a service the merchant-banker offered to the general public, traffic increased enormously, having a dynamic of growth apart from commercial activity. By the fifteenth century it was possible for anyone, by selling a bill and keeping it on the exchange, to take out a short-term loan from a merchant-banker, on which he was charged interest according to the usance, or he could, by buying a bill and keeping it on the exchange, in effect deposit money with a banker, on which he received interest regularly but at varying rates. Moreover, one could use the bill for pure speculation by collapsing the roles of remitter and drawer into one, thereby effecting change and rechange only for the purpose of making money on the difference in exchange rates. Trading was sufficiently intense to give rise also to arbitrage, and out of this growing traffic in the buying and selling of bills emerged a veritable international money market, including speculation, located in the principal commercial centers. It was because they dealt in money that mercantile firms came to be called "banks," and merchants "bankers" (words used for the business of manual exchange conducted over a counter, *banco*, in the local market), even when commercial operations were the more important part of their business. The bill of exchange did not circulate as paper, because it lacked negotiability and endorsement, features that can be found in isolation in Florence as early as the end of the fourteenth century but did not become widespread until the end of the sixteenth century in northern Europe.

The bill of exchange was, along with accounting, one of the most important instruments the international merchant-banker perfected in his effort to conduct his affairs with greater efficiency, and it was of a higher intellectual order than accounting. Indeed, it baffles many economic historians today, and even specialists find it difficult to explain the various ways in which it was manipulated for purposes other than straight exchange, especially to evade charges of usury. And the difficulties mount when one is pressed to explain the workings of the international money market, so long dominated by the Florentines, in which the bill was the principal instrument. Contemporaries themselves did not find exchange an easy subject to understand. In his manual on commercial practice in the mid-fifteenth century Benedetto Cotrugli, a Ragusan who grew up in the Venetian system but had worked for Florentines at both Ragusa and Valencia, recognized the importance of the bill as "a delicate invention, a condiment of all things mercantile, as necessary to commerce as air is to the human body," and he introduced the subject as "a most subtle activity to investigate."[35] Non-Florentines with less business experience than Cotrugli despaired of the subject. During the 1421–23 session of the estates of the kingdom of Aragon, Johan de Fontcuberta, the mayor of Barcelona, a major port city, condemned the way Florentines conducted business. After recognizing all the usual benefits of trade to the well-being of humanity, he condemned the Italians (though given the specifics of his indictment, it was clearly the Florentines he had in mind): "They distort and destroy the *ars mercantilis* by their subtle and depraved nature, depriving it of its utility; they make imaginary contracts for exchange, rechange, insurance and other similar things; and they know more about destroying the function of the *ars mercantilis* than about using it correctly."[36] Even a Florentine entrepreneur confronted with explaining the bill could be driven, if not to despair, to something else. In 1417 Antonio di messer Francesco Salutati, at the time an employee of the bank of Giovanni di Bicci de' Medici in Florence, copied out a merchant manual of an earlier date in which exchange is treated extensively, and at the very end he added his own comment that "he who deals in exchanges and he who deals in merchandise is always anxious and beset by worries. I will instead give you a recipe for lasagna and macaroni." He proceeds to do so and then concludes: "Let him who wants to draw on Bruges and remit to Paris do it. I, for my part, prefer to enjoy supper with my companions. Amen."[37]

[35] Quoted in Mueller, *Venetian Money Market*, 288.
[36] Quoted in Del Treppo, *I mercanti catalani*, 310.
[37] Quoted in Mueller, *Venetian Money Market*, 355.

The International Exchange Market

It is impossible to measure the growth of the international money market, not least because of the difficulty in distinguishing between the two functions of the bill in business documents.[38] Already in the 1330s the Florentine firm of Piero Del Buono & Partners operated in Venice for the explicit purpose of engaging in both exchange and commerce.[39] Over the following century the increased traffic in bills, in part arising from their use as a credit instrument, led to the streamlining of the market in two respects. First, merchants eventually concentrated exchange activity in a few international commercial centers where they assembled in large numbers, thereby facilitating book clearance of exchange operations among them. The more merchants assembled in one place seeking to shift money from one place to another, the easier it was for any one of them to find someone who had the credits elsewhere that he could use or someone who could use the credits he had, the hope of all of them being to reduce shipment of specie. Moreover, the greater the number of exchanges that took place in one marketplace, the easier it was for bankers elsewhere to use that place as a center for the bills of exchange they drew up to effect loans; and greater concentrated activity also gave rise to arbitrage. These exchange centers, therefore, were major international emporia. A second refinement was the substitution of a regular periodicity on the due dates of bills, legitimate or fictitious, in place of the varying usance between different trade centers. With this centralization and regularization of the international exchange market, following on the refinement in the manipulation of the bill as a credit instrument, Florentines consolidated their position as Europe's leading international bankers.

In the course of the fourteenth century Venice emerged as the first center where Florentines increasingly directed bills used as credit instruments. Its massive bullion market, supplied by silver from southern Germany and eastern Europe, was organized around the demand for silver arising at the time of galley departures for the eastern Mediterranean, where it was needed to balance payments. Since fluctuations in the demand for silver were thus subject to the fairly regular schedule of sailings, the general course of monetary exchange rates, on which depended the profits to be made in the bill market, was reasonably pre-

---

[38] The fundamental general surveys of the development of international exchange markets and banks, which include discussion of techniques, are those by Herman van der Wee: "Monetary, Credit and Banking Systems," in *The Cambridge Economic History of Europe*, ed. E. E. Rich (Cambridge, 1977), 5:290–392; and "European Banking in the Middle Ages and Early Modern Times (476–1789)," in *A History of European Banking*, by R. Bogaert, G. Kurgan-Van Hentenryk, and Herman van der Wee (Antwerp, 1994), 71–264. See also his *Growth and Development of the Antwerp Market and the European Economy (Fourteenth–Sixteenth Centuries)* (The Hague, 1963), 2:333–68.

[39] Mueller, *Venetian Money Market*, 264.

dictable. Venice receded in importance toward the end of the century, however, with the emergence of Geneva as a major European trade emporium on the overland route linking northern and southern Europe. Paris had earlier been on the southward route, but after it was isolated by the Hundred Years' War, it was sidestepped by the increased traffic on the route now going from the Low Countries through Burgundy to Geneva and on to the Mediterranean. The impressive growth of Geneva as a key place of commercial exchange between these two major areas made it the natural clearinghouse for the balancing of payments between north and south and for the consequent shipment of bullion to the south. The money market at Geneva, a market clearly dominated by the Florentines, grew rapidly after 1400. The gathering of so many merchants at the fairs facilitated clearance of exchange operations among them, while the seasonal timing of the fairs, each lasting about a week, at four equal intervals throughout the year made it possible for them to do this on four dates—Epiphany (6 January), Easter, at the beginning of August, and All Saints' Day (1 November). Merchants were thus able to regularize the terms of all bills, hence usance, into equal periods, since the fairs, not the travel time of the bills, now determined the dates for exchange transactions.

The success of an international money market depended on a stable currency in the place where the market was held, since a foreign currency was essential to the entire exchange transaction (for which reason the market could never have been in Florence itself). This had been one of the advantages of Venice, whose gold ducat was, along with the florin, the most stable coin in Europe. In promoting the new trade fairs of Geneva, the prince-bishop who ruled the city sought also to assure the success of the money market, and to this end he guaranteed the stability of the local gold écu, or scudo, by fixing the number that could be minted from a single mark of gold, a troy weight equal to 226 grams. Hence the mark became the money of account for international exchange operations, equal originally to sixty-four and later to sixty-six écus, each more or less equal to the gold florin. The mark as a fixed weight in gold independent of the value of minted gold coins became the standard, thus assuring a solid foundation for stability in international exchange operations for the traffic in bills.

The shift of this traffic from Venice to Geneva brought the bill market to a principal location on what was becoming, as we have seen, the major trade route overland between the Mediterranean and an area in northern Europe extending from the Low Countries to Germany. Geneva was thus more central than Venice to the Florentine commercial network in western Europe, and it attracted many merchants, above all from Italy, France, and Germany, who did not operate in Venice. The presence of so many merchant-bankers at the fairs simplified communications among them. Moreover, standardization of practice increased the possibility of arbitrage and hence greater exchange activity. The Medici worked through a factor in Geneva in the early 1420s and then advanced to a separate contractual arrangement (accomandita) in 1426 (under the name, however, of Giovanni Benci & Partners) and to a full-scale partnership in 1439. For the years that are documented down to the 1460s, it earned handsome profits, often representing better than a 30 percent return on capital, much of which took the form of specie or bullion that was shipped to Florence. The best-documented firm in the city, that of Antonio Della Casa, Simone Guadagni & Partners, executed an average of 632 exchange operations totaling *sc.*312,443 annually for three years in the 1460s. The firm's profits came as much from exchange operations as from commerce. For most of these firms, in fact, exchange was more important than trade.[40]

The international center of the bill market shifted from Geneva to Lyons beginning in the 1460s, following the emergence of Lyon as a major emporium under royal auspices (see chapter 2). Lyons opened yet greater commercial possibilities, being more accessible from both the Mediterranean and the urban markets of the French hinterland. Moreover, since the city became a center of much royal financial activity, with the court itself often in residence in the early sixteenth century, Florentine bankers found easy access to the business generated by the fiscal administration of a monarchy that was rapidly reasserting itself after the Hundred Years' War. The relocation of the bill market to a major commercial and financial center facilitated expansion of traffic in the bill utilized as a credit instrument, and, in fact, Lyons became a major banking center, not just an international emporium, attracting Italian bankers from other cities, especially Genoa, Lucca, and Milan. Although the Florentines thus lost the clear dominance they had had at Geneva, their preeminence at Lyons was manifest in the agreement of the others to conduct their clearing operations in the loggia of the Florentines. At the end of each fair, after the fifteen-day period of commercial activity, they all met there to validate bills and draw up general balances, to set the rates for the next fair, and, finally, to settle accounts (usually by simple book clearance, not by payment in specie). The emergence of Lyons as the first major center of the international bill market thus represented a further streamlining of the instrument in response to a growing demand from various other places. Unfortunately, for all the scholarly attention this international exchange market attracted in the twenty years immediately following the publication of Fernand

[40]Michele Cassandro, ed., *Il libro giallo di Ginevra della compagnia fiorentina di Antonio Della Casa e Simone Guadagni, 1453–1454* (Prato, 1976).

Braudel's study of the Mediterranean in 1949, we still have no major study of a Florentine firm there despite, or perhaps because of, what can only be described as an overwhelming abundance of surviving business records, especially for the sixteenth century.[41]

The refinement of the bill of exchange as a credit instrument, the international centralization of the bill market, and the standardization of usance are indicators of the growing importance of credit in local markets throughout Europe, both the need for it and the availability of savings to supply it, and their extensive network gave Florentines an advantage in exploiting this situation over a large geographic area. Since the bill was a major instrument for effecting what in reality was an outright loan, albeit in disguise, traffic in the bill became a major activity of many of these international merchants in the numerous cities west of the Rhine where they had branches or agents. By the fifteenth century the business of many of these Florentines revolved more around the bill market and other financial operations than around trade. They were, in fact, operating more as bankers than as merchants: they organized an international money market and effected transfers of funds across all of western Europe; they opened outlets for savings by accepting time deposits and selling bills of exchange; they provided the services of a current account to merchants; they made credit available generally through overdraft on current account and the bill of exchange; and they helped finance governments—all on an international scale.

The fairs at Lyons marked the high point of Florentine preeminence in the international exchange market.[42] Already in the second quarter of the sixteenth century challenges arose from Genoa in the south and from Antwerp in the north. Because of their close ties to Charles V, the Genoese found themselves caught up in the political rivalries between the emperor and Francis I, and this complicated their participation in the exchange fairs at Lyons. On the one hand, the French king was likely to penalize them at Lyons; on the other, the emperor tried to lure them away. Hence the Genoese, beginning in 1532, organized their own fairs, synchronized with those of Lyons and in the vicinity but at cities within the imperial orbit. After 1535 these fairs were, in fact, referred to as the fairs

[41] Roger Doucet, *La banque Capponi a Lyon en 1556* (Lyons, 1939), publishes and analyzes a fragment of an account book of Lorenzo and Piero Capponi, Tommaso Rinuccini & Partners found in the Lyons archives, without, however, consulting the abundant materials in Florence. Michele Cassandro, *Le fiere di Lione e gli uomini d'affari italiani nel Cinquecento* (Florence, 1979), utilizes materials of Carlo and Cosimo Martelli & Partners but does not present a complete business history. Cf. the study of a Lucchese firm by Françoise Bayard, "Les Bonvisi, marchands banquiers à Lyon, 1575–1629," *Annales: Économies, sociétés, civilisations* 26 (1971): 1234–69.

[42] On the exchange fairs in Lyons, see Richard Gascon, *Grand commerce et vie urbaine au XVIe siècle: Lyon et ses marchands (environs de 1520–environs de 1580)* (Paris, 1971), 1:237–62; José-Gentil Da Silva, *Banque et crédit en Italie au XVIIe siècle* (Paris, 1969), 465–528; and Cassandro, *Le fiere di Lione.*

of Besançon, the place where they were frequently, but not always, held in the early years. Eventually the Genoese built up their own international exchange network founded on their domination of the bullion shipments and the international transfers of funds they executed in conjunction with the extensive European interests of the Hapsburgs. In 1579 they moved the fairs to Italy, where, with the bullion flow close at hand in Hapsburg territories, they could better manage the exchange operations arising from the favorable balance many Italian merchants had with northern Europe. They could not organize them in Genoa itself because the entire exchange system depended on clearance in a foreign currency, so they met elsewhere, usually at the nearby Farnese capital of Piacenza but also in the Piedmont, in Lombardy, at Trent, "or wherever they wanted," commented the contemporary Florentine Bernardo Davanzati in his tract of 1588 on the subject, "so that they would have done much better to call the place Utopia, or fairs without a location."[43] Being movable, these fairs assured the international money market a certain freedom from the destabilizing effects of local political and military disturbances. They continued to be held somewhere in the vicinity of Genoa until at least 1763.

Florentines and other bankers participated in the Besançon fairs, but the Genoese alone controlled them, the final authority for resolving disputes being the senate at Genoa. This closed group saw to the monetary standard, the technical machinery, and the organizational procedures that assured the success of the fairs in making credit accessible throughout western Europe. And the Genoese did by far the greatest amount of the business there, now that they served the king of Spain in the financing of loans and in the international transfer of the vast amounts of bullion coming in from the New World. It was through exchange transactions between Piacenza and Antwerp that they managed to move much of this wealth to the Low Countries for military expenditures and, in the process, convert it from silver to the gold needed to pay the troops. Their handling of vast amounts of specie and bullion and their dealing in government credits in Spain allowed them to mold the fairs to their advantage and to make profits at every step along the way—from interest on loans to the king, from shipment and insurance charges, from differences in exchange rates.

The fairs of Besançon "or wherever they will be," as they were identified in Florentine ledgers at the time, were strictly financial, not tied to commercial trading as at Lyons. Hence they were attended by only from about 50–60 to 150 or so bankers, in contrast to the crowds of merchants at a Lyons trade fair. Their very

[43] Bernardo Davanzati, "Notizie de' cambi," in *Scisma d'Inghilterra con altre operette del signor Bernardo Davanzati Bostichi, gentiluomo fiorentino, tratte dall'edizion fiorentina del MDCXXXVIII* (Padua, 1754), 112.

existence, completely detached from commercial activity, testifies to how large the demand for credit had become by that time. In 1600 the annual total of bills handled amounted to about 40 million scudi. We can take the measure of the increased traffic in bills in the 1580s from a ledger of just one firm, Simone and Heirs of Giovanni Corsi & Partners, which had no branches outside of Florence. This firm dealt with thirty-five banks—fourteen at Lyons, seventeen at Besançon, and four with branches in both places—compared with the three in Lyons that appear over a period of seven years a century earlier on the profit-loss account of the firm of Filippo di Matteo Strozzi, one of the largest of its day. In 1582 the Corsi had assets under management that were approximately equal to the assets of the Medici banks a century earlier at Florence and Rome together. To better organize the mass of operations, their accountant had to refine earlier practice, opening separate accounts for each fair, for loans, for each client bank at the fairs, and for commission charges alone, with the result that the profit-loss account yields at a glance a precise breakdown of activity and hence a full picture of operating results, something rare in ledgers from an earlier period. Profits from the nominal commission charges for bills, which varied from a miniscule 0.33 percent to 0.35 percent, alone account for 10 percent of gross profits, an eloquent testimony to the number of operations handled by the firm. The massive Corsi ledgers, unlike anything found much before the mid-sixteenth century—so heavy that one needs a cart to get one of them to the study table in the archives and, once there, too unwieldy to be held up by a reading stand—themselves testify to a new scale of operations.[44]

The competition from "Besançon" was a principal cause of the eventual collapse of Florentine banking at Lyons, along with the decline of the commercial fairs (discussed in chapter 2) and the loss of financial business with the monarchy (discussed below).[45] In the exchange operations conducted by the Corsi firm at the fairs of both places from 1582 to 1588, 11 of the 21 firms it dealt with at Lyons and 8 of the 18 at "Besançon" were Florentine, and only 3 of these operated at both places.[46] By 1600 there were hardly any Florentine firms in Lyons, and at Besançon they numbered only 9 out of the 160 bankers who are documented as attending at least one of two fairs there that year. At these latter fairs, however, 6 Florentine firms were among the 28 that transacted more than sc.100,000 worth of business (far behind the Genoese, with 18, but ahead of Venice and Milan, each

[44] Richard A. Goldthwaite, "Banking in Florence at the End of the Sixteenth Century," *Journal of European Economic History* 27 (1998): 491–99.

[45] Marie-Thérèse Boyer-Xambeu, Lucien Gillard, and Ghislain Deleplace, in "La crise du système de change lyonnais à la fin du XVIe siècle," *Revue internationale d'histoire de la banque* 32–33 (1986): 145–66, discuss some technical aspects of how the shift of the international exchange market from Lyons to Besançon worked to the advantage of the Genoese over the Florentines.

[46] Goldthwaite, "Banking in Florence," 493.

with 2), and 1, the firm of Francesco and Piero Capponi, was second only to a Genoese firm in business transacted.[47] Not many Florentine firms, if indeed any, could even approach the scale of operations of the Balbi firm of Genoa, which cleared drafts totaling about a million scudi a year at these fairs from 1602 to 1605. In 1622, when the Genoese transferred their fairs to Novi, within their own territory, the Florentines took the initiative to organize their own fairs. Winning over the support of bankers from Milan, Venice, and Bologna, they had some success, but eventually, in 1638, they had to end their secession and return to the Genoese fold. By this time Florentine bankers were probably using the fairs much more for local credit operations in Florence than for international transfers.[48]

While in southern Europe the international exchange market shifted from the commercial fairs at Lyons, dominated by the Florentines, to the purely financial fairs in Italy organized by the Genoese, the market at Antwerp, now a central emporium in the expanding world economy of northwestern Europe, reached a level of activity that marked a new chapter in the history of financial markets, a chapter that takes the story beyond the Italian contribution. Antwerp was, like Lyons, a commercial trading center, but on a much larger scale, and it attracted more merchants from a much wider geographic range. The inflow of German silver following the establishment of a distribution center for Portuguese spices in 1508 made Antwerp a major money market as well, and later in the century this market underwent further growth and considerable refinement as a result of imports of Spanish bullion to pay for the religious wars of the Hapsburgs. On the one hand, the intensity of trade and the influx of bullion created an immense amount of capital in search of outlets. A sure sign of this situation was a feverish speculation of a kind not found in Venice, Lyons, and other earlier international emporia: people speculated in the purchase of spices before their arrival and in maritime insurance, they organized lotteries, and they placed bets on virtually anything, from the return of ships to the sex of unborn children. On the other hand, the intensity of trade also generated an enormous demand for commercial capital. Government officials learned that with so much wealth in circulation, they too could borrow funds in this market. And towns, provincial diets, tax receivers, and other government authorities throughout the Low Countries, as well as foreign

---

[47] Giuseppe Felloni, "All'apogeo delle fiere genovesi: Banchieri ed affari di cambio di Piacenza nel 1600," in *Studi in onore di Gino Barbieri: Problemi e modelli di storia ed economia* (Milan, 1983), 2:883–901. For the Florentines at the Genoese fairs in the seventeenth century, see Da Silva, *Banque et crédit en Italie*, 97–109.

[48] Edoardo Grendi, *I Balbi: Una famiglia genovese fra Spagna e Impero* (Turin, 1997), 54–55 (table 10).

rulers, including the emperor and the kings of England and Portugal, financed their floating debt through the sale of bonds in the Antwerp market.

Merchant-bankers of different nationalities formed syndicates among themselves for investments of this kind, and a professional class of intermediaries appeared to bring lenders and borrowers together. Moreover, with the opening of the Exchange in 1551, for the first time merchants had a permanent place open every day, not just quarterly, for international clearance and exchange. Practices arose to meet the insatiable need merchants and others had for credit—the writing of promissory notes (IOUs or letters obligatory) payable to the bearer, endorsement of bills of exchange, discounting of both notes and bills—and measures were taken to give these practices legal status. With this private paper passing through dozens and dozens of hands before being extinguished by cash payment, liquidity of credit far exceeded anything experienced in Italian markets. A major breakthrough in the history of financial markets occurred when the traffic in these instruments reached the point where clearance took place through the simple, even daily exchange of paper, not through periodic book entry as traditionally practiced by the Italians.

All this activity in the money market, well lubricated by new financial instruments and sustained by the appropriate institutions, boosted Antwerp as a financial center to a level much higher than that of any of the southern markets. The city attracted many players from Spain, Portugal, England, France, Germany, and elsewhere. The major rivals to the Italians at the beginning of the century were the southern German merchants, including the Fuggers and the Welsers, newly enriched by the imperial privileges they enjoyed over the mines in southeastern Germany and emboldened by their ties to the Hapsburgs. After the retirement of Charles V in 1555, however, most of them gravitated toward the Austrian Hapsburgs and away from Spain, with its ever-growing inflow of bullion from the New World. Under Philip II the Genoese gained preeminence in Antwerp, since they managed the king's search for credit there, as well as the transfer of much of the wealth sent from Spain to Antwerp through the exchange markets at Medina del Campo in Spain and at Piacenza.[49]

Notwithstanding the intensification of trade and the widening of its geographic scope in the sixteenth century, merchants and bankers were integrated more than ever in the great international exchange capitals at Besançon in the south and Antwerp in the north. In this growing "international republic of money," as it has been called, the Florentines found themselves outnumbered and

---

[49] Valentin Vásquez de Prada, "Gli uomini d'affari e i loro rapporti con la corona spagnola nelle Fiandre (1567–1597)," in *La repubblica internazionale del denaro tra XV e XVII secolo*, ed. Aldo De Maddalena and Hermann Kellenbenz (Bologna, 1986), 243–73.

outclassed.[50] They were no longer "the masters of the money of other countries," as they boasted in their defense against an attempt by the grand duke to regulate them in 1605.[51] They perfected accounting techniques and used paper instruments, both the check (as we shall see) and the bill of exchange, but they did not make more than tentative use of circulating negotiable paper. They did not use promissory notes, as northern merchants had as early as the fifteenth century, and since their bills did not have bearer clauses, negotiability was limited to specific assignment. Isolated examples of discount and endorsement have been found in the records of Florentine banking going back to the end of the fourteenth century, but these do not reflect general practice.[52] On the whole, Florentines had never needed to develop these new techniques: Florence itself was not an emporium of any more than local importance, and abroad Florentines operated at the upper end of the market and through a relatively small group of international merchants. They went to Antwerp, but they remained on the periphery of the growing market there with respect to the sheer volume of the traffic in goods and the soaring number of transactions that generated the need for more efficient techniques.

Florentine private banking remained at what A. P. Usher, the founder of modern banking history, called the primitive stage. Florentines did not take the final steps toward discount banking, banks of issue, and a central bank. The revolutionary advance occurred elsewhere, with the legal recognition of transferability, negotiability, and discount of private credit instruments, all of which led to a market in paper. When, how, and to what extent Florentine banks fell into line with the progress toward modern banking in Antwerp, and later in Amsterdam and London, is a story that has yet to be written.

Government Finance

Beyond these exchange and credit services, the merchant-banker found himself also drawn into financial administration for popes and princes, who offered him tax-collecting powers as security for loans as well as for payments he might make in advance for international transfer of funds. In fact, the possibility of profits from this kind of activity attracted some of these men away from the world

[50] The phrase is Aldo De Maddalena's, used for the title of the aforementioned book.

[51] Armando Sapori, "La registrazione dei libri di commercio in Toscana nell'anno 1605," in his *Studi,* 1:48. Jan Albert Goris, *Études sur les colonies marchandes méridionales (portugais, espagnols, italiens) à Anvers de 1478 à 1567* (Louvain, Belgium, 1925), has little on Florentines in Antwerp.

[52] See two articles by Federigo Melis, both reprinted in his *La banca pisana:* "Una girata cambiaria del 1410 nell'Archivio Datini di Prato," 295–306, and "Di alcune girate cambiarie dell'inizio del Cinquecento rinvenute a Firenze," 1–48.

of trade altogether. Many Italians followed this route from commerce to banking and state finance, but the Tuscans were the most numerous and successful, with the Florentines rapidly gaining international preeminence over all others by the beginning of the fourteenth century.

Loans to Rulers

Merchants made their largest loans by far to the governments of the places where they operated, from urban councils to local feudal lords. The loan Florentines made to Venice for payment of the indemnity required by the papacy for the lifting of the interdict imposed during the War of Ferrara has already been mentioned. In 1328 Donato di Pacino de' Peruzzi, a partner in the family bank, arranged for a loan of £20,000 *parisis* to the city of Bruges.[53] In feudal Europe, of course, ruling princes were much larger borrowers than communes. With poorly developed systems of direct taxes and no proper funding of debts, rulers targeted these prosperous merchants, seemingly flush with capital, as obvious sources for loans to get them through recurrent and inevitable liquidity crises, sometimes of considerable dimensions. The English kings, beginning with Edward I (1272–1307), repeatedly borrowed from Italians, and increasingly from Florentines, to finance their political ambitions in Sicily and wars in Wales and Scotland and then in France. The enormity of the credit of the Bardi alone with the English crown in the 1340s is almost inconceivable. Estimated as between *fl*.535,000 and *fl*.900,000, its value in real terms in the local market in Florence was equivalent to between one-fourth and one-third of the total liquid wealth in the city as reported in the 1427 catasto.[54]

For security the merchant might take as a pawn princely jewels, such as the precious miter that Giovanni di Bicci de' Medici accepted for money loaned to Pope John XXIII (Baldassarre Cossa), which was redeemed by Martin V in 1419; or the twenty-pound bejeweled tiara Ghiberti claimed to have made, which a consortium of bankers took for *fl*.40,000 loaned to Pope Eugene IV in 1439 and which almost twenty years later, in 1456, was pawned by Pope Calixtus to Tommaso Spinelli; or the tiara of Innocent VIII that the Genoese bank of the Centurioni passed on to the Medici bank, along with the transfer of a papal debt in 1489; or the nineteen-pound bejeweled reliquary, known as the fleur-de-lys of Bur-

---

[53] Raymond de Roover, *Money, Banking and Credit in Medieval Bruges* (Cambridge, MA, 1948), 84–85.

[54] The estimate is from Armando Sapori, *La crisi delle compagnie mercantili dei Bardi e dei Peruzzi* (Florence, 1926), 77. My conversion of it is based on what the florin could buy in the market for unskilled labor in Florence at the time as compared with that price in 1427.

gundy, that Archduke (later Emperor) Maximilian pledged to Tommaso Portinari, the former Medici agent in Bruges, who stored it in the hospital of Santa Maria Nuova in Florence.[55] Usually, however, security for loans and repayment took the form of privileged access to the sources of state income, which bankers had the technical expertise and the financial organizational network to handle better than the inchoate bureaucratic apparatus of most feudal states. This activity drew them into the administration of state finances, especially concessions to run specific tax farms for salt monopolies, customs, tolls, and other such charges imposed by governments.

With Edward I the English crown incorporated borrowing on these terms systematically into its fiscal system. The Frescobaldi firm in London, active about 1300, received royal contracts for operating a silver mine, for handling receipts from various royal estates, and for collection of port tolls (the major source of the crown's income). Moreover, Edward II freed the firm from any supervision by the Exchequer, making it responsible only to the Royal Wardrobe.[56] A few years later the Bardi and the Peruzzi regularly collected funds from sheriffs, bailiffs, and other local officials. The same firms, especially the Bardi, the Peruzzi, and the Acciaiuoli, moved into the fiscal administration of the Kingdom of Naples in a major way following its conquest by the Angevins with the victory of Charles of Anjou over the heirs of Emperor Frederick II in 1268. In return for their significant contribution to the financing of the invasion, they gained access to a variety of royal revenues, from local port taxes to the mint; these liens on royal income led them into the direct administration of fishing ports, the mint, tax collecting, and other fiscal activities. In addition, they acted as receivers of ecclesiastical revenues for the papacy, and they raised considerable funds from deposits by the nobility, a source that, in the light of what happened in the 1340s, appears to have been more important in Naples than in England. During the reign of Robert of Anjou (1309–43) the Bardi, Peruzzi, and Acciaiuoli firms gained virtually complete control over royal finances, first in competition with one another but eventually in cooperative arrangements involving all three, to the exclusion of other firms. The Florentines, in fact, eventually came to have a strong presence in the Angevin government as permanent, professional administrators, something they never had in England.[57]

[55] De Roover, *Medici Bank*, 15, 355–56; Melissa Bullard, "Banking on Reputation," in *Lorenzo il Magnifico: Image and Anxiety, Politics and Finance* (Florence, 1994), 169; Philip Jacks and William Caferro, *The Spinelli of Florence: Fortunes of a Renaissance Merchant Family* (University Park, PA, 2001), 71–75.

[56] Sapori, "La compagnia dei Frescobaldi," 872–88.

[57] David Abulafia, "Southern Italy and the Florentine Economy, 1265–1370," *Economic History Review* 33 (1981): 383, reprinted in his *Italy, Sicily and the Mediterranean, 1100–1400* (London, 1987).

The large international firms were not the only ones to move into government finance. Smaller operators can be found doing the same thing in more provincial places. For example, in 1279 Raimondo Della Torre, the patriarch of Aquileia, in the relatively remote feudal corner of Italy, negotiated a loan from Capponcino Capponi, a Florentine merchant-banker in Lombardy, offering him liens on certain state revenues. Capponi then moved to Friuli, and his family became closely involved in the patriarch's financial affairs. They took over management of forestland rights, the fishery monopoly, customs tolls at Udine and Cividale, the mint, and ecclesiastical revenues, and their administration probably contributed to bringing some kind of central control over a confusing welter of revenue sources in this provincial feudal state. In 1285 Lippo Capponi served as the patriarch's procurator in negotiating a treaty with Venice. The Capponi also engaged in trade and moneylending, but not as petty pawnbrokers, and although they earlier had had ties to the Rimbertini and Pulci banks, they do not seemed to have widened the scope of their activities beyond the confines of the region. They lost their position on the death of their protector, Della Torre, in 1299. There is evidence that later, in the 1330s, the Bardi had similar interests in Friuli.[58]

The credit merchant-bankers extended and the arrangements made for repayment thus tended to be directed toward supporting state finance, not toward stimulating economic activity within the private sector, although they might plow profits back into their commercial activities. On occasion, however, they made loans to rulers in exchange for opportunities to exploit certain local economic resources. The Medici firm was involved in two of the most notable enterprises of this kind. In 1466, once operations were up and running at the recently discovered alum mines at Tolfa, in the Papal States near Rome, the largest deposit ever found in Europe, the bank won the marketing contract for the output of this new operation. With papal support it attempted to gain a monopoly position for the sale of a product that was essential to the wool industry everywhere in Europe. In 1476 the Medici firm lost the contract to the Pazzi, and after the downfall of this family as a result of the conspiracy against the Medici two years later, the contract passed out of Florentine hands. In 1489 the branch of the Medici firm in Pisa made arrangements with the lord of Piombino for the marketing of iron ore from Elba delivered at Pietrasanta and Pisa, but after the exile of the family five years later, this business was taken over by other merchants. Neither of these Medici enterprises, however, reached the scale of operations achieved by the Genoese Bene-

[58] Donata Degrassi, "I rapporti tra compagnie bancarie toscane e patriarchi d'Aquileia (metà XIII secolo–metà XIV secolo)," in *I toscani in Friuli*, ed. A. Malcangi (Florence, 1991), 169–99.

detto Zaccaria, who, on the rights he gained at the end of the thirteenth century to exploit the alum mines of Phocaea, on the coast of Asia Minor, built an empire consisting in the working of the mines, shipment to Genoa, the operation of a dye shop in the city, and a virtual monopoly over the marketing of the product in European markets for almost two centuries.

One area in the industrial sector where Florentines found many opportunities with governments abroad was the minting of money and related mining operations. In a period of commercial expansion, from the twelfth century on, when rulers everywhere sought to establish their own monetary systems, there was a demand for men with the expertise many Florentines had in all matters regarding money, specie, and bullion, including, after the minting of the first gold florins in 1252, the technical knowledge required to run a mint. As men who knew about assaying and could deal in the market for metals and effect international exchange, they qualified as directors of mints. They themselves probably did not enter into the direct operation of mines but instead advanced loans to small operators, who repaid with metals. As early as 1218 a consortium of Florentines made a contract with the bishop of Volterra to take over his debts in return for rights to operate silver mines nearby at Montieri and to mint coins.[59] In 1278 Charles I of Anjou, newly installed in his Neapolitan kingdom, called on a Florentine to take charge of operations for the minting of gold and silver *carlini*, new coins named after him with the design of canceling the memory of the money of his imperial predecessors, and subsequent operations of the mint continued to be contracted out to Florentine bankers. In 1279 the Florentine Boniface Galgani became chief assayer in England, with deputies in the provincial mints; his nephews and their descendants, by now anglicized residents, remained active in the royal mints through to the 1340s. They were followed, from the 1360s to the 1390s, by another anglicized Florentine, Walter de' Bardi.[60] James Donati was one of the mint masters in Dublin in the early 1280s, and other Florentines held the position over the following years. Edward I put Florentines in charge of operations of Irish mines opened in 1289–90, although the actual mining was conducted by a Genoese.[61] A Florentine was mint master in Provence in 1301; in the 1320s Pope John XXII turned over the minting of imitation gold florins to a Florentine; and in 1341 a Tuscan was appointed master of the new mint in Lübeck. The Peruzzi were involved with the

[59] Davidsohn, *Storia di Firenze*, 1:1177–81, 1192–98; idem, *Forschungen zur Geschichte von Florenz* (Berlin, 1896–1919), 3:3, doc. 8.

[60] See Martin Allen, "Italians in English Mints and Exchanges," in *Fourteenth Century England*, vol. 2, ed. C. Given-Wilson (Woodbridge, Suffolk, 2002), 53–62, where almost all the Italians mentioned are really Florentines.

[61] M. D. O'Sullivan, *Italian Merchant Bankers in Ireland in the Thirteenth Century* (Dublin, 1962), 93–96, 97, 99.

royal mints in France, as were the Frescobaldi in England.[62] Across the fourteenth century Florentines of more modest stature operated mints in Germany, from Swabia in the southwest to Saxony in the northeast.

From the later thirteenth through the fifteenth century Florentines working in this sector had a particularly notable presence in the area extending east and northward from the Tyrol to Hungary, Bohemia, and Poland, where the most important copper and silver mines in Europe were to be found. In 1269 the bishop of Trent appointed a Florentine to handle the minting of money from his silver mines, and other Florentines followed, including the Frescobaldi, to run the operations of other princes throughout the region. In 1300 King Wenceslas II of Bohemia (1278–1305), in return for loans, granted privileges for the operation of both the Kuttenberg mines and the royal mint to the Donati brothers, Apardo (Alfredo), Cino, and Ranieri, a contract later renewed by John of Luxemburg (1310–46). As we have seen, Florentines were among the earliest mint masters at Kremnica, in Slovakia, where Europe's most important gold mines were opened in the 1320s. And under Louis I (1342–82) they were frequently involved in minting and mining activities. In Poland the mint master in Cracow in 1404 was Leonardo Bartoli, a Medici agent, and the Medici bank had major interests in the copper trade between that region and Venice. Many of these men who went to eastern Europe to run mints and mines moved into other areas of government finance, especially the collection of customs revenues and the management of salt monopolies, all these privileges being conceded in return for advances to rulers whose governments were at a relatively primitive stage of administrative development. Many, too, engaged in pawnbroking, sometimes with an official license, to serve a wider clientele, from feudal nobles to working people. Some also engaged in trade through contacts back in Italy, but commerce was secondary to these financial services until the end of the fifteenth century, when the market opened up for Florentine silks. By this time, however, the Hapsburgs were extending their dominion throughout much of this area, and they leaned heavily on the merchant-bankers of southeastern Germany for loans and financial services, including mining and mint operations. No Florentine ever got contracts as large as those conceded in 1490 and 1494 by the emperor Maximilian to Jacob Fugger for control of the output of the copper mines of both the Tyrol and Hungary.[63]

---

[62] Davidsohn, *Storia di Firenze*, 4, pt. 2:560–61, 632–33, 637, 656, 702–3, 786–87.

[63] Florentines as mint officials in central Italy down to the early fourteenth century are noted in ibid., 594–616. See also Winfried Reichert, "Mercanti e monetieri italiani nel regno di Boemia nella prima metà del XIV secolo," in *Sistema di rapporti ed élites economiche in Europa (secoli XII–XVII)*, ed. Mario Del Treppo (Naples, 1994), 337–48; and Wolfgang von Stromer, "Medici-Unternehmen in

Risks

As a result of ventures into state finance the figure of the banker has gained considerable visibility in the political annals of the period because it propelled him to the very center of power. Loans to princes, however, were always somewhat delicate arrangements. A loan in support of a government at war with another might endanger the merchant's operations in the other place. Florentines found this out in the 1330s, when their support of Edward III's campaign in France led to disruption of their maritime trade to the north as a result of the Genoese alliance with the king of France, and again a decade later, when, at home in Florence, their ambiguous support of pro-Ghibelline policies against the interests of the king of Naples led to a run on their banks in Naples that triggered the great banking crisis of the 1340s. In letting himself be drawn into the finances of a feudal lord, the merchant faced the very real prospect that the ruler would repudiate his debt, and in the end he had no way to protect himself from the personal whim of his powerful client or the machinations of the court. Moreover, he could find himself, as the Bardi and the Peruzzi did in the 1340s, in a situation where there was a concurrent demand for payment of debts in several places in Europe and not enough time to manage the problem through transfers, a potential danger inherent in their far-flung network. The history of the period is strewn with these merchant financiers who suffered heavy losses as a result of defaults on loans to sovereigns, ranging from the Tuscans whom the English kings sent into bankruptcy one after the other in the early fourteenth century—the Ricciardi of Lucca in 1301, the Bonsignori of Siena in 1302, and then the Florentine firms of the Mozzi in 1301–2, the Pulci and the Rimbertini in 1305, the Frescobaldi in 1311, the Scali in 1326, and the Bardi and the Peruzzi in 1342–46[64]—to those Florentines who, along with German bankers, suffered losses with the successive rescheduling of payment to participants in the Grand

---

den Karpatenländern: Versuche zur Beherrschung des Weltmarkts für Buntmetalle," in *Aspetti della vita economica medievale*, 370–97.

[64] On the Frescobaldi, see Armando Sapori, *La compagnia dei Frescobaldi in Inghilterra* (Florence, 1947); and Richard W. Kaeuper, "The Frescobaldi of Florence and the English Crown," *Studies in Medieval and Renaissance History* 10 (1973): 41–95. On the Scali, see Silvano Borsari, *Una compagnia di Calimala: Gli Scali (secc. XIII–XIV)* (Macerata, 1994); and Edmund Fryde, "The Bankruptcy of the Scali of Florence in England, 1326–1328," in *Progress and Problems in Medieval England: Essays in Honour of Edward Miller,* ed. R. Britnell and J. Hatcher (Cambridge, 1996), 107–20. On the Bardi and the Peruzzi, see *I libri di commercio dei Peruzzi*, ed. Armando Sapori (Milan, 1934). And on the Acciaiuoli, see Hidetoshi Hoshino, "Nuovi documenti sulla compagnia degli Acciaiuoli nel Trecento," in his *Industria tessile e commercio internazionale*, 83–100. Unfortunately, Edwin S. Hunt, *The Medieval Super-Companies: A Study of the Peruzzi Company of Florence* (Cambridge, 1994), is not reliable, inasmuch as it ignores the extensive literature in Italian, including published documents, and misunderstands many technical matters.

Parti of 1555, devised by the French crown to handle its enormous debt to them.

The willingness of these merchant-bankers to take the risks involved in royal finances sometimes grew out of larger economic considerations. The notorious series of royal debt repudiations that drove firms operating in early fourteenth-century England into bankruptcy reveal the complexity of the situation in which these men found themselves. They needed money in England to buy wool, and since it was not forthcoming from sales of the products they could import, the king's need for money to pay for his wars against the French played into their hands. On the Continent they had the resources from commercial profits to extend loans to him there, while the liens on his English revenues they received in exchange gave them the wherewithal to pay for the raw wool they exported. The arrangement, in other words, allowed for a balance of payments in the firm's relation with England without the physical movement of bullion and specie, a consideration of utmost importance in the management of international commercial activity at the time. In a sense these financiers were as dependent on the king as he was on them. Moreover, they were both at the mercy of fluctuations in the gold-silver ratio, which worked for or against them, the English sterling being on the silver standard, the Florentine florin on the gold.[65]

The many notorious sequences of debt repudiation should alert us to the consideration that the risks of such ventures on the part of merchant-financiers cannot always be assessed in the simple terms, too often used in the historiography, of the perfidy of princes on the one hand or the ruthless unscrupulousness of avaricious merchants on the other. Other concerns went into the rational calculations of those early capitalists who took their chances with loans of this kind. The direct advantage to be gained from such loans usually outweighed the calculated risks, and it should not be surprising that these men continued the practice despite what might seem to have been the lesson of experience. A primary concern was, quite simply, the cost of doing business in a foreign land, where merchants sought safe conduct, protection, licenses, tax advantages, and, perhaps most important, legal privileges and the support of the government for claims against private persons. Moreover, in part because of these special arrangements, they also had to deal with local political authorities for protection in foreign places. On the one hand, feudal princes could be only too arbitrary in administering the law in cases involving foreigners and, on the other, the presence of foreigners might arouse hostility from local merchants, resentful of their competition, from the

---

[65] Richard A. Goldthwaite, "Italian Bankers in Medieval England," *Journal of European Economic History* 2 (1973): 763–71.

high nobility, jealous of their influence at court, and from the public in general, outraged by their usurious activity. Hence, for a host of reasons the goodwill of a prince was often worth a risky loan. In this sense, the merchant may have found himself in a situation where he had no choice but to agree to a loan. Debt repudiation, with the possible consequence of bankruptcy, was a high price to pay, of course, but with respect to the sequence of them in early fourteenth-century England, after each firm left the scene in failure another showed up to take its place. Moreover, as Armando Sapori observed about the situation in the 1330s, the king, after the failure of his campaign on the Continent, was simply in no position to pay off his debts. There is no reason to believe that these merchant-banker-financiers did not learn how to deal with such risks, building them into their rational calculations as protocapitalists in the medieval world.

Who is to deny, therefore, that the arbitrary cancellation of debts by a monarch, so infamous in much of the historiography, was probably accepted as an inherent characteristic of the feudal regime under which these bankers operated in northern Europe? Whatever one might want to make of the rationalism of these early capitalists, it was conditioned by the feudal culture in which they immersed themselves to do business. The prestige of association with the great and powerful men of their times may have made good business sense, or it may have meant more to them than could be calculated by business interests. Moreover, as purveyors of all kinds of fine luxury goods, they often established personal relations with rulers. A few of these merchant-financiers found further advancement as officials in princely courts, generally in offices that gave them some control over taxes as security for loans. As early as the 1290s the merchant Giacomo "Scaglia" Tifi became receiver and treasurer of the counts of Montbéliard and a major figure in the diplomatic relations with Philip IV involving the crown's claim to the county of Burgundy.[66] The Frescobaldi in England were also absorbed into court life at the beginning of the fourteenth century. They received ecclesiastical prebends belonging to the king and concessions for collection of rents from royal fiefs, including some in France, with all the rights to administer justice. They had the right to hold public office and to appeal for royal absolution from certain criminal actions for themselves and for their clients and friends. The king gave gifts to members of the family and named one of them to the honorific post of royal councilor.[67]

The most notorious of this early generation of bankers abroad were the brothers Albizzo and Giovanni Paolo "Musciatto" de' Franzesi, who started out working

---

[66] Armando Sapori, "Un fiorentino bizzarro alla corte di Borgogna, Scaglia Tifi," in his *Studi*, 1:101–31.

[67] Sapori, "La compagnia dei Frescobaldi," 883–86.

for the Scali firm and ended up in France by the 1280s. They moved into the entourage of the Duke of Brabant and eventually into that of the king, Philip the Fair. They served the latter both as bankers, in charge of collecting various revenues, and as trusted representatives on diplomatic missions to Germany and to Rome. Both "Biche" and "Mouche" received knighthoods and exerted their influence at court to promote their self-interests against those of other Italian merchants, whose enmity they aroused. They alone survived the arrests and exiles the king imposed on all "Lombards" in 1291. Both brothers eventually returned to Tuscany and bought up land with the ambition of establishing a state of their own under imperial auspices at Staggia, in the Valdelsa, without, however, severing their ties with France. Mouche entered the fray of politics in Florence. The Franzesi were at the height of their power and influence, both in France and at home, when the bankruptcy of the Gran Tavola of the Bonsignori of Siena in 1303 left them in the lurch with a now worthless advance they had made to the firm with funds from the king of France. Everything then fell apart, and the first blow came in 1305, when the government in Florence condemned Mouche to death and ordered his property confiscated. Both brothers died before worse came to worst, and after their deaths, in 1307, the king confiscated their property in France in payment of earlier debts he claimed they still owed him. A surviving brother and his descendants continued to hold on to the mini-lordship in Staggia until 1360, when they conceded it to Florence in return for cancellation of debts that remained from the disaster more than a half-century earlier.[68]

Other Florentines who entered government service were more successful. In particularly striking contrast to the rise and fall of the Franzesi was the unimpeded ascent of the Florentine merchant who achieved the highest rank as a titled feudal lord abroad, Niccolò Acciaiuoli (1310–65). His father's firm rose to become one of the triumvirate, along with the Bardi and Peruzzi firms, that dominated trade and finance in the Angevin Kingdom of Naples; these personal family ties to the royal family smoothed Niccolò's rise to power. He was knighted at the age of twenty-five and appointed master of the royal household. And when he personally took over a fief assigned to his company in the principality of Achaea, he entered the feudal nobility, whence he went on to assemble vast landed estates and to become the Count of Melfi and the powerful Grand Seneschal. One gets the impression that Acciaiuoli left the banking world altogether to become an energetic supporter of the royal family against its enemies in both the political and military spheres, his power and influence apparently not compromised by

[68] Paolo Pirillo, *Famiglia e mobilità sociale nella Toscana medievale: I Franzesi Della Foresta da Figline Valdarno (secoli XII–XV)* (Florence, 1991), 50–67; idem, "Tentazioni signorili," in *Costruzione di un contado: I fiorentini e il loro territorio nel Basso Medioevo* (Florence, 2001), 85–99.

the failures of the 1340s. Yet he used much of his wealth to build the great Certosa back in Florence, which included his own tomb, and so in the end he too returned to his native city, although his heirs continued on their new social trajectory in the south.[69]

Almost as famous as Acciaiuoli was Filippo Scolari, known as Pippo Spano (1369–1426), who made his career almost a century later in the kingdom of Hungary following a different route, as legend has it, though still that of a businessman. Of modest origins, he went to Buda as a company employee, and he owed his first step to fame to his technical business training rather than to the wealth and power of a successful merchant. According to his contemporary biographer, Poggio Bracciolini, King Sigismund began planning major military operations against the Turks but remained perplexed by what it would cost him and how he could pay so many troops. Scolari, who was present at a planning session, having been recommended by the archbishop of Esztergom, took pen in hand and made all the necessary calculations with such speed that the king immediately took him into his service as an administrator. He rapidly advanced to become a royal adviser and successful commander in the king's many military adventures, for which he was rewarded with the title of count *(span)*. He too was remembered back in Florence—in a biography by the prominent humanist chancellor of the republic, in his depiction as a soldier (along with Acciaiuoli as a governor) among the illustrious persons of the time painted by Andrea del Castagno at the Pandolfini villa in Soffiano, and in the octagonal chapel designed by Brunelleschi at the monastery of Santa Maria degli Angeli (financed by his family through complicated hereditary arrangements in which he played a major role).[70]

Another merchant-banker who rose to prominence abroad was Tommaso Portinari, a major, if controversial, figure in Bruges under the dukes of Burgundy. Portinari arrived in the city in 1440, at the beginning of his career as agent of the Medici, and remained for more than a half-century, to 1497. He set up headquarters in an impressive mansion Piero de' Medici purchased in 1466 from the duke, who had had it built for his court treasurer. Portinari became a councilor of the dukes and engineered loans to them in exchange for control over customs tolls at the port of Gravelines and a monopoly on the distribution of alum, essential to the local cloth industry, and he was involved in their efforts to build a small galley fleet. It cannot be determined whether he did these things with the approval of the Medici back in Florence. In any event, Lorenzo de' Medici blamed his personal ambitions for the problems leading to the closing of the bank in Bruges in

---

[69] See the entry for Acciaiuoli in the *Dizionario biografico degli italiani*.

[70] Poggio's "Vita di Messer Filippo Scolari," trans. Bastiano Fortini, is found in G. Canestrini, ed., "Due vite di Filippo Scolari detto Pippo Spano," *ASI*, ser. 1, 4, pt. 1 (1843): 117–232.

1481. Portinari stayed on, despite continuing difficulties arising out of that clos-ing, to end his career on ambassadorial missions for the emperor Maximilian before retiring to Florence, where he died in 1501. No other Florentine resident had as conspicuous a presence in Bruges as Portinari, for the house he lived in and for his position at court.[71]

In sixteenth-century France the passage from merchant banking to royal ser-vice in the army or at court was a particularly notable social phenomenon. Some financiers of the French crown abandoned business and their native city alto-gether, putting down permanent roots for their descendants in the nobility of a foreign land. The most notable of these was Antonio di Antonio Gondi, who en-tered the nobility through purchase of estates and service to the king as collector of royal revenues. In 1550 he abandoned Lyons for the court in Paris. One son, Pierre, became bishop of Paris; the other, Albert, became maréchal de France; and the line continued through the dukes and cardinals de Retz. Other branches of the Gondi family, however, remained in Lyons as merchant-bankers.[72]

These personal successes, of course, were balanced by disastrous failures. However much these merchants were prepared to accept gestures of magnanim-ity and generosity as a fair return on their investment, bankruptcy was the risk they took as they tried to navigate through feudal society. The record of bank-ruptcies of international firms goes back to the thirteenth century, but there is no way of assessing the importance of loans to foreign governments as a general cause.[73] The danger for the great corporate firms of the late thirteenth and early fourteenth centuries, which simultaneously had close ties to various rulers, above all the kings of England and Naples and the papacy, arose from the chance coin-cidence of credit crunches in several places at the same time and not necessarily from one ruler's behavior. The failure of the Ricciardi in England in 1301 followed on the sequestration of their property in France by Philip the Fair in 1294 and heavy loans to Boniface VIII in support of his policy to buy out the Aragonese claims to Sicily. Whether the sequence of other bankruptcies in England at the beginning of the fourteenth century were isolated events or part of a similar pat-tern is impossible to say. However, the great concatenation of bankruptcies in the early 1340s that pulled down the very largest international merchant-banking

[71] Marc Boone, "Apologie d'un banquier médiéval: Tommaso Portinari et l'état bourguignon," *Le Moyen Âge* 105 (1999): 31–54, examines Burgundian materials in an attempt to modify de Roover's harsh judgment of Portinari. The earlier research on Portinari by Richard Walsh has only just re-cently been published: *Charles the Bold and Italy, 1467–1477: Politics and Personnel* (Liverpool, 2005), ch. 3.

[72] Jacqueline Boucher, *Présence italienne à Lyon à la Renaissance: Du milieu du XVe à la fin du XVIe siècle* (Lyons, [1994]), 99–106. On Italians in general, but especially Florentines, who moved into royal service, see Henry Heller, *Anti-Italianism in Sixteenth-Century France* (Toronto, 2003), chs. 3, 5.

[73] Bankruptcies are listed in Davidsohn, *Forschungen*, 3:xiv.

firms, including those of the Bardi, the Peruzzi, the Acciaiuoli, and the Buonaccorsi, was brought on, not by one ruler's debt repudiation, but by a coincidence of problems arising at the same time resulting from these firms' involvement in government finance in several places. It was an episode of a very different magnitude in the history of Florentine international banking for the shock it sent throughout the entire sector and, apparently, even beyond.

In fact, the real crisis came to a head on the local scene at Florence. When, from the late 1330s, Edward III began increasing the pressure on Italian bankers for loans to finance his campaigns in France, they found themselves also making heavy loans to their government at home in Florence to pay for a war against Lucca. The political machinations resulting in the expulsion of the Duke of Athens and the establishment of a popular government in 1343, however, precluded any foreseeable settlement of the claims of bankers who had been part of the preceding oligarchic regime. At the same time, ambiguities about the commune's Guelf loyalties raised by the war against Lucca antagonized King Robert of Naples, and this triggered a run on the principal banks by depositors of the Neapolitan branches. Meanwhile, in 1341 Benedict XII in Avignon began shifting papal banking away from the Florentines. This is the context in which Edward III's actions have to be understood: these firms were hit on all four of their principal bases at the same time. To make matters even worse, their situation in England was further aggravated by a completely extraneous economic factor: a fall in the silver-gold ratio, from about 14:1 to 11:1, in international markets precisely at this time, during the second quarter of the fourteenth century, resulted in a considerable drop in the value in florins of the debt the English king owed the Italians in sterling.[74] Under these extraordinary circumstances, taken all together, these bankers could hardly survive. In short, the coincidence of crises in England, Naples, Florence, and Avignon exposed an overextension of credit and triggered the disastrous series of bankruptcies throughout the network that precluded the possibility of satisfying claims through international transfers of credit.

One large company that did survive the crises of the 1340s was that of the Alberti, which had agents in both Naples and London but apparently no involvement in government finance in those places. In any event, despite everything, the Bardi were soon back on their feet. The sons of two of the bankrupt Bardi partners—Francesco, Biordo, and Iacopo di messer Vieri di ser Lapo and ser

[74] The most comprehensive analysis of the crisis is still Sapori, *La crisi,* but see also Michele Luzzati, *Giovanni Villani e la compagnia dei Buonaccorsi* (Rome, 1971), for a criticism of the chronicler's classic account of the matter. The problem of the gold-silver ratio, not mentioned by Sapori, is discussed by Frederic C. Lane and Reinhold C. Mueller in *Money and Banking in Medieval and Renaissance Venice,* vol. 1, *Coins and Moneys of Account* (Baltimore, 1985), 439–42.

Andrea di Gualtieri di messer Iacopo—went into business at the papal capital at Avignon, while the sons of another partner—Rodolfo and Filippo di Bartolo—regained the favor of the English king, albeit at a somewhat reduced level. They opened a new company in London in 1357 with the king's support, and Walter de' Bardi dominated the royal mint in England from the 1360s to the 1390s. Moreover, the crown never altogether repudiated its debt to the Bardi, and Richard II made a final settlement with them in 1391–92, a half-century after the crisis.[75] Following the crisis of the 1340s, however, Florentines in England were primarily merchants, not bankers. They were no longer heavily involved in royal finances, and by the fifteenth century they had also lost much of the traffic in ecclesiastical transfers to the papacy. For about a decade, from the late 1460s to the late 1470s, the Medici bank made large loans to the king through its agent Gherardo Canigiani, but this isolated episode was of greater significance to Lorenzo de' Medici's political ambitions and to the bad management in his London branch than to the larger history of Florentine banking abroad.[76]

Few of the Florentines involved in the debt of foreign rulers from the fourteenth to sixteenth centuries appear, in the end, to have had much more in mind than the interest of their business. The glaring exception is Lorenzo de' Medici, who patently used loans to princes through his family bank to promote his own political, not business, interests. The grand mansions where the Medici bank set up its headquarters in Milan and Bruges, the former a structure remodeled into a great Renaissance palace by the architect Michelozzo, the latter built by the Duke of Burgundy for his court treasurer and sold to the Medici, both conspicuously bearing the symbols of Medici ownership, went far beyond any purely business need to establish a conspicuous presence in an important princely capital. No other Florentine bank went this far. The crises the Medici bank underwent in the year 1477 to 1481 exposed how precarious its foundations were as a result of this policy of personal ambition, which left the bank unguarded on too many fronts. In 1477 the bank was forced to close down its branch in England because the cost of its heavy loans to the crown, in return for privileges and tax exemptions in its wool trade, created a problem in its balance of payments, and its debts were transferred to the Bruges bank. The death that year of the duke, Charles the Bold, however, left this branch, now burdened with the English debt,

---

[75] For the Bardi in Avignon, see Yves Renouard, "Le compagnie commerciali fiorentine del Trecento (dai documenti dall'Archivio Vaticano)," *ASI* 96 (1938): 63, 67. For those in London, see the entry for Bartolo Bardi by Arnaldo d'Addario in *Dizionario biografico degli italiani;* and Alice Beardwood, *Alien Merchants in England from 1350 to 1377: Their Legal and Economic Position* (Cambridge, MA, 1931), 4–9.

[76] George Holmes, "Lorenzo de' Medici's London Branch," in *Progress and Problems in Medieval England: Essays in Honour of Edward Miller,* ed. Richard Britnell and John Hatcher (Cambridge, 1996), 273–85.

suddenly even more exposed to unpaid loans from the duke and other nobles. To make matters worse, in the same year the Venetian branch went bankrupt and entered into liquidation. In the next year, 1478, the bank closed down its Milan branch, which by that time had little reason to exist, being almost completely dependent on the court for both sales and loans to the Sforza duke; already in 1459 the single largest item on its profit-loss account had been interest on these loans, larger, even, than sales of luxury objects. Meanwhile in Rome, the Medici were losing their influence with the pope: in 1474 the office of depositary was reassigned to a Genoese banker, and in 1476 they lost the Tolfa contract to Guglielmo and Giovanni Pazzi. The political repercussions abroad of the Pazzi conspiracy in 1478 brought all these problems to a head and created further problems for the bank of near-disastrous dimensions. The pope confiscated Medici property in Rome, while his ally King Ferrante of Naples shut down the branch in Naples and sequestered Medici property throughout the kingdom.

In this situation, with the branches in London, Milan, and Naples closed, the one in Venice in liquidation, the one in Bruges threatened with closure, and the one in Rome in a precarious situation, the bank found itself with hardly any flexibility to deal with these problems through the shifting of credits and debits from one branch to another. Only the personal intervention of Lorenzo at the political level saved the situation for the moment. Closings of other branches in the immediate aftermath of the debacle brought on by the Pazzi conspiracy, however, were symptomatic of a serious systemic problem: the company at Avignon (which did not carry the family name) closed in 1480, leaving behind as major debtors the king of France (as the heir of King René) and King Ferrante of Naples; the company in Bruges finally closed in 1481, its precarious state having been exposed by the recent death of the duke; and the liquidation in Venice continued to drag on. Over a period of only a few years the Medici network abroad shrunk to only Lyons outside of Italy and to Rome and Naples. Despite a major reorganization plan in 1482 to deal with this retrenchment, it is generally thought that the firm was on the verge of bankruptcy at the time of Lorenzo's death in 1492, but the expulsion of his family two years later suddenly ends its history, complicating an assessment of the situation.[77]

Bankruptcy was a frequent, if not regular, occurrence in an economy like that of Florence, but, as we shall see in chapter 6, nothing like the bankruptcy crisis of the 1340s occurred ever again in the history of Florentine banking. The crises of the Medici bank had little repercussion in the banking sector, let alone in the lo-

---

[77] The classic study is de Roover, *Medici Bank*. For additional bibliography down to 1987, see Richard A. Goldthwaite, "The Medici Bank and the World of Florentine Capitalism," *Past & Present*, no. 114 (1987): 3–31. See also above, chapter 1, n. 73.

cal economy in general, and even the exile of the family in 1494 did not pull any other bank down. The disastrous failures of the early fourteenth century may have left their mark on the collective memory as a lesson not to be repeated, but the times also changed. The circumstances leading to the extraordinary coincidence of debt repudiation and credit crunches throughout the network never arose again. In the course of the fourteenth century governments everywhere, from cities to feudal monarchies, confronted mounting expenses, mostly of a military nature, and they introduced innovations that brought greater discipline to the ad hoc, personal ways in which they had earlier handled their finances. They still relied heavily on bankers, but the nature of their relations changed. And just as governments became more sophisticated in managing their debts, banks became more sophisticated in handling this debt for them. The flexibility gained from the new arrangements reduced the risks involved in this kind of activity. After the mid-fourteenth-century crisis, Florentines concentrated their interest in government finance on the papacy, first at Avignon and then at Rome, and on the French monarchy, at Lyons; in both governments they worked through new institutional structures devised for handling their floating debt. The history of that involvement reflects one of the major themes in the historiography of later medieval and Renaissance Europe, the rise of the modern fiscal state.

The Papacy

The Papal Curia had revenues coming in from all over Christendom. The amounts involved were considerable, and the traffic increased as the papacy perfected its bureaucratic machinery. When the papacy began to impose taxes on dioceses and religious houses, churchmen throughout Europe found themselves facing practical problems of collecting income due them, dealing with diverse moneys and getting the money to Rome, not to mention their inability to pay immediately. They turned to international merchants to collect their taxes, effect transfers to wherever the income was needed, and advance loans in the meantime. By the end of the twelfth century Italian merchants from Rome itself and from elsewhere were serving the papacy for the exchange of money, holding of deposits, and transfer of funds from abroad. The earliest reference to Florentines among them dates from 1177,[78] and the first appearance of a Florentine officially identified as *campsor domini papae,* from 1232. During the middle two quarters of the thirteenth century the Sienese played the principal role, although the

---

[78] Pierre Toubert, *Les structures du Latium médiévale: Le Latium méridional et la Sabine du IXe siècle à la fin du XIIe siècle* (Rome, 1973), 1:618.

revenue-producing areas were divided among various bankers, including, besides the Sienese, the Lucchesi, and the Florentines, the Ammannati of Pistoia and the Scotti of Piacenza. The Florentines rose to prominence over the others toward the end of the century, in part thanks to their city's Guelf policy in support of the papacy's opposition to the heirs of imperial Ghibellinism (who included the Sienese). Their position in England at that time strengthened their hand. In pursuit of a vigorous anti-imperialist policy in Italy, Innocent IV (1243–54) sought heavy extractions especially from the English church and from Henry III, whom the pope lured into Italian affairs with the offer of the Sicilian crown to the king's son. The role played by Florentine merchants in effecting the related transfers and extensions of credit perhaps more than anything else brought them an ever-larger share of business with both the papacy and the English crown. By the end of the century they outnumbered Italians from other cities and superseded the Sienese as the *campsores* or *mercatores papae*. All the representatives sent by the various rulers to Rome on the occasion of the election of Boniface VIII in 1294 were Florentine,[79] and the Spini and the Mozzi, together with the Chiarenti of Pistoia, shared the keeping of the personal accounts of Boniface that survive in a fragment of 1302–3.[80] Bankers probably made up most of the crowd of Florentines Boniface famously addressed, on the occasion of the jubilee of 1300, as the fifth element. By that time the papacy had assigned to Florentines some of the most important areas in Europe for the collection of papal revenues, and this activity was the solid foundation on which the greatest of the bankers expanded their businesses to include the acceptance of deposits and the granting of loans. Some of these early papal bankers—Pulci, Rimbertini, Mozzi, Frescobaldi, Scali, Spini, Bardi, Cerchi (to put them in the order of their appearance in papal documents from 1282 on)—we have already encountered. The business in papal revenues in England brought in the funds they used for the purchase of wool, and their support of the papacy against the claims of the German emperors opened the way to their ascendancy in the commerce and finances of the new Angevin kingdom in the south.[81]

Florentines continued to serve the papacy in the international transfer of funds and exchange banking after its move to Avignon in 1305. The Scali, Buonaccorsi, Bardi, Peruzzi, and Acciaiuoli firms dominated papal business before they ended in bankruptcy. In the aftermath of the crises of the 1340s the popes turned

[79] Giovanni Cherubini, *Città comunali di Toscana* (Bologna, 2003), 18n.

[80] Bruno Dini, "I mercanti-banchieri e la sede apostolica (XIII–prima metà del XIV secolo)," in *Gli spazi economici della Chiesa nell'Occidente mediterraneo (secoli XII–metà XIV)* (Pistoia, 1999), 72, reprinted in his *Manifattura, commercio e banca nella Firenze medievale* (Florence, 2001).

[81] Still the best survey of this early evidence of Florentines serving the papacy is Davidsohn, *Storia di Firenze*, 4, pt. 2:ch. 5.

to others, especially the Lucchesi, but by the 1360s the Florentines had regained their strength, the Alberti being especially prominent, followed by the Guardi and the Soderini. Meanwhile, major changes in the administrative structure of the papacy that accompanied its establishment at Avignon very much enlarged business opportunities for merchant-bankers in residence. For the first time a large court of clerics from all over Christendom assembled around the pope, and this opened a major commercial and financial market. More important, however, was the formation of a comprehensive fiscal bureaucracy that resulted in a more efficient administration of international revenues. In addition, in 1353 the new pope, Innocent VI, initiated a vigorous military policy to carve out a secure territorial base in central Italy in anticipation of the return to Rome.

Avignon, in short, became a major center in the international money market, with church revenues flowing in from all over Europe and flowing out to pay for the military campaigns in central Italy. This traffic is epitomized in the ledgers of the firms of Bartolomeo and Iacopo di Caroccio degli Alberti, in the large remittances they register in the 1350s both from Bruges to Avignon, in the name of the archbishop of Riga, and from Avignon to the papal representative at Perugia, the center of military operations. Another company active in this decade, that of Niccolò and Martino di Simone Guardi, had branches only in Avignon and Perugia (with agents elsewhere, however), presumably to handle transfer of funds to pay troops in the field. Florentines were in a better position than bankers from other places to serve the papacy in this way because of their much more extensive network. Moreover, the papacy considered the Guelf sentiments of their home government more favorable to its Italian policy.[82]

The 1378 schism of the papacy into two allegiances, one centering in Rome and the other in Avignon, initially created problems for Florentines, who adhered to the Roman cause. They did not, however, abandon Avignon, which was a major regional market center, in contrast to Rome, which did not lie on trade routes of any importance. Already in 1381 Clement VII authorized their residence in the city, and they were soon back in business. The Italians, wherever they came from, still dominated papal finances, although the bankers the Avignon popes leaned on came from places other than Florence, above all from Lucca, Asti, Genoa, and Bologna; most of them had their main base at Paris or Barcelona, in the two kingdoms that fell into the Avignon allegiance. On the question whether the schism led also to a split in international finance between adherents of one side or the other, the evidence from papal documents is too much on the Roman side to

---

[82] Yves Renouard has documented the Florentines at Avignon in "Le compagnie commerciali fiorentine" and in *Les relations des papes d'Avignon et des compagnies commerciales et bancaires de 1316 à 1378* (Paris, 1941).

permit a clear answer. If one great Lucchese firm, the Rapondi, served Avignon and another, the Guinigi, served Rome, it was because each had its base of operations in its respective area of papal allegiance. The Medici, on the other hand, crossed allegiances. Andrea de' Pazzi in Barcelona, for instance, an agent of the Roman firm belonging to Francesco de' Bardi and Averardo di Francesco de' Medici, transferred ecclesiastical revenues to Avignon in the first decade of the fifteenth century, and through him the firm in Rome had other financial dealings with the rival claimant. It is hardly surprising that finance, like commerce, knew no ideological divide.[83]

The papacy's return to Rome, however, marks a watershed in the history of Florentine banking at the papal court. Already in the late 1360s, with the attempted return to Rome of Urban V to take control of the Papal States, the way was opened for Florentines to move into the financing of his political ambitions. The eventual relocation of the papacy in a city that was to emerge as the capital of a territorial state opened new opportunities in commerce and government finance. Business underwent a crisis during the War of the Eight Saints (1375–78), when Florence was under interdict, but picked up again with the schism, which left Urban VI, in Rome, cut off from much of his northern European revenues and facing problems of political instability in the city and in its highly decentralized territorial state. Merchant-bankers from all over Italy moved to Rome, and in the early years the Lucchese firm of the Guinigi almost monopolized business with the Curia, largely because of its ability to transfer ecclesiastical funds from its branches in Bruges and London, which fell into the Roman allegiance. In the 1390s, however, the Florentines emerged to dominate the scene, led by the Alberti, the Ricci, the Spini, and the Medici. Vieri di Cambio de' Medici, whose family had never numbered among the top merchant-bankers at home, made a fortune in Rome that, on his death in 1395, ranked him among the wealthiest men in Florence.[84]

The papacy's move to Rome resulted in structural changes in the handling of its finances that for bankers opened up possibilities of profit there that they had not had in Avignon. In Rome the papacy found itself deprived of the financial

<hr/>

[83] Jean Favier, *Les finances pontificales a l'époque du grand schisme d'occident, 1378–1409* (Paris, 1966), 517–18, differs with de Roover in maintaining that these two Medici firms worked closely together and indeed may have been one firm. Luciano Palermo thinks that there were two firms following a joint policy to satisfy both obediences. "Banchi privati e finanze pubbliche nella Roma del primo Rinascimento," in *Banchi pubblici, banchi privati e monti di pietà nell'Europa preindustriale* (Genoa, 1991), 1:458.

[84] For papal bankers in this period, see Favier, *Les finances pontificales*, esp. ch. 10; Arnold Esch, "Bankiers der Kirche im grossen Schisma," in *Quellen und Forschungen aus italienischen Archiven und Bibliotheken* 46 (1966): 277–398 (282–321 on Florentines); and idem, "Florentiner in Rom um 1400: Namenverzeichnis der ersten Quattrocento-Generation," ibid. 52 (1972): 496–525.

machinery that had been built up in Avignon; at the same time, it had to confront the immediate problems of ruling a territorial state and, hence, of diplomatic involvement in the turbulent political scene in Italy. It had no option but to lean heavily on bankers for loans to meet these heavy expenditures, and this dependence eventually led it to restructure the financial administration of the Curia around the office of the depositary. This official did not manage papal financial affairs; instead, he received major funds in deposit from the treasurer of the Apostolic Chamber, who handled income and expenditures through this office. Bankers were the obvious choice to be named depositary, since they could advance loans to the treasurer, in return for which they gained control over incomes from such things as customs, the salt monopoly, and other tax revenues in Rome and the Papal States. With this lien on the revenues deposited with him, the depositary in effect was able to tap the wealth of the church, and he could bring in other bankers by farming out the direct administration of these revenues to them. The office evolved slowly in its juridical and administrative definition, and it gained formal status among the officials of the Apostolic Chamber under Martin V (1417–31). From 1390 on, bankers held the office, thereby assuming an official role in papal finances, while the papacy gained the possibility of having access to long-term credit. The first depositaries were from Lucca and Bologna. The first Florentine was Niccolò de' Ricci, named in 1406, and he was followed in 1409 by Doffo di Neri Spini. Florentines continued to hold the office for about half of the fifteenth century, most of them being associates of the Medici. Tommaso di Leonardo Spinelli (1400–1471), who served as depositary from 1443 to 1447, rose to the office having made his fortune in Rome. The son of a dealer in furs and skins, Spinelli began his career in the city working for the Alberti and eventually built up his own firm, with branches in Bruges, Venice, and London, which engaged in trade all across Europe, from Spain to France and even Germany. In 1452, on the occasion of the last imperial coronation in medieval Rome, he hosted the emperor, Frederick III, in his villa at the foot of Monte Mario.[85]

The Roman company of Vieri di Cambio de' Medici was the foundation of the great Medici bank of the fifteenth century, and Rome always remained at the center of the family's business empire. Its special relation to the papacy grew out of the friendship Giovanni di Bicci de' Medici had with Baldassarre Cossa, the schismatic pope John XXIII (1410–15), whose vigorous policy to establish a politi-

---

[85] For the recent literature and consideration of the historiography on papal finances in this period and the evolution of the office of depositary, see two articles by Luciano Palermo, "Banchi privati e finanze pubbliche" and "La finanza pontificia e il banchiere 'depositario' nel primo Quattrocento," in *Studi in onore di Ciro Manca*, ed. Donatella Strangio (Milan, 2000), 349–78. Spinelli's career is summarized in William Caferro, "L'attività bancaria papale e la Firenze del Rinascimento: Il caso di Tommaso Spinelli," *Società e storia*, no. 70 (1995): 717–53.

cal base in Italy the Medici supported with heavy loans.[86] The 1420 articles of association for renewal of the partnership specifically stated the purpose of the firm as dealing in exchange, without mentioning commerce. Moreover, subsequent renewals mention no capital at all from the partners, since it was able to operate on funds raised from deposits and papal contracts. From 1420 to 1435 the Rome branch accounted for 63 percent of all profits earned by this international company agglomerate, and it was a major source of credit to branches elsewhere whenever they encountered problems. Under Lorenzo, as we have seen, political ambitions, more than business interests, tended to drive the firm's policy of making loans to the pope, and his premature death left the bank on the verge of bankruptcy.[87] The difficulties that faced the papacy when it turned against the Medici in the aftermath of the Pazzi conspiracy testify to its dependence on this one bank.[88]

The slow assertion of direct political control by the papacy throughout the Papal States resulted in a territory that by the mid-sixteenth century included Umbria, much of the Marche, the Romagna, and a foothold in Emilia at Bologna. The corresponding enlargement of the pope's temporal revenues provided him with the security he could put up in return for the loans he needed from merchant-bankers to handle perennial deficits. The papacy obtained loans in a number of ways. It borrowed directly at stated rates of interest, usually about 12 percent, offering liens on future revenues as security. It contracted out, for specified periods, the administration of revenue sources, such as customs tolls, the Roman port at Ripa, the mint, the salt monopoly, the alum mines at Tolfa, various depositories (including those for the Datary, for the works at the new St. Peter's, for monasteries and individual cardinals, as well as that for the Apostolic Chamber), the numerous provincial treasuries (Fermo, Camerino, Ascoli, Perugia, the Marche, Umbria, Parma-Piacenza, Patrimonio, and yet others in the territorial state), and a host of other treasuries for specific taxes. The papacy also raised funds from offices, offering some as security in return for loans and selling others outright; some carried the prestige of a title, some could be sold on the market, and virtually all carried an income or offered some other financial advantage. The fact that the titles of more than 258 offices passed through the hands

[86] George Holmes, "How the Medici Became the Pope's Bankers," in *Florentine Studies: Politics and Society in Renaissance Florence,* ed. Nicolai Rubinstein (London, 1968), 357–80.

[87] Lorenzo's personal involvement in the bank in Rome is recounted in Bullard, "Banking on Reputation," 155–88.

[88] On this point, see George Holmes, "The Pazzi Conspiracy Seen from the Apostolic Chamber," in *Mosaics of Friendship: Studies in Art and History for Eve Borsook* (Florence, 1999), 163–73.

of Filippo Strozzi during his service as banker to the Medici popes in the early sixteenth century indicates something of the traffic in this kind of investment.[89]

Finally, the funding of the debt opened up yet other opportunities to borrow. In 1486 the Apostolic Chamber took the first step toward regularizing the debt through an agreement with a consortium of bankers according to which they would advance loans over a number of years in return for their control over consolidated revenues. Nine bankers participated in the original pact, and over the next eight years, in the subsequent parceling out of shares, the number rose to forty-six, most of them Genoese and Florentines. A full funding of some of the debt occurred with the establishment of the Monte della Fede in 1526, and over the course of the century forty other *monti* were set up. These were funds raised through sale of shares that paid interest guaranteed by assignment of specific revenues for this purpose, some shares carrying a title of knighthood to attract buyers. These shares were essentially lifetime *rentes,* although some paid interest in perpetuity and were therefore inheritable. And since the bearer could reassign shares, a secondary market grew up around them. The funding of the debt by the papal government in the sixteenth century marked a significant improvement over the traditional way rulers, like the English and Neapolitan kings, borrowed money by making deals with private lenders on an ad hoc basis. Through the monti the papacy institutionalized its borrowing, creating a permanent funded debt that opened opportunities for investors outside banking circles. It did not, however, completely depersonalize borrowing, for the bankers came in through the back door, one might say, to take over the administration of the revenues assigned to the funds.[90]

All these devices arose from a situation in which papal finances were almost always in deficit, and the debt continued to rise to the point that in the early sixteenth century servicing it was the principal charge on papal income. Only a large money market could have sustained the proliferation of such a variety of devices to borrow money, and this market was in the hands of bankers. In addition, they provided the usual banking services of loans, deposits, and transfers to resident ecclesiastics and the Roman nobility. In the fifteenth century Florentines dominated this money market as bankers transferring ecclesiastical revenues from northern Europe, as lenders to the pope, and as administrators of papal revenues. Toward the end of the century the Genoese appeared in force, and then came the

[89] Melissa Bullard, *Filippo Strozzi and the Medici: Favor and Finance in Sixteenth-Century Florence and Rome* (Cambridge, 1980), 151–52.

[90] Peter Partner has written extensively on papal finances and has summarized his work, citing further references, in "The Papacy and the Papal States," in *The Rise of the Fiscal State in Europe, c. 1200–1815,* ed. R. Bonney (Oxford, 1999), 359–80. On the 1486 consortium, see Melissa Bullard, "Financing the Pope's Debt," in *Lorenzo il Magnifico,* 189–214.

Germans. The Fuggers, with a foundation in silver mines and the support of the Hapsburgs, were far richer than any single Italian firm. They took over the transfers from the German church to the papacy, and their loans to the pope brought them the usual portfolio of revenue-collecting privileges. The Germans, however, suffered from the growing hostility between Clement VII and Charles V over divergent policies on the wider European stage. The open rupture between the two in 1526 and the sack of Rome by imperial troops the next year in effect ended the short-lived prominence of the Germans, and of the Fuggers in particular, on the local scene.[91] In 1540 the creditors of the Apostolic Chamber were almost equally divided between Florentines and Genoese.[92]

Just as the papacy got its fiscal house in order with a more rational organization of its debt, the bankers organized themselves to handle their enormous collective business with the papacy. They did this, not through an institutional structure, but by more cooperation among themselves. This took the form of dividing contracts into shares distributed among different bankers; moreover, shares in any one contract might be taken out by bankers from different places. Hence, opportunities opened up for more participants, individual risktaking was reduced, and the international community of bankers became somewhat more integrated. All this can be illustrated by the career of Benvenuto di Paolo Olivieri (1496–1549), the only Florentine whose business records have been thoroughly studied. Olivieri did not come from a prominent family. His grandfather, who had modest artisan status as a goldsmith, left a patrimony consisting only of a farm with a peasant's house and another piece of rural property. And although nothing is known about Benvenuto's father, the fact that he and his numerous brothers also became merchants, scattered across Europe, suggests that their father, Paolo, had been on an upward economic trajectory. Benvenuto was in Rome by the time he was twenty and got his start working with Bindo Altoviti (as an employee and eventually as partner) and then Filippo Strozzi the Younger (as partner), two of the most prominent Florentine bankers at the papal court, both best known for their roles as exiles opposing the new regime of Cosimo I in Florence.[93]

[91] Philippe Braunstein, "Du nouveau sur l'activité des Fugger à Rome entre 1517 et 1527," in *Wirtschaftskräfte und Wirtschaftswebe: Festschrift für Hermann Kellenbenz,* ed. Jürgen Schneider (Nuremberg, 1978), 1:657–71.

[92] Francesco Guidi Bruscoli, *Benvenuto Olivieri: I "mercatores" fiorentini e la Camera Apostolica nella Roma di Paolo III Farnese (1534–1549)* (Florence, 2000), 105n, now translated as *Papal Banking in Renaissance Rome: Benvenuto Olivieri and Paul III, 1534–1549* (Abingdon, England, 2007).

[93] Melissa Bullard has studied both of these bankers. See *Filippo Strozzi and the Medici,* and "Bindo Altoviti, Renaissance Banker and Papal Financier," in *Raphael, Cellini, and a Renaissance Banker: The Patronage of Bindo Altoviti,* ed. Alan Chong, Donatella Pegazzano, and Dimitrios Zikos (Boston, 2003), 21–57. Neither, however, left behind a significant body of business records.

Olivieri held the post of depositary of the Apostolic Chamber from 1540 to 1543 and from 1545 to 1546. During these years his company was advancing loans to the papacy in about every possible way, usually jointly with other bankers. In 1539 he and two others bought the salt customs in Rome. In 1540 he bought a 25 percent share with five others in the salt customs in the Romagna, a 25 percent share with three others in the management of the Roman mint, and, for himself alone, a 25 percent share in the wine tax at Rome, which supported the university (*gabella dello Studio*). In 1541 he bought a 20 percent share with four others in the Treasury of Perugia; in 1542, a 30 percent share in the Treasury of Parma and Piacenza; in 1543, a 50 percent share with one other in three contracts for the customs of Rome; and in 1546 a 25 percent share with five others in the Treasury of the Romagna. Since each of these contracts had a duration of several years, there was much overlap. And if all this were not enough, in 1542 he received the venal office of an apostolic secretary as security for a loan and bought a second one. And all the while he was buying and selling credits in several monti, including the colleges of knights. During these same years his commercial business with the papal government included contracts for the importation of grain to the city of Rome—a major commercial interest of most of these bankers—and a subcontract for the exportation of alum from Tolfa to specified ports in France, which he purchased from the Genoese banker who had the primary Tolfa contract. This complex and variable web of Olivieri's credit ties to the papal government also extended underground, so to speak, through his contribution in 1542 to the capital of another company, Girolamo di Raffaello Ubaldini & Partners, set up "to engage in exchange, shipping, contracts for customs, the alum trade, [papal] treasuries, and other things," as stated on the occasion of the renewal of the partnership three years later, when the name of his four-year-old son was added to the firm's title.[94]

This intricate institutionalization of credit devices on the one hand and the large community of participating bankers sharing risks on the other assured considerable flexibility in the market that grew up around papal finances, precluding the kinds of disasters suffered by the Bardi, Peruzzi, and other firms in the relatively primitive credit market two centuries earlier. Bankruptcies were always occurring, of course, but there does not seem to have been a chain reaction, and some firms reopened afterwards. Of the known firms that went bankrupt in the period from 1566 to 1608 only about eight were Florentine, and the bankruptcies of four of these—Ubaldini, Tassoni-Orlandini, Antinori, Altoviti—occurred in

[94] All this is documented from Olivieri's extensive business archive by Guidi Bruscoli, *Benvenuto Olivieri*. The cluster of companies belonging to Olivieri's brothers is mentioned in chapter 1.

1588. The overall picture is not clear, however, although the rationale given at the time for the opening of Rome's first public deposit bank in 1605, the Banco di Santo Spirito, was that deposits of religious institutions in private banks were endangered by bank failures.[95]

With assets under management alone totaling *du*.302,000 in 1543, Olivieri's principal firm operated at a level three times that of the Medici branch in Rome in 1427 (considering both the appreciation of the florin-ducat and inflation), a clear indication of the growth of the financial market at Rome in the meantime. By Olivieri's time the enormous increase in the number of fiscal offices in the Papal States, of monti, and of other investment opportunities attracted bankers from many places. The Florentines by no means monopolized the scene. Of the thirty-one international exchange bankers who in 1550 signed an edict that moved the day for effecting exchange clearance to Fridays, only a dozen can be identified as Florentine with certainty. Other major bankers active in the city were from Pisa, Siena, Milan, Spain, and above all Genoa; among them was a converted Portuguese Jew, Giovanni Lopez. The Genoese, however, were the only group who competed seriously for papal business. Their rise throughout southern Europe at the time, encapsulated in Felipe Ruiz Martín's phrase "the century of the Genoese," is one of those central subjects in the economic history of early modern Europe that still lacks its historian. Genoese bankers had always been on the scene wherever the popes were, first in Avignon and then in Rome, and they were treated with particular favoritism at the end of the fifteenth century, when there was a sequence of Ligurian popes: Sixtus IV Della Rovere (1471–84), Innocent VIII Cibo (1484–92), and Julius II Della Rovere (1503–13). At various times they held the post of depositary of the Apostolic Chamber and had the contract for the alum mines at Tolfa, and they constituted the original consortium of 1486 that anticipated the funding of the papal debt. In the sixteenth century Florentines and Genoese alternated in holding major financial posts, and at times, rather than working in competition, they joined together in veritable consortia for the administration of papal revenues.

Symbolic of the importance to Florentines of their presence in the city is the church they began to think about building for their community in 1508. The project got under way with the election of the Medici pope Leo X in 1513 but was not completed until a century later. As mentioned in chapter 2, it was the most

[95] A general picture of money, finance, and banking in sixteenth-century Rome is to be found in Jean Delumeau, *Vie économique et sociale de Rome dans la seconde moitié du 16. siècles* (Paris, 1957), 2:845–937; his view of the extent and causes of the bankruptcies in this period, listed on 894–905, is somewhat contradictory. For a more recent bibliography, see Fausto Piola Caselli, "Banchi privati e debito pubblico pontificio a Roma tra Cinquecento e Seicento," in *Banchi pubblici, banchi privati,* 1:461–95.

monumental project the Florentines planned in any of the places within their network. It was to have a prominent location at the head of the fashionable new Via Giulia, just a few steps from the Ponte Sant'Angelo and in the immediate neighborhood of the new mint and the palaces of the Altoviti, the Gaddi, and other resident Florentine bankers.[96] At the end of the century there were about a hundred Florentine merchants and bankers, compared with thirty Genoese, who were the next most numerous group.[97] The Genoese, however, were dominated by only a few major families, including the Doria, the Negrone, the Pallavicino, the Spinola, the Sauli, and the Giustiniani, who over the course of the century took an increasingly larger share of the spoils; by the seventeenth century the Florentines clearly had lost out to them. The decline of the one, however, is as obscure in the historiography as the rise of the other.

Competition and Innovation in the Sixteenth Century

In the sixteenth century two challenges to Florentine preeminence in international banking arose, one from the southern Germans and one from the Genoese. Both had direct access to enormous supplies of bullion and operated under the umbrella of the Hapsburg emperors, which, beginning with Maximilian (1493–1519) and culminating with Charles V (1519–56), stretched across Europe from the Low Countries to Hungary and Bohemia in the north and took in Spain and the Neapolitan kingdom in the south.

The Germans, most of them from Augsburg and Nuremberg, built their commercial success on the intensification of trade across Germany stimulated by the rise of a strong fustian industry and by the growth of the great international emporia at Lyons to the southwest and Antwerp to the northwest. Of major importance also was the mining boom in copper and silver that got under way in the second half of the fifteenth century, first in Saxony and then in the Tyrol and Slovakia. The richest of these families, the Fuggers of Augsburg, built their fortunes on lucrative privileges in the administration of the mines in Hapsburg territories that they gained in exchange for loans to Maximilian for the pursuit of his political ambitions. They had an increasingly heavy hand in the collection of ecclesiastical revenues in Germany directed to Rome. Both they and the Welsers, also from Augsburg, rose to prominence in Antwerp, where they had strong in-

---

[96] The bankers' investment in this project has been documented by Francesco Guidi Bruscoli in "San Giovanni dei Fiorentini a Roma: Due secoli di finanziamenti tra pontefici e granduchi, prelati e *mercatanti*," *Quellen und Forschungen aus italienischen Archiven und Bibliotheken* 86 (2006): 294–320.

[97] Claudia Conforti, "La 'nazione fiorentina' a Roma nel Rinascimento," in *La città e i luoghi degli stranieri, XIV–XVII,* ed. Donatella Calabi and Paola Lanaro (Rome, 1998), 175.

terests in the spice trade from Lisbon, and in Lyons and other important centers in the western Mediterranean. The Welsers, after the Fuggers the most powerful of these families, had agents in Vienna, Antwerp, Lyons, Genoa, Milan, and Venice, in addition to administrators at mines in Bohemia. The Fuggers alone amassed capital far beyond the capability of any Florentine merchant-banker. In 1491 they had 54,385 Rhenish florins, or gulden (worth about a quarter less than the Florentine florin), invested in their company, and this figure rose to 196,791 Rhenish florins in 1511; the net value of their assets reached more than 2 million florins in 1527 and about 5 million in 1546.[98] Of the 851,000 Rhenish florins raised by Charles V to win his election as emperor in 1519, the Fuggers contributed 543,000 florins, the Welsers 143,000 florins, and the Genoese Vivaldi and the Florentine Gualterotti together only 165,000 florins. Although they, along with other German merchant-bankers, subsequently found themselves increasingly and inextricably entangled in the imperial debt resulting from the European ambitions of Charles V, they also rose to become major merchants and financiers in the Hapsburg lands of Spain and Naples in the first half of the sixteenth century. They thereby came into direct competition with the Italians, above all the Genoese and the Florentines. During Charles V's reign the loans these Germans made to the crown of Castile, the emperor's chief base, may have been as important as those made by the Genoese.[99]

Despite the enormous resources at the disposal of the Germans and their influence on the emperor, they could not, in the long run, compete with the Genoese in Spain: they were too tied to the Austrian Hapsburgs, and they lacked the broader commercial and financial structure of the Genoese.[100] Although no Genoese merchant-banking family was as rich as the Fuggers or perhaps the Welsers, many were much richer than those Germans at the rung beneath them. The extensive commercial interest of the Genoese merchant-bankers in Spain, where there were Genoese communities throughout the country, gave them greater flexibility in credit dealings with the crown; they had the ships to move the bullion to Italy; and they had their own exchange fairs at Besançon (later at Piacenza) to facilitate international transfers. In short, unlike the Germans, the Genoese

[98] Jacob Strieder, *Jacob Fugger the Rich* (New York, 1931), 86–89, 183.

[99] The general overview of the rise of German banking in Richard Ehrenberg, *Capital and Finance in the Age of the Renaissance: A Study of the Fuggers and Their Connections* (London, 1928), published in German in 1896, is still useful. Unfortunately, the English translation omits the chapter on the Genoese, which traces the ascent of the Genoese over the Germans in the Spain of Phillip II. For a table summarizing the debt obligations of the treasury of Castile, 1521–55, see James D. Tracy, *Emperor Charles V, Impresario of War: Campaign Strategy, International Finance, and Domestic Politics* (Cambridge, 2002), 101.

[100] Reinhard Hildebrandt, "I 'merchant bankers' della Germania meridionale nell'economia e nella politica del XVI e del XVII secolo," in Maddalena and Kellenbenz, *La repubblica internazionale del denaro*, 211–42.

had an extensive commercial, shipping, and financial network throughout the western Mediterranean, including the Spanish territories, and this solid foundation, along with superior business techniques, put them in a better position to serve the rulers of unified Spain in the handling of the bullion imports from the New World and the transfer of funds to pay for the Hapsburgs' military campaigns in northern Europe.

By the second half of the century the Genoese were the chief players, more important than the Germans, in financing Philip II's enormous floating debt, which was organized around the *asientos* (loan contracts for the floating debt). They were more successful than the Germans and the Tuscans in renegotiating that debt after the so-called royal bankruptcy of 1557, with the result that they gained ascendancy over the others in doing business with the crown.[101] From 1567 to 1574 the brothers Visconte and Nicola Cattaneo alone loaned *du.*1,125,000 plus *sc.*142,000, an astronomical figure by Florentine standards.[102] The loans the Genoese made to Philip III in the early years of his reign, from 1598 to 1607, added up to almost 23 million ducats, 88 percent of his total borrowing.[103] The Genoese also dominated the market in Antwerp, which remained a center for raising public funds even as it went into commercial decline at the end of the sixteenth century. At this level of royal finance the Genoese left the Florentines, as well as the Germans, far behind. Some Florentines invested in asientos, but collectively they could hardly challenge the commanding position of the Genoese. The firm of Zanobi Carnesecchi and Alessandro Strozzi underwrote two asientos for the grand duke, one for *sc.*250,000 in 1580 and the other for *sc.*300,000 in 1583. Only the largest of Florentine banks could take such risks, however, and it did so only in accord with the grand duke.[104] In the Antwerp market for asientos apparently only one

---

[101] For a revision of the negative view of the bankruptcies during these years, see Mark Steele, "The Management of Spain's Debts under Philip II, 1556–1598," in *Local and International Credit in the Middle Ages and the XVI Century* (Berne, 1986), 76–87. Giorgio Doria has shown how little these "bankruptcies" affected the personal fortune of one Genoese banker who had large investments in Spain during this entire period. See his "Mezzo secolo di attività finanziarie di un doge di Genova," in *Nobiltà e investimenti a Genova in Età Moderna* (Genoa, 1995), 175–88, reprinted from Schneider, *Wirtschaftskräfte und Wirtschaftswege*, 1:731–44.

[102] Enrique Otte, "Il ruolo dei genovesi nella Spagna del XV e XVI secolo," in Maddalena and Kellenbenz, *La repubblica internazionale del denaro*, 39. See also Grendi, *I Balbi*, ch. 2, for a detailed analysis of one Genoese firm's interest in asientos.

[103] Thomas Allison Kirk, *Genoa and the Sea: Policy and Power in an Early Modern Maritime Republic, 1559–1684* (Baltimore, 2005), 88.

[104] Felipe Ruiz Martín, *Lettres marchandes échangées entre Florence et Medina del Campo* (Paris, 1965), lvii–lxv. Scattered throughout this correspondence are references to other Florentines who invested in asientos, some together with non-Florentines. See Hermann Kellenbenz, "Die fremden Kaufleute auf der Iberischen Halbinsel von 15. Jahrhundert bis zum Ends des 16. Jahrhunderts," *Kölner Kolloquien zur internazionalen Sozial und Wirtschaftsgeschichte* 1 (1970): 283–84. Note the complete absence of Florentines, however, in Henri Lapeyre, *Simon Ruiz et les "asientos" de Philippe II* (Paris, 1953).

prominent Florentine, Luigi Capponi, was among the bankers who in 1589 joined the great Doria-Velluti-Amatto consortium, and only one or two were included in the renewal of the consortium in 1596.[105]

If the Florentines did not play a large role in the market for state funds within Spanish territories, at Antwerp and in Spain itself, at least one of them, Gaspar Ducci (b. ca. 1495, last documented in 1585), has emerged in the historiography as something like an archetypal figure of the new kind of speculator to which the Antwerp market gave birth. Ducci, however, did not belong to the Florentine business community, although he is always described as a Florentine merchant in the documents. Born in Pescia, near Lucca but in the Florentine state, he got his start working for the Lucchese company of Niccolò Nobili in Antwerp, and he remained there for his entire career, without, however, breaking family ties with his homeland. Eventually he was working on his own as an agent, intermediary, and financial entrepreneur. His commercial activity concentrated on trade in English wool, Portuguese spices, and precious metals. His chief activity, however, was as a financial entrepreneur, arranging loans as an intermediary and speculating on the exchange. He organized loans for the government of the Low Countries in return for contracts for collection of taxes. In 1542 he organized a massive loan to the emperor, successfully competing with no one less than the Fuggers. He bought a large estate, entertained the nobility, and in 1547, in return for his financial services to the emperor, was made a councilor of state and ennobled as lord of Crujbeck, where he had property. His professional reputation was truly international. He worked for German bankers as well as for Italians, he once served Cosimo I as agent in Antwerp, and he was asked by Francis I to go to Lyons as his agent to arrange for loans (he did not go). His dealings as a financier sometimes got him into trouble and antagonized other operators in the field, while his social ambitions aroused suspicion and dislike. For these reasons the older literature was unkind to him, but he has also been recognized as one of the first men who understood how changed conditions in the financial market made it possible for an intermediary to arrange loans for governments by recourse directly to the market—in Antwerp through the Bourse—so that they could avoid dependence on big bankers.[106]

The one place outside of Italy where Florentine bankers had considerable success as government financiers was France. Previously French kings, unlike their English counterparts, had never relied on loans from Italian merchants. After Philip the Fair freed himself from Mouche and Biche toward the end of his reign, the crown had little recourse to private bankers. The French kings did not have

---

[105] Valentin Vasquez de Prada, *Lettres marchandes d'Anvers* (Paris, 1960), 1:195–97.
[106] See the entry for Ducci, by Enrico Stumpo, in *Dizionario biografico degli italiani.*

access to the same kind of consolidated tax income to guarantee loans that the island kingdom of England had in its customs charges. Moreover, they tended to staff their bureaucracy with Frenchmen, not foreigners, since no place under their direct rule gave them access to as large a community of Italian merchant-bankers as was to be found in London or Bruges. With the end of the Hundred Years' War, however, greater financial pressures on the one hand and readier access to bankers on the other put the king in a different position. Having established Lyons as a major trade center that then became the most important market for international exchange, the crown found that the heavy concentration of Italians there gave it access to their banking services, and the king had increasing recourse to them to finance his costly rivalry with the Hapsburgs, which unsettled the international political order in western Europe for the better part of the century.

Francis I borrowed from the Lyons bankers in the usual way, granting them in return liens on various taxes. Of the 87 Italians out of the 127 known lenders during his reign, 45 were Florentines.[107] Florentines contributed half of a loan of 400,000 livres to the king in 1542, the Lucchesi contributed 100,000 livres, and both the Welsers and a group of French bankers contributed 50,000 livres each. When the Grand Parti was set up in 1555, the crown already owed three Florentine banks, those of the Salviati, the Guadagni heirs, and the Panciatichi-Rinuccini, a total of 1,073,344 livres (400,000 écus).[108] Many of these Florentines in Lyons had gone into exile after the fall of the last republic in 1530. With support from colleagues in Rome, such as Filippo di Filippo Strozzi and Bindo Altoviti, they formed an active pressure group only too willing to make loans to a ruler with whom they could find common ground, joining their anti-Medicean cause to his anti-imperialist policy in Italy.[109]

One of the most remarkable of these was Albizzo di Piero Del Bene (Albisse d'Elbène), who came from a large family of merchant-bankers long active at Lyons, some of whom held royal offices. In the 1540s his loans to the king brought him several tax farms and other financial privileges related to the importation of alum and spices, and in 1543 he became one of the executors named to run the most important bank in Lyons for making loans to the king, that of Tommaso di Tommaso Guadagni, who died prematurely, leaving behind several small children. Del Bene's success at organizing his fellow bankers into groups, or syndicates *(parti),* for the purpose of arranging collective loans won him the royal appoint-

[107] Philippe Hamon, *L'argent du roi: Les finances sous François Ier* (Paris, 1994), 140–41.
[108] Roger Doucet, "Le Grand Parti de Lyons au XVI siècle," *Revue historique* 171 (1933): 478, 490.
[109] The important link between the exiled bankers and the French monarchy is emphasized in Paolo Simoncelli, "Florentine Fuorusciti at the Time of Bindo Altoviti," in Chong, Pegazzano, and Zikos, *Raphael, Cellini, and a Renaissance Banker,* 285–328.

ment, in 1550, as superintendent of finances for the Italian wars, a post created for him, marking the first time a banker became a major financial officer in the royal bureaucracy. Del Bene was, in fact, known as the king's banker, in charge of financing the active political ambitions of Henry II (1547–59) in Italy. From 1551 to 1556 he raised more than 8 million livres for this purpose. His considerable skills as a banker who fully understood international monetary matters, both the exchange market and the movement of specie, enabled him to rationalize royal borrowing policy; at the same time, in dealing with his fellow bankers, albeit in the interest of royal policy, he fully recognized their legitimate interests as well.[110]

Henry II's borrowing continued unabated as the Hapsburg-Valois wars approached a climax; and it was most likely Del Bene who, in 1555, devised the scheme known as the Grand Parti de Lyon to deal with a debt that threatened to get out of control. According to this plan a large association, or syndicate, of bankers agreed to handle the debt of the crown in a way that represented considerable advance over the turbulent floating debt incurred through personal loans arranged by earlier rulers. On the one hand, the crown consolidated and funded the debt and financed interest and amortization through assignments of fixed income according to a regular schedule based on the exchange fairs. On the other hand, the bankers, including mainly Florentines and Germans whom the king pressed into financing the scheme, met the challenge in a more systematic way, sharing the investment as a consortium and then spreading the risk as widely as possible by seeking subscriptions from smaller investors, who in turn could sub-subscribe them yet further, in effect selling shares that could then be traded in a secondary market. The mechanism used to handle this consolidated debt thus shifted the basis of the floating debt from short-term to long-term lending, complete with an amortization plan with regular payments. Moreover, it gave the bankers considerable elasticity in dealing with it, so they could spread the risks widely throughout the banking community. For example, one of the Florentine investors in the scheme, Giovambattista Botti, whose family company operated through branches in Florence and Spain but did business also in Lyons, participated with five others in a consortium that invested a mere *sc.*11,085 from 1555 to 1559, a time when the king's debt exceeded 3 million scudi.[111]

---

[110] Marie-Noëlle Baudouin-Matuszek and Pavel Ouvarov, "Banque et pouvoir au XVIe siècle: Le surintendance des finances d'Albisse Del Bene," *Bibliothèque de l'École des Chartes* 149 (1991): 249–91, is a study of Del Bene based on new documents for the years 1555–59, which throw much light on the background to the Grand Parti.

[111] Angela Orlandi, *Le Grand Parti: Fiorentini a Lione e il debito pubblico francese nel XVI secolo* (Florence, 2002). This is the only microstudy of a participant in the Grand Parti based on the lender's accounts. For background on the scheme, see Hamon, *L'argent du roi*, 150–51, 166–70; Hamon's recent study places the floating debt of the king in the wider context of the development of royal financial institutions.

Del Bene's stature in France, incidentally, was formally recognized in the treaty of Cateau-Cambrésis in 1559, by which the French king effectively renounced his ambitions in Italy, for the treaty contained a specific clause that provided for the restitution to Del Bene of property in Florence that Cosimo I had confiscated. Del Bene's brother, in fact, was killed at Marciano, one of the last battles fought by the exiles against the Medici forces. Del Bene managed to put his children on the usual upward trajectory in his adopted country: his sons received honorific offices at court, and his daughters married into the nobility.

The Grand Parti, however, proved an illusory solution to the problem of gaining lenders' confidence because of the crown's insatiable need for money, given the political situation of the 1560s, making it difficult even to meet interest payments. The debt was repeatedly rescheduled, new loans were incorporated into it along with unpaid interest, and the value of the shares in it fluctuated at rates far below par. In short, the bankers found themselves facing the perennial dilemma of how to refuse to go along with what seemed to be an unending cycle. Threats from Florentines and Lucchesi to abandon Lyons went unheeded by the king, who knew how empty they were, although in the end he always had to bring them into a bargaining process over each new arrangement. In fact, it was probably the centrality of Lyons as a commercial and exchange market for their entire international network that compelled Florentines, even those not personally present in Lyons, to go along with the scheme. At least for those bankers operating in Lyons, however, it does not seem to have been a high price to pay. The investment of *sc.*11,085 by the consortium to which Botti belonged realized at least *sc.*2,713 in interest and *sc.*6,186 on the sale of the credits in 1564, leaving them with a real loss of *sc.*2,186 (as compared with the book loss of *sc.*8,867, calculated on the basis of the face value of the credits they sold, together with unpaid interest).[112] This works out to about *sc.*218 a year, of which Botti's share was only about *sc.*50. And the fact that the consortium had no problem in finding a buyer for its investment after nine years of such a performance, if at a price much below par, would indicate that other merchant-bankers were prepared to pay the cost of staying in business in Lyons and that some investors considered such shares a reasonable risk. In a 1576 list drawn up for the distribution of a loan of 340,000 livres to Henry III, the Florentines were down for the largest amount, 29 percent of the

---

[112] Orlandi, *Le Grand Parti*, documents these details from Botti's account. The author, however, considers only the paper losses of this investment (unpaid interest, depreciated market value, loss of earnings from alternative investments), not the real cost to Botti in the end, and hence much exaggerates the risks, the disillusionment, and even the irrationality involved. My calculations are based on tables 6 and 7, pp. 60–61 and 63. Much more light could be thrown on the whole matter if the substantial records of other Florentines operating in Lyons, most much more important than Botti, were studied with the same attention his have received.

total, followed by the Lucchesi, the Portuguese, the Germans, and the Milanesi, in that order.[113]

The decline of Lyons as a major commercial and banking center toward the end of the sixteenth century meant that the crown lost a community of bankers with whom it could negotiate loans. At the same time, however, it was establishing a more stable financial base in a system of tax farms and annuities tied to venal offices and centered at Paris, giving rise to a distinct class of French financiers. By 1600 the crown had largely closed the door to foreign bankers. Lyons was the last base Florentine bankers had for moving into special financial relations with a government outside of Italy.

[113] Richard Gascon, "Le couple Lyon-Milan dans l'Europe des affaires au XVIe siècle: La primauté milanaise," in *Histoire économique du monde méditerranéen, 1450–1650: Mélanges en l'honneur de Fernand Braudel* (Toulouse, 1973), 182.

PART II

THE URBAN ECONOMY

CHAPTER FOUR

The Textile Industries

General Performance: *The Wool Industry, The Silk Industry,*
   Linen Drapers.
Business Organization: *The Firm, Operations beyond the Firm.*
Production: *The Shop, The Work Force.*
Recapitulation.

The production of textiles gave the Florentine economy a solid industrial base that few other Italian cities enjoyed. More than any other activity, it generated the extraordinary growth of the city's wealth. In a 1321 ranking of sources of tax contributions the wool guild comes first, far above all the others, and the next highest was the guild that included manufacturers of silks and silk products.[1] Two and a half centuries later, in 1587, a report made to the grand duke on economic matters recognized the wool and silk industries as the forward sectors of the economy, "like two beautiful eyes in front of the head."[2] Not by chance the two oldest Italian treatises on silk and wool production date back to fifteenth-century Florence. The strength of the sector lay in its orientation to international markets for its products. Originally production was limited primarily to wool cloth, but in the later fourteenth century it expanded to silks in a major way, and for the next two centuries, down to the beginning of the seventeenth century, both industries successfully adapted their products to changes in the volatile international economy on which they depended. The dynamic that set off this remarkable performance was one that drove much Italian manufacturing in the Middle Ages: import substitution, that is, competition directed against high-quality products imported from outside of Italy. Although the Florentine wool industry had its origins in the exploitation of local resources, the boost that explains its initial success in international luxury markets came when it began directing production to compete with

---

[1] Giovanni Cherubini, "Le città della Toscana," in *La città del Mediterraneo all'apogeo dello sviluppo medievale: Aspetti economici e sociali* (Pistoia, 2003), 330.

[2] Quoted in Roberta Morelli, *La seta fiorentina nel Cinquecento* (Milan, 1976), 1.

luxury products from northern Europe. The production of silks, on the other hand, fell into line with all those other products—paper, metalwork, ceramics, soap, cottons—that Italians had originally imported from the Levant but then began producing for themselves.

In this process of retooling its local industry for import substitution Florence went well beyond the capabilities of the natural resources of the region. Tuscany had enough of the basic raw materials, both wool and dyestuffs, to give rise to a healthy local industry, but the wool was not of sufficient quantity and quality to support the industry on the scale it eventually achieved. That growth depended on imports from outside the region. The silk industry, by way of contrast, was built up from the beginning without any local sources of raw silk. Once up and going, the industry gave rise to the diffusion of sericulture in the Romagna and eventually throughout the Florentine countryside, but during the period covered in this book, down to the later sixteenth century, most of the raw silk consumed by the industry came from abroad. In short, to sustain the two major textile industries in a geographic location like that of Florence required merchants who could go far afield to find virtually all the necessary raw materials, bring them home, and then turn around to get the finished products onto international trade routes leading to markets abroad.

If merchants were thus the efficient cause of the success of the Florentine textile industry, the Arno was the permissive cause. While the region of Florence lacked the raw materials needed for a major wool industry, it had in the Arno a natural feature that was absolutely necessary for the growth of the industry. The Arno was the lifeblood of the city, a river unlike any other in Italy. A large, rapidly flowing stream fed by a vast watershed even before coming out of the hills to reach Florence, it provided two natural resources—power and water—necessary for the growth of a strong wool industry. Moreover, as a fluvial route out of Florence capable of facilitating commercial traffic to the sea and beyond, it provided this relatively isolated hinterland city with access to the markets abroad where its textile industries found raw materials and where they sent their finished products. The Arno was the precondition for Florence's becoming one of medieval Europe's great industrial cities.

The production processes for wool and silk, from the raw material to the finished textile, are completely different. Wool derives from animals, silk from insect larvae; the former passes through the hands of various workers with a wide range of skills, while the latter passes more directly from the hands of the cheapest kind of labor to relatively few highly skilled weavers; wool cloth requires major operations after weaving, while silk is finished on coming off the looms; wool textiles fall into a relatively simple typology, while the varieties of silk almost defy typological description. The two production processes have only two phases in common, dyeing and weaving, but there is no overlapping of the two industries at these points: different equipment and skills are required, and the labor forces are not interchangeable.

Despite these fundamental differences, the two industries were organized around the same basic structures. First was the partnership firm, the business enterprise that drove the industry, clearly separating capitalist investors and managers from the work force. Second was the guild, which incorporated everyone involved in the industry and institutionalized the subordination of the work force to the owners of the firms, who alone could buy the raw materials and sell the finished products. The guild, however, did not block outsiders, even those from modest social backgrounds, from investing in the industry and becoming themselves wool or silk producers.[3] A third structure that conditioned these industries was the putting-out system around which production was organized, giving some space for artisan enterprise, notwithstanding the restrictions of the abovementioned structures. Fourth was the international commercial and banking network built up by Florentine merchants, which served both industries in supplying raw materials and providing outlets for finished products. There was, finally, considerable interlocking of these structures within each industry and between the two industries, inasmuch as the owners of firms, the respective guild elite, and the importer-exporters were not mutually exclusive groups: some men were partners both in a wool and silk shop and in an international merchant-banking firm and were members of both guilds, and they all belonged to the same social, economic, and political upper class. These institutional structures facilitated the growth and flexibility of both industries, since their business and guild organization at home and the network abroad allowed producers wide latitude for maneuvering in adjusting to changing market conditions. Given the similarity of these organizational structures within the two industries, in this chapter, after a survey of the performance of each over the entire period, the two are treated together in a comparative approach. Throughout the discussion the Italian terms *lanaioli* and *setaioli* are used for the capitalist entrepreneurs who set up firms for the production of, respectively, wool and silk cloth.

General Performance
The Wool Industry

With the expansion of urban economies in Italy from the eleventh century on, many towns saw the growth of a wool industry directed to supplying ordinary

---

[3] For some examples, see below, chapter 7.

cloth in the local market, while the rising demand for better-quality cloth was met by imports from northern Europe, especially from the Flemish cities.[4] Only slowly did the industry in a few Italian cities develop higher-quality cloth to be sold in Near Eastern markets and in other places throughout the Mediterranean. Florence was one of these, along with some cities just south of the Alps, notably Milan, Monza, Como, and Verona. Growth was predicated on the diffusion of the basic technical innovations that largely fixed the parameters for productivity in the industry down to the industrial revolution: the water-powered fulling mill, dating from as early as the tenth century, the spinning wheel for weft yarns, the

[4]Virtually every aspect of the industry in its first three phases, down to the sixteenth century, is the subject of what has become a classic study in the historiography of Florence. A century ago, in 1901, Alfred Doren laid down the foundations for the subsequent historiography with his massive study of the wool industry. His view of the business and industrial organization of the industry has been corrected and enlarged by studies of specific firms: Raymond de Roover's classic study of a mid-sixteenth-century Medici firm, followed by Federigo Melis's research in the extensive Datini documents, Bruno Dini's article on the Del Bene firm, and Alessandro Stella's on the Strozzi. Hidetoshi Hoshino greatly deepened our knowledge of the industry through wide-ranging archival research, and he went on to lay out the broad picture of the international commerce in raw wool and finished cloth. Recently Franco Franceschi has rounded out the economic and social context of the wool workers' world during the half-century following the Ciompi revolt. In addition, a host of other monographic studies, especially those on the Ciompi revolt, which was spearheaded by wool workers, have filled in our picture of the industry with considerable detail. The vast bibliography on the subject, including the studies mentioned above (for which specific references can be found in the following notes), can be approached through the most recent major publication, Franco Franceschi, Oltre il "Tumulto": I lavoratori fiorentini dell'arte della lana fra Tre e Quattrocento (Florence, 1993). Useful also is the census of shops based on the 1427 and 1480 catasti made by Maria Letizia Grossi, Lucia Cristi, and Maria Luisa Bianchi in separate articles in Ricerche storiche 30 (2000).

We know much less about the sixteenth century. Hidetoshi Hoshino did not live to produce his projected second volume, but he presented a brief yet comprehensive sketch of his views in a published lecture, L'industria laniera fiorentina dal Basso Medioevo all'Età Moderna: Abbozzo storico dei secoli XIII–XVII (Rome, 1978). With little secondary literature to work with and some preliminary soundings in the archives, Patrick Chorley has made an overall assessment of the industry's performance over the course of the century in two articles: "Rascie and the Florentine Cloth Industry during the Sixteenth Century," Journal of European Economic History 32 (2003): 487–526, which also includes a technical discussion of rascia; and "The Volume of Cloth Production in Florence, 1500–1650: An Assessment of the Evidence," in Wool: Products and Markets (13th–20th Century), ed. G. L. Fontana and G. Gayot (Padua, 2004), 551–71. Raymond de Roover, "A Florentine Firm of Cloth Manufacturers: Management and Organization of a Sixteenth-Century Business," reprinted from Speculum 16 (1941) in Business, Banking, and Economic Thought in Late Medieval and Early Modern Europe, ed. Julius Kirshner (Chicago, 1974), 85–118, is a study of a specific firm. For structural analysis of the industry based on the study of one firm in the 1580s, see Richard A. Goldthwaite, "The Florentine Wool Industry in the Late Sixteenth Century: A Case Study," Journal of European Economic History 32 (2003): 527–54. Paolo Malanima, La decadenza di un'economia cittadina: L'industria di Firenze nei secoli XVI–XVIII (Bologna, 1982), surveys the industry over the following two centuries.

For an overview of the industry throughout Italy down to 1500, see Bruno Dini, "L'industria tessile italiana nel tardo Medioevo," reprinted from Le Italie del tardo Medioevo (Pisa, 1990) in Saggi su una economia-mondo: Firenze e l'Italia fra Mediterraneo ed Europa (secc. XIII–XVI) (Pisa, 1995), 13–49. The best recent guides to the larger European context are Patrick Chorley, "The Evolution of the Woollen, 1300–1700," in The New Draperies, ed. N. B. Harte (Oxford, 1997), 7–33; and John Munro, "I panni di lana," in Commercio e cultura mercantile, ed. Franco Franceschi, Richard A. Goldthwaite, and Reinhold C. Mueller, vol. 4 of Il Rinascimento italiano e l'Europa, ed. G. L. Fontana and L. Molà (Treviso, 2007), 105–41.

horizontal loom, and cards with iron teeth, all of which were in use by the thirteenth century. The subsequent growth of the Florentine industry did not see any more technical innovations of major importance but depended instead on the quality of both the raw material and the finished product and on the commercial network for marketing abroad.

Its geographic position gave Florence the potential for industrial growth. As observed in the introduction, the region had the resources to get an industry up and going in a number of towns—the possibility of transhumance of sheep and the availability of alum and vegetable dyes. In addition, Florence, more than any of the other Tuscan towns, had the advantages of the Arno—water, power, and transport. This geographic advantage also included easy access to a market area for sales that took in cities in northern Tuscany and central Italy that were less suitable for growth of a large local cloth industry. Hardly any materials survive to document the early history of the growth of the industry in the thirteenth century. The best circumstantial evidence for growth is the extraordinarily rapid rise in the city's population, since no other industry can explain how so many people were employed. As we have seen, the search for raw materials and markets abroad as the industry increased its output and improved the quality of its products generated one of the major dynamics, along with the search for grain to feed the population, driving the expansion of the commercial network abroad. Both searches extended throughout the western Mediterranean and hence overlapped. Florentines who are documented as settled in Messina in 1193 may have been there to procure raw wool from North Africa. Florentines are recorded in Tunis in 1245 as having received wool as security for a loan contract, and in 1269 they bought large quantities of North African wool in the Genoese market. The early documentation of the city's regional commerce, mostly dating from the second half of the twelfth century, does not specify what was being traded, but it most likely included cloth. A 1204 commercial treaty with Faenza has a reference to cloth, and in the second quarter of the century the geographic range of cloth exports took in Lucca and Genoa to the northwest, Venice to the north, Macerata to the southeast, Palermo to the south, and Ragusa and the Levant overseas. Moreover, Florentine textile workers are recorded as being lured abroad by other towns anxious to start up their own industry—to Bologna (1231), to Genoa (1234–40), and to Naples during the reign of Charles of Anjou (1268–85). In the meantime, the wool guild, for which the first secure date is 1212, emerged to become one of the major guilds. On the aforementioned list of sources of tax revenues in 1321 it ranked high above all the other guilds, and in 1331, when the decision was made to enlarge the barely begun new cathedral of Santa Maria del Fiore, the commune entrusted to it the patronage of this glorious symbol of the city.

The industry's early products were not of the highest quality. A 1246 document from Lucca records sales of Florentine cloth to rural markets in the countryside, and a 1299 document recording the value of cloth imported at Orvieto ranks Florentine cloth much lower than Flemish cloth.[5] The products were no challenge to the *panni franceschi*, the luxurious cloths of northern Europe, especially those from the northern French and Flemish cities, which enjoyed a virtual monopoly at the high end in Italian markets as well as in the markets of the rest of Europe at the time. The best Florentine cloths sold for only one-third to one-half the price of these northern cloths, but they may have been comparable to the cloths produced at Milan and other cities in northern Italy. Something of the variety of foreign products available in Italy in the last quarter of the thirteenth century is documented in the personal accounts of Florentines who recorded what they themselves bought in their local market. Purchases made by Baldovino Iacopo Riccomanni from 1272 to 1278 and by Bene Bencivenni from 1277 to 1296 included cloth from Paris, Caen, Arras, Ghent, Ypres, Lille, and Louvain in the north as well as from Bologna, Cremona, and the Romagna closer at hand in Italy. A generation later the sons of Stefano Soderini, partners and salaried employees of the Peruzzi company, had their current account with the firm, running from 1306 to 1325, debited for, among other personal expenditures, the purchase of says from Ireland, Caen, Hondschoote, and nearby Altopascio, other cloths from Genoa, Milan, Naples, and the Romagna, and blankets from Provence, Venice, and Cyprus.[6]

The transcontinental trade in northern European cloth had its impact on the local industry in Florence. With direct access to the industry in the north and to markets in the south, Calimala merchants began to import semifinished cloth from the north for dyeing, or redyeing, and finishing; they then exported the finished products to markets abroad around the Mediterranean, including the Levant, where they competed with finished Flemish products. Thus a distinct branch of the industry emerged, dependent on these merchants, to become a major activity through the first half of the fourteenth century. The economic sense of the operation lay in the fact that both the dyestuffs (especially woad, saffron, and kermes) and the mordant (alum) used by northern manufactures came from the south and were largely supplied by the very merchants who then purchased finished fabrics to sell in their home markets. Not all Calimala merchants

---

[5] Hidetoshi Hoshino, *L'arte della lana in Firenze nel Basso Medioevo: Il commercio della lana e il mercato dei panni fiorentini nei secoli XIII–XV* (Florence, 1980), 97–99 (tables).

[6] Both the Bencivenni and Riccomanni accounts are published by Arrigo Castellani in his *Nuovi testi fiorentini del Dugento* (Florence, 1952); the Soderini accounts are published by P. Manni in "Il libro del dare e dell'avere dei figli di Stefano Soderini (1306–1325)," *Studi di filologia italiana* 36 (1978): 67–155.

added this industrial activity to their commercial and financial business, and it probably constituted a minor part of the total operations of those that did, to judge from the firm of Francesco Del Bene, active from 1318 to 1323, the only Calimala cloth-producing firm whose records survive.[7] The process involved dyeing and the subsequent finishing of the cloth—napping and shearing, stretching, mending, pressing, and folding. In the manufacturing process for making cloth at this time, the cost of dyeing and finishing constituted probably about 20 percent of total manufacturing costs (exclusive of the cost of raw wool), most of this going for the dyeing itself, the stage, moreover, that required a high level of technical expertise.

Hidetoshi Hoshino suggested that the importation of superior northern cloths for refinishing and then sale in Italian markets may, in fact, have retarded the development of higher-quality production by the local industry. Eventually, however, the growth and refinement of these finishing stages of the manufacturing process must have been a factor in the improvement of the quality of locally produced cloth that is apparent by the 1320s. This was achieved by extending a supply channel to obtain top-quality English wool, which Florentine merchants were already exporting to the Flemish industry, and by producing cloths *alla francesca*, in clear imitation of northern types that they were designed to compete with. This initiative to orient the industry more to compete in foreign markets with high-quality cloth owed much of its ultimate success to economic circumstances of the moment, both in Flanders, the home of the competition, and in England, the source of the raw material. It was precisely at this time—the 1320s for the Flemish cities and some two decades later for the Brabantine cities—that these northern industries were faced with the crisis that led to the slow decline of the *grande draperie* over the rest of the century. Often cited as a major factor in this decline is the high incidence of war, which increased the risks and hence the costs of overland transport. The resulting higher prices in Mediterranean markets for both luxury cloths and the semifinished cloths imported by the Calimala merchants were an inducement for Florentine producers themselves to undertake the complete production of high-quality products. Moreover, by the 1320s the maritime voyages between the Mediterranean and the north had become regularized to the point that the Florentines had a direct line to the source of superior English wool. Having handled much of the supply of English wool to the Flemish and Brabantine industries, they could easily shift that export trade elsewhere. The financial context for this operation was sketched out in chapter 3: the purchase of wool in England for shipment to Italy was a convenient way for Florentine

---

[7] Armando Sapori, *Una compagnia di Calimala ai primi del Trecento* (Florence, 1932).

merchant-bankers, deeply involved with loans to the English crown for its campaigns in France, to channel profits accumulated there back home in the form of an industrial raw material. In short, the "industrialization" of Florence, to use Hoshino's term in talking about the rapid development of wool production in the 1320s (though it would be more accurate to speak of an upgrading within the industry), owed much to new opportunities that opened up as a result of favorable conjunctures on the economic scene in Europe in general about the first quarter of the century.

That the impetus for growth in the industry was import substitution can be deduced from the categorization of some of its products as being in the style of the cloth of specific Flemish and Brabantine towns, such as Douai, Brussels, and Malines, precisely those kinds of cloth that Florentines such as Baldovino Riccomanni and Bene Bencivenni were buying a generation earlier. Nevertheless, these Florentine cloths were different. The expensive cloths imported from the north were true woolens, both warp and weft made from carded, wheel-spun yarns, whereas the Florentines produced lighter, half-worsted fabrics, making the warp from rock-spun, combed wool. Although this seemingly retrograde technology raised costs, the result was a lighter fabric. The scattered evidence for rising prices of these new Florentine products has been used to document the rapid and steady growth of the industry in the second quarter of the century. What figures we have indicate that production on a per capita basis remained strong through the third quarter of the century, notwithstanding the dramatic population decline in 1348.[8] In fact, from what we know about the profits made by two wool producers at midcentury, it could be concluded that the industry's growth had reached boom proportions by that time. The company of Antonio di Lando degli Albizzi paid profits averaging just over 22 percent annually from 1346 to 1350, and the company of Francesco Del Bene, despite several bad years, averaged 11.7 percent from 1355 to 1370.[9] By the end of the century, in addition to the Florentines, other Mediterranean producers, especially Lombards and Catalans, had greatly reduced the share at the high end of the market heretofore held by Flemish and Brabantine woolens, and in the market area extending from Spain and southern France into Italy and across the Mediterranean to the Near East, Florentine cloth came to enjoy the distinction of being the most luxurious and costly of all.

---

[8] On prices, see the various tables in Hoshino, *L'arte della lana;* on output, see Franceschi, *Oltre il "Tumulto,"* 6–13.

[9] Hidetoshi Hoshino, "Note sulla compagnia commerciale degli Albizzi del Trecento," *Annuario* of the Istituto Giapponese di Cultura in Roma 7 (1969–70): 9–10; idem, *L'arte della lana,* 213.

The highly luxurious products made from English wool were identified locally as San Martino cloths, a name that came from the convent of San Martino, in the center of the city (between the cathedral and the Palazzo Vecchio), where most of the producers were located. The industry also produced lower-quality cloths made from wool imported from around the western Mediterranean; these products were identified as Garbo cloths, a name derived from a place in northwestern Africa from which some of the wool came. Each branch imported different kinds of wool from its source and produced a variety of cloths of differing quality, but the overall qualitative distinction between San Martino and Garbo cloths remained, the former, sold mostly in Spain and Italy, selling for about twice the price of the latter, sold mostly in the Levant. As a result of the rapid growth of these two branches, the finishing operation of the Calimala merchants was largely closed down by the second half of the fourteenth century, and the industry remained organized around the manufacture of these two kinds of cloths well into the sixteenth century.

The San Martino branch long retained its monopoly position as a producer of luxurious fabrics, yet overall production began a slow decline in the later fourteenth century owing, it is generally thought, to problems of supply. Difficulties in the export of wool from England arose from cartel practices among wool exporters there and from royal policies designed to protect the growth of domestic production through a rise in export taxes on raw wool. Meanwhile, the Garbo branch too faced increasing problems of supply from its sources in Catalonia and southern France. These problems have been attributed to the interruption of maritime trade due to intermittent military hostilities extending from the end of the fourteenth century through the 1420s, but this explanation does not accord well with the picture, presented earlier, of the intensification of regional trade in this area precisely at this time. In any event, problems of supply of the basic raw material in both branches have been cited as a reason for a slump in the industry beginning after the Ciompi revolt and reaching a low in the 1390s. Production was clearly rising, however, by the second quarter of the fifteenth century and soon returned to earlier levels. One significant indicator of this revival was the immigration of wool workers from beyond Tuscany and even Italy; by 1480 they constituted perhaps as much as one-eighth of all wool workers, with a much higher proportion among weavers, the most skilled.[10]

In part the revival of the industry in the fifteenth century was led by demand: in the course of the century, three major new markets for prestige products

[10] The German immigrants have been exhaustively studied by Lorenz Böninger. See his *Die deutsche Einwanderung nach Florenz im Spätmittelalter* (Leiden, 2006).

opened, all in capital cities undergoing rapid population growth following the establishment of reinvigorated and expansive political regimes. Two of these were in Italy, at Naples and Rome, both growing capitals of newly consolidated territorial states with large princely courts, the former the residence of the conquering ruler of the trans-Mediterranean Aragonese kingdom and the latter the residence of the papacy, now firmly reestablished in Italy and vigorously promoting the growth of its territorial state into one of the peninsula's five major powers. A third market opened up in the capital of the newly formed Ottoman Empire at Constantinople, which rapidly grew to become the largest metropolis in the Mediterranean. On the supply side, the Garbo branch found a successful response to problems with its traditional sources by shifting increasingly to wool imported from central Italy, chiefly from the Abruzzi region. There in the 1440s Alfonso, the new Aragonese king of Naples, reorganized the transhumance of the kingdom and bred a new type of sheep that produced better-quality wool much like the Spanish wool that Florentines were using at the time. This *matricina* wool led to some improvement in the quality of Garbo cloths. In the course of the fifteenth century the ratio of these to San Martino cloths rose from 3:2 to 3:1, and their higher price as compared with the earlier products of this branch of the industry made up for the decline in sales of the more expensive San Martino cloths, with the result that the value of the total output of the industry reached earlier levels.

Over the final two decades of the fifteenth century a major transformation of the industry got under way with yet another shift by some manufacturers in the Garbo branch to Castilian wool, recently developed in Spain. This wool was of better quality than that from the Abruzzi, and with it the industry developed a new product, *rascia* (sometimes called *rash* in English). These cloths fell into the category of exceptionally fine serges, which were much lighter and of much higher quality than the traditional second-line Garbo cloths made from matricina wool. Eventually the producers of San Martino cloths also shifted almost entirely to the better Spanish wool to make rascia; and with the increased concentration of production on this new luxury, lightweight cloth throughout the second half of the century, the distinction between the two traditional branches faded away. This production change in the industry followed yet another major shift in markets. During the second quarter of the sixteenth century, traditional Garbo cloths began to lose their Near Eastern markets, the result partly of the decline of the counterbalancing trade in raw silk from the region and partly of increasing competition from an invigorated Venetian industry, not to mention the difficulties, already discussed, of the political relations between Cosimo I and the Ottoman Empire. Venetian cloths, though probably somewhat inferior, were directed almost entirely to Near Eastern markets, where the Venetians had a much stronger trade network than the Florentines had ever had; by the 1560s the Venetians had largely eliminated the competition from Florentines. While the Garbo branch of the industry thus lost a major outlet for its traditional product in the Levant, the rascia branch was for the first time capturing major new markets in Europe, which it reached through the great fairs of Castile and Lyons and the new emporium at Antwerp. These fabrics, mostly black in color, enjoyed much prestige in these northern markets, where they were known as "serges de Florence" and "rashes of the flowers people." Florentine cloths sold well also in Italian markets; along with Venetian cloths, they are virtually the only such products that show up in the accounts of the papal court throughout the entire century.[11]

Down to the end of the sixteenth century the number of wool shops remained at over a hundred, about the level of a century earlier. The evidence, as feeble as it is, indicates a short period of expansion in the third quarter of the century, when rascia and other quality products may have constituted as much as three-fourths of the industry's total production. Shops numbered 152 in a 1561 survey. Guild registration of apprentices also increased, and the employment records of the only firm that has been studied for this period—Cristofano di Tommaso Brandolini & Partners, active in the 1580s—testify to the large number of immigrant weavers in the city, most now coming from the more remote areas of Tuscany and from bordering regions. Moreover, many weavers were now women, and wages were as high as they ever had been.

With all these positive indicators, it is not surprising to learn that investor confidence in the industry remained high. The official register of limited-liability accomandita contracts records more capital going into wool companies down to the end of the century than into any other sector, including the silk industry. Profits of the Brandolini firm, whose capital came almost entirely from two Strozzi brothers, averaged only a modest 6 percent for the nearly two decades of its activity, from 1580 to 1597, but this return was apparently sufficient and steady enough to justify three renewals of the original partnership over this period. Other patrician families have been documented as having large investments in the industry at the end of the century. Agnolo di Girolamo Guicciardini (d. 1581) built up a fortune in wool, silk, and dyeing, and his sons continued investments in the cloth industry. Antonio di Bernardo Gondi, who had started off life working as a clerk for a Spanish importer of wool and knew the industry well, had *fl.*6,000 invested in each of three shops at the time of his death in 1591. The Corsi, whose long engagement in trade in southern Italy and in banking in Lyons gave

---

[11] Hoshino, *L'industria laniera fiorentina,* 6. For the rise of rascia production, see Chorley, "*Rascie* and the Florentine Cloth Industry."

them a knowledge of foreign markets, had four wool shops by the turn of the century. Likewise, the Riccardi, on their way to becoming the wealthiest family in Florence after the Medici, increased their investment from *fl.*4,000 in 1568 to *fl.*8,000 in two shops in 1591 and then to *fl.*19,000 in four shops in 1600, making wool more prominent than silk in their investment portfolio down to the end of the century.[12]

Finally, the last thirty years of the century saw a surge in proposals regarding technical and mechanical aspects of the industry that would seem to demonstrate a widespread interest in ideas about how to cut costs and improve quality in the production process. Requests were made for patents on inventions for the weaving of new kinds of fabrics and for virtually all stages in the production of cloth, from carding, combing, and spinning wool to fulling, dyeing, stretching, pressing, and shearing finished cloth. Artisans within the industry came up with some of these ideas. The profit motive was clear, and competition among inventors could be keen. Although in the final analysis these inventions probably made little impact on the performance of the industry, the enthusiasm for them manifests a confidence about the continuing potential of the industry, if not its vitality, at the end of the sixteenth century.[13]

To recapitulate, the variables determining distinct phases in the history of the wool industry from the fourteenth through the sixteenth centuries are (1) the sources for raw wool (the western Mediterranean in general, England, central Italy, Spain); (2) the markets for its products (Italy, the Levant, northern Europe); and (3) the quality of these products (Garbo, San Martino, rascia). These variables, moreover, came into play in a complex and ever-changing international market in which Florence was just one agent, and everywhere Florentines faced competition to a greater or lesser extent. No surviving documents lend themselves to close statistical analysis for the purpose of quantifying the performance of the industry through these three centuries. Records of gate gabelles and customs receipts do not survive, and the archives of the wool guild have yielded only isolated and fragmentary figures. Nevertheless, some rough short-term trends in

---

[12] Richard A. Goldthwaite, *Private Wealth in Renaissance Florence: A Study of Four Families* (Princeton, NJ, 1968), 153–54 (Guicciardini), 184 (Gondi); idem, "Florentine Wool Industry" (Brandolini); Hidetoshi Hoshino, "Messina e l'arte della lana fiorentina nei secoli XVI–XVII," in *Studi dedicati a Carmelo Trasselli*, ed. Giovanna Motta (Soveria Mannelli, 1983), 427–46 (Corsi); Paolo Malanima, *I Riccardi di Firenze: Una famiglia e un patrimonio nella Toscana dei Medici* (Florence, 1977), 59, 74.

[13] Luca Molà, "Artigiani e brevetti nella Firenze del Cinquecento," in *La grande storia dell'artigianato*, vol. 3, *Il Cinquecento,* ed. Franco Franceschi and Gloria Fossi (Florence, 2000), 57–79. The applications for patents are listed in Daniela Lamberini, "'A beneficio dell'universale': Ingegneria idraulica e privilegi di macchine alla corte dei Medici," in *Arte e scienza delle acque nel Rinascimento,* ed. Daniela Lamberini, Alessandra Fiocca, and Cesare Maffioli (Venice, 2003), 60–66.

total output have been somewhat precariously constructed from this material, and if estimates of product quality and population—data that are equally fragile—are factored in, a general picture of the performance of the industry emerges. Table 4.1 assembles estimated production figures, values of products, and population to calculate per capita production in this industry from the late fourteenth to the early seventeenth century. In a first step this table renders the sporadic monetary values for total output *(a, b, c)* into the number of work years of unskilled labor represented by that production *(d, e)*, thus building in an inflation factor. In a second step, this index to input in the economy is evaluated against total population at the time *(f)* in order to measure the per capita value of industrial production *(g)*.

The results, tentative as they are, confirm scholars' general impressions about the performance of the industry. Sharply falling production in the last quarter of the fourteenth century led to a slump that lasted through the first quarter of the fifteenth century, caused presumably by problems of supply of raw material. By the second half of the century, however, production was back at a high level, reflecting both the reinvigoration of the industry following the shift of supply to matricina wool from the Abruzzi and new growing markets, especially in the capital cities of Naples, Rome, and Constantinople. The continuing production at this level through the sixteenth century marks the success of the industry's transition to another distinct phase with the manufacturing of a new luxury cloth made now from Spanish wool. Above all, what is to be noted in the data presented in the table is that notwithstanding the decline of total output in the industry, the better quality of the product pushed the value of that production to a higher level than it had reached in the later fourteenth through the fifteenth century. And as we shall see, the greater value of these fabrics represents greater labor input as well as more costly raw materials. As a result of having to adjust its products to very different kinds of wool as it shifted its sources from the western Mediterranean to England, to central Italy, and then to Spain, the industry may have gained a certain technical know-how that allowed it to maintain a generally high level of performance, notwithstanding occasional crises, over three centuries, in contrast to the relatively turbulent history of the industry in the Low Countries during the same period.[14]

Yet within this generally positive picture of the global performance of the industry signs began to appear toward the end of the sixteenth century that all was not well. Inventors may have been enthusiastic and investors extraordinarily

---

[14] A notion suggested by Herman van der Wee, "The Western European Woolen Industries, 1500–1750," in *The Cambridge History of Western Textiles,* ed. David Jenkins (Cambridge, 2003), 1:407.

TABLE 4.1
The Wool Industry, 1373–1619:
Production as Investment in the Local Economy

Year	(a) Bolts produced	(b) Gross value of production in florins (scudi)	(c) £ per florin (scudo)	(d) Net value* of production in lire: 60% of (b) × (c)	(e) Daily wage† (soldi)	(f) Value of production in work years of 260 days: (d) ÷ (e)/20 ÷ 260	(g) Population	(h) Per capita value of production in work years: (f) ÷ (g)
1373	30,000	1,050,000	3.4	2,142,000	10	16,477	60,000	0.27
1381–82	19,000	679,250	3.6	1,467,180	10	11,286	55,000	0.21
1391–95	13,000	455,000	3.8	1,037,400	10	7,980	60,000	0.13
1425–30	11,000	437,662	4.0	1,050,389	10	8,080	40,000	0.20
1488	17,000	471,075	5.8	1,639,341	10	12,610	42,000	0.30
1526	18,000–24,000	600,000	7.0	2,520,000	10	19,385	70,000	0.28
1553–54	—	470,000	7.5	2,115,000	13	12,515	60,000	0.21
1558–59	—	540,000	7.5	2,430,000	13	14,379	60,000	0.24
1560–61	—	945,000	7.5	4,252,500	13	25,163	60,000	0.42
1570–71	—	927,000	7.5	4,171,500	16	20,055	60,000	0.33
1591–1605	13,437	850,000	7.5	3,825,000	20	14,712	65,000	0.23
1619	10,717	500,000	7.5	2,250,000	20	8,654	75,000	0.12

CALCULATIONS AND SOURCES:

1373: *Calculation:* 40% San Martino @ *fl.* 50 and 60% Garbo @ *fl.* 25. *Sources:* Franco Franceschi, *Oltre il "Tumulto": I lavoratori fiorentini dell'arte della lana fra Tre e Quattrocento* (Florence, 1993) 13 (citing Pucci), for production. Hidetoshi Hoshino, *L'arte della lana in Firenze nel Basso Medioevo: Il commercio della lana e il mercato dei panni fiorentini nei secoli XIII–XV* (Florence, 1980), 175: median price of about *fl.* 50 for 322 panni of San Martino cloths; I have estimated Garbo at one-half that.

1381–82: *Calculation:* 19,000 bolts, with 43% San Martino @ *fl.* 50 and 57% Garbo @ *fl.* 25. *Source:* Hoshino, *L'arte della lana,* 227, which sees this figure as probably low.

1391–95: *Calculation:* 40% San Martino @ *fl.* 50 and 60% Garbo @ *fl.*25. *Source:* Franceschi, *Oltre il "Tumulto,"* 13.

1425–30: *Calculation:* 37% San Martino @ £219 and 63% Garbo @ £124. *Sources:* Franceschi, *Oltre il "Tumulto,"* 13 (10,000 cloths); Hoshino, *L'arte della lana,* 204–6, 229 (11,000–12,000 cloths).

1488: *Calculation:* 24% San Martino @ £277 and 76% Garbo @ £124. *Sources:* Prices: Archive of the Ospedale degli Innocenti, ser. 144 (Estranei), 332 (record book of Attaviano di Contuccio & Partners, 1456–61 [San Martino]); ibid., 756 (record book of Lorenzo di Antonio Ridolfi & Partners, 1464–67 [Garbo]).

1526–1605: *Source:* Patrick Chorley, "Rascie and the Florentine Cloth Industry during the Sixteenth Century," *Journal of European Economic History* 32 (2003): 515–19.

1619: *Source:* Maurice Carmona, "La Toscane face à la crise de l'industrie lainère: Techniques et mentalités économiques aux XVIe et XVIIe siècles," in *Produzione, commercio e consumo dei panni di lana (nei secoli XII–XVIII),* ed. Marco Spallanzani (Florence, 1976), 158–59.

* Net value is gross value less the amount spent for imported raw wool, which was about 40% of total costs; it represents manufacturing costs spent within the local economy.
† The wage rate is that of an unskilled worker in the construction industry.

confident, but they had an eye only on performance in the short run; the former were looking for a quick profit, and the latter had nothing tied up in plant and equipment and could shut down operations at any time without a loss. Anyone taking a longer view, however, would have noted the problems, and some did. The percentage of output constituted by rascia fell slowly with the increased production of lower-quality products. After 1590 imports of Castilian wool by the Ruiz company in Florence, for example, began to decline. A sensibility to competition manifested itself in measures to protect the industry in the local market through legislation directed toward blocking imports, on the one hand, and, suppressing any competition arising from rural production within the territorial state, on the other. The grand-ducal government felt the need to attend to problems in the industry by opening several investigations of the situation and to take certain initiatives. Underlying these problems were profound structural changes that very rapidly, after the turn of the century, brought to an end this last phase in the history of the industry. Whereas up to the end of the fifteenth century supply had always been largely in the hands of Florentine merchants operating abroad, the shift at that time to the better-quality Spanish wool led to gradual dependence, now for the first time, on foreigners, namely Castilians. These merchants were able to take the initiative because they and the wool they sold came from an area in Spain that fell somewhat outside the Florentine network. Some thirty Castilian merchants were active in Florence as early as the 1490s, and their presence in the city a century later has already been noted.[15] With the Castilians came also the Genoese, who thus brought Florence into their expanding commercial and banking network in Spain. By the end of the sixteenth century a few large operators from Genoa and from Spain, including the well-known company of Simón Ruiz, had a virtual monopoly on supply. For a while these foreigners made their base in Tuscany a center for the distribution of wool to other Italian cities, but in the early seventeenth century they shifted their operations to Venice, attracted by more favorable port and trade arrangements as well as a more thriving local industry.

In addition to the contraction of the Florentine commercial system abroad, the international market to which the industry was oriented underwent fundamental changes in the course of the century that eventually locked the Florentines out. Just as they had encountered problems in supply from England once the local industry there began to grow, in the sixteenth century they confronted challenges in Spain once the expanding production of wool generated the growth of

---

[15] Bruno Dini, "Mercanti spagnoli a Firenze (1480–1530)," in *Saggi*, 289–310. See also Lorenz Böninger, "Politics, Trade and Toleration in Renaissance Florence: Lorenzo de' Medici and the Besalú Brothers," *I Tatti Studies* 9 (2001): 142–44.

a competing local cloth industry. Local producers in France too were making imitation rascia by the third quarter of the century. Competition, however, did not stop with import substitution in local markets abroad. In the increasingly complex international market of the expanding economy of northwestern Europe, where demand was volatile and competition keen, producers were stimulated to vary their products, to innovate, and to find new markets, and they created a wide range of fabrics of various quality and at all price levels. The development of successful new fabrics was, in fact, a major factor in the extraordinary growth of the English economy that got under way at the end of the sixteenth century. Cloth imported from northwestern Europe, including England, and from Catalonia and Provence in the western Mediterranean showed up in virtually all Italian markets. Competing industries also arose in Italy itself, across the north from Milan to Venice, in part invigorated by access to the new Spanish merino wools; these industries directed production to the higher end of the market within Italy as well as in the Near East. The Venetians, in addition to increasing production of the kind of cloth that sold well in the Near Eastern markets, to the detriment of Florentine sales, began to imitate rascia to compete also in Italy. The final challenge came from the "new draperies," the lighter, cheaper fabrics developed in the north with which the Dutch and English began flooding all the Mediterranean markets beginning about 1570.

By the turn of the century Florentines found themselves selling a narrow range of expensive products in an increasingly complex international market where there were more competitors and a greater variety of products of varying quality. After the departure of Spanish merchants, the industry turned again to Italian sources for wool, with the result that quality declined. It made efforts to adjust to the new conditions by imitating not only Venetian cloth but also the new draperies being imported from the north and by producing lower-quality rascia, and it found outlets in Italian markets beyond Tuscany. Nevertheless, in the first quarter of the seventeenth century production for international markets fell off rapidly. Ducal inquests into the situation reveal an awareness of the fundamental structural problems, as well as the economic and social consequences of an industry in crisis. Some efforts were made to address these problems, especially through regulatory policy, but nothing could arrest a decline that came so fast as to justify describing it as a collapse. From the turn of the century to the 1620s the number of shops fell from about one hundred to fewer than half that, and the decline in the number of looms was even greater. Not only did total production fall by more than one-half but the 2:1 ratio of quality cloths to mediocre ones was reversed to 1:2.[16]

---

[16] Malanima, *La decadenza*, 289–305, reviews the available statistical data.

What brought the wool industry down at the beginning of the seventeenth century was the failure to meet the competition from producers of import substitutes for rascia in ultramontane markets, from northern producers of the new lighter cloth invading Italian markets, and even from expanding industries in northern Italian towns. From the fourteenth to the early sixteenth century the Florentine industry had prospered probably without facing much competition in the markets of the relatively undeveloped economic areas to which it directed its products, and it had been in a better position than any other to capture for itself the demand concentrated in the new and rapidly growing capital cities that sprung up in these areas in the fifteenth century. When in the sixteenth century, however, the industry reoriented production to markets in northern Europe, it found itself operating under the completely different conditions of the most vigorously growing and developing economy that Europe—indeed, the world—had ever seen. The incipient globalization emanating from the north engulfed Italy and relegated its economy evermore to the sidelines. The Florentine industry had never faced the kind of competition this new world economy generated, and its presence in international markets simply collapsed over a period of only two decades, unable to resist sufficiently to go instead into a slow decline.

In a certain sense, this inability to face keener competition is not surprising. As we shall see, the subordination of artisans to producers precluded the kind of flexibility in adjusting to changing conditions that characterized the industry in some places in northern Europe in the early modern period where craftsmen, organized in their own guilds and less subordinate to capitalist investors, had more control of the manufacturing process.[17] Industrial policy, however, eludes us. Within the complex structure of miniscule firms, guilds, artisan enterprises, and trade networks in which the industry operated it is difficult to locate where strategies were formulated to meet challenges and where initiatives arose to introduce innovations. Guild records reveal much about problems facing the industry in the efforts to find solutions through regulations but little about innovative ideas for change. The vast archives of private business records consist almost entirely of accounting materials, with no hint of entrepreneurial strategies; correspondence, where one might expect to find references to policy and problems, was not part of the paperwork of a wool firm. Not even the government's keen interest in the problems of an industry in crisis aroused anyone to come up with a clear line of action. Some historians have pointed to higher labor costs as the main structural straightjacket that rendered enterprise everywhere in Italy less

---

[17] Robert Du Plessis and Martha C. Howell, "Reconsidering the Early Modern Urban Economy: The Case of Leiden and Lille," *Past & Present,* no. 94 (1982): 49–84.

competitive in the expanding global economy, but no one has gone on to check the evidence in a comparative context.

It has been argued, however, that Florentine lanaioli could not have reduced costs by moving to cheaper labor in the countryside, following the route of "proto-industrialization," which gave a new lease on life to many urban cloth industries in northern Europe. Because of the integration of the rural and urban economies, labor was not much cheaper in the countryside, and the diffusion of sharecropping in the countryside around Florence limited the availability of wage labor even on a seasonal basis. Given the kind of mix cropping that characterized Tuscan agriculture, sharecroppers were busy working their land throughout the year, and there was not a landless class of day laborers of any size available for employment. In any event, the city's protectionist policy had long precluded the rise of a rural industry of quality that might have been a basis for a shift of the industry from town to countryside. In this respect, a structural barrier separated the city from its countryside.[18]

In considering the factors that led to the loss of foreign markets by the wool industry after more than three centuries of success, it remains an open question how much weight to give to inadequate policymaking mechanisms and internal structural barriers to adjustment and change as against the external market forces arising from the globalization of the economy of northwestern Europe.

The Silk Industry

It was not until the fifteenth century that Florence became a major producer of silk cloth.[19] The industry had a long tradition in Lucca, going back probably

---

[18] The problem of the rural labor market was raised by Judith C. Brown, "The Economic 'Decline' of Tuscany: The Role of the Rural Economy," in *Florence and Milan: Comparisons and Relations* (Florence, 1989), 2:101–15; and Stephan R. Epstein discusses the structural problem in Tuscany, putting it in the wider Italian and European context, in "L'economia italiana nel quadro europeo," in Franceschi, Goldthwaite, and Mueller, *Commercio e cultura mercantile*, 37–43.

[19] The classic work on the industry in the fifteenth century is Florence Edler de Roover, "Andrea Banchi, Florentine Silk Manufacturer and Merchant in the Fifteenth Century," *Studies in Medieval and Renaissance History* 3 (1966): 223–85, where there is a full bibliography of the earlier literature. A bibliography of her work on the subject, which includes the pioneering study of the industry in medieval Lucca, is included in the volume of her posthumously published papers, *L'arte della seta a Firenze nei secoli XIV e XV*, ed. Sergio Tognetti (Florence, 1999). The Banchi article remains the only business history of a Florentine firm, but presumably the accounting system used by the firm did not lend itself to a drawing up of a general balance of its performance. William Caferro's study of the Spinelli firm, "The Silk Business of Tommaso Spinelli, Fifteenth-Century Florentine Merchant and Papal Banker," *Renaissance Studies* 10 (1996): 417–39, does not enlarge the picture; based only on inventories and balances, not accounts, it follows Edler de Roover's model. Bruno Dini has studied particular aspects of the industry in the fifteenth century and has made attempts to measure its growth (in these studies he refers to *tesi di laurea* on several early sixteenth-century firms, but these are not generally available and cannot be checked); see the references to his collected studies mentioned above. Sergio Tognetti deals with the commercial aspect of selling silk fabrics abroad in

as far as the eleventh century. The Lucchesi made notable improvements in the technology of silk-throwing devices and forged a backward linkage to the raw material through the promotion of sericulture in the immediate countryside, including the Valdinievole, an area that came under Florentine dominion in the fourteenth century. By the thirteenth century Bologna, Venice, and Genoa had also become centers of production, albeit to a lesser extent. The rise of the industry is to be seen as a component of a dynamic that drove much of the Italian economy in the later Middle Ages, import substitution. In the earlier period Italians imported both Byzantine and Islamic silks from the eastern Mediterranean; and, in fact, some of the textiles that first came off Italian looms sought to imitate these products from the Levant. Slowly, the industry replaced imports and went on to sell its own products, even in Eastern markets, and in this process the Italians adapted foreign designs to their own taste and eventually abandoned them altogether as they developed their own styles.

The history of the development of the industry in northern Italy outside the four urban centers of production has largely centered on its diffusion from Lucca

---

Un'industria di lusso al servizio del grande commercio: Il mercato dei drappi serici e della seta nella Firenze del Quattrocento (Florence, 2002). For an excellent general survey of all aspects of the industry fully informed by the most recent literature, see Franco Franceschi, "Florence and Silk in the Fifteenth Century: The Origins of a Long and Felicitous Union," Italian History and Culture 1 (1995): 3–22. The history of what came to be known as the silk guild is summarized in Piero Pieri, Intorno alla storia dell'arte della seta in Firenze (Bologna, 1927).

As with the wool industry, hardly any archival research has been directed to a study of the industry much beyond the fifteenth century. Although by the sixteenth century there are dozens of ledgers of silk companies more complete than those of the Banchi firm, there is no study of the internal operation of any Florentine shop as thorough as Paola Massa's study of the small Genoese firm in the early sixteenth century: Un'impresa serica genovese della prima metà del Cinquecento (Milan, 1974). For overviews, see Morelli, La seta fiorentina; and for the sixteenth through the eighteenth century, see Malanima, La decadenza, and Tamara Boccherini and Paola Marabelli, "Sopra ogni sorte di drapperia . . .": Tipologie decorative e tecniche tessili nella produzione fiorentina del Cinquecento e Seicento (Florence, 1993). For the seventeenth century there are three articles by Jordan Goodman: "Financing Pre-Modern European Industry: An Example from Florence 1580–1660," Journal of European Economic History 10 (1981): 415–35; "Tuscan Commercial Relations with Europe, 1550–1620: Florence and the European Textile Market," in Firenze e la Toscana dei Medici nell'Europa del '500 (Florence, 1983), 1:327–41; and "Cloth, Gender and Industrial Organization: Towards an Anthropology of Silkworkers in Early Modern Europe," in La seta in Europa, sec. XIII–XX, ed. Simonetta Cavaciocchi (Florence, 1993), 229–45. See also Jordan Goodman and Judith C. Brown, "Women and Industry in Florence," Journal of Economic History 40 (1980): 73–80. For the subsequent period, see two articles by Jean-Claude Waquet: "Pour une histoire de l'industrie de la soie à Florence aux dix-septième et dix-huitième siècles," Ricerche storiche 13 (1983): 235–50; and "Quelques considerations sur l'industrie et le commerce de la soie à Florence aux XVIIe et XVIIIe siècles," in Cavaciocchi, La seta in Europa, 760–70. Sericulture in the Tuscan countryside has found its historian in Francesco Battistini: Gelsi, bozzoli e caldaie: L'industria della seta in Toscana tra città, borghi e campagne (sec. XVI–XVIII) (Florence, 1998); see also his "La produzione, il commercio e i prezzi della seta grezza nello Stato di Firenze, 1489–1859," Rivista di storia economica 20 (2005): 233–72. Luca Molà, The Silk Industry of Renaissance Venice (Baltimore, 2000), includes a concise, recent survey of the industry in general throughout Italy in the late Middle Ages and the early modern period. See also Sergio Tognetti, "I drappi di seta," in Franceschi, Goldthwaite, and Mueller, Commercio e cultura mercantile, 143–70.

in the fourteenth century. The emigration of Lucchesi silk workers, included among some three hundred Guelf families exiled in 1314 as a result of internal factional politics, presumably provided the principal motivation behind this expansion, and emigration continued for the next half-century as a result of subsequent political problems at Lucca arising from the rule of Castruccio Castracani (1316–28) and the conquest by Pisa in 1342. It was not until a century later, in the second quarter of the fifteenth century, that the industry emerged as a notable presence in the urban economies everywhere across northern Italy and began the remarkable growth that made it a leading industry of the Italian economy for the next several centuries. In part this growth is to be explained as demand led. The redistribution of wealth following the demographic crises in the fourteenth century boosted spending on luxury goods, among which textiles were a major item, while the increased stability of princely courts, especially the many small ones scattered about central and northern Italy, resulted in a greater concentration of this demand.

While the diffusion of this new industry was a general Italian phenomenon, Florence had a bit of a head start and went on to move into the top rank of the Italian centers of the industry. The industry could hardly have found a more fertile economy in which to put down roots. The city had the capital available for investment, a long tradition of entrepreneurial know-how, and an international commercial network to facilitate the supply of raw materials and the marketing of finished products. Although the industry got up and running in a period when there was a considerable slump in the output of the wool industry, in the last quarter of the fourteenth century and the first quarter of the fifteenth, it is difficult to see much more than a coincidence in the two phenomena. There was no crossover of skills between the two industries or any overlap in the production process, as we shall see. The contemporaneous slump in the wool industry certainly meant that more capital was available for alternate investment, but how, and if, this led to a transfer from one industry to the other has not yet been worked out. It would seem, however, that the industry required an entrepreneur of a rather different stamp. On the one hand, the silk industry presented much less of a management problem, since the putting-out system for organizing labor was not nearly as extensive as that of the wool industry and involved many fewer independent male workers and many more female workers living in the closed environment of the home or convent. This feature may, in fact, have had its appeal in the aftermath of the Ciompi revolt, which left behind a strong suspicion, if not a fear, on the part of the ruling elite in general of the political ambitions of wool workers. On the other hand, the setaiolo took a much greater risk, for he needed more start-up capital, his investment in materials and labor was tied up much longer in the production process, his finished product was more subject to the variables of taste in faraway markets, and, finally, he himself often had to take the initiative for getting his products to markets abroad. It is not surprising that two-thirds of the setaioli registered in the 1427 catasto were new men in the sense that their families did not have a long record, if any at all, of officeholding at a high government level (and therefore, presumably, of high economic status).[20]

Already in the thirteenth century Florence had a certain number of artisans working with silk. By midcentury they had become absorbed into one of the city's guild conglomerates, the Arte di Por Santa Maria, and the eventual transformation of this corporation into what was, in effect, the silk guild is the best documentation we have for the rise of the industry. The Arte di Por Santa Maria, like most other guilds following the formation of the guild republican constitution, was a heterogeneous conglomerate of artisans most of whom worked on cloth in one form or another. In 1346 it had three official membership groups: setaioli, retail cloth dealers, and a composite group of men in other categories that included tailors, embroiderers, and makers of vestments, mattresses, coverlets, stockings, doublets, and a variety of other products. A major group were the *ritagliatori*, retailers who worked and sold every type of cloth for the local market. Some ritagliatori engaged in finishing operations for the Calimala merchants, and a few achieved considerable wealth. Setaioli were a minor but distinct group within the guild. In the statutes of 1335 they appear less as manufacturers of fabrics than as shopkeepers and producers of threads, ribbons, purses, and other such haberdashery. Manufacturers of finished fabrics probably appeared on a modest scale only with the immigration of exiled Lucchesi silk workers in 1314. In 1322 the guild admitted gold- and silversmiths, some of whom also worked in the textile sector as manufactures of metallic threads. It is likely that production of high-quality fabrics was limited to specific orders for personal use, such as the four velvets ordered by the Peruzzi in 1333 as gifts to the Countess of Flanders, and did not include fabric for export.[21] In short, although the Arte di Por Santa Maria enjoyed the status of being one of the major guilds, its membership did not include the kind of capitalist entrepreneurs who controlled the guilds of wool manufacturers (Lana), local bankers (Cambio), and the international importers of semifinished wool cloth (Calimala). Its importance lay not in the level of wealth of individual members but in the links some of them had with the Calimala

---

[20] John F. Padgett and Paul D. McLean, "Economic Credit and Elite Transformation in Renaissance Florence," forthcoming in the *American Journal of Sociology* (available on the Internet at http://home.uchicago.edu/~jpadgett/, table 5).

[21] Bruno Dini, "L'industria serica in Italia, secc. XIII–XV," in Cavaciocchi, *La seta in Europa*, 109 (reprinted in *Saggi*).

merchants as well as in their collective presence as operators in the clothing and jewelry industry supplying a large and wealthy city.

In the second half of the fourteenth century the guild underwent some trans-formation in the relative importance of its constituent groups. In part this re-sulted from the decline of industrial operations by the Calimala merchants, but more important was the growing number of silk manufacturers within the guild. Giovanni Villani ignores the industry altogether in his famous description of the city in 1338. Yet the renewed guild statutes of 1352 include provisions relative to the entire process of the production of silk textiles, and setaioli appear on the several rosters of citizens compiled for fiscal purposes in the following years, although they constitute no more than 1 percent of those who are identified by a profession as compared with 33 percent for lanaioli. In the 1390s and continuing into the next century Florentine silk workers show up abroad—weavers, especially weav-ers of velvets, in Venice and others active in the commerce and production of silk in Bologna.[22] In 1404 guild records for the first time make a clear distinction between true manufactures of silk cloths, that is, setaioli, and small retailers and petty artisans who made objects with silk, *setaioli a minuto*. Revisions in 1411 refer to the entire gamut of luxury silks that were presumably being produced at the time, including taffetas, satins, velvets, and brocades (although Florence appears to have been less important than Bologna as a supplier of silk for the vast opera-tions abroad of Francesco Datini). Some thirty-eight silk companies show up in the 1427 catasto, about one-fourth the number of wool firms.

After the turn of the century the commune took wide-ranging initiatives to pro-mote this new and expanding industry. Legislation was enacted making it easier to import raw silk (1406 and 1408), discouraging emigration through penalties levied on both entrepreneurs and artisans within the sector who operated in other cities (1419), attracting specialized silk workers to the city (1423), limiting the sale of im-ported silks in the local market (1426), and facilitating the repatriation of those workers who had fled the city because of indebtedness (1429 and repeatedly thereafter).[23] Further legislation was directed to encouraging sericulture in the countryside, thereby forging a backward linkage to supply within the Florentine state itself. In 1408 the commune levied a tax on exports of silkworms, mulberry leaves, and raw silk, and in 1423 it exempted imports into the city of mulberry leaves. In 1441 it ordered peasants to plant a minimum of five mulberry trees on the land

---

[22] Iacopo Volpi, "Mercanti e setaioli a Bologna intorno al 1400," *Archivio storico italiano* (hereaf-ter *ASI*) 154 (1996): 583–604.

[23] This legislation is reviewed in Franco Franceschi, "Istituzioni e attività economica a Firenze: Considerazioni sul governo del settore industriale (1350–1450)," in *Istituzioni e società in Toscana nell'Età Moderna* (Rome, 1994), 76–117.

they farmed, and it took measures to encourage the immigration of workers of raw silk. In 1443 it forbade the exportation of raw silk from Florentine territory.

The success of the industry and the rise to prominence of setaioli is best marked by the growing public presence of the guild of Por Santa Maria on the local scene. Although long one of the major guilds, it had never had quite the same stature as the others, since its constituent crafts included few men of high economic and social status, but this changed with the increasing number of silk manufacturers. By the beginning of the fifteenth century these entrepreneur-producers constituted the largest constituent group *(membrum)* within the membership, followed by the ritagliatori and the goldsmiths. Since many of these men did not come from the ranks of established upper-class families, their ascent probably explains the guild's vigorous promotion of its growing public status. The guild, in short, became an outlet for the public affirmation of the wealth and status of a new industrial class.

In 1377 work began on a new guildhall conspicuously located just off the Mercato Nuovo, where the international merchant-bankers were concentrated, and adjacent to the palace of the Parte Guelfa, the powerful political organization; the building was enlarged in 1423. Also in 1377 the guild purchased the marble block for the sculpturing of the figure of St. John the Evangelist that was to become the first of the great statues to decorate the niches of Orsanmichele, the former grain hall newly remodeled as a monument to the guild constitution of the city. The grandest assertion of the guild's status came in 1419 with the foundation of the Ospedale degli Innocenti, the famous monument designed by Brunelleschi, as original in its early Renaissance architecture as it was in the function it performed as the city's first orphanage. Something of the importance of this project for the assertion of the guild's newly gained status can be read into the haste with which the building committee saw immediately to the completion of the impressive loggia opening on the square long before the church and the residential buildings behind were ready for the opening of the orphanage.

By this time the guild of Por Santa Maria had come to be more popularly known on the local scene as simply the silk guild, the Arte della Seta. Its members included some of the most successful local entrepreneurs; under their auspices the guild's patronage of public monuments could now challenge that of the Calimala and the Lana, whose traditional importance to the economy of the city was symbolized by their patronage as official sponsors, respectively, of the Baptistery and the cathedral, obviously the city's most prestigious monuments.[24] The patronage by the silk guild was a fitting token of the city's arrival in the early

---

[24] Richard A. Goldthwaite, "La fondazione e il consenso della città," in *Gli Innocenti e Firenze nei secoli: Un ospedale, un archivio, una città,* ed. Lucia Sandri (Florence, 1996), 7–11.

fifteenth century as the fifth major center of the industry in Italy, taking its place alongside Lucca, Bologna, Genoa, and Venice. The silk workers have left behind their own architectural monument as another visible testimony to the success and importance of this industry: the grandiose, five-bay loggia constructed at the end of the century for the new hospice of their confraternity, by far the most impressive project undertaken by any artisan group in the city.[25]

The reality behind communal legislation promoting the industry, and behind the architectural manifestations of the status of the setaioli, is somewhat less distinct, albeit clearly discernible. Statistical data documenting the performance of the industry are fragmentary and diverse, but together they point to a growing trend. Taxpayers' declarations of wealth include shops working silk, but it is not easy to distinguish those producing for the international market from small local operators. The ratio of silk to wool firms in the 1427 catasto is about 1:4, but the ratio of total capital invested in the two industries was closer to 1:2 since the average capital of a silk firm was much higher than that of a wool firm. Total production figures for silk that exist for the period 1430–47 show a fourfold increase, from 498 to 2,002 pieces, although it is not at all clear what constituted a piece, since these luxurious fabrics varied so much in length and value. The value of output has been estimated to have grown from about fl.270,000 in 1451–53 to about fl.400,000 in 1490, a figure that is almost at the level of the value of output in the wool industry. This growth was reenforced by the concurrent development of a sub-branch of the industry, the manufacturing of gold and silver threads, which were used in the most luxurious fabrics. The number of these battiloro companies increased from 9–10 in the 1460s to about 16–20 in the 1490s. Some battilori expanded operations to become themselves producers and major exporters of finished silk cloths indistinguishable from setaioli. In the early 1460s the Cambini import-export firm made higher profits from its trade in silk, between importing raw silk and exporting finished products, than from its trade in wool.[26]

In his survey of the city's resources in 1470, Benedetto Dei claims that there were eighty-three silk shops and that the industry employed no less than one-third of the population. His statistics are hardly reliable, but his emphasis on the major importance of the industry to the city's economy contrasts with Villani's utter

---

[25] The hospice was built opposite the monastery of San Marco on what today is Via Cavour. Later in the sixteenth century the buildings were purchased by the Medici to expand their holdings northward from the "garden" of San Marco, and the loggia was eventually moved to its present location on Via San Gallo.

[26] The data come from Gino Corti and José-Gentil Da Silva, "Note sur la production de la soie à Florence, au XVe siècle," *Annales: Économies, sociétés, civilisations* 20 (1965): 309–11 (production estimates based on fees to the Innocenti); and Bruno Dini, "La ricchezza documentaria per l'arte della seta e l'economia fiorentina del Quattrocento," in Sandri, *Gli Innocenti e Firenze*, 161 and 166–69, reprinted in *Manifattura, commercio e banca nella Firenze medievale* (Florence, 2001).

silence about the sector in his more reliable survey of 125 years earlier. The two Italian princes ruling over the largest capital cities turned to Florentines to get the industry going in their states: in 1441 Duke Filippo Maria Visconti granted privileges to Pietro di Bartolo to set up a shop in Milan, and in 1474 King Ferrante I of Aragon induced the merchant Francesco di Nerone to organize operations in Naples, including the opening of a shop to produce gold and silver threads.[27] The vitality of the industry also found expression in a comprehensive and highly technical treatise on the craft written about 1450, the only one to survive from anywhere in Renaissance Italy.

In this phase of expansion firms like those of Andrea Banchi and Tommaso Spinelli (the only firms studied) produced the most luxurious kinds of fabrics, including patterned varieties of the lampas category, figured velvets with piles of different heights, and brocades enhanced with gold and silver threads and elaborate embroidery. Of the silk fabrics purchased by the Cambini merchant-banking firm from 1459 to 1480, 47 percent were velvets at the top of the market and another 20 percent were damasks.[28] Florentines exported these products to lay and ecclesiastical courts everywhere across the Mediterranean, from Pera and Alexandria in the Near East to Spain and Portugal, but the chief markets were within Italy itself, in the growing capital cities of Rome and Naples. Moreover, silk fabrics were the first major products made in Florence that sold also in the markets throughout the Florentine commercial network in northern Europe. They were shipped to the traditional outlets in Bruges and London, and new markets opened up with the organization of the great international fairs, first at Geneva, then at Lyons and, in the sixteenth century, at Antwerp. The search for new markets was a principal dynamic behind Florentine merchants' push into central Germany, an area that until then had been on the periphery of the Florentine commercial and banking system. Florentine silks were present at the Frankfurt fairs in 1495. In 1499 Raffaello di Iacopo Vecchietti set up a company in Nuremberg explicitly for the sale of silks,[29] and others followed, as we have seen. In 1536 a company of battilori was organized under the name of Gherardo Bartolini for the specific purpose of producing silk fabrics for this new German market.[30]

---

[27] Luca Molà, "Oltre i confini della città: Artigiani e imprenditori della seta fiorentini all'estero," in *La grande storia dell'artigianato*, vol. 2, *Il Quattrocento,* ed. Franco Franceschi and Gloria Fossi (Florence, 1999), 90–99.

[28] Sergio Tognetti, *Da Figline a Firenze: Ascesa economica e politica della famiglia Serristori (secoli XIV–XVI)* (Florence, 2003), 114.

[29] Edler de Roover, *L'arte della seta,* 116.

[30] Marco Spallanzani, "Le compagnie Saliti a Norimberga nella prima metà del Cinquecento (un primo contributo dagli archivi fiorentini)," in *Wirtschaftskräfte und Wirtschaftswege: Festschrift für Hermann Kellenbenz,* ed. Jürgen Schneider (Nuremberg, 1978), 1:607. For Florentines in Germany, see above, chapter 2.

Changing conditions in international markets led to a significant transformation within the Florentine industry beginning in the sixteenth century, namely, the sharpening of competition and the ever-increasing variability of demand. Competition resulted from the rapid growth of the industry in at least a half-dozen other cities within Italy by the end of the fifteenth century. Reference has already been made to the establishment of the industry in Milan and Naples, partly with the help of Florentine immigrants; these cities soon joined Lucca, Bologna, Genoa, and Venice as major centers of production. The industry in some of these places (to the extent that we can judge) reached production levels far above that of Florence.[31] Florentine products, in fact, accounted for only a small percentage of total output in Italy, and that percentage probably shrank during the sixteenth century as the industry continued to expand to yet other cities. Florence, in short, never enjoyed anything like the near monopoly in silk that it had long enjoyed in luxury wool cloths. The competition became all the keener with the loss of the commercial advantage the city had long held in some of the most important markets for silk. Merchants from Genoa, with their own products to sell, moved into the markets of the western Mediterranean, including Rome and Naples, in a major way. Building up a superior commercial and banking system that had a solid foundation in maritime power, the Genoese were in a position to sell fabrics from other Italian cities as well as their own. The appearance of other merchants operating on a larger international scale, such as the Castilians and the southern Germans, further improved marketing opportunities for producers of silks in other Italian cities. By the 1580s Genoese, Castilian, and even German merchants had a notable presence in Florence itself as no foreigners had had a century earlier. One setaioli firm, Baccio Martelli, Pierfrancesco Del Giocondo & Partners, sold 29 percent of its output from 1584 to 1590 to no fewer than twenty-seven foreigners present in the local market.[32] In this restructured international commercial system, Florentine setaioli no longer sold their products exclusively to local Florentine merchants. This more fluid and efficient market generated keener competition, a dynamic that had repercussions on the industry everywhere.

Competition was further enlivened by the very nature of the demand for silk fabrics. Whereas the wool industry, turning out San Martino cloths and then rascia, concentrated on a highly prestigious but standardized product that came close to assuring the industry a monopoly, at least for a while, in the luxury market for woolens across the fifteenth and sixteenth centuries, the silk industry was subject to a highly volatile demand linked to an increasingly rapid change in

---

[31] See Molà, *Silk Industry*, 14–19.
[32] These results are from my yet unpublished study of the firm.

fashion. Silks came in a far greater variety than woolens, there being seemingly infinite possibilities for different combination of threads, weaves, textures, designs, colors, and even luminosity and three-dimensionality, all variables that could be used in any number of combinations and in conjunction with other materials, from linen to gold and silver threads. A 1519 inventory of the company of Bernardo Acciaiuoli and Bernardo Saliti in Nuremberg lists 267 different fabrics. These came in sixteen weaves, in different designs, and in ten colors in various combinations; some were made with gold and silver threads; and some were described as "alla lucchese," while others were described as "alla veneziana." So great was the variety that it is virtually impossible even to categorize them.[33] Production of this kind gave rise to more experimentation and innovation in the search for greater variety and, at the same time, lower costs. Moreover, the variety of the fabrics, along with their lightness, opened up seemingly endless possibilities for tailoring. For the rich, clothing became a means of fashioning the presentation of self that had not existed earlier, and demand became all the more vigorous as the rich became richer at a time when the European economy was expanding into the Atlantic and around the entire globe. The demand for silk, in short, was subject to many variables and driven by the dynamic of change we today associate with fashion. Competition intensified in response to this new kind of demand, and production standards shifted continually with the introduction of new techniques and new products.[34]

All this competition among producers operating in a more efficient international market, the wide range of their expensive products, and the increasingly rapid changes in fashion combined to create a market situation in the sixteenth century that probably had not existed anywhere in the West much before then. Rascia, a lighter luxury product dependent on high-quality imported raw material, was the wool industry's response to this market, but its success was short-lived, in large part because the high end of the market increasingly abandoned wool for lighter, more luxurious and varied silk fabrics, and the industry was incapable of shifting to the cheaper lightweight cloth introduced by the Dutch and the English. The Florentine silk industry, however, followed a different tact. Faced with competition in a market driven by a highly volatile demand that imperiled the sale of extremely costly products with designs or weaves that were likely to go out of

---

[33] Marco Spallanzani, "Tessuti di seta fiorentini per il mercato di Norimberga intorno al 1520," in *Studi in memoria di Giovanni Cassandro* (Rome, 1991), 3:995–1016.

[34] Recent surveys of the increasing use of silks include two exhibition catalogs: *Velluti e moda tra XV e XVII secolo* (Milan, 1999), esp. the contributions of Roberta Orsi Landini, and *Arte e lusso della seta a Genova dal '500 al '700*, ed. Marzia Castaldi Gallo (Genoa, 2000). The notion of fashion is treated in Ann Rosalind Jones and Peter Stallybrass, *Renaissance Clothing and the Material of Memory* (Cambridge, 2000). See also the conclusion of Molà, *Silk Industry*.

fashion in a short time, the industry shifted to reduce the production of highly luxurious velvets and brocades enriched with gold and silver threads. This downscaling occurred rapidly. In a 1525 survey of the city's shops only 4 of the 121 weavers are described as weavers of taffetas. In 1546 the Venetian ambassador to France, remarking the large profits the Florentines (along with the Genoese) earned from the sale of damasks and satins, reported that "they produce things that suit the desires and tastes of the French, that is, cloths that cost little and last even less, which is exactly what that nation wants, because it would get bored if a garment lasted too long."[35] By the end of the century production had descended to even simpler fabrics, such as plain satins, sarcenets *(ermisini)*, and, to a lesser extent, taffetas (the latter two of the tabby category), which were directed to the lower end, if not the bottom, of the luxury market. These fabrics constituted the bulk of the production of Martelli, Del Giocondo & Partners, mentioned above, active from 1584 to 1608. During the firm's first partnership, from 1584 to 1591, no less than two-thirds of its production consisted of satins (44 percent) and sarcenets (20 percent), and most of the rest fell into the same general category. Brocades account for only 1.34 percent of sales, and velvets a mere 0.90 percent, both probably manufactured on special order. In the mid-seventeenth century the silk guild reported that 90 percent of the industry's production consisted of less costly items, and it found that only one "master" in the city knew how to weave designs into cloth of gold.[36]

Faced with increasing competition from other Italian producers, the industry took the easy way out, redirecting production to a secure niche market with a standardized and less costly product that would sell in any market and be less subject to changes in fashion. This strategy would seem to have paid off, for notwithstanding the lowering of the quality of its products, investment in the industry remained strong, and profits were high. In a survey made in 1561 there were ninety-one setaioli shops plus twenty battiloro shops, many of which may also have been setaioli shops. In the course of the century the annual importation of raw silk increased from 27–30 tons to 60–65 tons, and the number of looms doubled, from about one thousand to more than two thousand.[37] This success can be measured in the expanding place of silk in the investment portfolio of the Riccardi at the end of the century, a family noted for its rapidly growing wealth at the time. The Riccardi had *sc.*4,500 invested in a single silk company in 1590; *sc.*17,000 in two companies in 1600; and *sc.*48,000 in five silk companies and one battiloro company in 1610, by which time it was divesting in the wool industry, as we have

[35] Quoted in Molà, *Silk Industry,* 96.
[36] Goodman, "Cloth, Gender and Industrial Organization," 239.
[37] These statistics come from Battistini, "La produzione, il commercio e i prezzi," 235–37.

seen.[38] The net annual return on the investment in the Martelli, Del Giocondo firm, which specialized in simpler fabrics, averaged 15 percent from 1584 to 1591, 9 percent from 1591 to 1605, and 10 percent from 1605 to 1608; this was not an outstanding performance by the standards of a century earlier, but at a time when interest rates were falling all over Europe, it was a better than respectable return. Moreover, the importance of the industry in the local economy, as measured by the few figures we have for output, was greater than it had been in the fifteenth century (see table 4.2). In 1546 Cosimo I, barely ten years into his reign, took initiatives to set up a silk industry in Pisa as well; in 1549 the Arte della Seta was established there, independent of the Florentine guild.

In short, whereas the wool industry, aiming at the top end of the market, lost its competitive position and virtually collapsed in the second decade of the seventeenth century, the silk industry, aiming instead at the low end, continued to grow, remaining strong through the seventeenth century, a time when the industry underwent a crisis at Milan, Naples, and Genoa. And this despite the disintegration of the international commercial-banking network, which had been the necessary precondition for the foundation and early growth of the industry.

The industry was also strengthened in the sixteenth century to the extent that backward linkages to supply of raw materials were forged within the local economy, a development that never took place in the wool industry. In the Middle Ages the Near East was the major supplier of raw silk to the Italian industry, but this changed beginning in the fourteenth century with the rapid diffusion of sericulture in the western Mediterranean. About the time the Florentine industry began to grow, Spain was a source of raw silk for the industry in Lucca. In the fifteenth century sericulture spread rapidly throughout Italy, from Calabria in the south to the Marche, the Abruzzi (especially at Sulmona), Romagna (at Modigliana), Lombardy, and the Veneto. By the sixteenth century governments everywhere in Italy, from the Kingdom of Naples to Venice and Savoy in the north, were vigorously promoting sericulture to support local industry, and by the end of that century all the raw silk consumed by Italian producers came from within Italy itself. Cities such as Florence and Genoa, whose hinterland could not satisfy the demand of the local industry, came to depend chiefly on the Kingdom of Naples, where production was centered around Naples itself, in Calabria, and in Sicily. Genoese merchants were particularly aggressive in promoting this expansion of production in the hinterland.

In Tuscany sericulture had a modest tradition in the Valdinievole, dating from the fourteenth century, as an extension of the industry in Lucca. In the

[38] Malanima, *I Riccardi*, 74, 97.

TABLE 4.2

The Silk Industry, 1436–1629:
Production as Investment in the Local Economy

Year	(a) Gross value of production in florins	(b) £ per florin	(c) Net value* of production in lire: 35% of (a) (b)	(d) Daily wage† (soldi)	(e) Value of production in work years of 260 days: (c) ÷ (d) / 20 ÷ 260	(f) Population	(g) Per capita value of production in work years: (e) ÷ (f)
1436	233,000	4.15	338,433	10	2,603	40,000	0.07
1451–53	270,000	4.25	401,625	10	3,089	40,000	0.08
1461–62	300,000	4.50	472,500	10	3,635	40,000	0.09
1490	400,000	5.80	812,000	10	6,246	42,000	0.15
1527	400,000	7.00	980,000	10	7,538	70,000	0.11
1588	1,000,000	7.00	2,450,000	20	9,423	65,000	0.14
1628–29	1,172,280	7.00	2,872,086	20	11,046	75,000	0.15

SOURCES:

1436–90: Bruno Dini, "La ricchezza documentaria per l'arte della seta e l'economia fiorentina del Quattrocento," in *Gli Innocenti e Firenze nei secoli: Un ospedale, un archivio, una città,* ed. Lucia Sandri (Florence, 1996), 29, with explanation of calculation on p. 17 n. 33.

1527: Venetian ambassador, quoted in Dini, "La ricchezza documentaria," 19.

1588: Venetian ambassador, quoted in Paolo Malanima, *La decadenza di un'economia cittadina: L'industria di Firenze nei secoli XVI–XVIII* (Bologna, 1982), 313.

1628–29: Jordan Goodman, "Tuscan Commercial Relations with Europe, 1550–1620: Florence and the European Textile Market," in *Firenze e la Toscana dei Medici nell'Europa del '500* (Florence, 1983), 1:332.

* Net value is gross value less the amount spent for imported raw silk, which on the average was 65% of total costs; it represents manufacturing costs spent within the local economy.

† The wage rate is that of an unskilled worker in the construction industry.

early fifteenth century, with the rise of the industry in Florence, as we have seen, the government took steps to encourage the planting of mulberry trees, but domestic production did not see major expansion until the Medici dukes made a more vigorous effort to strengthen the industry. In legislation of 1546–47 Cosimo I took the first steps toward what became ducal policy to promote sericulture beyond the Valdinievole, especially in the Valdelsa and the Valdipesa. Directives were issued ordering the planting of mulberry trees along certain roads and streams and even along the walls of Florence itself; at the same time, efforts were made to subject sericulture to rigorous standards and strict controls. It has been estimated that in the course of the sixteenth century the share of raw silk produced locally in Tuscany to meet the needs of the industry rose from 10 percent to 35 percent, an impressive performance considering the overall increase in the amount of raw silk the industry absorbed over the century.

The shift in the source for the supply of raw materials can be traced in the histories of specific firms that have been studied. In the early fifteenth century Andrea Banchi imported raw silk from, in order of importance, the Caspian Sea area, southern Spain, and central Italy, with only a miniscule portion from Tuscany. At the end of the century the Serristori firm took only one-third to one-half of its raw silk from the Caspian Sea area and virtually nothing from Spain, with the rest coming from Italy itself, almost one-fourth from Calabria alone.[39] A century later, in the 1580s, the firm of Martelli, Del Giocondo & Partners used only Italian silk, with slightly less than half coming from the Kingdom of Naples (mostly from Calabria) and about a quarter from its home region of Tuscany.[40] Inasmuch as the raw material constituted about 60 percent of total production costs for silk fabrics, this backward linkage to supply very much enhanced the strength of this industry within the economy as a whole (and by the eighteenth century Tuscany was self-sufficient in the supply of raw silk to the industry). The concentration of sericulture in the area of Pescia gave rise to the opening of throwing mills there at the end of the sixteenth century—there were five in 1590 and twenty in 1615—and hence the transfer of some of the industrial processing from Florence to the place where most of the raw silk was produced.[41]

[39] Tognetti, *Un'industria di lusso*, 88, 98.

[40] The Ruiz letters of the 1580s, published by Felipe Ruiz Martín, *Lettres marchandes échangées entre Florence et Medina del Campo* (Paris, 1965), make no reference to silk exports. Earlier, in 1537–41, the Rovereto firm in Genoa took only about 16 percent of its silk from Chios, the rest coming from southern Italy and the Veneto. Massa, *Un'impresa serica genovese*, 50.

[41] Battistini, *Gelsi, bozzoli e caldaie*, 178.

Linen Drapers

Linen drapers constituted what was one of the most numerous categories of tradesmen after the lanaioli and the setaioli. The 1427 catasto names forty-nine linen drapers' shops, and the 1480 catasto names fifty-four, approximately the same number as those of setaioli. Nothing has been written about these men, however, and the few extant records of their businesses have not been studied. Hence we are hardly in a position to assess the importance of this industry in the local economy.[42]

Flax was one of the most common agricultural crops in the countryside around Florence, and a cottage industry producing linen grew up organized around the households of the people who worked the land. This production, almost all of it for local consumption, surfaces in many of the 1427 catasto reports submitted by urban residents who owned land in the countryside.[43] Use of the banks of the Arno for processing flax and hemp was, in fact, so extensive as to create problems for navigation. In other words, there was a well-developed rural industry. Cloth production in the city seems to have been limited. In her search through the catasto documents extending from 1427 to 1480, Florence Edler de Roover found only twenty-five to thirty linen weavers in the city, and most of these worked not for linen drapers but for landowners who cultivated flax on their farms. Moreover, she identified only one dyer of linen in the 1427 catasto. However, drapers could organize production of these cheaper cloths by putting out linen, cotton, and other vegetable fibers to women; to this end they utilized the cottage industry in the countryside as well as the considerable resources of female labor in the city's convents. One indication of this traffic is the decision of the commune in 1474 to eliminate gate duties on linen and cotton going into the countryside to be worked, the motivation being to encourage more production and thereby secure employment for the finishing process in the city.[44] The 1550 shop inventory of the linen draper Tommaso Fiaschi lists a great variety of cloth but no clothing or cloth products; and the list of his debtors includes cross references to a manufacturing journal *(libro di manifattori)*. The total value of his

---

[42] The most intelligent statement about them is found in Edler de Roover, *L'arte della seta*, 84–85, which does not altogether accord with the view of the Florentine industry one gets from the scattered remarks in Maureen Fennell Mazzaoui, *The Italian Cotton Industry in the Later Middle Ages, 1000–1600* (Cambridge, 1981). Mazzaoui's study, however, is an essential guide to the international trade in linen and cotton. Luciana Frangioni, "Sui modi di produzione e sul commercio dei fustagni milanesi alla fine del Trecento," *Nuova rivista storica* 61 (1977): 493–554, also has much general information about the industry in Italy.

[43] Amanda Lillie, *Florentine Villas in the Fifteenth Century: An Architectural and Social History* (Cambridge, 2005), 30.

[44] Sergio Tognetti, "Problemi di vettovagliamento cittadino e misure di politica annonaria a Firenze nel XV secolo (1430–1500)," *ASI* 157 (1999): 439.

gross assets, divided about equally between inventory and debtors, was *fl.*2,145, a figure that gives us some sense of the scale of operations such a business could reach.[45] Unlike the wool and silk industries, however, the manufacture of products in these cheaper cloths was not directed to export markets.

Linen drapers were also retailers who sold products made of linen, cotton, and fustian (a linen and cotton hybrid), such as undergarments, summer clothing, towels, tablecloths, scarves, handkerchiefs, and the complete line of bedding. Much of this production was of poor quality to satisfy mass demand at the low end of the market, but the materials could also be made into goods of the highest quality, for which there was substantial demand from people who were better off. Moreover, linen was often used in combination with silk, and the growth of the silk industry in the fifteenth century may have had a significant impact on the traffic in these cheaper fibers. Linen drapers were incorporated together with secondhand dealers *(rigattieri)*, tailors, and makers of doublets and mattresses in a single guild, the Arte dei Linaioli e Rigattieri, and there may have been considerable overlap between linen drapers' activity as retailers and that of secondhand dealers. The surviving account books of the linen draper Tommaso di Donato, who headed a partnership spanning the last decade of the fifteenth century, yield hardly any evidence for the production of cloth other than occasional payments to "our weaver." He imported some materials from Germany and sold everything from cloth to rugs and eyeglasses.[46]

Some of these kinds of cloth were imported from abroad. Linen was the most important product the Neapolitan company of Alessandro Gondi exported from that region to Florence in the late 1480s.[47] A principal center for the working of cotton was central Italy, in Umbria and the Marche; the raw material was imported from the Levant, and finished products, including threads, linings, and veiling, were exported to markets outside the region. Florentine merchants were active in this trade, directing much of it to markets abroad but some also to Florence. It seems, however, that they brought some of this cloth, both linen and cotton, to the city to be put through a bleaching process and then reexported to foreign markets, but this aspect of the industry, perhaps a spin-off of the wool industry, has not been studied.[48] During the fifteenth century an increasing amount of cotton imported to Italy ended up being sent to Germany, where a vigorous fustian industry took root, eventually invading Italy with its products.

[45] ASF, Libri di commercio, 2197.

[46] Archive of the Ospedale degli Innocenti, Florence, ser. 144 (Estranei), 869–77.

[47] Alfonso Leone, "Rapporti commerciali fra Napoli e Firenze alla fine del secolo XV," in *Studi in memoria di Giovanni Cassandro,* 2:494–96.

[48] Bruno Dini, *Arezzo intorno al 1400: Produzioni e mercato* (Arezzo, 1984), 53–69.

The 1578 statutes of the guild mention imports of linen cloth from Flanders, Germany, Venice, Mantua, and Naples.

Linen drapers, therefore, dealt with importers and handled a large variety of cloth. With their interest in this trade, they probably had opportunities that few other local operators had for expanding their business into the network abroad. The economic history of one family of linen drapers, the Cambini, documents such a trajectory. The linen draper Francesco Cambini, who died in 1400, left a patrimony worth *fl.*950 in 1414, when it was divided among his sons, enough to put the family solidly in the middling class (as we shall define it in chapter 7). Two of his sons, both having already reached employment age, had been placed in international firms abroad, and the business they set up later on their own has been frequently referred to in these pages. Two younger sons, taking their father's shop as their share of the estate when it was divided in 1414, opened their own firm with a corpo of *fl.*500, but a year later they dissolved this firm and joined with two outside partners to set up another with a corpo of *fl.*1,400. Over the next nine years, down to the founding of a new company in 1423, one partner left and two others were added, the corpo grew to *fl.*5,000 (the share of the Cambini brothers having doubled, from *fl.*1,150 in 1415 to *fl.*2,300), and a branch was opened in Rome. In the eleven years from 1415 to 1425 these firms yielded profits amounting to *fl.*12,555, well over *fl.*1,000 a year. In the 1427 catasto each of the two brothers had a net worth of just over *fl.*1,500, the chief asset of each being his share in the firm. Each brother set a son up in a separate firm, one of whom subsequently shifted to the wool business and then to silk. When this grandson of Francesco died in 1468, however, he had divested himself of this interest and was living as a rentier from real-estate holdings worth *fl.*2,204. Unfortunately, no records survive to give us any idea of the internal history of these firms, but clearly somewhere early on in this history the Cambini, while still linen drapers, branched out well beyond the confines of the ordinary shop. They did this as merchants, however, not as producers.[49]

Business Organization
The Firm

THE GUILD CONTEXT   The business organization of the textile industry was highly fragmented among individual firms, each of which was a miniscule operation in the overall structure of the industry. However, neither the lanaioli nor the

---

[49] Sergio Tognetti, *Il banco Cambini: Affari e mercati di una compagnia mercantile-bancaria nella Firenze del XV secolo* (Florence, 1999), 25–40.

setaioli were completely on their own in running their businesses. They enjoyed the corporate protection of their respective guilds—the Lana, which was exclusively a guild of wool manufacturers, and the Seta (Por Santa Maria), which was a guild conglomerate including members other than the setaioli. All regulation of the industries, such as it was, emanated from these two guilds. Manufacturers controlled the affairs of the guild, including enforcement of its regulations, administration of justice over workers, and admission into membership. The Lana also did for the lanaioli collectively what the individual firms could not always do for themselves: it operated fulling mills and tenter sheds, manufactured soap, and maintained a warehouse for dyes. The guild also made efforts to assure the industry an adequate supply of dyes and oil for the making of soap. After the suppression of the revolt at Volterra in 1472, at a time when the supply of alum from the Levant had been cut off, the wool guild gained the authority from the commune to search for alum mines in the area and to contract out the operation of them. Given the silk industry's different and more limited production process, the setaioli did not require such help from their guild, which, in any case, was a conglomerate that included other economic groups (we have already reviewed the many ways that communal legislation supported the industry during its initial growth stage at the beginning of the fifteenth century).

In the management of their firms in both industries, manufacturers were very much on their own, with ample room to conduct their business as they wished, subject only to certain industrial standards regarding mostly quality controls that they all accepted through guild regulation. They enjoyed monopoly control over the factors of production within the industry inasmuch as none of their workers were allowed to organize themselves into autonomous—and potentially recalcitrant—guilds (although a few groups were given subordinate status in their respective guilds) and they alone owned the basic raw materials of the industry during the entire process of production.

CAPITAL NEEDS   Organized as partnerships called companies *(compagnie)*, manufacturing firms represented the major concentration of investment capital in the industry, and they incorporated the entrepreneurial energy and management skills that drove the industry. Generally at least two parties came together as *compagni* to set up a company: a major partner (or a family group), who put in most of the capital, and a managing partner, who contributed his services *(persona)* and perhaps also some capital. Other investors, but generally not more than two or three, might also join the partnership. The formal contractual agreement in the articles of organization followed a standard form in setting down the basic business arrangements, giving the duration (usually three to five years), the prerogatives of the major partner, the responsibilities of the managing partner, the rules of business conduct, and the procedures for early termination in case of a death and for liquidation and division of profits. The firm took the name of the major partner, who generally supervised the bookkeeping; the managing partner dealt with production. All these arrangements incorporated in the articles of association are typically limited to what we might call matters of business administration common to any enterprise, be it a bank or a cloth firm; they are not concerned with the particulars of textile production. The articles of organization remained unchanged over the fifteenth and sixteenth centuries.[50]

The investment needs of a firm included little fixed capital—nothing for plant and hardly anything for tools and equipment. The firm rented its premises, and since production was organized around the putting-out system, it could leave the purchase of tools and equipment to the workers who contracted for the various stages of production. A wool firm supplied its shop only with the inexpensive tools used in the initial stage of beating, combing, and carding the wool, but this required a miniscule outlay of capital. Almost all the equipment and tools needed for the subsequent stages of production of wool and virtually all those needed for silk were owned by the workers themselves. A dyer's equipment was probably worth about *fl.*50, and a silk-throwing machine, about *fl.*25. Looms for weaving silk ranged in value according to the type of fabric, the most expensive, used for figured brocades and velvets, costing as much as *fl.*25–35, while a loom used for wool was worth only about *fl.*5. A shearman's shears cost up to *fl.*8, a high-quality carding comb around *fl.*1. These figures come mostly from the 1427 catasto or other fifteenth-century sources; given the level of earnings of skilled artisans at that time, which ranged from *fl.*35 to *fl.*70, the cost of none of these things was beyond their reach. Moreover, there is hardly any evidence that cloth firms— unlike the drapers in the Low Countries—had capital tied up in significant liens on equipment and tools as a result of extending credit to workers for the purchase of these things.

Plant represented by far the largest investment in the fixed capital of the industry, but the capital did not come from the wool and silk firms. Ownership was highly fragmented and widely diffused throughout the society. Firms rented their premises, sometimes from one of the partners,[51] and the workspaces outside the shop, where almost all the manufacturing process took place, were either

---

[50] For summaries of partnership arrangements, see de Roover, "Florentine Firm of Cloth Manufacturers," 87–91; and Caferro, "Silk Business," 423–24.

[51] According to the survey of shops in the 1427 catasto made by Maria Letizia Grossi, only five wool shops and six silk shops were owned by the men who used them for this purpose. "Le botteghe fiorentine nel catasto del 1427," *Ricerche storiche* 30 (2000): 29.

owned or rented by the people who worked there. Many craftsmen, especially spinners and weavers, worked at home, and given the high incidence of home-ownership in the 1427 catasto, much of this workspace probably belonged to workers themselves. The industry was far from being a domestic cottage industry in a literal sense, however, for many workers worked in places outside the home; and these work places together constituted a large body of urban real estate. Most of these nondomestic workspaces, including the shops of the manufacturing firms, were just that: places to work, without any other particular requirements with regard to investment. Only three stages in the production of wool cloth—scouring, fulling, and stretching—required relatively heavy investment in a specially outfitted facility. The wool guild, besides being a regulator and ad-judicator, played an active role as an investor in these more expensive properties to assure smoother operations for private firms. In the fifteenth century it oper-ated workshops for scouring wool, a shop for the making of soap, and a ware-house to supply the industry with woad, the most basic dyestuff. Most tenter sheds and, at least in the earlier period, fulling mills were in private hands, some probably belonging to lanaioli personally. In 1498, however, the guild owned six tenter sheds, and over the fifteenth and sixteenth centuries it bought up many, if not most, fulling mills. The guild leased these properties out to the craftsmen working on contract from lanaioli. Tenter sheds were massive structures that, although of no great complexity, required a heavy investment. In his record book Buonaccorso Pitti mentions that his father, Neri, who had investments in the wool industry, spent *fl.*3,500 to put one up about the middle of the fourteenth century. There were many tenter sheds scattered all around the city, a notable cluster of them being located behind the cathedral in an area extending from Borgo degli Albizzi to Via della Colonna.[52] Besides mills along the riverbanks, tenter sheds were the only industrial buildings that had a distinct architectural identity on the urban scene. They have all since disappeared, but to anyone look-ing over the cityscape at the time, they alone revealed something about the indus-trial life of the city.

Fulling mills required by far the largest investment in plant and equipment. They were located in large, multifunctional mill complexes outside the city, along the river, in part because of the noise and stench they generated. They usually belonged to wealthy landowners. One of these families, the Albizzi, assembled a notable cluster of fulling mills along the Arno between Nave a Rovezzano and Le Sieci, just upstream from Florence, where they had their ancestral lands.

[52] E. Salvini, "Gualchiere e tiratoi a Firenze nel Medioevo," *L'universo* 67 (1987), esp. 442–59 on tenter sheds, with a census of the known ones.

Beginning in 1322 the five sons of Lando degli Albizzi bought up four mills and built a fifth *ex novo* at Remole in 1326. This latter was a major industrial complex costing *fl.*5,000 (some of which was borrowed from the wool guild). It had twenty sets of hammers and accommodations for the fullers, including an oven and stables, all enclosed by crenellated walls with two massive towers, giving rise to the name by which the place was known from the sixteenth century on, the castle of Remole. A church was projected but never built. The place must have been something like a modern factory town. The brothers organized the operation as a partnership, dividing the property among themselves into five shares, each with four sets of hammers. The staff consisted of five fullers, one for each share, and a supervisor, who directed them and attended to general maintenance of this complex industrial structure. The partnership lasted until at least 1429, by which time ownership, through generational fragmentation, had become divided into sixty shares, each yielding a revenue of *fl.*10 annually. This heavy investment in such a large fulling-mill operation may, in fact, have given the five brothers a near monopoly over this stage of production within the entire industry.[53]

If the strength of the two textile industries together is estimated roughly as consisting of 150 wool and silk firms and 1,500 weavers (which it appears to have been through most of the fifteenth century), one might estimate that the total fixed capital in tools, equipment, and plant (excluding domestic space) probably did not amount to much more than *fl.*75,000, about the value of the capital of the Medici agglomerate at the time.[54] None of this capital, however, came from the lanaioli and silk firms as such (excepting the small investment wool firms had in tools). What these manufacturers needed was almost exclusively start-up capital so that they could buy raw materials and pay workers to get operations going to the point where income from sales was sufficient to meet ongoing costs. The basic raw material constituted a major proportion of their total expenditures. For wool the cost was 40 percent, a level that remained constant throughout the history of the industry regardless of the source of the raw material and the quality of the final product. For silk the cost was much higher, ranging from one-half to two-thirds and in some instances even higher, its variability a function of the complex typology of the finished fabrics in contrast to the standardization of wool cloth. Firms paid the relatively small costs of the soap and dyes they supplied to

---

[53] Ibid., 404–41; Lorenzo Fabbri, "*Opus novarum gualcheriarum:* Gli Albizzi e le origini delle gualchiere di Remole," *ASI* 162 (2004): 507–61 (with references to some recent articles on technical aspects of these fulling mills).

[54] The estimate is based on the following data: 400 silk weavers, each with a loom worth *fl.*20 (for a total value of *fl.*8,000); 1,000 wool weavers, each with a loom worth *fl.*5 (*fl.*5,000); 150 shops, each worth *fl.*300 (*fl.*45,000). Other data can be found in Edler de Roover, *L'arte della seta,* and in Franceschi, *Oltre il "Tumulto."*

dyers, and silk companies had the additional expense of gold and silver threads, as well as more costly dyes.

Besides this outlay for materials, liquidity for current expenses also required a certain amount of capital. Ready cash was needed to pay rent and meet payroll demands whenever the cloth returned to the shop as it passed through the stages of the putting-out system, most stages lasting only a few days. When it was out for long periods, workers, most notably the weavers, required advances. Since production time extended up to two months for wool cloth and longer for silk, depending on the type of fabric, it could be several months before a new firm reached the point at which income from sales was sufficient to meet the continual need to pay for materials and labor. Once investment capital was exhausted and the firm was up and running, the main administrative task was to balance expenditures for raw materials against income from sales in order to have the cash flow needed to pay ongoing production expenses.

A firm bought its raw materials as needed and sold its products immediately to any merchant-exporter who would buy them; any slack in demand could be met simply by ceasing production. At any one time, therefore, a firm had relatively little capital tied up in materials, and claims from its payroll extended to no more than the several weeks—somewhat longer for silk firms—it had to pay advances to weavers while they had cloth on the looms. By buying only enough raw wool to keep the level of output at two to three bolts a week, so that it had no more than eight to twelve bolts in various stages of being woven at any one time, the wool firm could stop production immediately at virtually no cost. Within his own operation as a manufacturer, however, there was no flexibility. Completed work that came in from the people who were employed through the putting-out system required cash payment on the spot, and advances, usually weekly, had to be made to those workers, such as weavers, who needed more time to finish their task. In the inevitable moments when liquidity was threatened, two main instruments were available to give the firm respite through short-term credit: overdraft on current accounts with a bank or clients, and direct borrowing through short-term time deposits by outside investors or other instruments such as bills of exchange with international merchant-bankers. Since the firm owned the basic raw material as it went through all stages of the production process, it always had collateral to put up for a loan, even when the silk or wool was temporarily out to subcontracted workers. In general, the easy availability of short-term credit assured a reasonably smooth cash flow. A convention of business practice at the time allowed delayed payments for goods sold, an instrument that could be used by a buyer to gain credit for up to a year. But for the cloth producer, who, on the one hand, bought raw materials and, on the other, sold finished products, this arrangement cut both ways: while he could gain time to pay for raw wool, he had to give a buyer of finished cloth time to pay.

These circumscribed conditions in which a firm found itself—investing in raw materials but having very little in fixed capital and a kind of hand-to-mouth existence between outlay for raw materials and income from sales in the attempt to maintain liquidity—limited its scale of operations. The firm sought to avoid risks by minimizing both the demand on the liquidity needed to meet ongoing expenditures and the capital tied up in the production process. The very largest wool companies in the 1427 catasto had capital of *fl.*4,000 to *fl.*6,000, and a decade later one of the largest of the new silk companies, that of Andrea Banchi, had capital of *fl.*9,000. In the wool industry the ceiling did not go much higher in the fifteenth century, and the capital of many firms was below *fl.*2,000, while the silk industry saw a slight trend toward ever higher capitalization in the course of the century as a result of forward commercial operations (discussed below). By the fifteenth century wool companies numbered more than a hundred, and the rise of the silk industry saw the opening of another fifty or so firms. Given these numbers, it is not unreasonable to think that total capital investment in the two textile industries reached at least a half-million florins; it probably went much higher. At this level of operation probably no wool firm accounted for more than 1–2 percent of total production, and although some silk firms exceeded this share of the market, none approached a commanding position over the others. The business organization of the industry remained fragmented more or less to this degree through the sixteenth century. If the capitalist who had either a wool or a silk firm wanted to increase his investment in the sector, he opened a second firm rather than enlarging the operations of the one he already had. Some men invested in both industries. On the whole, however, few investors possessed as many as two wool firms, and fewer still had both a wool and a silk firm. In the fifteenth century a family as rich as the Medici never had more than one silk and two wool firms, none of them any larger than many others in the city and all three together amounting to no more than about one-fifth of the family's investment in banking and commerce. At the end of the sixteenth century there were men, such as the Riccardi and Corsi, who had as many as three or four firms in each of both industries operating concurrently, but there does not seem to have been a trend toward the rise of an elite with anything like a commanding position in either of the textile industries. Investment in textile production, in short, was highly fragmented with respect to both business structure and ownership of capital.

RELATIONS WITH INTERNATIONAL MERCHANTS   For both the purchase of raw wool and the sale of finished products the firm had recourse to the local import-export merchants who commanded the vast commercial network Florentines had built up abroad. Since Florence was not an international emporium, the market was not organized around periodic trade fairs or centralized in a guild or in a merchants' hall like those in the Flemish wool-producing towns, nor were merchant importer-exporters organized through a state transport facility, except for the city's halfhearted galley system. With no focus on a place or schedule and in the absence of a single mediating agency, the market was highly fragmented and unfixed in its timing. As buyers and sellers cloth manufacturers were on their own, and they worked through guild-approved brokers *(sensali)* to forge the necessary links to the import-export merchants. These men simplified the commercial side of a manufacturer's operations, and the easy access they provided to the supply of raw materials and to outlets for finished products also cut the risks of excessive losses.

In a market with this fragmented business structure, relations between cloth producers and their clients were fluid, not subject to strong ties of dependency, especially given the former's unrelenting need for liquidity. Even if a firm belonged to an agglomerate of companies (like that of Francesco Datini) or was part of a larger holding structure that included trading operations abroad (like that of the Medici), it bought raw wool or silk only as needed and from whoever had it for sale, just as it sold its finished cloth as soon as it could and to whomever it could. Likewise the import-export firm dealt with any client it could find. Neither party did any stockpiling, given the high value of the goods involved. Since firms were relatively small in size, no one firm in either the wool or the silk industry came close to having a significant share of the market. Nor were individual firms, let alone the industry, dominated by the importer-exporters on whom they depended for the supply of raw materials and the marketing of their products, not even when there were ties of common ownership between the two.

For example, the Salviati wool firms in the second quarter of the sixteenth century sold only a small part of their production to the family merchant-banking firm—31 percent from 1518 to 1522, 20 percent from 1525 to 1532, and 7 percent from 1538 to 1544. Likewise, over the period from 1580 to 1597 the wool firm of Brandolini & Partners sold 30 percent of its production to twenty-three foreign firms and 70 percent to local buyers, none of whom bought more than 4 percent of total production. In the same period, from 1584 to 1591, the silk firm of Martelli, Del Giocondo & Partners bought silk from one hundred different suppliers, and only 11 percent of this supply came from the Martelli family firm of international merchant-bankers, which had clients in southern Italy (the source of most raw silk at the time) as well as throughout Europe, from Paris to Vienna. Of the firm's sales of finished silk, 17 percent went to one of the partners, and only 10 percent went to the Martelli commercial firm, the rest going in lesser amounts to any number of other clients.[55] This fluidity is confirmed by the accounts of the merchant-banking firms serving the cloth industry. In 1451 Francesco and Giovanni Salviati & Partners imported 466 pokes of English wool, which it sold in small amounts to forty-four different companies, the largest single sale consisting of only 39 pokes.[56] Two ledgers of the Strozzi firm in the 1480s have accounts for a total of twenty-one wool firms and six battiloro (probably silk) firms, but none of these continue from one ledger to the next, and of the thirty-nine silk firms with accounts, only seven appear in both ledgers. Likewise, in the two Corsi ledgers a century later, in the 1580s, none of the seventeen wool firms and only four of the forty-nine silk firms that have accounts appear in both ledgers.[57] The situation in the market for raw wool, however, changed in the course of the sixteenth century, when, with the shift to Spanish wool, a few Spanish and Genoese merchants came to dominate imports of this raw material. Over seventeen years, from 1580 to 1597, the Brandolini firm mentioned above bought 47 percent of its wool from just one Spanish importer, Baltasar Suares & Partners, and 28 percent from only nine other foreign firms. The Florentine merchants' share of the market, by contrast, was still highly fragmented, with 25 percent of Brandolini's supply provided by some thirty companies.[58]

CONCLUSION   The flexibility of business structures allowed the wool firm in particular to remain solvent even in the worst of times. Its fortunes varied according to the vagaries of demand abroad, and in moments of crisis in the industry partners might find it difficult to recover their capital, but with reasonable management they could avoid being hounded into ruin by creditors. The Florentine correspondent of the Spanish merchant Simón Ruiz considered the later-sixteenth-century wool market—which as an importer of raw wool he knew very well—stable and unperturbed, a good place to do business: "It is the safest of all such markets, for the buyers of wool are solid, and in a thousand years not one failure has been seen."[59] In fact, it is difficult to find a bankruptcy of a wool

[55] Data for the Salviati firm come from Bruno Dini, "Aspetti del commercio di esportazione dei panni di lana e dei drappi di seta fiorentini in Costantinopoli, negli anni 1522–1531," in *Studi in memoria di Federigo Melis* (Naples, 1978), 4:20 (reprinted in *Saggi*); for the Brandolini firm, from Goldthwaite, "Florentine Wool Industry," 535–36; and for the Martelli firm, from the company accounts, ASF, Archivio Martelli, 165–70.

[56] George Holmes, "Anglo-Florentine Trade in 1451," *English Historical Review* 108 (1993): 374–75.

[57] References to the Strozzi and Corsi firms are cited in Richard A. Goldthwaite, "Banking in Florence at the End of the Sixteenth Century," *Journal of European Economic History* 27 (1998): 486.

[58] Goldthwaite, "Florentine Wool Industry."

[59] Ruiz Martín, *Lettres marchandes*, cxx, 289.

firm in the annals of the industry. However, if risks were low to nonexistent, profits were not exceptionally high. Perhaps during the expansion of the industry in the fourteenth century, when wool companies also engaged in trade, large profits were to be made, but by the fifteenth century, when its activity was limited to manufacturing, a wool firm was not a road to great wealth. The rich invariably invested in one or two wool firms, but these constituted a small fraction of their overall portfolio. For great entrepreneurs such as Francesco Datini and the Medici, a miniscule part of total business profits came from wool. In short, wool was a conservative investment, sound and less risky if only moderately profitable. A setaiolo in his strict capacity as a manufacturer (setaioli more than lanaioli were likely to extend their activity to sales abroad, as we shall see) took more risks, in part because the raw materials were much more expensive and the weaving process much longer and in part because selling the variety of fabrics they produced was more problematic than was selling the standardized cloth of the wool industry.

The protagonist in Leon Battista Alberti's treatise on the family, when asked whether trade would be an honorable occupation for the head of a family, responded that

> for greater peace of mind I would elect something certain, which in my own hands I might see get better day by day. Perhaps I would supervise the working of wool or silk or some similar activity that is less demanding and gives much less bother; and I would willingly engage in the kind of activity that requires many workers because thereby money gets distributed among more persons, so that it benefits many poor people.[60]

Here the capitalist investor in the textile industry appears more an extremely cautious but socially conscious investor than a capitalist entrepreneur.

In conclusion, the textile industry was highly fragmented, with many relatively small wool and silk shops. There was also much fluidity in and out of the ranks of the men who ran these businesses, in part because, guild membership not being closed to outsiders, it was relatively easy to open a business in either industry. In the next chapter we will encounter, among other artisans, a brickmaker, Benedetto da Terrarossa, who set his nephews up in a wool partnership, and a painter, Neri di Bicci, who set his sons up in the silk business. The history of the silk industry reveals the economic conditions that favored social mobility: it was a new industry in the early fifteenth century; it opened entirely new markets for Florentine merchants; it paid very high profits; and it created new fortunes.

---

[60] Leon Battista Alberti, *I libri della famiglia*, bk. 3.

The first generation of prosperous setaioli, as identified by their level of wealth reported in the 1427 catasto, were mostly new men. A 1451–52 list of setaioli who paid obligatory contributions to their guild's confraternity for silk workers includes 26 different surnames; a list just ten years later, in 1461–62, has 35 surnames, 18 of which were not on the earlier list; and a half-century later the list of the 103 firms bearing 46 surnames for whom the silk weaver Iacopo di Tedesco worked from 1490 to 1538 has only 9 surnames found on the 1461–62 list.[61] The city's textile industrialists did not organize themselves as a closed elite.

In short, the structural fragmentation of the power of capital in the textile industries was complete. The industries consisted of many small firms that came and went with much frequency, relations these firms had with the great international merchant-banking firms on which they depended were highly fluid, capital was not concentrated in the hands of a few investors, and there was much mobility in and out of the ranks of investors.

Operations beyond the Firm

THE WOOL INDUSTRY   The discussion above of the Albizzi fulling complex at Remole raises a question about the private integration of the various stages of production and marketing within the wool industry, for the Albizzi were a prominent lanaiolo family with investments throughout the industry. Their initiative in constructing the fulling mill appears as part of a larger project to build up a comprehensive conglomerate of properties and firms that embraced the entire production process, as well as marketing operations abroad. In 1347 Antonio di Lando degli Albizzi, one of the five brothers who undertook the project at Remole, formed a partnership with four sons that had a corpo of *fl.*6,897 (£10,000 a fiorini), which was augmented by time deposits that on occasion more than doubled the original investment. This single company, of the earlier corporate kind, operated two wool shops producing San Martino cloths and a warehouse for distribution abroad, in northwestern Europe and at Venice, where Lando had a merchant-banking firm. At the same time, two of Lando's sons were partners along with seven cousins, all sons of three of Lando's brothers, in a large dyeing establishment, and the family, probably including some of these members, owned a number of tenter sheds located in the immediate vicinity of the family's urban residences, behind the cathedral. After Lando and three of his sons died in the plague of 1348, the surviving son renewed the partnership of the wool firm in 1354

---

[61] The lists are published in Dini, "La ricchezza documentaria," 15, 18; for Iacopo di Tedesco, see Richard A. Goldthwaite, "An Entrepreneurial Silk Weaver in Renaissance Florence," *I Tatti Studies* 10 (2005): 69–126. The phenomenon of new men in the silk industry at the beginning of the fifteenth century is documented in the unpublished paper by Padgett and McLean cited in n. 20, above.

with a corpo of *fl*.13,200, double that of the earlier firm, but the two shops were now reduced to one. With these properties and their cluster of firms, the Albizzi had direct control over the entire production process as well as marketing (and probably the supply of raw wool as well). It could hardly have been coincidental that their wide-ranging venture came at the time when the industry was undergoing a major shift to make a superior product from English wool.[62]

The Albizzi enterprise remains, at least for the moment, the only example of such a comprehensive industrial conglomerate, but other evidence exists, especially from the fourteenth century, for the extension of a lanaiolo's interest beyond that of a typical manufacturing firm. The earliest, Calimala phase of the wool industry had been merchant led, and these firms embraced the entire cycle, from supply to sales: they purchased semifinished cloth abroad, organized industrial operations in Florence to have it finished, and then sold the final product abroad. The Alberti, major Calimala merchants at the middle of the fourteenth century, had a warehouse for imported cloth and owned at least eight tenter sheds in the vicinity of their residences, at San Iacopo dei Fossi, and it would not be surprising to learn that they also possessed a dye house along the street of the dyers, the Corso dei Tintori, which ran by their properties. In 1387 the lanaiolo Bartolo di Cercie had a partnership with a major woad merchant from Arezzo, Simo d'Ubertino, whose operation extended to Pisa.[63] The Castellani, who had a firm for the production and export of wool cloth, probably owned the enormous tenter shed known as "dell'Arno" or "dei Castellani," which as late as the eighteenth century dominated river views of the city looking toward what today is the area behind the Uffizi, where the family palace (now housing the Museum of the History of Science) was located. In 1366 Mazza Ramaglianti and seven other partners, with capital of *fl*.12,000, set up a company operating a wool shop in San Martino and a warehouse for exports.[64] In 1372 the brothers Piero and Stefano di Bindo Benini, together with Andrea di Betto Filippi, invested *fl*.12,000 in a similar company to operate a wool shop in San Martino, a warehouse for exports, and possibly a second shop and additional commercial activity as the partners saw fit.[65] Some medium-sized companies had their own agents abroad, especially in ports with trade to the eastern Mediterranean, and some sent agents on voyages to the Near East. For example, Cione and Neri di Buonaccorso de' Pitti & Partners,

[62] Hoshino, *L'arte della lana*, 311–16; the following pages extend the history of the Albizzi wool firms through successive generations. To identify relationships within this family, consult the genealogical tables in Fabbri, *"Opus novarum gualcheriarum."* According to Hoshino, the Albizzi had a monopoly on fulling mills. Conversation with the author.

[63] Dini, *Arezzo intorno al 1400*, 33.

[64] Hoshino, "Note sulla compagnia commerciale degli Albizzi," 13n.

[65] *Il libro segreto della ragione di Piero Benini e comp.*, ed. P. Ginori Conti (Florence, 1937), 34–35.

active in the 1340s, had an agent in Naples to sell its cloth. And the Del Bene company, which operated only as a wool shop from the mid-1350s to 1370, sent a partner to Venice and later to Naples to open a commercial operation for the sale of the company's cloth.[66]

A lanaiolo, in short, could extend his investment in the industry to include purchase of a plant where specific operations took place outside the firm's shop, but he did this not through his wool firm, which did not own real estate, but on his own or with relatives or through a partnership agglomerate of which his firm was just one element. Given the limited number of such properties, however, there could not have been many men, or families, who did this. Moreover, lanaioli who extended their firm's activities to include forward sales operations abroad become rarer in the second half of the fourteenth century, perhaps because enterprise in general came to be channeled through the more articulated business structures of the partnership agglomerate, which emerged at this time. Only eighteen wool firms in the 1427 catasto have been identified as operating outside of Florence, two of these outside of Italy. By this time most wool firms were organized as essentially that, manufacturing enterprises with no commercial activity outside the local market and completely dependent on importer-exporters.[67] The opening of the market for wool cloth in the Ottoman Empire in the second half of the century prompted some producers themselves to take initiatives to send cloth to the market in Constantinople, as we have seen, and this involved them in a return trade, but they generally did this as a venture through an accomandita, not as a full-fledged commercial operation of the manufacturing firm. By this time commission agents rather than resident branches of merchant-banking firms were handling sales in the Levant. Still, examples of comprehensive conglomerate structures occasionally turn up in the sixteenth century, perhaps inspired by the growth of the strong market for rascia in northern Europe. In 1548 Giuliano di Piero Capponi, who had a commercial company in Pisa as well as a silk firm, put up two-thirds of the capital for a holding company, Vincenzo Violi & Partners, which invested in separate partnerships for a warehouse, a dye shop, and a wool firm.[68]

THE SILK INDUSTRY   Although Alberti puts silk and wool manufacturing in the same business category, a silk firm was not necessarily as strictly confined

[66] Hidetoshi Hoshino, "La compagnia commerciale de' Pitti in Napoli nel 1341: Un commento per la storia dell'arte della lana di Firenze del Trecento," in *Studi in memoria di Federigo Melis* (Naples, 1978), 2:222; idem, *L'arte della lana,* 173 (on Del Bene).

[67] A phenomenon noted also by Dini for the early sixteenth century. "Aspetti del commercio di esportazione," 240–42.

[68] Goldthwaite, *Private Wealth,* 220–33.

to production as was a wool firm, and it could make more demands on its owners. There was a strong impulse for more expansive operations, especially because many kinds of silk fabrics could not be marketed in the same way as wool cloth. Wool cloth was highly standardized: in the fifteenth century it fell essentially into two categories—Garbo and San Martino—which came in about a half-dozen weaves. Manufacturers produced wool cloth in bolts of regulated size for a generalized market and could leave the marketing to the export merchants, who knew what sold in foreign markets. Silks, as already observed, came in infinite variety and ranged considerably in cost at the highest end of the luxury market. In the second half of the sixteenth century simple, unfigured velvets were two and a half times as costly as rascia, the most expensive woolen the Florentine industry ever produced, and the addition of figured patterns and gold and silver threads pushed prices of silk fabrics very much higher. The most luxurious silks, therefore, were produced in shorter lengths, sometimes no longer than a few yards, and targeted to particular clients, especially feudal and ecclesiastical princes, and indeed they were often made on commission. The prospect of tying capital up in such highly individualized luxury products, which required special efforts, and therefore a longer time, to sell, made marketing silks through the ordinary channels of the commercial system more problematic.[69] The setaiolo himself, therefore, was likely to take the initiative to engage in forward marketing operations.

Letter books in the surviving records of silk manufactories testify to the importance of direct links between the producer and his market abroad, while their accounts, in keeping track of single operations, often list the specific clients abroad to whom their products were delivered. In the diary recording his career as a silk manufacturer, Gregorio Dati recounts how often in his early years, during the 1390s and into the fifteenth century, he went to Valencia, at least once for several years, to conduct the commercial end of the company business.[70] A generation later Andrea Banchi, whose firm is the only one that has been thoroughly studied, took an active interest in selling his products, with only about a third of them going to local export merchants. He dealt with commission agents throughout Italy. Several times he sent a partner to L'Aquila, and then he went into partnership with an employee whom he sent there as a resident agent. On occasion he sent personal agents to fairs at Barcelona, Geneva, Paris, Bruges, and the eastern Mediterranean, and one of his partners opened a shop in Rome. Another manufacturer, Tommaso Spinelli, a late contemporary of Banchi's, came to the business as an established international merchant-banker and so was able to market

---

[69] Morelli, *La seta fiorentina*, 82, cites correspondence of the Strozzi firm in Lyons in the 1520s remarking on the problems of following the French court in order to make sales.

[70] Leonida Pandimiglio, *Il libro di famiglia e il "Libro segreto" di Goro Dati* (Alessandria, 2006).

his own products, dealing through intermediaries in Rome, Milan, Geneva, and Lübeck. In 1441 another prominent banker, Giovanni Rucellai, along with Giovanni di Francesco della Luna, the son of the richest setaiolo in the 1427 catasto and a cousin of Andrea Banchi, set up a company in Venice for banking and the production of silk.[71] By the end of the fifteenth century many silk companies were also active in international merchant banking. This scale and range of operations was by this time inconceivable for a wool-manufacturing firm. A wool firm had no need to engage in any correspondence at all, since it left sales to the exporter. Extant records of these firms, besides not including letter books, reveal nothing about where products went after they were sold to local exporters, let alone who the eventual customers were.

The setaiolo had less possibility than the lanaiolo for vertical integration because the stages of silk production were fewer and offered fewer investment opportunities. In 1434 three setaioli—Benedetto di Giuliano Gini, Leonardo di Ridolfo de' Bardi, and Luca di Matteo da Panzano—who previously had had a partnership *(chonpangnia d'uno filatoio)* with the throwster Michele di Pelo, set up another partnership *(chonpangnia di filare e torciere seta)* with the throwster Filippo di Bartolomeo, but nothing is known about the arrangements.[72] In 1457 Bartolomeo di Zanobi Del Giocondo was a partner in both a dye shop and a firm of setaioli.[73] With only about a half-dozen dye shops and fewer throwing mills in operation, however, this kind of expansion was limited. Instead, some setaioli had close ties with manufacturers of gold and silver threads. The artisan enterprises that worked with beaten gold *(battilori)* to make such products as gold leaf for use in the backgrounds of paintings turned to making metallic threads but did not produce these in sufficient quantity to satisfy the growing demand from the industry once it sought to make the more luxurious "cloth of gold." In the early 1420s three setaioli set up a partnership for this special purpose and actively sought to attract qualified artisans from Genoa and Venice in an effort to promote the craft in Florence. Fusion of the two kinds of firms also occurred. By the end of the fifteenth century many battiloro companies were indistinguishable from manufacturers of silk cloth, some identifying themselves as companies of both or alternatively as battilori and setaioli. Extending its activity in yet another direction, toward the local market, a silk firm might go beyond the production of fabrics to engage in the manufacture of finished products ranging from ribbons

[71] Molà, "Oltre i confini," 87.
[72] ASF, Archivio Ricasoli, Libri di amministrazione, 111 (accounts and record book of Luca da Panzano), fol. 173v.
[73] Edler de Roover, *L'arte della seta*, 34–35.

and belts to fine liturgical garments and take yet the next step to open up a retail outlet for local sales as a setaiolo a minuto.

One of these comprehensive vertical partnerships was that organized in 1444 by Niccolò di Piero Buonaccorsi and the brothers Zanobi and Guglielmo di ser Martino Martini along with one of the most prominent non-Italian businessmen of the century, Jacques Coeur, and his associate, Guillaume de Varye. In his catasto report of 1451—the year of Coeur's arrest in France—Buonaccorsi declared the company as "a silk shop . . . and with this shop we have a battiloro shop and a certain *accomanda*," the latter being a contract made, also in 1444, with Lodovico di Francesco Strozzi in London for sales there. In 1454 Coeur's French colleague, acting through Buonaccorsi, invested in another silk shop with one of the most prominent merchant-bankers in Florence, Tommaso Spinelli; both partnerships lasted until 1457. Coeur's association with these shops served them in directing finished products to his warehouse in Tours and hence to other markets in France.[74] In the last quarter of the fifteenth century Ristoro Serristori and his brothers had an even more extensive conglomerate of companies for the production and sale of silks. One of the brothers, Antonio, organized both a company of battilori and a company of dyers; the brothers also opened a retail shop for the sale of their products in the local market. Meanwhile, the company itself, as a legal personality, expanded its activities abroad: in 1482 it made an accomandita investment with Antonio di Piero Gualterotti for a company in Bruges; in 1485 it made another with Lodovico Cavalcanti for a commercial company in Lyons; and in 1495 or 1496 the brothers' battiloro company itself became a partner of a company operating in London. Finally, the family rounded out its investment portfolio in the industry with initiatives to establish sericulture on its rural properties in the upper Valdarno, and it also entered the market for raw silk in the Valdinievole, in the lower Valdarno.[75] Another network of companies for the production and sale of silks was that of Niccolò di Tommaso Antinori, who had bought what is now the family palace from the Martelli in 1506. In 1519 he had a setaiolo company, a battiloro company, a company in the Abruzzi for the purchase of raw silk, and, for sales, a company in Lyons, a company with Raffaello Torrigiani in Germany, and, through the setaiolo company, a company with Bernardo Uguccioni in Spain.[76]

---

[74] Michel Mollat, "Les affaires de Jacques Coeur à Florence," in *Studi in onore di Armando Sapori* (Milan, 1957), 2:761–71; idem, *Jacques Coeur, ou l'esprit d'entreprise au XVe siècle* (Paris, 1988), 91–99. The Spinelli company is the subject of Caferro, "Silk Business," which, however, does not mention the Frenchman's investment.

[75] Tognetti, *Da Figline a Firenze*, 136, 151–52, 159.

[76] Piero Antinori, "Gli Antinori fra documenti d'archivio e memorie di famiglia," in *Futuro antico: Storia della famiglia Antinori e del suo palazzo* (Florence, 2007), 67.

This extension of silk firms into sales abroad also led them into the market for raw silk. Andrea Banchi bought raw silk in the Near East (in the regions of the Caspian Sea and the Aegean), in southern Spain, and in central Italy (the Romagna, the Marche, and the Abruzzi). Since some of these were areas where he sold cloth, he could in effect barter products for raw silk. In this way the setaioli engaged in supply as well as sale operations. These markets, however, overlapped only slightly, and the overlap shrunk in the course of the century. By the sixteenth century virtually all raw silk came from Italy, while the expanding markets for finished products were in northern Europe, which was not a silk-producing region. Hence manufacturers of silks became, for the most part, dependent on suppliers, and the market relations between importers and silk companies were as fluid as those in the wool industry. From 1480 to 1483 the merchant-banking firm of Filippo Strozzi sold 30 bales of silk to sixteen different setaioli, the largest sale being 4 bales to one firm, while only nine of these firms were among the twenty-two from whom he bought finished silk for export.[77] The Olivieri agglomerate of companies mentioned in chapter 1 organized the commercial side of the business at both ends, marketing raw silk it imported from its firms in southern Italy and buying finished silk fabrics for export to its firm in Nuremberg, but the agglomerate did not itself enter into production.[78] Later in the century, from 1582 to 1588, the Corsi firm sold 82 bales of silk to thirty-nine setaioli, the largest purchase being only 5.5 bales.[79] Martelli, Del Giocondo & Partners, setaioli, operating in the same years as the Brandolini wool firm, bought raw silk from no fewer than a hundred suppliers. Many of these were individuals, since some raw silk came from the surrounding region, but half are identified as companies.[80]

It is an open question how much initiative setaioli in the fifteenth century, such as the Serristori, took to control the sources of supply by investing in sericulture in the countryside. Giovanni Rucellai planted between three thousand and four thousand mulberry trees in two to three years on the estate he built up at Poggio a Caiano in the 1450s and 1460s. However, he is not known to have invested in a silk-producing firm in Florence, although he made such an investment in Venice and had a commercial interest in the export of finished silk. His investment in the textile industry was limited to the production of wool.[81] When Flo-

---

[77] ASF, Carte strozziane, ser. 5, 36 (ledger F).

[78] For further details, see Francesco Guidi Bruscoli, "Drappi di seta e tele di lino tra Firenze e Norimberga nella prima metà del Cinquecento," *ASI* 159 (2001): 359–94.

[79] ASF, Archivio Guicciardini Corsi Salviati, 109 (ledger P, 1582–88).

[80] This information is from my yet-unpublished study of this firm, the accounts for which are in ASF, Archivio Martelli, 165–70.

[81] F. W. Kent, "Lorenzo de' Medici's Acquisition of Poggio a Caiano in 1474 and an Early Reference to His Architectural Expertise," *Journal of the Warburg and Courtauld Institutes* 42 (1979): 251 and n.

rentine patricians began to build up landed estates in the later sixteenth century, some did this as a commercial investment, since prices of agricultural products were rising rapidly; we do no know to what extent the promotion of sericulture on their land figured into their calculations.

The upward mobility of the early generations of setaioli has already been remarked. In the 1427 catasto only two setaioli ranked among the top 1 percent of the city's wealthiest men, but the high profits to be earned in silk as compared with wool made the industry a vehicle for the accumulation of a large fortune, especially if the setaiolo moved into the marketing of his products abroad. On lists of setaioli compiled in 1451–53 (34 men) and in 1461–62 (51 men) only a few seem to represent older wealth.[82] By the second half of the century investors in the industry included some of the city's great international merchant-bankers, such as Cosimo de' Medici, Tommaso Spinelli, the sons of Antonio Serristori, Gino Capponi and his son Piero, Iacopo Salviati, and Filippo Strozzi the younger. The enormous profits that could be made in silk have been documented for several setaioli: Andrea Banchi became in the course of his career, from 1427 to 1457, one of the ten top taxpayers in the city;[83] Tommaso Spinelli's company consistently yielded high profits, at times more than 20 percent annually;[84] and the Serristori earned profits totaling *fl.*57,688 over the period from 1471 to 1492.[85] A century later, Martelli, Del Giocondo & Partners paid a return on invested capital that averaged 15 percent annually over twenty-four years; during the same years, with the wool industry at its all-time high, the Brandolini wool firm earned only about 6 percent.

An investor in silk, however, faced higher risks than did the lanaiolo. The capital of a silk firm, like that of a wool firm, served primarily for start-up liquidity, but the silk manufacturer's higher investment in raw materials and longer production time made it somewhat more difficult for him to maintain liquidity. On the one hand, with so much capital tied up in operations, the firm's flexibility was compromised. On the other hand, demand for its products was highly variable, being subject to the taste, habits, and personal financial fortunes of the clients at the very top end of the market it targeted. The problem is reflected on the balance that Martelli, Del Giocondo & Partners drew up in 1591, after seven years of operations, where the inventory of raw silk and unsold cloths (*fl.*20,365) exceeded by far the firm's capital investment (*fl.*12,500). Besides problems inherent in the

[82] Dini, "La ricchezza documentaria." Compare these names with those on the lists published by Anthony Molho in *Marriage Alliance in Late Medieval Florence* (Cambridge, MA, 1994), app. 3.

[83] This despite his firm's continuing difficulties as documented in Edler de Roover, "Andrea Banchi."

[84] Caferro, "Silk Business," 432–33.

[85] Tognetti, *Da Figline a Firenze*, 129.

industry, a firm's venture into international commerce, while designed to facilitate marketing, carried its own risks. It was not unusual for a silk firm to fall on hard times, as that of Andrea Banchi did, and some faced bankruptcy. Of the eight firms that Alamanno Rinuccini listed as going bankrupt in 1464, the most serious crisis since the crash of the 1340s, five were setaioli.[86]

During the sixteenth century the business of operating a silk firm probably contracted considerably, at least for many firms, as a result of the shift of production from the very top end to the lower end of the market. By concentrating on simple cloths, such as plain satins, sarcenets, and taffetas, the industry targeted a market for standardized products that cost less and sold more easily at a time when demand was rising with the increased use of such cloths for household furnishing and changing fashions in clothing. Local merchant-exporters were willing to handle bolts of standardized silks of this kind. Hence, a firm like Martelli, Del Giocondo & Partners, which concentrated more exclusively on production of the less expensive line of fabrics, found itself in a position analogous to that of wool manufacturers that engaged in few forward operations. One of this firm's journals contains a letter book documenting correspondence with companies at Venice, Bologna, Lucca, Ancona, and Macerata, as well as at Burgos and the imperial court in Vienna. During the three years the book covers, however, this correspondence fills only about five folios and concerns mostly modality of payment, with no information about the products themselves; most of the correspondence is directed to the firm's major local suppliers of raw silk at Pescia and Castelfranco di Sotto. The firm sold almost all of its products to local buyers; of the 60 percent sold to exporters, almost half—27 percent—went to foreign merchants present on the local scene. Its single most important client was the separate merchant-banking firm of the principal partner, Iacopo Martelli, but this activity accounted for only just over 11 percent of the supply of raw silk and 10 percent of sales of finished cloth. It is not surprising to learn that in the seventeenth century silk firms worked mostly on commission from local merchants executing orders from abroad.[87]

It is important to note, in conclusion, that none of what has here been called vertical integration involved a single business enterprise, let alone the manufacturing process organized by either the wool or the silk firm operating within the traditional parameters of the putting-out system. The integration of these activi-

---

[86] *Ricordi storici di Filippo di Cino Rinuccini dal 1282 al 1460, colla continuazione di Alamanno e Neri suoi figli fino al 1506,* ed. G. Aiazzi (Florence, 1840), xciv–xcv. See also Edler de Roover, "Andrea Banchi," 285n.

[87] Goodman, "Cloth, Gender and Industrial Organization," 235. Some firms still took initiatives to find customers abroad. Malanima, *La decadenza,* 264–65, cites an example of an agent sent abroad in 1685 who traveled from London to Vienna in search of commissions.

ties was more a function of a diversified investment strategy in the private interest of the lanaiolo or setaiolo or a commercial strategy for sales than an operational strategy to improve the efficiency of production and therefore industrial productivity.

Production

A cloth firm organized production through the putting-out system. It had only a few salaried employees on the payroll who worked in the shop under the control of the management; it dealt with the others either through intermediaries (especially in the wool industry) or directly through contracts for work paid on a piece-rate basis. The firm owned the raw materials as they passed from one worker to another in the process of being transformed into cloth; to the extent that it contracted with them at each stage in the production process, it determined the availability of work. With few exceptions, the firm left the worker on his own to supply himself with tools and equipment, to find a place to work, and to determine his own rhythm of work once he was on contract. The labor force was, therefore, highly fragmented into many separate, semiautonomous operations, with no overlap between the two industries.

The Shop

Central management of the shop rested in the hands of one of the partners, who often had been brought into the firm for precisely that reason. Instead of capital, however, he contributed his personal service, or persona, which was given a nominal capitalized value and added to the invested capital of the company, so that his compensation took the form of a partner's share of the profits as well as a share in the division of capital at the dissolution of the partnership. These managing partners usually received a salary as well. Individual variations exist, but these general arrangements are usually the same. For example, the silk firm of Martelli, Del Giocondo & Partners, founded in 1581, made the usual arrangement with its partner-manager, Gherardino di Antonfranceso Gherardini, capitalizing his persona at fl.2,500, to be added to the fl.10,000 of invested capital, but it gave his claim to profits priority over any distributions to the investing partners, who shared only what was left according to their share of the capital of the firm. The contemporary wool firm of Cristofano di Tommaso Brandolini & Partners, organized in 1580, went one step further in tying the manager's earnings to profits. It paid its manager, Brandolini himself (who was not an investing partner, although the firm took his name), in two ways: instead of a salary, it gave him a one-sixth share of the profits as a prior claim before any distributions were made to the investors (permitting him to take advances on this claim in the meantime); and it capitalized his persona at *fl.*400, which entitled him to a share in the distribution of the remaining profits proportional to the nominal capital of *fl.*7,000 (*fl.*400 for his persona and *fl.*6,600 from the investors). On the first renewal of the partnership Brandolini's share of profits before distribution was raised to one-fifth, a 20 percent increase.

Partnership contracts generally spell out the responsibilities of the manager. He was considered a full-time employee who was to work only for his own firm, and he employed all workers and directed daily operations subject to accounting controls and policy decisions by the investing partners. Unfortunately, we have no career studies of company managers. Some were sons of upper-class families who took on management as an apprenticeship to the trade, and some were sons of artisans working in other sectors who, presumably, hoped the job would lead to modest wealth, if not also upward social mobility. Probably something like a class of professional managers existed. Cases in point may be the two managers mentioned above. Brandolini's father had been a simple *lanino,* one who worked on contract with wool firms for the putting-out of wool to spinners of the weft.[88] Gherardini, who contributed only his persona to the silk firm organized in 1584, invested the considerable sum of *fl.*4,000 when the partnership was renewed in 1591, and over the next seventeen years he tripled his investment. A list of families that were historically members of the guild drawn up in 1570 includes his name, and later two sons and two collateral relatives were added.[89]

The central shop in the putting-out system contracted for each stage in the process of manufacturing cloth. Shop employees handled the materials as these came in and went out during the various stages of the manufacturing process, and some had the skills required for sorting and quality control during this processing. The managers themselves, even those of upper-class status, engaged in this "most vile and dirty work," as a Venetian ambassador reported in 1527, probably just as surprised as Giovanni di Tommaso Ridolfi had been a few years earlier, in 1522, when in Venice he noted that there "gentlemen do not work with wool and silk but have the work done."[90] This salaried staff, which could number between six and a dozen employees at any one time, was for the most part divided into two categories, *garzoni* and *giovani*. The former, who might be young boys in

[88] He is so documented in de Roover, "Florentine Firm of Cloth Manufacturers."
[89] ASF, Arte della Seta, 30 ("Libro vecchio delle casate").
[90] *Relazioni degli ambasciatori veneti al senato,* ed. Arnaldo Segarizzi (Bari, 1912), 1, pt. 1:17; P. J. Jones, "Travel Notes of an Apprentice Florentine Statesman, Giovanni di Tommaso Ridolfi," in *Florence and Italy: Renaissance Studies in Honour of Nicolai Rubinstein,* ed. Peter Denley and Caroline Elam (London, 1988), 280.

their early teens going through an informal apprenticeship, started at low salaries that increased annually but hardly ever reached what an unskilled construction laborer could expect to earn if he worked full time, while a *giovane*'s salary might rise to the level of a moderately skilled artisan. Typically, rosters reveal considerable fluidity within the ranks of a staff, it being rare to find an employee who remained with one firm for as long as the duration of even one partnership contract.

The putting-out system for wool was more complex than that for silk. Wool went through many stages both before and after weaving. Raw wool arrived in bales and had to be washed, carded, and combed before being put out to spinners, and the spinners were themselves divided into two groups, one for the weft and one for the warp. After weaving, the cloth went through a long finishing process consisting in burling, scouring, fulling, and stretching, and at various points along the way it required napping, shearing, mending, and pressing. Finally, dyeing took place somewhere during the preparatory or finishing process, either in the wool or in the cloth. There were two distinct kinds of dyers, those using only woad and those, called *tintori di arte maggiore,* using other dyestuffs for supplementary dyeing if required. In organizing the processing of the wool and the spinning of threads down to the point at which these were consigned to weavers, wool shops resorted to four different intermediaries: *capodieci* supervised the beating and oiling of the wool once it had been washed; *fattori* got the wool to the carders and combers; *lanini* dealt with the wheel-spinners of the weft from carded wool *(lana);* and *stamaiuoli* dealt with the rock-spinners of the warp *(stame)* from combed wool. These intermediaries—capodieci, fattori, lanini, and stamaiuoli—were paid on a piece-rate basis, and with the possible exception of the capodieci, the workers they supervised—carders, combers, and spinners—worked outside the firm's shop. To make direct contact with other workers, firms might use brokers registered with the guild.

Silk production required fewer stages, essentially only winding and unwinding of threads, dyeing, and weaving. The initial preparation of silk took place at the source, and the raw product arrived in Florence already transformed into skeins of filaments reeled together. The process of transforming these into threads consisted in winding on spools, a throwing and twisting process, unwinding in preparation for degumming and dyeing, and, finally, rewinding and warping. At this point threads went to the weavers, and the woven fabric returned was the finished product, ready for the market.

In the wool industry the low level of output of any one firm and the short duration of work in most stages of the manufacturing process precluded an attempt to organize labor in any other way than through the putting-out system. Producing an average of 100 to 120 bolts of cloth a year, barely 2 bolts a week, a wool firm could have offered full-time employment to eight to ten weavers taking from three to four weeks to produce a bolt and to more than twice as many spinners. Given this level of production, however, the work that went into processing the wool and then into the finishing of the cloth was not enough for a firm to offer full-time employment to anyone else. The cost breakdown for one bolt of cloth in the 1580s reveals the problem: to finish the cloth that a weaver produced in three to four weeks for £65, the firm paid rates per bolt that amounted to no more than £4 for each of the stages of burling, scouring, and shearing, to only £1 for fulling and the same for stretching, and to less than £1 for mending. These rates take on meaning with respect to the employment opportunities offered by a firm when related to the daily wage of £1–2 paid to a skilled construction laborer. In short, a firm receiving only two or three bolts of cloth each week from its weavers could offer only a day or so of work to the workers needed to finish the cloth, and the employment opportunities it offered in the preparatory stage of processing raw wool needed for this amount of cloth were only slightly better. It is not surprising, therefore, that the firm worked through intermediaries for the beating, carding, and combing of wool and for spinning and then contracted out the weaving and finishing of the cloth. The technology of the industry made it unlikely that any savings could have been achieved by recourse to direct employment at any stage of production. Moreover, direct management of a labor force presented problems of a different magnitude, related above all to the disciplining of workers, that entrepreneurs in the preindustrial world were not prepared to confront. The refusal to engage in micromanagement of workers was an obstacle to a firm's growth, as was, as already observed, the problem of liquidity, which imposed constraints on the commitment that could be made to a labor force that demanded payment in cash.

The earliest documented firm, that of Francesco Del Bene, operating from 1355 to 1370, employed day laborers in its shop on salary, not on a piece rate, for processing raw wool through the stages preceding spinning, which suggests that there may have been an earlier stage in the history of the industry when some work was organized around direct employment rather than being put out on contract. Franco Franceschi suggests that at this time there was, indeed, a "turning point" in the organization of the industry away from a strong—one might even say modernizing—tendency toward a centralized workshop with a salaried work force and toward the completely decentralized putting-out system as described above. He suggests that the former trend was at least partly a consequence of a booming market for wool cloth. Guild legislation indicates, in fact, that in the mid-fourteenth century firms were producing as many as two hundred and even more bolts a year, far higher than later production levels. The "turning point" came in a period toward the end of the century when there was a depression in the industry. If such a structural change in the industry occurred, it would provide a new context in which to see the Ciompi revolt, spearheaded as it was by wool processors seeking to make their voices heard as a corporate group united in their own guild. Franceschi further suggests that the Ciompi revolt may have made the lanaioli aware of the potential danger of a class of workers too dependent on daily wages and too concentrated in workplaces, and this fear may have motivated them to turn away from a centralized manufacturing system to a more thorough putting-out system.[91]

To put into relief these characteristics of the textile industries in Florence, it is useful to consider the contrast with the industry elsewhere. In the Low Countries, the most important center in Europe for the production of wool cloth throughout the Middle Ages, the industry was subject to the constraints of local corporatism. The most important workers had their own guilds, and they did not work under the control of local commercial capital, since marketing was largely in the hands of foreign merchants. Moreover, a weaver could become a producer, buying the cloth of other weavers, shepherding it through the finishing process, and selling it all directly in the local market. These weaver-drapers were the entrepreneurs who dominated the industry, and they were distinct from the foreign merchants to whom they sold their finished cloth for export. In some cities of Italy and Spain weavers in the silk industry also had their own guild and worked within an industrial structure that allowed them to buy raw materials and sell the finished product, thus giving them the space for entrepreneurial advancement that wool weavers had in the north. In Milan a silk weaver could control much of the entire production process by bringing throwing mills for the reeling of threads and the looms for weaving together in the same establishment, where he could also have a shop for selling the finished fabrics. Entrepreneurial weavers who gained both wealth and high social status have been documented in both Milan and Valencia. In Florence, however, the structures of industrial organization of both the wool and the silk industry worked very much against the mobility weavers had in these other places.[92]

[91] Franco Franceschi, "L'impresa mercantile industriale nella Toscana dei secoli XIV–XVI," *Annali di storia dell'impresa* 14 (2003): 229–49. The Del Bene firm has been studied by Bruno Dini. See "I lavoratori dell'arte della lana a Firenze nel XIV e XV secolo," reprinted from *Artigiani e salariati: Il mondo del lavoro nell'Italia dei secoli XII–XV* (Pistoia, 1984) in *Manifattura, commercio e banca*, 141–71.

[92] For careers of specific weaver-entrepreneurs in Milan, see two articles in *Studi storici* 35 (1994): Paolo Grillo, "Le origini della manifattura serica in Milano (1400–1450)," 897–916; and Consuelo Roman, "L'azienda serica di Leonardo Lantieri, imprenditore a Milano nel XV secolo," 917–42. On weavers in Valencia, see Germán Navarro Espinach, "Los negocios de la burguesía en la industria

Florentine capitalist investors in the textile industries seem never to have organized production in any other way than through the putting-out system. They took commercial initiatives for the marketing of their products, but they did not seek to integrate and centralize the production process along the lines followed by the wool drapers in the Low Countries and in England or by the silk manufacturers in Venice, Milan, and Valencia. One Florentine setaiolo who brought the entire industrial process together in a single workplace was Piero di Bartolo, but he did this in Milan, not Florence. In 1442 he accepted a contract from Duke Filippo Maria Visconti for starting up the industry in Milan, in return for which he was given a ten-year monopoly on the production of silk, customs privileges for importing the necessary materials and equipment, tax exemptions and citizenship for his workers, and above all a handsome monthly subsidy. Armed with all these advantages, he showed up in the Lombard capital with spinners, dyers, and weavers. Before long he had organized a partnership that raised capital from several prominent local investors and was running a business that possessed all the plant and equipment required for the entire production process—a spinning establishment, a throwing mill, a dye house, and looms.[93] As far as we know, no firm of setaioli back in Florence ever achieved anything like this kind of industrial integration. Gains in efficiency might not have counted for very much so long as firms were producing luxury products at the top end of the market, but that favorable situation changed once competition arose, as it did in the sixteenth century. How this industrial failure impinged on whatever comparative advantage their products had in international markets is a problem yet to be researched.

The Work Force

STRUCTURE   Both the wool and silk industries were organized around the same basic production procedures, and they resembled each other with respect to business organization, shop activity, and labor relations. Beyond the shop were the workers, and in both industries the work force was structurally fragmented according to different skills roughly corresponding to the stages of production. Workers could not take initiatives to combine these stages in order to improve their productivity, so they were blocked structurally, if not also for lack of sufficient means, from moving upward within the industry to become industrialists themselves (although, as we shall see, they could achieve this by following other routes). Moreover, they did not own the wool or silk they worked with. Beyond

---

precapitalista valenciana de los siglos XIV–XVI," *Revista d'història medieval* 11 (2000): 88–98. See also Molà, *Silk Industry,* 301–2; and Massa, *Un'impresa serica genovese,* 81.

[93] Molà, "Oltre i confini," 90–93.

this basic structural similarity, however, the wool and silk industries in Florence had different labor forces with no overlap of skills. For the most part, we can study these workers only through their employers' records, and given the detachment of the putting-out system, this precludes a very clear view of workers' life on the job. Even earnings, the most essential tool of analysis, elude us, since the basis was piecework, not a daily wage; we have only the employer's record of what he paid out, not the employee's record of what he earned from the various employers for whom he worked. Nevertheless, the general profiles of the two work forces emerge clearly enough, and they reveal considerable difference in the variety and level of skills, in wages, and in gender.

Somewhat less than half the labor costs in the wool industry went to manual and low-skilled laborers in the preliminary processing of the raw material, which absorbed about 20–25 percent of total manufacturing costs, and to women spinners, who account for another 20 percent of costs. Weaving and finishing, which constituted more than 50 percent of labor costs, involved workers with a variety of skills, the most highly skilled of which were the weavers. Wages accordingly fell into line with traditional standards, ranging from what an unskilled manual laborer earned in the construction industry to roughly twice that. This maximum 2:1 ratio represented the traditional ceiling for wages of the most skilled workers throughout the economy as compared with the wages of an unskilled manual laborer. The only significant group of workers who might have fallen outside this range were the weavers, at the top, whose earnings rose with the introduction of rascia in the sixteenth century, and women spinners, at the bottom, who, working at home to supplement the family's income, probably earned less than the minimum wage as defined by that of an unskilled manual laborer. On the whole, however, the labor force in the wool industry probably represented a fair cross section of the working classes with respect to the artisanal organization of work and the range of earnings. The one significant change in that work force noted in the historiography is the replacement, toward the end of the fourteenth century, of female weavers, who seem to have had a dominant presence, by male weavers (a strong component of these being immigrants from Germany and the Low Countries), a change that has been explained by the greater strength required to handle the more difficult kind of looms—using longer reeds, needed for finer cloth—that the industry adopted at the time.[94]

In the wool industry women did all the spinning and some of the weaving, but men dominated the initial processing of raw wool and then the finishing stages. In

[94] Dominque Cardon, *La draperie au Moyen Âge: Essor d'une grande industrie européenne* (Paris, 1999), 549–50. For the community of immigrant German weavers, see Böninger, *Die deutsche Einwanderung nach Florenz*.

the silk industry women and even children have a much larger presence. The mass of workers other than weavers were women, and they performed an essential function in the preweaving stages of the production process. They did the preliminary winding of the silk they received in skeins from the setaioli; the reels then went off to the throwsters, after which the silk was returned for a second winding before it went off, finally, to the weavers. Some women were also warpers, weavers, and even throwsters. In a certain sense, these women were marginal workers. Many probably worked to supplement the earnings of men in the family, and many lived in convents. There is evidence from the later sixteenth century that some of the institutions that took in orphans put their charges to work on the preparation of silk threads. The houses of St. Catherine of Siena and the Conservatorio della Pietà had well over fifty girls, and sometimes even more, working at winding silk. Likewise, the foundling house of the Innocenti put some of its girls to work at winding reels; the boys could be sent out as apprentices, but the girls had to be kept on the premises.[95] Male children too have a large presence as apprentices of silk weavers, who needed more help than wool weavers in operating their complex looms. In the 1525 census of shops, the nine silk weavers with the largest workshops employed all together no fewer than 121 apprentices and helpers. These were probably all boys between the ages of ten and twenty whose earnings ranged from below that of a household servant to a maximum, even after ten years of apprenticeship, of no more than the wage of an unskilled manual laborer.

High above this mass of low-paid women and children in the silk industry were the few men who had the shops for the throwing and twisting of threads and the weavers. Little is known about the former. In the mid-fifteenth century the setaiolo Andrea Banchi did business with four to seven throwsters in any one year, and there were probably not many more. Throwing mills must have required more capital investment than the usual artisan enterprise; by the same token a throwster probably had greater earning potential. The two throwsters who went into partnership with the setaioli Benedetto di Giuliano Gini—Leonardo di Ridolfo de' Bardi and Luca di Matteo da Panzano—have already been mentioned. In his 1427 catasto report, one throwster, Michele di Pelo, declared real-estate holdings worth fl.1,078 and a net worth, after deducting debts, of fl.978, enough to rank him in the top quarter of the population. Among his assets was a credit of fl.307 with another throwster, Bello di Niccolò.[96]

---

[95] Nicolas Terpstra, "Making a Living, Making a Life: Work in the Orphanages of Florence and Bologna," *Sixteenth-Century Journal* 31 (2000), esp. 1071–73; Maria Fubini Leuzzi, "Vincenzio Borghini spedalingo degli Innocenti: La nomina, il governo, la bancarotta," in *Fra lo "spedale" e il principe: Vincenzio Borghini, filologia e invenzione nella Firenze di Cosimo I* (Padua, 2005), 53–54.

[96] ASF, Archivio Ricasoli, Libri di amministrazione, 111 (accounts and record book of Luca da Panzano), fol. 173v; ASF, Catasto 66, fol. 109v.

The skill of silk weavers exceeded by far that of their counterparts in the wool industry. The standardization of wool cloth fixed the skill of the weaver in that industry. Changes in the nature of the wool cloth made for the export market over the centuries probably did not require much retraining on the part of weavers, and the limited range of weaves did not give rise to a high degree of specialization. The high-quality rascia, a distinctively innovative product that enjoyed much success in the last phase of the history of the industry, probably put more demand on the weaver's time than on his skills. Silk cloths, instead, required more elaborate and diverse looms and took many months to finish. Hence silk weavers collectively represented a much greater variety of skills than was to be found among wool weavers, and their shops were highly specialized with respect to the kinds of fabric they wove. Moreover, they were responsive to the increasingly rapid shift of tastes in the market, and there was even room for taking the initiative themselves to introduce innovations—how many were of a technological nature has yet to be studied. Weaving accounted for 50–60 percent of manufacturing costs; given the cheap child labor weavers used, most of this ended up in the hands of the weavers. When they were at the journeyman stage, their earnings fell into the normal range of artisan wages, reaching even the upper end, and once they became full-fledged weavers, they could earn two, three, and even more times what an artisan in any other sector of the economy earned.

The production of silk gave rise to employment opportunities for workers outside the industry, and in this respect silk had more extensive ramifications throughout the urban economy than did wool. This peripheral work force consisted of both independent artisans who were called in only occasionally for one job or another during the production process and others whose jobs were created by the uses of silk once it came off the looms. Among the former were the battilori. They traditionally produced gold leaf for a variety of uses, and they also produced thinly hammered sheets of gold and silver for making metallic threads to be woven into the most luxurious of silk fabrics. With the growth of the production of silk in the later fifteenth century, the number of battilori increased; and as already observed, some became setaioli. The battilori, however, contracted out the work for the actual making of the threads, most of this to women, who cut the thinly hammered sheets of metal into strips and wrapped these around silk threads. Most of these women lived in convents, and these institutions may have supplied as much as three-fourths of the metallic thread used by the industry. Painters also found occasional employment with setaioli and weavers, making designs and working with the latter to set the looms accordingly. Many setaioli, operating essentially as setaioli a minuto, gave work to women, many of them nuns, who made the many objects of silk haberdashery sold in their retail shops. The industry's products also opened up new employment opportunities for the makers of vestments *(banderai)* and tailors, who explored the infinite possibilities of adapting silk fabrics to the many uses demanded by consumers, from liturgical accessories to luxury clothing.

In short, the labor forces in the two textile industries contrasted sharply. The labor force in wool included workers at all skill levels, from manual laborers to weavers, and wages in the industry corresponded to the traditional range of earnings in working-class society in general. The silk industry had a mass of women and children—perhaps 90 percent of the entire work force—at the bottom, relatively few weavers at the top, and not many workers of any kind in between, and most wages fell outside the general range of workers' wages at both ends. At the bottom end, women and children earned well below what we have called the minimum wage, and at the top end, weavers' earnings reached heights that could only have been considered extravagant by artisan standards at the time. These structural differences between the work forces in the two industries and the lack of any interchangeability between them had profound implications for their impact on the economy as a whole. The rise of the wool industry in the fourteenth century strengthened the working classes of the city by offering employment to workers with a wide range of skills, and the work force remained stable despite changes in the industry's products over the course of its history. The rise of the silk industry at the end of the fourteenth century brought into existence a completely different kind of work force. Given the utterly different work forces in the two industries, it would be difficult to argue, without considerable qualification, that any slack in the performance of one could have been taken up by the other. In fact, the collapse of the wool industry at the beginning of the seventeenth century left the city with a very different work force in textiles from the one it had had in the fourteenth century, before the production of silk got under way. If the rise of the silk industry raises questions about where all the women and children came from, what they had been doing previously, and how their employment affected the economic and social life of the city, the collapse of the wool industry more than two centuries later raises questions about where all the male employees went.

WORKERS   Workers were not subject to the regulation and discipline of factory employment, but they were completely dependent on the cloth manufacturers, who not only provided them with work but also owned the raw materials they worked with. The guild, controlled by the manufacturers, fixed the official rates they could charge for work, although it remains to be seen to what extent these rates corresponded to the realities of the market. Dyers and silk weavers—but not wool weavers—had a subordinate but official status in their guilds, but most workers had no guild status. This lack of status among cloth workers was much more a reality in the wool industry, given the relatively few male workers in the silk industry other than weavers and dyers, both highly skilled, and given also the complete domination of the wool guild by the lanaioli. Some categories of guild workers—washers and carders, beaters, weavers, shearers, dyers—had their own confraternity, but with the exception of the dyers', these existed under the tutelage of the guild. For lack of documentation, we know hardly anything about the internal administration of the silk guild, but it must have had much less a presence in the work force of the industry than the wool guild did in the work force of the wool industry. On the one hand, the many women and children in the silk industry, working at home or in institutions, required less active disciplinary intervention than did skilled wool workers; on the other hand, the guild, lacking the homogeneity of the wool guild, consisted of full-fledged members who did not work in the industry, most of whom were artisans and shopkeepers.

Occasionally in the course of the fourteenth century the low-skilled wool workers agitated to win some kind of guild status. Under the very brief lordship of Walter of Brienne, 1342–43, the dyers were organized into a new guild, and other worker groups gained a certain legitimacy, though not guild status. But these innovations were thrown out after Brienne's expulsion by the new popular government based on the traditional guild structure. Wool workers were eventually successful in spearheading the extraordinary outbreak in July 1378 against the upper-class guild regime known as the revolt of the Ciompi, the name that collectively identified this category of workers. There is much controversy about the real nature of this event in the history of the republic, especially since in the course of the agitation leading to the revolt the movement picked up support from other wool workers and members of the fourteen minor guilds, thereby taking on an economic and social complexity that still is not well understood. The revolt was briefly successful in establishing three new guilds—one for the Ciompi, which now included also the weavers; one for dyers; and one for doublet makers *(farsettai),* which included finishers of cloth, tailors, and a few other categories of artisans outside the wool industry—and these guilds increased the collective weight of the minor guilds in the government. There was an immediate reaction against the extremists in this popular movement, however, and by September the new guild of the Ciompi was suppressed. In 1382 the leaders of the major guilds finally got the upper hand again, and the two other new guilds were also liquidated, although some of their members were accommodated in the traditional guilds. This reaction to the Ciompi revolt is regarded as the moment when the republic finally came under the firm domination of the political elite representing the major guilds that would govern into the age of the Medici.[97]

The revolt had no apparent effect on the wool industry. In fact, the specific program for reforms put forward by the Ciompi in July 1378, the most extreme moment of the revolt, made no reference to the organization of the industry, to the firms these men worked for, to the conditions of their employment, or even to the level of their earnings. They demanded their own guild autonomy, complete with a headquarters and officials, so that they could participate in government. They were especially insistent about getting out from under the onerous judicial authority exercised by the wool guild to force workers into compliance with industry regulations. Justice was administered by a foreigner appointed by the guild, and he meted out a severe and cruel justice. Workers were brought before him for delays in consigning work, working illegal wool, theft of materials, resisting the police authority of the guild, and other contraventions of guild regulations, for which penalties included corporal punishment, torture, and even maiming.[98] It seems that after the revolt the guild reduced the authority of the foreign official and took a more collegiate, and more flexible, approach to the enforcement of guild regulations with respect to the workers, although the guild retained its authority to impose corporal punishment and even torture.

Otherwise, the program put forward by the Ciompi in July 1378 appears to have been very much a popular taxpayers' revolt directed not so much against the level of taxation as against the system of forced loans the commune was using in lieu of direct taxation. Most of the concerns voiced in the petitions regarded the direct, rather than the indirect, tax system. Notwithstanding a strong current in the historiographical tradition, it is not clear whether the Ciompi, who were the most poorly paid among the rebel groups, had other economic concerns. Wages, in fact, had risen considerably since the Black Death, and economic discontent has been seen as arising not so much from desperation as from the dashing of aroused expectations resulting from a relatively slight fall in wages during the 1370s (we shall return to this problem below, in chapter 7). Some have seen a proto-proletarian movement in the Ciompi revolt, and there is no question that the impressive ability of these men to organize themselves, complete with a shadow government and a well-articulated program of objectives, suggests a strong sense of class consciousness, something quite remarkable for the period. But their

---

[97] Franco Franceschi, "I Ciompi a Firenze, Siena e Perugia," in *Rivolte urbane e rivolte contadine nell'Europa del Trecento: Un confronto* (forthcoming), offers the best introduction to the vast literature on the Ciompi, along with a fresh interpretation.

[98] Franco Franceschi, "Criminalità e mondo del lavoro: Il tribunale dell'Arte della Lana a Firenze nei secoli XIV e XV," *Ricerche storiche* 18 (1988): 551–90.

work, their economic status, and the industry in general seem to have been far from the forefront of the concerns that molded that consciousness. Ironically, the consciousness of class engendered by this episode may have been stronger among the elite than among the poor, for one of the most lasting consequences of the revolt, political historians tell us, was the memory of its violence and its radical popular program that survived through the following generations, keeping alive a fear of, and even what some have called contempt for, the lower working classes. It may have been this fear that reversed the modernizing trend in the organization of production in the wool industry.

One of the most characteristic features of the working life of textile workers, whether in the wool or the silk industry, was the fluidity and instability of employment with any one employer resulting from their dependency on the episodic putting out of work to them by the manufacturers. Over three years, from 1580 to 1583, the Brandolini wool firm paid 71 weavers for the 450 cloths it produced, whereas 12 or 13 weavers working full time could have done the job. Only 2 of the firm's weavers had steady employment (32 and 35 months); only 7 worked regularly, without interruptions, during the period they were employed; and 16 wove only one bolt each. The roster of weavers paid by the contemporary Martelli, Del Giocondo silk firm reveals the same fluidity. Of the 84 weavers who made 889 deliveries to the firm in three years, from 1587 to 1589, 18 made just 1 delivery, and only 13 showed up with any regularity for as long as 30 out of the 36 months documented. The only records we have for the weaver's side of an employment history, the accounts of the silk weaver Iacopo di Tedesco, reveal the same fluidity: each of the seven ledgers documenting his shop activity from 1499 to 1526 has accounts for about a dozen setaioli for whom he worked, and he was not dependent on any one of these clients for more than a quarter of his production at most.

In part, this fluidity in the labor force of any one firm was structural, inherent in the business organization of the industry inasmuch as it responded to the exigencies of the employer. It was the corollary to the flexibility that governed his organization of production, imposed primarily by the concern for liquidity. Once up and running, as already observed, a firm operated on a short margin dependent on cash flow. With few exceptions—weaving being the longest process—contracts for work involved a short-term commitment, and hence the firm could stop contracting for production without much cost immediately when demand lagged. The employer could dip into the labor market as needed, sometimes relying on a broker to find the appropriate workers, and he had no need to make workers dependent on him through extension of credit. The lack of the kinds of ties between employer and employee, even personal acquaintance, that might have come from steady work explains a situation that surfaced in a report made to Cosimo I in the early 1540s: weavers were going about collecting wool and a cash advance on work from as many as six lanaioli at the same time and then fleeing town with the money (and perhaps with the wool as well).[99]

This fluidity of workers in and out of employment rosters is not to be seen in an entirely negative light, however. If it reveals a degree of precariousness in their lives, at least as seen from the employment record of the employer, it may have been a consequence of the worker's own volition. Flexibility in the job market made it possible for the worker to take time off, something that appealed to a worker in a preconsumer economy, whose earnings could buy him little else once basic needs had been satisfied. Fluidity may, therefore, be an index also to employment possibilities and to wages. In any event, fluidity would seem to indicate that employees were not tied to employers by credit dependency. Unlike weavers in northern Europe, Florentine weavers were not bound to the firm by liens on their looms for credit advanced to them. Franceschi found evidence for this kind of indebtedness in the early fifteenth century, and guild documents in the mid-1540s indicate that this was becoming a problem, but that this situation was a general characteristic of the industry over the period surveyed here has not yet been confirmed by evidence from the credit side of such arrangements as recorded in the many personal and business accounts of lanaioli that have been studied. Indebtedness on weavers' accounts in company books is almost always a function of the length of time it took them to do the work, during which they were being paid advances.[100]

However much the worker was circumscribed by guild regulations, the putting-out system gave him some maneuverability for taking the initiative in organizing the forces of production within his craft to his own advantage. Those who needed a workspace outside the home often joined forces to work in partnership with one another. Most of these artisan-entrepreneurs were wool workers, especially those involved in the preparatory stages of processing raw wool and the final stages of finishing cloth, for they needed a specific place to work, perhaps outfitted with special equipment, as well as help, if for nothing else than handling heavy materials. Silk throwsters and weavers also formed partnerships. These associations assured help in tasks from co-workers and the sharing of the financial burden of paying an assistant or two and meeting the commitment to a rental

---

[99] Marco Spallanzani, " 'Modo da crescere l'entrate di Firenze': Un progetto presentato a Cosimo I," *Annali della Scuola Normale Superiore di Pisa: Classe di lettere e filosofia,* 3d ser., 16 (1986): 522.

[100] Franceschi, *Oltre il "Tumulto,"* 74, 76, 187–88, 281–82; Bruno Dini, "Le ricordanze di un rammendatore (1488–1538)," reprinted from *Nuova rivista storica* 74 (1990) in *Manifattura, commercio e banca,* 196; Malanima, *La decadenza,* 126–27.

contract for a workspace. Above all, partnership assured them, through a common effort, a certain continuity of employment. Even lower-skilled laborers in the wool industry—washers, carders, combers, burlers, nappers, menders, shearmen—are commonly identified on manufacturers' accounts as having partners. Franceschi has documented such partnerships for some categories of wool workers from guild, court, and notarial records. Partners generally sealed their accord in a formal contract, identifying their association with their names followed by the words *e compagni*, the same terminology (translated here as "& Partners") the manufacturers, as well as merchant-bankers, used to identify their firms. The articles of association were often registered with the guild, and arrangements generally were made for as long as three to five years. Like many Florentine craftsmen, they probably kept accounts, but accounts documenting the internal operations survive for only two of these enterprises: the shop of makers of combs and loom reeds during the years 1372 to 1378 and the company of the silk weaver Iacopo di Tedesco, active in the early sixteenth century. To find work, these men looked to brokers in the pay of capitalist firms, but we know of at least one wool shearman who himself paid a broker to put him into contact with a manufacturer.[101]

In these initiatives workers were, for the most part, not blocked by lack of capital. Few activities required much investment in equipment and plant beyond simple tools. The most expensive equipment—a dyer's cost about *fl.*50, and a silk loom or a silk-throwing machine cost from *fl.*25 to *fl.*35—amounted to little more than a year's earnings of the men who used them. The capital of two recorded partnerships of makers of cards and teasels, used for the purchase of tools, barely reached the uppermost level of what the most skilled craftsman could hope to earn in a year—190 lire (*fl.*51) for a partnership of two set up in 1389 and 250 lire (*fl.*66) for another set up in 1404. In 1388 two brothers organized a three-year partnership for shearing cloth with presumably no capital other than the shop and tools contributed by one of the brothers for two-thirds of the profits, the other brother putting in only his persona for one-third of the profits. In the 1427 catasto the best-equipped throwster of silk had four machines for spinning and throwing silk worth all together *fl.*100,[102] and an instance has already been cited of throwsters going into partnership with a manufacturer of silk cloth. As to plant, workers who could not work at home could find workspace, even that outfitted for specialized tasks, readily available for rent at rates ranging from 20 lire (*fl.*5) to 80 lire (*fl.*20) in 1427, which workers of middling skill operating in partnership

[101] Franceschi, *Oltre il "Tumulto,"* 47–66 (on partnerships and the surviving shop book), 186 (on the broker).
[102] Franceschi, "Florence and Silk," 8.

could easily afford. Fullers, scourers, and stretchers of wool often joined forces to pay the high rent on the specialized spaces they needed for their work, and the rental contract could involve them in a partnership with the owner, be it the guild or a private person, that defined responsibilities for maintenance of equipment, expenses, and sharing of profits. In 1589 one man alone was renting out no fewer than four of the wool guild's tenter sheds, but unspecified problems resulting from this arrangement prompted the guild to make new contracts with eight men.[103] Finally, manufacturing firms provided the expensive raw materials these men worked with, and the practice of paying workers weekly advances, mostly in cash, for work lasting more than a week or so precluded major problems of liquidity.

Of all these cloth workers, weavers of silk showed the strongest proclivity for enlarging the scale of their operations. The infinite varieties of the fabrics they produced required highly specialized skills and looms with different specifications, and both skills and techniques were continually challenged by the relatively rapid change in taste that characterized the growth of the market for silks at the time. Such challenges might induce a weaver to enlarge the scale of operations if for no other reason than to widen the range of the products he could offer to his clients, the setaioli. The more looms he had and the larger his work force of assistants, the better position he was in to increase the variety of his output and thereby to improve his competitive position for getting commissions. This also put him in a better position to offer product innovations, such as the new kind of cloth Vincenzo di Lorenzo Casini, a weaver with fourteen looms, experimented with making and for which he sought a patent in 1584.[104] In 1427, when the industry was still in an early stage of its growth, the catasto returns of thirty-eight out of the ninety-five silk weavers from the quarter of Santo Spirito, the area with the heaviest concentration of weavers, reported more than a single loom, and two reported 7.[105] A century later almost two-thirds of all silk weavers in the survey of 1525 had more than 2 looms, nine had more than 7 and one had no fewer than 25. Most of these weavers worked in shops with several boy apprentices (garzoni and fattori), and the nine shops with more than 6 boys had a total of 121 all together. Some of these places must have had something of a factory atmosphere about them, if we are to believe Vasari's anecdote about the shop next door to Botticelli: the operation of its eight looms so shook the entire building and made

---

[103] *Legislazione toscana raccolta e illustrata dal dottore Lorenzo Cantini socio di varie accademie,* 32 vols. (Florence, 1802–8), 12:322–68.

[104] Molà, "Oltre i confini," 60.

[105] Franceschi, *Oltre il "Tumulto,"* 181.

so much noise that the painter could not stay at home, let alone work there. The exceptionally high earnings of silk weavers have already been remarked.

The greatest success story that can be told about anyone within the city's artisan ranks, inside or outside the textile industries, is that of the silk weaver Iacopo di Tedesco. Iacopo went into partnership with other weavers, and the ten companies he organized over a long working life that spanned almost a half-century, from 1490 to 1539, are documented by account books that, in all respects, meet the highest standards of the city's leading capitalist enterprises. The company shop was the largest silk-weaving operation listed in the 1525 survey; and with twenty-five looms and thirty-two boy apprentices on the payroll, it may have been the largest private employer in the city. The advantage of size was not in productivity gains in the actual weaving of fabrics but in Iacopo's improved chances of getting work by being able to offer his clients, the setaioli, a greater range of products. In his best years Iacopo's earnings reached several hundred florins, exceeding by far the *fl.*100 salary paid Brunelleschi as director of the cathedral workshop. As a weaver completely dependent on commissions from setaioli, he did not own the materials he worked with and could not sell the finished product of his labor, but he was able to invest freely in other branches of the industry. He put most of his savings in real estate, including the shop rented out to his company, but occasionally he also put money into other enterprises—a partnership of ritagliatori, a battiloro shop, a venture to buy raw silk in the Valdinievole, and even a silk firm. At the time of his death Iacopo, the son of a woodworker, left an estate that probably ranked him close to the upper 5 percent of all Florentines.[106] Having worked for almost a half-century, during which time he dealt with more than a hundred setaioli and invested in several branches of the industry, he probably could have set up a son, had he had one, as a setaiolo.

By way of contrast, weavers of wool, the most highly skilled workers in their industry, had little to gain from increasing the scale of their work. The cloth they wove was highly standardized. It came in a few basic weaves, all of relatively simple construction, and production required no more than two or three different kinds of looms. Producing standardized products that came in only a few varieties and required less complex looms, wool weavers did not reach as high a level of skill and specialization as silk weavers. They did not have to adjust their work and their equipment to meet a demand that arose from continual changes in fashion; by the same token, they could not take the initiatives silk weavers could to capture demand by specializing and varying products. Without technical innovations wool weavers did not have the possibility of making significant

[106] Goldthwaite, "Entrepreneurial Silk Weaver," 108.

productivity gains through increasing the scale of operations much beyond the household, although legislation in 1560 permitted them to operate as many looms as they wished.[107] The weaver of wool, therefore, had little to gain from leaving his home to set up a shop with other weavers, although he might have more than one loom at home being worked by family members or paid assistants.

Of all these artisan-entrepreneurs, dyers stand out as a distinct group. In the fourteenth century the wool guild itself was deeply involved in dyeing. It saw to the importation of woad, the principal dye used by the industry, and it operated some establishments in partnership with dyers that were large enough to handle a significant percentage of the cloth produced annually. At the end of the thirteenth century dyers had their own confraternity, dedicated to Sant'Onofrio, which, unlike the confraternities of other guild workers, did not come under the control of the guild, and during the fourteenth century they built their own hospice *(ospedale)*. When the industry expanded its production of quality cloths, dyers were among the more aggressive groups that tried to gain separate guild statues. They achieved this for only a few months in 1343, under Walter of Brienne, but in 1361 they gained the statutory right to hold office in the guild alongside the lanaioli. They gained guild status again during the few years of the Ciompi regime but lost it in the wake of the oligarchic reaction in 1382. By the fifteenth century wool dyers appear as autonomous small-scale entrepreneurs within the capitalist class, alongside the manufacturers themselves and merchant-bankers. Toward the end of the fourteenth century silk dyers emerge as a completely separate group of artisans, eventually numbering about half as many as wool dyers. Although they did not have the status in the silk guild that wool dyers had in theirs, some silk dyers were every bit as successful, to judge from catasto documents.

Dyeing was a major enterprise requiring vats and other equipment, as well as a special place to work, and dyers had to be prepared to meet a small payroll of workers. For some colors, two different processes and therefore two dye houses were required, and the cost could constitute about one-fifth of all direct manufacturing costs for a bolt of rascia. Both kinds of dyers usually worked through formal partnerships. A firm needed only about *fl.*50 for equipment, and often the manufacturer supplied the expensive dyes and soap, both of which differed for the two dyeing processes. Some firms, therefore, could operate with a capital of only about *fl.*400–500, but the five largest firms documented in the 1427 catasto had capital ranging from *fl.*1,000 to *fl.*1,600, somewhat below that of the average wool firm. The list of debits and credits that one of these, Bartolomeo di Lorenzo

---

[107] *Legislazione toscana*, 4:78.

di Cresci, presented in his report, totaling, respectively, *fl*.4,374 and *fl*.5,163, conveys an idea of the scale of operations this kind of enterprise could reach. Some instances of upper-class entrepreneurs going into partnership with dyers have already been mentioned. To these can be added the firm organized in 1508 by the dyer Giovanni di Ridolfo and the three sons of Giuliano di Giovenco de' Medici and Bartolomeo Bernini, in which Giovanni put in his persona to become the manager and the others put in the capital, totaling *fl*.800.[108] Most firms we have information about, however, were entirely artisan enterprises. Many ledgers of these small dye firms survive, some with the usual array of subordinate account books, but none have been investigated. A study of the extant accounts of a dyer in late fourteenth-century Siena, however, documents, besides the technical nature of the craft in all its aspects, how in a nearby Tuscan city the business provided upward economic mobility for at least one entrepreneurial craftsman.[109]

Wool dyers sometimes went into partnership with their suppliers. In the 1370s the dyer Bancozzo di Giovanni was a partner with Simo d'Ubertino, the major supplier of woad from Arezzo (whom we encountered in chapter 1), whose business included a wool shop in Arezzo and a commercial firm in Pisa.[110] In the 1360s and 1370s Giovacchino di Gucciarello Pinciardi (also encountered in chapter 1), an immigrant from Borgo Sansepolcro who had a partnership for importing woad from his native city, worked with a partner in Borgo, Bartolo d'Uguccio, to extend operations to a dye house in Florence, a wool firm in Borgo, and the commerce in wool cloth. The two together had *fl*.2,000 invested in a dyeing establishment in Florence with a third partner, probably the dyer. In Borgo the two had an investment, perhaps amounting to as much as *fl*.6,500, in a partnership including Bartolo's two sons for the production and marketing of wool cloth. One of Bartolo's sons was to set up a wool shop in Borgo, the other was to manage a warehouse in Urbino for regional sales, and Pinciardi was to operate a dyeing establishment in Florence and send cloth to Borgo. The firm marketed both Florentine and locally produced cloth throughout central Italy. The entire arrangement was probably set up primarily to finance the commerce in woad directed to Florence.[111]

[108] De Roover, "Florentine Firm of Cloth Manufacturers," 99n4.

[109] Information from catasto documents on both silk and wool dyers is collected in Edler de Roover, *L'arte della seta*, 31–47. Data on firms from the 1427 catasto can be found in the survey made by John Padgett, cited in n. 20 above. The study of the Sienese dyer is Piero Guarducci, *Un tintore senese del Trecento: Landoccio di Cecco d'Orso* (Siena, 1998).

[110] Dini, *Arezzo intorno al 1400*, 33.

[111] Giuliano Pinto, "Giovacchino Pinciardi da Borgo San Sepolcro, mercante e tintore di guado nella Firenze del Trecento," in *La Toscane et les Toscans autour de la Renaissance: Cadres de vie, société, croyances; Mélanges offerts à Charles-M. de La Roncière* (Aix-en-Provence, 1999), 95–110. For the accounts of a contemporary merchant of Arezzo who exported woad to Florence, working in partnership with a lanaiolo there, see Dini, *Arezzo intorno al 1400*, 32–35.

These various initiatives reveal something of an entrepreneurial spirit on the part of at least a few craftsmen. Working within the putting-out system, they entered into formal partnerships and kept accounts. They owned the tools of their trade, and what plant they did not own they could rent. To be assured of regular work, they had to contract with any number of cloth firms simultaneously, and they employed their own work staff. Although the structure of the industry limited the parameters of their operations, they had institutional protection for contractual arrangements, and it is not a foregone conclusion that the more successful of these workers—such as the silk weaver Iacopo di Tedesco—could not have risen to the top of the hierarchy as manufacturers. In the next chapter we shall see how relatively open these ranks were to artisans working in other sectors of the city's economy.

Recapitulation: Wool, Silk, and the Economy

Textile production represented by far the city's most important industrial activity, although taking the measure of its impact on the economy is not easy. Nevertheless, trends can be perceived, and they suggest a hypothesis for the consideration of larger issues. The basic data presented in tables 4.1 and 4.2, relative to the wool and silk industries, respectively, are compared summarily in table 4.3 in an attempt to measure something of the impact the two industries together had on the local economy. The wool industry went through several stages as it adjusted its products to the kind of wool it was able to import; although its performance had its ups and downs, the trend was generally upward. It reached its height in the later sixteenth century, when, for the first time, it found a major outlet in northern Europe, the most competitive market within the European and Mediterranean economic region, then undergoing dynamic expansion. The trend of silk was clearly upward in the fifteenth century and then more or less stable through the sixteenth century, notwithstanding the shift from products directed to the top end of the market to those directed to the bottom end.

The trend of both industries taken together suggests several hypotheses about the performance of the industries in general. First, by 1420 the production of silk was sufficient to compensate for the difference between the level of production of wool at that time and its level in the 1390s, so that the total production of the textile industries was back to its previous high levels. Moreover, the continuing rise in the production of silk fabrics in the fifteenth century raised the performance of the sector as a whole even higher by close to 50 percent. Finally, the level of production of both industries reached its all-time high in the second half of the

TABLE 4.3
The Wool and Silk Industries, 1373–1629:
Production as Investment in the Local Economy

| | | Gross sales in lire | | Value in work years | | | |
| | | | | Number | | Per capita | |
Year	Population	Wool	Silk	Wool	Silk	Wool	Silk
1373	60,000	2,142,000		16,477		0.27	
1381–82	55,000	1,467,180		11,286		0.21	
1391–95	60,000	1,037,400		7,980		0.13	
1425–30	40,000	1,050,389		8,080		0.20	
1436	40,000		338,433		2,603		0.07
1451–53	40,000		401,625		3,089		0.08
1461–62	40,000		472,500		3,635		0.09
1488–90	42,000	1,639,341	812,000	12,610	6,246	0.30	0.15
1526–27	70,000	2,520,000	980,000	19,385	7,538	0.28	0.11
1553–54	60,000	2,115,000		12,515		0.21	
1558–59	60,000	2,430,000		14,379		0.24	
1560–61	60,000	4,252,000		25,163		0.42	
1570–71	60,000	4,171,500		20,055		0.33	
1588	65,000		2,450,000		9,423		0.14
1591–1605	65,000	3,825,000		14,712		0.23	
1619	75,000	2,250,000		8,654		0.12	
1628–29	75,000		2,872,086		11,046		0.15

NOTE: See tables 4.1 and 4.2 for calculations and sources.

sixteenth century despite the uncertainties that increasingly threatened the wool industry and the decline in quality of the products of the silk industry.

Investment by the two industries in the local economy went above all for labor, and the index used to measure performance in table 4.3 is the per capita value of that investment. The amount spent by both industries together about the middle of the sixteenth century was sufficient to pay half of all the residents of the city—men, women, and children—a year's minimum wage (as defined by what an unskilled manual laborer earned). The impact of the textile industries on the economy as a whole, however, goes somewhat beyond what firms spent in the domestic market in manufacturing costs as represented in the table. If a high percentage of total costs—40 percent for wool, 65–70 percent for silk—went for raw materials procured from abroad, this is not to say that this capital left the economy altogether. Some of those expenditures ended up in the hands of Florentines engaged in related commercial operations and transport. Moreover, the profits of these merchants were brought home, to be injected into the economy through reinvestment or consumption. Finally, the diffusion of sericulture in Tuscany, especially in the sixteenth century, kept some of the money spent for raw materials within the regional economy.

Table 4.3 illustrates the much greater importance of the wool industry to the local economy. In the second quarter of the fourteenth century, according to

Villani, about a third of the population lived off the industry, and in the 1427 catasto about 40 percent of all declarants who stated the nature of their employment worked in the industry. For all the prestige and luxury of the products of the silk industry, its performance, as measured in the value of investment in the local economy, not in the value of gross sales, did not reach the level of output of the wool industry until well into the seventeenth century, by which time the wool export industry had collapsed. Despite the much larger investment a silk entrepreneur needed, up to 70 percent of his investment left the urban economy to buy raw materials, as compared with 40 percent of the wool entrepreneur's, and what was left for manufacturing never reached much more than 50 percent of what the wool industry spent.

The impact of the investment in the production of wool, moreover, resulted in a more balanced labor force. The production of wool comprised many stages and required a variety of skills ranging from simple manual labor to weaving, and some wool workers took modest entrepreneurial initiatives within their sphere of activity. The work force in silk, instead, was extremely polarized between a mass of workers at the very bottom, many of whom were women and children, and an elite few, the weavers, whose earnings soared well above the traditional ceiling for artisan wages; such a skewed labor force left little room for entrepreneurial maneuvering. For every *fl.*100 spent for the production of wool cloth, *fl.*60 went for manufacturing, about *fl.*40 of that for skilled labor of one kind or another; for every *fl.*100 invested in silk, *fl.*30 went for manufacturing, probably not more than *fl.*10–15 of which went for skilled labor, above all highly paid weavers, and the rest went to people working at or below what here has been called the minimum wage (table 4.4). In other words, the share of every *fl.*100 spent for production that went to skilled wool workers was three to four times the share that went to skilled silk workers. Over the course of the fourteenth, fifteenth, and sixteenth centuries the basic structure of this work force in the two industries remained fairly stable. In the course of the sixteenth century, with the downgrading of the quality of its products, the silk industry saw a lowering of the general level of skill among weavers, whose numbers, however, were relatively few. What changed was a narrowing of the gap in the polarity between weavers and the mass of workers at the bottom of the wage scale. In the wool industry variations in the quality of products over the centuries probably required little adjustment among its workers.

The collapse of wool production for export at the beginning of the seventeenth century must have had widespread repercussions, perhaps even reaching crisis proportions, given the rapidity with which it came and also the high level of output in the years immediately preceding the crisis. The city saw its major industry drastically reduced in scale, leaving it with many fewer skilled and entrepreneur-

TABLE 4.4

Percentage Breakdown of Production Costs in the Wool and Silk Industries,
Fifteenth and Sixteenth Centuries

Wool	%	Silk	%
Raw material	40	Raw material	70
Manufacturing		Manufacturing	
Processing	9	Reeling, throwing, dyeing	15
Spinning	16	Weaving (including a	
Weaving	13	component of child and	
Finishing, dyeing	22	apprentice labor)	15
Total	100	Total	100

SOURCES: For wool, Richard A. Goldthwaite, "The Florentine Wool Industry in the Late Sixteenth Century: A Case Study," *Journal of European Economic History* 32 (2003): 533 (table). For silk, estimates vary more widely: Paola Massa, "Technological Typologies and Economic Organization of Silk Workers in Italy from the XVIth to the XVIIIth Centuries," *Journal of European Economic History* 22 (1993): 546–47; Bruno Dini, "L'industria serica in Italia, secc. XIII–XV," in *La seta in Europa, sec. XIII–XX,* ed. Simonetta Cavaciocchi (Florence, 1993), 113–14; Sergio Tognetti, *Un'industria di lusso al servizio del grande commercio: Il mercato dei drappi serici e della seta nella Firenze del Quattrocento* (Florence, 2002), 89–91, 99–103 (tables).

ial craftsmen. With this loss in the wool industry and the lowering of the level of skill in the silk industry that had occurred in the sixteenth century, Florence lost the solid industrial base that had been the strength of its economy during the Renaissance. The city found itself with a very different working class from the one it had had in the fifteenth century. To repeat an earlier question, where did these wool workers find reemployment?

The underlying condition that characterized the organization of the textile industry was fragmentation, both of ownership and of operations. Cloth production, both wool and silk, was controlled by numerous, relatively small businesses set up as formal partnerships. No one firm had a significant share of the market, and very few investors had interests in as many as three or four firms between the two industries. The rhythm of industrial activity was, therefore, the collective result of short-term micromanagement decisions as each firm sought, almost on a daily basis, to maintain liquidity by balancing ongoing operating costs with income from the sale of finished products. For all the fragmentation of business organization, firms nevertheless operated within two larger structures. Entrepreneurs had a formal corporate organization in the guild that assured their domination as capitalist investors, set standards for the industry, regulated operations and, with respect to the wool guild, supplied the capital for investment in the more expensive forms of fixed capital. A second structure within which the industries functioned was the international commercial network of Florentine merchant-bankers, which supplied raw materials and marketed finished products. Wool firms eventually became dependent on import-export merchants, while silk firms tended to insert themselves into the international network to forge for themselves these backward and forward linkages. In other words, by the fifteenth century the wool industry and international merchant banking were two distinct if interdependent spheres of business, whereas the silk industry and international merchant banking overlay one another. The entrepreneurs who ran these businesses might, however, invest in all three activities, and they all came from the same economic and social class.

The organization of the Florentine textile industries is consistent with our understanding of capitalism at this early stage of its development prior to the industrial revolution. Lanaioli and setaioli invested capital in their partnerships and could be found working hard on the scene in their shops. They organized the forces of production around the putting-out system based on the cash nexus, and they directed their products to markets abroad. Moreover, through their guilds they monopolized production by blocking cloth workers from access to raw materials and from the sale of finished products. Yet these Florentine entrepreneurs did not invest in fixed capital; they minimized the direct management of labor through the putting-out system; and in the end, limiting their investment to start-up capital and keeping production levels within the parameters that liquidity permitted, they took little, if any, risks. Bankruptcy was not much of a threat, and those setaioli who had to face it probably owed their difficulties to their forward marketing operations abroad. These men were a far cry from those clothiers in England who forged backward linkages to supply by investing in sheep pastures and who abandoned the putting-out system to take direct control of production by buying fulling mills, spinning houses, and dyeing establishments and by assembling a labor force under their own roof.[112] Entrepreneurial energy of this kind did not manifest itself during the long history of the textile industry in capitalist Florence. Instead, lanaioli and setaioli used the guild to confine both the corporate autonomy and the entrepreneurial energies of artisans, while they worked through a business structure that gave them maximum flexibility to adjust to changing market conditions. For all the conservatism of their investment strategy, as Alberti implied in giving advice about what was the most suitable business for the head of the kind of upper-class family he envisaged, these men nevertheless succeeded in keeping the industry on a steadier course and over a longer time—more than three centuries for wool and more than two centuries for silk—than was the case in most other centers of textile production at the time.

---

[112] Christopher Dyer, "Were There Any Capitalists in Fifteenth-Century England?" in *Enterprise and Individuals in Fifteenth-Century England,* ed. Jennifer Kermode (Wolfeboro Falls, NH, 1991), 19.

CHAPTER FIVE

Artisans, Shopkeepers, Workers

The Work Force: *Guilds, Artisans, Workers on the Margins of the Market.*
Performance of the Artisan Sector: *Demand-Driven Growth, Parameters of the Local Market.*

The previous chapters have dealt with the leading sectors of the economy that were controlled by capitalist investors—international commerce and banking and the textile industries. The people in this chapter worked in many activities, but they can be lumped together in one composite sector of the economy that produced goods and services primarily, if not exclusively, for the local market, not for export. The performance of this sector was a function of the distribution and structure of wealth. The sector grew as a result of the increased demand for consumer goods that arose from the wealth that flowed into the city in the form of profits from textile exports and merchant banking abroad. The success of the sector lay in its ability to satisfy that demand, especially for the wide range of luxury products at the top end of the market desired by the rich, so that only a small percentage of those profits were spent on foreign-made goods. As a result, the profits brought home from abroad were, in effect, reinvested in human capital. To some extent, the initiative and enterprise that drove this performance must have been inspired by the desire of many of those who worked within the sector to improve their economic status. We therefore need to understand how the artisan—by which is meant here both shopkeeper and skilled craftsman—conducted his affairs in this particular marketplace: the extent to which institutions defined the parameters of his activity, how he prepared himself to confront the market, what instruments and practices he utilized to deal with market conditions, the degree of success he could hope to achieve. Through these structural and technical aspects of work we can hope to penetrate to the economic realities of the lives of men who made their living in one of the principal centers of capitalism in its preindustrial form.[1]

---

[1] Much of what follows is taken from Richard A. Goldthwaite, *The Building of Renaissance*

The Work Force
Guilds

According to the traditional historiography, the economic life of most skilled workers and shopkeepers in medieval Europe revolved around guilds.[2] An exclusive organization, the guild—at least according to the stereotype that emerges from generalizations in the historiography—regulated the training of the apprentice, established the role of the master within the corporation, and defended the interest of the group in the marketplace. In addition, guild religious activities, welfare concerns, and family traditions reinforced the economic ties that bound members together. In the preindustrial period the working life of the worker centered on this restricted corporate life, not on the marketplace. His economic culture consisted in a strong sense of the exclusiveness of his craft, the dominance of the master within the craft, pride in his work, and the protective comfort of a closed religious and social body. These cultural norms are the antithesis of those generated by the so-called free market, in which the individual operator is on his own. In the historiography, in fact, guilds are regarded as an obstacle to the development of the modern economy, especially in the textile industries, the leading sector in the development of industrial capitalism. In sixteenth-century Italy the resistance of guilds to lowering quality presumably destroyed the ability of the industry to compete with less expensive products imported from abroad, and later, in northern Europe, the flight of the industry from the city to the countryside in order to escape guild conservatism is seen by some as a step toward the industrial revolution, a development known, in fact, as protoindustrialization. These grand historiographical schemes, however, often appear disembodied from studies of specific situations in which guildsmen confronted market conditions. A difference between rules and reality has been noted in late medieval Bruges, for instance, where guilds appear to have been relatively open institutions and artisan entrepreneurs fairly successful in circumventing guild regulations.[3]

Florence: An Economic and Social History (Baltimore, 1980), ch. 6. The social world of the working-man is best approached through the studies of Giovanni Cherubini and Franco Franceschi. For Cherubini, see *Scritti toscani: L'urbanesimo medievale e la mezzadria* (Florence, 1991); and *Il lavoro, la taverna, la strada: Scorci di Medioevo* (Naples, 1997). For Franceschi, "La mémoire des 'laboratores' à Florence au début du XV siècle," in *Annales: Économies, sociétés, civilisations* 45 (1990): 1143–67; and *Oltre il "Tumulto": I lavoratori fiorentini dell'arte della lana fra Tre e Quattrocento* (Florence, 1993).

[2] Guilds dominate the discussion (with little about Italy, however) in the contributions to *Les métiers au Moyen Âge: Aspects économique et sociaux,* ed. P. Lambrechts and J-P. Sosson (Louvain-la Neuve, Belgium, 1994), although in concluding remarks R. van Uytven observes that artisan production has not received much attention. The traditional view is also presented in the recent general European survey of James R. Farr, *Artisans in Europe, 1300–1914* (Cambridge, 2000), ch. 1.

[3] Peter Stabel, "Guilds in Late Medieval Flanders: Myths and Realities of Guild Life in an Export-Oriented Environment," *Journal of Medieval History* 30 (2004): 187–212.

Likewise, a focus on the behavior and mentality of workers at Florence—a place better documented than any other by accounting materials, which are nothing if not the direct record of market activity—reveals a picture that hardly accords with the European stereotype.

In Florence the reorganization of the guilds for political purposes at the end of the thirteenth century led to a radical modification of the role of guilds in the economic life of workingmen. Until that time the city, like most others in medieval Europe, saw the formation of many guilds corresponding to the rapid growth of its population and the emergence of distinct occupational groups large enough to unite institutionally to protect their common economic and social interests. Thirteenth-century documents reveal hints of the organization of such small groups of workers as overland carriers, river transporters, and makers of millstones, and eventually guilds may have numbered more than seventy. In 1293 the major players in the political life of the city, all men of a certain economic standing, managed to organize the government on the basis of a constitution, known as the Ordinances of Justice, which defined the republic as a kind of confederation of guilds. Power was concentrated in their own, so-called major guilds, seven in number, but over time other guilds were brought in as minor participants. This process of defining guilds for political purposes set limits on the number of guilds and resulted in the merging of some guilds into others and the incorporation of men with different economic interests together in what might be called guild conglomerates. The major guilds were controlled by men of relatively substantial means: international merchants who imported cloth for finishing and reexport (Calimala); moneychangers (Cambio); manufacturers of wool cloth (Lana); cloth retailers, who were concentrated in the street of Por Santa Maria (Por Santa Maria); furriers, both dealers and manufacturers (Vaiai e Pellicciai); physicians, apothecaries, and speziali (Medici e Speziali); and finally, judges and notaries (Giudici e Notai). The Calimala and the Cambio were completely homogenous in their membership, and the Giudici e Notai and the Vaiai e Pellicciai reasonably so, but others absorbed men in very different occupations and of varying economic and social status. The Por Santa Maria and the Medici e Speziali were, in fact, conglomerates with men in different occupations organized in several official membership groups, or divisions *(membra);* these included the speziali, who dealt in drugs, spices, and a variety of chemical substances. In the Lana guild, in contrast, only the lanaioli themselves constituted the governing membrum; some workers in the industry had a subordinate status, and the entire work force of the industry was subject to guild regulation.

Many artisans were initially excluded from these arrangements, and subsequent to the Ordinances of Justice other occupational groups joined together in organizations resembling guilds—stonecutters at the quarries of Fiesole, sellers of herbs, hat makers, horse merchants, renters of pack animals, bell casters, producers and sellers of glass, parchment makers, and bookbinders. Eventually fourteen more official guilds, themselves conglomerates to a greater or lesser extent, were brought into this constitutional structure as the so-called minor guilds: construction workers (Maestri di Pietra e Legname), butchers (Beccai), shoemakers (Calzolai), blacksmiths (Fabbri), linen drapers and secondhand dealers (Linaioli e Rigattieri), wine retailers (Vinattieri), innkeepers (Albergatori), tanners (Cuoiai e Galigai), armorers (Corazzai e Spadai), ironworkers (Chiavaioli), woodworkers (Legnaioli), bakers (Fornai), strap and belt makers (Correggiai), and grocers (Oliandoli). Other groups were accommodated in one of the official guilds, usually according to a certain logic; for example, painters, to mention one group that contributed prominently to the fame of the city, in 1316 found a place in the Medici e Speziali, which included the dealers from whom they bought their colors. The heterogeneity of membership of some of these guilds was considerable. In 1346 Por Santa Maria had three membership divisions, one of which comprised distinct subgroups. Doctors, speziali, and mercers constituted the three divisions of the Medici e Speziali, but the membership also included saddlers, painters, barbers, food dealers, waxworkers, makers of belts and purses, and others (table 5.1).

By 1320 legislation reaffirmed the exclusive status of twenty-one major and minor guilds and abolished all other formal organizations. Any professional group that aspired to a role in the political life of the commune had to find a place in one of these original guilds. The guild that underwent the greatest internal change as a result of subsequent developments within the local economy was the Por Santa Maria. As we have seen, it absorbed the impact of the growth of the silk industry in the fourteenth century, elevating the position within the total membership of both investing entrepreneurs and those skilled workers with subordinate status—weavers, dyers, battilori. The only modification to this constitutional guild structure of the state came temporarily with the Ciompi revolt in 1378, which, in fact, was instigated by three different groups of workers—dyers, shirtmakers, and wool workers (the Ciompi)—who wanted their own guilds, but by 1382, when the oligarchy returned to power, these new guilds had been eliminated.

The guild conglomerates that emerged from this political process lacked the homogeneity of membership that characterizes the stereotypical medieval guild, and this weakened their ability to intervene in economic and social matters. In classic medieval fashion guild statutes, most dating from the early fourteenth century, laid down the basic standards for the practice of the craft, restricted entry, and established a hierarchy of members within each guild, but for the most

TABLE 5.1
Florentine Guilds and Their Membership

Guild*	Members
Food	
Beccai	Butchers; importers of animals and fish
Fornai	Bakers
Oliandoli, pizzicagnoli	Grocers and dealers in agricultural goods from the countryside
Vinattieri	Wine sellers, taverners
Cloth	
LANA	Wool manufacturers and all subordinate workers
Linaioli e rigattieri	Dealers in used goods; linen drapers; tailors
POR SANTA MARIA	Silk manufacturers and all subordinate workers; goldsmiths, battiloro; makers of silk clothing, vestments, and accessories
Skins, leather	
Calzolai	Makers and sellers of shoes
Correggiai	Makers of belts, straps, and shields in leather; saddlers
Cuoiai e galigai	Tanners, leather workers
VAIAI E PELLICCIAI	Dealers and workers in furs, skins, and leathers
Metals	
Chiavaioli	Locksmiths and others working and selling iron products
Fabbri	Blacksmiths, makers of tools and utensils in metal
Spadai e corazzai	Makers of arms and armour
Construction and woodworking	
Legnaioli	Woodworkers; makers of furniture and utensils in wood
Maestri di pietra e legname	Construction workers, stonecutters, brickmakers, carpenters
Miscellaneous	
Albergatori	Hostellers, overland transporters
CALIMALA	International import-export merchants; originally finishers of imported cloth
CAMBIO	Local bankers
GIUDICI E NOTAI	Lawyers; notaries
MEDICI, SPEZIALI E MERCIAI	Physicians, barbers; dealers in spices, medicines, dyestuffs, wax; stationers; mercers; painters, potters

*The names of major guilds are fully capitalized.

part they did not closely regulate the economic activities of their members. The notable exceptions were the wool and silk guilds, which subordinated the many workers in these industries to the capitalist investors, both within the guild and in the workplace. It is hardly surprising that, given the lack of a cohesive identity among members, their religious and social-welfare activities were also limited, although some groups—for instance, the painters, silk weavers, and, as already remarked, different groups of wool workers—had their own confraternities, which served these functions. Some men belonged to guilds only for political reasons, having no economic interests in common with other members; and, indeed, men in sectors with no guild organization had to matriculate in one of the official guilds in order to participate in the political life of the city. For instance, Dante, whose father was perhaps a moneychanger, was a member of the Medici e Speziali. Moreover, multiple guild membership was possible and not at all unusual. In these circumstances guilds, including the wool and silk guilds, did not seriously block outsiders from access to their ranks and to the practice of their respective trades; in fact, their matriculation rosters are by no means indicative of the number of practitioners in a given occupation.[4] For this reason, too, the guild lost much disciplinary control over its members. The imprecise, even deceptive terminology used in guild statutes and in the records of artisans themselves for the designation of apprentices and of shop trainees and assistants reflects a reality rather different from the guild stereotype. Nor do we hear anything about the "masterpiece," or trial work, that an apprentice had to present in order to gain his credentials as a master in his craft. Nor, indeed, do we encounter many artisans who refer to themselves, or are called, "master." This title was used universally for masons, and it is often assumed that a man identified only as a *maestro* was in fact a mason, although he could also have been a teacher. Nor, finally, did many artisans "sign" their products with an individual, guild-approved mark. Masons' marks, for instance, so common in northern Europe, are not found in this city of stone.[5]

The weakening of the guild as an economic force within the practice of a particular craft resulted also from external political pressures in line with the trend toward more centralized government in the fourteenth century, notable in the reaction to the popular government of the 1340s and fully confirmed in the oligarchic restoration of 1382 after the Ciompi episode. By the end of the century the guilds' role in government, as well as their freedom to legislate in their internal affairs, became subject to the authority of the commune. The incorporation of much of the substance of guild statutes into the 1415 compilation of communal legislation indicates how much the state had preempted traditional guild authority in such economic matters as setting standards and prices and regulating trading practices that were in the general interest of the entire community. Moreover, the guilds' role in adjudicating disputes was subordinate to the supreme authority of the tribunal of the Mercanzia. Guild membership remained the essential qualification for election to political office, but the electoral process was organized through the guilds under

---

[4] For the speziali, for example, compare the figures from the 1427 catasto with those from the matriculation rosters, as reported by Antonella Astorri, "Appunti sull'esercizio dello speziale a Firenze nel Quattrocento," *Archivio storico italiano* (hereafter *ASI*) 147 (1989): 37–38, 43.

[5] Franco Franceschi, "Intervento del potere centrale e ruolo delle Arti nel governo dell'economia fiorentina del Trecento e del primo Quattrocento: Linee generali," *ASI* 151 (1993): 863–909, surveys the decline of the economic role of artisan guilds in this period.

the supervision of the Mercanzia, so that guilds became the routes to political activity rather than themselves agents in the political process. Positions on government committees and councils were distributed between the major and minor guilds, with the former collectively much more represented than the latter.

Given this history, it makes little sense to categorize workers according to guilds. Of the twenty-one guilds, eighteen included both artisans and shopkeepers: four for food workers, four for those dealing in skins and leather, three for cloth and clothing workers, three for metalworkers, two for those providing miscellaneous services, one for construction workers, and one for woodworkers. The remaining three guilds—the Cambio for local bankers, the Calimala for cloth importers, and the Giudici e Notai for judges and notaries—had no artisan members. The anomalies in this system are striking. The different kinds of workers involved in construction—layers of brick and stone, stoneworkers from quarriers to sculptors, carpenters, brickmakers—each of which had its own guild in most other medieval cities, belonged to just one guild, whereas metalworkers, who were not nearly as numerous, were divided into no fewer than four different guilds. Three had their own guild, while gold- and silversmiths, who also worked in base metals, were subsumed in Por Santa Maria. Woodworkers who made furniture and other highly crafted objects had their own guild, but wood sculptors belonged to the guild of construction workers, which also included sculptors in stone. Painters found themselves with a heterogeneous mix of mercers, stationers, speziali, and doctors, whereas in many other cities where they had their own guild—Venice and Bruges, for example—they themselves were subdivided into several distinct categories. Some guilds, especially those of leather- and metalworkers, overlapped with respect to some crafts, and it is possible to find artisans with the same skill in different guilds. Makers of drinking glasses, for instance, turn up in the rosters of the Oliandoli, the Chiavaioli, and the Medici e Speziali. By way of contrast, retailers and craftsmen who could be classified under the general rubric of those dealing in food products were more homogeneously divided among four guilds. Some of these artisans did not have full guild status but were nevertheless autonomous practitioners of their craft. In contrast, those in the wool and silk industries, even the most skilled and entrepreneurial, such as dyers and silk weavers, were not only subordinate members of their respective industrial guilds but also completely dependent on the capitalists who controlled the industry. In this situation, some artisans managed to evade membership in the appropriate guild, fathers could easily enough put their sons on a career path in a guild other than their own, and multiple memberships were also possible. This fluidity within the guild system had implications for the economic behavior of artisans.

Given this situation, and given the inadequate coverage of it in the scholarly literature, it is difficult to assess what guild membership meant to artisans and shopkeepers. Before the establishment of the Medici principate in the 1530s, guilds had some political significance for those who had full membership status, since, being the conduits to political office, they defined citizenship. This political status was symbolized by the oratory of Orsanmichele, where each of the seven major guilds and six others, along with the Mercanzia, had its own niche with a statue of its patron saint. The process of selection to political office, however, was controlled, not by the guilds, but by the oligarchy that secured its power over the state after the Ciompi period. Some guilds had their own courts to settle disputes among members, but these were subject to appeals to the tribunal of the Mercanzia. Moreover, this latter tribunal was often the court of first appeal in matters of debt claims. Each guild had its own hall, but only those of the industrial capitalists—merchants, bankers, setaioli, lanaioli—had a monumental presence on the urban scene in the immediate vicinity of the Mercato Nuovo, the banking center of the city. The butchers' guild was a notable exception: they rebuilt their hall in the Renaissance style, much enhancing its prominent position opposite Orsanmichele. Only a few guilds opened hospices for their aged and sick members, and very little is known about the history of any of them.

In short, whatever role guilds played, the economic lives of their members seem not to have been deeply embedded in institutional relations tied to guild affiliation. In the fifteenth century some consideration was given to the further agglomeration of the artisan guilds to reduce their number, and by this time such a measure would have had few repercussions outside the political sphere. One of the first measures the new government of Duke Alessandro de' Medici took against the traditional republican constitution of the city in 1534 was, in fact, to consolidate the fourteen artisans guilds into four new guild *università:* the construction, wood, and ferrous-metal workers (Maestri, Legnaioli, Fabbri, Chiavaioli, Corazzai) into the Università dei Fabbricanti; the purveyors of food (Fornai, Oliandoli, Beccai) into the Università di Por San Piero; the leatherworkers (Calzolai, Cuoiai, Correggiai) into the Università dei Maestri di Cuoiami; and the hostellers, wine dealers, and linen drapers (Albergatori, Vinattieri, Linaioli) into the Università dei Linaioli. Under Cosimo I these new conglomerates were all brought together under one roof at the new building of the Uffizi, the bureaucratic center of the ducal government. In 1583 the government took yet another step in streamlining the administration of these worker organizations by merging the Università dei Fabbricanti and the Università di Por San Piero, creating the unlikely agglomeration of workers in the heavy industries and food services, men who a century earlier had been organized in eight of the fourteen minor guilds.

Artisans

PREPARATION FOR THE MARKET   Florentine guilds lacked strong authority in areas of fundamental importance to the stereotypical medieval guild: mandatory membership, protection of quality, limits on competition among members, a closely regulated apprenticeship program. Moreover, the ranks of any particular group of craftsmen were not protected by a guild oligarchy in an effort to secure access for sons as a hereditary right. Market forces had dissolved guild structures to the extent of transforming apprenticeship into a more explicit form of paid child labor. A boy who went to work for a master rarely had a written contract, let alone a notarized one, defining his position. The master agreed to teach the boy the craft and to pay a salary (whereas in many places he was paid by the boy's father to take him in), but he did not assume paternal authority, rarely taking the apprentice into his own family.[6] All this meant that a youth found himself making his way in the marketplace without much protection and little regulation by his colleagues; by the same token, he was relatively free to go his own way. A young Florentine, less bound by the guild ties, and hence family traditions, so characteristic of guild society elsewhere, had the possibility, at least in theory, of selecting the trade he wanted to practice (or entering the one his father wanted to direct him to). The dozens upon dozens of boys who went to work as helpers and apprentices to the silk weaver Iacopo di Tedesco, who himself was not the son of a weaver, were put there by fathers who represent virtually the entire range of the city's occupations, hardly any of them being weavers. The printer Filippo di Giunta, the son of a retail cloth dealer, did an apprenticeship with a goldsmith and later opened a stationer's shop. The father of the noted stone and wood sculptors Giuliano and Benedetto da Maiano belonged to the carpenters' guild and had two brothers who, as stonecutters, belonged to the guild of construction workers; Giuliano belonged to the carpenters' guild, Benedetto belonged to the construction workers' guild, and a third son belonged to the guild of doctors and speziali. The son of another stoneworker, Andrea di Nofri Romoli, started off as a mercer and went on to become a setaiolo. The brickmaker Paolo da Terrarossa set his sons up as lanaioli. The painter Neri di Bicci placed one son with a lanaiolo

---

[6] In his survey of urban life throughout Europe at the end of the Middle Ages and in the early modern period, Marino Berengo found this Florentine practice so exceptional as to be unbelievable. *L'Europa delle città: Il volto della società urbana europea tra Medioevo ed Età Moderna* (Turin, 1999), 443.

and another with a banker. The painter Botticelli had one brother who became a goldsmith and another who became a banker, and their father was a tanner. The son of another painter, Taddeo Gaddi, somehow became a merchant-banker. Professional mobility thus made economic ascent a possibility.

The consequent weakness in family occupational traditions that resulted from this kind of fluidity is best illustrated by what is perhaps the city's most well known group of artisans, the painters, who at the time, for all their fame today, had no more economic, social, or cultural status than most other artisans. Almost none of the most famous of these men came out of a family tradition in the craft, and in contrast to the situation of painters in, for instance, Venice, Milan, and Bruges, the ranks of Florentine artists include virtually no dynasties. In fact, not many of them were sons of painters.[7] The father of Brunelleschi was a notary, as was the father of Leonardo da Vinci; fra Filippo Lippi's father was a butcher, Botticelli's was a tanner, fra Bartolomeo's was a muleteer, Andrea del Sarto's was a tailor, the Pollaiuolo brothers' was a poulterer, and Verrocchio's was a brickmaker. The story told by Vasari about how Cimabue, while traveling through the countryside, came across the young Giotto drawing on a rock can be taken as the primordial myth of the rise of the Florentine artist, whose talent was not blocked by either family traditions or guild corporatism. Family traditions among the artisans of Florence were likely to have been strongest in those crafts where a relatively high investment determined a continuity from father to son through the inheritance of a property such as a kiln (the Della Robbia), a foundry (the Ghiberti), or the shop inventory of a speziale or goldsmith (the Dei). Yet family groups did not dominate even these crafts. A study of family traditions in the speziali, the only such in-depth study of any occupational category, reveals that notwithstanding the high value of the stock some kept on hand, only 17 of the 60 speziali who appear in the 1480 catasto descended from one of the 113 speziali who appeared in the 1427 catasto, two generations earlier.[8]

In this situation of relatively ready access to guild ranks, the prospect for work was not confined to a sector circumscribed by any individual guild. The freedom to work in more than one trade or craft is best illustrated, again, by those artisans we today call artists. Painters, sculptors, and architects at least in theory belonged to different guilds, but in practice these crafts were not exclusive occupational categories. There is even some question that artisans were obligated to belong to the appropriate guilds. Brunelleschi had been head mason at the cathedral for

---

[7] Werner Jacobsen, in his *Die Maler von Florenz zu Beginn der Renaissance* (Berlin, 2001), 131, identified only 85 out of 296 painters who had a father or son who was a painter.

[8] Astorri, "Appunti sull'esercizio dello speziale," 41, 43.

years when, in 1434, the guild of construction workers had him thrown into jail for never having paid the matriculation fee in the guild. (The powerful cathedral works committee retaliated by having one of the guild consuls thrown into jail for his audacity.) In fact, some prominent artists—from Brunelleschi, Ghiberti, and Mino da Fiesole in the fifteenth century to Cellini in the sixteenth century, and including the painters Piero di Cosimo and Botticelli—were tardy or altogether negligent in the matter of membership in the appropriate guild. For instance, Antonio del Pollaiuolo, the son of a poulterer (one of his brothers continued in that trade) did his apprenticeship with a goldsmith and became an established sculptor and painter with his own shop before matriculating, at the age of thirty-five, in the goldsmiths' guild. Like Pollaiuolo, many painters and sculptors did their apprenticeship with goldsmiths. In fact, for lack of full professional training, some Florentine bronze sculptors had to contract out much of their casting, and their work often reveals an inadequate knowledge of the technical problems involved. The goldsmith Ghiberti created his most famous sculptures in base metals, a possibility forbidden by goldsmiths' guilds in many European cities at the time, and his son and grandson continued the tradition of his foundry, specializing in munitions, objects far removed from the liturgical utensils and jewelry typical of goldsmiths' production. Ghiberti, moreover, executed designs for painters and glassworkers, and the painters Uccello, Benozzo Gozzoli, and perhaps Masolino came out of his shop. He also claimed to be an architect and for a while directed works at the cathedral. Brunelleschi, another artisan trained as a goldsmith, worked as an architect and master mason. Indeed, no architect is known to have emerged from the ranks of the masons. The Pollaiuolo brothers and Verrocchio were both painters and sculptors. Many artisans thus followed an *iter* that freely crossed guild confines. Versatility, in fact, is a noted characteristic of Florentine artists, in contrast to the Venetians and those from virtually any other Italian city. In economic terms, versatility translates into a greater range of possibilities, freedom of choice, and greater potential; it promotes the free exchange of ideas among occupational groups and valorizes creativity and virtuosity.

Freed from guild ties, the artisan worked within a political and juridical system that, if not directly responsive to his particular interest, at least assured him a high degree of protection in the marketplace. Those artisans who did not have subordinate status in a major guild had at least a collective presence in the councils of government, since the minor guilds had a minority representation on all the many political bodies that determined policy and administered the city's business, including the Signoria. (Their actual input in political affairs, however, has not been studied.) The government, in any event, limited its interference in the marketplace to taxes on goods coming and going through the city's gate and to regulations in matters of wider public interest, such as provisioning of grain, measurement standards, and protection against fraud. Moreover, with respect to the enforcement of regulations on work laid down by the major guilds in which artisans had a subordinate status, it was not a foregone conclusion that the capitalist investor enjoyed any favoritism. When the silk weaver Iacopo di Tedesco once produced a damask fabric that was not of regulation width, the guild fined both him and the silk manufacturer who had commissioned it: "he too was condemned" was the comment Iacopo squeezed into the margin next to the account book entry in which he had already recorded payment of his fine.[9]

More importantly, the system of justice seems to have assured the workingman considerable objectivity in adjudicating disputes about property rights and contracts. Such was their confidence in the legal system that in going about their business artisans and shopkeepers, like capitalist entrepreneurs, had largely abandoned the notary by the fourteenth century. Although we have no studies of the social aspect of the administration of justice by the city's courts, in the few known cases of disputes about breach of contract between artisans and capitalist the former had no reason to be unhappy with the decision. In 1392 Agnolo Gaddi, Niccolò Gerini, and another painter were summarily dismissed from a job they were doing in the house of the rich merchant Francesco Datini, leaving their work unfinished and them unpaid; after much haggling over the matter, their appeal to the court of the Medici e Speziali to force Datini to pay was successful. In 1431 the barber-poet Burchiello was arrested and thrown into jail (though immediately released) for being in arrears in the rent for his barbershop owed to Giovanni de' Nobili; however, the eventual judgment against him by the tribunal of the Mercanzia was not altogether unfavorable despite the upper-class status of the creditor, inasmuch as what he was ordered to pay was somewhat less than what he owed. In 1458 Federigo di Iacopo Federighi, a member of one of the city's most illustrious families, brought the sculptor Luca Della Robbia before the court of the Mercanzia for being three years behind in meeting the deadline for the completion of the tomb of Federighi's uncle, Benozzo, bishop of Fiesole (d. 1450). The contract was complex and the issues numerous, and the case dragged on for a year. In the end the court appointed as arbitrator another sculptor, who concluded that Della Robbia was to have the maximum recompense allowed in the contract.

[9] Richard A. Goldthwaite, "An Entrepreneurial Silk Weaver in Renaissance Florence," *I Tatti Studies* 10 (2005): 76.

In 1481, in a case involving two stationers and the son of a prominent banker, Michele di Antonio di Messer Niccolò da Rabatta, the roles were reversed: it was the artisans who took the patrician to court. Da Rabatta, the stationers' landlord, wanted to raise the rent for their shop. To strengthen his position against any eventual protest by the tenants, who had been there ten years, he arranged a fictitious transfer of the ownership of the property to his son, a canon, presumably thinking that an important ecclesiastic—and one from a prominent family— would count for something in any forthcoming dispute. But he was wrong, for the tenants, the brothers Antonio and Giovanni di Niccolò di Lorenzo, did, in fact, bring suit against da Rabatta in the court of the Medici e Speziali, the major guild to which they belonged, arguing that they had not been given advance notice and that during their long tenancy they had paid for substantial improvement to the property. They won their case, as well as an award for damages. In 1497 another artisan, the painter Filippino Lippi, won his suit against one of the richest families in the city. Lippi, who had been working many years on his contract with Filippo Strozzi (d. 1491) to fresco the banker's chapel in Santa Maria Novella, sued Strozzi's heirs for an increase in his contracted fee. Although the Strozzi, who had already paid him almost two-thirds of his fee, had every right to be much distressed with Lippi's slow progress on the job, he claimed that the cost of materials was so high that he could not continue working. The court of the Medici e Speziali, to which the painters belonged, agreed, significantly increasing the contractual fee the Strozzi were to pay Lippi from *fl.*250 to *fl.*350; the painter, however, had to pay the small legal fee.[10]

Freed from traditional corporate bonds, the artisan was well prepared to deal in the marketplace of one of the most advanced centers of capitalism at the time. He knew how to read and write. The high rate of literacy in Florence and the other Tuscan towns in the fourteenth century has often been remarked, with particular reference to Giovanni Villani's observation, made in 1338, that from eight thousand to ten thousand youths were to be found in the city's elementary reading and writing schools at any one time. Even if one wants to dispute the reliability of Villani's statistical analysis of the city's population, the evidence that literacy

[10] Renato Piattoli, "Un mercante del Trecento e gli artisti del tempo suo," *Rivista d'arte* 11 (1929): 553–60 (Datini); Luca Boschetto, "Burchiello e il suo ambiente sociale: Esplorazioni d'archivio sugli anni fiorentini," in *La fantasia fuor de' confini: Burchiello e dintorni a 550 anni dalla morte (1449– 1999)* (Rome, 2002), 44; Hannelore Glasser, "The Litigation concerning Luca Della Robbia's Federighi Tomb," *Mitteilungen des kunsthistorischen Institutes in Florenz* 14 (1969–70): 1–32; Alessandro Guidotti, "Indagini su botteghe di cartolai e miniatori a Firenze nel XV secolo," in *La miniatura italiana tra gotico e Rinascimento* (Florence, 1985), 2:492–93 (Da Rabatta); Eve Borsook, "Documents for Filippo Strozzi's Chapel in Santa Maria Novella and Other Related Papers," *Burlington Magazine* 112 (1970): 737–45, 800–804. The extraordinarily abundant trial records of the Mercanzia are finally being studied by Luca Boschetto; his study will give us a better idea of how objective this court was.

extended to the working classes, even to its lowest levels, exists today in the written records these men left behind in account books and in their 1427 catasto declarations. The surviving documents of shopkeepers and craftsmen well justify the description of late medieval Tuscany, and not just Florence, as "a region with pen in hand."[11]

Literacy included numeracy. According to Villani's statistics, the youths in attendance at an abacus school, the place where they learned the basic arithmetic they needed to solve practical problems involving the monetary and measurement systems, numbered from a thousand to twelve hundred at any one time. Considering all the variables—population, age cohorts, sex ratio, duration of the course of study—this estimate would suggest that a vast majority of boys, and not just those belonging to the upper class, attended these schools.[12] In their 1427 catasto reports many artisans and shopkeepers declared that their children were at that time enrolled in an abacus school.[13] From numeracy learned in the schools they went on to accountancy picked up on the job. In his *Ricordanze* Bartolomeo Masi, son of a coppersmith, noted that when he was only slightly over eight years old, in 1489, he and his older brother, then just over ten, entered such a school. His brother left after eight months and went to work in their father's shop. Bartolomeo remained another year, perhaps because he had started so young, and then, when he was almost ten, he too entered the family shop. A year later, at the age of eleven, he began keeping the shop journal of income and expenditures.

Knowledge of accountancy was particularly important for organizing economic activity and for shaping the mentality with which Florentines confronted economic matters. The statutes of many of the artisan guilds, including those of the speziali, the grocers, the tailors, the wine merchants, the smiths, and the dealers in furs and skins, required that their members keep an accounting record of their affairs. The evidence that they did so is overwhelming. The minutes of the

---

[11] The phrase is the title of a chapter in Duccio Balestracci, *La zappa e la retorica: Memorie familiari di un contadino toscano del Quattrocento* (Florence, 1984); see also idem, *Cilastro che sapeva leggere: Alfabetizzazione e istruzione nelle campagne toscane alla fine del Medioevo (XIV–XVI secolo)* (Pisa, 2004). For the diffusion of accountancy and business techniques among local merchants in the Florentine countryside, see Charles Marie de La Roncière, *Firenze e le sue campagne nel Trecento: Mercanti, produzione, traffici* (Florence, 2005), 247–50, 269–78. See also Cristiane Klapisch-Zuber, "Le chiavi fiorentine di Barbablù: L'apprendimento della lettura a Firenze nel XV secolo," *Quaderni storici* 57 (1984): 765–92; A. Petrucci and L. Miglio, "Alfabetazzazione e organizzazione scolastica nella Toscana del XIV secolo," in *La Toscana nel secolo XIV: Caratteri di una civiltà regionale,* ed. Sergio Gensini (Pisa, 1988), 465–84; and Ronald Witt, "What Did Giovannino Read and Write? Literacy in Early Renaissance Florence," *I Tatti Studies* 6 (1995): 83–114.

[12] The relevant statistics are a population of 100,000; a sex ratio slightly in favor of males; the age pyramid in 1427 constructed by David Herlihy and Christiane Klapisch-Zuber (*Les toscans et leurs familles: Une étude du catasto florentin de 1427* [Paris, 1978], 370–84); an age of about 11 to 14 for the boys in these schools; and a duration of less than a year for the course of study.

[13] Armando Verde, *Lo studio fiorentino, 1473–1503: Ricerche e documenti* (Pistoia, 1977), 3:1005–1202.

tribunal of the Mercanzia record that these men, when summoned to court, hauled their books before the judges to make their case. Only by recourse to written records of this kind could artisans have submitted long lists of debtors and creditors on their 1427 catasto returns. Indeed, their extant account books constitute an impressive archival patrimony that is unique in all of Europe for the documentation of the economic life of workingmen. Account books dating from before 1400 survive for a painter, a seller of wine, a dealer in kitchenware, and a maker of combs for the wool industry, while for nearby Prato they exist for a mercer, a cloth dealer, a tailor, a hosteller, a waller, an apothecary, a butcher, a stationer, a grocer, and a cheese dealer.[14] For the fifteenth century there is hardly a major craft that cannot be documented by a practitioner's accounting record of one kind or another.

These documents testify to a mastery of all the accounting techniques that characterize the ledgers of the capitalist entrepreneur: articulated accounts; separation of debit and credit entries; division of entries into text at the left and figures in a column at the right; use of jargon;[15] cross reference for double entry; and the hierarchical organization of material into the complete array of account books one would find in a merchant's office, from the cashbook, various journals, and the record book to the ledger, each successive series identified in the same standard way by the color of the cover and a letter indicating the place in the series. When the grandsons of the painter and sculptor Antonio del Pollaiuolo found themselves called before the tribunal of the Mercanzia in a dispute over his inheritance, they presented as evidence for their case an archive of no fewer than twelve account books for four different partnerships the artist had had with two other goldsmiths over the years—three journals, three income-and-expenditure books, and six ledgers, including a *libro segreto*.[16] The ledgers of these men were recognized as legal documents, providing the written record an artisan needed to be assured of the inviolability of the various contracts he entered into during the course of a day's work. Unseen in these ledgers, but looming over all the relatively petty activities they record, is the larger institutional structure that ultimately regulated the marketplace for artisans and shopkeepers, just as it did for merchant-bankers and textile manufacturers. The system of justice clearly instilled into the modest operator that confidence about economic relations with others that underpins the capitalist system.

---

[14] The most comprehensive study of these books is Richard K. Marshall, *The Local Merchants of Prato: Small Entrepreneurs in the Late Medieval Economy* (Baltimore, 1999).

[15] For example, *de' dare* and *de' avere*, *portò* and *recò*, *posto in questo a*, *come apare a*, *a dì detto*, *monta in tutto*, *per lui a*, *per lui da*, *per una sua ragione*, *infrascritto*, *contrascritto*.

[16] Doris Carl, "Zur Goldschmiedefamilie Dei, mit neuen Dokumenten zu Antonio Pollaiuolo und Andrea Verrocchio," *Mitteilungen des kunsthistorischen Institutes in Florenz* 26 (1982): 165–66.

Indicative of how deeply this culture penetrated into society are the payment instructions that a brickmaker wrote out and sent along with the carrier who delivered four different loads of bricks to a client in the city in 1473. What the brickmaker, Papi del Compagno, wrote were, in effect, orders of payment that have all the characteristics of a check one might have written on a bank account: small slips of paper of the same size, the client's name on one side and the order itself on the other presented in the standard format, with the date centered at the top and Papi's signature at the bottom right, written out using the accountant's jargon—"give to the bearer," "post to my account"—and stating the charge in a money of account, not as so many coins. Notwithstanding his crude handwriting and the diverse spelling of his own name, Papi, out in the countryside, had clearly gone through some kind of educational program that gave him the tools he needed, although we do not know whether he, in fact, kept accounts for the operation of his kiln in Signa. His four orders of payment survive thanks to the client, who tucked them into his ledger at the page where an account was opened in Papi's name. They are eloquent testimony to the preparation even modest artisans had for dealing in the marketplace.[17]

Accountancy was more than just a technical instrument in the hands of the artisan that allowed him to clarify the organization of his affairs: it transported him to the world of credit and provided him with all the rules that were needed to play the game of shifting debits and credits through various other players simply by a stroke of the pen. He could offset credits and debits on his books, and he could effect such offsetting on the books of others through transfers from one party to another, sometimes via written orders, such as those Papi sent his client. Monetary exchange thus became a matter of book entry. And in this process it conditioned men such as the brickmaker Papi di Compagno to think about money, the most basic of economic tools for dealing in the marketplace, as a pure abstraction. The actual coins that passed from hand to hand in the marketplace—quattrini, soldini, grossi, grossoni—are rarely mentioned in the written record of their transactions, whether their own or that of capitalist clients. Instead, workingmen fixed the prices of their products and of their labor, in effect placing a value on their own human capital, in terms of a ghost money, as Carlo Cipolla called moneys of account. Most prices and wages in the local market came to be stated, not in so many coins of any specific kind, but as so many denari or soldi or lire—the principal money of account used in the local market—even though these denominations had no exact equivalent in coins.

---

[17] Goldthwaite, *Building of Renaissance Florence,* 310–13, where the orders are reproduced along with Papi's account in his client's ledger.

Ordinary Florentines, in short, thought in terms of this money of account, and this made it easier for them to accept book transfers in lieu of payment in coin. All this transported the workingman into the world of credit. In the next chapter we shall see how well prepared he was to handle himself there.

THE ARTISAN AS ENTREPRENEUR   Relatively unbound by corporate ties and protected by the legal system, workers plied their trade subject more to market forces than to guild constraints. Their relations to the market varied. Some, like those working in the food and clothing sectors, produced goods for direct sale in the market; some, like painters and woodworkers, worked on commission; some, like construction workers, sold their labor or services; and some, like those in the textile industry, worked in the constricted market defined by capitalist producers. Whatever his orientation, the worker had a certain freedom to maneuver on his own. "With pen in hand" he was well prepared to enter into the web of debit-credit relations that a monetized market generates. There is plenty of evidence, moreover, that many of these men, in trying to make their way in the market, demonstrated a certain entrepreneurial energy informed by the ways of the capitalist who dominated the economy—what we might call the spirit of capitalism.

Inside his shop the artisan organized the labor force he had at his disposal according to what the market permitted, not what a guild prescribed. In contrast to the situation in many other towns, in Florence he could take on apprentices without committing himself to a long, precise program of training on the job that also required him to accept the youth into his own household. What emerges from the fourteenth-century statutes of some of the Florentine guilds is an image of apprenticeship that conforms to the medieval stereotype, of the kind that the painter Cennino Cennini perhaps had in mind when, in his shop manual written about 1390, he prescribed a long training program, noting that his apprenticeship with Agnolo Gaddi had lasted twelve years. In the fifteenth century, however, the system loosened up, to judge from the record book of another painter, Neri di Bicci, kept from 1453 to 1475. This book records the coming and going of more than twenty employees in as many years; many left the shop before the end of the term fixed by their employment contract. Some of the city's painters who today enjoy a certain fame remained "giovani" for years, working for different "masters" and never opening a shop of their own.

In the workshops of the silk weaver Iacopo di Tedesco, documented for almost half a century, from 1490 to 1538, and of the goldsmith Zanobi di Lorenzo Cambi, documented for the following forty years, from 1532 to 1572, contracts for the numerous youths whom these men employed had hardly any uniformity:

the period of employment was from one to four years; entry-level salaries differed; raises did not follow any pattern and were unrelated to seniority; absences were frequent and fully anticipated; and fluidity in their ranks was considerable, with many leaving long before the termination of their contracts and few renewing their contracts. During the nine years of one of Iacopo's partnerships, from 1504 to 1513, there were sixty-three youths on the payroll; of these, only twelve worked four or more years, and just one worked for the whole period, while thirty-five worked less than a year, some for only a few weeks. Workers showed up in the morning, left at the end of the day, and collected their wages on Saturday. Contracts for the employment of youths often obligated the employer to training on the job, but otherwise they were simple, unnotarized hiring agreements with nothing of the paternal arrangements associated with apprenticeship in the medieval guild. Neither the weaver Iacopo di Tedesco nor the goldsmith Cambi received his employees into his home. By the fifteenth century the guilds had withdrawn from any attempt to control the labor market in the traditional way, leaving laborers floating around in a pool that the employer could dip into at will; and employment contracts between the two were based on the cash nexus.[18]

Many artisans at all levels went into business by forming partnerships, or *compagnie*, their objective being to expand the potential of their business and to find some kind of protection from the perils of the market by joining forces with fellow workers. There was hardly an occupation for which such partnerships did not exist, whether craftsman or shopkeeper. Artisans who entered into partnerships ranged from the modest makers of combs for the processing of wool mentioned in the preceding chapter, whose enterprise is documented by a *libricciuolo* of accounts from 1372 to 1378, to the three teachers who in 1370 pooled their intellectual property to run an abacus school.[19] These men entered into arrangements that had all the characteristics of the firms of international merchant-bankers and of wool and silk producers: a written contract, limited duration of usually three to five years, capital often divided into complex shares, and an accounting system. They too presented themselves to the public as a formal collective entity identified by their names followed by *e compagni* even when there were no partners other than those mentioned in the name of the firm; for example, Iacopo di

[18] Neri di Bicci's shop is described in Anabel Thomas, *The Painter's Practice in Renaissance Tuscany* (Cambridge, 1995), esp. ch. 3; Iacopo di Tedesco's in Goldthwaite, "Entrepreneurial Silk Weaver," 90–99; and Zanobi Cambi's in Rita Maria Comanducci, "Fattori e garzoni al lavoro nelle botteghe d'arte," in *La grande storia dell'artigianato*, vol. 3, *Il Cinquecento*, ed. Franco Franceschi and Gloria Fossi (Florence, 2000), 41–55.

[19] Elisabetta Ulivi, "Per una biografia di Antonio Mazzinghi, maestro d'abaco del XIV secolo," *Bottettino di storia delle scienze matematiche* 16 (1996): 117–19.

Tedesco, Pasquino dell'Incaglia & Partners, silk weavers, had only the two named partners. And they did all this without recourse to a notary.

Artisans demonstrated considerable ability at using the partnership as a malleable instrument that provided flexibility in the conduct of their business and opened up possibilities for expansion. They were ready to change partners with successive company reorganizations: of the ten partnerships Iacopo di Tedesco organized from 1490 to 1537, five were with one other silk weaver and five with three; and only three of the eleven different partners he had over the period show up a second time, and only one of these a third time.[20] During some of this time, moreover, Iacopo was also working on his own, outside his firm. Likewise for painters, being a partner did not preclude accepting commissions on their own. Some partnerships, however, severely restricted autonomous activities by a partner. Sometimes two or more artisans, each with his own shop, went into partnership to execute a specific joint project. In 1427 the painter Pesello, besides operating his own shop, was a partner with two others in a firm that had its own shop, and in 1431 this firm joined with another, also with three partners, that likewise had its own shop.[21] The brickmaker Benedetto da Terrarossa, active in the second quarter of the fifteenth century, expanded his business through a holding-company arrangement exactly like that found in the partnership agglomerates of international merchant-bankers. He owned a three-eighths share in his firm, Benedetto da Terrarossa & Partners, and a two-thirds share in the kiln that the firm rented for its operations. The firm itself, as a collective entity, became a partner for a 17.5 percent share in a second firm of brickmakers along with three persons, two of whom were also associated with da Terrarossa in the parent firm of da Terrarossa & Partners.[22] The three da Maiano brothers, working along with their sons in a fraterna and then in a formal partnership, at one time operated three shops for the working of stone and wood. They had something like their own sales agent abroad in the person of their brother Giuliano, who on his travels about Italy working as an architect obtained commissions for both wood and stone products from the family shop at home. In contrast to the da Maiano brothers, the Rossellino brothers and Desiderio da Settignano and his brothers divided their patrimonies and operated separate shops.[23] In short, artisans had innumerable possibilities for joining with others in order to make their way in the marketplace.

[20] Goldthwaite, "Entrepreneurial Silk Weaver," 77.

[21] Ugo Procacci, "Di Iacopo di Antonio e delle compagnie di pittori del Corso degli Adimari nel XV secolo," *Rivista d'arte* 35 (1960): 18–23; this article describes some of the complex partnership arrangements made among painters in the fifteenth century.

[22] Goldthwaite, *Building of Renaissance Florence*, 192–94.

[23] Margaret Haines, "Giuliano da Maiano capofamiglia e imprenditore," in *Giuliano e la bottega dei da Maiano*, ed. D. Lamberini, M. Lotti, and R. Lunardi (Florence, 1994), 131–42; Doris Carl, *Benedetto da Maiano: A Florentine Sculptor at the Threshold of the High Renaissance* (Turnhout, 2006), 25–35.

The need for investment capital was a primary reason for going into partnership. One partner might put up the entire capital and the other only his services, or persona, which was capitalized for purposes of defining the latter's share of the profits. Sometimes what the investor committed as his share of the capital was not cash but equipment, stock, or some other form of fixed capital, such as the two mules a hosteller contracted out to a carrier in 1465 or the shop one perfumer consigned to another in 1563.[24] Some set up their firms with capital from outside investors raised through the limited-liability accomandita. More than one-third of the extant contracts of this kind registered from 1450 to 1530 were executed for men such as tanners, smiths, soapmakers, brickmakers, mercers, speziali, and secondhand dealers. In the fifteenth century the capital required by most craftsmen to open a shop probably was not more than several hundred lire, the amount a skilled worker could hope to earn in a year or two of work or to receive from his wife's dowry. Artisan firms rarely needed investment capital for plant and equipment, since the former could be rented, perhaps from one of the partners, and the latter could be supplied by the partners themselves, perhaps as their contribution to the capital. Most needed only a space to work; and judging from the 1427 catasto, virtually all (96.7%) were renters, not owners, of their shops. Just over half of these paid no more than sixty lire in rent.[25] They may have had to put up capital, however, to buy what was called *entratura,* the sellable right to a rental contract for a shop but separate from the rent, guaranteeing the tenant use of the place for a given period or in perpetuity.[26]

In any event, the capital outlay for tools and equipment was not beyond the reach of the vast majority of these men. Probably no piece of equipment cost more than a loom for weaving the most complex kind of silk fabric, the most expensive of these, costing about two hundred lire, amounted to less than what a weaver could hope to earn in a year. Looms for weaving wool, the basic equipment of the city's leading industry, cost much less, and it will be recalled that indebtedness of weavers to their employers for the looms they worked was not a characteristic of the industry in Florence as it was in northern Europe (although many instances can be found). Finally, for circulating capital to build up stock and to provide liquidity for meeting daily operating expenses, they had recourse to the same instruments that the city's wealthier investors used, that is, advances

[24] Bruno Dini, "L'economia fiorentina dal 1450 al 1530," in *Saggi su una economia-mondo: Firenze e l'Italia fra Mediterraneo ed Europa (secc. XIII–XVI)* (Pisa, 1995), 209–10: Gino Corti, "Le accomandite fiorentine nel XV e XVI secolo" (Tesi di laurea, Facoltà di economia e commercio dell'Università degli Studi di Firenze, 1937).
[25] Maria Letizia Grossi, "Le botteghe fiorentine nel catasto del 1427," *Ricerche storiche* 30 (2000): 39.
[26] *Legislazione toscana raccolta e illustrata dal dottore Lorenzo Cantini socio di varie accademie,* 32 vols. (Florence, 1802–8), 1:168–69; Florence Edler, *Glossary of Mediaeval Terms of Business: Italian Series, 1200–1600* (Cambridge, MA, 1934), 112; Procacci, "Di Iacopo di Antonio," 18.

on contracted work, delayed payment, overdraft, book transfers, not to mention payment in kind and barter. These instruments were generally available to anyone "with pen in hand," as we shall see in chapter 6 (where a major theme, in fact, is the wide use of these instruments throughout the economy, and where a particular effort is made to use illustrative material drawn from the working class).

The partnerships with the largest capital investment, sometimes reaching several hundred florins, were those of craftsmen who had special requirements for expensive stock or high labor input—a speziale's shop, a dye house, a furnace for making glassware, a brick kiln, a quarry, a mill, a foundry. In the 1457 catasto one maker of glassware *(bicchieraio)* declared an investment of *fl.*100 in a firm with two other partners, and in the 1480 catasto another reported an investment of *fl.*230 in a firm with one partner. In 1427 another maker of glassware, Prospero di Goro, then residing in Pisa though filing his declaration in Florence, reported an investment of *fl.*340 in a firm with a fellow craftsman in Florence, in addition to investments worth *fl.*800 in Pisa that included another firm producing glassware.[27] The capital investment of tools and equipment in the firms the silk weaver Iacopo di Tedesco had with two other weavers, which may have been among the largest in the city, amounted to £7,863 in 1514 and £4,335 in 1522; and his firms paid out as much as £3,000 to £4,000 a year in shop expenses and salaries, putting him at the level of a small wool-producing firm. Patricians too went into formal partnership with artisans for the operation of a facility they owned, such as a mill or a kiln, and occasionally invested directly in an artisan enterprise. In 1429 Carlo di Marco degli Strozzi entered into an accomandita contract with Bartolomeo di Bernardo Benzi, a glassworker, to make drinking glasses for five years. Strozzi invested *fl.*300 and made a house available for the kiln; Benzi provided all the equipment and tools, valued at *fl.*100, and was to pay all expenses; and at the termination of the contract each was to get back his investment (Strozzi being guaranteed on this score) plus half the balance. In 1490 Francesco di Antonio Antinori made a collective three-year contract with no fewer than twenty-three potters in Montelupo for the marketing of their entire production.[28]

The artisan, in short, did not lack a certain space within the market where he could operate as an entrepreneur, and the spirit that drove his enterprise was informed by a sophisticated economic culture. He had the technical education to

[27] These and other catasto documents are published in Guido Taddei, *L'arte del vetro in Firenze e nel suo dominio* (Florence, 1954).

[28] Marja Mendera, "I centri di produzione in Toscana," in *Il vetro in Toscana: Struttura prodotti immagine (secc. XIII–XX)*, by S. Ciappi, A. Lugli, M. Mendera, and D. Stiaffini (Poggibonsi, 1995), 34 (glassworks); Galezzo Cora, *Storia della maiolica di Firenze e del contado, secoli XIV–XV* (Florence, 1973), 422–23 (Antinori).

deal with many of the problems he confronted in the marketplace: he could write, do calculations, play the game of balancing debits and credits, and organize his affairs according to the contemporary standards of business practice. Moreover, he could make his way through the market relatively free from guild and government interference and reasonably assured of the validity of contracts and the objectivity of the law even in his relations with the men of the ruling class. The full rein he could give to his creative imagination as an economic operator in this environment is manifest in the many products some of these men put on the market that we still admire today for their beauty and craftsmanship.

Workers on the Margins of the Market

A not insignificant portion of the city's work force could be found on the margins of the marketplace. They ranged from simple manual laborers who for lack of skills and collective organization had little or no bargaining power to the many residents of religious houses, some with considerable skills, who produced for the market behind the protective walls of their communities. This marginal work force consisted of women and children as well as men. Because the earnings of most of these people put them at the low end of the market, the total monetary value of the product of their labor was probably not very high. But their labor was essential, whether it was the hard work manual laborers contributed to get many jobs done throughout the city or the delicate tasks women performed in the production process of the textile industries, the leading sector of the economy. To appreciate the economic importance of this marginalized labor and the degree of its marginalization is to recognize the limits to the full development of the market and, by the same token, to raise questions about the extent to which the economy was a capitalist one.

DAY LABORERS   Most skilled laborers, including those in the textile industries, worked for piece rates and were paid for finished work; many worked on their own, in shops or at home, beyond the direct supervision of their employers. On the whole, day laborers, who worked for a daily wage, probably did not constitute a large segment of the labor force. They undoubtedly were to be found doing odd jobs requiring only muscle power for artisans and shopkeepers in all sectors of the economy, but since much of their employment was occasional, they rarely have enough presence in the documents to be noted. Construction was the one industry that employed a mass of day laborers, both skilled and unskilled, although for some construction workers too it was the task, not the time, that served as the basis for their compensation—so much cubic volume for the digger of foundations, so much square area of wall for the bricklayer or stonemason, so many finished columns, capitals, corbels, or other decorative elements for the stonecutter. Because construction work in Florence, like that in most late medieval towns, is so well documented, we are best informed about day laborers in this industry. The terms of employment were those found in the industry just about everywhere in Europe at the time. Already by the fourteenth century Florentine workers were thoroughly acclimated to the market. The basis of their relation to employers was the cash nexus, with little else thrown into the bargain. They worked an average of about five days a week (having Sundays and many other official religious holidays off), with less work and lower wages in the winter, and they collected their wages in cash on Saturdays. The length of the workday is not well documented, but it is presumed that it extended to ten to twelve hours. Since the conditions of their employment were not embedded in a system of social relations dominated by any kind of paternalism on the part of the employer, they had no safety net of social welfare. Whether they showed up for work or not depended more on their volition or economic necessity than on anything else; in fact, in Florence as just about everywhere else in Europe at the time, nothing characterizes the employment roster of a construction project more than the fluidity in this labor force. Construction work required hard labor, and availability of work was subject to seasonality of activity and to the vicissitudes of the builder's finances. Otherwise the basic terms of employment in this industry obtained for day laborers in other sectors as well.[29]

Although the construction worker's contract was based on the cash nexus, he was in some sense marginalized in the market. The market functioned imperfectly at his expense, for the going wage seems not to have been determined by a simple supply-and-demand mechanism. In Florence, as elsewhere in Europe through the entire period for which wages are documented down to the industrial revolution, wages were sticky, lagging behind prices, presumably held back by traditional notions of what constituted the just price of labor and generally not responsive to temporary rises in demand or temporary shortages of supply or to slow inflation of prices. The one moment when wages did respond immediately to a sudden change in supply was in 1348, at the time of the Black Death. The plague struck suddenly and hard in the spring, and the effect on the labor market must have been dramatic. It did not last long, reaching its climax in June and July, and by September the economy was back in full swing. But the demand for labor

---

[29] For the wool industry, see Bruno Dini, "I lavoratori dell'arte della lana a Firenze nel XIV e XV secolo," in *Artigiani e salariati: Il mondo del lavoro nell'Italia dei secoli XII–XV* (Pistoia, 1984), esp. 32–53, reprinted in his *Manifattura, commercio e banca nella Firenze medievale* (Florence, 2001); and Franceschi, *Oltre il "Tumulto,"* 212–13.

now was confronted with such radically reduced supply that wages shot up immediately. For the unskilled laborer the daily rate doubled, fluctuating between 8 and 9 soldi di piccioli. It remained absolutely stable within the range of 8 to 10 soldi until the 1530s, when it began a rise that continued steadily to about 20 soldi, or 1 lira, at the end of the century, stabilizing once again for the following century. In other words, the nominal wage rate, after doubling within a few months, remained stable for almost two centuries and then doubled again over the last three-quarters of the sixteenth century. The daily wage rates paid to skilled construction workers were, of course, higher, varying according to skill but hardly ever, even for a project foreman, more than twice the rates paid to unskilled workers. This 2:1 ratio remained fixed during the entire period covered in this volume, as indeed it did throughout most of Europe at the time.

Unfortunately, we do not have comparably thorough price studies to evaluate real wages, that is, the purchasing power of the nominal wage in the local market. Data have been assembled for the period from the second half of the fourteenth century to the end of the sixteenth, although as one goes forward during this period they thin out considerably with respect to both frequency and the number of items in the basket of consumables documented. Good series have been assembled for wheat prices alone but hardly provide an ideal index, since they fluctuated much more erratically than other foodstuffs, and such fluctuations upward, coming suddenly and radically as a result of shortages, could have disastrous consequences for the poor in particular. In the long run, however, the other prices that have been collected conform to wheat prices, and taken together these data suggest certain trends. Figure 5.1 plots, on an index scale, the wage of an unskilled worker based on the wheat it could purchase, in other words, something approximating his real wage. This wage also shot up in 1348, although somewhat less than the nominal wage, because prices rose as well. The trend, based on eleven-year averages, which iron out fluctuations, thereby hiding disastrous drops, was as follows: high in the later fourteenth century; a rise of close to 50 percent toward 1400, continuing on to reach a high in the period 1420–60, when the wage was about double what it had been after 1348; then a steady fall, followed after the 1520s by a rapid decline until toward the end of the century it was where it had been before 1348 (and during this latter period the annual wage frequently fell below that level). In other words, the unskilled manual laborer found himself much better off in the second half of the fourteenth century than he had been before 1348 and still even better off in the early fifteenth century, but after about 1460 his situation began a steady decline, reaching the point where he was no better off than he had been before 1348. The real wages of skilled construction workers followed the same trend, but at a level that rarely exceeded the ratio of two to one.

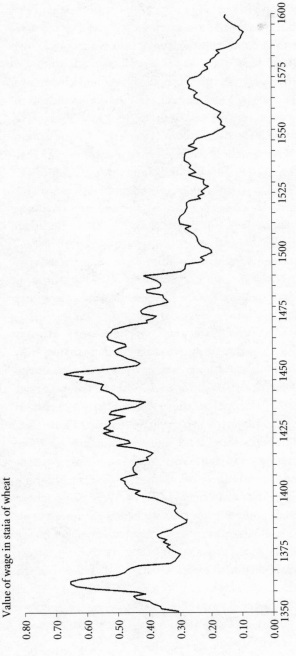

Value of wage in staia of wheat

Figure 5.1 The real value of an unskilled construction worker's daily wage, 1350–1600, expressed in the staia of wheat he could buy with it (11-year moving average)

Sources: The data base of wheat prices is principally that in Richard A. Goldthwaite, "I prezzi del grano a Firenze dal XIV al XVI secolo," reprinted in *Banks, Palaces and Entrepreneurs in Renaissance Florence* (Aldershot, 1995), appendices (1354–1567). To this have been added data from Sergio Tognetti, "Prezzi e salari nella Firenze tardomedievale: Un profilo," *ASI* 53 (1995): 317–18 (1336–1414); Biblioteca Riccardiana, Florence, 2312, fols. 234–35 (1522–84); and Giuseppe Parenti, *Prime ricerche sulla rivoluzione dei prezzi a Firenze* (Florence, 1939), app. 1 (1567–1600). The wage data are from Richard A. Goldthwaite, *The Building of Renaissance Florence: An Economic and Social History* (Baltimore, 1980), app. 3.

Note: A staio was equal to 24.7 liters or about 0.7 bushel.

We shall consider the validity of this wage of the unskilled construction worker as a general index of poverty in chapter 7. The concern here is with the behavior of the nominal wage and its lag behind prices, most strikingly in the sixteenth century, a situation certainly not unique to Florence. The phenomenon raises fundamental questions about how the labor market functioned: why the long inertia, and why the lag? As far as we know, there were no effective wage controls, but there must have been a fixed notion about what constituted a day's wage, a cultural norm subject to the inertia characteristic of a preindustrial economy. The norm was broken in 1348 because of the drama of the situation: a sharp fall in the supply of labor while demand remained high. This situation, however, was unique in the entire period covered by this survey. No event after that had such an observable effect on the demand-supply mechanism of the market. In an economy with relatively few day laborers, scattered about in different workplaces, a labor crisis was not likely to occur. Demand, moreover, was highly fragmented and notoriously soft. In such a labor market the unskilled laborer had no skills to give him any bargaining power, while the skilled construction worker was locked into an occupation with no possibility of technological or organizational improvement in his productivity or of refinement of his skill; and neither had the kind of organization to provide a collective voice for bargaining.

Another dynamic that has to be factored into the labor contract at the time is flexibility with respect to work and leisure. As we have had more than one occasion to observe in these pages, nothing better characterizes a work force of any kind, whether day laborers at a construction site or weavers working at piece rates at home, than fluidity in its ranks. All rosters of employees that have been studied reveal their coming and going and the lack of a work discipline, not to say a work ethos. This instability in some sectors was built into the putting-out system, dominated as it was by the employer, who wanted flexibility as much as he sought to avoid the direct supervision of work. However, study of the construction site of the Strozzi palace, begun in 1489, shows that even when workers had the chance to work full time, because the employer wanted to see the job finished and had no problem in financing the project, workers were casual about showing up on the job with any regularity.[30] As has often been observed, preindustrial economies were not yet driven by consumerism and offered few outlets for modest savings, so the day laborer, after providing for his basic needs, may have desired nothing more than time off from hard work. The margins within which he had the flexibility

---

[30] Richard A. Goldthwaite, "The Building of the Strozzi Palace: The Construction Industry in Renaissance Florence," *Studies in Medieval and Renaissance History* 10 (1973): 173–77.

to do this depended on his earning power, and this obviously contracted from the later fifteenth century on.

In short, there were no dynamics from the supply side of the labor market strong enough to break the inertia of the nominal wage for the two centuries following the Black Death, and we know nothing about the process, or mechanism, that finally broke this inertia and slowly increased the nominal wage, step by step, to the point that it doubled over the last three-quarters of the sixteenth century. We assume that it was pressure from below, impelled by greater need in view of the rise in prices during the so-called price revolution. But we know nothing about how the cultural norm fixing a traditional wage was modified by a rise in prices that, despite its "revolutionary" nature, was almost imperceptible, hardly exceeding, on the average, 1 percent a year. We have, alas, no documentation for a bargaining process.[31]

In any event, day laborers were marginal workers with respect both to their small numbers and to the functioning of what is considered a normal market process.

CLOISTERED WORKERS   The monasteries and convents of Florence housed communities of men and women who, notwithstanding their seclusion, contributed much to both the economic and the religious life of the city. In 1427 there were about forty-four such houses in Florence and thirty-three more in the immediate environs, some with only a few residents and some with very many; their total population approached fifteen hundred men and women, equivalent to about 8 percent of the total adult population recorded in the catasto, in which they were not included. These communities, especially those with women, grew over the next century. Some of these establishments were well endowed, others not; and their additional income from the religious services performed by their members for the public depended much on their size. Most, however, had grown to the point that they could not survive from these resources alone. Inasmuch as work of some kind was central to the disciplined life the orders imposed on their communities, and inasmuch as most of them

---

[31] For a recent statement about wage stickiness in the expanding economies of Holland and England before the industrial revolution, see John Munro, "Builders' Wages in Southern England and the Southern Low Countries, 1346–1500: A Comparative Study of Trends in and Levels of Real Incomes," in *L'edilizia prima della rivoluzione industriale, secc. XIII–XVIII*, ed. Simonetta Cavaciocchi (Florence, [2005]), 1013–76. On the role of custom in determining such behavior, see Donald Woodward, *Men at Work: Labourers and Building Craftsmen in the Towns of Northern England, 1450–1750* (Cambridge, 1995), 205–7. And a comprehensive overview of the problem of leisure preference on the part of the worker is offered by Peter Mathias, "Wages and Leisure in the Eighteenth Century," in *Domanda e consumi: Livelli e strutture (nei secoli XIII–XVIII)*, ed. V. Barbagli Bagnoli (Florence, 1978), 7–19.

had marginal endowments, it is hardly surprising that these communities channeled at least some of the productive energy of their members into an activity that would pay off in the local market, especially given their location in one of Europe's wealthiest cities. Unfortunately, despite an enormous amount of surviving archival material for the monasteries and convents of Florence, much of it consisting of account books, we have no economic study of any one of these institutions.

Women far outnumbered men in the total population of these communities. In 1427 there were 20 convents with about 1,000 women residents; in 1552 there were 47 with a total population of about 3,400.[32] The essential role of these women in the production of silk—reeling and unreeling threads and making metal threads—has already been remarked. Many of the other things nuns made that they sold in the consumer market were the products of what is considered traditional women's work, above all sewing, embroidery, and the related needle arts. These included the kinds of linens to be found in a home or in a bride's trousseau. The wife of Francesco Datini, the merchant of Prato, once wrote to him about the towels she had bought at one convent and tablecloths ordered to be made at another. Nuns and other women attached to convents have also been documented as making a large variety of completely different kinds of objects, some of luxury quality requiring highly developed skills. The convent of San Iacopo di Ripoli invested in a printing press that turned out thousands of books from 1476 to 1484; although a friar directed the enterprise, nuns did some of the compositing. The nuns at the Paradiso, where the community numbered 63 in 1509, did a little bit of everything: their ledgers for the mid-Quattrocento have accounts for earnings from sales of cloth, embroidery work (for whose patterns they paid a painter), passamaneria, gold threads, breviaries, and other books with devotional and moral content. Many of these items they sold directly to the public, but they also received prestigious commissions, including some from abroad, for embroidered liturgical vestments and furnishings. Likewise, the nuns at the convent of Santa Maria del Fiore (known as Lapo), who numbered from 25 to 30 in the fifteenth century, produced finely carded wool, ribbons, silk purses, linen sheets and undershirts, as well as devotional books for women; and they operated a school for teaching girls the needle arts. When the convent of Le Murate was rebuilt after a fire in 1471, it had ten cubicles in its scriptorium; at the end of the next century these numbered twenty-six. It is not known whether their manuscripts were produced on commission or directed to the market. In the later

[32] Richard C. Trexler, "Celibacy in the Renaissance: The Nuns of Florence," reprinted from *Annales: Économies, sociétés, civilisations* 27 (1972) in his *Dependence in Context in Renaissance Florence* (Binghamton, NY, 1994), 348–54.

fifteenth century the full range of objects produced at Le Murate—metallic threads, needlework, linens, sculptural pieces in gesso, liturgical and devotional books—generated an income of *fl.*500, not much per capita for the many women who lived there but equivalent to the profits of several wool firms. The largest and most prestigious of these houses, Le Murate was something of a tourist site for distinguished visitors to the city. In the later sixteenth century the community at St. Catherine of Siena, which included the painter Suor Plautilla Nelli (1523–88), produced, besides the usual needlework objects, paintings and sculptural works of devotional figures in papier-mâché and terra cotta. In 1586 the silk guild claimed that about three hundred pounds of artificial gold and silver threads were imported into the city every year from Bologna and consigned to convents, where nuns used them to make flowers, wreaths, and other such decorative objects.[33]

Convents, in short, were centers of production. Nuns were highly skilled in several crafts, and many convents set aside special workspaces for them. Many of the things they produced were sold in the local retail market, although there is no way to assess what share of that market their production had. In the silk industry, nuns played a major role in the phases of the production process that saw the preparation of threads for weaving. The income all their different kinds of work generated probably contributed only a small part to the total budget of even the most industrious of convents, but given the fragile economic foundations of most of these institutions, this extra income may have made survival possible. In fact, it has been argued that the growth of their endowments in the sixteenth century, rendering them more self-sufficient than they had been earlier, explains, at least in part, their withdrawal from productive activity directed to the market even as their total population grew, at midcentury reaching two to three times what it had been in 1427. Hence they were under less pressure to earn extra income and

---

[33] The only significant discussion of nuns as workers in the market is in Sharon Strocchia, *Nuns and Nunneries in Renaissance Florence* (Baltimore, forthcoming). In the meantime, see the comments in the following articles on women's work in convents: idem, "Learning the Virtues: Convent Schools and Female Culture in Renaissance Florence," in *Women's Education in Early Modern Europe: A History, 1500–1800,* ed. Barbara J. Whitehead (New York, 1999), 5–46; Melissa Conway, *The "Diario" of the Printing Press of San Jacopo di Ripoli, 1476–1484: Commentary and Transcription* (Florence, 1999); Catherine Turill, "The Nun-Artisans of Santa Caterina da Siena and Their Clients," in *The Art Market in Italy, 15th–17th Centuries,* ed. M. Fantoni, L. C. Matthew, and S. F. Matthews-Grieco (Modena, 2003), 95–103; K. J. P. Lowe, "Rainha D. Leonor of Portugal's Patronage in Renaissance Florence and Cultural Exchange," in *Cultural Links between Portugal and Italy in the Renaissance,* ed. Lowe (Oxford, 2000), 228, 244–45; idem, "Women's Work at the Benedictine Convent of Le Murate in Florence: Suora Battista Carducci's Roman Missal of 1509," in *Women and the Book: Assessing the Visual Evidence,* ed. J. Taylor and L. Smith (London, 1997), 133–46; idem, *Nuns' Chronicles and Convent Culture in Renaissance and Counter-Reformation Italy* (Cambridge, 2003); Maria Cristina Improta and Anna Padoa Rizzo, "Paolo Schiavo fornitore di disegni per ricami," *Rivista d'arte* 41 (1989), esp. 45–54 (on Il Paradiso). The reference to the importation of artificial gold and silver comes from Luca Molà, "Artigiani e brevetti nella Firenze del Cinquecento," in Franceschi and Fossi, *La grande storia dell'artigianato,* 3:63.

had the time for pursuits more in line with their calling—in the spirit of the Council of Trent, which sought to recall nuns to their vow of poverty and to discourage work directed to production for the market.

Residents of monasteries also produced for the market, although there were fewer of them. The Umiliati friars, who established something like wool-producing factories throughout northern Italy in the early thirteenth century, came to Florence in 1239 and set up a large operation on the Arno, in the area where the church of Ognissanti is today. They did washing, spinning, weaving, and fulling. Some forty years later, in 1277, they leased out the riverside property where much of this work was done and closed down production to retire into a more traditional monastic life. Other than this episode of the Umiliati, none of the city's male religious communities had strong ties to the textile industries. They produced any number of other things, however, including illuminated manuscripts, a characteristic luxury product turned out by monasteries everywhere in medieval Europe. In the early fifteenth century the Camaldolesi, at Santa Maria degli Angeli, enjoyed international fame for their richly illustrated editions of humanist texts. In the second half of the fifteenth century the residents at the house of the lay confraternity of the Gesuati at San Giusto made window glass for many churches and produced pigments, which they sold to painters. Those at the monastery of the Paradiso sold lenses to local makers of eyeglasses. Notable also is the number of Florentine Renaissance painters who had taken religious orders, such as the Camaldolese Lorenzo Monaco, the Carmelite fra Filippo Lippi, and the Dominicans fra Angelico and fra Bartolomeo. Although they were members of religious communities, these painters accepted commissions from private persons, and some operated their own shops outside the monastery without renouncing their orders. At the end of the sixteenth century fra Domenico Portigiani (d. 1602) operated a full-scale foundry at the Dominican house of San Marco. Although not a sculptor, he commissioned artists for wax models of decorative details on the pieces he cast. He did all the casting for major pieces of bronze sculpture, including the doors of the cathedral at Pisa and the bronzework in the Salviati chapel.[34]

WOMEN   We know as little about workingwomen outside convents as we do about those inside.[35] It is generally thought that their place in the work force de-

---

[34] Avraham Ronen, "Portigiani's Bronze 'Ornamento' in the Church of the Holy Sepulchre, Jerusalem," *Mitteilungen des kunsthistorischen Institutes in Florenz* 14 (1969–70), esp. 430–33.

[35] This void in the historiography is addressed by Isabelle Chabot, "La reconnaissance du travail des femmes dans la Florence du bas Moyen Âge: Contexte idéologique et réalité," in *La donna nell'economia, secc. XIII–XVIII*, ed. S. Cavaciocchi (Florence, 1990), 563–76, where the statistical data cited here are to be found, along with a bibliography.

clined from the thirteenth century on, but the evidence for workingwomen in the earlier period is slim. After the Black Death, when workers' real wages rose, women and children were particularly targeted for the alms distributed by Orsanmichele, the city's principal charitable organization. The 1427 catasto documents reveal few female workers of any kind. At that time most adult unmarried women without the support of a household either resided in convents or worked in private households as servants. Although servants, like cloistered nuns, escaped the reach of the 1427 catasto, it is likely that they numbered about twenty-five hundred. Many servants came from the countryside, and many were children. The notable characteristics of their employment in the fifteenth century are their low wages—twenty to forty lire annually[36]—and their short time on the job, most staying less than a year. Many private record books have entries for the employment of a servant, always on a year-long contract, with the added note, entered only a few weeks or months later, that she had left the job. The servant population increased beginning in the latter part of the century, and by 1552 one-sixth of the population (8,890 persons) was employed in this sector, with 47 percent of the city's households employing at least one servant. The great families had, on the average, many more than their ancestors had had in the early fifteenth century: no fewer than 140 households had six or more.[37] By this time, however, there had been a strong influx of men into the ranks of household servants.

Other than those in convents and in domestic service in private households, almost all women either were or had been married. In the 1427 catasto only 16 percent of households were headed by a woman, and 93 percent of these were widows, few of whom declared an occupation. Many of these married women worked in some kind of activity that impacted on the market, most of it indirectly by helping their husbands in their work or directly through the putting-out system. In either case, they worked hidden within the sanctity of the household, and hence the documents provide hardly any hint of what they were doing. The 1578 statutes of the Linaioli, in fact, remark that the many women working as tailors were not registered with the guild.[38] In Florence, as elsewhere, many were probably to be found working in service occupations, in food production, in retail shops, or in the needle arts. Very few women worked independently in their own shops outside the home. Only just over 1 percent of the shops used as workplaces reported in the 1427 catasto were run by women. To judge from guild records

[36] Their salaries were quoted in florins *di* £4 and ranged from *fl*.5 to *fl*.10.
[37] The figures come from Pietro Battara, *La popolazione di Firenze alla metà del '500* (Florence, 1935), 70. The estimate of 2,500 female servants in 1427 is based on the assumption that 25 percent of the nearly 10,000 households in the 1427 catasto employed at least one servant.
[38] *Legislazione toscana*, 9:62.

and, above all, from the massive number of private accounts where personal household expenditures of all kinds are recorded, women had virtually no presence in the ranks of the major categories of the city's artisans.

As we have seen, it was in the textile industries that women constituted a work force of major importance to the economy. In the wool industry they did all the spinning, some weaving, and little else. Spinning alone constituted about 20 percent of labor costs (not including dyeing), and inasmuch as they were paid at the lowest rates, spinners probably constituted an even higher percentage of the total labor force in the industry. These women worked secluded in the home, some doing wheel spinning in the city and some spinning on the distaff in the immediate countryside.[39] In the silk industry, between those inside and those outside convents women worked in every stage—spinning and reeling silk threads, winding metallic threads, working with throwsters, and weaving the less complicated fabrics. Moreover, the employment of women in both industries apparently increased toward the end of the sixteenth century; and after 1600, with the lowering of quality in both industries, women came to dominate weaving in the wool industry and all stages in the silk industry. If one is to believe that in the course of the sixteenth century nuns inside convents withdrew from market-directed production, this rising female labor force in the textile industries must have represented new employment opportunities for women outside convents. The increased employment of women in the textile industries at a time when population was growing raises the question where the men who had previously done this work were going. In any event, most of these women worked inside their homes to supplement the income of the household, and materials were brought to them through the putting-out system. Hence they too worked on the margins of the market.

CHILDREN   Child labor has been as little studied as female labor.[40] Undoubtedly many children went to work as their parents' helpers, both inside and outside the home. Some may have been put out as assistants and apprentices at about age seven. Most children of about this age, however, entered a reading-and-writing school, and many of these went on to study in an abacus school for about a year. Then, at the age of about eleven to thirteen, they went to work as apprentices, whether in the office of an international merchant-banking firm,

---

[39] For comparative data, see Federigo Melis, *Aspetti della vita economica medievale: Studi nell'Archivio Datini di Prato* (Siena, 1962), 561 (for 1396–99 and 1556–58); and Richard A. Goldthwaite, "The Florentine Wool Industry in the Late Sixteenth Century: A Case Study," *Journal of European Economic History* 32 (2003): 553 (for the 1580s).

[40] The problem is raised by Franco Franceschi, "Les enfants au travail dans la manufacture textile florentine du XIVe et XVe siècle," *Médiévales* 30 (1996): 69–82.

the shop of a lanaiolo or a setaiolo, or the workshop of an artisan. An artisan might have one or two boys working alongside him, a weaver one or two on every loom, a cloth producer or merchant-banker two or three on his staff of a half-dozen or so clerks and helpers. In other words, boys in their early teens or younger, both rich and poor, were to be found doing essential work in all sectors of the economy. And they must have constituted a massive labor force. According to statistics derived from the catasto documents in the fifteenth century, about 40 percent of the population was younger than 14, by which age many boys had been working for several years, and those between 14 and 19 constituted 10 percent of the total population of the city. Moreover, the sex ratio of male to female children of working age was high—123 for those aged 13–17, 117 for those aged 18–22.[41] Inasmuch as virtually all boys in their early teens, if not earlier, were thus in the labor market, to label this constituency of the work force "child" labor is to impose on the past a term loaded with our own prejudices. Indeed, the terms used in the documents to identify these employees— *discepolo, fattore, garzone, giovane, lavorante*—are imprecise and not age specific; only diminutives such as *fattorino* and *fanciulli,* which are found less frequently, hint at the youthfulness of the boy.

Apprenticeship is usually thought of as a transition in the life of a boy on his way out of the family to his eventual entrance into the labor market, a stage spent in on-the-job training in the family of a master craftsman. Given the weak corporate structure of guilds in Florence, however, this transitional stage introduced the boy much more abruptly to the realities of a labor market dominated by the cash nexus. Written contracts made by the aforementioned silk weaver Iacopo di Tedesco specified little more than the annual salary for the term of employment, which could vary from one to five years. Neither the virtually complete set of accounts for the operation of Iacopo di Tedesco's shop nor the record book of the shop of the painter Neri di Bicci yields any evidence that boys moved in with the family of their employer. Nor do we know what the father's responsibility for his son was during this period of transition. Those relatively few boys who started out working in an artisan's shop or a firm were usually assigned the cashbox, a particularly onerous responsibility, especially for a boy who might be only about eleven years of age. Andrea di Carlo Strozzi had an agreement with Lorenzo and Filippo di Filippo Strozzi & Partners, lanaioli, that his son Smeraldo, once out of the abacus school, would take over the firm's cashbox, and early in 1505 Smeraldo, just fifteen, went to work for this prestigious firm. When, a year later, a shortfall of *fl.*100 was discovered, Andrea agreed to make up for it in three annual

---

[41] Herlihy and Klapisch-Zuber, *Les toscans et leurs familles,* 333, 375.

installments. (In his own ledger he opened an account in Smeraldo's name and debited it for *fl.*100 against any future claims the boy might have against his father's estate.)[42] In the contract Tommaso di Bernardo Tossi made in 1584 for placing his son Cosimo as cashier with Martelli, Del Giocondo & Partners, setaioli, he agreed to reimburse the firm for any shortfalls in the cashbox and to make an interest-free deposit of *fl.*500 with the firm as security for his son's behavior.[43] Eventually, of course, fathers, including artisans, had recourse to the formal act of emancipation, by which they legally recognized their children as adults with full economic autonomy. This legal act brought about, finally, the transition to adulthood at the age of eighteen or older.

All the characteristics of the children who worked in the shop of Iacopo di Tedesco, discussed above—imprecise terminology; entry into the labor market at a very early age, perhaps as young as seven years; short-term contracts based on the cash nexus; employment as manual laborers, but at substandard wages and with no apprenticeship arrangement; separation of the workplace from the household of the employer; fluidity in the children's ranks; lack of discipline concerning attendance—confirm everything we know about the labor market in general. With virtually no fixed program imposed on their lives, and thrown into the market at an early age, these youths could become a public nuisance. They were free to roam the streets in bands and often engaged in violent behavior. This may explain the prominence in fifteenth-century Florence, more so than for any other city, of confraternities founded exclusively for children and adolescents, from all economic and social classes, in an attempt to socialize them.[44] Youth groups also figure prominently in the Savonarolan movement in the 1490s. In 1542 Cosimo I took direct action to deal with the problem of child vagabonds by imposing discipline on them through the Bigallo, one of the city's oldest charitable confraternities, which he appropriated to set up a magistracy for public welfare in general throughout the state. However, his successor, Francesco I, abandoned this project for children as being too complicated.[45]

The oldest and most prestigious of the city's orphanages, the Innocenti, was founded in 1419 with a program for taking care of abandoned children that in-

[42] ASF, Archivio Strozzi Sacrati, 524 (accounts and record book of Andrea di Carlo Strozzi, 1500–1510), fols. 158, 250, 257v.

[43] ASF, Archivio Martelli, 151 (journal and record book A of the firm, 1584–87), fol. 151.

[44] Ilaria Taddei, *Fanciulli e giovani: Crescere a Firenze nel Rinascimento* (Florence, 2001), 233–34, 287.

[45] Filippo Fineschi, "I 'Monellini' della Quarconia: Controllo pubblico e disciplinamento dei fanciulli in un istituto fiorentino del Seicento," in *Infanzie: Funzioni di un gruppo liminale dal mondo classico all'Età Moderna,* ed. Ottavia Niccoli (Florence, 1993), 252–86, reviews the literature on the earlier period; and Lorenzo Polizzotto, *Children of the Promise: The Confraternity of the Purification and the Socialization of Youths in Florence, 1427–1785* (Oxford, 2004), studies a specific boys' confraternity in the wider social context of these institutions.

cluded preparing them to enter the world on their own. It sent the boys out as apprentices, and presumably they eventually disappeared into the crowd. The girls, being "the weaker sex and more exposed to dangers," remained in the institution, some until their thirties, where they were put to work, probably doing spinning and reeling for the silk industry (the place being under the patronage of the silk guild) or needlework of one kind or another. By the mid-sixteenth century, when the number of wards in the Innocenti's care rose to about a thousand, it may have become a center of production of some consequence. There is evidence that residents engaged in carpentry, shoemaking, and weaving. The accounts open on its books to keep track of "the income of our women and girls," however, have yet to be analyzed. After a financial crisis in the late 1570s put it on the verge of bankruptcy, the Innocenti undertook a more direct utilization of its labor potential to earn badly needed income. It opened a workshop for the production of tapestries and rugs explicitly directed to competing with imports in the local market; and in an entrepreneurial spirit, its director experimented with the use of goat's hair rather than wool to reduce the cost of both raw materials and weaving.[46]

After the Innocenti opened its doors, orphans were taken in by other hospices, most being very small operations under the patronage of a confraternity or comparable organization. During Cosimo's reign the most significant effort to confront one of the problems presented by children in the streets was the opening of institutions that offered a comprehensive program for taking care of orphans and preparing them for work. The Ospedale degli Abbandonati opened its doors to boys in 1542, and by the 1550s it had over a hundred residents. It provided the boys a home, gave them the rudiments of an education, and, at the appropriate age, sent them into the marketplace as apprentices and helpers in the expectation that eventually they would be able to go off on their own. The Abbandonati was followed in the 1550s with the opening of three orphanages for girls—Santa Maria Vergine in 1552, the Conservatorio della Pietà in 1555, and San Niccolò in 1556, whose wards by the turn of the next decade numbered, respectively, 20, 80, and possibly 160. A fourth orphanage for girls, Santa Caterina, was opened in the 1590s. Unlike the boys at the Abbandonati, these girls were brought up in a completely cloistered environment. To ward off idleness, and to bring in income for

---

[46] Luciano Marcello, "Andare a bottega: Adolescenza e apprendistato nelle arti (sec. XVI–XVII)," in Niccoli, *Infanzie*, 244–46; Philip Gavitt, "An Experimental Culture: The Art of the Economy and Economy of Art under Cosimo I and Francesco I," in *The Cultural Politics of Duke Cosimo I de' Medici*, ed. Konrad Eisenbichler (Aldershot, 2001), 205–21; Maria Fubini Leuzzi, "Vincenzio Borghini spedalingo degli Innocenti: La nomina, il governo, la bancarotta," in *Fra lo "spedale" e il principe: Vincenzio Borghini, filologia e invenzione nella Firenze di Cosimo I* (Padua, 2005), 37–64 (quotation from 53–54).

the institution, they were put to work, some being sent out as domestic servants but most remaining within their cloistered community, usually doing something within the needle arts, such as spinning, making metallic threads, or weaving. The larger of these places have, in fact, been called factories. The staff included a salaried female superintendent, who might come in from the outside, to train the girls and direct their work. Specific rooms were set aside as workspaces, and the work could be highly specialized. Merchants usually dealt directly with the establishment for commissions and purchases, and they might seek to monopolize its production. The Pietà had by far the largest workshop and turned out the highest-quality products. Its girls were famed for their brocaded silks. Over a period of a dozen years, from 1566 to 1578, their work provided the institution with an income that averaged more than *fl.*750 annually, or 40–50 percent of its total income. In other words, the Pietà's gross earnings from this workshop were about two to three times the profits of a large wool shop.[47]

SLAVES   The most marginal of all workers were slaves. Florentine merchants, like their colleagues throughout the Mediterranean, dealt occasionally in slaves, but probably only a few, such as the Marchionni in Lisbon, had direct access to native populations along the African coast and handled them in any quantity. Spanish cities were the most important markets, though the number of slaves was not large. Many of these were males who entered the work force individually as the property of artisans and others, and they had certain legal rights. As a rule, they did not end up in gangs of laborers. The market in Italy was much smaller. Slaves began to appear in Florence in the course of the fourteenth century. A register of sales in 1366–68 lists 222, and 294 were recorded in 261 households documented in the 1427 catasto, almost all of them women. In the years 1474–76 the Cambini firm imported 27 female slaves from Lisbon, most of whom were sold in Florence itself. Florentines bought females for personal domestic service, not males to be put to work in any of the productive sectors of the economy. Slaves were considered private property and as such could be rented out and resold. Most of these women were eventually freed, often with a dowry on the occasion of marriage. The principal reason for this particular market for slaves seems to have been the prospect they offered of permanence on the household staff of their owners, a substitute for salaried servants, whose brevity on the job is so well documented in personal record books of the period. The number of slaves seems to have declined by the end of the fifteenth century, perhaps because employed

---

[47] Nicholas Terpstra, *Abandoned Children of the Italian Renaissance: Orphan Care in Florence and Bologna* (Baltimore, 2005), 125–30, 141–47, 231.

women became more reliable and hence the investment of *fl.*30–50 in a slave became less attractive.[48]

In the second half of the sixteenth century the slave population increased, but now they were all male, they all belonged to the grand duke, and they served an entirely different function. They were the victims of the religious clash between Christians and Muslims in the Mediterranean, most of them having been seized by the maritime knights of the ducal order of Santo Stefano in attacks on Muslim ships and in raids in North Africa. The grand dukes sold some of these slaves in the growing market outside of Tuscany for forced labor and traded others for ransom. Most of those they kept for themselves ended up working on the state galleys. Slaves were never employed in productive economic enterprises, although they do show up along with soldiers and peasants, both the dukes' own subjects, pressed into forced labor on corvées at numerous construction sites, especially those for the new fortifications undertaken throughout their new state at key places along the coastline, at points of entry into the duchy, and, as a symbol of authority, at many major towns. At Florence both slaves and forced labor were used at the Fortezza da Basso and the Medici villa at Pratolino, just outside the city.[49]

Performance of the Artisan Sector
Demand-Driven Growth

DEMAND   It was local, not foreign, demand that stimulated the growth, diversification, and specialization of the artisan sector during the fifteenth and sixteenth centuries. This demand was fed by the enormous wealth that accumulated in the city almost continually from the second half of the fourteenth century. And after the first third of the following century, with the falling off of the military costs of territorial expansion, the tax burden on private wealth lessened considerably (of which more in chapter 7). At the same time, the cultural climate changed in a way that released inhibitions people may have had about directing greater disposable wealth into consumption. The stabilization of the internal political scene, especially after Cosimo de' Medici's return from exile in 1434, confirmed once and for all the ruling elite's control of the complex republican structure

---

[48] The classic article on the subject is Iris Origo, "The Domestic Enemy: The Eastern Slaves in Tuscany in the Fourteenth and Fifteenth Centuries," *Speculum* 30 (1955): 321–66. For a more recent bibliography, see Monica Boni and Robert Delort, "Des esclaves toscans de milieu du XIVe au milieu du XVe siècle," *Mélanges de l'École française de Rome: Moyen Âge* 112 (2000): 1057–77. The Cambini traffic in slaves is documented in Sergio Tognetti, "The Trade in Black African Slaves in Fifteenth-Century Florence," in *Black Africans in Renaissance Europe,* ed. T. F. Earle and K. J. P. Lowe (Cambridge, 2005), 213–24.

[49] Franco Angiolini, "Slaves and Slavery in Early Modern Tuscany (1500–1700)," *Italian History and Culture* 3 (1997): 67–86.

of government. The formalization of objective procedures for assessing taxable wealth, incorporated in the 1427 catasto, may have played a part in freeing the rich from the fear that conspicuous consumption made them vulnerable to taxation. It is a good guess that the earlier arbitrary methods to assess private taxable wealth had been susceptible to personal impressions and therefore that any kind of conspicuous consumption in public, whether a grand palace or luxurious clothing, might have been a liability. The principle underlying the new system was that taxable wealth consisted of income-producing investments and marketable assets, not consumption and not earned income from salaries, wages, and profits (more on this too in chapter 7). Nor was sumptuary legislation directed against consumption in the private sphere; rather, it was directed only against the use of certain kinds of goods, mostly wearing apparel, for conspicuous public display. Inhibitions about spending, moreover, were being eroded by a new ethic of magnificence promoted by some of the most prominent humanists on the local scene. Inspired by classical writers, they argued that private wealth, in reinforcing ties of family and friendship and conditioning public behavior in ways that strengthened the body politic, could be a conduit to civic virtue.

Nor is there any evidence that this wealth was held back from the market by hoarding. On Filippo Strozzi's death in 1491, his heirs found an enormous treasury of 52,000 gold florins stored away in bags, probably accumulated over many years in the hope that he could meet the eventual costs of building his monumental palace through to completion. A generation earlier, however, another banker, Francesco Sassetti, had qualms about protecting a hoard of cash: after noting in his ledger that over time he had depleted the *fl.*4,400 hidden away in his privy, he added, "I no longer want to put myself to this trouble, because I don't know whether I could succeed in watching over them for a long time—in fact, I don't believe so."[50] Moreover, Florentines, unlike the rich in northern Europe, did not hoard capital in the form of expensive jewels and an abundant stock of plate. Not one of the hundreds of inventories and private account books that survive from about 1400 on reveals much of anything in the form of cash, plate, or jewels in the possession of these men—certainly nothing like the quantity of these things, worth an astounding *fl.*30,000 (£5,000 sterling), left behind by the well-known contemporary English merchant Richard Whittington (d. 1423).[51] Wealthy Florentines had few silver objects other than knives, forks, and spoons, and hardly any had as many as a dozen of these items. A few had parade armor for their

[50] Richard A. Goldthwaite, *Wealth and the Demand for Art in Italy, 1300–1600* (Baltimore, 1993), 36.
[51] Christopher Dyer, *Standards of Living in the Later Middle Ages: Social Change in England, c. 1200–1520* (Cambridge, 1989), 194.

occasional chivalric games, but they did not tie up much capital in it; in any event, it was all probably made in Florence, not purchased from abroad. For the famous joust of 7 February 1469 organized by Lorenzo the Magnificent, the banker Benedetto Salutati outfitted himself with extravagant splendor, utilizing ten kilograms of gold and fifty-eight of silver, worth about *fl.*4,500. But after the event was over, he had the gold and silver objects melted down to convert the bullion back to money.[52]

Beginning in the fifteenth century, when the documentation becomes particularly rich, and increasingly through the sixteenth century, much of the wealth that accumulated in the city ended up being used for consumption in the local market. Heading the list of what the rich spent their money on were buildings—their houses and chapels, and the furnishings for both. These expenditures are evident today in the physical aspect of the city, and they constitute that patrimony of art and architecture encapsulated in our concept of the Florentine Renaissance. Men built in part because they wanted to assert the status of their family and to assure that status for their descendants. Their dynastic sense of family manifests itself in the coats of arms and personal emblems they had built into the structure of their homes and, above all, in their testamentary provision that the buildings were to remain forever in the hands of their descendants. These urban palaces, not their villas on ancestral properties in the countryside, were the primary seats of their social status. And they could build their enormous houses right in the center of the congested city, where many of their families had long resided, in the process absorbing not an insignificant amount of the available real estate. From 1442 to 1467 Giovanni Rucellai bought up seven properties to be incorporated, along with his residence, in the famous palace that Alberti designed for him. In preparation for the construction of his great palace, begun in 1489, Filippo Strozzi engaged in a major urban clearance project in the area, buying up four small houses, nine shops, some with living quarters, and two large buildings, one with three shops and the other, formerly belonging to the counts of Poppi, with a tower. Strozzi razed all these properties, along with his own residence, to build a completely new palace, whereas many others, like Rucellai, remodeled preexisting buildings and fitted them together behind a single facade. Already by 1462, according to Alamanno Rinuccini, "the building of so many beautiful and large houses of noble and powerful men" was creating such a housing crisis for the people that the commune took measures to promote new building.[53]

---

[52] D. A. Covi, "Nuovi documenti per Antonio e Piero del Pollaiuolo e Antonio Rossellino," *Prospettiva* 12 (1978): 61–64.

[53] Filippo di Cino Rinuccini, *Ricordi storici di Filippo di Cino Rinuccini dal 1282 al 1460, colla continuazione di Alamanno e Neri suoi figli fino al 1506*, ed. G. Aiazzi (Florence, 1840), xc.

Contrary to what some historians have argued, speculating on the functions of the vast spaces these men created for themselves in their palaces, nothing in the mass of surviving chronicles, private record books, and accounts of personal and household expenditures documents much spending for elaborate entertainment on any but the most occasional event.[54] Consumption instead manifested itself in durable goods, not only in more of them but also in their elaboration and even in new kinds of goods, while a more rapidly changing sense of style or fashion generated additional demand for renewal of goods in both the domestic and ecclesiastical spheres. Today we are only too familiar with these dynamics, but they appeared with significant force, perhaps for the first time, in the behavior of Italian elites in the later Renaissance, especially in the furnishing of homes and churches. Earlier, the principal rooms of a house were multifunctional and identified more by size than by anything else. The central room in an upper-class residence was the owner's chamber, a relatively small space used for sleeping and receiving that was often richly furnished with wall paneling and hangings, massive pieces of basic furniture, and decorative objects—"ornate woodwork and elegant wall hangings and elaborate moldings and Virgin Marias and other things, which cost over *fl.*800—a most unseemly thing," complained Bartolomeo Cerretani at the beginning of the sixteenth century.[55] This space represented an extraordinary concentration of consumption, often the investment in a kind of counterdowry by the owner, since it was usually furnished on the occasion of his marriage. Other rooms were multifunctional and relatively sparsely furnished. Furniture tended to be massive and confined to a very limited typology of beds, chests, tables, and benches, and decorative furnishings consisted of wall hangings, wainscoting, small tabernacles, and other devotional objects.

During the Cinquecento the interior of the household began its slow evolution toward its modern form, driven by two dynamics that directed consumption of the rich in different but complementary directions. First, they wanted more objects, both more elaborate and innovative, to satisfy their expanding taste for everything from increasingly larger and more complicated meals to works of art. Second, they required a more articulated division of domestic space according to the different functions of a more complex lifestyle. Already in the third quarter of the sixteenth century Vasari considered the older chamber out of fashion, a thing of the past. By the early seventeenth century a palace of the rich was a different place from what it had been in the Quattrocento. Now it had separate

[54] Cf. F. W. Kent, "Palaces, Politics and Society in Fifteenth Century Florence," *I Tatti Studies* 2 (1987): 41–70; and Brenda Preyer, "Planning for Visitors at Florentine Palaces," *Renaissance Studies* 12 (1998): 357–74, both of which cite little evidence beyond that for the Medici.

[55] Bartolomeo Cerretani, *Ricordi*, ed. Giuliano Berti (Florence, 1993), 127.

rooms for eating and for sleeping, most likely a chapel for private worship, and possibly a library for books and a gallery for works of art. The greater variety of objects that filled these spaces, from tableware to furniture, as well as pictures on the walls, increased to the point of defying an easy typological classification, while at the same time they were subject to replacement with changes in taste. Inventories of the Strozzi palace at the end of the sixteenth century reveal a house with separate rooms for receptions, guests, games, dining, sleeping, the art collection, and the family archives, as well as two chapels and a sacristy. The inventory drawn up on the death of Piero d'Agnolo Guicciardini in 1626 lists 230 paintings and 165 sculptures distributed in sixteen rooms, one with 151 pictures; and like many others at the time, the house also had a private chapel. Writing in 1665, Tommaso Rinuccini, now an old man, commented on how much the private home had changed from earlier times: walls of many rooms were covered with rich stuffs, as were pieces of furniture and doorways; the principal room was blanketed with pictures in gilded frames; the older, built-in stone water basins, supplied with a bucket for washing hands, had been walled up, as had the fireplaces, to be replaced by braziers; ceramics and pewterware were still used at table, but now supplemented with silver plates, bowls, forks, spoons, and saltcellars. No wonder there was a much greater need for household servants, including more men, some attired in livery.[56]

Two other areas of consumption in which expenditures increased were clothing and ecclesiastical furnishings. Little survives today as material testimony for the changing and growing wardrobe of Florentines, or for Europeans in general, in the Renaissance, but the written evidence, accompanied by illustration in the pictorial arts, is overwhelming. The rich spent even more on personal adornment than on furnishings for their homes, and the difference becomes ever more notable through the sixteenth century—even more so if jewelry (as distinct from jewels) is included. After jewelry, clothing constituted the most important single category of personal expenditures of the rich. The increased production of silk textiles over the period surveyed in this volume expanded the variety of fabrics available for clothing to virtually an infinite degree, while the lightness of the material lent itself to a comparable expansion of the possibilities for tailors. Clothing also became more adorned with embroidery, gold and silver buttons,

[56] Goldthwaite, *Wealth and the Demand for Art*, 235–54. Three households of the earlier kind, dating from 1488 to 1511, are described by Jill Burke in *Changing Patrons: Social Identity and the Visual Arts in Renaissance Florence* (University Park, PA, 2004), 49–61; the interior of the Strozzi palace, by Richard A. Goldthwaite in "L'interno del palazzo e il consumo dei beni," in *Palazzo Strozzi: Metà millennio, 1489–1989* (Rome, 1991), 164–65; and the Guicciardini inventory, by John Kent Lydecker in "The Domestic Setting of the Arts in Renaissance Florence" (PhD diss., Johns Hopkins University, 1988), ch. 5. Tommaso Rinuccini's "Considerazioni sopra l'usanze mutate nel passato secolo del 1600" is published in Filippo di Cino Rinuccini, *Ricordi storici*, 270–89.

pearls, and other such ornaments. As a consequence, fashion became ever more perceptible in the marketplace, generating such an "infinite variety" of wearing apparel that "confusion" about dress reigned in the marketplace (as Giuliano de' Medici observed in the second book of *The Book of the Courtier*). At the same time, fashionable clothing extended to a larger social base. What men wore began to rival in luxury what women wore. The taste for more elaborate clothes became so diffused throughout the society that sumptuary legislation took a new direction, defining the rules not just according to economic and moral criteria but also according to social categories. Status is a principal concern of the sumptuary legislation promulgated by Cosimo I in 1546, 1562, and 1568. If on the one hand this reflects a growing sense of nobility among the elite, on the other hand it responds to an increasingly diffused conspicuousness in dress throughout society.[57]

The greater spending for ecclesiastical furnishings was directed not so much to changes in the traditional liturgical apparatus as to more objects of this kind, some reflecting changing tastes and some more luxuriously crafted and decorated. From the later fourteenth century on there was a boom in the construction of private chapels in Florentine churches to the extent that most churches ended up being completely restructured, while new ones were planned as chapel-lined spaces. And these chapels could cost twenty, thirty, and more times what the most skilled craftsman in the construction industry could hope to earn annually (about *fl*.50 in the mid-fifteenth century). In 1464 Bongianni Gianfigliazzi (whom we encountered in chapter 1) estimated that his new chapel in Santa Trinita could be built and decorated for between *fl*.2,600 and *fl*.2,700, half of what he considered the worth of his recently built palace to be.[58] Moreover, these new spaces required the full array of liturgical furnishing and appropriate decoration. Devotional objects became more conspicuous inside the home as well; by the later sixteenth century the rich were building chapels in their homes, a space not found earlier and one requiring furnishings appropriate to the function. A major dynamic behind these kinds of expenditures was the church's proclivity for luxury, vigorously, even defiantly, reaffirmed by Counter Reformation zeal. The sumptuousness with which religious space was outfitted required enormous expenditures

---

[57] Giulia Calvi, "Abito, genere, cittadinanza nella Toscana moderna (secc. XVI–XVII)," *Quaderni storici* 37 (2002): 477–503. Carole Collier Frick, *Dressing Renaissance Florence: Families, Fortunes and Fine Clothing* (Baltimore, 2002), does not go beyond the late Quattrocento. Maria Giuseppina Muzzarelli, *Guardaroba medievale: Vesti e società dal XIII al XVI secolo* (Bologna, 1999), 268–349, notes the trend in Italian sumptuary legislation in general.

[58] Brenda Preyer, "Around and in the Gianfigliazzi Palace in Florence: Developments on Lungarno Corsini in the 15th and 16th Centuries," *Mitteilungen des kunsthistorischen Institutes in Florenz* 48 (2004): 66, 94n84.

for all those things needed for Catholic religious practice in its innumerable forms.[59]

Illustrative of that difference in scale with respect to costs is the elaborate chapel that the Salviati built at San Marco in the 1580s. For this chapel, which is completely documented by detailed accounts, the sons of the merchant-banker Filippo di Averardo Salviati anticipated expenditures of no less than *fl*.34,000 florins, a sum equal to about half of what the Strozzi paid a century earlier for their palace, which at the time was the largest the city had ever seen and which has rooms larger than the Salviati chapel. Whereas the money spent for the Strozzi palace ended up in the hands of construction workers—wallers, brick-makers, stonecutters, manual laborers—what the Salviati spent for their chapel went to pay all the skilled workers it took to produce the frescoes, painting, bronze reliefs, marble statues, stone intarsia work, and the liturgical furnishings that enrich this space, all of whom were Florentines. To make a more exact compari-son, the Salviati chapel cost about eight times as much as one of the most elabo-rate private chapels built in the entire Quattrocento, that of the Portuguese car-dinal at San Miniato al Monte (1473), commissioned for the son of a king and employing artists of the caliber of Luca Della Robbia, Alesso Baldovinetti, and the Rossellino and Pollaiuolo brothers.[60] The chapels built by the Gaddi at Santa Maria Novella (1574–77) and the Niccolini at Santa Croce (1585), with all their work in *pietre dure*, may have cost as much as the Salviati chapel. Even more ex-pensive were the altar and ciborium built in inlaid stone at Santo Spirito from 1599 to 1607, said to have cost the patron, Giovambattista di Tommaso Michelozzi, a partner in the great Ricci bank, *sc*.100,000, equivalent to the entire patrimony of the two or three richest men in Florence in 1427.

In short, the extraordinary rise in private expenditures for household furnish-ings, for clothing, and for religious objects resulted in a virtual boom in the local market for luxury goods as defined in all of the calibrations and degrees of the term, and at Florence this extraordinary demand for durable goods was satisfied almost entirely by the city's artisans. And there is plenty of anecdotal evidence that they too were spending. Their demand stimulated the serial production of less costly devotional objects made for the home, such as paintings, tabernacles, and relief sculptures in wood, gesso, papier-mâché, and terra cotta. Almost a quarter of Neri di Bicci's customers, the buyers of his cheaper line of products,

---

[59] Goldthwaite, *Wealth and the Demand for Art*, 138–58.

[60] The accounts for the Salviati chapel are published in Ewa Karwacka Codini and Milletta Sbrilli, *Il quaderno della fabbrica della cappella di Sant'Antonino in San Marco a Firenze: Manoscritto sulla costruzione di un'opera del Giambologna* (Pisa, 1996). The estimate for the chapel of the Portuguese cardinal is based on documents published in Frederick Hartt, Gino Corti, and Clarence Kennedy, *The Chapel of the Cardinal of Portugal, 1434–1459, at San Miniato in Florence* (Philadelphia, 1964).

were from the artisan class. Buyers of the books printed by the Ripoli press, active from 1476 to 1484, which were primarily of a religious nature, included four gold-smiths, three metalworkers, two carpenters, a baker, a flax worker, a hosier, a mason, and a weaver (these were about half of the buyers whose professions are identified).[61] The customers for the pieces of imported Hispano-Moresque ce-ramics that mercers bought by the hundreds included the entire range of workers—shoemakers, leatherworkers, saddlers, blacksmiths, carpenters, butch-ers, vintners, barbers, wallers, armorers, weavers, dyers. One weaver of wool cloth had thirteen bowls, thirty-four plates, and seven jars.[62] In 1527 a cloth shearer, a fuller, and two contractors who put out wool for spinning paid *fl.*4 for Oriental rugs from the wool firm of Carlo Ginori (the fuller and the contractors each bought two rugs).[63] The Cambio broker Guasparre del Lama commissioned Bot-ticelli to paint his *Adoration of the Magi,* now in the Uffizi, for his chapel in Santa Maria Novella. Within a few months in 1520 the vestment maker Bartolomeo di Lorenzo Banderaio bought a terra-cotta St. Jerome, a terra-cotta Mary Magdalene, a painted terra-cotta relief of the Pietà, a gesso tondo of the Madonna, and a gesso plaque of nudes in battle; and it is unlikely that religious zeal alone inspired this minor spending spree.[64] Later in the century Vasari commented in a letter to Benedetto Varchi that there was not a shoemaker's house in the city that did not have a Flemish painting. Activity in the secondhand market also increased; by the early sixteenth century the Officials of Wards (the Pupilli), who handled the liquidation of estates of minors, were prompted to make their storage and auction facilities available to the general public.[65] Bartolomeo Cerretani, writing at the beginning of the sixteenth century, commented on the *fl.*150–200 *di monte* the poor were spending for dowries and how much artisans were spending to dress themselves and their wives and to decorate their houses.[66]

PRODUCING FOR THE MARKET   All this consumption stimulated artisan activity. Its impact on the economy was especially strong because it was di-rected almost exclusively to the internal market, with the result that there was a greater diversification of the work force and increased specialization. We have no way of measuring precisely the growth and development of this artisan sector—the number of skilled workers, their distribution in various activities,

---

[61] Conway, *"Diario,"* 71–72, 77–78.
[62] Marco Spallanzani, *Maioliche ispano-moresche a Firenze nel Rinascimento* (Florence, 2006), 21–22.
[63] Marco Spallanzani, *Oriental Rugs in Renaissance Florence* (Florence, 2007), doc. 127.
[64] Goldthwaite, *Building of Renaissance Florence,* 403.
[65] Lydecker, "Domestic Setting of the Arts," 214–19.
[66] Cerretani, *Ricordi,* 127.

their relative importance in the economy as a whole, their improved economic standing, their efforts at innovation, their improved productivity. Villani, writing in the first half of the fourteenth century, has little to say about artisans in his otherwise comprehensive survey of the city's economic life. Dei, on the other hand, writing in the 1470s, boasts about the city's painters, carvers of stone and marble, makers of wax figures, gold- and silversmiths, battilori and intarsia artists, along with the producers of wool cloth in many colors and of "magnificent and prestigious" silks sold throughout Europe and the Mediterranean—all these he touts as glories of his "Fiorentia bella." The catasto returns for 1427 and 1480 have been mined to yield the number and nature of "shops" (*botteghe*), which included places used for retail sales and productive activity, and specific surveys for these places exist for 1551 and 1562, but little can be learned from them about change over time.[67] At the most, several new or more specialized activities appear in these documents: in 1480, makers of frames, *cembali*, and chairs and two "sculptors"; in 1561, book dealers, printers, perfumers, operators of kilns for alabaster, and—the big difference that comes to light in this source—two to three times as many tailors and more specialized tailors. Another indicator of a widening consumer market is the rise in the second half of the sixteenth century of inventors seeking to profit from the situation, a phenomenon notable enough to prompt the government to accommodate them by granting patents. Those who made official applications included makers of mirrors, buttons, damascene needles, masks, crystal, and liqueurs, as well as men who had ideas about how to pierce pearls, to work silver, to produce brass, and to raise flowers in greenhouses.[68] Thanks to the strength of the long artisan tradition of the city, the growth of the luxury crafts during the fifteenth and sixteenth centuries resulted predominately from dynamics internal to the sector, not from the immigration of foreigners from abroad as in seventeenth-century London and Paris.[69]

[67] For 1427 and 1480, see Maria Luisa Bianchi and Maria Letizia Grossi, "Botteghe, economia e spazio urbano," in *La grande storia dell'artigianato*, vol. 2, *Il Quattrocento*, ed. Franco Franceschi and Gloria Fossi (Florence, 1999), 27–63; for 1561, P. Battara, "Botteghe e pigioni nella Firenze del '500: Un censimento industriale e commerciale all'epoca del granducato mediceo," *ASI* 95 (1937): 3–28 (more useful for rents than for the categories of labor); and for 1631 and 1642, Judith C. Brown and Jordan Goodman, "Women and Industry in Florence," *Journal of Economic History* 40 (1980): 73–80. A 1562 survey has been published in a facsimile edition that includes an index of trades: Silvia Meloni Trkulja, ed., *I fiorentini nel 1562: Descritione delle Bocche della Città et stato di Fiorenza fatta l'anno 1562* (Florence, 1991). And a survey for 1525 is being prepared for publication by Franco Franceschi.

[68] See the references cited in chapter 4, n. 13.

[69] Linda Levy Peck, *Consuming Splendor: Society and Culture in Seventeenth-Century England* (Cambridge, 2005), 19–20; François Crouzet, "Some Remarks on the *Métiers d'Art*," in *Luxury Trades and Consumerism in "Ancien Régime" Paris: Studies in the History of the Skilled Workforce*, ed. R. Fox and A. Turner (Aldershot, 1998), 264.

What happened in the construction industry from the later fourteenth to the sixteenth century encapsulates in many ways the development of the artisan sector as a whole: diversification and specialization of the work force. In other words, there was an increase in human capital, without, however, any significant innovations in construction techniques or in industrial organization that might have increased productivity. The building boom, if one can use that term, in Florence was not sufficiently strong to inspire an entrepreneur to take initiatives to increase the scale of operations, as Gilbert van Schoonbeke would in sixteenth-century Antwerp and any number of building entrepreneurs and speculators would in later seventeenth-century London. The industry underwent rapid expansion at the time in both these cities, in Antwerp to accommodate the enormous increase in population that accompanied its transformation into an international trade and exchange emporium, in London to rebuild after a disastrous fire. New demand for building in Florence did not arise from such a sudden and generalized need. Instead, the building of palaces by the well-off and the remodeling of most churches to satisfy the desire of these same people for chapel space were responses to a new demand for architecture, not just building, a demand notable for the quality and not just the quantity of resources it generated. These men wanted their buildings embellished throughout with all the kinds of decorative stonework—columns, capitals, corbels, the variety of moldings—that constitute the vocabulary of classical architecture. Some wanted facades in rusticated stone, some wanted them frescoed, and others wanted them decorated with sgraffiti; and not a few sought out architectural talent for overall planning of their projects. All this generated more jobs for men with skills, especially those that required artistic talent.[70]

At the artisan level within the industry there is considerable evidence for expanded production by single operators to meet this demand for building. We have already cited the relatively sophisticated business structure the da Terrarossa brothers used to increase their share of the market. They owned a part of a brick kiln, organized a partnership that rented and operated it, and through a holding-like arrangement used this company to organize a second partnership for the independent operation of another kiln. It was the stoneworking branch of the industry, however, that underwent the greatest development, for expansion included also improving the quality of its products to meet the requirements of the new taste in architecture. These decorative architectural elements were made out of *pietra serena*, a stone not otherwise suitable for construction. With this raw

[70] The construction industry is the subject of Goldthwaite, *Building of Renaissance Florence;* the material in the following discussion comes from chs. 4 and 7.

material at hand in plentiful quantities on the hillsides extending from Settignano to Fiesole, just a few miles north of the city, a new branch of the industry opened up that expanded employment opportunities for stoneworkers and resulted in an impressive rise in the skilled component of the work force. These were the sculptors who carved not only highly decorative architectural elements but also monumental fireplaces, water basins, coats of arms, tabernacles, and other furnishings that were built into palaces and chapels. Some, like Niccolò di Romolo, a contemporary of the da Terrarossa, became veritable entrepreneurs: they owned the quarries they worked and organized the entire process of production, opening a workshop in the city, where they were prepared to accept orders for a variety of items and deliver finished pieces to the building site. As we shall see, the success of the da Terrarossa brothers and Niccolò di Romolo enabled them to place the next generation of the family on an economically and socially upward trajectory.

Out of all this building activity that got under way in the fifteenth century emerges the new figure of the architect, but these men did not come out of the ranks of construction workers strictly speaking. In the cities of the Po valley, an area of brick architecture, the first generation of Renaissance architects—Biagio Rossetti at Ferrara, Alessio Tramello at Piacenza, Aristotele Fioravanti at Bologna—were trained as bricklayers. In Florence, however, not one architect is known to have been a waller, literally *muratore,* the Florentine term for a man who laid bricks and stones and could go on to supervise building projects as a foreman. There the men who somehow presented themselves to patrons with design ideas and were ready to assume the responsibility of a foreman at a building site had had artistic training. The painter Giotto and the painter and sculptor Orcagna are the notable figures from the fourteenth century. In the fifteenth century the ranks of architects were filled with men trained as goldsmiths, stone sculptors, or woodcarvers, such as Brunelleschi, Michelozzo, and Giuliano da Maiano, and in the sixteenth century painters too found work as architects. These men had developed a talent for design and acquired a knowledge of classical architecture. Once active in the planning and supervision of building, they developed the techniques of communicating ideas to both patron and workers through models and drawings, and they identified teams of stoneworkers who could execute their ideas for decorative details. Although they might assume the responsibility of foreman of the works at one site, they could also work exclusively as an architect at another site, selling their ideas, drawing up plans, and hiring themselves out as consultants, perhaps doing no more than stopping by occasionally to check on building progress. Brunelleschi worked this way at the Ospedale degli Innocenti while employed full time as foreman of the cathedral works. At the end of the century Cronaca was, at least at one point, employed by the cathedral workshop, the commune, and the Strozzi, and he may have had other jobs as well. Likewise, in the 1520s Baccio d'Agnolo, trained as a woodworker, was paid only a small consultant's fee for the Bartolini and Da Gagliano palaces and the bell tower at San Miniato al Monte, all being built concurrently, and together these hardly constituted full-time work for him. In short, during the fifteenth century, amidst a boom in prestige architecture, a new artistic profession began to take its modern shape in Florence.

One index to the wider consumer market that opened up over the course of the fourteenth and fifteenth centuries is the growth of the glass industry and the production of inexpensive, everyday objects. In 1306 Florentines first heard about the invention of eyeglasses from the pulpit, in a sermon by the Dominican Giordano da Rivalto at Santa Maria Novella; and in 1315 makers of glass tableware *(bicchierai)* were members of the Medici e Speziali. A century later both products were being mass-produced for a wide consumer market. Technical progress in the making of eyeglasses reached the point where lenses could be ground for the farsighted and the nearsighted, with gradations in progressive powers calculated according to five-year intervals for people of thirty to seventy years of age. At the same time their price fell to the level where, at two soldi a pair, anyone could afford them, even an unskilled laborer working for ten soldi a day. The Florentine industry gained considerable fame abroad; eyeglasses were exported in the hundreds and thousands all over Italy and to northern Europe and the Levant. Not to be overlooked in the economic assessment of this industry is the extra cost that could be expended on these cheap objects for frames, which could be embellished with carving and precious materials to be made into something fit for a king, like the silver-gilt frames and gold-gilt and silver-nielloed cases Cavalcanti, Bardi & Partners supplied to two of the highest officials in the court of Henry VIII in 1527—Thomas Wolsey, cardinal archbishop of York and chancellor, and Henry Wyatt, treasurer of the Royal Chamber.[71]

The production of glass tableware also increased in the second half of the fourteenth century, one of Italy's most important centers of the new industry being the Valdelsa (on which more in chapter 7). Many artisans from this area moved to Florence, where they established glassworks and opened shops for direct sale to the public. These enterprises could require considerable investment by artisan standards, as we have observed, and they produced objects in impressive quantities for general consumption, not art glass. Seventy-five percent of the production by the firm mentioned above in which Carlo di Marco Strozzi in-

---

[71] The definitive work on the production of eyeglasses in Florence is Vincent Ilardi, *Renaissance Vision from Spectacles to Telescopes* (Philadelphia, 2007).

vested consisted of drinking glasses. The 1435 inventory of the shop belonging to Niccolò di Ghino lists no fewer than 99,980 drinking glasses, 14,305 pitchers, 2,400 flasks, 1,000 inkwells, and a variety of other items. Niccolò's son, Bartolomeo, also a glassworker, in 1457 had an estate worth *fl*.2,000 between land and outstanding credits. Eighteen of these shops are documented in the 1552 census, and ten inside the walls of the city in the census of 1662.[72]

Sculptors responded to this growing consumer market in the fifteenth century by finding new ways to make less costly products. They turned out a broad range of objects—altarpieces, baptismal fonts, tabernacles, devotional pieces, statues, busts, armorial shields—in a variety of materials, including terra cotta, stucco, cartapesta, gesso, and wax. Moreover, since these materials were inexpensive and could be molded, and therefore worked easily and quickly, production was less labor intensive and pieces could be produced in series. Ghiberti's shop produced some images in tens of copies. A Madonna by Donatello is known in at least fifteen copies; another, by Benedetto da Maiano, in more than thirty copies; and the *Madonna della Candelabra*, by Rossellino, in more than fifty copies.[73] It cost little to make these products more attractive by having them glazed or painted. Over a period of fewer than four months in 1510–11 the painter Bernardo Rosselli received more than 116 objects of this kind to be painted—large and small, round and rectangular, most representing the Virgin Mary, with and without the Christ Child, and 2 "for women"—along with two busts of emperors.[74] Luca Della Robbia invented the technique of glazing terra cotta, and production evolved into a family tradition that continued into the next century, famed for its relatively inexpensive but highly visible objects for the popular market in both ecclesiastical and domestic furnishings. The shop produced low-cost items in series, some with empty spaces left for a buyer's coat of arms to be added in a second firing. In 1524 Cappone di Iacopo Capponi, having entered what one critic wrote had by then become the "mere potter's factory" of the Della Robbia to buy a Madonna relief, observed that "there is one for two florins and another for three, with space to include the arms."[75] Hundreds of such armorial shields by the Della Robbia shop still exist. Portrait medals too were turned out "ready made" in series for ordinary

---

[72] Guido Taddei, *L'arte del vetro;* Alessandro Guidotti, "Appunti per una storia della produzione vetraria di Firenze e del suo territorio pre-Cinquecentesca," in *Archeologia e storia della produzione del vetro pre-industriale,* ed. Marja Mendera (Florence, 1990), 167 (for the Niccolò di Ghino inventory); Gabriella Cantini Guidotti, *Tre inventari di bicchierai toscani fra Cinque e Seicento* (Florence, 1983).

[73] Giancarlo Gentilini, *I Della Robbia: La scultura invetriata nel Rinascimento* (Florence, 1998), 24–32, emphasizes the exceptional social and geographic diffusion of these objects.

[74] Rita Comanducci, "Produzione seriale e mercato dell'arte a Firenze tra Quattro e Cinquecento," in Fantoni, Matthew, and Matthews-Grieco, *Art Market in Italy,* 108.

[75] F. W. Kent, "Art Historical Gatherings from the Florentine Archives," *Australian Journal of Art* 2 (1980): 47.

buyers who wanted a religious portrait, the reverse sometimes left blank to be finished on order for the more demanding client.[76] Likewise, the rise in demand for small bronzes led to the development of techniques for reproducing them from a single model.

The extraordinary artistic, if not economic, success of Florentine painters can be understood as emblematic of the entrepreneurial spirit that drove some of these artisans in the marketplace. They worked primarily to satisfy a local demand that was widely diffused throughout the society, not concentrated either in the court of a prince or in trade fairs frequented by merchants from abroad. They were not removed from the market as was a painter such as Mantegna, who worked to satisfy a prince and was subject to the whims of a patron; nor were they lured into standardization, specialization, and mass production, as the painters of Bruges and Antwerp were, in order to satisfy the large but anonymous demand of an international fair. In the Florentine market the painter went from one private commission to another. It is possible to read the dynamic that drove the remarkable stylistic developments of Florentine Quattrocento art—the powerful urge of the painter to demonstrate his mastery of anatomy, classical architecture, *disegno*, geometrical composition, linear and aerial perspective, narrative content (*istoria*)—as a market technique to improve his ability to attract commissions. At the same time, to meet the growing popular demand for devotional paintings, he sought to increase production by standardizing images, making copies, and working from cartoons to facilitate replication.[77] The painter Neri di Bicci, the most affluent member of his profession to show up in the 1480 catasto, like most painters produced major altarpieces on commission, but he expanded his production by making small devotional objects in series, which he sold to the general public across the counter in his shop.

In the introduction to his life of Perugino, Vasari raised the question why it was that "in Florence, more than elsewhere, men became superior in all the arts." His answer lies partly in his analysis of the market situation in which they found themselves: Florentine "artisans" were driven by "the need to be industrious . . . [and] to know how to make a living, [and] competition . . . is one of the nourishments that maintain them." Vasari was one of the very first writers in the Italian language to use the word *competition*, especially in its economic sense, and he used the term—*concorrenza* and also *concorrente*—repeatedly. From this perspective,

---

[76] Arne R. Flaten, "Portrait Medals and Assembly-Line Art in Late Quattrocento Florence," in Fantoni, Matthew, and Matthews-Grieco, *Art Market in Italy*, 127–39.

[77] Megan Holmes, "Copying Practices and Marketing Strategies in a Fifteenth-Century Florentine Painter's Workshop," in *Artistic Exchange and Cultural Translation in the Italian Renaissance City*, ed. Stephen J. Campbell and Stephen Milner (Cambridge, 2004), 38–74.

the release of creative imagination that we call the Renaissance in art was, at least in part, a manifestation of an economic culture driven by the entrepreneurial energy of artisans in the marketplace, who, through stylistic innovation, shaped and renewed taste and thereby generated further demand for their own products. In this way the economic system was a permissive, if not effective, cause of the vigor of the market for the arts in Renaissance Florence.[78]

The single most conspicuous consumer in the sixteenth century, unlike anything the city had seen earlier, was the new Medici court. The first dukes accumulated an enormous private fortune. Although the Venetian ambassadors at the end of the century were much impressed with how much Francesco and Ferdinando managed to save,[79] what these dukes spent was even more impressive. Their acquisition went well beyond the ordinary needs of a court since their demand was prompted largely by their personal interest in artisan crafts and technology. Besides inducing the printers, armorers, and tapestry weavers mentioned above to come to the city and set up their own shops, Cosimo sent spies to Venice to learn the secret of making quality glass. And he attracted one Murano glassmaker to Florence, offering him a furnace, all the necessary materials, and *sc.*1,000, along with privileges and a monopoly on the production of Murano-type glass.[80] Cosimo and the two sons who succeeded him also opened workshops under their personal supervision, creating, in effect, a state enterprise for the production of objects of great luxury and prestige. To these they attracted the best craftsmen they could find in Italy and in northern Europe—engravers from France, tapestry weavers from Flanders, clockmakers from Germany, glass artists from Venice. Cosimo I put various artisans, including cutters of hard stone, goldsmiths, jewelers, weavers, and distillers, to work in rooms of the Palazzo Vecchio, his first official residence. In 1568 Francesco, then regent for his father, bought the land on which he then constructed the Casino di San Marco, which by 1577 had become what we might call a center of the arts and crafts. It included a foundry, a distillery, facilities for alchemical research, and workspaces where craftsmen of various kinds perfected their skills. Their research into the tempering of steel resulted in the first tools sufficiently strong to carve porphyry, the hardest of stones; they succeeded in melting rock crystal so that it could be blown as glass was; and they learned how to make soft-paste porcelain, the closest anyone in the West came to producing true porcelain before the eighteenth century.

[78] The authoritative study of painting for the market in fifteenth-century Florence is Susanne Kubersky-Piredda, *Kunstwerke-Kunstwerte: Die Florentiner Maler der Renaissance und der Kunstmarkt ihrer Zeit* (Norderstedt, Germany, 2005).

[79] *Relazioni degli ambasciatori veneti al senato*, ed. Arnaldo Segarizzi (1916; facsimile repr., Bari, 1968), 3:20, 129, 158, 161.

[80] Cantini Guidotti, *Tre inventari*, 33.

Later Francesco transferred many of these shops to the top floor of the new Uffizi, in what came to be known as the Gallery of Works (Galleria dei lavori), where there were also galleries for the display of ancient sculpture. When Ferdinando became grand duke in 1587, he went one step further by imposing a formal organization on these activities, placing them all under the supervision of a general superintendent and naming the prominent Roman musician and composer Emilio de' Cavalieri to the post. Florentine tapestries were the envy even of the Flemish, according to the Venetian ambassador, and the production of objects in pietre dure was the most important in Europe. Also significant, given the interest in research as one of the defining characteristics of the scientific revolution, was the production of such things as clocks, quadrants, compasses, armillary spheres, terrestrial globes, astronomical and geographical maps, glass instruments, and lenses, all made with great precision and richly adorned.[81] In addition to these court artisans, the Medici employed many painters, sculptors, and architects for various construction and remodeling projects—the Palazzo Vecchio, the Uffizi, the Palazzo Pitti together with its garden, and numerous villas throughout the territorial state.[82] If this was not the first program of its kind in the history of Europe, it marked a qualitative difference from anything that went before with respect to range, centralization, and overall success. It anticipated the royal manufactories set up a century later, on a much larger scale, and with explicit commercial objectives, at Versailles.

Yet this ambitious and prestigious enterprise of the grand dukes has not yet found a historian to bring together in a comprehensive overview all the specialized studies dedicated to many of the particular crafts that constituted the whole. In that absence it is difficult to evaluate the full impact all this artisan activity had on the economy. Ducal policy was directed largely to political ends: to furnish the court of these newly arrived princes with an appropriate aura of luxury, to supply gifts in accordance with the contemporary culture of diplomacy, to boost the international prestige of the new state in the courts of Europe. Some of this production ended up in the market, but hardly to the extent of enjoying what could be called commercial success. In any event, the two products that did occasionally find buyers, both abroad and at home, were tapestries and furniture in pietre dure, both involving an investment in materials and time that was well beyond

[81] R. S. Westfall, "Science and Technology during the Scientific Revolution: An Empirical Approach," in Renaissance and Revolution: Humanists, Scholars, Craftsmen and Natural Philosophers in Early Modern Europe, ed. J. V. Field and F. A. J. James (Cambridge, 1994), 63–72.

[82] Suzanne B. Butters, " 'Una pietra eppure non una pietra': Pietre dure e botteghe medicee nella Firenze del Cinquecento," in Franceschi and Fossi, La grande storia dell'artigianato, 3:145ff., surveys this ducal activity and cites the bibliography. For a list of the artisans working under Cavalieri, see Marco Spallanzani, Ceramiche alla corte dei Medici nel Cinquecento (Modena, 1994), 175–78.

the reach of an artisan in the private sector working on his own or in partnership. In the final analysis, the historical importance of this ducal enterprise lay in its reinforcement of the long Florentine tradition of highly skilled and artistically talented craftsmen. The grand-ducal Gallery of Works represented the culmination of that development. Government policy in consolidating this tradition was certainly successful in promoting the prestige of what was emerging as one of the most visible sectors of the economy. In a significant public gesture, symbolic of what all this meant to the city, Ferdinando I in 1593 cleared the Ponte Vecchio of the indecorous butchers' shops that had long been there in order to bring all the city's goldsmiths together in this prestigious spot right in the center of the city, where they remain today.

The more concrete success of the sector—if these crafts can be brought together under one rubric—lay in its ability to satisfy local demand for manufactured objects, so that recourse to imports, especially those at the high end of the market, was largely precluded. It kept in the home market much of the wealth increasingly being spent on luxury, which otherwise might have flowed out of the economy; and it resulted in increased investment in human capital, from which the city still benefits. Local workers met the demand for luxury textiles, for furniture, for jewelry, and for high-quality utensils and decorative objects of all kinds. The large collection of merchandise journals that survive for Datini's import-export business in Pisa at the end of the fourteenth century and for the Salviati company there a century later document how little incoming traffic from abroad there was in manufactured products of quality. Merchants imported principally raw materials and semiworked materials for the local textile and leatherworking industries, along with other natural products ranging from foodstuffs, nonferrous metals, wax, and furs to spices, amber, and ostrich feathers. The few manufactured goods they supplied to the local market consisted mostly of the cheaper cloths—cotton, linen, fustians—and nonferrous metalwork, much of it ordinary tools and utensils but some of it quality products, such as pewterware from England and wrought ironware from Germany. In the earlier period Florentines imported costly goods produced in the Levant, but by the fifteenth century they had substituted their own products for these and in some instances were selling their products in Levantine markets.

One example of this change is Hispano-Moresque ceramics made in Valencia. This was about the only manufactured product of any quality that Datini imported from the western Mediterranean area. And as we have seen, his company records document every step taken in the market in which these goods were handled, from commissions received in Florence for pieces of these ceramics decorated with the client's coat of arms to the orders Datini's agent consigned to the potters in Valencia and the customs records of the arrival of the finished product at Genoa, then at Pisa, and finally at the gates of Florence. By the end of the fifteenth century, however, even this traffic, never more than a drop in the bucket in the total import-export business, had ground to a halt, as local artisans in Montelupo and Cafaggiolo succeeded in capturing the market with their own products.[83]

Two other products, tapestries and Oriental rugs, also illustrate how the local market reacted to quality imports. Probably the most luxurious manufactured items imported from abroad were the tapestries produced by the industry that grew up in Flanders in the late fourteenth and fifteenth centuries as a result of the successful restructuring of the textile industry there. These prestigious products, which usually came in costly ensembles, found buyers in Italy, mostly rulers and governments. Italians took the initiative to send specific orders to the Low Countries, sometimes accompanied by artists' designs. Occasionally a Flemish tapestry merchant made the journey to Italy in search of commissions, and many weavers came looking for work. In the mid-fifteenth century immigrant weavers found employment working for the Gonzaga in Mantua and the d'Este in Ferrara. When they set up shop in Siena, Bologna, Perugia, and a few other towns without a major court, however, they were not able to stay in business for more than a few years. Local demand in republican Florence too was limited. Through their agent in Bruges, the Medici arranged for many commissions and sales, including some major series for their own use, but other than the Medici, probably few men had as many fine tapestries as did the banker Benedetto di Antonio Salutati, who in 1477 sent some forty pieces to Pisa to be put at the disposal of Alfonso of Aragon on his stopover there while on his way to Catalonia.[84] Flemish weavers came to the city to execute several large public commissions—for the Palazzo Vecchio, the cathedral, the baptistery—but left on the completion of their commissions. For the famous vestments of San Giovanni, designed by Antonio del Pollaiuolo for the baptistery and produced in the 1460s and 1470s, only one Florentine worked along with two embroiderers from Flanders, one from Spain, and one from Venice during the first phase; and the partnership organized for the later phase consisted of two Florentines along with a Fleming, a Venetian, and a Veronese. Apart from a few commissions, local production in the weaving and embroidering of tapestries never got under way.[85]

In this light it would be interesting to know what the merchant Bernardo di Zanobi Saliti had in mind when, in 1545, he made a case to Cosimo I for establish-

[83] Spallanzani, *Maioliche ispano-moresche a Firenze,* 139.
[84] Spallanzani, *Oriental Rugs,* 107–8.
[85] L. Becherucci and G. Brunetti, eds., *Il museo dell'Opera del Duomo a Firenze* (Milan, 1971), 2:261.

ing the industry in Florence. Saliti, whose experience in the silk trade in Nuremberg is recounted in chapter 2, argued that it would boost employment, pointing
out that the industry in Brussels employed fifteen thousand people and that production would both cut into imports and find clients abroad, especially in the
great courts at Rome and Naples. The duke found the argument persuasive, probably because the project also appealed to his protomercantilist ambitions to promote prestigious state industries in competition with the other courts of Italy.
Within a year Cosimo had made contracts with two Flemish tapestry weavers for
setting up two shops in the explicit hope of establishing the industry in Florence,
and official production got under way. These initiatives were not economically
successful; and in 1568, a few years after the death of both of these men, the two
shops were consolidated into one. Local demand for these very special products
seems not to have been forthcoming, and production was directed primarily to
supplying the ducal court. The appointment of Guasparre Papini as head of the
works in 1588 raised some expectation of earning profits on commissions from
abroad, and in 1611 business was successful enough that a catalog listing the workshop's products was circulated abroad. In any event, the industry did not attract
capitalist entrepreneurs from the private sector; and given the heavy initial investment required to buy the expensive equipment needed for production and to
sustain long-term production costs, not to mention the problem of sales, artisans
could hardly have built up the industry on their own.[86]

Oriental rugs were the one imported quality product that Florentines made no
effort to produce for themselves, despite the healthy local demand for them. Merchants imported them in large numbers for sale across the counter in the local
market, and they also accepted commissions for specific products, some with the
client's coat of arms, which they then ordered to be custom-made in the Levant.
With prices fluctuating around several florins, rugs were not cheap for the ordinary Florentine, but neither were they extravagantly expensive. Linen drapers and
mercers handled the retail trade in this product, and their customers ranged from
the wealthy to ordinary artisans. Oriental rugs show up on the inventories of the
houses of people in all classes, and they were also omnipresent in the liturgical
furnishings of churches. Although not a major item in the local market, rugs
clearly elicited some demand. One might have thought that in a city with highly

---

[86] Thomas Campbell, *Tapestry in the Renaissance: Art and Magnificence* (New Haven, CT, 2002),
85–101, offers a good recent summary, with full bibliography, of the fifteenth century; see also Paula
Nuttall, *From Flanders to Florence: The Impact of Netherlandish Painting, 1400–1500* (New Haven,
CT, 2004), esp. 100–102. For the early ducal period, see Lucia Meoni, "L'arazzeria medicea," in Fran-
ceschi and Fossi, *La grande storia dell'artigianato*, 3:225–63; and idem, *Gli arazzi nei musei fiorentini:
La collezione medicea; Catalogo completo*, vol. 1, *Manifattura da Cosimo I a Cosimo II (1545–1621)*
(Livorno, 1998).

developed wool and silk industries, well supplied with all the necessary raw materials, not to mention a sales network abroad, someone might have attempted to go into the business of producing rugs. Yet there is no evidence that anyone ever did—except, as might be expected, the Medici dukes, ever ready to extend the range of luxury objects produced in their state. A request presented by Bernardo Saliti in 1567 to set up a manufactory in Pisa was rejected. In 1581, Francesco I himself took the initiative in granting a ten-year monopoly on rug production to be organized at the Innocenti, partly to provide employment for the children and women who lived there, but after a few years the project was abandoned. Presumably, in the Renaissance, no less than today, production of Oriental rugs was better left to an undeveloped or command economy, well supplied with cheap labor, especially that of women and children. Rugs, in any event, were about the only quality manufactured products imported into Florence with some regularity from the fourteenth through the sixteenth century.[87]

Parameters of the Local Market

The Florentine labor force, if broken down into its constituent parts, probably looked quite different from that found in most other European cities. Florence was a large industrial city, producing textiles for export; wool workers may have made up as much as 30–40 percent of the working population, and silk workers another 4–5 percent. Moreover, construction workers probably numbered somewhat higher than elsewhere, since the city underwent considerable building and rebuilding in the course of the fifteenth and sixteenth centuries. Because so much of this building was in stone, the industry required correspondingly more workers, from manual laborers to stone carvers. Construction workers may have accounted for more than 15 percent of all workers, the upper range of their numbers in other cities at the time. Finally, the number of highly skilled artisans, especially those in the luxury crafts, was probably also much higher than in the average European town, given the greater demand for consumer goods generated by the rich, who were becoming ever richer during the fifteenth and sixteenth centuries. However, we have no reliable way to break the work force down into measurable occupational categories and to factor into the calculation the mass of women and children, many of them in institutions, who constituted such a large part of that work force.[88]

[87] Spallanzani, *Oriental Rugs.*

[88] The percentage of textile workers has been estimated by Franco Franceschi in *Oltre il "Tumulto,"* 114, and in "Un 'grande artigianato': L'industria laniera," in *La grande storia dell'artigianato,* vol. 1, *Il Medioevo* (Florence, 1998), 129; and by Florence Edler de Roover in *L'arte della seta a Firenze nei secoli XIV e XV,* ed. Sergio Tognetti (Florence, 1999), 113. See also the shop surveys of Bianchi and Grossi, "Botteghe, economia e spazio urbano," in Franceschi and Fossi, *La grande storia*

For purposes of economic analysis directed to assessing the importance of workingmen in the total economy, we can divide them into two general functional categories, although the distinction will become blurred as the discussion progresses. The basic distinction is between those who produced for export and those who produced to satisfy local demand. The former contributed to the economy inasmuch as the product of their labor brought wealth into the economy; the latter contributed to the economy to the extent that their labor satisfied the consumer demand generated by this wealth, thereby precluding its reexport. Textile workers constituted the vast majority of those working for the export market; although they had a degree of maneuverability, they were subordinate to the highly circumscribed structure dominated by capitalist investors that was described in the preceding chapter. Workers whose labor was directed to satisfying demand in the local market were, by contrast, autonomous operators, be they shopkeepers selling to the public, artisans producing on commission or for the generalized market, or those working in the service sector. They had little possibility for expanding production to foreign markets. This, in fact, is why they were not subordinated to capitalist investors: the product of their labor, by and large, did not offer enough potential for profits in foreign markets to make the attempt to organize them worthwhile. Hardly any of these local producers had a direct outlet to foreign markets, and few could have handled sales abroad on their own. The Florentine marketplace, as we have seen, was anything but a great entrepôt of international trade: it had nothing of the ongoing traffic of a port city, nor were there large periodic fairs, such as those at Bruges, Lyons, and Antwerp, to bring foreign merchants and local producers together in the local marketplace.

The one clear exception to the generalization that the products of these artisans were not primarily directed to foreign markets is the book. Even before the advent of print, Florentine scriptoria were turning out humanist manuscripts that aroused demand from abroad, and the humanist script they developed at the end of the fourteenth century had become the norm throughout Italy by the 1430s. The Camaldolesi monks at Santa Maria degli Angeli, in particular, enjoyed considerable fame for their manuscripts. Moreover, the presence of the pope in the city from 1434 to 1443, and especially the arrival of the church council in 1439, helped to bring the quality of locally produced manuscripts to the attention of the many churchmen who came from abroad. Some of the city's stationers served as agents who saw to the execution of commissions from abroad by contracting with local copyists. The most noted of these, Vespasiano da Bisticci, emerged as an

---

dell'artigianato, 37. A general survey of the division of labor in European cities can be found in Farr, *Artisans in Europe,* 99–107.

independent stationer and copyist in the 1440s. He built up a clientele throughout Europe among the rulers, popes, collectors, and scholars who commissioned work from him, providing him with a range of acquaintances that allowed him to write his famous *Lives* after he retired. Vespasiano has also been singled out as the first to extend his business beyond that of middleman between client and copyist in the attempt to exploit the commercial potential of this growing market. He took the initiative to arrange for the production of uncommissioned manuscripts for eventual sale, even anticipating the later use by printers of the colophon to advertise his business. Moreover, in at least two instances he himself entered the export market, albeit with dubious success: in 1457 he consigned some eighteen books to a Florentine merchant for sale in Naples, and in 1459 he tried to arrange for sales in Mantua during the church council there.[89]

With the introduction of printing, book production expanded exponentially, sometimes exceeding what demand in any local market could absorb. Here, in short, was the one business that, unlike any other in Florence outside the textile industry, was potentially oriented to production for foreign markets. The first printing press appeared in Italy in 1465; six years later, in 1471, the first book was printed in Florence, and some eighteen presses have been identified as operating sporadically through to the end of the century, most turning out short books directed to the general public. By 1500 the city ranked fourth in Italy—after Venice, Rome, and Milan—for the number of titles printed. Florentine publishers, however, could not count on a strong local demand such as that generated by the large clerical population in Rome, nor did they have the ready access to foreign markets to be found in a great international emporium such as Venice. In 1476 Cappone di Bartolomeo Capponi, a merchant and member of a prominent patrician family, entered into a five-year partnership (with how much capital we do not know) with the resident German printer Niccolò di Lorenzo, the first serious initiative in Florence to establish a publishing business. In the next year Capponi became involved in a venture, the details of which are not known, with the sculptor Matteo Civitale to set up the first printing press in Lucca. Not surprisingly, other capitalist investors seem not to have been forthcoming. The one other documented Florentine patrician investor in the industry, the merchant Girolamo di Carlo Strozzi, ventured into the business, at Venice, in 1475–76, with the intention of opening a new market by sponsoring and publishing Italian translations of

---

[89] Vespasiano's business practices have been best analyzed by Albinia de la Mare in "New Research on Humanistic Scribes in Florence," in *Miniatura fiorentina del Rinascimento, 1440–1525: Un primo censimento*, ed. Annarosa Garzelli (Florence, 1985), 395–476. For his venture in Naples, and the most recent bibliography on Vespasiano as publisher, see Luca Boschetto, "Una nuova lettera di Giannozzo Manetti a Vespasiano da Bisticci, con alcune considerazioni sul commercio librario tra Firenze e Napoli a metà Quattrocento," *Medioevo e Rinascimento*, n.s., 15 (2004): 175–206.

three books, two of which—Leonardo Bruni's and Poggio Bracciolini's histories of Florence—might have been expected to have their biggest market in Florence.[90]

For the most part the history of Florentine printers is that of ventures that hobbled along, from one contract to another, until the Giunti appeared on the scene at the end of the century. Filippo di Giunta (1456–1517), the son of a retail cloth dealer, had two brothers who remained in that business, another who became a tailor, and two others who went to Venice, where they became stationers and printers. Filippo did his apprenticeship in the shop of the goldsmith Antonio del Pollaiuolo, but eventually, in 1489, he too opened a stationer's shop in Florence. In 1491 he had enough capital from the estate of his father to invest in a partnership with his brother Luc'Antonio in Venice; when the partnership was reorganized in 1499, the net value of all assets was *fl*.11,000. Meanwhile, in 1497 Filippo published his first book in Florence as a capitalist investor, not as a printer. The business grew both in Venice and in Florence, but the brothers dissolved their partnership in 1509, although disagreements between the two delayed the final settlement until 1517. At that time Luc'Antonio's share of the assets was *fl*.13,806 and Filippo's, *fl*.6,102, a division that reflects where the center of gravity in the new industry was. Nevertheless, in 1513 Filippo's son Giovanni went to Spain, where he set up a business that had shops in Salamanca and Burgos; eventually, in the 1590s, Giovanni's heirs also had a firm at Madrid, which gained recognition as printer for the king. The family business survived in Spain until 1668. Meanwhile, Luc'Antonio in Venice went on to open a company in Lyons, another international emporium, with a capital of *fl*.2,000 (through an accomandita registered in Florence by a nephew). These two branches, often working together, continued to expand into an agglomerate with a veritable international sales network, including agents throughout Italy and warehouses in Paris, Antwerp, Frankfurt, and Lisbon, as well as those in Spain.[91]

[90] A recent general survey of the industry, with further bibliography, is Renzo Sabbatini, "Cartolai, librai, tipografi ed editori nella Firenze del Quattro-Cenquecento," in Franceschi and Fossi, *La grande storia dell'artigianato*, 3:94–95. On Capponi, see Lorenz Böninger, "Ein deutscher Frühdrucker in Florenz: Nicolaus Laurentii de Alemania," *Gutenburg-Jahrbuch 2002* 77 (2002): 95–99; and idem, "Ricerche sugli inizi della stampa fiorentina (1471–1473)," *La bibliofilia* 105 (2003): 225–48. On Strozzi, see Florence Edler de Roover, "Per la storia dell'arte della stampa in Italia: Come furono stampati a Venezia tre dei primi libri in volgare," ibid. 55 (1953): 107–17.

[91] William A. Pettas has studied the various branches of this family business. See the following by him: *The Giunti of Florence: Merchant Publishers of the Sixteenth Century* (San Francisco, 1980), which documents their business arrangements in the early sixteenth century; "The Giunti and the Book Trade in Lyon," in *Libri, tipografi, biblioteche: Ricerche storiche dedicate a Luigi Balsamo* (Florence, 1997), 169–92; and *A History and Bibliography of the Giunti (Junta) Printing Family in Spain, 1626–1682* (New Castle, DE, 2005), with a long introduction that summarizes the history of the entire family.

The Florentine branch of the Giunti, which passed into the hands of Filippo's heirs, was on the periphery of this network, but locally in Florence it often enjoyed a near monopoly until the business was finally closed down in 1604 (at which time it had 13,685 books in its inventory). A few other presses came and went in the course of the century, but the only other major publisher was the Brabantine Lorenzo Torrentino. Torrentino was attracted to Florence in 1547 by official privileges and a salary granted him by Cosimo I, who considered publishing an instrument for propaganda to strengthen his program of cultural politics. Torrentino remained in business until his death in 1563, surviving the limited market conditions in Florence only because of support from the duke. His business closed down in 1570, when its inventory was bought by the Giunti. Another foreigner, the Frenchman Giorgio Marescotti, set up a shop in the city; although he failed to gain the ducal privileges enjoyed by Torrentino, he managed to remain in business until his death in 1602. Of all the books printed in Italy over the following fifty years, through the first half of the seventeenth century, those printed in Florence account for only 6–9 percent. In Florence publishing, the one enterprise outside of textiles oriented at least in part to foreign markets, was not a business that could attract big investors.[92]

Another group of craftsmen whose work may have been exported in significant quantity, given the importance of the natural resources of the region for the industry, were metalworkers. As remarked at the outset of this book, Tuscany had the natural resources for a thriving metalworking industry, and furnaces were scattered all along the slopes of the Apennines, extending across the Valdinievole to Pistoia. In Florence metalworkers were divided into four separate guilds—the Arte de' Corazzai e Spadai (armorers and sword makers), the Arte de' Chiavaioli (ironworkers and locksmiths), the Arte dei Fabbri (blacksmiths), and the Arte dei Medici e Speziali, which included gold- and silversmiths, who also worked in base metals. The measure of the importance of the first three of these can be taken from the fact that despite their miniscule size, they managed to retain their separate guild identity in face of the merging of other craftsmen into the large, often heterogeneous guild conglomerates at the end of the thirteenth century. Metal products of all kinds, from buttons, buckles, knives, and pliers to military gear, were, after cloth, the most important Florentine products that Datini exported throughout the western Mediterranean from his firm in Pisa and sold directly on

---

[92] Antonio Ricci, "Lorenzo Torrentino and the Cultural Programme of Cosimo I de' Medici," in Eisenbichler, *Cultural Politics of Duke Cosimo I de' Medici*, 103–19; Giampiero Guarducci, *Annali dei Marescotti tipografi editori di Firenze (1563–1613)* (Florence, 2001), 103–19; Brendan Dooley, "Printing and Entrepreneurialism in Seventeenth-Century Italy," *Journal of European Economic History* 25 (1996), table on 585.

the market out of his shop at Avignon, far more important than the occasional luxury items he handled.

Although little is known about this industry, the prestige Florentine armorers in particular enjoyed abroad is clear. Already in the mid-thirteenth century major figures on the Italian political scene—the emperor Frederick II, Charles of Anjou, and Alfonso IV of Aragon—sought their products.[93] At the time of Dante the Dominican preacher and writer Remigio de' Girolami included armaments as one the three industries (along with the cloth and construction industries) on his list of the seven gifts God had bestowed on Florence. A century later Datini's shop in Avignon did a major business in the entire range of military arms and armor, both offensive and defensive, from swords, daggers, lances, pikes, and hatchets to shields and the panoply for a knight and his horse.[94] Many such items made in Florence during this period, notable above all for their design, are to be found today in museum collections throughout Europe.[95] The guild of Corazzai e Spadai was the only lesser guild among those at the lowest level within the hierarchy of the lesser guilds to be assigned one of the tabernacles added in the early fifteenth century to the exterior of Orsanmichele, the great civic monument to the guild republic. Forty-seven declarants in the 1427 catasto identified themselves as armorers, and seven of these had a net worth of more than *fl*.1,000.

We know virtually nothing, however, about the link between armorers and the export market. It has been thought that Florentine capitalists, unlike those in Siena and Milan, were interested only in the marketing of these goods and that production remained highly fragmented in the hands of specialized artisans. This lack of industrial organization has been cited as an explanation of why the Florentine arms industry did not make the successful transition to the new military technology developing around firearms and artillery in the fifteenth century.[96] Yet we know about two Florentine investors at the beginning of the sixteenth century—the brothers Paolo and Giovanni Vettori—who operated a furnace at Buti, on the Monti Pisani above Pisa, for the production of arms and ammunition, which they sent to Rome and to England as well as to Florence.[97] The Florentine industry, however, failed to keep up with developments in Milan and

[93] Robert Davidsohn, *Storia di Firenze* (Florence, 1956), 4, pt. 2:43–46.

[94] Luciana Frangioni, *Chiedere e ottenere: L'approvvigionamento di prodotti di successo della bottega Datini di Avignone nel XIV secolo* (Florence, 2002).

[95] Mario Scalini, "L'armatura fiorentina del Quattrocento e la produzione d'armi in Toscana," in *Guerra e guerrieri nella Toscana del Rinascimento,* ed. F. Cardini and M. Tangheroni (Florence, 1999), 83–126.

[96] Scalini, "L'armatura fiorentina," 85; Mario Borracelli, "Siderurgia e imprenditori senesi nel '400 fino all'epoca di Lorenzo il Magnifico," in *La Toscana al tempo di Lorenzo: Politica, economia, cultura, arte* (Pisa, 1996), 3:1218–19.

[97] Rosemary Devonshire Jones, *Francesco Vettori, Florentine Citizen and Medici Servant* (London, 1972), 4–5.

Brescia in the sixteenth century. In these major Lombard centers of production, which had access to iron of superior quality, the technology was developed for making harder armor to meet the challenges of gunpowder, and considerable entrepreneurial energy went into the organization of the industry. It was to these Lombards, not to Florentine producers, that Cosimo I turned to procure arms for his new militia and for the knights of his Order of Santo Stefano; he also sought to induce some of them to move their production to Florence. Eventually, in 1568–69, he succeeded in attracting the prominent Milanese armorer Matteo Piatti by offering him a seven-year contract for the operation of a shop.[98]

Florentine merchants occasionally bought other products from local artisans for sale abroad, either taking the initiative to supply the markets where they did business or acting as agents for foreign buyers. In his shop in Avignon in the second half of the fourteenth century Datini sold devotional pictures, painted chests, and abacus boards made in Florence. The ledgers of the Cambini merchant-bankers document the occasional traffic in luxury goods conducted by one medium-sized firm during the third quarter of the fifteenth century. To Rome the firm sent a tondo with the Madonna by Botticelli, a black satin purse with gold threads and pearls, and a bread knife in its red satin sheath with silver ornamentation executed by Antonio del Pollaiuolo; and to Lisbon it sent glazed terra cotta, eyeglasses, grammar books, and a Ptolemy. Customs records in Rome for the second half of the fifteenth century document the importation of eyeglasses, popular devotional paintings, books, intarsia work, cembali, and other products from Florence, while records of imports into England mention the more luxurious work of the city's goldsmiths, including silver buckles and buttons, golden spoons and ladles with silver ornamentation, and gold and silver basins decorated with branches and leaves in coral.[99]

Some artisans worked on commissions that came from abroad. In his 1433 tax return the painter Giuliano d'Arrigo, listing the contents of his shop, mentions a ceremonial standard being made for the lord of Faenza and two shields for Count Francesco Sforza. In 1445 the bronze slab of the tomb of Nicholas V in San Gio-

[98] Suzanne B. Butters, *The Triumph of Vulcan: Sculptors' Tools, Porphyry, and the Prince in Ducal Florence* (Florence, 1996), 1:254–62.

[99] Frangioni, *Chiedere e ottenere* (on Datini's shop in Avignon); Gino Corti and Frederick Hartt, "New Documents concerning Donatello, Luca and Andrea della Robbia, Desiderio, Mino, Uccello, Pollaiuolo, Filippo Lippi, Baldovinetti and Others," *Art Bulletin* 44 (1962): 155–67; Sergio Tognetti, *Il banco Cambini: Affari e mercati di una compagnia mercantile-bancaria nella Firenze del XV secolo* (Florence, 1999), 184–85; Arnold Esch, "Roma come centro di importazioni nella seconda metà del Quattrocento ed il peso economico del papato," in *Roma capitale (1447–1527)*, ed. Sergio Gensini (San Miniato, 1994), 119; Doris Esch, "Musikinstrumente in den römischen Zollregistern der Jahre 1470–1483," in *Studien zur italienischen Musikgeschichte*, ed. F. Lippmann (Laaber, 1998), 63; Alwin A. Ruddock, *Italian Merchants and Shipping in Southampton, 1270–1600* (Southampton, 1951), 73–74.

vanni in Laterano was sent from Florence to Rome. Local woodworkers probably prefabricated the elaborate paneling decorated with inlay that was then sent to Urbino and Gubbio to be assembled into the famous private studies *(studioli)* of the Duke of Montefeltro. The da Maiano shop of woodworkers sold furniture to the king of Hungary and sent elaborate daybeds *(lettucci)* decorated with inlay and carved woodwork to the king of Naples and to other nobles in that kingdom. Verrocchio's shop produced two reliefs representing Alexander and Darius that Lorenzo de' Medici presented to the king of Hungary, and the artist received an order for a decorative fountain from the king himself, Matthias Corvinus. In 1472 Antonio del Pollaiuolo, on a commission from the government of Florence, made a display helmet for Federigo da Montefeltro (which he may have delivered himself); and the Signoria commissioned a luxurious bed from another woodworker for the sultan in Egypt. In 1476 books purchased in Venice were brought to Florence for binding and then sent on to Siena. Iacopo di Tedesco's shop wove silk fabrics for ecclesiastical garments with the coats of arms of the king of Spain, Emperor Charles V, and Pope Paul III.

Not all these exported products fell into the luxury category. Eyeglasses, which cost no more than two soldi each, enjoyed a certain success in world markets extending from London to Constantinople, to judge not only from the orders for them recorded in surviving merchants' ledgers but also from what foreign ambassadors wrote about them in their reports. From 1462 to 1466 Duke Francesco Sforza and his son Galeazzo Maria sent orders to Florence for hundreds of these inexpensive products. In 1488 Giuliano da Maiano, in Naples, requested that his brother send him twenty thousand glazed floor tiles, products that obviously could not be supplied by the da Maiano brothers' shop, and in 1518 the painter Raphael in Rome ordered floor tiles from the Della Robbia shop for the loggia in the Vatican. Pieces produced in the Della Robbia shop are documented as having been sent to Spain, Portugal, Provence, Flanders, and England, as well as throughout Italy, including the Florentine territorial state. It has in fact been claimed that in the second half of the fifteenth century Florence had almost a monopoly in the production of the devotional terra-cotta reliefs of the Madonna and Child that are found throughout Italy.[100]

---

[100] References to the more obscure of these exports are found in Rita Comanducci, "'Buono artista della sua arte': Il concetto di 'artista' e la pratica di lavoro nella bottega quattrocentesca," in Franceschi and Fossi, *La grande storia dell'artigianato*, 2:157–58 (Giuliano d'Arrigo); Arnold Esch, "La lastra tombale di Martino V ed i registri doganali di Roma," in *Alle origini della nuova Roma: Martino V (1417–1431)* (Rome, 1992), 625–41; Sergio Tognetti, "'Fra le compagnie palesi et li ladri occulti': Banchieri senesi del Quattrocento," *Nuova rivista storica* 88 (2004): 54 (binding in Florence); Gino Corti, "Relazione di un viaggio al Soldano d'Egitto e in Terra Santa," *ASI* 116 (1958): 247–66; Goldthwaite, "Entrepreneurial Silk Weaver," 84–85; Francesco Quinterio, *Maiolica nell'architettura del Rinascimento italiano* (Florence, n.d.), 31 (tiles to Naples); Vincent Ilardi,

All this represented only occasional production in the overall history of these artisan shops. Virtually none of them produced primarily for the export trade. Artisans themselves, however, traveled widely throughout the Italian peninsula. The painter Benozzo Gozzoli carved out a market for himself in the minor towns of Umbria and Tuscany, and numerous painters went off to Rome on commission from the great ecclesiastical princes or journeyed farther afield to the royal court of Hungary in the early fifteenth century. Donatello went to Padua to work on the equestrian monument to Gattamelata, Verrocchio went to Venice to work on the one dedicated to Colleoni, and Leonardo had such a project in mind for the Sforza when he went to Milan. The architect Giuliano da Maiano traveled to Siena, Faenza, Loreto, and Naples; Michelozzo received a major appointment as architect at Ragusa; and yet other architects made their careers abroad, as did Luca Fancelli at Mantua and Iacopo Sansovino at Venice. The Pollaiuolo brothers spent their final years in Rome working on the tombs of Sixtus IV and Innocent VIII. By the second half of the fifteenth century Florentine stonemasons working abroad had a presence throughout Italy comparable to that of the Lombards in quantitative terms but much greater as measured by the higher-quality sculptural work they did. The many terra-cotta sculptors and woodworkers who went abroad were, however, in a class by themselves. Florentine mosaic artists, trained in the cathedral workshop, also found work abroad through the fourteenth century; in 1432 Paolo Uccello went to Venice to work as a mosaicist. In 1479–80 the commune received a request from the Ottoman ruler in Constantinople to send him sculptors working in bronze and craftsmen specializing in woodcarving and inlay. One of the consequences of the successive invasions by the French kings, beginning in 1494, was the trek many artisans made to France in the train of a returning king, especially Francis I. Among these were ceramic artists, who had a notable presence in early sixteenth-century Lyons. In 1518 Girolamo di Andrea Della Robbia established his own shop in France, where he remained active until his death in 1566. This veritable diaspora of Florentine artists from the fourteenth through to the early sixteenth century was facilitated by the extensive network built up by Florentine merchant-bankers, and their work abroad accounts for the preeminence of the Florentine school throughout Italy in the history of early Renaissance art. The metaphor the Duke of Urbino used when, searching for an

---

"Firenze capitale degli occhiali," in Franceschi and Fossi, *La grande storia dell'artigianato,* 2:195, 199; Gentilini, *I Della Robbia,* 35; Ronald G. Kecks, *Madonna und Kind: Das häusliche Andachtsbild im Florenz des 15. Jahrhunderts* (Berlin, 1988), 154; and J. V. G. Mallet, "Tiled Floors and Court Designers in Mantua and Northern Italy," in *The Court of the Gonzaga in the Age of Mantegna: 1450–1550,* ed. C. Mozzarelli, R. Oresko, and L. Ventura (Bologna, 1997).

architect to rebuild his capital, he called Tuscany a "fountain of architects," could be applied more widely across the spectrum of Florentine artisans.[101]

Artisans' travels abroad, of course, did not contribute directly to the local economy, except in the modest profits they might have brought home. It is possible that they were paid more abroad than at home, both in provincial markets, where artisans with their skills were not likely to be found, and in the numerous courts in Italy, where they might enjoy the largesse of a princely patron and also receive commissions much larger than anything that came their way in Florence.[102] Mino da Fiesole started his career in Florence sculpting mostly portrait busts, but it was in Rome, where he went in 1454, that he matured as a prominent sculptor with a large workshop that produced major public monuments. And within a year of his return to Rome in 1474, after ten years back in Florence, he was busy working on three tombs.[103] It is unlikely that Antonio del Pollaiuolo and his brother would have found the kind of lucrative commissions in Florence that kept them busy for a dozen years in Rome working on two papal tombs. In the 1480 catasto, just five years before leaving for the papal capital, Antonio declared land he had purchased for *fl.*415 and seven other pieces of rural property (besides his house in the city, which was exempt), but he claimed that all this did not balance the lien against his estate for his wife's dowry of *fl.*800. Sixteen years later, in 1496, after eleven years in Rome, he was in a position to include in his will a provision for dowries of *fl.*1,000 for each of his two daughters. Moreover, the brothers won posthumous recognition in the form of a prominent funerary monument with sculpted relief portraits of both at the entrance to San Pietro in Vincoli in Rome, a public recognition no contemporary artist received in Florence.[104]

Probably no artist anywhere in sixteenth-century Italy, let alone Florence, could challenge the size of the fortune Michelangelo built up in Rome. He arrived there in 1496, just twenty-one years old. By 1506 he had started work on the

[101] Roberto Bartoli, "I toscani fuor di Toscana: Viaggi d'artisti," in *Storia delle arti in Toscana: Il Quattrocento,* ed. Gigetta Dalli Regoli and Roberto Paolo Ciardi (Florence, 2002), 223–46; S. Danesi Squarzina, ed., *Maestri fiorentini nei cantieri romani del Quattrocento* (Rome, 1989); Eve Borsook, "Un mistero musivo," in *La grande storia dell'artiginato,* 1:163–71; Henri Amourice and Lucy Vallauri, "L'introduction du décor bleu de cobalt dans le Midi française, de la fin du Moyen Âge à l'époque modern," in *XXX Convegno internazionale della ceramica* (Albisola, 2002), 79–88.

[102] Michelle O'Malley, *The Business of Art: Contracts and the Commissioning Process in Renaissance Italy* (New Haven, CT, 2005), 133–34, 136, 142, argues that at the end of the fifteenth century Florentine painters were paid more abroad than at home.

[103] Shelley E. Zuraw, "Mino da Fiesole's Forteguerri Tomb: A 'Florentine' Monument in Rome," in *Artistic Exchange and Cultural Translation in the Italian Renaissance City,* ed. Stephen J. Campbell and Stephen Milner (Cambridge, 2004), 75–95.

[104] Alison Wright, *The Pollaiuolo Brothers: The Arts of Florence and Rome* (New Haven, CT, 2005), 16–17, 21; Maude Cruttwell, *Antonio Pollaiuolo* (London, 1907), 236–40 (which publishes the 1480 catasto return).

fl.10,000 contract for the tomb of Julius II and had purchased land back in Florence for *fl*.1,000, more than the highest assessment of any artist in the 1480 catasto. He certainly had not accumulated the money to buy so much land from what he was paid for work on his return trips to Florence—an annual stipend of *fl*.72 plus a bonus for the marble *David* in 1501–2 and an annual stipend of (presumably) *fl*.120 for frescoes in the Palazzo Vecchio in 1504–5. By 1523, at the age of forty-eight, he had purchased land worth almost *fl*.8,000, and when he died in 1564 he left an estate worth *fl*.22,000, having earned during his lifetime perhaps as much as *fl*.50,000.[105]

Merchants were probably responsible for the many prestigious commissions from abroad that artisans working in the luxury sector of the so-called decorative arts—and not just painters and sculptors—received during the fifteenth century. A century later Vasari, whether knowledgeable about the matter or not, took it for granted, in explaining the travels of earlier Florentine artists abroad and the export of their work, that the intermediary responsible had often been a merchant.[106] The export trade in their products, even those of the most luxurious kind, counted for very little, however, either at the level of the output of individual artisans or in the overall operations of the merchants who handled commissions from abroad or who themselves took the initiative to sell such goods abroad. Certainly no merchant made a major investment in the attempt to organize production of these goods more efficiently with the objective of improving his profits. Merchants did not, therefore, intervene directly in the operations of the artisans who produced these goods.

In short, no segment of the artisan sector of the economy was export driven. This is not to say, however, that traffic of this kind did not have a powerful indirect impact on the economy. On the one hand, merchants who handled these goods—such as the Cambini in Portugal, Filippo Strozzi in Naples, or the Medici in various places—may have used the occasional sale of such prestigious luxury goods to improve their standing, and therefore to promote their commercial and banking interests, with foreign clients who were major figures in the places where they did business. On the other hand, some artisans in Florence must have taken much inspiration from the prestigious, relatively lucrative and artistically challenging commissions that they received from abroad: the knowledge that they and their products enjoyed a certain fame among the great and powerful throughout Italy, and even Europe, meant that the world they worked in was less provin-

---

[105] Rab Hatfield, *The Wealth of Michelangelo* (Rome, 2002), assembles all the data.
[106] Martin Warnke, *Artisti di corte: Preistoria dell'artista moderno* (Rome, 1991), 136–39.

cial and insular as a result. But how is one to measure the economic importance of such intangibles?

In conclusion, the strength of the artisan sector lay not in its direct contribution to the balance of payments through production oriented to exports but in its ability to meet local demand in just about every respect, so that the market had little recourse to imported manufactured goods. The few raw materials it needed to import for its production aimed at the high end of the market—nonferrous metals, pigments, dyes, semiprecious and precious stones—hardly weighed in the overall balance of payments, while the availability of gold and silver was a direct consequence of that balance. Florentine artisans, probably more than artisans anywhere else, had the flexibility to respond to the growing demand for all kinds of objects, perhaps even the ability to generate demand for them. On the one hand, they were less bound by traditional guild structure and had a sophisticated knowledge of how to operate in the market and, on the other hand, the demand for their products kept rising through much of the period as a result of the considerable wealth that flowed into the city. In this situation the artisan had greater potential for improving the quality of his production, however much technology limited productivity gains. In chapter 7 an attempt is made to draw up a final balance for the performance of this sector through the fifteenth and sixteenth centuries by approaching the subject through a discussion of the distribution, and redistribution, of wealth in Florentine society as manifested in demand. Suffice it to conclude here that the growth of the sector can be seen in the perfection and elaboration of skills, the development of new skills, and the enlargement of the creative imagination, all of which add up to growth in human capital. And that, in the long run, marks the greatest success in the performance of any economy.

CHAPTER SIX

Banking and Credit

Banking Institutions through the Fifteenth Century:
*Historiographical Problems, Local Banks, Pawnbrokers, Welfare
Institutions, Banks and the Government, Lack of a Banking
System.*

Performance of the Banking Sector: *Practices, Economic
Functions, Bankruptcies.*

Banking outside of Banks: *Offsetting, The Private Credit
Market.*

New Directions in the Sixteenth Century: *A Public Savings-
and-Loan Bank, A Central Clearance Bank? Conclusion.*

Banking Institutions through the Fifteenth Century
Historiographical Problems

The basic function of banking is to attract deposits from private persons with
more money than they need and then to put this money to use by loaning some
of it out to persons who need it. A bank pays interest to attract deposits; it as-
sumes that not all depositors will want their money back at the same time, so
that it can risk loaning some of it out; and it makes its profits on the difference
between what it pays depositors and what it charges on its loans. In managing
this business a bank also offers various services to attract depositors and lenders, on some of which it might make additional profits. These include, to keep
the discussion within the confines of the historical period of interest here, safekeeping of money, current accounts, book transfer of debits or credits, extension of short-term credit through overdraft on current accounts, manual exchange of coins, and international transfer of funds. Through these various
activities a bank performs three important functions that stimulate economic
activity in general: it channels savings into consumption and investment; it
enlarges the money supply by creating bank money (to the extent that both
borrower and depositor are using the same money); and it increases the velocity

of the circulation of money, and hence the money supply, by facilitating payment in bank.

The documented history of full-service banking in Florence begins late. Notarial records in Genoa from the early thirteenth century document the development of deposit banks that offered overdraft and payment through transfer as well as international exchange, and good records also survive for banking in Lucca and Catalonia from the thirteenth century on. The first extensive accounting records of a deposit bank date from fourteenth-century Bruges.[1] Although banking practices had clearly emerged in Florence by this time, it is not until late in that century that we have sufficient documents of the banks themselves to study comprehensively all the essential banking functions for local banking, as distinct from international banking. The history of those practices and the subsequent evolution of banking, however, cannot be recounted in a straightforward narrative. On the one hand, institutions were diverse and not necessarily related to one another, so there is no institutional unity to the subject. International merchant banks offered banking services to their clients in Florence, and alongside these firms were local deposit banks, some opened by international merchant-bankers and others having evolved from the completely different activity of money-changing. In addition, with the passing of time other institutions appeared—pawnbrokers, the depository service of welfare organizations, the Monte di Pietà—that, though not banks strictly speaking, performed some of these functions. There was, moreover, no structural cohesion among these institutions and no central banking agency. Completely outside this amorphous institutional structure, on the other hand, most banking functions could be found in the practices of private persons dealing with one another on their own. Indeed, collectively these private practices may have had a greater impact on the local economy as a whole than did the institutions calling themselves banks.

In addition to the lack of institutional clarity, other problems confront the historian of Florentine banking. One problem, especially prominent in the historiography of the subject, is the illusion that technical progress in accounting and banking practices necessarily is a sign of progress in the role of banking in the economy at large. From the perspective of the sixteenth century, which is well beyond the range of the traditional historiography, one cannot say of banking in the fifteenth century that the future lay altogether with private banks, for all their much-touted technical proficiency. Another problem is that any history of local banking in Florence has to be constructed on the precarious discrepancy, so

---

[1] See Raymond de Roover, *Money, Banking and Credit in Mediaeval Bruges* (Cambridge, MA, 1948); for the evidence from Genoa, see 294.

characteristic of the economic history of the city, between the rich archival sources and the scant historiography. The following discussion is based largely on the only local bankers whose books have been studied—Bindaccio di Michele de' Cerchi and the sons of Niccolò Cambini, active in the third quarter of the fifteenth century, and Luigi di Lorenzo Calderini, a century later.[2]

Finally, a problem inherent in the history of banking during this period is the constraint imposed on economic activity by the usury doctrine, which subjected the extension of credit to moral imperatives. Thirteenth-century notarial contracts for loans never mention interest, whereas contemporaneous accounts are usually explicit about it. But beginning in the early fourteenth century the usury restriction began to raise problems about the charging of interest. The growth of the economy and the development of instruments for utilizing capital for business enterprises generated practices that patently went against the doctrine and by the same token aroused a more vigorous defense of the doctrine. This dialectic process generated compromise on both sides—that of practice, with recourse to circumvention, and that of theory, with recourse to reservations, refinements, and exceptions—but it was a precarious compromise and one that created many ambiguities in practice. On the one hand, some capitalists at the end of their career, confronting the ultimate destiny of their souls and repentant of their usurious activity, made testamentary provisions for restitution to all their victims, sometimes collectively through a charitable bequest and sometimes individually. On the other hand, some clerics were always ready to reject any compromise and rant and rave against the illicit practices they saw all around them. The compromise and tensions were probably felt more keenly in fifteenth-century Florence than anywhere else, since credit instruments that lubricated the economy reached a high level of technical refinement there and since two of the most important late medieval religious thinkers who addressed the subject, the popular Sienese preacher Saint Bernardino (1380–1444) and the bishop of the city, Saint Antonino (1389–1459), were prominent figures on the public scene at the same time. Of course, the economic realities were not to be denied, and the operators in the credit market found ways to largely circumvent the usury restriction without erasing the bottom line, the fixing of the interest rate at the beginning of a contract. Moreover, the state recognized manifest usury in licensing Christian moneylenders, although it pulled back when, in 1437, it shifted the licenses to Jewish

---

[2] Richard A. Goldthwaite, "Local Banking in Renaissance Florence," *Journal of European Economic History* 14 (1985): 5–55; idem, "Banking in Florence at the End of the Sixteenth Century," ibid. 27 (1998): 504–9; Sergio Tognetti, "L'attività di banca locale di una grande compagnia fiorentina del XV secolo," *Archivio storico italiano* (hereafter *ASI*) 155 (1997): 595–647. For an overview of local banking in the early fourteenth century, see Charles Marie de La Roncière, *Un changeur florentin du Trecento: Lippo di Fede del Sega (1285 env.–1363 env.)* (Paris, 1963), ch. 4.

pawnbrokers, who fell outside the Christian community. For its part the church too recognized the legitimacy of modest interest charges at the beginning of a contract as a fundamental principle in the foundation of the Monte di Pietà, initially, one by one as they were founded, beginning with Pius II's approval of the Monte at Orvieto in 1464, and then as a general sanction in a bull issued by Leo X at the Fifth Lateran Council in 1515.

Banks both charged and paid interest, and the devices they used to cover up their illicit activities are well known. The bill of exchange has already been mentioned, and other subterfuges will be encountered in the following discussion of banking practices. The circumvention of the usury restriction lay in the technicality that the interest charge was established at the time of the repayment of the loan, not at its issue. On a bill of exchange it depended entirely on exchange rates in the future (and sometimes these could work against the lender), whereas on what was called a discretionary deposit it depended, in theory, on the discretion of the borrower. Nevertheless, account entries for the former, whether in the lender's or the borrower's ledger, usually contain enough basic information about the transaction to make it possible to calculate the interest charge; and most records of discretionary loans explicitly state the rate. On other kinds of loans, however, banks practiced a complete cover-up. Their records for loans made on the security of a pawn, a promissory note, or simply the legal authority of an account entry rarely yield a hint about the interest charged. Bankers probably did what notaries did: they entered in their record book and ledger only what the borrower owed when the loan fell due, not what he actually received. In short, bankers—and others—had no difficulty in circumventing the usury restriction, but at what cost? Economic historians are not agreed on what effect the doctrine and the ensuing practices had on the economy in the long run.[3]

Local Banks

International merchant-bankers performed many banking functions for their clients at the local level. They offered the service of a current account, including assignment to third parties and transfer of funds outside of the bank and beyond the local market to just about anywhere in western Europe; they extended credit through overdraft, the bill of exchange, and arrangements for delayed payment; and they accepted interest-bearing time deposits. All these features can be found, to a greater or lesser extent, in the accounts of the ledger of the Covoni company

[3] For a positive view, see Frederic C. Lane, "Investment and Usury," reprinted from *Explorations in Entrepreneurial History,* 2nd ser., 2 (1964), in *Venice and History: The Collected Papers of Frederic C. Lane* (Baltimore, 1966), 67–68.

in Padua, open from 1336 to 1339.[4] International merchant-bankers usually conducted their business in Florence from an office inside their place of residence. They did not deal with the general public beyond their circle of clients, who, however, included many local firms, especially lanaioli and setaioli, as well as other merchants. As a rule, they did not engage in deposit banking at the local level.

Deposit banking, like international banking, arose from the activity of money-changing, but in the local market. Manual exchange was an essential service in any urban market exposed to the continual influx of diverse coins at a time when a town of any size had its own mint and when there was considerable monetary instability resulting from lack of any uniform standards and from frequent and often irresponsible debasements. Under these conditions, uncertainty about coins abounded, and speculators were always ready to exploit the situation. The record book of Lippo di Fede del Sega (ca. 1285–ca. 1363) documents the kind of traffic in coins that took place in the market at the beginning of the fourteenth century. Taking advantage of variance in the value of coins from one place to another, he bought foreign coins to have them reminted at the local mint as Florentine coins, at times receiving back not coins but blanks suitable for minting elsewhere. He also carried coins, and perhaps such blanks from the Florentine mint itself, to the provincial mint of Volterra for reminting as Florentine coins notwithstanding legislation against such foreign production of the city's coins. Del Sega traveled extensively throughout Tuscany and farther afield to Perugia, Bologna, and Venice to buy and sell coins. His record book includes a list of coins from many different places, some of them clearly designated as coins of one place but minted in another. Del Sega was not an official moneychanger; but in a market flooded with so many foreign coins, some official and some not and many of doubtful intrinsic value, the commune had to recognize the necessity of providing the public with official moneychangers, who performed the essential function of ascertaining the value of coins. These men also engaged in the related activity of dealing in precious metals, and they were important suppliers to the mint.[5]

It is not difficult to see the logic in the steps that led from simple moneychanging to dealing in money on a larger scale—the use of security facilities to attract deposits for safekeeping, the transformation of these deposit arrangements into current accounts complete with transferable credits and overdraft, and the lending out of any capital on hand in return for pawns of a relatively high value, above

[4] Giulio Mandich illustrates them all in his introduction to *Libro giallo della compagnia dei Covoni*, ed. Armando Sapori (Milan, 1970), cxxiv–clv.

[5] De La Roncière, *Un changeur florentin du Trecento*. See also Lucia Travaini, *Monete, mercanti e matematica* (Rome, 2003), 26–27, 144–46.

all jewelry. The evolution from simple moneychanging to these additional activities cannot be traced in the documents; but at the point where they were attracting capital, loaning it out, and facilitating transfer, moneychangers were operating as full-fledged bankers. They had their own guild, the Arte del Cambio, setting them off in a sphere of local activity distinct from that of international merchant-bankers. The earliest guild statutes are dated 1299, but sections therein were clearly copied from earlier versions. Their importance in the local economy at the time is manifest in their status as one of the major guilds in the hierarchy of the guild republic. Moneychangers *(cambiatori)* came to be called also bankers *(banchieri* or *tavolieri)*, from the counter *(banco* or *tavola)* across which they did business with the public. Since they confined their activity exclusively to the local market and did not engage in international banking, they will be referred to here as local bankers to distinguish them from international merchant-bankers. For all the official status they had as members of one of the major guilds, they were regarded with some suspicion as usurers. For this reason the 1294 statutes of the confraternity of the Madonna of Orsanmichele forbid the deposit of any of the organization's moneys with them.[6] A century later, in 1398, when Francesco Datini consulted his associates about opening a local bank, he received some negative reactions. His factor in Florence reported that when people heard the news, they told him that Datini "wants to lose his name as the biggest merchant of Florence to become a money-changer, since there is not one of them who does not make usurious contracts" and that "they will say he is a *chorsino* [usurer]." To these warnings the factor replied in his employer's defense that none of this was true, because "what he has he will leave to the poor." And Datini's partner in Valencia wrote that "it does not seem to me that you have the best advice about the bank, because I see that most moneychangers tend to take up commerce and leave moneychanging, since they make more profit and also because it is more just in the eyes of God."[7]

What little we know about these men before the second half of the fourteenth century derives mostly from the records of their guild, the Cambio. The guild statutes, like guild statutes everywhere, are concerned mostly with internal organizational matters and professional standards, especially about money and relations between members, rather than with the actual conduct of business. Moreover, guild statutes are often outdated by subsequent practice. The guild required registration of all banks, and some of these rosters survive. The earliest, dating from about 1300, lists 130 banks; Giovanni Villani, writing about two generations

[6] Arrigo Castellani, ed., *Nuovi testi fiorentini del Dugento* (Florence, 1952), 2:659.
[7] Federigo Melis, *Aspetti della vita economica medievale: Studi nell'Archivio Datini di Prato* (Siena, 1962), 212–13.

later, says that there were 80. After the Black Death, which left the city with a much-reduced population, the number of banks on surviving rosters fluctuates between 60 and 70 until the early fifteenth century and then falls to about 50 toward the end of the century. On the rosters these banks appear as companies, or partnerships: they are officially identified by the name of the banker followed by the words *e compagni,* "and partners," even though many, in fact, were one-man businesses with no partners, and few had more than two partners.

According to the early fourteenth-century guild statutes, these banks were concentrated in the business center of the city, in an area extending from the Mercato Vecchio (now the Piazza della Repubblica) to Orsanmichele and the Mercato Nuovo, and there were also a few across the river. Most of those operating in the fifteenth century for which we have evidence were located in either the Mercato Nuovo or the Mercato Vecchio. Nothing is known about any measures taken for police protection of the area to make it secure for local banking operations. The shop housing the bank of Paolo di Alessandro Sassetti was described in 1375 as closed from outside by a green iron-chain curtain over the entrance and furnished inside with a large counter covered with a carpet—the public sign of the moneychanger—and containing a built-in strongbox and a bench behind, permitting the banker to sit at a higher level than his clients. Its equipment probably included what Francesco Datini bought on opening his bank in 1398: an inkwell, account books, a box with a lock to hold papers, a money dish for the counter, money bags with locks and seals, and a variety of other locks and keys.[8] Other expenses included materials for assaying and refining precious metals. Some bankers employed a boy as cashier, and all conducted their business through brokers who had official guild status. Brokers were essential agents in the banking business since they identified potential clients and brought them together with the banker. We have already encountered Botticelli's brother, Giovanni di Mariano Filipepi, who began his career as a broker and then went on to become a partner in the international bank of Tommaso Spinelli in Rome. Another broker commissioned Botticelli to paint his *Adoration of the Magi,* now in the Uffizi, for his chapel in Santa Maria Novella. Bankers themselves could serve as brokers to people who wanted to make a personal loan to another party but presumably preferred to go through the formal channel of a bank. Thus in 1465 the painter Neri di Bicci had recourse to Francesco Bagnesi & Partners to arrange a loan of forty lire to a tenant on his land outside the city; the loan was registered on the banker's books and repaid through the bank.[9]

---

[8] These details come from Goldthwaite, "Local Banking," 11. The carpet covering the counter is discussed in Marco Spallanzani, *Oriental Rugs in Renaissance Florence* (Florence, 2007), 53.

[9] Neri di Bicci, *Le ricordanze (10 marzo 1453–24 aprile 1475),* ed. Bruno Santi (Pisa, 1976), 257, 262.

The firm of Bindaccio di Michele de' Cerchi, open from 1472 to 1485, is the best-documented local bank that has been studied. Like many of these bankers, Cerchi was in business on his own, but the bank had a formal organization at least in name. "I have no partners," Cerchi once noted, "but the bank is known as Bindaccio and Partners"; and he used the plural *we* in recording his dealings with clients. It was a small business. Many of his clients were artisans and shop-keepers, and the balance Cerchi drew up in August 1482 shows total assets of only just over *fl.*500. In fact, Cerchi worked alone for eight years before employing a sixteen-year-old cashier. In his ledger of deposit accounts he made no more than one entry a week during one six-month period, all together filling up only forty-one pages. Nevertheless, his activity embraced the basic banking functions, if on a very small scale. His books document two time deposits for six months, on which he paid interest of 9 percent. He accepted deposits for safekeeping pay-able on demand and opened current accounts, but activity on them consisted of little more than a single deposit and a subsequent withdrawal or two after only a few weeks; the accounts reveal relatively few transfers to third parties, and they were seldom overdrawn. Cerchi made small loans ranging from *fl.*2 to *fl.*50, gener-ally repayable in no more than six months. Most of these were secured only by a promissory note, but for some he accepted a lien on a government obligation (a credit in the Monte, the state debt) or claims on future interest payments on such obligations or, to a lesser extent, a relatively valuable pawn, such as jewels, jewelry, silverware, or clothing accessories. Loans of all kinds averaged *fl.*1,170 annually during the period 1480–84.

As moneychangers these local bankers had to have expert preparation in the assaying of coins. One of the employees who filed a claim for back salary from the firm of Taddeo dell'Antella & Partners when it went bankrupt in 1345 stated that he had started out his employment with the firm, working eighteen months at the counter and at the furnace refining gold.[10] Since they loaned on pawns, bankers also had to know something about "rings and jewels, as the profession requires," as we learn from the apprenticeship of Giovanni da Empoli, the merchant who traveled to the Far East, in his father's bank in the late 1490s.[11] Indeed, Raymond de Roover described the bank of Francesco di Giuliano de' Medici (d. 1528), active in the early sixteenth century, as essentially a high-level pawn bank, lending on the security of jewelry and other valuable objects.[12] The books of Luigi Calderini,

---

[10] Armando Sapori, "Il quaderno dei creditori di Taddeo dell'Antella e compagni," *Rivista delle biblioteche e degli archivi*, n.s., 3 (1925): 179–80.

[11] From his uncle's biography of him, printed in Marco Spallanzani, *Giovanni da Empoli: Un mercante fiorentino nell'Asia portoghese*, 2nd ed. (Florence, 1999), 125.

[12] Raymond de Roover, *The Rise and Decline of the Medici Bank, 1397–1494* (Cambridge, MA, 1963), 15.

Giuliano Guiducci & Partners *del banco,* open from 1580 to 1587, show that it dealt almost exclusively in the buying and selling of gold, silver, jewelry, and other luxury objects, including the consignment of gold to goldsmiths for the manufacture of chains and buttons. In fact, one of the partners contributed only gold valuables as his share in the capital of the firm. The bank also engaged in manual exchange and lending for pawns; however, the relative importance of this kind of over-the-counter business as compared with dealing in valuables cannot be assessed, since it left little evidence in the firm's accounts. The bank had only a few deposits, and collectively these did not constitute a significant activity. Calderini, Guiducci & Partners, however, was by no means a small business: it had a capital of *fl.*5,000, and it returned slightly more than that in profits to its partners in just seven years.[13] Its activity appears as a branch of the jewelry business, but it identified itself as a "bank" and falls into a tradition that can be seen as a logical evolution from the moneychangers of the thirteenth century. Although in the fourteenth century moneychangers were distinct from goldsmiths, each having a separate guild identity, sixteenth-century legislation directed specifically to regulating the guild of Por Santa Maria, which included goldsmiths, frequently refers to the two professions as virtually one and the same.[14]

Among these local banks were some set up by international merchant-bankers who wanted to move into this sphere of activity in the local market as an extension of their business abroad. To open a local *tavola* merchant-bankers had to become members of the Cambio, where they registered their business on the official guild roster. The Cambio, however, made no distinction between local banks operated by international banks and those that were strictly local operations, since it concerned itself exclusively with those activities in the local market that derived from manual exchange. In the following discussion, therefore, it will be useful to distinguish between these two kinds of Cambio banks; to that end, those that belonged to international bankers will here be referred to as international Cambio banks, and the others, as local banks.[15] One notable difference between the two categories of Cambio banks could be the scale of operations. In contrast to Cerchi's miniscule operation, for instance, were giants such as the bank of the brothers Agnolo, Giovanni, Niccolò, and Galeazzo di Lapo da Uzzano,

---

[13] Goldthwaite, "Banking in Florence," 504–9.

[14] For example, *Legislazione toscana raccolta e illustrata dal dottore Lorenzo Cantini socio di varie accademie* (Florence, 1802–8) 8:215, puts "orefici o banchieri che tenghino orerie o argenterie o altre cose attententi allo esercizio dell'orefice" in one category of guild membership for purposes of setting matriculation fees (1575).

[15] De Roover called the strictly local Cambio banks *banchi a minuto* and those set up by international bankers *banchi grossi.* Both terms seem to have been his own invention, but the latter is found in Benedetto Dei, *La cronica dall'anno 1400 all'anno 1500,* ed. Roberto Barducci (Florence, 1984), 82, where it has the precise meaning intended by de Roover.

whose extant records from the 1360s show that it had branches in Pisa, Bologna, Genoa, Venice, Rome, and Naples and that it almost daily made loans ranging from less than one to over a thousand florins.[16]

International Cambio banks were located in the Mercato Nuovo, undoubtedly because this put them in the immediate vicinity of the shops of setaioli and many lanaioli, the producers whom they dealt with as importer-exporters. These local banks of international merchant-banking firms were organized in one of two ways: either they were set up as autonomous firms operating within the larger business agglomerate of their owners or they were direct extensions of the international merchant-banking firm in the local market. The wealthy Prato merchant Francesco Datini, whose agglomerate of companies and agents extended all around the western Mediterranean from Pisa to Avignon, Barcelona, and Majorca, organized his bank as a partnership separate from his other companies operating abroad. Others, however, such as the Cambini, had no autonomous organizational structure: the merchant or parent firm simply opened a separate set of books for local operations (this was to meet a guild requirement) and integrated them into their larger accounting system. It is not clear whether the distinction between these two kinds of Cambio merchant banks was functional or merely organizational. Like the da Uzzano bank mentioned above, the *tavola* of the Cambini, the only international Cambio bank to have been studied, was clearly tied into the wider commercial activity of the firm. The *tavola* of Datini, which has not been studied, notwithstanding the most complete set of accounts to survive for any of these local banks, appears to have been a more autonomous business. The two kinds of international Cambio banks probably did not differ, however, in the services they offered to the general public.

Opening a local *tavola* involved the merchant-banker in a different kind of banking, one that was not without its moral stigma, as Datini was warned. Yet by moving into this sphere the merchant-banker opened what was, in the context of banking at the time, a comprehensive, full-service bank. International Cambio banks performed the same functions as the other Cambio banks, though they may have dispensed with certain petty activities, such as small-scale pawn banking, but unlike the local banks, they could also offer the services of their parent merchant-banking firm. Merchant-bankers may have opened local banking offices because it allowed them to raise further capital by attracting deposits from the public in general; to this extent they were appendages of their owners' wider commercial activity. Hence as Cambio banks they operated on a much larger

---

[16] Victor I. Rutenburg, "La compagnia Uzzano (su documenti dell'archivio di Leningrado)," in *Studi in onore di Armando Sapori* (Milan, 1957), 1:689–706.

scale than the local banks. The Cambini bank annually extended credit through overdraft alone that amounted to more than ten times what the Cerchi bank put out in all its loans. Local banking also gave the merchant-banker a solid credit foundation at his headquarters in Florence to better counterbalance the firm's indebtedness from commercial operations abroad, which usually required much time before transactions were completed and profits realized. In fact, the Cambini bank's overextension of borrowing in the local market to compensate for credits abroad that it was having difficulty in bringing home led to the firm's bankruptcy in 1482.[17]

If merchant-bankers could open a local bank, a local banker presumably could have moved into international merchant banking. The way was not blocked by guild barriers. The father of Boccaccio, Boccaccino (or Boccaccio) di Chellino, whose family immigrated to Florence from Certaldo in 1297, is documented as a moneychanger in Paris in 1313, perhaps also functioning as a "Lombard" money-lender; the next year he was back in Florence, where he enrolled in the Cambio. He operated a bank with partners and was active in guild affairs. At some point, however, he went to work for the Bardi, who sent him to Naples in 1327, where he remained until 1338, occasionally traveling abroad to Paris, Venice, and back to Florence. As a factor in an international firm he could easily have become, with sufficient financial means, a merchant-banker himself.[18] At the end of the century, to judge from what Datini's partner in Valencia wrote to him in the letter cited above, many local bankers were entering into international merchant banking. Two later examples have already been cited: Botticelli's brother, Giovanni di Mariano Filipepi, and Paliano di Falco Falcucci.

In conclusion, there were three kinds of Cambio banks: local banks, international Cambio banks that were autonomous firms within a larger merchant-banking agglomerate, and international Cambio banks that were simply extensions of the activity of a merchant-banking firm to the local market. All these Cambio banks were local operations, the first kind being strictly that and the latter two part of a larger international business. Moreover, one could pass from the ranks of one to the ranks of another. It is important to note, however, that by no means all international merchant-bankers opened a local bank. The Medici business agglomerate long included a local bank, but Filippo Strozzi (d. 1491), one of the wealthiest merchant-bankers in the city, never opened one. Datini opened his bank only toward the end of his long career, in 1398, and then closed it down after less than two

---

[17] This failure is documented in Sergio Tognetti, *Il banco Cambini: Affari e mercati di una compagnia mercantile-bancaria nella Firenze del XV secolo* (Florence, 1999).

[18] Reinhold Mueller, "Boccaccino, Giovanni Boccaccio, and Venice," *Studi sul Boccaccio* 25 (1997): 133–42.

years. Merchant banks that did not open a local bank, however, also performed important banking functions for their local clients, as observed above.

Pawnbrokers

With the development of a monetary economy came a need, felt most keenly in the lower economic classes, for a relatively easy way to obtain short-term credit, and borrowing in exchange for pawns was the obvious solution.[19] As we shall see, many Florentines were prepared to make personal loans depending on particular circumstances, and moneylending of this kind was widespread throughout the society. The demand for money, however, far exceeded what individuals operating in a private capacity could satisfy, and some men established themselves in the moneylending business by opening a pawn bank that engaged in the sole activity of making loans in exchange for the security of a pawn, the standard rate of interest being about 20–30 percent. Because of the canonical ban on usury and outcries against this kind of activity that mounted in the early fourteenth century, the commune eventually sought to exercise some control over the situation. In 1351 it in effect licensed the business by limiting it to twenty-one bankers in return for payment of fines imposed on them collectively. In 1367 the Cambio forbade its members from engaging in the practice, but this meant only that those who continued in the business no longer had guild membership. Thereafter, guild bankers who, like Cerchi, made loans in exchange for pawns limited this practice to the relatively high end of the market, as we have seen, far above the level of working people, who needed some access to credit in moments of distress.

Lenders of money at interest, whether individuals or pawn bankers, were of course concerned about the usury prohibition. In their wills they often made bequests to atone for their illicit activity, some even calling on their executors to do restitution, that is, to return their ill-gotten gains to their victims. The earliest known testament of this kind is that of Pagno Bordone, who in 1295–96 left £1,600 for this purpose. A sampling of testaments before the mid-fourteenth century reveals that about 12 percent stipulated restitution of ill-gotten gains, and although by the fifteenth century this usually took the form of some kind of

[19] On pawnbroking, see the articles of Armando Sapori in vol. 1 of his *Studi di storia economica: Secoli XIII, XIV, XV,* 3 vols. (Florence, 1955–67); Umberto Cassuto, *Gli Ebrei a Firenze nell'età del Rinascimento* (Florence, 1918); Marino Ciardini, *I banchieri ebrei in Firenze nel secolo XV e il Monte di Pietà fondato da Girolamo Savonarola* (Florence, 1907); Marvin Becker, "Three Cases concerning the Restitution of Usury in Florence," *Journal of Economic History* 17 (1957): 445–50; and Riccardo Fubini, "Prestito ebraico e Monte di Pietà a Firenze (1471–1473)," in his *Quattrocento fiorentino: Politica diplomazia cultura* (Pisa, 1996), 159–216.

blanket bequest to finance a religious or social service, instances have been found of restitution to specific victims.[20]

Estate records that survive from the end of the fourteenth century for two Christian usurers, Bartolomeo di Bartolo Cocchi Compagni (d. 1389) and Agostino di Dino Migliorelli (d. 1396 or 1397), reveal this concern and complement one another in what they tell us about how executors proceeded in the matter. Neither of these men appears on the guild rosters of local bankers. Cocchi was a lanaiolo, at least in his earlier years, and had some prominence as a political figure, having been elected to the priorate in 1374. In 1377 the Parte Guelfa publicly admonished him as "an evil man and usurer," but the conferment of a knighthood on him by the government of the Ciompi would indicate that he was considerably esteemed by the masses, notwithstanding, or perhaps because of, his profession. Migliorelli, who was not matriculated in either of the guilds of major economic importance at the time, the Lana or the Calimala, operated a pawn bank, at one time having two places of business in the city. He left an estate assessed at *fl.*35,990, including government obligations (Monte credits) worth *fl.*45,000 on paper, which must have been one of the largest in the city.

The records for the settlement of Cocchi's estate document the procedures by which the executors identified the persons who were objects of his usurious activity. What survives for Migliorelli is a ledger kept for the inventory and disposition of his wealth, which includes separate accounts for each person paid restitution. The executors of Cocchi's estate paid a total of *fl.*2,164 to more than 100 borrowers, including the abbot of Santa Trinita and the Lana guild. The executors of Migliorelli's estate, for whom it took five years to complete the task of making restitution, paid *fl.*3,175 to 259 borrowers, 13 of whom, including the bishop of the city and the abbots of San Salvi and (again) Santa Trinita, received between *fl.*50 and *fl.*200, and the rest an average of *fl.*8, far above the level of petty distress loans to the desperately poor. The amounts paid out for restitution represent significant loans, since restitution involved some negotiation—*per sua chortesia* is a recurring phrase in the Migliorelli account entries—and was probably made only for what was considered in excess of an acceptable rate, *ad donum honestum* (the term used by the Cocchi executors without specifying what that might have been). If restitution is calculated at a rate of 10 percent, these loans possibly added up to about *fl.*20,000 for Cocchi and *fl.*30,000 for Migliorelli, not including those that could not be proved usurious. Although we do not know the length of time for which they provided these loans, it is clear that these two private moneylend-

---

[20] George Dameron, *Florence and Its Church in the Age of Dante* (Philadelphia, 2005), 170 (the early fourteenth-century samples); Nicola Ottokar, *Il comune di Firenze alla fine del Dugento* (Florence, 1926), 96 (Bordone).

ers, whether licensed or not, performed an important function in maintaining liquidity in the local market. The level of their business, in short, exposes a serious limitation to the service provided by local banks, an impression that is confirmed by the prestige of some of their clients.[21]

Toward the end of the fourteenth century the rising tide of mendicant preaching against manifest usury made the situation ever more difficult for Christian moneylenders. In 1394 some guilds made provisions in their statutes against lending of this kind. The state too began trying to clamp down on them more seriously, continuing to impose fees in the form of fines and limiting the maximum rate of interest they could charge. In addition, it empowered the Monte officials, who managed the state debt, with the sole authority to settle the estates of manifest usurers to assure restitution to the people who had borrowed from them. The government, however, could not close down these businesses altogether until it found another mechanism for performing their essential function. This happened in 1437, when, after many years of bargaining, the commune made a contract with the Jew Abramo da San Miniato for the organization of a consortium of fellow Jews who agreed to open four pawn banks with a total capital of *fl.*40,000. Only at this point did the government not renew the licenses of the Christian moneylenders. By this time, however, few of these may have been practicing, since the preamble to the legislation indicated that one of the reasons for this new arrangement was the absence of public lending, which forced many who sought loans to go outside the city. If this was true, then it is clear that these Jewish pawn banks were set up to serve others apart from the poor at the lowest economic rung, who could hardly have made the trip to a nearby city to pawn whatever modest valuable they might have had.

The concern in the above legislation that people were going outside the city to find someone who would lend money to them indicates that moneylenders were operating in the countryside. In fact, long before confronting the problem in the city the government had recognized the legitimacy of Jewish pawn banks in the provincial towns of the territorial state. Since about 1300 Jews from Rome had been spreading out northward to open pawn banks in Lazio, Umbria, and Tuscany. In

---

[21] Armando Sapori, "L'interesse del denaro a Firenze nel Trecento (dal testamento di un usuraio)," in his *Studi,* 1:223–43 (Cocchi); Sergio Tognetti, "'Aghostino chane a chui Christo perdoni': L'eredità di un grande usuraio nella Firenze di fine Trecento," *ASI* 164 (2006): 667–712 (Migliorelli). I am indebted to John Padgett for the information about these two men in guild records. A testament from the end of the fifteenth century requiring restitution to specific victims has been studied by Florence Edler de Roover; see "Restitution in Renaissance Florence," in *Studi in onore di Armando Sapori,* 2:775–89. Another testator, from earlier in the century, instructed his heirs to follow any future official church decision on the matter of restitution for usury. Lawrin Armstrong, "Usury, Conscience and Public Debt: Angelo Corbinelli's Testament of 1419," in *A Renaissance of Conflicts: Visions and Revisions of Law and Society in Italy and Spain,* ed. John Marino and Thomas Kuehn (Toronto, 2004), 173–240.

Tuscany they first showed up at Siena and in other nearby places; in the second half of the century they moved also to Pisa, to Lucca and then into the Valdinievole, and to various places in the Valdichiana. In the early fifteenth century they were to be found throughout the Florentine state—at San Gimignano, San Miniato, Empoli, Volterra, Pisa, Pescia, Pistoia, and Prato to the west and at Arezzo and Castiglion Fiorentino to the southeast. In return for the contracts admitting Jews to these provincial centers with the right to open pawn banks, the state gained access to new revenues, but it must also have recognized the problem caused by a growing need for credit in small towns that lacked institutions to make it available.

Opposition to this usurious activity, however, was more effective in delaying such a concession in the capital city itself. It has generally been claimed that the commune made the decision to admit Jewish pawn banks in part as a response to mendicant pressures against Christian pawnbrokers and in part as a device to raise badly needed funds from the license granted to Jews. In addition, the literature hardly fails to mention the economic distress among the poor that gave rise to the business in the first place. The commune's rationale, stated explicitly in requests to the pope for approval of its eventual policy in favor of a contract with the Jews, emphasized the need of the poor for such a service not otherwise provided, while also admitting that it was not an altogether good thing.[22] The city fathers were up against popular mendicant preachers like San Bernardino, who were making pawnbroking more untenable for those Christians engaging in it, but they knew that any contraction of the business would create a social crisis. The Jews were called in to fill this widening gap, not just to provide the state with a fiscal expedient.

Within a month of the 1437 contract, Jews were operating four pawn banks, each a separate business with its own area of the city. They kept more or less this number open throughout the century. The commune periodically renewed what was essentially a license, or charter, but only after considerable consternation in the legislative councils. Yet in 1491, when the charter was renewed for twenty-five years rather than the usual ten, the government in effect recognized them as permanent institutions. The charters granted the Jews a monopoly privilege to lend for pawns (but forbade lending for promissory notes) and allowed them to charge 20 percent interest; in return, they were obliged to pay a fee and on occasion to make loans to the government. These Jewish pawnbrokers had access to large amounts of cash. One of them, Salamone di Bonaventura da Terracina, having been condemned in January 1441 for violation of the contract, was able to pay

[22] Gene Brucker, "Ecclesiastical Courts in Fifteenth-Century Florence and Fiesole," *Medieval Studies* 53 (1991): 248n.

the enormous fine of *fl.*20,000 in only five months, in May. Another, Vitale da Montalcino, who was given four years to pay a fine of *fl.*22,000 imposed on him in 1461, was reduced to poverty; whether he ever paid the fine is not known.

The Jewish pawnbrokers seem to have assumed other banking functions. In 1481 the commune granted them the right to engage in manual exchange. They also accepted interest-bearing deposits from Christians; indeed, some Florentines may have privately contributed to the *fl.*40,000 capital that the Jews agreed to invest in their original operation.[23] The articles of association for a pawn bank set up in 1491 as a partnership between the Jews Abramo di Dattilo da San Miniato and Elia di Dattilo da Vigevano, with a capital of *fl.*3,000, permitted the partners to add up to *fl.*3,000 more as *sopraccorpo* paying 12 percent interest and to raise up to *fl.*2,000 more by accepting deposits paying 10 percent. The names of some depositors were to be kept secret, presumably to protect Christians from being exposed for their involvement in manifest usury.[24] Yet in the accounts of one Christian who in 1493 loaned *fl.*550 to the Jewish moneylender Datero di Salamone da Camerino for one year at 10 percent, the nature of the transaction is clearly explained in the debit entry opened in Datero's name, although the account was eventually balanced by credits only for cash repayments of the capital, without any indication of payment of interest.[25] There is some evidence, too, that these outside depositors could open current accounts.[26] How extensively Jewish pawn banks engaged in these other activities, from moneychanging to acceptance of interest-bearing deposits and the services of a current account is unknown, but to the extent that they did, they would have functioned as full-fledged local banks.

In making the 1437 contract with Jewish moneylenders, the government recognized a basic fact of the economic life of the city. It imposed a comprehensive organization on an area of activity that had heretofore operated haphazardly and hesitantly owing to the usury restriction, and it assured the smooth functioning of the credit market at its lowest level. If it did not lower the cost of credit to borrowers, the state at least brought that cost under control and, through fees, appropriated some of the profits from this activity for the public good. Jewish pawn banks, in short, were an essential part of the Florentine banking scene. They used capital from the Jewish community, with its networks abroad, to operate at the low end of the credit market, where other banks never entered. Moreover, the scope of their business, as we shall see, extended well beyond distress loans understood in

[23] This has been suggested by Fubini, "Prestito ebraico e Monte di Pietà," 176–80; to date, however, no evidence to this effect has been found in the private records of Florentines.

[24] Michele Luzzati, "Firenze e le origini della banca moderna," *Studi storici* 28 (1987): 433–34.

[25] ASF, Gondi, 263 (anonymous ledger, 1491–96), fol. 73.

[26] Luzzati, "Firenze e le origini della banca moderna," 433–34.

the narrow sense often used to decry the misery presumably underlying the demand for them.

Welfare Institutions

Florentines occasionally deposited cash and jewelry for safekeeping with the city's leading welfare institutions, especially when they fled the city to escape the plague or internal violence.[27] The local Benedictine monastery, the Badia, and the city's largest hospital, Santa Maria Nuova, seem to have been the most popular places for such deposits. The service was probably used only on occasion, and procedures were of the simplest kind. In 1436, for example, Santa Maria Nuova accepted *fl.*84 from the setaiolo Lapo di Pacino and wrote out a receipt that was then torn into two pieces, one of which was put into a bag with the money, while the other was given to Lapo, to be presented by him or anyone else whenever the money was to be returned.[28] In the third quarter of the fifteenth century, however, both Santa Maria Nuova and the recently founded orphanage of the Innocenti advanced beyond this primitive kind of safekeeping to open ledgers for the sole purpose of keeping track of a growing traffic in cash deposits. By the beginning of the next century the Badia, the place the Monte di Pietà, founded in 1495, first used as a depository, was also maintaining a "book of deposits." Depositors at Santa Maria Nuova included artisans and others of the middling classes who had no other outlet for savings or investment, such as Leonardo da Vinci and Michelangelo.[29] Some deposits were for nothing more than safekeeping; others were conditioned by being tied to dowry payments, property transfers, or estates of minors. Most of the deposits in Michelangelo's account were made in cash, including one made by a local bank and another by a bank in Rome; debits consisted of cash withdrawals and payments made in his name by the hospital to third parties.

Both the hospital and the orphanage paid interest on some deposits, usually 5 percent, a practice that grew after the turn of the century; however, we do not know how, or whether, funds collected in this way were used to generate the income necessary to pay interest. According to the contemporary historian Giovanni Cambi, in 1527, a year of growing political and military crisis, the hospital loaned money to the government at 12 percent and 14 percent interest—the

---

[27] For much of the following discussion, see Goldthwaite, "Banking in Florence," 512–14. The reference to the Badia's "Libro de' dipositti . . . segnato C," open in 1509, comes from Bruno Dini, "Le ricordanze di un rammendatore (1488–1538)," reprinted from *Nuova rivista storica* 74 (1990) in *Manifattura, commercio e banca nella Firenze medievale* (Florence, 2001), 194.

[28] Goldthwaite, "Local Banking," 44–45.

[29] Both of whose accounts are published in Rab Hatfield, *The Wealth of Michelangelo* (Rome, 2002), ch. 3 and 279–90, 426–52.

normal rates paid on the floating debt—while paying only 5 percent and 8 percent interest on its deposits. Although deposits do not seem to have added up to a significant activity within the overall operations of either the hospital or the orphanage, separate books were opened for this sole purpose; and as we shall see, deposits grew rapidly in the course of the early sixteenth century. The surviving books of both institutions, as well as any relevant Badia materials, await study to assess the operation as a business activity in the overall administration of the property of an institution dedicated to the performance of social services. Their very existence, however, is an indicator of a major change in the local money and credit market that transformed banking in the sixteenth century.

The opening of these depositories by the city's most prominent welfare institutions, all of which had close ties to the ecclesiastical establishment, along with the virtually permanent status that Jewish pawn banks came to enjoy on the local scene, contributed to a softening of the traditional prejudice against usury in many of its forms. Church intellectuals slowly came to terms with the problems occasioned by the payment of interest on the public debt; they also recognized the validity of certain business practices involving payment of interest. Some of these practices, as we shall see, were now out in the open, or barely disguised, and the welfare institutions were explicit about payment of interest on some of their deposits. In fact, after the death of the bishop and later saint Antonino in 1459, the episcopal court became less zealous in prosecuting usurers, and the number of cases declined.[30] Moreover, the rapid spread of the Monti di Pietà throughout central and northern Italy in the second half of the century, recounted below, also represented a qualified legitimization of interest. In 1473, when the foundation of a Monte was first being considered at Florence, the archiepiscopal court determined that the practice of these institutions was not usurious. In 1495 a Monte di Pietà opened in Florence. Finally, in 1515 a papal bull recognized the legality of low rates of interest for Monti di Pietà. The standard was 5 percent, the rate long used by welfare and public institutions and the rate Calvin later accepted, without, however, denying the illegitimacy of usury in principle. The bull did not justify usury as such but instead recognized the legitimacy of charges to cover operating expenses of a Monte di Pietà, from rent for space to employees' salaries. The usury doctrine remained intact, but practices and attitudes had slowly changed.

We shall see below how in the sixteenth century the Florentine Monte di Pietà developed into an institution that served the functions of both Jewish pawn banks and the depositories of welfare institutions and how the growing importance

[30] Brucker, "Ecclesiastical Courts."

of those functions leading to their fusion in the Monte represented a response to an important development in the Florentine economy.

Banks and the Government

No one has studied the relations between the Florentine government and the banking industry, and it may be that the subject offers limited research prospects because those relations were, in fact, minimal. As far as we know, Florence never saw an attempt on the part of the government to move into the sphere of private banking in a major way. It did not fall into line with the cities that set up public deposit banks in the first decade of the fifteenth century—Barcelona in 1401, Genoa in 1408, Valencia in 1409—in the attempt to attract capital that could then be appropriated, in one way or another, by the state. Of these the Banco di San Giorgio at Genoa was the most advanced in that it allowed transfers on current account in bank and made loans in the private sector to everyone from artisans and shopkeepers to private bankers; in the end, however, it was not successful and closed down in 1445. The phenomenon of public banks seems to have been temporary, however, for the others also lost their importance in the later fifteenth century.

These banks, all in major centers of the Florentine international commercial system at the time, may have been models for the proposal made about 1430 by the silk merchant Andrea di Francesco Arnoldi to establish what would have been a public bank in Florence. Or Arnoldi may have drawn on his direct knowledge of banking in Venice, where he is known to have spent some of his career. Venice did not have a public bank, but banking practice there, which in many respects resembled that in Florence, may have suggested to Arnoldi ways a fully developed private banking system could be incorporated in a public bank. Venetian deposit banking, as big an industry as that of Florence with respect to total assets, if not to its widespread use by the population, was entirely in the hands of a half-dozen or so gigantic banks located at the Rialto. The government could hardly have ignored this extraordinary institutional concentration of both capital and power over depositors' interests, especially in view of the frequency of bankruptcy that pulled all of them down, and it found ways to regulate the activity of these banks in order to protect depositors. Moreover, the government pressed them into service as major supporters of the floating debt. The opening of a new bank, in fact, occasioned a public ceremony. Arnoldi may have devised his plan for Florence thinking that it would have been a logical step to organize this state-regulated industry in Venice into a public bank along the lines of those already established in other cities.

Whatever the inspiration, Arnoldi's plan was prompted by pressing concerns in Florence about how to deal with the rapidly growing public debt in the 1420s. As he saw it, all government obligations in the hands of citizens—the credits in the funded public debt, or Monte, that they received in return for forced loans—could be transformed into current accounts on which they could make transfers among themselves for the settlement of private debts. The government would thus be able to avoid repayment of its obligations. Moreover, to attract further capital through deposits, it could go one step further and require that all debts over *fl*.10 be paid by transfer in these current accounts on its books. In effect, this monetization of the public debt would have produced a considerable supply of official fiduciary money (in the form of credits on the government's books) moving about at high velocity as a mandatory substitute for specie in transactions above *fl*.10 (equivalent at the time to about four months' earnings for an unskilled manual laborer but well within the range of operations of many of the city's artisans and shopkeepers). As Arnoldi explained, "Money and bank credit are both the same thing as cash." He knew very well that most of the money circulating in Florence at the time was in fact bank money, not actual coin, for, as he went on to ask, how else could a city with no more than 150,000 florins in coin on hand at any one time ever have paid out the 4 million florins that the recent war with Lucca alone had cost? Following this logic, it would have taken just one more step to move to paper money issued by the commune. We do not know whether Arnoldi ever presented his plan. Clearly, it would have called for an enormous accounting apparatus that would have seemed a bit overwhelming even to Florentines, for all their deeply engrained habit of keeping accounts; yet its very conception rested on the assumption of widespread familiarity with payment in bank. Such a bank would have radically reduced the sphere of operations of local banks, although it presumably would not have interfered in the private business of moneylending.[31]

The Florentine government followed a laissez-faire policy toward private banks. The comparison with banking in Venice, with its high concentration of banks in only a few very large businesses, helps to explain why the government was not more intrusive. The fragmentation of the banking sector in Florence among so many operators and its lack of any structural cohesion precluded the kind of government regulation banking was subject to in Venice. In contrast to the situation in Venice, bankruptcies in Florence after the crisis of the 1340s were scattered and isolated occurrences, so that the state hardly felt a pressing need to

[31] Richard A. Goldthwaite, *The Building of Renaissance Florence: An Economic and Social History* (Baltimore, 1980), 316–17.

regulate the industry in order to protect depositors. Not even the pressures of the public debt, no less urgent for Florence than for any other state at the time, led to a policy to incorporate banks, as many and diverse as they were, into the fiscal system. We have seen that Florentine merchant-bankers operating abroad were often targeted by governments to supply emergency funds and that they were thus enticed into the area of fiscal administration, sometimes to their immense profit, despite all the risks involved. Their government at home in Florence too found these men a ready solution to pressing needs for money, at least before the funding of the public debt in the 1340s. Such local pressures, as we have seen, was a factor leading to the bankruptcy of the Bardi and the Peruzzi. With the founding of the Monte and the funding of the public debt in the 1340s, however, the government set up a fiscal system that allowed it to gain better control over its floating debt. By the fifteenth century it was obtaining short-term loans from wealthy men—not banks, although some of these men were bankers—by offering them a high rate of interest and a term of several years as an official of the Monte, which managed state finances. These arrangements had nothing to do with banks as such and led to no structural ties between these businesses and the government.

Although the state thus found little occasion to regulate banks, some government offices used the services of individual banks. For example, in the fifteenth century the Monte handled the traffic in government obligations through a private banker; the Pupilli officials, who served as executors of estates for orphans, deposited cash with banks and used current accounts in bank to administer their extensive property holdings; and during military campaigns the Twenty of the Balìa, the supervising magistracy, used banks to handle finances in the field. The subject of relations between the state and banks, however, awaits research. The principal issues are where the profits were in these kinds of arrangements, whether such arrangements involved contracts and loans in advance, and the extent to which bankers, in turn, exploited the state for their own benefit. Those who served as Monte officials, for instance, had considerable control over the state fiscal machinery during their tenure in office. Yet to judge from the almost complete turnover from one term to another on the rosters of the officials—not all of whom, as stated above, were bankers—over the second half of the fifteenth century, there was nothing like a financial oligarchy.[32] Moreover, the few extant accounts of bankers in office do not document major involvement in state finances during their tenure or at any other time. Indeed, bankers' accounts that

---

[32] Richard A. Goldthwaite, "Lorenzo Morelli, Ufficiale del Monte, 1484–88: Interessi privati e cariche pubbliche nella Firenze laurenziana," *ASI* 154 (1996): 626–27.

have been studied reveal hardly any activity with the state at all. The Medici clearly used their diplomatic role in the state to promote the interest of their bank abroad, especially in Milan and Rome, but for all the contemporary charges of corruption against Lorenzo the Magnificent, the bank's involvement in the state's fiscal administration has not yet come to light.[33]

Lack of a Banking System

As a group of businesses banking was an amorphous sector with no unifying institutional structure. The Cambio embraced all local banks, including those belonging to international merchant-bankers, but it had few regulatory powers, its main function being to maintain standards of practice. Moreover, by the later fourteenth century it, like all guilds, functioned more as an appendage to the city's political system than as a force in its economic life. The Cambio, in any event, did not extend its authority into international banking, and international merchant-banking firms that did not have a local bank remained outside its jurisdiction. Nor did international Cambio banks represent a particular force as an interest group within the community of local bankers, since international merchant-bankers, as already remarked, had no cohesive corporate organization: they were most likely members of the Lana, the Seta, or the Calimala guild, and some belonged to more than one. The government also left them alone, free from the close inspection of a regulatory policy. Finally, there was no central bank nor even a dominant bank. Bankers did not operate collectively through formal interlocking business structures, and it does not seem that they were bound closely together by debit-credit relations. In the early fifteenth century they may have been somewhat tied in to the Medici banking complex, which was so much bigger than the others. An analysis of some 4,835 transactions recorded on the debit-credit balances of forty-eight banks reported in the 1427 catasto has revealed that 24 percent of these involved just two Medici banks, that of Averardo di Francesco de' Medici and that of Cosimo and Lorenzo di Giovanni de' Medici.[34] The Medici may, however, have lost this commanding position in the course of the century notwithstanding their rise to political power. In the dozens of both business and personal ledgers that survive for the later period, one finds hardly any accounts opened in the name of the Medici bank. In fact, the expulsion of the family in

---

[33] Some of the evidence is discussed in Alison Brown, "Lorenzo, the Monte and the Seventeen Reformers: Public and Private Interest," in *The Medici in Florence: The Exercise and Language of Power* (Florence, 1992), 151–211.

[34] Paul D. McLean and John F. Padgett, "Was Florence a Perfectly Competitive Market? Transactional Evidence from the Renaissance," *Theory and Society* 26 (1997): 226.

1494 and the failure of the bank seem not to have had repercussions, let alone to have led to any bankruptcies, on the banking scene at home or abroad.

Performance of the Banking Sector
Practices

Between international merchant banks, local banks, and pawn banks, Florentines had access to the most basic banking services. Although these same services were to be found, to a greater or lesser extent, in other major financial and commercial centers—some documented earlier than in Florence—the survival of so many accounting records of both banks and their clients makes it possible to study these banking practices in Florence as in no other city. One of the most striking characteristics of banks that emerges from these records is the widespread familiarity throughout the society with banks and their services. The illustrative material utilized in the following discussion has been selected specifically to make this point—that Florentines from all classes, including artisans, shopkeepers, manual laborers, and even farmworkers, appeared on the premises of the city's banks. In dealing with all these people, moreover, bankers reduced transaction costs by dispensing with the notary for the validation of deposits, promissory notes, and other kinds of transactions. Private records of the respective parties, especially account books, constituted sufficient documentation for disputes in the courts.

MANUAL EXCHANGE   Although local banking had its origins in manual exchange, bankers' books, which survive only from the later fourteenth century on, reveal hardly any activity of this kind. In an economy that had not yet evolved a fully established token currency, however close to it Florence may have come, anyone handling cash in the local market—and this is to say all Florentines—had to face the problem of knowing the real, intrinsic value of coins, which underwent debasement in the course of reissue and were ever subject to clipping, erosion, and counterfeiting. Moreover, Florentines had to confront a variety of foreign coins in local circulation. Hence manual exchange was essential for the smooth execution of even the smallest transaction in the local market, and banks performed this function. Bernardo Machiavelli (Niccolò's father), for example, noted in his record book that in 1480 a dealer to whom he sold olive oil paid in gold coins from Florence, Genoa, and Rome, along with "five pieces of Bolognese gold," and that he then took these coins to the banker Donatino to exchange them for florins.[35] A century later, in 1589, legislation specified no fewer than thirty-two

---

[35] Bernardo Machiavelli, *Libro di ricordi*, ed. C. Olschki (Florence, 1954), 122.

types of coins as being legal tender in the city; two years later the list numbered sixty-two.[36] Thus bankers performed a major service as moneychangers. They had no reason to record these across-the-counter transactions, however. In fact, activity of this kind in the cashbox is not documented in surviving bankers' accounts, except for the occasional inventory of the contents of their cashboxes; or, rather, scholars have yet to examine these records with this problem in mind.[37] Had Florentines such as Machiavelli not occasionally noted such events in their private record books, we would know nothing about this essential role banks played in their lives.

CURRENT ACCOUNTS   By definition the most important way a bank attracts capital is to offer, instead of interest, certain services: safekeeping of cash, restitution of it on demand, and the administration of an account that the principal can use for assigning credits to and from third parties. Thus was born a current account, or *conto corrente,* and the term had entered the accounting jargon by the fifteenth century. An individual could open an account in a bank by depositing cash or by transferring credit with a third party to the banker; and if he were paid through a bank, he could use the credit to open a current account. The principal could order the banker to pay cash or transfer a credit to a third party; he could request that third parties make payments into his account either in cash or by transferring credit; and he could withdraw his money any time he wished. Anyone who made a deposit with a specific purpose in mind could specify that withdrawals must be subject to certain conditions, such as for use only to settle an estate or to pay for a dowry. Moreover, since overdrafts were permitted, the current account made available a limited line of credit.

A great many Florentines, from all walks of life, appear in the current accounts on a banker's book, and their private record books are replete with memoranda about banking transactions. The evidence that workers of all kinds went to banks to be paid is overwhelming. In 1394 the painter Piero di Nello acknowledged receipt of *fl.*22 from Iacopo di Bardo Altoviti, which he says was paid by the bank of Primerano de' Pilli; in the 1450s Desiderio da Settignano was paid by a client with written orders on the Cambini bank that either he or an assistant presented to the bank for payment; in 1463 the farmworker *(lavoratore)* Lorenzo di Panicale sent his son to the bank of Bernardo Bonaguisi to collect £14 that his employer, Filippo di Antonio Michi, was loaning him; in 1476 the workers employed on the construction of the house of Giovanni Zampini were all paid by Filippo di

Giovanni Corbizzi out of an account with the Cambini bank; in 1478 a farm-worker who had sold an ox to Bernardo Machiavelli was paid by Machiavelli's banker, Niccolò di Lorenzo Lorenzi. Finally, many workingmen themselves had a current account in bank. In 1456 Donatello, finding himself with an account opened in his name with the Cambini bank resulting from a payment of *fl.*100 to him through the bank, used the account over the following months to make payments in bank to third parties. Likewise, the painter Benozzo Gozzoli, who rented a house from the hospital of San Paolo, paid the rent for nearly twenty years, from 1458 to 1476, mostly through the Rucellai bank rather than in cash.[38]

It was probably as a memory aid that entries on current accounts in bank often included the client's reason for making a transaction—for example, that the principal had ordered payment to a third party in order to pay his rent or to buy something—even though such information was otherwise of no interest to the banker. Thanks to this practice, bankers' accounts can be a veritable chronicle of heterogeneous information about his customers that is often invaluable for the modern researcher. Art historians have been particularly zealous in mining these records for details about the production of artists not otherwise documented. Accounts of clients of the Cambini bank reveal payments made from 1454 to 1460 to Vespasiano da Bisticci, the famed bookseller, copyist manufacturer, and biographer, for "a Dante," for illuminating a manuscript of Livy's *Decades*, for a missal for Cosimo de' Medici, and for books from Bologna.[39] The executors of the testament of the cardinal Jaime of the royal house of Portugal used the Cambini bank to pay for the building and decoration of his burial chapel in San Miniato al Monte; and entries for payments in their current accounts document details about the work of Alesso Baldovinetti, Antonio and Piero del Pollaiuolo, Antonio and Bernardo Rossellino, Luca Della Robbia, and Desiderio da Settignano.[40] Likewise, entries recording Michelangelo's transactions at the bank of Giovanni Balducci & Partners contain abundant information extraneous to any essential banking function but important for documenting the work he did during his early years in Rome.[41] Like the early catasto reports, which Florentines submitted for tax purposes, fifteenth-century bankers' books are frequently chronicles of

[38] These examples are cited in ibid., 21 (Piero di Nello); Richard A. Goldthwaite, "L'arte e l'artista nei documenti contabili dei privati (sec. XV)," in *Gli Innocenti e Firenze nei secoli: Un ospedale, un archivio, una città*, ed. Lucia Sandri (Florence, 1996), 184–85 (Desiderio); Archive of the Ospedale degli Innocenti, ser. 144 (Estranei), 617 (record book of Antonio di Benedetto Michi and his son Filippo, 1446–77), fol. 26v; Goldthwaite, *Building of Renaissance Florence*, 306–7 (Corbizzi, Gozzoli); and Machiavelli, *Libro di ricordi*, 74.

[39] Goldthwaite, "L'arte e l'artista," 187–88.

[40] Frederick Hartt, Gino Corti, and Clarence Kennedy, *The Chapel of the Cardinal of Portugal, 1434–1459, at San Miniato in Florence* (Philadelphia, 1964).

[41] See the references in Hatfield, *Wealth of Michelangelo*.

the time; but as with the later catasto and decima reports, this quality was lost as practice became ever more habitual, giving way to a more rigorous formality and the exclusion of extraneous matter.

The current account generated a certain amount of paperwork apart from the posting of the banker's ledger. In theory, the depositor did not need a receipt, let alone a notarized act, since the banker's ledger was a legal record and proof enough of the transaction. The depositor might, however, enter into his own record book a reference to the page in the banker's book where the transaction could be found, or he might open a specific account on his own books. The banker might write a note to a client to inform him of a payment into his account by a third party, such as the one the lanaiolo Andrea di Cresci de' Cresci received from the Rucellai bank that is still preserved in one of his account books:

> Andrea di Cresci: you are a creditor in our cash book, fol. 201, for six fiorini larghi, received in your name from Bettino di Guelfo.
>
> Giovanni Rucellai & Partners on 26 October 1475[42]

The bank could supply a client with a statement of his account at any time. In 1481 Lorenzo di Matteo Morelli, for example, had no problem obtaining a statement from his bank, Bartolomeo di Leonardo Bartolini, Francesco di Piero Del Tovaglia & Partners, which he needed to bring his own records up to date; and he had to accept it despite doubts about its accuracy. Years later the bank was able to provide Morelli's son with a copy of his father's active accounts for a period of thirty years, from 1478 to 1508.[43]

Paperwork also included written orders of payment. Entries in the banker's ledger generally do not explain the mode of orders from his clients, but it is generally thought that the parties conducted most of their transactions in the banker's presence, as they most certainly did in Venice and Bruges, two places where the documentation leaves no doubt about the matter. The fact that in Florence entries sometimes state that the client "said" *(disse)* this or that would confirm the practice for Florence as well. It is just as clear, however, that bankers often dealt with third parties rather than directly with the client. In the record Filippo di Cante Cavalcanti kept of his account with the Scali company from 1290 to 1325, perhaps the earliest extant document of this kind, he almost always stated that payments into his account had been made by third parties and that debits on his account had been for payments made by the banker to third parties. The same is true of the few transactions he had with the local

---

[42] Marco Spallanzani, "A Note on Florentine Banking in the Renaissance: Orders of Payment and Cheques," *Journal of European Economic History* 7 (1978): 162.

[43] Goldthwaite, "Local Banking," 23–24.

moneychanger, identified only as Alberto. That he himself was not present at the time of these transactions to check the recording of them on Scali's books would explain his occasional perplexity about the banker's record. Once, in July 1317, since he could not remember the amount the bank had paid to messer Attaviano de' Brunelleschi out of his account, he had to go to the bank to see for himself (it was *fl.*301, no small amount); on the balance the bank sent in January 1306, he found one charge against his account that left him "marveling that it was so high"; and a balance sent to him in April 1305 seemed "to be truly deceptive."[44]

By the end of the century clients were commonly using written orders of payment to third parties, or checks. Such *polizze* are mentioned frequently in account entries, and enough of them have been found, generally between the pages of the banker's ledger, to round out the documentation of the practice dating from the later fourteenth century. The widespread familiarity with the instrument is confirmed by the standard format and formulaic language of many of these checks: on the recto the name of the bank; on the verso the date centered at the top, followed by the text—often including the standard wording *pagate a* (pay to), *portatore* (bearer), and *ponete al mio conto* (post to my account)—and, below on the right, the signature. Given that they often measured no more than about two by eight inches, it is surprising that any have survived. No fewer than eighty-three orders of payment written by the mattress maker *(coltriciaio)* Matteo del Tegghia in the name of his partnership survive in the records of his banker, Francesco Datini.[45]

A notable documentation of the practice of making checks out to workingmen is the current account opened in 1473 for the payment of construction costs for the apse of the church of San Martino a Gangalandi, just outside Florence. Leon Battista Alberti, who had been prior there, provided for the financing of this project in his testament; and his executors, who were in Rome, charged the Florentine canon Niccolò Corbizzi to supervise construction according to the architect's design and arranged for payments to him through the local bank of Guglielmo Rucellai, Matteo Baroncelli & Partners. Corbizzi paid the woodworkers

---

[44] M. Vitale, "Il quaderno di ricordi di Messer Filippo de' Cavalcanti (1290–1324)," *Studi di filologia italiana* 29 (1971): 5–112. Silvano Borsari lists the references to the transactions with the Scali bank in *Una compagnia di Calimala: Gli Scali (secc. XIII–XIV)* (Macerata, 1994), 42n. Borsari correctly observed that, contrary to the archival inventory's identification of him, Cavalcanti was not a banker. The date of the first record of transfers in bank to and from third parties can perhaps be pushed back to 1211, the date of a fragment of what is taken to be a banker's ledger. See Mario Chiaudano, *Studi e documenti per la storia del diritto commerciale italiano nel sec. 13* (Turin, 1930), 61.

[45] Federigo Melis, "Sulla non-astrattezza dei titoli di credito del Basso Medioevo," in *La banca pisana e le origini della banca moderna*, ed. Marco Spallanzani (Florence, 1987), 346. For the most recent discussion of the check, see Spallanzani, "A Note on Florentine Banking," and further bibliography therein, especially to other articles by Melis.

and stonecutters, who were working outside the city, out of this account with checks written on the bank.[46] Artisans too wrote checks on their own accounts to other artisans. In Vespasiano da Bisticci's account with the Cambini bank mentioned above, entries record checks he sent to the bank ordering payments to a manuscript illuminator and a stationer.[47] Two checks made out to workers even lower on the economic and social scale actually survive, tucked away in the ledger of the banker who paid, where the corresponding debit entry on the check writer's account also can be found. One of these, written on 8 February 1481 by Leonardo di Filippo Bisticci, was made out for £3 10s. payable to a farmworker, Luca di Niccolò, who cashed it the next day at the Cambini bank.[48] The other, in perfect format, was written by the haberdasher Piero di Giovanni di Piero to pay Antonio di Antonio, called "il Mugnaio" (the Miller), for emptying a privy *(neciesario)*. On the recto is the banker's name, Cione di Antonio di ser Bartolo, and the order reads:

On the day of 19 June 1477

Give to the bearer of this, who will be "the Miller," £ two, s.2, for the privy that he emptied: £2 s.2—

Piero di Giovanni[49]

Below the signature the banker, or his accountant, penned in the reference in the bank's books where the appropriate entry was made when "the Miller" cashed his check.

With banking so firmly grounded in refined accounting practice, the written order of payment was an instrument that made it easy enough to effect transfer and retransfer in bank. The standardization in the language of accounting of such phrases as *da noi a* (from us to) and *per noi a* (for us to)—using the impersonal first person plural—with reference to bank transfers testifies to how routine the practice was. Transfers could be extended beyond one party and beyond one bank. On 28 March 1467 Filippo Strozzi, on an order from Piero de' Medici & Partners, made an entry in his ledger crediting the account of Carlo Guasconi for *fl.*130 (and accordingly debiting the Medici's account), and he noted that the Medici had informed him that the credit had been advanced to them from Bono Boni, who in turn had done this in the name of

---

[46] Marco Spallanzani, "L'abside dell'Alberti a San Martino a Gangalandi: Nota di storia economica," *Mitteilungen des kunsthistorischen Institutes in Florenz* 19 (1975): 245.

[47] Goldthwaite, "L'arte e l'artista," 185.

[48] Tognetti, "L'attività di banca locale," 640. One might question whether this is a true check written to a third party or simply an order of payment to a dependent of the principal.

[49] Spallanzani, "Note on Florentine Banking," 156.

Zanobi Dietisalvi & Partners.[50] The account entry does not furnish enough information to make it possible to reconstruct the actual sequence of events in a multiple transfer of this kind—whether Boni had ordered the Medici to pay Dietisalvi, who then had transferred the credit to Guasconi, who in turn had transferred it to the Strozzi, or whether Dietisalvi had ordered Boni to pay Guasconi, who then had transferred the credit through the Medici to Strozzi. Whatever the sequence, five parties were involved, and no cash passed through anyone's hands. Two of the five parties are identified as banks, and a third, the Dietisalvi company, was probably a merchant bank; of the two individuals, Boni was one of the city's most prominent bankers, and Strozzi was a merchant-banker. Many accounts document transfers such as this one involving three, four, or five parties; and as this example shows, transfer extended well beyond the scope of one bank's clientele. In other words, there was a degree of interbank clearance. Moreover, interbank transfer extended to people outside the sphere of the city's most prominent businessmen. To cite just one example, the active account the notary ser Girolamo di ser Giovanni da Colle had with Antonio di Vittorio Landi & Partners, bankers, records, from 1468 to 1473, eighteen credits transferred from three other banks, where payments had been assigned to him by third parties.[51]

It remains a mystery, however, how the parties involved in these transfers communicated with one another, whether through checks or through another kind of written order for a simple transfer of funds (what the Italians call a *giro conto*) or through personal encounters (although it is difficult to imagine Strozzi, to refer to the example cited above, and the four other men involved working out a transfer among themselves while huddled over a *banco*). Although no example has been turned up, endorsement of a check may have been one means of effecting transfers through more than two parties, since we know of some examples of endorsed bills of exchange dating back to 1410.[52] In any event, interbank transfers were made through direct contact between banks, not through a central clearing bank.

There is no evidence that banks in Florence—any more than those in Bruges, Venice, Genoa, or anywhere else—paid interest on deposits, presumably because these services in and of themselves were sufficiently attractive to the depositor. Nor do they seem to have charged for overdrafts. In his treatise on accounting, Luca Pacioli states that bankers could charge a service fee for bank transfers or cash transactions, and some Florentine evidence suggests that bankers may indeed have levied a small service charge for transfers to and from places abroad

[50] Ibid., 161.
[51] ASF, Conv. sopp. 111 (S. Lucia), 141, fol. 32ff.
[52] See the references to the articles by Federigo Melis in chapter 3, n. 52.

(exclusive of the bill of exchange).[53] Banks probably profited from cash transactions by taking advantage of their authority to determine the price of both coins and the money of account in which the firm kept its books. Variations in the market price of coins and the *aggio*, or premium, of the gold florin were minimal at any one moment, but within these margins even the smallest variation could be magnified into a significant profit by the number of transactions. Florentines from all walks of life were aware of this basic condition of their monetary system, and bankers, if anyone, surely knew how to turn the situation to their own profit. This aspect of banking, and of market transactions in general, however, has yet to be investigated.

Evidence of the diffusion of practice does not necessarily indicate anything about the frequency of use. There is no question about the broad social spectrum represented by holders of current accounts in bank, but it is another matter to speculate on the centrality of such accounts in the lives of these people. Many accounts on bankers' books were open only for brief periods of safekeeping, usually no more than a few days or weeks and rarely as long as a year; they record nothing more than an initial cash deposit and then its depletion through cash withdrawals, with few, if any, transfers to third parties. Some of the most active accounts with giro transfer were set up to make payments for a specific purpose, such as the construction projects mentioned above, so that the banker was really serving as a paymaster. Rare is the account as active as that of Lorenzo Morelli, mentioned above, which extends over five years, from 1478 to 1483, but even this account registers little more than cash deposits on the average of less than once a month and cash withdrawals on the average of once a week. Yet, contradicting all these reservations is the current account of Nofri di Palla Strozzi with the bank of Luigi di Manetto, Arrigo de' Davanzati & Partners. Open for eight years, from 1405 to 1413, it takes up forty-one of the ninety-seven folios in Strozzi's ledger. Besides cash withdrawals, entries record payments the bank made in Strozzi's name for taxes, land, farm animals, and a variety of other purchases from ordinary people such as notaries, goldsmiths, blacksmiths, brickmakers, druggists, clothiers, shoemakers, and even wet nurses and farmworkers. Francesco Datini also had an account with the Davanzati bank, on which he wrote checks, and there is no reason to think Strozzi did not make payments out of his account in the same way.[54]

DEPOSITS The most basic function of banks is to attract dormant savings and put them to work through loans to people who need the funds either for

---

[53] Tognetti, "L'attività di banca locale," 617–18.

[54] ASF, Carte strozziane, ser. 3, 281. Melis notes Datini's extant checks in "Sulla non-astrattezza dei titoli di credito," 348n.

consumption spending or for investment. Money is thereby kept in circulation, stimulating economic activity, and the bank profits from the difference in the interest rates it charges borrowers and those it pays depositors. By itself the corpo of a Florentine merchant bank, being limited by the small number of partners and by what they were willing to invest in the firm, did not give it much potential for lending, even if profits were poured back into it as sopraccorpo. To attract additional funds the firm could open the corpo to outside investors who were prepared to share the risks of the business as sleeping partners. This device was refined by the accomandita contract, legislated in 1408 but not used extensively until the sixteenth century, which limited the liability of the investor to the amount of his investment. By offering the services of a current account, discussed above, and accepting the interest-bearing deposit, however, banks could enlarge their working capital beyond their corpo. We have seen how the international merchant-banking firms succeeded in enlarging working capital much beyond their corpo by attracting deposits from rich nobles and ecclesiastics throughout Europe wherever they did business. They, as well as local banks, offered the same possibility to Florentines back home.

Interest-bearing deposits with firms can be documented back to the earliest surviving private and business accounts of Florentines from the thirteenth century. In March and April 1273 the executors of the estate of Baldovino di Iacopo Riccomanni opened deposits with six firms totaling £2,109 (ca. *fl.*1,400), and over the next two years, besides renewing some of these, they made deposits in four more firms.[55] Most deposits were made for over a year; separate entries explicitly state the amount of interest *(prode)* paid but rarely the rate, which ranged from 7 percent to 14 percent, averaging about 10 percent. Over the course of the fourteenth century the time deposit's name changed, though its essential character did not, in response to mounting concern about the usurious nature of interest charges. It came to be called a discretionary deposit *(deposito a discrezione)*, the notion being that anything earned on the deposit was not determined at the outset by the lender but left to the discretion of the borrower as a gift. The real nature of the contract, however, was not to be denied, and by the fifteenth century discretionary deposits almost always stated the rate of interest at the outset. Thus, on the account of one such deposit with the bank of Palla di messer Palla Strozzi, Orsino di Lanfredino Lanfredini & Partners the credit balance in 1428 is described as "the capital and *discrezione* of his money deposited at the rate of 8 percent per annum."[56] In the instance of another borrower, Francesco Castel-

---

[55] Castellani, *Nuovi testi fiorentini*, 1:268–78. These deposits are discussed in Chiaudano, *Studi e documenti*, 65–69.

[56] Goldthwaite, "Local Banking," 32.

lani, the loan from the banker Bono Boni took the form of a time deposit for six month with interest "at my discretion," or, as he repeats, "at that discretion that might please me, which we estimate to be about *fl.*8 per hundred at the highest."[57] The term became a mere euphemism for any kind of interest-bearing deposit with a fixed duration, usually six months or a year, be it with a bank or any other kind of business or even with a private party. The practice of making discretionary deposits seems to have waned in the sixteenth century, giving way to a preference for deposits to keep money on the exchange, a safer subterfuge against the charge of usury.

A merchant-banking firm could significantly enlarge its working capital by accepting time, or discretionary, deposits. The middle-sized Cambio merchant bank for which we have the most detailed information, the Cambini bank—Francesco and Carlo di Niccolò Cambini & Partners, then, from 1462, Francesco and Bernardo di Niccolò Cambini & Partners—attracted considerable capital through such deposits. On closing its books in 1462, it had 27 deposit accounts totaling *fl.*16,279 di suggello, eight times the firm's capital of *fl.*2,000; in 1473, deposits numbered 62 and totaled *fl.*21,174, twelve times its capital of *fl.*1,667 at that time. In both instances deposits constituted about one-third of the firm's total liabilities (not including capital and profits owed to partners).[58] An international firm, however, could attract much larger deposits from wealthy nobles and ecclesiastics in their branches abroad than it could from anyone back home in Florence. The figures cited above for deposits in the Cambini bank shrink to insignificance in comparison with the funds deposited in the foreign branches of the Medici bank (see chapter 3). The largest depositors of the Cambini were, in fact, foreigners, in places where the bank did business.

Another kind of deposit emerged during the fifteenth century with the development and refinement of the international exchange market and the increased traffic in bills of exchange utilized as credit instruments. The bill of exchange sold by the merchant-banker could function as a short-term deposit, for its evolution into fictitious exchange transformed it into a disguised interest-bearing time deposit. The term lasted as long as the travel time of the bill (or the quarterly periods of the fairs), and it could be extended indefinitely by rechange. The depositor opened his account with a bank on the purchase of a bill, and he could keep the money in deposit through successive fictitious exchanges and rechanges. For the banker, recordkeeping of this kind of interest-bearing deposit involved (besides the necessary correspondence to agents abroad) nothing more than entries

---

[57] Francesco di Matteo Castellani, *Ricordanze,* ed. Giovanni Ciappelli (Florence, 1992), 1:132.
[58] Tognetti, *Il banco Cambini,* app. 3 and pp. 213, 270.

on his books recording the fictitious exchange-rechange transactions, along with
the profit (or loss, if any) and his commission fee. Money kept on the exchange,
of course, did not pay a fixed rate of interest, and the inherent volatility of the
market could at times work against the depositor. In compensation, money kept
on the exchange earned interest compounded according to usance, an advantage
earlier forms of deposit did not offer. In 1415 the Aretine merchant Lazzaro Bracci,
living in Florence, bought nine bills through different local bankers for periods
of three to five months, all together putting to work in the hands of bankers
fl.2,096, on which he earned an average of 6–7 percent.[59] In 1582, by which time
bankers were explicit about what they were doing, the bank of Simone and Heirs
of Giovanni Corsi & Partners had thirteen such deposits, almost all of them from
relatives or persons with close ties to the family, adding up to 40 percent more
than the capital of the firm and kept open for years.[60] By this time private banks
attracted capital even from the Monte di Pietà, now a public bank: in 1582 the
Monte had *fl*.123,058 in deposit on the exchange with just two private banks.[61]
This kind of deposit became widespread in the sixteenth century as exchange
rates became less volatile in the more centralized international markets of Lyons
and Besançon, lowering the cost to the banker of money from this source. His
commission fees, which he charged even on fictitious exchange, reduced somewhat further the cost to him of accepting money for a deposit of this kind; these
fees could be a significant element of the banker's profits when exchange rates
were low and quantity high.[62] The extensive and more complete records of
sixteenth-century banks await examination to determine the frequency and importance of this kind of deposit. It is likely that by the end of the century most
traffic in bills by Florentine banks involved credit activity in the local market
rather than international transfer of funds.

The weakness of Florentine local banks was their failure to attract modest
savings through something like what today we would call the simple savings
account. To holders of current accounts, many of whom were working people,
banks offered security and the services of a current account but not interest.
They paid interest only on the time deposit, but the small number of such deposits turned up in the records of the few banks that have been studied, along
with the relatively stable interest rate paid on these deposits over a century and

[59] Raymond de Roover, "Cambium ad Venetias: Contribution to the History of Foreign Exchange," reprinted from *Studi in onore di Armando Sapori* in *Business, Banking, and Economic
Thought in Late Medieval and Early Modern Europe: Selected Studies of Raymond de Roover,* ed. Julius
Kirshner (Chicago, 1974), 250.
[60] Goldthwaite, "Banking in Florence," 489.
[61] Ibid., 516.
[62] For an analysis of costs, see ibid., 527–29.

a half, would suggest that banks generated little demand for them except to meet exigencies of the moment. In any event, banks seemed to have accepted only deposits of *fl.*50–100 and higher, amounts well above the modest savings of most people. In 1473 the Cambini bank had only two depositors identified as artisans (both woodworkers). The ordinary artisan or shopkeeper with a little extra cash on hand would probably not have thought about depositing it with a bank. One might wonder, of course, how much of a limitation this was in a preindustrial urban economy that limited the downward distribution of wealth and made it difficult for ordinary working people to accumulate modest savings. In Florence, however, the active effort to attract modest savings undertaken in the mid-fifteenth century by at least three of the city's leading welfare institutions must signal that something was changing in the economic life of this city. But if the opening of these depositories can thus be seen as an economic indicator, their growing success, modest at first but ever more successful during the sixteenth century, when they were joined by the Monte di Pietà, exposes one of the weaknesses of private banking, for all its technical accomplishments.

Jewish pawn banks also were conduits through which the savings of Jews and some Christians got channeled into the local credit market. Savings pooled from within the Jewish community came from family consortiums with networks extending well beyond Florence throughout Italy and perhaps even across the Alps. Given the restrictions most governments imposed on the purchase of real estate by Jews and the limited possibilities for alternative investment in the forward sectors of the economy, these funds had hardly any other outlet. Savings were thus put to work in a way that served a genuine economic function performed by no other institution. And these savings were significant: the *fl.*40,000 the consortium of Jewish pawnbrokers were able to make available for lending within three years of their original 1437 charter ranked their banks collectively with the corpo of the largest international merchant banks, only the Medici company being appreciably larger; and their collective capital remained at this level throughout the century. At this scale of operation, the money these pawn banks injected annually into the local economy may have amounted to as much as 15 percent of what the entire wool industry spent in local production costs; in fact, the percentage was probably higher, depending on how much of this capital was recirculated in new loans during the course of a year.[63] This amount grew over the century to the extent that these pawn banks plowed back into their businesses the 20 percent profits on loans, less operating costs (including the

[63] This rough calculation is based on the figures for the wool industry reported in table 4.1.

high government fee for the license to operate) and what the community may have exported through its familial networks.

EXTENSION OF CREDIT   Essential to the definition of a bank is the lending out of the money that it attracts in the form of deposits. For the banker, interest on loans is the major source of profit. For the economy, such loans activate otherwise dormant savings; at the same time, they increase the money supply, since the lenders are now using the depositors' money. The banker takes his risks, on the one hand, with the trustworthiness of the people to whom he has lent out the money and, on the other hand, with the calculation of how much cash he needs to hold back in reserve to meet his depositors' demands for repayment. The danger for the economy of this kind of business lies in the possible failure of the banker to gauge his risks correctly, for bankruptcy results in the loss of money by many people and in a general credit crisis.

Local banks loaned money out in a number of ways. Cerchi, the local banker mentioned above, made loans on the kinds of surety that one would expect to find in this period, namely, valuable pawns, especially jewelry and costly clothing accessories, and promissory notes. The latter took the form of signed statements written out in the banker's record book, often countersigned by a guarantor. In the thirteenth century such notes were often notarized, but by Cerchi's time bankers had long abandoned the notary. Cerchi's accounts document the importance of another source of surety for Florentine bankers in the fifteenth century—government obligations. These credits came from forced loans the state imposed on its citizens in lieu of direct taxes (they sometimes had the option of paying less if they renounced such claims). Although these credits could not be cashed in, they could be assigned to other parties through a secondary market and encumbered as surety for loans. Cerchi also purchased assignments on future interest payments on these Monte credits belonging to private persons, in effect extending loans on the surety of a lien on future fixed income from government obligations.[64]

Sometimes a bank did not require surety at all. Given the legal standing of the banker's ledger, an account opened in the name of the lender (presumably someone to be trusted) with a debit entry for the loan sufficed as binding evidence of the bank's claim. In the entry on his books, therefore, the banker had no need to specify that the debit was a loan. He credited the account for repayments and balanced it when the debt was paid off, disguising the interest by the

---

[64] On the legal status of title to Monte credits, see Julius Kirshner, "Encumbering Private Claims to Public Debt in Renaissance Florence," in *The Growth of the Bank as Institution and the Development of Money-Business Law,* ed. Vito Piergiovanni (Berlin, 1993), 19–75.

standard practice, long followed by notaries, of including it in the amount of the loan as stated in the debit entry in his ledger, although he had in fact paid the lender somewhat less, the difference being the interest. The reality of such fictitious loans, as they are called, was exposed, perhaps inadvertently, by one of Cerchi's clients, Monte di Bardo di Cesare di Bardo, when, on 4 January 1482, he wrote out and signed a statement in the banker's record book recognizing his debt of *fl.*67 10s. di grossi (a loan effected through a temporary transfer of Monte credits) to be paid in a year: he managed to slip into his statement the observation that he had in fact received only *fl.*55 larghi.[65] Cover-ups of this kind could be denounced anonymously by depositing a note with all the details in a box at the Cambio. In 1476 the guild officials noted one such denouncement laying out the details and naming the borrower, Giovanni di Bartolomeo Federighi, his guarantor, Iacopo di Niccolò Federighi, and the lender, Giovanni di Bartolo, identified as a ropemaker, who, however, had a small bank in the Mercato Vecchio. Federighi's loan, taken out for one year in 1471, was for *fl.*15, but the amount was recorded as *fl.*18 in the written contract; and in June 1472 and again in June 1473 Federighi paid Giovanni *fl.*3, each time receiving from the banker (Giovanni is so described) a written promise not to demand the *fl.*18 for the following year.[66] The guild's action in this instance is not recorded. Prosecutions of manifest usury of this kind, however, have not yet been turned up in the archives, whereas the evidence for use of this device for disguising interest is only too abundant.

In theory the banker's procedure of entering only the amount owed on a loan, not the amount paid, created an accounting problem, since in a true double-entry system the difference in expenditures and receipts would show up somewhere, presumably in the cash account. The banker's principal account book, the official book of record that is referred to in the guild roster of banks, was called a cashbook *(quaderno di cassa)*, not a ledger *(libro di debitori e creditori* or *libro mastro)*. It recorded cash transactions in individual accounts, but since it was not kept in double entry and had no cash account, a balance sheet could not be prepared without an inventory of the cashbox. For a local bank there was no need to keep a ledger as a book of higher synthesis. For an international Cambio bank, in contrast, whose primary book of synthesis was a double-entry ledger that included its commercial activities as well, the cashbook for banking operations alone was not fully integrated into the accounting system.

[65] ASF, Cerchi, 315, fol. 34v.
[66] ASF, Arte del Cambio, 19 (Deliberazioni, 1462–76), unfoliated but at 5 April 1476.

In his record book, Filippo d'Antonio Michi, a setaiolo, copied out a number of accounts opened with various bankers debited for a cash withdrawal and subsequently credited for repayments. He was thus credited *fl.*100 di suggello by Zanobi Girolami & Partners in 1465, *fl.*6 by Bono di Giovanni Boni & Partners in 1467, *fl.*8 by the Boni bank in 1468, *fl.*4 by Donato di ser Francesco & Partners in 1474, *fl.*2 by Mariotto Buti & Partners in 1476, *fl.*18 £5 in three payments by Piero Mellini & Partners in 1476, *fl.*30 in four payments by the Mellini bank in 1477, and *fl.*30 by Francesco di ser Iacopo Bottegari & Partners in 1477. All these firms are identified as banks, and twice Michi states explicitly that they loaned him the money. For loans he had from private persons, Michi mentions whether he left a pawn or wrote a promissory note, but only for two of the loans from banks does he refer to a guarantor *(a preghiera di);* for the other loans, presumably the account in the bank's books was itself sufficient guarantee. Michi paid back most of these loans in a matter of weeks, without indicating any interest. His accounting procedures were exactly those of the bank: he credited the bank for what he owed, not what he actually received, the difference reflecting the interest owed.[67]

Merchant banks, whether local Cambio banks or not, loaned money through the bill of exchange, as already explained. By the fifteenth century this standard credit instrument, complete in all of its subterfuges, was widely available to persons outside the circle of international merchants and local capitalist entrepreneurs. Of the twelve loans extended by the merchant Lazzaro di Giovanni Bracci through purchase of bills of exchange in 1415, nine were made to bankers, but two were made to a lanaiolo, and one was made to a setaiolo.[68] Filippo Michi once had recourse to the instrument, and it is worth describing the transaction in all of its detail, for it reveals something about how the instrument could be handled in the marketplace by someone who was completely outside the circle of capitalist entrepreneurs.[69] On 25 January 1475 Michi "took one gold mark" on the exchange of the Easter fair at Lyons, that is, he borrowed florins in exchange for a mark (the standard monetary unit used in the exchange fairs in Lyons), presumably to be delivered in Lyons at the Easter fair, but at the time of payment at the fair the mark was to be used to buy florins at the subsequent August fair payable in Florence by Michi. On the surface, what is involved here is a standard exchange-rechange transaction used to disguise a loan: only what was paid back, and not the amount of the loan, is mentioned. What is curious, if not indeed significant, about this transaction is that neither party was a banker. Indeed, the "remitter" (or lender)

---

[67] Archive of the Ospedale degli Innocenti, ser. 144 (Estranei), 617 (record book of Antonio di Benedetto Michi and his son Filippo, 1446–77), fols. 31v, 44v, 47, 79, 90v, 95, 96.

[68] De Roover, "Cambium ad Venetias," 250.

[69] See Michi's record book, cited above in n. 67, fols. 81, 83v.

was a woodworker *(legnaiolo)* named Iacopo di Cerbino, who, according to the entry in Michi's record book, "directed the bill" to Amerigo Corsini, Giovanni Falconieri & Partners in Lyons. The document does not tell us who sent the bill or whether one was sent at all, whether and how a banker in Florence was involved, or what was earned on the exchange-rechange operation. What we do learn, however, is that an artisan used the most sophisticated credit instrument at the time to loan money. Even if he did nothing more than loan Michi the money and left it to Michi—who, as a setaiolo, would have had much familiarity with merchant banks—to devise how the transaction was to be formally disguised, the woodworker must have known how such things worked.

What happened to this bill documents the flexibility of the instrument as well as the complexities arising from its use as a subterfuge. On 7 July, before the due date of his obligation to pay on the (theoretical) return of the bill after the August fair, Michi "took" another gold mark on the August exchange fair, this time from the bank of Francesco Martelli, Antonio Corsini & Partners, and had this gold mark, or bill, "consigned" *(si chonsengniò)* to the woodworker in exchange for the previous bill. As a result of this transaction, the bank extinguished Michi's debt by paying the woodworker *fl*.57 (what Michi owed at this point was *fl*.58, but he received a discount of *fl*.1 for having "given back the said gold mark" in advance) and then debited Michi's account for this amount. In other words, the bank assumed the credit from the woodworker, paying him off and debiting Michi. This second gold mark (i.e., the bill) returned on 9 September worth *fl*.58, and six weeks later, on 25 October, Michi ordered the bank of Francesco Cambini & Partners to pay Martelli, Corsini & Partners the *fl*.58 he owed them plus two-thirds of a florin for their commission fee *(provvisione)*. This fee, amounting to 1.16 percent on the sum Michi paid back, was much larger than the miniscule commission charged on normal, straightforward exchange transactions, real or fictitious, which were usually expressed in thousandths, not hundredths; it may represent the bank's higher handling charges for the subterfuge used by parties outside the bank. Note that (1) a bill, though not negotiable, could be bought and sold, although on the surface what was being bought and sold here was a gold mark of Lyons, not a bill (the word is never used); (2) there is no way to know whether these transactions were fictitious exchange; (3) we only know what Michi owed, not what he received, so that no interest charge can be calculated; (4) neither the lender nor the borrower was a bank, although both had recourse to a bank; and last but certainly not least, (5) the lender was an artisan. Stripped of the subterfuges, these transactions consist of a loan and then the lender's sale of the credit at discount to a third party, for which a fee was charged.

Apart from direct loans, whatever form they took, banks in the normal course of their business extended credit by permitting overdrafts on current accounts. On balances of the Cambini bank drawn up in 1461 and in 1472, more than half of all current accounts open at the time—101 out of 177 for the former, 133 out of 255 for the latter—were overdrawn. Moreover, the total credit the bank had extended to these clients almost equaled the total on accounts not overdrawn: in 1461 the difference was only *fl*.530 in the bank's favor; in 1472, *fl*.1,322 against the bank. In the former these credits constituted 25 percent of the firm's assets, in the latter, 21 percent; and these assets, it is to be noted, were those of a local merchant bank with extensive commercial operations.[70] Such a notable presence of overdraft on the balances of this one firm, the only one for which we have significant data, justifies the hypothesis that this may have been the most important credit function banks performed. Yet this credit was apparently free, for no one has found evidence of any interest charges on overdrafts, either in Florence or in Venice. In the early fourteenth century firms like the Peruzzi and the Covoni either paid or charged interest on current accounts opened in the name of the partners (and their relatives), depending on whether the balance showed a credit or a deficit, but this practice, limited to this one sector and to privileged clients, seems to have been abandoned later on.[71]

Hardly to be overlooked among credit instruments, finally, is the simple pawn. It was the principal access, if not the only one, to credit for the masses of artisans, shopkeepers, and workers, not just for the desperately poor. A measure of the importance of Jewish pawnbrokers to the local economy of a city with about ten thousand households can be taken in the only extant journal (kept in Hebrew) of one of these, belonging to Isacco da San Miniato and open from 1473 to 1475. The da San Miniato pawn bank averaged about fifty transactions a day, which is to say that it had from twelve thousand to thirteen thousand clients in a year. Loans ranged from 20 soldi to *fl*.45–50, most being about 50 soldi (about half a florin, or the equivalent of a week's wages for an unskilled laborer) and very few higher than *fl*.10. In the course of a year the bank loaned out about *fl*.15,000. At the high end of this schedule of loans, the da San Miniato pawn bank operated at the level of the Cerchi local bank, but its massive business at the low end makes the Cerchi bank pale by comparison with respect to both number of clients and cash turn-

---

[70] Tognetti, "L'attività di banca locale," 602, 604.

[71] On the perplexity about this issue of interest on overdrafts, see ibid., 617–18; and Goldthwaite, "Local Banking," 27. In Venice, no interest seems to have been charged for overdrafts on Barbarigo's account. Frederic C. Lane, *Andrea Barbarigo, Merchant of Venice, 1418–1449* (Baltimore, 1944), 25. The subject is not mentioned in Reinhold C. Mueller, *The Venetian Money Market: Banks, Panics, and the Public Debt, 1200–1500*, vol. 2 of *Money and Banking in Medieval and Renaissance Venice*, by Frederic C. Lane and Reinhold C. Mueller (Baltimore, 1997).

over. Only 9.7 percent of borrowers asked for a renewal of their loans, and a mere 3.5 percent defaulted on their obligations, resulting in the sale of their pawns.[72] The success of this pawn bank testifies to the economic importance of these institutions in meeting liquidity problems of the lower classes, just as the low renewal and default rates on their loans, especially in view of the high interest rates, testify to how temporary those problems were in the lives of the borrowers.

The literature on Jewish pawn banks somewhat distorts their function in the economy by emphasizing their traffic in distress loans. *Distress,* however, is a relative term, too often used with prejudice as an absolute state. These clients of Jewish pawn bankers, after all, had some personal property worth pawning. They preferred to pawn it for a loan of much less than its market value rather than sell it, they were prepared to pay the high interest rate (usually about 20 percent), and almost all of them were eventually in a position to redeem their pawns. Many of these borrowers needed credit not just for consumption in moments of distress but for capital investment in tools and equipment or simply for the liquidity needed to get through the working day. Delays in payment until the completion of work and irregularity of employment were endemic to the preindustrial economy based on the putting-out system, and workers often had to confront temporary shortages of cash. Even a prosperous artisan such as the painter Neri di Bicci, who operated one of the busiest shops in the city and ranked as the wealthiest painter in the 1480 catasto, occasionally pawned pieces of clothing and clothing accessories. In his record book he noted some dozen transactions in the years 1453–57 with three different Jewish pawn banks to obtain loans mostly ranging between one and three florins (the highest was for *fl.*11).[73] He was able to exchange an object already pawned for a different one, adjusting his debt accordingly; he once pawned a piece of clothing with a Jew to get the money to redeem a pawn left with another Jew; and he is always explicit about the amount (though not the rate) of interest he paid. For an artisan such as a painter, who was not fully paid for commissioned work until the end of the long time it took to complete it, problems of liquidity to pay ongoing expenses must have been frequent, and for the relatively small amounts he needed, the pawn bank was the only recourse available. Pawn banks, in short, made it possible for workers, artisans, and shopkeepers to fit a credit line into the management of their domestic and working lives. The "distress" these businesses relieved has to be understood in the context

[72] These data come from an analysis of two months' activity in the surviving ledger: Flavia Careri, "Il 'Presto ai Quattro Pavoni': Dal libro-giornale di Isacco da San Miniato (1473–75)," *ASI* 159 (2001): 395–421.

[73] Neri di Bicci, *Le ricordanze*, 4–5, 16–17, 20, 28, 32, 36–37.

of a preindustrial economy, uncontaminated by modern prejudices about this kind of business.

Account books of people in the more substantial upper classes also document recourse to Jewish pawn banks. One of these men was Giovanni di Iacopo Strozzi, a battiloro, whose ledger, open from 1443 to 1474, reveals a man of substantial means: it records, among other things, payment of most of his guild matriculation fee through a bank, the ownership of a slave, credit claims against the ruler of Rimini, Sigismondo Malatesta, money put on the international exchange market, and the administration of real-estate holdings.[74] Notwithstanding this level of activity, Strozzi occasionally borrowed from Jewish pawn banks; and his recourse to them became very frequent in the period from February 1453 to July 1454. No fewer than twenty-one times during this year and a half he carried expensive personal clothing and silver forks and spoons to the three pawnbrokers on his side of the Arno for loans ranging from several lire to *fl.*12, with most about *fl.*1. He redeemed many of these items in a few months, only to pawn them again for another loan. During the first six months of 1454 alone he took out ten loans, and at any one time he had at least six loans running concurrently (one a renewal of an earlier loan, on which occasion he paid the interest due up to that point with a rug from his private chamber). One wonders why men of means such as Strozzi, including even the occasional cleric,[75] had recourse to Jewish pawnbrokers rather than to official banks, which would have cost less in interest charges. Was it a matter of the limited development of banking, or reluctance to be involved with fellow Christians engaged in an illicit activity?

Economic Functions

By the fifteenth century Florentines had access to as large an array of banking services as could be found anywhere in Europe at the time. On the one hand, they had a place to put any surplus cash they might have. They could deposit it, payable on demand, for safekeeping or for the convenience of opening a current account on which they could write checks and effect book transfers of debits and credits to and from clients of other banks. They could also place savings in a discretionary deposit or purchase fictitious bills of exchange, and they could speculate in the international exchange market. On the other hand, they had access to credit to meet all needs, from momentary distress in their personal affairs to lack of liquidity in their business: they could borrow money on the security of

---

[74] ASF, Carte strozziane, ser. 3, 275.
[75] See Brucker, "Ecclesiastical Courts," 248.

any valuable they had at hand, from a piece of cloth or jewelry to future interest payments on government obligations, or they could write a promissory note, or they could take out a fictitious bill of exchange, and they could count on temporary credit through overdrafts on current accounts in bank. Finally, they had no problem in exchanging debased and foreign coins or in transferring money to and from just about any place in western Europe. The people who used these banking services came from a wide spectrum of Florentine society, extending well below the capitalist classes of merchant-bankers and cloth manufacturers to include artisans, shopkeepers, and even ordinary laborers, as many of the examples cited above demonstrate.

Many of these banking practices were probably to be found in other major European economic centers. Deposit banking, complete with interbank transfer and overdraft, has been abundantly documented for both Bruges and Venice, although in Bruges it apparently disappeared from the scene in the fifteenth century. And although we know much less about private banking in Genoa, a number of checks written on the public Banco di San Giorgio have survived from the fifteenth century to testify to the development of banking there. If deposit banks in these places did not traffic in bills of exchange, not being international merchant-banking companies, resident Florentines were probably available to provide all the services linked to this instrument. As to the social extent of banking practice, the Banco di San Giorgio extended credit to artisans and shopkeepers during its short life, from 1408 to 1445, and there is no reason to think that in Venice the Rialto banks did not also serve the same kinds of people. In nearby Padua a surviving banker's ledger, open from 1435 to 1437, contains current accounts for a tailor, a woodworker, a stone carver, a smithy, and other artisans.[76] Nor can it be asserted with absolute certainty that the accounting practices of Florentine bankers assured greater efficiency, inasmuch as the extant bankers' books from fourteenth-century Bruges, the most complete accounts of private bankers to have survived from any of these other places, appear to have all the refinements of comparable records in contemporary Florence.[77] It is the extent of the documentation from both the bankers' and the clients' records that gives Florence a clear preeminence in the history of local banking during this period.

We do not yet have sufficient data to measure the importance of deposit banking in the city's economy. No one has yet turned up a book of a Florentine banker

---

[76] Edoardo Demo, "'Tengho dinari li quali trafego in lo me bancho': L'attività di Giovanni Orsato, banchiere padovano del XV secolo," *Studi storici Luigi Simeoni* 54 (2004): 348–49. Demo refers to these current accounts without, however, presenting clear supporting evidence that they were indeed that.

[77] Raymond de Roover, "Le livre de comptes de Guillaume Ruyelle, changeur à Bruges (1369)," *Annales de la Société d'Emulation de Bruges* 77 (1934): 15–95.

comparable to the one surviving from Bruges that contains eleven hundred accounts opened in just five months, from December 1368 to the following May, and records as many as thirty transactions a day.[78] And certainly no local bank approached the scale of operations of any of the four Rialto banks that together had more than a million ducats in deposits in 1498.[79] When one of these banks—the Lippomano—failed the next year, it owed money to 1,248 creditors. In making comparisons like these, however, the terms have to be spelled out. In Florence at any one time in the later fifteenth century there were at least 50 local banks, whereas contemporary Venice, whose population was two to three times that of Florence, had only 4 or 5 banks; and fourteenth-century Bruges, which was about the same size as Florence in the fifteenth century, had no more than 16 or 17 banks. Moreover, both these cities were large international emporia crowded with foreign merchants, who were important clients of local deposit banks, whereas Florence was strictly a regional market center, attracting few foreign merchants and serving the local population almost exclusively.

Florentine banks varied so much in size, ranging from the miniscule business of Cerchi to that of the Medici, one of the largest international firms in Europe, that comparisons with these other cities on the basis of what we know about any one of these banks is difficult. The problem is further complicated by the fact that the Cambio merchant banks, like the Medici firm, were part of larger international commercial operations, not strictly deposit banks such as those in Bruges and Venice. Yet if put in context, data from the Cambini bank—the only one studied—look impressive, at least on the surface. In 1461 it had 177 accounts on the books of its local bank, and it opened 285 new accounts over the next eighteen months. In 1472 it had 255 accounts, and it opened 325 more over the next eighteen months; and during this decade its obligations to depositors with current accounts alone went from *fl.*13,000 di suggello to *fl.*17,000 larghi (worth 20 percent more than the fiorino di suggello).[80] These are not insignificant numbers for just one medium-sized bank out of fifty or so in a city with about ten thousand heads of households. Unfortunately, any statistical analysis of these data is vitiated by the organizational indivisibility of the Cambini company's local banking activity and its international commercial business. We still have no study of a local merchant bank like that of Francesco Datini (for which a complete set of books survives), which had its own autonomy as a local deposit bank within the larger business structure of its principal partner.

---

[78] De Roover, *Money, Banking and Credit in Mediaeval Bruges,* ch. 13.
[79] Frederic C. Lane, "Venetian Bankers, 1496–1533," *Journal of Political Economy* 45 (1937): 190, reprinted in *Venice and History: The Collected Papers of Frederic C. Lane* (Baltimore, 1966).
[80] Tognetti, "L'attività di banca locale," 639.

Banks performed a major economic function in making credit available for investment in productive activities. One reason why an international merchant bank opened a local bank was undoubtedly to help finance its own business in one way or another, but it also extended much credit more widely in the local economy. To juxtapose the capital of the Cambini bank—*fl.*2,000 di suggello in 1461, *fl.*1,667 larghi in 1472—with the credit it extended through overdrafts on current accounts alone—*fl.*14,898 di suggello in 1461, *fl.*14,704 larghi in 1472—is to emphasize the power of a bank to put other people's money to work outside the banker's own business activity.[81] The major need for credit in this economy was to meet short-term problems of liquidity, not capital investment. Merchants had to confront the slowness of both transport and communications in the conduct of foreign trade, and local textile producers, who depended on these merchants for raw materials and for marketing finished products, had to meet weekly payrolls. For these entrepreneurs, overdraft and delayed payment in particular served an essential function in day-to-day operations. Balances on the first of every month for a year on the accounts of several of the clients of the Cambini bank illustrate the extent of the problem in the textile industry. In 1462 two companies of lanaioli were overdrawn every month for an amount that averaged *fl.*532 di suggello for one and *fl.*773 di suggello for the other, and in 1473 another was overdrawn nine months for an average of *fl.*260 larghi. One company of setaioli was overdrawn nine months during 1462 for an average amount of *fl.*190 di suggello, and another was overdrawn for four months in 1473 for an average of *fl.*63 larghi.[82] Many of Cerchi's loans, most of which were under *fl.*50 and some as low as *fl.*2, probably served the same purpose for more modest operators inasmuch as the availability of even *fl.*2, which at the time was equivalent to about a month's earnings for an unskilled manual laborer, could make a big difference in a day's business of the stationers, notaries, bakers, weavers, and secondhand dealers who numbered among his clients. That large banks like the ones the setaiolo Michi dealt with—most of which carried patrician names—also made such small loans points to the important function local banks, large and small, played in the economy of the city. Pawnbrokers performed the same function in the vast area at the lowest level of the market by facilitating the temporary monetization of personal possessions.

---

[81] See the two balances in Tognetti, *Il banco Cambini,* 213, 270. Since at this time the fiorino largo was worth 20 percent more than the fiorino di suggello, the difference in the comparisons is somewhat greater than the figures by themselves represent. There may be some slippage in my calculations using the data from these balances since they were not collected to illustrate the aspects of local banking discussed here.

[82] Tognetti, "L'attività di banca locale," 621–29.

Banks by definition also increase the supply of money. By effecting monetary transactions through transfers on its books, they create fiduciary money as a legal means of payment; and as long as their clients, both depositors and borrowers, accept this way of making transactions, banks can reduce cash holdings. The money supply is increased to the extent that banks extend credit in bank money beyond their ability to meet their obligations to depositors in cash. Arnoldi, as we have seen, recognized the phenomenon: he built his argument for setting up a public bank on the premise that, as he said, bank money *(schritura di banco)* was in fact the same as money *(denari)* and cash *(contanti)*. Obviously there is no way of knowing to what degree this banking practice increased the money supply. The scattered data that have been collected for the cash reserves of particular banks, all of which need considerable qualification, reveal that the ratio of cash reserves to the balance of all active accounts in their banking operations varied considerably, usually at a level well below 100 percent.[83] Moreover, the use of credit for transactions increases the velocity of the circulation of money, and this too impinges positively on the supply of money. However inconsistent and unreliable the data, there can be little doubt that banks, through the current account and the facilitation of transactions in bank, created money, the spending of which stimulated that much more economic activity.

Still, in the end we are confronted with the relatively small size of the local-banking sector of the economy. There were many firms, perhaps one for every four textile firms, and people from all walks of life used them in one way or another at least occasionally, but the small scale of deposit-and-loan banking leads one to wonder about the importance of banks to the economy at large. And their importance shrinks even more on consideration of the alternatives Florentines had in the private credit market, as we shall see when we take up the subject of banking outside of banks.

Finally, it is impossible at this stage of research to say anything about the course of interest rates in the credit market and therefore about the cost of money. We have bits and pieces of runs of exchange rates in the international money market, but these do not necessarily reflect conditions in any local market. The interest rate on discretionary deposits fluctuated between 6 percent and 10 percent throughout the entire period from the late thirteenth to the early sixteenth century. Why the cost remained so stable over these two centuries is not at all clear. Demand and supply in the money market must occasionally have fluctuated beyond this range. Perhaps the discretionary deposit, with its explicit rate of

---

[83] For the Cambini bank, see ibid., 602–6; for Cerchi and two other banks, see Goldthwaite, "Local Banking," 53–54.

interest, was too precariously close to manifest usury to go beyond a certain ceiling. The same reasoning may explain why welfare institutions, such as the hospital of Santa Maria Nuova, kept the interest they paid on deposits at 5 percent. In any event, one suspects that here, as in so many other places in this economy, the force of tradition belies the logic of modern economic behavior based on a perfect demand-and-supply mechanism. Interest charged on private loans not identified as deposits could go well above this range, not uncommonly exceeding even the 20 percent permitted to Jewish pawn banks. Abroad, too, rates could be much higher. For instance, the fragment of the ledger Rinieri Fini kept at the Champagne fairs from 1296 to 1299 shows that loans put out to other, mostly Florentine, operators (which were not petty loans of the kind made by pawnbrokers and "Lombards") earned 20–25 percent, more than twice the going rate in the home market.[84]

Bankruptcies

Banks of all kinds had to face problems endemic to the money market in which they did business, from insufficient cash reserves to overextension of credit. International banks were especially vulnerable because their assets were in relatively long-term commercial ventures and precarious loans abroad, while their liabilities were in demand, hence short-term, deposits. Any failure of a local bank, by the very nature of its business, had repercussions throughout the population commensurate with the extent of its operations; and the failure of an international merchant-banking firm, even one without a local bank, could also have severe local repercussions since its principal clients were local cloth manufacturers and it operated in a tightly woven network with other Florentine firms.

Bankruptcies of international firms were not infrequent events, but no one has tried to assess their local repercussions in Florence itself. Creditors from abroad, however, counted for much more than those at home. When the Scali firm failed in 1326, the claims of Florentine creditors, fifteen in all, amounted to *fl.*35,646, an impressive amount per capita but probably not more than 10 percent of the firm's total liability and hardly enough to create a major liquidity crisis in the population at large.[85] A very different situation was created by the series of bankruptcies in the early 1340s, one of the great dramatic events in the history of banking as well as in the history of republican Florence. The largest international firms—the Bardi, the Peruzzi, and the Acciaiuoli—and a host of others

---

[84] Arrigo Castellani, *Nuovi testi fiorentini*, 2:674–96.
[85] Borsari, *Una compagnia di Calimala*, 85–89.

collapsed, and a chain reaction drove several hundred local operators to declare themselves bankrupt.[86] Local claims filed by seventy-one creditors against the company of Taddeo dell'Antella totaled more than *fl.*30,000, and this multiplied many times spells a real disaster with wide repercussions. Villani considered the crisis one of the worst in the history of the city, one that could only be understood as some kind of divine retribution for the evils of the time.

Yet, curiously, for all the attention his observations on the crisis have received, Villani has little to say about the matter and offers no particulars about the dynamics that linked these bankruptcies in a chain reaction—all the more curious because he was himself a partner in the international merchant-banking firm of the Buonaccorsi. Historians too have made much of these bankruptcies, but they hardly go beyond registering Villani's observations. Armando Sapori, who wrote the classic account of the crisis, documented the flood of claims that poured into the Mercanzia from all over western Europe, including even remote Sardinia and Corsica, but local claims go unremarked. Unfortunately, we have no information about the relative importance of local depositors as distinct from other creditors in the claims filed following the bankruptcies of the Frescobaldi, Bardi, Peruzzi, Acciaiuoli, and all the other firms at this time. They probably did not number very many or represent a very broad cross section of society, notwithstanding the impression one gets from reading about this great crisis. Among the seventy-one claims filed against the bankrupt firm of Taddeo dell'Antella in 1345 (the only list published), only one refers to his credit as a deposit, and two others refer to it as "capital." Only three claimants—two speziali and one stamaiuolo, all probably clients of the firm—are identified as men outside the circle of the city's upper class.[87]

In much of the historical work on the period these bankruptcies of the 1340s appear as little more than a rhetorical device to heighten the drama of a turbulent decade, extending through a sequence of political crises—the war against Lucca, in 1336–38; the tyranny of the Duke of Athens, in 1342–43; the victory of a popular government over the oligarchy, in 1343—to one of the most severe famines in the city's history in 1347 and then the Black Death, amidst which the sharp fall in the ratio of gold to silver (referred to in chapter 3) reduced the value of credits in florins for people who needed silver money to spend in the local market. These events taken together justify the grim view of these years one finds in the traditional literature. Yet the 1340s were the very years that saw the funding of the

---

[86] Gene A. Brucker, *Florentine Politics and Society* (Princeton, NJ, 1962), 16–17, refers to a partial list (from A to S) of 350 Florentines who went bankrupt over the period from 1333 to 1346, but he does not indicate whether the list distinguishes between individuals and companies.

[87] Sapori, "Il quaderno dei creditori," 159–80.

state debt and the emergence of a lively secondary market, including major speculation, in the new government obligations (to be discussed in chapter 7). These were also the years when the mint's production of gold florins reached its highest documented level. We still have no study that isolates the bankruptcies in this complex picture with the objective of learning something about the structure of the local credit market, that is, about the ties that bound together the social constituency of that market.[88]

However serious these bankruptcies were, economic activity picked up again in the immediate wake of the Black Death, as is manifest, above all, in the extraordinarily rapid rise of wages in the autumn of that year (see chapter 5). Moreover, international banking was no longer dominated by such giants as the Bardi, Peruzzi, and Acciaiuoli firms, which were so irretrievably tied into government finance abroad. The highly decentralized structure of the banking system in the fifteenth century precluded anything like the disasters of the 1340s. Hardly any of Florence's numerous chroniclers mentions the subject. The largest concentration of failures any modern scholar has recorded occurred in the decade 1366–76, but the annual average was only from seven to eight.[89] The chronicler Pagolo Petriboni recorded six failures in the last two months of 1425, presumably related to the severe fiscal problems of the state at the time and bankers' involvement in the floating debt.[90] A few contemporaries remarked a rash of failures in 1464–65, Benedetto Dei recorded seven in 1474, and Bartolomeo Cerretani recorded another in 1502.[91] None of these, however, led to a general run on banks with repercussions throughout the economy.

The bankruptcies of 1464–65 were the most commented on by contemporary writers (as they are by modern historians). Even by this testimony, however, the disturbance appears to have been largely contained with respect to both the number of firms involved and its duration. Alamanno Rinuccini, the writer with the most specific information, mentions total losses of *fl.*310,000 incurred by the failure of eight firms in November 1464, most of which are not known to have been in the top rank of merchant banks.[92] Dei also notes financial difficulties about

[88] The most comprehensive survey of the literature directed to throwing light on the local economic scene during these years of crisis is Carlo M. Cipolla, *The Monetary Policy of Fourteenth-Century Florence* (Berkeley and Los Angeles, 1982), ch. 1. But in this literature, including the work of Nicola Ottokar, Gene Brucker, and Marvin Becker, the specific problem of the bankruptcies is not explored even minimally; and Sapori has virtually nothing to say about local depositors and creditors in *La crisi delle compagnie mercantili dei Bardi e dei Peruzzi* (Florence, 1926).

[89] Brucker, *Florentine Politics and Society*, 15 (citing *provvisioni*).

[90] Pagolo di Matteo Petriboni and Matteo di Borgo Rinaldi, *Priorista (1407–1459)*, ed. Jacqueline A. Gutwirth (Rome, 2001), 181.

[91] Dei, *La cronica*, 98; Bartolomeo Cerretani, *Ricordi*, ed. Giuliana Berti (Florence, 1993), 38.

[92] Filippo di Cino Rinuccini, *Ricordi storici di Filippo di Cino Rinuccini dal 1282 al 1460, colla continuazione di Alamanno e Neri suoi figli fino al 1506*, ed. G. Aiazzi (Florence, 1840), xciv–xcv.

this time with reference to sixteen merchant-banking families, including the Medici and other prominent ones. In December 1464 Filippo Strozzi, in Naples, received several letters with news of these failures from his mother and from friends. His mother wrote that "there is much turbulence in the land," and Alamanno Acciaiuoli judged the situation the worst since 1339, one that left "the poor without bread, the rich without brains, and learned men without good sense." Yet the next month, in January 1465, Strozzi's mother wrote that "for the moment the matter of these failures seems to have settled down . . . and I have not heard anything from others. . . . I believe it is a good thing for one who has debts."[93] In none of these comments is there any hint about causes, although the coincidence of these failures with Cosimo's death in 1464 and the ensuing challenge to his son Piero's political authority has not gone unobserved, even by contemporaries. One chronicler at the time blamed Dietisalvi Neroni, who, for his own political motives, put pressure on Piero to call in his loans and hence precipitate a crisis, a notion picked up later by Machiavelli but rejected by Raymond de Roover (who, however, was not aware of this earlier source).[94] A contemporary, Marco Parenti, also exonerated the Medici but went on to comment that whereas Cosimo, had he been alive, might have done something about the affair, Piero took some pleasure in the misfortunes of others.[95] According to de Roover, these failures more likely resulted from direct Venetian action against Florentine interests in the Near East arising from the prolonged war that broke out in 1463 between Venice and the Ottoman sultan; and, indeed, Dei also commented on failures about this time with a characteristically inflammatory tirade against the Venetians, whose perfidy he blamed for losses suffered by Florentines in the Near East. This situation may have contributed to the move of the principal Florentine banking center abroad from Venice and Geneva to Lyons about this time.

For the most part, bankruptcies were isolated and occasional events, and at least after the 1340s they were largely confined to merchant banks. The textile industry, the backbone of the economy, was less subject to bankruptcies since, as we have seen, firms could easily avoid overextension of credit by adjusting production schedules to any temporary lack of liquidity or to fluctuations in the demand for their products in international markets. Those textile firms that went bankrupt were most likely also operating as international merchant banks, a phenomenon found among wool firms in the fourteenth century (but not later) and

---

[93] Alessandra Macinghi negli Strozzi, *Lettere di una gentildonna fiorentina del secolo XV ai figliuoli esuli*, ed. Cesare Guasti (Florence, 1877), 333, 336, 342, 350 (letter from Acciaiuoli), 351 (letter from Bernardo Salviati), 354, 358, 379, 421.

[94] Rab Hatfield, "A Source for Machiavelli's Account of the Regime of Piero de' Medici," in *Studies on Machiavelli*, ed. M. Gilmore (Florence, 1972), 317–33; de Roover, *Medici Bank*, 358–60.

[95] Marco Parenti, *Ricordi storici, 1464–1467*, ed. Manuela Doni Garfagnini (Rome, 2001), 72–74.

not uncommon among the larger silk firms that sprung up in the fifteenth century. As to the international banking sector, it operated independently of what was happening in Florence. Few Florentines other than the partners themselves had an interest in this business as either investors or creditors. The city benefited from the enormous profits bankers brought home, but it suffered hardly any loss at all when they went bankrupt. Not even the collapse of an extensive family network of companies operating abroad, such as that of the Alberti in the 1430s or, more dramatically, that of the Pazzi after the conspiracy of 1478, seems to have had repercussions throughout the business world. Nor did the decline and eventual collapse of the Medici bank, by far the city's largest, pull other banks into its vortex, let alone shake up the banking system as a whole. For all the prominence of the Medici both as bankers and as politicians, there is no indication, certainly not in the extensive scholarship on their political machinations, that the several challenges to Medici authority from within the oligarchy sent serious reverberations throughout the banking community. Not even the exile of the family in 1494 seems to have created difficulties for other merchant-bankers; and it would probably not have come about so smoothly had there been that prospect. The Medici bank was very far from having anything like the centrality within the banking system that the Bardi and the Peruzzi had had a century earlier.

The relative tranquility of the Florentine banking scene stands in stark contrast to that in Venice.[96] There failures were frequent and all the more disastrous because of the concentration of deposit banking in just a few firms that were giants compared with Florentine banks. The fragility of the Venetian system can be attributed to conditions peculiar to Europe's largest port city, where banks were more directly exposed to failures of merchants and disruptions in international trade, especially in the bullion market. The Florentine firms operating there do not seem to have been pulled down by the havoc these failures created in the Venetian money market, not even during the massive collapse of the Venetian banks on the Rialto in 1499.[97] Local banking in Florence was built on the foundation of an inland city with a strong industrial sector. In the short run at least, the commercial sector, oriented around the export of textiles, could usually adjust to temporary disturbances in foreign markets without much difficulty. Serving a local economy of this kind, the banking industry enjoyed a certain stability, especially because it was fragmented among so many relatively small firms.

---

[96] See Mueller, *Venetian Money Market,* pt. 2.

[97] A Venetian commentator on these bankruptcies considered them worse than the loss of Brescia would have been, observing that "in tanto moto, quanto è stà quel de fiorentini, tutti i so banchi, che son 10, è stà saldi." Domenico Malpiero, "Annali Veneti," *ASI* 7 (1843–44): 715.

Banking outside of Banks

The above survey illustrates banking practices with references, when possible, to artisans and other people outside the sphere of the upper classes in order to emphasize the widespread familiarity with banks in Florentine society. To put this social world of banking in perspective, however, we need to look at the banking functions that were performed outside of banks. The essential demand for credit in the Florentine economic system arose from the need to meet temporary problems of liquidity. As we have seen, the business community, from artisan to textile manufacturer and international merchant, had its own mechanisms for providing certain banking functions outside of banks. Moreover, through offsetting on one another's books other people too had worked out a way to provide themselves with almost all the basic services a bank offered—a depository for surplus funds, book transfer of debits and credits on current account, and loans—without recourse to a bank. In not one of these services did banks have a monopoly.

Offsetting

Offsetting on private accounts is another way of effecting transfer, and in Florence this practice was widespread and highly sophisticated. Florentines were meticulous and disciplined recordkeepers. Even artisans kept detailed accounts according to the highest contemporary standards of accounting practice, including double entry. In their extensive economic relations with one another as both private persons and businessmen these people were forever substituting book transfer of debits and credits for cash payment. Personal accounts in private ledgers, therefore, functioned somewhat like current accounts in bank. In 1503 the notary ser Andrea Nacchianti used the term in noting that he had paid the expenses for his new family chapel through two speziali, "who paid the major portion of the said moneys for me in the current account I have with them at their shop."[98] One could draw on his credit by written order for transfer to a third party, and the transfer could be passed on to a fourth party and even on to others by mere book entry. All the practices linked to a current account in bank can be documented abundantly in the private relations between Florentines, even those in the lower ranks of the economic and social order. In fact, to protect the creditor who did not want to be paid in book credit, legislation was occasionally enacted to require payment in cash.[99]

[98] Dario A. Covi, "A Documented Altarpiece by Cosimo Rosselli," *Art Bulletin* 54 (1971): 238.
[99] See Mario Bernocchi, *Le monete della Repubblica fiorentina* (Florence, 1974), 1:48–50 (1519) and 463–66 (1524).

It was standard practice of partners to open a personal current account on the firm's books, on which they drew against future earnings, and many of these accounts richly document how people spent their money in the ordinary course of their lives outside of their business. Likewise, workers, instead of taking all their wages in cash, commonly used credits on their wage account with their employer to pay for ordinary living expenses. Luca di Pippo, a manual laborer at the construction site of Santo Spirito from 1477 to 1479, had his salary account with the monastery debited for rent, wheat, wood, a bed, a hat for his son, and a dowry for his daughter.[100] The silk weaver Iacopo di Tedesco used credits from sales to his setaioli clients in the same way, in effect opening a current account on their books on which he drew in ordering payments to third parties; in 1522 one of these firms, Giovanni Popoleschi, Simone Guadagni & Partners, sent him a statement of the activity on the account.[101] The landlady of the stone- and metalworker Maso di Bartolomeo occasionally, in 1451–52, ordered him to use the credit she had with him for his rent to pay shoemakers on her behalf.[102]

Offsetting could be extended by transfer to a third party and even beyond. Just how complex this game could become is illustrated in an entry in the record book of the painter Neri di Bicci.[103] In 1466 one of Neri's tenants, a silk weaver, wanting to pay £40 toward his rent, asks a spinner with whom he had credit to pay Neri; the spinner, in turn, instead of paying Neri directly, asks a setaiolo firm with whom he had a credit to pay Neri; the setaiolo informs Neri of the credit, and Neri makes the appropriate entries in his ledger, crediting his tenant's account and debiting the setaiolo's account. At this point Neri, wanting to pay a debt he has with the heirs of a battiloro, who have instructed Neri to make the payment to their banker, orders the setaioli firm, with whom he now has the credit from his tenant, to pay the banker, thus extinguishing his debt with the heirs of the battiloro. The confusion a reader may have in trying to straighten out this chain of transfers indicates how intricate the network of offsetting debits and credits could become. Here, in the payment of rent by a tenant to a landlord, we have a series of credit transfers beginning with one party (the tenant-weaver) that then passed through two other parties (the spinner and the silk manufacturer) for the purpose of paying a fourth party (Neri, the landlord-painter), who in turn transferred the credit to a fifth party (the banker) to pay yet another party (the heirs

---

[100] Goldthwaite, *Building of Renaissance Florence*, 309.

[101] Richard A. Goldthwaite, "An Entrepreneurial Silk Weaver in Renaissance Florence," *I Tatti Studies* 10 (2005): 104.

[102] Goldthwaite, *Building of Renaissance Florence*, 307. Florence Edler de Roover also notes that workers could use their accounts with their employer to make transfers to third parties. See "Andrea Banchi, Florentine Silk Manufacturer and Merchant in the Fifteenth Century," *Studies in Medieval and Renaissance History* 3 (1966): 253.

[103] Neri di Bicci, *Le ricordanze*, 278.

of the battiloro). No cash changed hands; instead, payment was effected through transfers that involved six parties in all—four artisans and two firms—ranging from a simple spinner to a bank.

As an engrained habit, offsetting taken to the extent illustrated by this example from an artisan's record book presupposes not just literacy and numeracy but also knowledge of accountancy. Simple tallies and other such memory devices could not have guaranteed that all the parties involved in the many transfers of the Neri di Bicci example would remember what was happening, especially since the sum being transferred—£40—was determined by the decision of just one of the six parties and could hardly have resulted in the settlement of accounts between any of the others except Neri. Each must have kept some kind of accounts to know where he stood with respect to his individual balance of debits and credits after recording the transfer or at least had the confidence that the other parties' accounts would be readily available for reference, perhaps in a form approximating the bank statement, such as the one mentioned above sent to the silk weaver Iacopo di Tedesco. The long lists of debtors and creditors ordinary working people attached to their 1427 catasto presupposes some kind of written record of these complex relations. The stoneworker Andrea di Nofri di Romolo, for example, filed a list of no fewer than 130 debtors, adding at the end a single collective entry for the 90 more who owed him less than a florin.[104]

All these people must have been assured that private records were sufficient legal evidence in the event of a dispute. The abundant accounting material that survives for both creditors and debtors, from bankers and other capitalist entrepreneurs to artisans and shopkeepers, testifies to the extraordinarily widespread practice of accounting precisely for the purpose of keeping track of the complex and fluid record of offsetting. Their universal adoption by the end of the fourteenth century of the bipartite system (*alla veneziana*) to keep their accounts, listing debits and credits opposite, rather than above, each other, allowed them to record increased activity more efficiently; hence this innovation in accounting practice can itself be considered an economic indicator. Accounting, in fact, was an essential element of the economic culture of Florentines. Arnoldi could hardly have conceived his plan to require that all payments above a certain level—the amount transferred in the Neri di Bicci example was almost at that level—be made in current accounts on the state's ledgers if he had not assumed that many Florentines already knew how the procedures worked. The problem Arnoldi's project posed to the city fathers may have come down to whether they could

---

[104] Goldthwaite, *Building of Renaissance Florence*, 313.

manage such a gigantic accounting operation, not to whether Florentines would know how to use it.

The practice of offsetting became even more sophisticated with the use of written orders to effect transfers of credit. Neri di Bicci does not report how all the people involved in this one multitransfer of funds communicated with one another to make these orders of payment; although one imagines that transmission in most instances was oral, many written orders of payment, in effect checks written on current accounts with private parties just like those written on banks, have survived. The oldest extant order yet found, dating from 1368, was written by Tommaso and Zanobi Tornaquinci drawing on credit that the estate of a certain monna Dea had with Michele Castellani to pay £3 15s. a fiorini to a cloth dealer for cloth needed for her funeral. In another order, dated 18 September 1433, the notary Bindo d'Agnolo drew on his account with the cloth dealer Lapo di Pacino da Castelfiorentino to pay *fl.*4 to Giovanni Lenzi (and Lapo in turn ordered a haberdasher, with whom he presumably had credit, to make the payment). Bindo's order has the formal characteristics of a check written on a bank. It is a small piece of paper with the name of Lapo on one side and on the other the formulaic text in the standard format:

> Give to the bearer of this, who is Nencio di Giovanni Lenzi, *fl.* four d'oro.
>
> yours, ser Bindo d'Agnolo
>
> on 18 September 1433[105]

Both of these orders (and others) were found tucked away in the ledger of the party who received the check, but no mention of this mode of communication is made in the relevant entry on the account of the person who wrote the check. Silence on this point in the abundant accounting evidence for private offsetting does not, therefore, preclude the possibility that orders of transfer were often transmitted in written form.

How is the economic importance of offsetting to be assessed? In generating credit outside of banks, offsetting must have had the effect of increasing the money supply. In fact, it is often considered one of the recourses people had to compensate for shortages and debasement of coins, problems endemic to the European economy at the time; however, as we have seen, bullion was imported to this city, and the mint followed a purely defensive debasement policy. The scale of transactions recorded in Florentine accounts, both the amounts involved and the number of them, suggests that offsetting was more a matter of preference than a response to market constraints. To the extent that offsetting was executed

---

[105] These and other checks are published in Spallanzani, "Note on Florentine Banking."

through a written record of something approximating the current account complete with a sophisticated instrument for transfer of debits and credits, the practice served a banking function. The extensive practice of offsetting provided many Florentines at all social levels with what in effect were current accounts on which overdraft or delayed payment was a possible solution to temporary liquidity problems. Within this vast and amorphous network, retail shops dealing in the things people needed every day appear as microcenters for the generation of credit within their circle of clients. Tradesmen readily permitted delayed payment for weeks and sometimes months even for petty sales, they permitted clients to use their accounts as current accounts complete with transfer and overdraft privileges, and they were prepared to make loans.[106]

Both overdraft and delayed payment were, in fact, such universal practices, common among all operators, from artisans and tradesmen to merchants and bankers, as to suggest that time was not yet charged with the discipline of the modern market, notwithstanding Jacques Le Goff's thesis about the replacement of liturgical time by the merchant's more precise sense of time. The above example taken from the record book of the painter Neri di Bicci is instructive about the casualness toward time in the matter of paying one's debts. The original payment that set off the successive credit transfers was for rent owed by a silk weaver, and since it amounted to *fl*.7–8, one suspects that the renter was much in arrears at the time (*fl*.5 being a normal rent paid by a poor person for a house). We are not told when the weaver made the first move, but Neri was informed by the setaioli firm, the third party in the chain, on 19 August 1466 that he had this credit but that it would not be payable until four months later, on 19 December. It was only on 7 January 1467, several weeks after the promised date and five months after original notice of the credit, that Neri reassigned the credit to the heirs of the battiloro. These monetary relations probably cannot be considered apart from the myriad personal relations—between relatives, friends, neighbors, clients, partners, and employers—that must have counted for much in this casual attitude about time. The transfers from the silk weaver to the spinner and to the setaioli firm that constituted two of the sequences recorded by Neri, for instance, may have involved debits and credits incurred in working with one another.

In short, extensive networks of personal relations held together by informal arrangements, a sense of trust, and a mentality not yet disciplined by the imperatives of modern industrial capitalism made for a casual credit regime operating

---

[106] No study of this kind has been made of the accounts of a Florentine tradesman, but for fourteenth-century Prato see the discussion of "a world of credit and trust" in Richard K. Marshall, *The Local Merchants of Prato: Small Entrepreneurs in the Late Medieval Economy* (Baltimore, 1999), ch. 5.

outside the institutional constraints of banks and pawnbrokers. Hence the greatest significance of offsetting is probably to be found in the economic culture the practice represented. In fact, the endless maze of debit-credit relations may have been a major force inducing the accounting mentality that produced the extraordinary documentary record for the economic life of the city. Moreover, offsetting took place in a market where relations were subject to highly personal considerations and not yet conditioned by the discipline of formal institutional arrangements.[107] This "culture of credit" was quite different from the one that emerged in sixteenth-century England, elucidated by Craig Muldrew. There, litigiousness arising out of the expanding web of complex and increasingly problematic credit relations generated the social value of creditworthiness, shifting the prevailing ethic from passive honesty on the debtor's side to an aggressive sense of trust and reputation on the creditor's side. Muldrew makes the case for this ethic, not just the Weberian values of thrift and hard work, as a driving force that gave birth to the spirit of modern capitalism. In this as in so many other ways, the economic culture of England was evolving in a direction that left Florence far behind.[108]

The Private Credit Market

By now it should be clear that local banks did not have a commanding position in the local credit market. On the supply side of that market, the weakness of these banks in attracting deposits was exposed by their failure to provide an outlet for the savings that began to accumulate in the hands of artisans and shopkeepers in the second half of the fifteenth century. The depositories opened by the Innocenti, Santa Maria Nuova, and the Badia, in contrast, responded to this void in the market, signaling the new direction banking was to take in the following century. But it is when we turn to the demand side of the market that we can see banks' relative inability to attract capital. Local banks and especially pawnbrokers served the general public as sources for direct loans, but they were hardly the only conduit to credit. Direct loans were also readily available outside of banks. Evidence for loans from private persons abounds in the city's oldest notarial records. In the registers of the late thirteenth century that have been published, loans outnumber by far all other kinds of contracts. One notary, ser Matteo di Biliotto, drew up documents for loans—most of them not from moneychangers—amounting to between *fl.*11,000 and *fl.*12,000 in just twenty-five months, from 1294 to 1296, when there

---

[107] For one view of offsetting in seventeenth-century Rome, see Renata Ago, *Economia barocca: Mercato e istituzioni nella Roma del Seicento* (Rome, 1998), 57–60, 108–9.

[108] Craig Muldrew, *The Economy of Obligation: The Culture of Credit and Social Relations in Early Modern England* (Houndmills, UK, 1998).

were five hundred to six hundred notaries inscribed in the guild. Moreover, debits and credits recorded in these official documents could be reassigned through another notarial act, although it is difficult to say that traffic of this kind constituted a secondary market. Almost all of these notarized loans are for small amounts, since by this time businesses had replaced the notary with their own account books as the official record of larger credit transactions. Since interest could not be included, the notarized act had to be manipulated to protect the lender. Hence interest might be disguised as a straight interest-free loan or a deposit contract that stipulated what was owed rather than what the borrower actually received. A common device was to draw up one document for the sale of a property and then another for its repurchase at a different price. Today it is often impossible to unmask the disguise to reveal the true nature of these documents, and obviously hardly anything can be learned about interest rates.[109]

Loans are also a principal activity recorded in the earliest accounting materials, both business and private, dating from the thirteenth century. These accounting entries for private loans often make reference to an accompanying notarized agreement and witnesses (though rarely to pawns), but in the accounts the nature of the transaction is explicit in a way that reveals, already by this time, the sophistication of the culture of credit. The accounts, unlike notarial acts, record interest—*bene, costo, dono* (or *donamento*), *guadagno, interesse, merito, pro* (or *prode*), and *usura* are the terms already in use in the thirteenth century—but usually without mentioning rates. When stated, the rate is expressed either as so many denari per lira for a month or as a percentage, for example, *undici del centinaio* (11 percent). In a ledger open from 1274 to 1310 Gentile di Ugo Sassetti occasionally reveals how the loan was disguised in an accompanying notarial agreement with the borrower by stating only the amount owed, not what was lent. In his own accounting record Sassetti is explicit about the interest payments, which he isolates in separate entries. In several entries he goes on to add that the borrower "has forgiven us the interest charge" (*àcci perdonato il merito*).[110]

By the fourteenth century lenders had largely dispensed with the notary, and loans made by private persons could take the several forms mentioned in the above discussion: a witnessed transaction, pawning valuables, the promissory note, the bill of exchange, or the discretionary deposit (so called even when arranged with a private person). For people at the lowest level of the economic scale

---

[109] Franek Sznura discusses credit in notarial documents in the introduction to *Ser Matteo di Biliotto notaio: Imbreviatura*, vol. 1, *Registro (anni 1294–1296)*, ed. Manila Soffici and Franek Sznura (Florence, 2002), lxii–lxxviii.

[110] Almost all extant accounts in Italian before 1300 are published in Arrigo Castellani, *Nuovi testi fiorentini*.

pawning an object with a private party was one way to obtain a lira or two, and some shopkeepers had a little business on the side in pawnbroking—for example, the linen draper Tommaso di Donato, whose heirs sold the pawns they found in his shop, "which belonged to many persons," to another firm of linen drapers and a speziale for £170 in 1499.[111] At the same time there was a greater sensibility to usury. In the accounting record itself interest is generally disguised by the classic notarial technique, used also by banks, as noted above: entering the debt as what the borrower owed when repayment came due, not what he had actually received. Sometimes, however, the cover-up is revealed, as it was in the instance cited above taken from the books of the Cerchi bank. In 1360 Lippo di Fede del Sega recorded three loans in his ledger that he said appeared larger in the written agreement with the borrower—*fl.*20 instead of *fl.*10, *fl.*15 instead of *fl.*10, *fl.*9 instead of *fl.*6.[112] In 1450 Francesco Castellani stated in a personal memorandum of a promissory note he had signed for a loan of *fl.*110 that he had in fact received only *fl.*100.[113] Most of these private loans were for only several florins, larger than the average loan from a pawn bank but not large enough to make a significant investment. Most probably allowed the borrower to meet a temporary liquidity problem in either his personal or business affairs. The only major investment use of large loans would appear to have been the purchase of real estate.

We have already seen the small role banks played as sources for credit in the forward sectors of the economy. They did not provide start-up capital to entrepreneurs in the commercial and industrial sectors, who founded their enterprise on capital raised through limited partnerships, not loans. To judge from the relatively small number of merchant-bankers who opened local banks, much of the demand for capital for international trade was also satisfied without recourse to the general public through banks. They could raise much more capital by accepting deposits from the rich and powerful abroad, wherever they had branches. Nor was the textile industry, the foundation of the economy, tied into the banking system. Since manufacturing firms invested little in plant and equipment, entrepreneurs needed capital only to get production to the point where income could, at least under the most favorable circumstances, meet ongoing costs. They could provide the necessary capital from their own resources or by going into partnership, generally with no more than one or two others. A firm inevitably needed additional credit to meet temporary liquidity problems once operations were up and going, but the putting-out system gave it the flexibility to keep the problem from getting out of control, and structural arrangements existed within the business

[111] Archive of the Ospedale degli Innocenti, Florence, ser. 20, 41, fol. 4.
[112] De La Roncière, *Un changeur florentin,* 197n.
[113] Francesco Castellani, *Ricordanze,* 1:131.

community to make the necessary short-term credit available, primarily overdraft on account and delayed payment on goods, whether raw materials provided by import-export firms to textiles producers or finished cloth going the
other way. Delayed payment in the cloth industry, for either raw materials or
finished products, was allowed for several months, even up to a year, usually at
a rate of about 8–9 percent, and the creditor could not refuse to settle in advance
of the due date if the debtor so chose. International merchant-banking firms, as
importer-exporters, made these arrangements possible, but they too depended
on short-term credit from producers to pay for the products they exported. If
worse came to worst and the firm needed a considerable amount of ready cash,
there was always the discretionary deposit. The 1457 catasto declaration of the
setaiolo Giuliano di Antonio Gondi, the builder of the great family palace, reveals
that while he had borrowed *fl.*1,300 from banks through money put on the
exchange, he had also raised the extraordinary sum of *fl.*4,240 through discretionary deposits from nine private persons.[114] In short, local banks were not a
necessary part of the structure of credit relations within the forward sectors of
the economy.

Viewed from the perspective of people who wanted to invest savings passively
in the hope of earning some return on their capital, the credit market offered few
outlets besides a direct personal loan of the kind mentioned above, and bank
deposits were not prominent among these. Potential investors had few choices. By
far the most popular investment instrument by the fifteenth century was the
time, or discretionary, deposit, which was the same as the short-term time deposit at a fixed rate of interest offered by banks. Wool and silk firms commonly
carried a deposit or two of this kind on their books. The abovementioned Luca di
Buonaccorso Pitti, whose grandfather Luca had built the family palace, seems to
have been a rentier living off such investments. Over the fifteen years from 1467
to 1482 he had discretionary deposits with from three to seven companies, divided about evenly between international merchant banks and textile firms, both
wool and silk; at any one time his investment amounted to between *fl.*1,000 and
*fl.*2,000 and was earning 6–10 percent interest. When he transferred his accounts
to a new ledger in 1493 he had seven such deposits, totaling *fl.*6,000, with a battiloro firm, a silk firm, and several international merchant-banking firms.[115] If he
had the right connections, the investor might become a passive minor partner in
a business, sharing profits but risking full personal liability if the firm failed. Few
companies, however, had more than three or four partners. The 1408 legislation

---

[114] Florence Edler de Roover, *L'arte della seta a Firenze nei secoli XIV e XV,* ed. Sergio Tognetti
(Florence, 1999), 89.
[115] Goldthwaite, "Local Banking," 33–34.

enabling the accomandita brought the investor into the business as a silent partner with limited liability: he shared profits as a partner but risked only his capital
in the event of losses or eventual failure. The instrument seems to have been used
infrequently, however, until well into the sixteenth century, by which time even
artisans were using it as both investors and borrowers. In 1544, for example, the
silk weaver Iacopo di Tedesco invested *fl.*200 in an accomandita contract with a
linen and secondhand dealer in Prato that assured him a prior claim of 9 percent
on profits and the right to withdraw his investment at any time.[116]

In the normal course of their economic relations with one another, privately
and in the course of their work, Florentines had all the essential services of a bank
without recourse to a bank. They had current accounts with persons and businesses on which they could make giro transfers to third parties using written
orders of payment, and they had access to credit through overdraft and the con-
ventional business practice of delayed payment as well as through direct borrowing from personal acquaintances. Indeed, recourse to a bank was unnecessary for
most businesses, from textile firms to artisan enterprises like that of the painter
Neri di Bicci, whose shop book reveals hardly any transactions with banks. Banks
fully prepared to handle the full panoply of functions inherent in their business
were available, and just why they did not move into this private sphere, and why
people did not have more recourse to them, is not clear. Florentines were not held
back by horizontal credit ties binding them to family and institutions,[117] and use
of the centralizing services of banks would presumably have reduced transaction
costs. As it was, these banking practices outside of banks arguably had a much
greater impact on the economy at large in facilitating transfer and even enlarging
the money supply. In any event, banks clearly had a minor role in channeling
direct investments to productive sectors of the economy.

One credit instrument Florentines did not have that was widely used in local
markets in northern Europe was the private *rente,* an annuity that could be purchased from someone who guaranteed its payment through a lien originally on a
piece of real estate and could be contracted to last for one or more lifetimes. The
debtor encumbered income from a specified property for payment of the annuity,
but he had the right to redeem his commitment. The *rente,* therefore, was a long-
term loan, something like a bond. The creditor, moreover, could sell his *rente,* so
that it evolved as a negotiable credit instrument. It arose in the predominantly

---

[116] Goldthwaite, "Entrepreneurial Silk Weaver," 103–4.

[117] Ulrich Pfister, "Gérer les fortunes et les infortunes dans le milieu urbain, XVII–XIXe siècles,"
in *Des personnes aux institutions: Réseaux et culture du crédit du XVIe au XXe siècle en Europe,* ed. L.
Fontaine, G. Postel-Vinay, J.-L. Rosenthal, and P. Servais (Louvain la-Neuve, Belgium, 1997), 328.
Commenting on three essays in this volume, Pfister finds this characteristic of credit ties among
lower classes and asks whether this is a general situation.

agricultural economies of northern Europe, and recourse to it increased considerably from the sixteenth century on. Already at the time of the growth of the Antwerp market the use of the *rente* extended far beyond the ranks of merchants and capitalist investors. A mason, for example, could use the *rente* for speculation, taking out a loan on property he wanted to build on and then redeeming it after selling the building he had erected. Many of the people who bought annuities were craftsmen, small shopkeepers, and widows.[118]

Florentines did not have this investment outlet in the private sphere until the later sixteenth century.[119] The commune created something like it when it funded the state debt in the 1340s and imposed forced loans on its subjects in lieu of direct taxation, and the enterprise initially attracted voluntary loans. After a few years, however, irregularity in the payment of interest and the impossibility of redeeming capital discouraged voluntary loans. Inasmuch as the system of direct taxation was based on forced loans in return for which the "lender" was given credit in the Monte, many Florentines came to hold title to such government obligations over the years (in the 1427 catasto more than 20 percent of the households declared them as assets). Credits for both the principal and unpaid (and future) interest were assignable to third parties, and a busy secondary market arose in them that reveals considerable sophistication in the many ways Florentines managed to utilize these forced investments in the state for their own private purposes to guarantee loans, to make purchases, and to obtain cash. It was not until the sixteenth century that the fiscal system was put on a secure enough foundation for government obligations to attract voluntary investments. This is a subject that will be taken up in chapter 7.

New Directions in the Sixteenth Century
A Public Savings-and-Loan Bank

The above descriptions of the banking system and the credit market pertain to the period extending from the mid-fourteenth through the fifteenth century. Except for the substitution of Jews for Christians as pawnbrokers, they seem to have undergone little change during this time. The one new, if modest, institution was the depository service opened in the third quarter of the fifteenth century

---

[118] On all this see Herman van der Wee, "Monetary, Credit and Banking Systems," *The Cambridge Economic History of Europe* (Cambridge, 1977), 5:303–5. The early history of *rentes* in Italy can be approached through Manuel Vaquero Piñeiro, "Die Rentenkaufverträge im spätmittelalterlichen und frühneuzeitlichen Italien," *Quellen und Forschungen aus italienischen Archiven und Bibliotheken* 86 (2006): 252–93, on their sale in early modern Rome.

[119] Lorenzo Polizzotto is currently studying the *rente* in the investment portfolio of the Vettori family at the end of the sixteenth century.

by Santa Maria Nuova, the Innocenti, and possibly the Badia. By the second quarter of the sixteenth century, however, both Santa Maria Nuova and the Innocenti were growing rapidly; global figures from their records point to deposits averaging about *fl.*100–150. Indicative of the growth of Santa Maria Nuova is the activity of the account of its most famous depositor, Michelangelo, through which passed *fl.*11,252 in seventeen years, from 1505 to 1522. The hospital closed down this operation in 1553 for reasons that are not clear, but by this time business was picking up at the Innocenti. In 1564 the orphanage had 293 deposit accounts on its books totaling *fl.*45,010 from workers of all kinds, as well as from women and servants, some from the countryside.[120] In that year its new director, Vincenzo Borghini, reformed the bank (as it was now called) in the hope of increasing its business, and by 1579 he had succeeded in tripling the number of deposits (to 1,013) and doubling its capital (to *sc.*97,755). His program was badly conceived and badly managed, however, for it ended in bankruptcy in that year with debts of about *sc.*100,000, an event probably brought on also by opposition from certain religious quarters to usurious practice of this kind by a semiecclesiastical institution under the direction of a cleric.[121] The growth of the deposit banks of Santa Maria Nuova and the Innocenti points to something new in the economy: the mounting disposable wealth in the hands of people of middling status and the emergence of institutions seeking to attract these funds for their own purposes.

Both these welfare institutions, one a hospital, the other an orphanage, presumably sought funds to finance their activities. Until their records are studied, however, we cannot say anything about their strategy for investing their borrowed capital in ways to increase their income even enough to pay the interest owed on deposits. Surely the merchant-bankers who sat on the boards that directed these institutions knew that funds raised from interest-bearing deposits could not be used exclusively to meet internal operating expenses, although the disastrous bankruptcy of the Innocenti in 1579 would suggest otherwise. It is intriguing to think that perhaps they were counting on, first, limited withdrawals and, second, a continuing flow of money into deposit accounts at a rate that would be more than sufficient to meet ongoing—and mounting—interest obligations. Such a strategy, however improbable, would be another indicator of the growing disposable wealth—or at least of the perception of such wealth—in the

---

[120] Lucia Sandri, "L'attività di banco di deposito dell'Ospedale degli Innocenti di Firenze: Don Vincenzo Borghini e la 'bancarotta' del 1579," in *L'uso del denaro: Patrimoni e amministrazione nei luoghi pii e negli enti ecclesiastici in Italia (secoli XV–XVIII)*, ed. Alessandro Pastore and Marina Garbellotti (Bologna, 2001), 153–78.

[121] Maria Fubini Leuzzi, "Vincenzio Borghini spedalingo degli Innocenti: La nomina, il governo, la bancarotta," in *Fra lo "spedale" e il principe: Vincenzio Borghini, filologia e invenzione nella Firenze di Cosimo I* (Padua, 2005), esp. 51–52, 57–64.

hands of a middling class of Florentines, who had no alternative investment outlet.

These depositories enlarged the sphere of deposit-banking activity well beyond traditional banks and set the new direction banking took in the sixteenth century. This situation in the credit market is the context for understanding the evolution of the Monte di Pietà into a public bank, although it is generally not considered in this economic context. The movement that brought Monti di Pietà into existence throughout central Italy in the second half of the fifteenth century was the mounting clamor, especially on the part of Franciscans, against the manifest usury of Jewish pawn banks. In the half-century following the foundation of the first Monte at Perugia in 1462, some seventy others sprung up in towns all over Italy, including Siena and Lucca in Tuscany. Many places in Florentine territory—Volterra, Pistoia, Prato, Cortona, Montepulciano, Arezzo, Borgo Sansepolcro, and San Giovanni Valdarno—had a Monte di Pietà before the one opened in Florence. For the most part, however, the Monti did not immediately replace Jewish pawnbrokers, despite the often rabid condemnation of them by popular Franciscan preachers; in some places the Jews kept their banks open until well into the sixteenth century, when they had to confront the even harsher atmosphere brought about by the Counter Reformation. In any event, the aim of the movement against them was not to destroy pawn banking but to bring it under control through a new, presumably morally responsible management.

Although it was the government that permitted the opening of Monti in its provincial towns, Florence lagged behind in setting up its own Monte, just as it had in the legalization of Jewish pawn banks early in the century, because of practical problems inherent in the larger urban market of the capital city. The low end of the credit market was simply too large to permit tampering with the Jewish pawn banks that sustained it, and the taxes these institutions paid through their charters were not to be renounced easily. Moreover, the debate over the issue was more informed and more passionate in the capital city than in smaller provincial centers. If the Franciscans were vigorous in promoting their solution to what they regarded as a problem with Jewish pawn banking, the Dominicans were adamant in their position that the government could not itself sponsor usurious activity in this way. The government also had to confront the practical problem of financing a Monte: where was the capital to come from? In 1473 a project to set up a Monte got so far as to have collection boxes placed in major churches in the hope that people fired up by religious zeal would make contributions toward raising the necessary capital, but nothing came of this because funds were not forthcoming either from the government or from the public. It seems, too, that Lorenzo the Magnificent, aware of the social function they served, was anything but hostile toward these Jewish enterprises. Franciscans did not let up in their campaign, however, and in the charged political and religious atmosphere in the city following the expulsion of the Medici in 1494 and the rise of Savonarola, the project to set up a Monte rapidly took concrete form. No little credit for final approval of the scheme must go to the personal support of Savonarola himself, who, as a Dominican, tempered the traditional opposition of his order to the setting up of a publicly funded Monte.

The founding of the Florentine Monte di Pietà, however much it was driven by religious concerns, was built on assumptions that reflect the realities of the economy at the time: the widespread need for credit at the low end of the market, the validity of pawn banking, the availability of loose capital in the market, and the prospect of attracting this capital as deposits to finance the new enterprise. The acceptance of pawn banking, including the charging of interest as a necessary evil, points to the essential role the practice performed in the crowded low end of the credit market, which was largely ignored—or avoided—by other kinds of banks. Credit played an essential role in the lives of everyone, and it had to be supplied one way or another. When a Monte was finally set up in 1495, the plan for financing the enterprise explicitly rejected public funding and called instead for deposits in the form of private donations and free loans. In their hope of being able to finance pawnbroking by attracting funds from the public, the founders of the Monte, undoubtedly aware of what Santa Maria Nuova and the Innocenti had been doing for a generation, also assumed that much loose capital was available in the hands of Florentines. Deposits, however, were not forthcoming in large numbers. From 1496 to 1499 the Monte attracted all together fl.7,008 in deposits from 60 persons (18 of them anonymous), while it loaned out about fl.7,000 a year in exchange for pawns, far below the level of the Jews' operations, even though it brought the interest rate down from 20 percent to only 5 percent. The balance of April 1499 had only 21 open deposit accounts. After the turn of the century, as it lost something of the novelty of a new institution, donations fell off; two subsequent ledgers documenting activity to 1527 saw no more than about 65–70 accounts opened in the three-year period covered by each ledger. Moreover, many depositors, considering it a place for the temporary placement of funds, did not leave their money in for very long. Occasionally the state too ordered funds to be deposited with the Monte, of special importance being funds confiscated from Pisan rebels, but it was just as likely as private depositors to make frequent withdrawals from its accounts. The state also instructed the Monte di Pietà, in accord with its essential function as a charitable institution, to use some of its profits for contributions to support local welfare institutions. Under these circumstances, being subject to high turnover among depositors and to constant repayment of deposits, the institution lacked the financial stability to make much headway and limped along at a very modest level of activity. In the aftermath of the disastrous siege of 1529–30 and the fall of the last republic, the Monte found it ever more difficult to stay afloat, at one point even doubling the interest it charged on its loans.[122] In fact, Jewish pawn banks remained in business alongside the Monte di Pietà, a testimony to their essential role in the urban economy as a credit institution serving the general population, as well as, undoubtedly, a source of revenue for the state. Their survival, however, has not yet been studied.[123]

This early history of the Monte reveals the one mistaken assumption of its founders: the possibility of attracting deposits from a public willing to make charitable gestures with no expectation of interest, a hope probably explained by the charged religious atmosphere of the Savonarolan years in which they set up their enterprise. Eventually, the officials came around to recognizing the necessity of offering payment of interest on deposits as the only way to attract the necessary funds to finance the credit market it was serving, something the deposit operations of both Santa Maria Nuova and the Innocenti had been doing for a generation at the time when the Monte di Pietà opened its first ledger. Duke Alessandro de' Medici took the initiative to make this possible for the Monte di Pietà as well in 1533, by which time the supporters of the Monte had accepted a basic condition of economic life in Florence. Despite the long history of the usury restriction, no one could ignore the fundamental role that interest played in the money market.

Once it went down this route, the Monte had no problem attracting deposits. Its success was manifest in the rapid growth in the service it was designed to perform—pawnbroking. Whereas from 1531 to 1533 it had taken in only 5,500 pawns, by the mid-1540s it had close to 50,000 pawns in storage, and a generation later, in the period 1567–69, it took in 170,899 pawns in return for loans totaling *fl.*370,150. The balance of operations drawn up on 1 January 1582 records 88,293 pawns in storage at that moment, for which *fl.*280,809 had been lent out. This growth was nothing less than spectacular, even factoring in the population growth and inflation, and it boosted the operation of the Monte di Pietà to a level far above that of the Jewish pawn banks of the fifteenth century. All this traffic—which was only a part of its activity, as we shall see—was founded on

---

[122] Carol Bresnahan Menning, *The Monte di Pietà of Florence: Charity and State in Late Renaissance Italy* (Ithaca, NY, 1993). Most of the figures cited herein come from data published in Menning's book, esp. in ch. 3. For the Monte in the 1580s, see also Goldthwaite, "Banking in Florence," 509–22; and an overview of its subsequent history can be found in Guido Pampaloni, "Cenni storici sul Monte di Pietà di Firenze," in *Archivi storici delle aziende di credito* (Rome, 1956), 1:525–600.

[123] Cristina Galazzo, "Banchi ebraici e Monti di Pietà in Toscana," in *Monti di pietà e presenza ebraica in Italia (secoli XV–XVIII)*, ed. Daniele Montanari (Rome, 1999), 159–80.

2,784 interest-bearing deposits totaling just short of a million florins (*fl.*924,056). Most of these deposits came from the kind of people who had supported the banks of the welfare institutions—not the rich (although a few made some large deposits) but the middling class of shopkeepers, artisans, widows, and even people from the countryside. Although by 1582 the Monte had some very large deposits, the average amount of the 1,747 deposits under *fl.*1,000 was only *fl.*163; more than half of these were under *fl.*100, with 42 under *fl.*10. Some of these people conditioned their deposits by limiting withdrawals through arrangements tied to a dowry or to a testamentary disposition, but many were what today we would call ordinary savings accounts earning interest, subject only to a waiting period once a request for withdrawal was made. Separate ledgers were kept for these two categories of deposits.

The Monte di Pietà, in contrast to the banks of the hospital and the orphanage, thus evolved from a pawn bank into a genuine savings-and-loan bank. With the capital it attracted in deposits paying 5 percent interest, it began to loan out money independently of its pawn business at rates of up to 7 percent according to a schedule relative to the size of the loan. This activity soon far exceeded pawn lending in value, although it remained far behind in the number of transactions. Of the million florins under management at the time of the balance of 1582, only *fl.*280,809 were loaned out in exchange for pawns, compared with *fl.*629,882 in 882 larger loans. At the time the Monte also had *fl.*123,058 on the exchange with private banks and *fl.*19,696 in current accounts with three private banks. Moreover, it was tied into state finances. On the one hand, it became a mandatory depository for certain public bodies, including the guilds, the Office of the Works (*Opera*) at the cathedral, and, from 1590, the hospital of Santa Maria Nuova, and it occasionally received funds from the grand-ducal treasury. On the other hand, it also made loans to the grand duke, who used his account as a current account out of which he ordered transfers and payments for a variety of expenses involving both the state and his household. Profits came from interest the Monte charged on loans, from a small surcharge on all loans, and from earnings made from the money it had on the exchange. It took a sizable bureaucracy of forty-two employees to run the enterprise—nine at each of its three branches (at the Canto de' Pazzi, in Borgo SS. Apostoli, and, across the river, in Piazza San Felice) and fifteen in the central office, all working under the management of a superintendent in conjunction with a board of eight directors, called protectors. The extraordinarily bulky but comprehensive accounting apparatus needed to keep track of all of its activities survives virtually intact, untouched by historians of banking. The Monte di Pietà continued to grow: by 1620 it had tripled its assets to reach a total of 3 million ducats, it had become a depository for much of the state's revenues, and it was extending loans to foreign princes. Also by this time, it was issuing printed shares *(luoghi di monte)* of sc.100 earning 5 percent interest, and a secondary market had opened up in which these were traded. It remains to be seen to what extent it was a full-scale deposit-and-transfer bank, offering its clients the services of a current account as well.

The growth of the Monte di Pietà in the sixteenth century revolutionized Florentine banking. As in so many other places in Italy at the time, it had evolved into a public bank. It served the basic banking function of channeling savings from a wide spectrum of society back into the economy. It directed these savings to three outlets: first, petty loans through its pawn operations, its major activity by far with respect to the number of clients but now absorbing only a part of its resources; second, larger loans to private persons outside the pawn banks, by far its major use of funds; and finally, loans to the government. The economic impact of this rechanneling of private wealth must have been considerable, although, yet once again, the current state of research on the subject precludes anything but a hypothetical assessment. We can only assume that the loans made outside the pawn banks, given their larger size, averaging well over *fl.*100, with some over *fl.*1,000, were taken out not, for consumption needs, but to meet temporary cash-flow problems endemic to many productive activities or to make an investment of some kind. The pawn business assured access to liquidity for the working poor, and legislation in 1574 setting a limit of *sc.*150 on any loan obtained by pawning jewels indicates that the better-off also had recourse to the Monte.[124] It is usual to refer to these loans as distress loans, but as already observed, that term has to be understood in the context of a preindustrial economy, in which employment and payment for work were highly irregular. In this respect, the statistics from the Monte di Pietà confirm what has already been reported about the loans of the bank of the Jew Isacco da San Miniato in the 1470s. Almost all the loans were made to people who had a temporary need for cash; borrowers were willing to risk losing personal property in exchange for a loan of much less value; and they anticipated being able to pay interest to repossess it, for 90 percent of the 170,899 pawns the Monte di Pietà took in from 1567 to 1569 were redeemed. The Monte di Pietà did not have a monopoly on pawnbroking: the contemporary Calderini-Guiducci local bank engaged in the business, as we have seen. Moreover, Jewish pawn banks, although outlawed in the provincial cities, seem still to have been open in the capital, to judge from the occasional reference to them in the documents.[125]

---

[124] *Legislazione toscana,* 8:199.
[125] For provincial cities, see ibid., 7:253–56 (1570) and 389–91 (1571).

The Monte di Pietà also directed funds into public finance to help stabilize the fiscal system by meeting the government's short-term needs for money. By thus providing the state with a way to finance its floating debt, the Monte di Pietà helped put the state fiscal system on a sounder structural foundation than it had had during the republican period, when the government was forever borrowing from a few wealthy men at high rates of interest to meet temporary liquidity problems (see chapter 7). This function is not to be obscured by the personalization of the state in the figure of the grand duke, who in any event seems to have paid off his loans, along with interest, in a regular fashion. The Monte di Pietà also served as an instrument of economic policy. For example, in an effort to protect the threatened wool industry at the beginning of the seventeenth century, the Monte di Pietà moved into the market to buy wool for resale to lanaioli, presumably at a price more convenient than that offered by Spanish importers—a policy that in the end, as we have seen, could not save the industry.[126] The Florentine Monte di Pietà, however, seems not to have gone as far along the route to becoming a public bank as did the welfare deposit institutions in contemporary Naples. There three hospitals, an orphanage, and a hospice for poor girls, in addition to the Monte di Pietà, issued deposit certificates *(fedi di credito)* in different values and assignable to third parties that the state recognized as valid for meeting all obligations to it, and in 1594 they became mandatory depositories for all state agencies.

The Monte di Pietà, now functioning as a public bank, brought an order to the credit market that it had never known under the amorphous banking system of the past. In the final analysis, however, the institution is to be regarded as something more than a phenomenon in the history of financial and political institutions: its very existence is an indicator of changing economic conditions. Both the phenomena linked to its growth and transformation—more deposits of relatively modest sums and more lending for pawns—point to an economy with more liquid wealth. The Monte di Pietà succeeded because, on the one hand, it offered an outlet for much of this wealth, which was widely distributed throughout society and had no other outlet beyond consumption, and, on the other hand, it met the greater need for liquidity at the low end of the social order arising from precarious working conditions and greater consumption wants and needs. Moreover, as a deposit-and-loan bank the Monte increased liquidity by operating on fractional reserves. The genealogy of the Monte di Pietà goes back to both the deposit operations of welfare institutions and to pawn banks, both

---

[126] Maurice Carmona, "La Toscane face à la crise de l'industrie lanière: Techniques et mentalités économiques aux XVIe et XVIIe siècles," in *Produzione, commercio e consumo dei panni di lana (nei secoli XII–XVIII)*, ed. Marco Spallanzani (Florence, 1976), 161–62.

Christian and Jewish. The new function it performed in the credit market points to the failure of the traditional banking system to adjust to the changing economic conditions that had brought these other institutions into existence.[127] To what extent similar conditions are relevant to the rise of Monti di Pietà, and then the emergence of public banks, elsewhere throughout Italy in the late sixteenth and early seventeenth centuries—in Palermo, Messina, Naples, Rome, Genoa, Milan, Venice—is a subject yet to be explored; the context is barely adumbrated in the recent literature on both subjects.[128]

It is a matter of no little curiosity, in conclusion, that in contrast to the many contemporary Monti di Pietà in northern Italian cities housed in monumental quarters built for them and still prominent on the urban scene, the Monte di Pietà of Florence, for all its importance in the economic lives of Florentines, had no architectural presence whatsoever on the streets of this, the preeminent Renaissance city.

A Central Clearance Bank?

The Monte di Pietà evolved into a public deposit-and-loan bank that, besides serving the public in general, assumed a central role in the grand-ducal state as a mandatory deposit institution for some government agencies and as a source for credit. It was not, however, either a bank of transfer or a central clearance bank, at least in the sixteenth century, and it seems not to have had structural ties to the industrial, commercial, and international banking sectors of the economy. Private banks in their various forms continued to serve capitalist entrepreneurs, but during the sixteenth century something happened in the sector that has yet to be explained. Ducal legislation and chronicles document a liquidity crisis that arose in the late 1560s, when banks began making payments through giro operations to other banks, with the result that creditors found themselves being sent from one bank to another with "carte di credito" and having to pay a premium if they wanted cash.[129] Bankruptcies occurred, but at the same time several firms rose to such a commanding position in the local market that in 1578 the grand-ducal government had to take regulatory action specifically against them. A ducal proc-

[127] The contemporary growth of funds in the Monte delle Graticole (see chapter 7), with its three categories of deposits, paying 3 percent, 4 percent, and 7 percent, should be studied in this same light.

[128] For the recent literature on public banks, see the excellent articles by Ugo Tucci on Venice, Luigi De Rosa on Naples, and Luigi De Matteo on Rome in *Gli inizi della circolazione della cartamoneta e i banchi pubblici napoletani nella società del loro tempo (1540–1650)*, ed. Luigi De Rosa (Naples, 2002).

[129] The liquidity problem is discussed in Cipolla, *Money in Sixteenth-Century Florence*, with reference to the chronicle sources. See also *Legislazione toscana*, 7:26–27, 8:88–90, 9:130–33.

lamation issued at that time referred to four firms as "public banks"—Federigo de' Ricci & Partners, Luigi and Alessandro Capponi & Partners, Averardo and Antonio Salviati & Partners, and Zanobi Carnesecchi, Alessandro Strozzi & Partners. The latter three have left behind business records, which, however, have never been studied; and what we know about the Ricci, for which no business records survive, comes from other sources.[130]

Of these "public banks," the Ricci firm came to have what seems to have been a commanding position in the local banking world after 1552. During the war with Siena the bank made interest-free loans to Cosimo, in return for which it received much of the business of the ducal treasury. In the 1560s it was the largest supplier of bullion to the mint. On its reorganization in 1575 it had a capital of *fl.*40,000—*fl.*30,000 from Ruberto di Filippo Ricci for half the profits and the remaining *fl.*10,000 from Piero and Alessandro di Marcello Acciaiuoli, who apparently managed the firm, since they were to receive the other half of the profits. According to the chronicler Giuliano de' Ricci (not a close relative), "All moneys, both public and private, poured into the bank," so that it in effect controlled liquidity in the marketplace: it "was really everyone's cashier: it expanded and restricted the market at will, and one can venture to say that there were no other banks that moved cash around except the Ricci's." It is enough to open the ledger of any business enterprise in the 1580s to find the documentation for this bank's looming presence in the local market by that time. The current account with the Heirs of Federigo di Ruberto de' Ricci & Partners is the most active external account in the ledgers of the principal late sixteenth-century firms that have been studied—the international merchant-banking firm Simone and Heirs of Giovanni Corsi & Partners, open from 1582 to 1588; the local bank Luigi Calderini, Giuliano Guiducci & Partners, open from 1580 to 1587; the wool producers Cristofano di Tommaso Brandolini & Partners, open from 1580 to 1585; the silk producers Baccio Martelli, Pierfrancesco Del Giocondo & Partners, open from 1583 to 1605. The account the Corsi bank had with the Ricci records a level of activity far above anything found in any bank ledger of a century earlier, including those of the Medici bank: almost a thousand entries per year, filling

---

[130] The following discussion is derived from Goldthwaite, "Banking in Florence," based primarily on Giuliano de' Ricci, *Cronaca (1532–1606)*, ed. Giuliana Sapori (Milan, 1972), and Cipolla, *Money in Sixteenth-Century Florence*. Although no Ricci archive of business documents is known to have survived, the grand-ducal commission set up in 1594 to keep the bank solvent left behind a rich collection of papers documenting its extensive activity over the following years and into the seventeenth century (which I have only scanned to collect the material used herein). See ASF, Libri di commercio, 4308–17. See also *Legislazone toscana*, 14:87–96, 101–2, 111–12, 162–63, 200–215; and Giuseppe Vittorio Parigino, *Il tesoro del principe: Funzione pubblica e privata del patrimonio della famiglia Medici nel Cinquecento* (Florence, 1999), 173–74. The extant materials for the other banks are ASF, Libri di commercio, and BNF, Archivio Capponi, libri di commercio (Capponi); Pisa, Scuola Normale, Archivio Salviati, ser. 1 (Salviati); and ibid., ser. 4 (Carnesecchi, Strozzi).

more than forty-nine folios in the firm's ledger and amounting to almost four times the entries and twenty times the value of the activity in the cash account. Both the Calderini Guiducci and the Corsi firms used the Ricci almost exclusively for bank clearance. Likewise, the extensive use of a current account in the Ricci bank by both the Brandolini wool firm and the Martelli Del Giocondo silk firm for the purchase of raw materials and the sale of finished cloth has no counterpart from a century earlier, when textile firms tended to deal directly with import-export merchant-bankers.

This evidence indicates that current account in bank had become the normal instrument for effecting transfers of funds for payment among capitalist enterprises and, further, that this one bank had come to dominate the field. Serious problems in the 1590s, apparently owing to bad management by the Acciaiuoli partners and to squabbling among heirs, brought action from the grand duke himself. To help keep the bank afloat, he granted it a mint contract in 1591. And when it reached the verge of bankruptcy in 1594, he took official action to set up a commission to help it handle claims from creditors and followed this up with a loan of *fl.*100,000. Alessandro Acciaiuoli was declared personally bankrupt, and his properties were confiscated. The Ricci, however, were ready to do whatever was required to meet their responsibilities, including selling of their properties, even to the point of breaking hereditary entails and dowry restrictions. The ducal commission recognized the reorganization of "a new public bank," to be known as Giovambattista Michelozzi, Vincenzo de' Ricci & Partners (later Lorenzo and Francesco Michelozzi & Partners), and charged it with executing a complicated settlement with the creditors of the earlier firm. According to the repayment scheme, creditors could settle either by accepting immediately a flat payment of a percentage of what was owed them or by agreeing to be paid in installments, to be determined according to the number of years they were willing to wait (with interest on all unpaid claims in the meantime). Total claims seem to have reached several hundred thousand scudi, and the fact that creditors included hundreds scattered throughout the Florentine territory indicates that the firm did not confine its business to the city but functioned as a veritable state bank in line with the polity of the newly formed grand duchy. That status is confirmed by the seriousness with which the grand duke worked out arrangements for the bank's survival.

To what extent the Ricci, or any other banking "house" (the chronicler Ricci uses the term *casa*), continued as a central transfer bank is a question only future research can answer. It would seem that none did, since a proposal was made in 1601 to set up such a bank where all accounts could be cleared. At that time a problem of liquidity had been raised by lanaioli and setaioli, who complained about the difficulty in meeting weekly payrolls. The cause was understood to be not a lack of specie but the inability to obtain it from banks, thereby forcing employers to look elsewhere, even to Jewish moneylenders, for the cash they needed to meet payrolls. As they saw it, the public was no longer putting money in banks, and the Capponi and the Michelozzi Ricci banks, singled out probably because they were the two largest, no longer wanted to clear debits and credits with each other.[131]

Conclusion

The benchmarks in the history of Florentine banking from the beginning down to the end of the sixteenth century are indicators of the changing money and credit market. New banking institutions arose in response to the continual increase in liquid capital and its ever-wider distribution. Moneychangers and pawnbrokers served an essential function in a nascent money economy, and the former expanded into deposit banking to take advantage of both the increasing availability of disposable capital and the need for it. International merchant-bankers opened local banks for the same purpose. These banks, however, failed to keep up with the exigencies of a market that, in the course of the fifteenth century, was involving an ever-larger share of the population in the problems of liquidity, and two new institutions moved in to take advantage of the situation. On the one hand, the growing need for liquidity at a lower level in the credit market prompted the government to intervene with a more systematic, regulated approach to the problem by replacing Christian moneylenders through a comprehensive contract with Jews. On the other hand, the growing surplus of capital in the hands of the middling classes found an outlet in the three (and perhaps more) deposit operations set up by welfare organizations. It is no coincidence that these two institutions—the pawn bank and the depository—came into existence at the same time, in the middle decades of the fifteenth century, for they arose as responses to the same phenomenon. The Monte di Pietà was born out of the logic of fusing the two institutions into one; once freed of its initial economic ideology, it evolved into a public savings-and-loan bank serving the state and the population at large, rich and poor alike. Its expansion in the second half of the sixteenth century is an indicator of the further growth of the money and credit market, both the need for liquidity and the availability of it. It is worth emphasizing that public savings-and-loan banking in Florence did not evolve from private banks,

---

[131] ASF, Misc. medicea, 26, insert 35, fols. 13–30 ("Scritture in materia della strettezza di monete").

for all their long history of accomplishments in the development of modern banking techniques much emphasized in the literature.

During the sixteenth century banking underwent an extraordinary structural transformation. Earlier there had been no real banking system: diverse organizations had performed banking functions, credit transfers had taken place through private and business accounts as much as through banks, banks themselves had varied in kind and not been incorporated in a larger institutional structure, interbank exchanges had lacked a central mechanism, and the state had played hardly any role at all in the sector. In the sixteenth century three institutions emerged that brought considerable centrality to much of this banking activity. At the international level, as remarked in chapter 3, the strengthening of the great exchange fairs at Lyons and Besançon tied merchant banks into a more efficient and vastly expanded network abroad through which they performed their essential functions at the upper end of the local credit market, serving businesses and people of property. Notwithstanding Florentine merchant banks' loss of international status with the rise of the Genoese and the shift from Lyons to Besançon in the south and to Antwerp and then Amsterdam in the north, they continued to perform the function of international exchange banking in the local credit market. At the local level, a second institution, the Monte di Pietà, evolved into a public bank: it served the general population as a savings-and-loan bank, and it served the state as a depository and a source of credit, bringing a degree of order heretofore unknown to the fiscal system with respect to the floating debt. A third centralizing institution, finally, seems to have emerged, albeit murkily, given the current historiographical situation, in the form of one private bank—the Ricci— operating as a major central clearance bank for capitalist entrepreneurs that had significant influence on the money supply. By the end of the sixteenth century Florentines had a much clearer sense of banking than they had had earlier: legislation reveals a sophisticated awareness of problems of liquidity and bank money and identifies some firms as "public banks"; the chronicler Bastiano Arditi uses the name Mercato Nuovo as synonymous with the local banking community; the chronicler Giuliano de' Ricci uses *piazza* in the same way but with reference to international banking centers and refers to the great firms as banking *houses*.

Further structural changes reflecting more general economic conditions probably underlie another characteristic of banking at the end of the sixteenth century: the increase in the scale of operations, exceeding any reasonable expectations for growth that men in the fifteenth century might have had. Notwithstanding their more limited activity, as well as the general contraction of merchant banking abroad, both the private banks that have been studied were operating at a scale unimaginable before 1500. In the 1580s the Calderini Guiducci local bank had a capital that, taking into account both the rise in the price of the florin and inflation, was comparable to that of the Cambini international merchant-banking firm a century earlier. The contemporary Corsi firm had a working capital that, between partners' equity and deposits, amounted to *sc*.122,000, far exceeding in real value that of most fifteenth-century firms. The sheer physical size of the Corsi ledgers, along with considerable refinement in the organization of the accounts to handle the increased traffic, testifies to the larger scale at which the firm operated. The growth of the Monte di Pietà is especially impressive. In 1582 it had gross assets alone amounting to just over a million florins, equivalent to between one-fourth and one-third (in real value) of all the investment capital of the city (i.e., all wealth except real estate and credits in the state debt) as recorded in the 1427 catasto, and its assets increased threefold over the following half-century.

Two dynamics drove these developments in the Florentine banking sector throughout the fifteenth and sixteenth centuries. One was the increase in disposable wealth, and the response this elicited in the market took the form of depository institutions and the transformation of the Monte di Pietà into a public bank of deposit. The second dynamic was the growing need for credit, which gave rise to the public (Jewish) pawn banks and the Monte di Pietà, as well as, toward the end of the sixteenth century, increased business for the international exchange banks, whose operations by that time were probably oriented more to the local credit market than to transfer of funds in the service of international commerce. Increased liquidity was a general phenomenon throughout sixteenth-century Italy, documented in the rapid growth of Monti di Pieta, public banks, and the funding of state debts, but the larger economic context that made it possible for these institutions to prosper and multiply is rarely remarked. The papacy was especially zealous in taking note of the situation to fund its debt by attracting interest-bearing deposits in various Monti. These numbered eleven by 1585, and Sixtus V (1585–90) opened eight more, bringing in five and a half million scudi. Many people outside the ranks of international banker-financiers and from all over Italy put money in these and similar institutions that appeared in other cities. The portfolio of rich Florentines dating from this period usually includes shares in papal Monti and sometimes similar deposits with other states. These new investment opportunities attracting capital from a public throughout Italy are an index to the growth of disposable wealth, which, at least for Florence, cannot be explained by disinvestments linked to an economic slowdown. To what extent banks rechanneled this wealth as capital back into the more productive sectors of the economy, one of the essential functions of a modern banking system, remains to be seen.

The observation made during the 1601 investigation into the complaint that people were no longer putting money in banks suggests that private banking in Florence had undergone some kind of transformation by the end of the sixteenth century, as it seems to have done everywhere in Italy. The banking sector was still populated with private banks, both local and international merchant banks; but the only two firms that have been studied—the aforementioned Calderini Guiducci and Corsi firms, both of which used the Ricci as their primary clearance bank—while organized and managed very much as they had been earlier, now had more specialized functions. The Calderini Guiducci local bank limited its activity to trading in jewelry and gold and to petty pawnbroking, while the Corsi bank, which had neither a local bank nor branches abroad, used its capital almost exclusively to operate on the exchange at the Lyons and Besançon fairs. Moreover, neither bank had significant deposits, apart from those the Corsi accepted mostly from a narrow circle close to the family; and in striking contrast to earlier practice, neither carried much by way of current accounts on its books. The Monte di Pietà had apparently attracted savings away from private banks, but it is not at all clear what people were doing about current accounts. It remains to be seen how all this fits into the general pattern in Italy of public banks' emerging at the expense of the private banking sector, which, racked by frequent bankruptcies and general instability, lost investor confidence during the sixteenth century. In Venice, the foundation of the Banco della Piazza di Rialto in 1587 as a public deposit and transfer bank followed on the heels of the bankruptcy of the last major private bank; in Naples the emergence of no fewer than seven public banks at the end of the century spelled the end of private banking there; and in Rome the opening of the Banco di Santo Spirito, the city's first public bank, was presumably occasioned by bank failures in the private sector.

In the history of institutions, private deposit banking in Florence, for all its seeming modernity, appears almost as an anomaly, hardly central to the economic life of the city; and in the light of the emergence of the Monte di Pietà, its history even seems to have been a dead end. Indeed, it is not altogether clear how Florence fits into the evolution and development of modern banking in general. Historians have not failed to use the Florentine evidence to chart the progress of banking techniques, from the bill of exchange to the check and from double-entry accounting to giro transfers on current account. One cannot help but be impressed by the many relatively sophisticated devices ordinary Florentines handled, at least in the context of what we know about credit in northern Europe at the end of the Middle Ages. Although even in Italy its preeminence may well be an illusion due to the overwhelming abundance of the documentation compared with the void elsewhere, Florence nevertheless stands out from other major cities.

The contribution of Florentine practices to the evolution of modern banking, however, has yet to be documented. In any event, the contrast with Antwerp suggests how much Florence was being left behind by the end of the sixteenth century. In Antwerp people at the level of artisans and shopkeepers crowded into the market for private *rentes* as both investors and borrowers, and negotiable paper could pass through dozens of hands before arriving at a cash settlement, whereas in Florence neither instrument existed. In the final analysis, a stark contrast of this kind exposes two basic problems in the historiography of banking: the chronological barrier that separates economic historians of medieval Italy from those of Italy in the early modern period, and the geographical barrier that divides economic historians in general between north and south Europe.

CHAPTER SEVEN

Contexts

Government and the Economy: *Economic Policy, Fiscal Policy, Business Interests and Government.*
The Region and the City: *Urban Geography, Industrial Resources, Agriculture, Economic Integration.*
Private Wealth: *Social Mobility, A Profile of Wealth Distribution in 1427, Redistribution of Wealth in the Fifteenth and Sixteenth Centuries.*

Government and the Economy
Economic Policy

In surveying the economy of Florence we have often encountered many ways in which the government impinged on economic activity, and now it is time to take up this theme alone and to evaluate the role of the government in the economy. Hence the following discussion includes much material scattered throughout the preceding chapters that is relevant to government economic policies and initiatives, but it is brought together here to be seen in the light of the context government provided for economic activity.

In the course of its evolution from the thirteenth to the beginning of the six-teenth century—the period of the republic—the government underwent a profound transformation. The locus of power evolved from a loose corporate structure of institutions to a reasonably coherent elite, yet old institutions survived, holding on to their identity while undergoing redefinition in function and even relegation to the periphery of power. The overriding trend emerges clearly not-withstanding the obfuscatory survival of a plethora of obsolescent institutions and a government still run less by a central bureaucracy than by innumerable citizen committees and overlapping legislative councils, with all the attendant features of broad participation in the political process and complex electoral pro-cedures. It is the mark of the genius of three generations of Medici in the fifteenth century—Cosimo il Vecchio (1389–1464), his son Piero (1418–69), and his grandson Lorenzo the Magnificent (1449–92)—that from behind the scenes, without holding any formal political position, they were able to assert their leadership of the elite by manipulating the state's ramshackle constitution while leaving it intact. However, Cosimo's descendant and namesake, Duke, later Grand Duke, Cosimo I (1519–74), clarified the matter by cleaning out the political stables—in the manner of Hercules, his personification in art—and laying the foundations of a truly absolutist state. Most of the republican institutions were thrown out, and those that survived, including two of the most important economic institutions, were redefined in altogether new terms: the Mercanzia, now pushed out of the political sphere and confined to a strictly judicial function; and the minor guilds, most of which were merged into even larger agglomerates, with their headquarters relocated under one roof, the Uffizi, where they were absorbed into the new ducal bureaucracy.

In the early fourteenth century both the guilds and the Mercanzia, along with the official organs of the commune, were the agencies that made decisions and took actions of an economic nature. Economic policy was therefore a composite of the ideas and objectives that drove these bodies, each of which had its own interests. The origin of the guilds is lost in the obscurity of the early history of the city. By the time we have some precise notion of them, they were already undergoing that process of agglomeration that made Florence a distinctive guild republic. Florentine guilds did what guilds did everywhere: they controlled their matriculation rosters and therefore entrance into the crafts and trades within their separate spheres; they adjudicated disputes among their members; they regulated the practice of their respective activities, especially with regard to quality; they provided certain social and welfare services to their members. The very process of agglomeration, however, meant that the more complex ones lost something of the distinctive identity associated with separate crafts and trades. Moreover, during the fourteenth century guilds became ever more subordinated to the centralizing authority of an increasingly assertive government. Much of the internal politics of the city revolved around the struggle between the minor and major guilds for representation in the councils of government, resulting in periods of widening or narrowing of the popular basis of the government. The most democratic regime came with the revolt of the Ciompi in 1378, when low-skilled wool workers (the *ciompi*), dyers, and doublet makers succeeded momentarily in gaining guild status and representation in the government. But the oligarchic reaction that followed in 1382 brought a return to the original guild structure. From then on, political power rested in the hands of an elite that assured the domination of the major guilds in the councils of government. It did not abolish the fundamental role of the guilds in the electoral procedures followed to name men to political office, but it did manage to control that process. In other words, the locus of political power shifted from the guilds to an oligarchy and, within the government, from the legislative to the executive and ad hoc bodies. In this process the guilds became subordinated to the higher authority of the government in the economic sphere as well. They maintained certain economic functions, such as control of quality and jurisdiction over disputes among members, but they performed them as branches of the state, not as autonomous institutions.[1]

The Mercanzia underwent the same transformation. The guild of merchants, known as the Arte dei Mercatanti, or more commonly, the Arte di Calimala, is first documented in treaties in the 1180s with Empoli and Lucca, which refer to consuls from this organization. During the rapid commercial expansion of the thirteenth century, however, many men who were not members of the Calimala ventured out as international merchants; by the end of the century international merchants had interests that did not coincide with this or any other single guild. With the foundation of the guild republic, these men must have felt a need to have their own collective voice in government, apart from the different guilds to which they belonged, and these interests came to a head in 1308 with the founding of the Mercanzia. The Mercanzia appears to have been an attempt to create a supraguild controlled by merchants. It asserted itself aggressively to pursue the interests of merchants in the commercial sphere abroad, for instance, in matters regarding reprisals, brigandage, security of transport, and reciprocal trade arrangements with other states. Indeed, their model may have been the merchant guilds that dominated the governments in many other Italian cities at the time. However that may be, the Mercanzia, like the guilds, gradually became subordinated to the centralized oligarchic government that emerged in the fourteenth century and lost most of its economic functions. It survived as a tribunal for the settlement of debt claims and an institution through which the oligarchy controlled election to political office. This elite, which had consolidated its control over the government by the end of the century, by no means consisted exclusively of international merchants and bankers. Florence had an industrial base in the manufacture of wool, which gained strength in these years; lanaioli and, later, setaioli also became major players in the political life of the city. By the fifteenth century the six councilors of the Mercanzia, who had executive powers, no longer represented just the city's merchants operating abroad.

[1] The economic role of the state in the early fifteenth century has been delineated by Franco Franceschi in two articles: "Intervento del potere centrale e ruolo delle Arti nel governo dell'economia fiorentina del Trecento e del primo Quattrocento: Linee generali," *Archivio storico italiano* (hereafter *ASI*) 151 (1993): 863–909; and "Istituzioni e attività economica a Firenze: Considerazioni sul governo del settore industriale (1350–1450)," in *Istituzioni e società in Toscana nell'Età Moderna* (Florence, 1994), 76–117.

Notwithstanding this institutional structure, a coherent and comprehensive economic policy emerged in the course of the fourteenth century. There was little exceptional about it: it was not unlike the protomercantilist policy of most cities at the time. It defined the rules that regulated activity in the local marketplace. It laid down standards for weights and measures. Through courts it established the legal context for the validity of contracts and the handling of litigation arising from debt claims. In recognition of the growing need for credit at the beginning of the fifteenth century, it moved from a policy of regulating Christian money-lenders to the institutionalization of Jewish pawnbroking, and at the end of the century it went one step further in setting up the Monte di Pietà. A vigorous provisioning policy assured the availability of grain, including, in times of scarcity, subsidies for purchases abroad, bounties to merchants who imported grain, suspension of import duties, surveys of private stocks on hand, and action against speculators. The commune built the monumental central grain market at Orsanmichele, begun in 1336 (the market was transferred to behind the Palazzo Vecchio in 1365, having lost the centrality in the lives of Florentines that it had had before the Black Death). It supervised what has been called a flour factory, which in the later fourteenth century employed a staff of from eight to thirteen millers and more than twenty other workers at grain mills concentrated around a dam crossing the Arno between Porta San Niccolò and what today is the Ponte alle Grazie. Other basic foodstuffs were also subject to regulation, but the objective was neither to monopolize the market nor to impose strict price controls.[2]

The government's monetary policy was essential to the health of the economy. It impinged directly on market activity of all kinds and thereby helped shape the economic culture of Florentines. All Florentines were aware that monetary policy could serve interest groups. A bimetallic system in which silver was used to pay for the production of cloth at home that sold abroad for gold obviously has strong social implications, and the government's control over the price of florins of account could be used to reduce its fiscal burden, not to mention its impact on business activity. Unfortunately, these and other related subjects have never been comprehensively studied with the objective of uncovering either underlying economic principles or political objectives. As we have seen, the communal mint, one of the largest workshops in the city, maintained a stable currency, never compromising the purity of the gold florin, which was essential to the success of its

[2] See Giuliano Pinto, *Il libro del biadaiolo: Carestie e annona a Firenze dalla metà del '200 al 1348* (Florence, 1978), 107–30; Sergio Tognetti, "Problemi di vettovagliamento cittadino e misure di politica annonaria a Firenze nel XV secolo (1430–1500)," *ASI* 157 (1999): 419–52, surveying the fifteenth century, with reference to older literature; and for mills, John Muendel, "The Internal Functions of a 14th-Century Florentine Flour Factory," *Technology and Culture* 32 (1991): 498–520.

merchants in international markets; and an assayer's office (Saggio) set up in the central Mercato Nuovo assured the public of the purity of coins. Although Florence had a bimetallic system, it recognized that the gold-silver ratio was an international phenomenon over which it had no control; hence, it did not try to maintain a bimetallic standard, issuing silver coins on the basis of a fixed ratio between them and the florin. It faced a serious monetary problem when, in the second quarter of the fourteenth century, the gold-silver ratio fluctuated radically, but from midcentury on, the government followed a strictly defensive debasement policy with respect to silver coins so as not to disrupt the local market. The debasement of coins was slow, almost imperceptible, amounting to only about 1 percent every two or three years from the mid-fourteenth through the fifteenth century. New coins therefore did not disrupt the market, where older coins, which had lost some of their intrinsic value as a result of natural wear, circulated. Florence thereby avoided some of the shocks of the kind that often disturbed markets in late medieval England and the Low Countries, where the anger of workers over wages paid in coin that had been significantly debased could lead to labor unrest and even violence.[3]

The conservative monetary policy of the Florentine government may in fact have led ordinary Florentines to think about coins, not in terms of their intrinsic value, but in terms of their price, that is, in terms of the lira, a money of account. And this may not have been very far from thinking about coins as token money or even about money in general as an abstraction. Indeed, Arnoldi's plan in the 1420s to monetize the public debt would have been one step toward the acceptance of paper money simply on the basis of its ascriptive value. In any event, as we have seen, the widespread acceptance of moneys of account—"ghost moneys"—and the practice of accounting were essential components of the economic culture of this city. Moreover, Florentines used the monetary system, with its terminology of *denaro* for 1/240 and of *soldo* for 1/20, for everything from measuring lengths of bricks to subdividing shares of capital and dividing profits in a capitalist enterprise. For all kinds of measurements—lengths, weights, quantities—they used three and four as divisors as naturally as we use ten. In business documents, however, one notices a tendency in the fifteenth century to

---

[3] For a historical survey and analysis of Florentine moneys, with further bibliography, see Richard A. Goldthwaite and Giulio Mandich, *Studi sulla moneta fiorentina (secoli XIII–XVI)* (Florence, 1994), where real and nominal values of moneys are presented in tables and graphs. Mario Bernocchi, *Le monete della Repubblica fiorentina*, 5 vols. (Florence, 1974–85), is essential for its publication of mint documents and its collection of some basic numismatic data. The problem of the 1340s is treated in Carlo M. Cipolla, *The Monetary Policy of Fourteenth-Century Florence* (Berkeley and Los Angeles, 1982).

use percentage calculations, especially for stating interest rates and shares of profits.

The government assured security within the walls and defense beyond, depending on contracts with private condottieri for the conduct of war. For the protection of trade in and out of the city, it oversaw maintenance of roads and bridges and the navigability of the river to the sea. In dealing with the neighboring cities of Siena, Lucca, and Pisa (before acquiring them) it sought to gain access to ports and to facilitate the passage of merchandise. It made trade treaties to gain privileges for merchants abroad and to secure their protection against reprisals, and its ambassadors concerned themselves with specific problems individual merchants might have with foreign governments: "You represent us and our interests, especially our merchants, in general and in particular," the ambassador going off to Naples in 1484 was instructed.[4] The registers recording diplomatic correspondence from the second half of the fifteenth century contain many letters sent to foreign governments to request assistance in solving problems encountered by Florentine merchants operating under their jurisdiction: protection against reprisals, recovery of seized and stolen goods, information about missing goods in transit, retribution for unjust taxes imposed on them or for other damages they suffered, reconsideration of onerous customs charges, help in collecting credits and payment of debts, intervention in difficulties arising from relations with the local population, appeals in cases involving conflicts of jurisdiction between Florence and a foreign government, requests for privileges. Most of these letters were occasioned by specific instances regarding particular merchants; to what extent favoritism was a factor remains to be seen.[5]

How commercial interests impinged on foreign policy, however, is a theme that has never been tracked through the complex history of the city's involvement in the kaleidoscope of continually shifting relations that constituted the Italian state system. What is needed is not just a summary of trade treaties and policies but a political history of economic expansion that shows how political events and institutions shaped the performance of the economy.

The government also took some positive initiatives to promote economic activity and to support certain economic interests. It supported the university, first in Florence and then in Pisa, in part on the grounds that student spending was good for the local market.[6] To protect the textile industries, it sought to reduce competition within the state by forbidding production of comparable products in

---

[4] *Corrispondenza di Giovanni Lanfredini, 1485–86*, ed. Elisabetta Scarton (Naples, 2002), xxxiii.
[5] See, for example, ASF, Signori, Carteggio, Missive, I Cancelleria, 47 (1474–84).
[6] Jonathan Davies, *Florence and Its University during the Early Renaissance* (Leiden, 1998), 68, 71, 133.

subordinate towns; the legislation was somewhat less comprehensive for wool inasmuch as some towns had industries that had developed before their incorporation into the territorial state. The government also sought to protect these industries through import and export controls on raw materials and finished products, encouragement of the immigration of skilled workers, and restrictions on their emigration. But the state hardly intruded into the labor market. While it limited workers' collective action and occasionally sought to attract skilled workers from abroad, there is little evidence that it interfered to regulate wages or impede the normal functioning of the labor market in any other way. It left quality controls to the guilds. The wool industry had long had its own protective agency in the form of the guild under the secure control of the manufacturers, which performed a number of functions for their common benefit, including the storage of woad, the manufacture of soap, the operation of stretching sheds. In general, the state assumed an attitude of laissez faire toward the textile industries, the mainstay of the economy and by far the largest employers in the city. In fact, the state is largely absent in the many individual studies of the city's businesses, whatever the sector.

The one moment when the commune took especially aggressive action to support the textile industries came in the first quarter of the fifteenth century, by which time the ruling elite was firmly in control of the state following its reaction to the Ciompi revolt and had warded off the threats of conquest by Giangaleazzo Visconti. At a time when the wool industry was undergoing a slump in production and the silk industry was just getting started, the government made vigorous and costly efforts to promote both. It conquered Pisa, purchased Livorno, and launched a full-scale state galley system that included shipbuilding, sailmaking, and supervising a fleet, the main economic objective being to facilitate both the supply of raw materials—wool from England—and the marketing of products in the Levant. The prestigious florin was redesigned, the first time in about 175 years, so that it could compete against the Venetian ducat in Levantine markets. The Sea Consuls, who operated the galley system, extended their authority to the imposition of duty charges on imports and exports for the protection of the home industry. The galley system, however, was the only effort by the state to assume a supply or marketing function for the textile industries; in the end it failed partly because of lack of support from the merchants themselves. In these same years the state was also aggressive in promoting the silk industry, with numerous legislative measures to facilitate the importation of raw silk, to encourage the planting of mulberry trees, to attract foreign craftsmen to the city, to forbid the emigration of craftsmen, and to impose protective gate gabelles—none of which, however, required the cash outlays the commune was making to support the wool industry.

The reorganization of the state by the Medici princes in the sixteenth century resulted in the transformation of the government of the republic, with its patchwork constitution of legislative bodies, citizen committees, and territorial magistracies, into a centralized bureaucracy. Something of the spirit with which Cosimo I approached the government of his new state manifested itself in the surveys he had made in 1551 and again in 1562 to obtain a comprehensive overview of the situation in which he found himself. These surveys included precise information about the population and shops in the city, government offices within and without the city and their stipends, the various sources of revenue, data about the consumption of grain, meat, and salt in the subject towns, the number of oxen used to work the fields, the number of births each year, the number of ships of different kinds using the port at Livorno, the number of soldiers, the artillery available at different fortresses, and the supply of munitions. The Abbondanza, previously an ad hoc office active only in times of need, became a permanent agency for provisioning with authority throughout the territory. Regulations were issued to assure the supply of basic necessities, to attract artisans, and to fix working standards (although it is not clear whether policy impinged on how business was actually conducted). Monetary policy was directed to putting into place a more rational and articulated system of coins, and efforts to maintain the stability of the silver standard resulted in the best managed monetary system in Italy by the end of the century. The statutes of both the wool and the silk guild were rewritten; and the fourteen minor guilds were consolidated into four conglomerates, now called università, and eventually moved into the new building of the Uffizi, which housed the central magistracies of the state. The Monte di Pietà evolved into the city's first public bank.[7]

Besides these reforms by way of consolidating their control over the state, the Medici dukes pursued a vigorous policy of promoting an amazing variety of economic activities. From the very beginning of his rule Cosimo I set the pace of these initiatives. He attracted foreign artisans to the city to set up workshops for weaving tapestries, to modernize the local armory industry, and to increase the production of printed books, not to mention the many artisan activities he organized in his own ducal workshops. He contracted with foreign experts for the building of a factory for the production of saltpeter, granting them a twenty-five-year monopoly.[8] Moreover, he initiated a policy, continued by his successors, of offering patents *(brevetti)* to inventors. Although many quacks came forth with ideas that

---

[7] Furio Diaz, *Il Granducato di Toscana: I Medici* (Turin, 1976), 127–48; Arnaldo d'Addario, "Burocrazia, economia e finanze dello Stato Fiorentino alla metà del Cinquecento," *ASI* 121 (1963): 362–456; Carlo M. Cipolla, *Money in Sixteenth-Century Florence* (Berkeley and Los Angeles, 1989).

[8] Diaz, *Il Granducato di Toscana*, 145, citing archival sources.

can only be described as fanciful, his encouragement of innovation in an artisan population as large and varied as that in Florence must have heightened interest in the possibility of linking technology and economic rewards.[9]

With respect to the city's forward sectors—the wool and silk industries and international merchant banking—ways in which the ducal government was prepared to intervene when the public interest was at stake have already been recounted. It did so with substantial support when the Ricci bank appeared to be going under. From the 1590s on, it ordered investigations into the problems the wool industry was beginning to face; we do not know, however, whether in the end it took any decisive actions in the attempt to reverse the industry's eventual demise. The government was also zealous in promoting sericulture in its territories. It continued the earlier policies of the republic, but now with more vigor, providing strong central direction to the effort to circumvent local privileges and to regulate the internal trade in raw silk. In 1575, in an effort to gain a better sense of the extent of sericulture in the countryside, it issued legislation ordering precise recordkeeping of all the trade in locally produced raw silk—a measure of rigorous control that marked how different the ducal government was in spirit and in practice from its republican predecessor.[10]

Cosimo and his two sons were prepared to do what they could to boost the flagging international trade in the hands of the city's merchants. Cosimo seems to have been fairly obsessed with finding a role for the state as a maritime power, in part motivated by the need for defense from the Muslim pirates who infested the waters off the coast of his state. He proceeded to build a miniscule fleet to protect the coastline, he defined his new military Order of the Knights of Santo Stefano as an aggressive naval force in the Mediterranean theater of operations for war between Christians and Turks, and he gained possession of Portoferraio, on Elba, from Charles V, which he fortified. His initiatives at Livorno, however, reveal commercial maritime ambitions as well. For a moment in 1570 he considered an extraordinary plan to build a canal from Florence to the Adriatic. In 1576 his son Francesco I tried, but failed, to obtain from Portugal a monopoly on the pepper trade. Francesco also thought seriously about establishing trade colonies in Brazil and Africa, and his brother, Ferdinando I, succeeded in making a commercial treaty with Morocco in 1604. And all the while

---

[9] Luca Molà, "Artigiani e brevetti nella Firenze del Cinquecento," in *La grande storia dell'artigianato*, vol. 3, *Il Cinquecento*, ed. Franco Franceschi and Gloria Fossi (Florence, 2000), 57–79; Paolo Malanima, *La decadenza di un'economia cittadina: L'industria di Firenze nei secoli XVI–XVIII* (Bologna, 1982), 148–52.

[10] *Legislazione toscana raccolta e illustrata dal dottore Lorenzo Cantini socio di varie accademie,* 32 vols. (Florence, 1802–8), 8:215–17.

the dukes persisted in their efforts to reach some kind of trade agreement with Constantinople in the hope of opening its markets to Florentine wool cloth.

Livorno, of course, was their single greatest accomplishment in the commercial sector. Their objective was to facilitate the export of Florentine textiles and to establish a distribution center for imports directed throughout Italy, including wheat from the Baltic, to assure supply in Tuscan markets in moments of scarcity. Ferdinando offered fiscal exemptions, immunities, and other privileges to attract the Jewish, Greek, Armenian, and other Levantine merchants who were beginning to emerge as prominent players in Mediterranean trade. In issuing the famous Livornine laws to assure these immigrants religious toleration and in negotiating a navigational treaty with Protestant England, he was even prepared to risk his relations with the Counter Reformation papacy.[11]

These initiatives of Cosimo and his sons defined an activist role for government in the economy that went well beyond, in degree if not in kind, the proto-mercantilist legislation that characterized the economic policy of the medieval commune, including republican Florence. They clearly anticipate what became a major theme in the history of the early modern state. We can imagine that Cosimo became interested in economic matters as a prince of a new state who was anxious to find revenues that would free him from dependence on direct taxation of his subjects. We do not know, however, where he got his ideas or who the men were who advised him on these matters; nor, with respect to the underlying principles that drove policy, do we know anything about his understanding of what an economy was. Nor has anyone ever bothered to survey all the evidence of the economic policy of these early Medici princes, bringing together in a comprehensive overview all their various activities, from the organization of luxury crafts under the auspices of their court to the building of the free port of Livorno and land reclamation throughout the territorial state. Hence, we cannot evaluate what all these measures added up to with respect to the general course of the Florentine, and Tuscan, economy in the sixteenth century.

Meanwhile, the verdict is still out on the economic role of Cosimo I, who set the ducal government on this course. In the eighteenth century he was both praised as an absolutist monarch seeking to strengthen the economy and, in the new spirit of liberalism, criticized for the control he tried to assert over economic life. In our own time Furio Diaz has emphasized the "repressive, police-state" quality of Cosimo's economic policy, which he justifies as a natural reaction to demographic and industrial crises, while Judith Brown has proposed that what is

---

[11] Cesare Ciano, *I primi Medici e il mare: Note sulla politica marinara toscana da Cosimo I a Ferdinando I* (Pisa, 1980), surveys the maritime and commercial interests of these early Medici dukes. For their development of Livorno, see above, chapter 2.

involved here is instead the emergence of a notion of political economy that was a "radical departure" from the republican tradition in that it was directed to "the transformation of the entire economy."[12] Whatever their economic policy was, the Medici, seeking to leave no doubt in their subjects' minds about the spirit that drove their policies, stamped the urban landscape with the symbols of their presence—the headquarters of their bureaucracy at the Uffizi, their own residence at the enlarged Pitti Palace, and the Corridoio Vasariano crossing the river to link the two, as well as monuments to their military victories, equestrian statues in central squares, and busts of themselves scattered everywhere about the city on the facades of private palaces.

Fiscal Policy

If the republican government followed a laissez-faire policy toward the forward sectors of the economy, this is not to say that the men who ran the city were anything like free-market capitalists. Most, after all, were merchant-bankers and textile industrialists. If the state they in large part dominated, especially after 1382, did not assume a more active role, it was because they wanted things that way, which is to say, in turn, that they saw no other way the state could help them in their enterprise. Except, perhaps, through the fiscal system.

In the earliest period Florence, like the other Tuscan towns, imposed direct taxes on its residents, the first dating from 1202. But about 1300, with expenses mounting as a result of territorial expansion and increased involvement in foreign affairs, it changed its policy. In 1290 it first imposed indirect taxes, recognizing that the rapidly growing population increased the potential of this kind of revenue from market transactions, and in 1315 it abandoned direct taxation altogether for the mechanism of a forced loan. With this device, the commune assessed the wealth of those citizens it thought were in a position to pay, and on the basis of these assessments it levied forced loans on them and encumbered certain future incomes, mostly from indirect taxes, for the payment of interest and the liquidation of the principal. Both interest and maturity varied as dictated by the occasion. Over time the system underwent two refinements: the debt was consolidated into a permanent, interest-bearing fund; and efficient and objective procedures evolved for the assessment of private wealth, on which forced loans were based. Fiscal policy has been studied only for the republican period, and interest has concentrated either on internal technical procedures of fiscal admin-

---

[12] Diaz, *Il Granducato di Toscana*, 127–48; Judith C. Brown, "Concepts of Political Economy: Cosimo I de' Medici in a Comparative European Context," in *Firenze e la Toscana dei Medici nell'Europa del '500* (Florence, 1983), 1:279–93.

istration or on political aspects of policy, especially policy as an instrument of power for the political elite and policy as a theme in the emergence of the modern state. Studies of the public debt and the tax system have rarely raised questions about the implications of either for the economy in general.

THE PUBLIC DEBT   In 1343–45 the state debt was detached from the ad hoc arrangements used up to that time and amassed into what was called a "mountain" of debt, the Monte, becoming, in our terms, a permanent funded public debt. With this device the state could augment its indebtedness through the usual procedure of *prestanze,* or forced loans, and maintain it indefinitely by ongoing arrangements, primarily by assignment of indirect taxes, for payment of interest—originally at the fixed rate of 5 percent—and periodic reduction of principal. The other great commercial city-states, Genoa and Venice, being maritime and colonial powers long burdened with heavy military expenditures, had funded their public debt much earlier. It was only in the early fourteenth century that Florence began facing similar fiscal pressures from the rising costs of military operations incurred by a more aggressive expansionist policy and its emergence as a major territorial state within central Italy. Moreover, it is no coincidence that the first steps toward the funding of the state debt were taken at the moment when, after the expulsion of the Duke of Athens, the ruling oligarchy had to widen participation in the government to include the minor guilds and when the city was in the throes of a credit crisis of extraordinary proportions following widespread bankruptcy in the international banking sector. The Monte, in short, had elements of a social as well as a fiscal reform. It is interesting to note that the communal government did not adopt the fiscal practices of the princely states that its merchant-bankers were serving at the time, namely, the alienation of income, the contracting out of mint and other operations, and the sale of offices and life annuities. In the fourteenth century the government contracted out indirect taxes, but over the following century it largely abandoned this practice in favor of direct collection by its own officials. Rich Florentines could not make money by investing in their government at home in the ways that the international merchant-bankers among them made their fortunes working for governments abroad.[13]

With the Monte, Florentines for the first time had the possibility of investing in government obligations, something like long-term interest-bearing state bonds, and they could reassign their credits on the Monte books to others. There is

---

[13] For background and comparative study, see Maria Ginatempo, *Prima del debito: Finanziamento della spesa pubblica e gestione del deficit nelle grandi città toscane (1200–1350 ca.)* (Florence, 2000).

evidence that as early as 1339, before the establishment of the Monte, people even at the bottom of the economic and social scale were selling to speculators the credits they received in return for forced loans, and the foundation of the Monte further stimulated the lively secondary market in these titles. The Monte, however, did not issue certificates, and hence these assignable credits were nothing like fully negotiable bonds; they were transferable on request by the holder, usually after sale to another party.[14] Initially the state established public confidence in the enterprise: voluntary loans were forthcoming, the number of creditors grew, and a lively secondary market, populated with speculators and brokers, arose in titles to both the principal and interest payments. In 1347 one otherwise unknown person, Piero di Vannozzo Baroni, made 150 purchases, increasing his holdings to *fl*.16,000. The Monte was an instant success, perhaps in part because it appeared on the scene precisely at the moment when the great banking crisis must have eroded confidence in the private credit market, a coincidence of events that has been little remarked in the literature and leads one to wonder just how serious the "crisis" really was at the local level. However that may have been, the impact the Black Death in 1348 had on the money supply, leaving in its wake higher per capita wealth and higher wages, must have been a stimulus to this new market. This situation, however, does not seem to have lasted very long. During the second half of the century the government had to face the mounting costs of an ever-expanding territorial state, and the public debt began to get out of control. The state could not always meet interest payments out of its regular income from indirect taxes; and to counter the consequent negative effect on voluntary loans, it increased the interest rate to attract loans, which only added to the burden on the state's income. Moreover, credits ceased to be payable on demand. Already in the 1360s Florentines must have begun to have doubts about the validity of this kind of investment. During that decade one prominent lanaiolo, Francesco Del Bene, made sporadic purchases in Monte credits totaling more than *fl*.5,000, but in the end his losses were significant. At some point the state introduced the option of having one's tax bill reduced in exchange for renuncia-

---

[14] Bernardino Barbadori, *Le finanze della Repubblica fiorentina: Imposta diretta e debito pubblico fino all'istituzione del Monte* (Florence, 1929), 603–9. On speculators, see Roberto Barducci, "Politica e speculazione finanziaria a Firenze dopo la crisi del primo Trecento (1343–1358)," *ASI* 137 (1979): 177–219; Anthony Molho, "Créanciers de Florence en 1347: Un aperçu statistique du quartier de Santo Spirito," in *La Toscane et les Toscans autour de la Renaissance: Cadres de vie, société, croyances; Mélanges offerts à Charles-M. de La Roncière* (Aix-en-Provence, 1999), 89–91 (for the period 1347–51); Armando Sapori, "Case e botteghe a Firenze nel Trecento (la rendita della proprietà fondiaria)," in *Studi di storia economica: Secoli XIII, XIV, XV*, 3 vols. (Florence, 1955–67), 2:347–52 (on Francesco di Iacopo Del Bene, 1361–71); and Alessandro Stella, "Fiscalità, topografia e società a Firenze nella seconda metà del Trecento," *ASI* 151 (1993): 837–41 (for 1378).

tion of a credit on the Monte's book, at which point the forced loan became a direct tax.

On the occasion of the prestanza of April 1378 no fewer than 5,186 persons—61.6 percent of the total—paid speculators to take their assessment at a reduced price, leaving it to these speculators to pay the assessment to the state and so get the credit for themselves; in other words, they paid a lower tax by selling its potential credit value, and the speculators in effect were able to buy state obligations at a reduced price. The buyers numbered only 262, just 30 of whom dealt with 92 percent of the sellers; these speculators included a tailor, a grocer (*pizzicagnolo*), and two women, along with some prominent bankers, the largest purchaser being Vieri di Cambio de' Medici. The selling price was low, 20–25 percent of par, perhaps reflecting widespread anxiety in a political situation that several months later would explode into the revolt of the Ciompi (although the speculators obviously had a different view). It was probably this kind of traffic in Monte credits that prompted the Ciompi to take action against the policy of forced loans and the speculative market it had given rise to and against a monetary policy that inflated these credits. It is rarely pointed out that what the Ciompi agitated for was not reduced taxation but the abandonment of the policy of forced loans altogether and a return to a direct tax. Two years later, with the reassertion of an oligarchic government, confidence in the public debt was much higher, to judge from an observation by the chronicler Marchionne di Coppo Stefani.[15] He claimed that when the Monte offered a return of 10–15 percent, almost 5,000 people invested in it, many of them selling their land and houses and closing their shops to raise the funds. By the end of the century, however, when the debt was well above 1 million florins, no Florentine was making voluntary loans to the state through the Monte. The public debt ceased to be an investment outlet.

During the 1360s, with the debt mounting, the state took the initiative of attracting loans from non-Florentines and gave these private investors in the Monte special treatment. Since these were mostly political figures, it was in the state's interest to offer them the security of preferential status as creditors. In 1363 Mastino della Scala invested *fl.*50,000, and in 1367 Giovanna, daughter of the Duke of Durazzo, invested *fl.*40,000. Abroad the state presumably established its reliability as a debtor, for it continued to receive funds from other prominent foreigners who were looking for investment outlets or simply for a secure depository abroad for their wealth. These later investors included Luchino Novello Visconti, who had at least *fl.*20,000 credit at the time of his death in 1400; King John of Portugal, who

<hr>

[15] Marchionne di Coppo Stefani, *Cronaca fiorentina*, ed. Niccolò Rodolico (Città di Castello, 1903), rubric 883.

put in *fl.*20,000 in 1410 and eventually increased his holdings to *fl.*41,582; and Pope Eugene IV, who invested *fl.*100,000 in 1432. A few years later some of the foreign ecclesiastics residing in Florence to attend the church council bought these government obligations.[16]

From the 1390s through the 1420s the city, now growing into a significant territorial state on the wider Italian scene, had to confront the mounting costs of frequent wars with the other major Italian states, and the debt rose much higher, to 3 million florins in 1415 and to more than 4 million in 1427, where it remained for the next half-century.[17] The government, unable to bring this mounting debt under control in a way that assured regular payment of interest, let alone redemption of capital, had to devise ways to deal with the problem. One measure was a monetary policy directed to limiting the inflation of the nominal value of the debt by periodically fixing the price of the florin of account used to keep communal records. The government ended the practice of assigning prices of coins put in purses (see chapter 1) but continued to use the fiorino di suggello, now exclusively as a money of account, the price of which it fixed. Since it kept its accounts in this florin, the government was thereby able to temper the inflationary effect on its debt of the relatively rapid rise in the price of the gold florin, over which it had little control. Whereas the fiorino di suggello went from 80 soldi di piccioli in the early fifteenth century to 98 soldi at the beginning of the sixteenth century (a rise of 22.5 percent), the gold florin went from 86 to 140 soldi (a rise of 62.8 percent). In other words, at the beginning of the century the gold florin was worth only a few percentage points more than the fiorino di suggello, but by 1500 it was worth 42 percent more. Had the government used the gold florin, or a money of account more closely linked to it, its debt burden, as well as other fixed costs, would have steadily increased at a much higher rate. To fully appreciate this situation, one should keep in mind that the prices and wages in the local economy were quoted in lire (or soldi di piccioli), not florins. The relatively well off Florentines who had accumulated credits in the state debt as a result

[16] Marvin Becker, *Florence in Transition* (Baltimore, 1967), 178–79 (della Scala, Giovanna di Durazzo); Julius Kirshner, "Privileged Risk: The Investments of Luchino Visconti in the Public Debt (*monte comune*) of Florence," in *Politiche del credito: Investimento consumo solidarietà* (Asti, 2004), 32–67; Lawrin Armstrong, "Usury, Conscience and Public Debt: Angelo Corbinelli's Testament of 1419," in *A Renaissance of Conflicts: Visions and Revisions of Law and Society in Italy and Spain,* ed. John Marino and Thomas Kuehn (Toronto, 2004), 199 (Eugene IV); Eric Apfelstadt, "Bishop and Pawn: New Documents for the Chapel of the Cardinal of Portugal at S. Miniato al Monte, Florence," in *Cultural Links between Portugal and Italy in the Renaissance,* ed. K. J. P. Lowe (Oxford, 2000), 199–200 (King John); Luca Boschetto, *"Quando papa Eugenio fu a Firenze": Cortigiani, mercanti e umanisti nella città del Concilio, 1434–1443* (in preparation). Other loans are noted in Anthony Molho, *Florentine Public Finances in the Early Renaissance, 1400–1433* (Cambridge, MA, 1971), 144–48.

[17] For the debt in the early fifteenth century, see Molho, *Florentine Public Finances;* for that at the end of the century, see Louis F. Marks, "La crisi finanziaria a Firenze dal 1494 al 1502," *ASI* 112 (1954): 40–72.

of the heavy burden of forced loans at the beginning of the century saw the steady erosion of the real value of those credits, as exchanged into gold florins, throughout the century. It bears mentioning, however, that these were the very people who made monetary and fiscal policy.

Along with this depreciation in the value of the state debt, the irregularity of interest payments and the inability to cash in one's obligations depressed the market value of government obligations, which fell during the fifteenth century from about 50 percent of par to often well below 20 percent. By the second half of the century, in fact, there even seems to have been a certain lack of interest on the part of some to keep a record of the credits they had in the Monte. Many ledgers of private administration no longer had accounts open for this asset, and many declarants of the 1457–58 catasto expressed ignorance of exactly how much they had in Monte credits.[18] In contemporary Venice, however, notwithstanding even greater loss in the market value of credits in the state debt and in interest payments over these same years, Nicolò Barbarigo, who died in 1500, kept a careful record of all his government obligations, as did his heirs for the next two generations. By 1576 the descendants had collected what the government owed them, albeit much reduced in value by inflation in the meantime.[19]

Another device adopted by the state in the early fifteenth century to face the problem of a rising service charge on its debt was the Monte delle Doti, a scheme for selling future dowries, set up in 1425.[20] This was a fund into which a father could deposit cash that would mature into a dowry after seven and a half or fifteen years. Within a few years the dowry fund assumed the additional function of retiring the state debt by requiring purchases of dowries to be paid partly in Monte credits at market, not par, value. However, over the next half-century, with the obligations of this new fund rising, the state found it increasingly difficult to make dowry payments, and in a series of reforms dating from 1478 it began manipulating the fund to meet these problems. The measures taken to lighten the burden included limiting the size of the dowry, making payments of the dowry in installments, and paying part of the dowry in reassignable credits in a new fund paying 7 percent, called the 7-percent Monte. To this latter fund were eventually added two others, one paying 4 percent and the other 3 percent, and credits passed upward from one to the other according to a fixed schedule. These funds eventually replaced the Monte as depositories of the public debt, and they remained

[18] Anthony Molho, "Tre città-stato e i loro debiti pubblici: Quesiti e ipotesi sulla storia di Firenze, Genova e Venezia," in *Italia 1350–1450: Tra crisi, trasformazione, sviluppo* (Pistoia, 1993), 202.

[19] Frederic C. Lane, *Andrea Barbarigo, Merchant of Venice, 1418–1449* (Baltimore, 1944), 41–43.

[20] Anthony Molho, *Marriage Alliance in Late Medieval Florence* (Cambridge, MA, 1994), ch. 2 (with references to Molho's earlier articles on this subject).

open through the sixteenth century. The dowry fund as such, however, had lost its appeal by the end of the century and slowly declined.

This summary hardly reveals the considerable technical complexity of the various mechanisms designed over the years to deal with the public debt and with the dowry fund at a time when expenses, mostly for war, were draining the resources of the state; for the most part these problems were confined to the internal administration of state finances, a subject that need not detain us here. These manipulations had an impact on the credit market, however, to the extent that they permitted the use of government obligations to pay taxes or buy a dowry and allowed the transfer of credits and future credits (from interest due) by assignment from one party to another. These practices gave rise to a secondary market in these credits inasmuch as they circulated among private parties as a limited medium of exchange, completely outside the sphere of the fisc, the market being driven primarily by the value of Monte credits at the Monte office, not for redemption, but for meeting obligations to the state, including payment of forced loans. The market was large given the size of the debt; it was lively, since market values fluctuated incessantly; and it was complex, since assignment of these credits, which did not take the form of negotiable paper, often required procurators, notaries, and brokers. Moreover, one had to assess the risks involved—the immediate political situation and hence chances of default on interest payments, the declining price of the florin di suggello (the money of account used by the government), and the future behavior of the secondary market. Yet the sophistication in dealing in this market was evident throughout the society and is yet another testimony to the ease with which Florentines handled credit in general. And the bookkeeping required for the state to keep track of the fluidity in the ranks of its creditors was no small operation, as is evident in the immensity of the Monte archive that survives today.

So went the market, up and down, and it attracted many players from all strata of society. There is hardly a fifteenth-century account book kept for personal affairs that does not record the use of these credits, not just to pay taxes or buy into the state dowry fund but to put up collateral for a loan, to make an outright purchase, to offer security for deferred payment, or simply to speculate. Just to refer to some printed sources: the record book of the painter Neri di Bicci reveals the ease with which even an artisan bought and sold Monte credits, including those for interest payments, and could use them as security in the acquisition of a house or as money for purchases; in letters to her son Alessandra Macinghi degli Strozzi shows a keen sensibility to the fluctuations in the market price of Monte credits and an awareness of the consequent investment possibilities through speculation (as well as qualms about the morality of dealing in instruments that might be tainted as usurious); and Marco Parenti mentions a certain Matteo di Giorgio di maestro Cristofano, who suffered heavy losses from speculating on the course rates would take on the news of Cosimo il Vecchio's death.[21] Traffic in these credits was sufficiently intense to induce the banker messer Andrea de' Pazzi and eight others to organize a company in 1448—identified as a *maona*—to deal in this market of what they called Monte money *(danari),* each partner committing himself to invest *fl*.4,000 in Monte credits.[22] At some point the Monte began issuing certificates *(polizze)* for credits on its books, and these very much enlivened the market, to judge from a concern in the early 1540s that speculators were taking advantage of "poor widows and other sorts of people" who were not in a position to know the real value of the certificates they held.[23]

Although the handling of the public debt had some modern features—permanence, assignable (if not fully negotiable) credits, a secondary market in credits freed from government control—it was not adequately financed and failed to inspire the confidence of the private investor looking for a regular and secure income. It therefore did not attract wealth away from more productive kinds of investment and thereby induce a *rentier* mentality (as has been claimed). In other words, Florentines failed to effect a true financial revolution, one of the themes in the historiography of the emergence of the early modern state.[24] Yet as an administrative body the Monte evolved into an effective organ of the modernizing state run by an oligarchy that was fully entrenched following the reaction to the Ciompi revolt. Besides the collection of taxes, the Officials of the Monte (Ufficiali del Monte), the body that managed the Monte, took over the administration of indirect taxes, the supervision of state expenditures, and the administration of virtually all fiscal activities, including punishment of offenders.

Moreover, the Monte Officials brought the floating debt—that is, the arrangements that all states make for handling liquidity crises, when they need quick access to funds through short-term loans obtained directly from private parties at high interest rates—under control. The government had always leaned heavily

---

[21] Neri di Bicci, *Le ricordanze (10 marzo 1453–24 aprile 1475),* ed. Bruno Santi (Pisa, 1976), 111, 144, 149, 158, 160, 234–35, 296–97; Alessandra Macinghi negli Strozzi, *Lettere di una gentildonna fiorentina del secolo XV ai figliuoli esuli,* ed. Cesare Guasti (Florence, 1877), 353–43, 357, 573–74; Marco Parenti, *Ricordi storici, 1464–1467,* ed. Manuela Doni Garfagnini (Rome, 2001), 72–73.

[22] This enterprise is known only through a case brought before the tribunal of the Mercanzia involving credit claims by the partners: ASF, Mercanzia, 7164, fols. 293v–395v. My thanks to Luca Boschetto for bringing this document to my attention.

[23] Marco Spallanzani, "'Modo da crescere l'entrate di Firenze': Un progetto presentato a Cosimo I," *Annali della Scuola Normale Superiore di Pisa: Classe di lettere e filosofia,* 3d ser., 16 (1986): 526–27.

[24] To see how Florence's handling of the public debt compared with that of other places in Europe, see John Munro, "The Medieval Origins of the Financial Revolution: Usury, *Rentes,* and Negotiability," *International History Review* 25 (2003): 505–62.

on bankers for such loans, and these ad hoc personal arrangements could get out of control. It was one of the problems that compounded the crisis of the 1340s, as we have seen. In the fifteenth century the Monte Officials took hold of the situation: they individually assumed personal responsibility for these loans, each with his own quota, their security being the control over the state's fiscal operations that came with the office. The officials were selected for their ability to arrange these loans. Some were rich merchant-bankers who loaned their own money; others were able to work the market by subcontracting for loans of various kinds at lower rates of interest. The officials profited from both the emoluments of office and the high rates of interest, usually about 14 percent, the state paid for this kind of temporary loan. The tenure of the officials was several years, but the periodic renewal of the body and the high turnover among officials precluded the emergence of a financial oligarchy organized around this office alone.[25]

We know little about the fiscal system of the Medici dukes in the sixteenth century.[26] They let the dowry fund diminish away but kept the 3 percent, 4 percent, and 7 percent funds in place, now subsumed under what was called the Monte delle Graticole (*graticole,* or "gratings," referred to grids through which funds passed from one level to another according to a given schedule), considerably streamlining the administration of them, to judge from surviving accounts. Thanks to the general peace that resulted from the assertion of Hapsburg dominance over the peninsula in the 1530s, these early Medici did not have to resort to taxation to sustain heavy military expenses. Moreover, Cosimo began building up an enormous private fortune, profiting personally from some of his initiatives in economic policy; in the process, he managed to erode distinctions between his personal private wealth and that of the state.[27] Hence, he and his successors succeeded in putting the public debt on a sound foundation, so that it attracted voluntary investments even from the rich. From 1549 to 1568 the Riccardi family raised their holdings in the 7 percent fund to *sc.*13,090, more than they invested in land in the same period.[28] In the 1580s the three Monte funds had a balance of

---

[25] On the handling of the floating debt in the early fifteenth century, see Molho, *Florentine Public Finances,* 163–82; for the later period, see Louis F. Marks, "The Financial Oligarchy in Florence under Lorenzo," in *Italian Renaissance Studies,* ed. E. F. Jacob (New York, 1960), 123–47. Richard A. Goldthwaite, "Lorenzo Morelli, Ufficiale del Monte, 1484–88: Interessi privati e cariche pubbliche nella Firenze laurenziana," *ASI* 154 (1996): 605–33, illustrates how one of the officials advanced none of his own money but used his office to arrange for loans from others.

[26] The only specific study is Anna Teicher, "Politics and Finance in the Age of Cosimo I: The Public and Private Face of Credit," in *Firenze e la Toscana dei Medici,* 1:343–62.

[27] For the growth of Cosimo's personal estate, see Giuseppe Vittorio Parigino, *Il tesoro del principe: Funzione pubblica e privata del patrimonio della famiglia Medici nel Cinquecento* (Florence, 1999), esp. 68–73 for his financial dealings with bankers.

[28] Paolo Malanima, *I Riccardi di Firenze: Una famiglia e un patrimonio nella Toscana dei Medici* (Florence, 1977), 39–40.

*fl.*3,033,798, on which interest was being paid every four months. Credits were in part fully assignable but also in part conditioned by liens on property, dowry claims, charitable obligations, and inalienable patrimonial rights (through *fedecommessi,* or entails), which testify to its function as an outlet for savings and investment.[29] In 1558, in the aftermath of the conquest of Siena, the duke had recourse to Monte officials for short-term loans, but with the transformation of the Monte di Pietà into what was in effect a public bank in the sixteenth century, the Medici had an impersonal institutional device for handling any floating debt without direct recourse to local bankers.

Or the dukes resorted instead to foreign bankers. When they needed money to finance the one major military operation during this period, the war to conquer Siena in 1554–55, Cosimo I borrowed from Genoese bankers and the Fuggers rather than from Florentines, obtaining guarantees for these loans from those Florentines with close personal ties to him. One of these bankers, Bernardo di Giovanni Vecchietti, noted for his patronage and scholarly interests, repeatedly arranged loans from the Fuggers throughout Cosimo's reign. On occasion he went off to Venice and even to Augsburg for this purpose, and at least once he went to Genoa to arrange a loan from Niccolò Grimaldi. After Cosimo's death, Vecchietti continued to perform this service for both Francesco I and Ferdinand I down to his death in 1590.[30] At the same time that the Medici were borrowing, they were also loaning out funds to political figures abroad, for their financial situation permitted them to use the promise of credit as an instrument of foreign policy; as already noted, they sometimes arranging these loans through the Monte di Pietà.

When Ferdinand I needed to finance emergency efforts to get grain to the city in 1591, he did not resort to either borrowing in the usual way or to taxation. Instead, he set up a fund (another Monte) to raise *sc.*100,000 from the pubic by offering an 8.5 percent return to those who bought into it, with the provision that the account would be extinguished at death, with no reimbursement. In other words, they bought a lifetime annuity, or *rente.* The minimum was set at *sc.*100, with interest payable every two months, both capital and interest being free of any charges by the fisc. Credits could be transferred and sold, subject, of course, to the lifetime limitation of the original "montista," and the state reserved the

[29] An undated balance, but made sometime after 1582, is to be found in ASF, Carte strozziane, ser. 1, 22, fols. 56–58. Stefano Calonaci, *Dietro lo scudo incantato: I fedecommessi di famiglia e il trionfo della borghesia fiorentina, 1400 ca–1750* (Florence, 2005), 139, documents the application of fedecommessi to Monte funds for the preservation of a family patrimony.

[30] Francesca Carrara, "Il magnifico Bernardo Vecchietti, cortigiano e committente in un inedito epistolario privato," in *Giambologna: Gli dei, gli eroi,* ed. Beatrice Paolozzi Strozzi and Dimitrios Zikos (Florence, 2006), 302–14. See also Parigino, *Il tesoro del principe,* 68–73, for Cosimo's financial dealings with bankers.

right to extinguish the debt, with just compensation, in advance of death.[31] Here
we have perhaps the first rumblings of a "financial revolution" in Renaissance
Florence; but it involved nothing like the "colossal public debt which, in turn,
nurtured a state-*rentier* complex" among the urban elites in the later stages of the
development of the Dutch economy.[32]

TAXATION   A second refinement in the republic's fiscal system came in the
way it determined how assessments for forced loans were to be made and what
the tax base was to be. In the early fourteenth century neighborhood committees were set up to make assessments, a system that became more complex as
the procedure was fine-tuned over the following years in the name of objectivity. With the 1427 catasto, the government changed its strategy altogether by
having direct recourse to Florentines themselves for assessments of their wealth:
taxes were based no longer on an estimate made by others but on a concrete
inventory *(catasto)* of assets submitted by the person to be taxed. The catasto
officials required all heads of households, whether male or female, to submit
what today we would call a return and defined how this was to be done. The
procedures for calculating one's net worth were quite sophisticated. First, each
declarant listed all assets—real estate, animals, merchandise, business investments, government obligations (credits in the Monte), and all outstanding
credits from private parties (which had to be listed individually). Real estate
was precisely located, and the income it generated, whether in the form of rent
or produce, was fully explained; its value was then determined by the capitalization of the income at 7 percent. All assets, in other words, were listed in great
detail, although the residence of the reporting heads of households was exempt
from an assessment and Monte credits could be discounted by 50 percent. From
this total gross wealth the declarant then subtracted all outstanding debts and
ongoing obligations (both of which had to be individually listed if they exceeded a minimum figure), the capitalized value (at 7 percent) of rents paid for
a residence or workplace, and deductions for each member of the household
(*bocca*, "mouth," in the terminology of the enacting legislation), whose name,
relationship, and age also had to be entered. The result was total net worth as
defined for fiscal purposes. This figure became the basis for assigning an assessment of 0.5 percent in the city, less in the territory, which then was subject to

---

[31] *Legislazione toscana*, 13:255–60.
[32] Jan de Vries and Ad van der Woude, *The First Modern Economy: Success, Failure, and Perseverance of the Dutch Economy, 1500–1815* (Cambridge, 1997), 129. Luciano Pezzolo, "Elogio della rendita:
Sul debito pubblico degli stati italiani nel Cinque e Seicento," *Rivista di storia economica*, n.s., 12
(1995): 283–330, discusses aspects of the financial revolution in Italy.

collection as often as the government determined. What the head of household paid was a forced loan, in return for which he received credit in the Monte; if he agreed to forgo the credit, he could pay at a lower rate, in effect transforming the forced loan into a direct tax.[33]

Perhaps no other government, even down to the present, has ever sought to complete such a wide-ranging survey of the wealth of its subjects. A similar Venetian survey presumably served as the model for the catasto, but the resulting documents no longer survive. For Florence, however, all the original returns survive—nearly ten thousand for the city—along with full copies of them, with corrections made by government notaries during the course of verifying them. They constitute a unique source for the statistical study of both the demography and the wealth of a preindustrial city. Moreover, these returns often read like a rich chronicle of the life of the city at the time inasmuch as many declarants, never having been asked to submit anything of the kind before, entered all kinds of information about themselves and their affairs that was not required but that they thought might be relevant, especially for gaining some mercy from the officials.

Unfortunately, as expert as Florentines were in keeping accounts, they could easily enough doctor their records. Although the 1427 returns are generally considered to be reasonably accurate, subsequent efforts to have Florentines submit updated returns resulted in evasions and outright dishonesty. It was too easy to hide liquid wealth in particular, and the task of handling and checking this material and then dealing with fraud was enormous. Besides, it was always possible to make appeals, and one can only guess at how much friendship, relationship, and political allegiances counted in negotiating a final settlement in one's favor. One notable instance of a vast cover-up comes to light in a memorandum made on 23 February 1429 by Luca di Matteo Da Panzano in his private record book. Da Panzano was in business with two partners, Giuliano di Bartolo Gini and Leonardo di Ridolfo de' Bardi; and since the former was extraordinarily wealthy—he ranked sixteenth in the category of net taxable wealth in the 1427 catasto—the partners devised a way to avoid being hit *(gravati a botte)* by high taxes in the likelihood that the tax officials subjected such a wealthy man and his firm to a particularly close scrutiny. They recorded their balances in a private journal that Gini always took home, and their official company books did not record profits. Moreover, they debited Gini's personal account on the company books for all the silk they sent out to Valencia, Barcelona, and Avignon—worth *fl.*18,000—so that the company could show that it had not yet realized any of its profits and he could demonstrate that he had a large

---

[33] Elio Conti, *L'imposta diretta a Firenze nel Quattrocento (1427–1494)* (Rome, 1984), is the most thorough study of direct taxation in the fifteenth century.

debt to the firm. Another setaiolo, Andrea Banchi, made what seems to have been, as checked against his accounts, an accurate report in 1427, but on his second return, in 1430, he cheated to cover up the real value of even his real-estate holdings, the most difficult possession to hide. Although the authorities had their suspicions and inspected his books, they found his accounts in so much disorder that they ended up accepting Banchi's return, since "they could not spare the time needed to clear up the matter." Later Banchi, to protect himself against such inspections, doctored the secret ledger of his prosperous silk firm—"for love of the catasto," as his partner, who kept these accounts, sarcastically put it.

Later returns are replete with excuses for not reporting the desired information. The rich international banker Tommaso Spinelli, since 1443 depositary of the Apostolic Chamber, took a simpler and more direct approach, blatantly declaring in his 1446 return, "I find myself with nothing, neither property nor income." Gino di Neri Capponi, in contrast, declared all the various enterprises of his vast partnership agglomerate in his 1480 return but then went on to explain why no value can be assigned to any of them: the company in Lyons had been shut down, and a report on its status would be forthcoming; a company in Pisa could no longer be kept in operation, and it was hoped that all its creditors could be paid off; no value could be put on a share in a copper mine near Volterra, since the expenses involved in such a venture were enough to ruin one; the bank in Florence was suffering from such heavy expenses and taxes that virtually no capital was left, although the books were still open; and finally, as for the silk company managed by his son, there was only hope that it would remain solvent after all the debts and disorders were cleared up.[34]

The authorities thus learned in the course of the fifteenth century that in the end the only valid tax base was real estate. Citizens could not be relied on to report their liquid wealth, and there was no other way to find out what that was. An attempt was made in 1451 to narrow the tax on all forms of liquid wealth to the capital of all partnerships, which presumably was more easily verifiable, but this seems to have been a one-time effort.[35] As to Monte credits, they were clearly a matter of public record, but the state eventually had to recognize that it could not tax them, first, because they were patently no longer considered investments, and second, because their market value had fallen so much that subjecting them to

[34] ASF, Archivio Ricasoli, Libri di amministrazione, 111, fol. 173 (record book of Luca da Panzano); Florence Edler de Roover, "Andrea Banchi, Florentine Silk Manufacturer and Merchant in the Fifteenth Century," *Studies in Medieval and Renaissance History* 3 (1996): 281–82; William Caferro, "L'attività bancaria papale e la Firenze del Rinascimento: Il caso di Tommaso Spinelli," *Società e storia*, no. 70 (1995): 751; Richard A. Goldthwaite, *Private Wealth in Renaissance Florence: A Study of Four Families* (Princeton, NJ, 1968), 196n.

[35] Anthony Molho, "The Florentine 'Tassa dei Traffichi' of 1451," *Studies in the Renaissance* 17 (1970): 73–118.

taxation would only add insult to injury. What remained was land, and in fact the 1427 catasto was most successful as the first serious attempt at a complete land survey. Subsequent returns had to indicate where all pieces of property reported had appeared in the earlier returns (including, if the property had changed hands since the last return, on whose return it had appeared previously), and the authorities had little problem verifying everything. In 1495 the state finally abandoned the catasto and initiated the decima, which required everyone to file only a list of all income-producing real estate. This system of periodic property surveys for tax purposes, complete with internal cross references to that property in previous reports regardless of ownership, for all practical purposes remains intact today notwithstanding subsequent modifications made by the different regimes to which the city has been subjected over the centuries. Given this long tradition of tax reporting from the time of the 1427 catasto, and the survival of virtually all the documents, it is today a relatively simple matter to trace the ownership of any property in the city back over more than half a millennium. With the introduction of the decima, however, the individual return became a strictly formal inventory of real-estate holdings. Gone from these documents are all those other kinds of information that make the catasto, even its ever more diluted manifestations after 1427, a unique source in the annals of European history for details about private wealth, family genealogy, and demographic statistics, not to mention the rich chronicle content of the earlier returns.

The mechanisms of the tax system and of the administration of the public debt are of less interest here than the impact of taxes on the economy. In 1427 taxes hit the main categories of wealth—real estate, government obligations, and business investments. Moreover, since the rich (those with assets of more than *fl.*5,000) owned 61 percent of all Monte credits, most of which represented loans forced from them in the past, they were clearly paying a heavy tax burden, if not anything like their fair share (whatever that might have been). There is no reason to think that the less exacting assessments on wealth made for tax purposes before the 1427 catasto did not also include business investments. It has been estimated that Francesco Datini paid more than *fl.*1,000 in taxes annually during the dozen years before his death in 1410, no little amount even for a man of his wealth.[36] Nevertheless, there is no question that after the 1427 catasto business investments slipped away altogether from the control of the tax officials; as it evolved, the system clearly favored business interests and therefore the rich, who, as a whole, were not large property owners.

[36] Giovanni Ciappelli, "Il cittadino fiorentino e il fisco alla fine del Trecento e nel corso del Quattrocento: Uno studio di due casi," *Società e storia*, no. 46 (1989): 828–44.

Ownership of real estate was widespread throughout the urban population: two-thirds of the declarants of the 1427 catasto owned some kind of taxable property (which did not include one's residence). The rich owned only 22 percent of all real estate, while they owned 43 percent of the other two categories of wealth. And only 18 percent of these households had more than half of their wealth in land, whereas 51 percent had less than a quarter of their wealth in land. Moreover, the deduction allowed for "mouths" was high enough to more than cancel out the value of the land that people of more modest wealth were likely to own. Large landowners who had no other source of income would have had difficulty in paying their tax bill during the 1420s and the 1430s, given the particularly heavy burden during those years. These early taxes imposed on real estate alone—the 1480 catasto and subsequently the early decima—hit the wealthy landowner all the harder since they were graduated, so that the more property one had, the higher the rate he paid. The preamble of the 1495 decima was explicit about the objective "not to interfere in the businesses and trade of our city."[37] To the extent that the rich built up larger and more coherent landed estates in the sixteenth century, they came in for a greater share of the tax burden. But inasmuch as real estate remained the one investment people of modest means could make, they too suffered from a tax system that failed to strike the forward sectors of the economy.

Much has been written about the heavy burden of taxes in the first half of the fifteenth century, when the city was frequently involved in war, sometimes in its own territory. The case studies that have been presented as evidence, however, have little documentary evidence other than a sequence of catasto returns of specific persons showing declining wealth. While these declarations contain many complaints and cries of distress, they do not provide any concrete evidence of the extent to which these losses depended on the internal administration of patrimonies.[38] Much also has been written about how the ruling elite used the system to its own advantage, gaining tax favors for friends and relatives and penalizing political opponents. The notable example here is Matteo di Marco Palmieri, a speziale, who left a record book with all the details of his and his father's transactions regarding taxes they paid for half a century, from 1427 to 1474. Elio Conti's study of this extraordinary document illustrates how Palmieri, while heavily burdened with forced loans during the earlier years, when the city had to face the high cost of war, succeeded during the following years of lighter taxes in using his accumulated Monte credits to get back every-

---

[37] Quoted in Marks, "La crisi finanziaria," 54.
[38] The best arguments have been made by Conti, *L'imposta diretta*, 341–53. Ciappelli, "Il cittadino fiorentino," presents another case study.

thing he had paid in forced loans plus a net profit of *fl.*777.[39] He was able to do this, we are told, because he had the right connections within the ruling elite.

A generalization from this instance, however, has to be balanced with some consideration of the extent of these practices and the size of the elite. The people with means ran the state, and in the end they had to recognize that they were the ones who had to foot the tax bill. In the 1427 catasto Palmieri's father possessed 0.06 percent of the total taxable wealth of the city, and yet, as Conti has shown, the taxes paid by Palmieri from 1431 to 1440 amounted to between 0.92 percent and 1.55 percent of total income from this source. In any event, one can hardly go beyond the observations about the misuse of the system for personal and political interests to argue that the tax system in any way strapped economic activity, for these were the years that saw considerable economic expansion—the growth of the silk industry, the purchase of the ports of Livorno and Porto Pisano, the launching of the galley system, the organization of the first exchange market at Geneva, the initiatives to open the market for wool cloth in the new Ottoman state. And it was during the years, from the mid-1420s to the mid-1430s, that the city was footing the large bill for the building of the massive cupola of the cathedral, which immediately became the symbol of the city.

The burden of paying for wars lightened toward the mid-fifteenth century, not to rise again until the end of the century. From the mid-1430s through the third quarter of the century the burden of direct taxes fell by more than 50 percent, and thereafter it fell again to only slightly more than a third of what it had been at the time of the 1427 catasto.[40] The 1494 invasion triggered the long-drawn-out rebellion of Pisa (1494–1509) and pulled Florence into the political struggles among the rulers of Europe over the dominance of Italy, which did not end until the disastrous ten-month siege of 1529–30 and the return of the Medici, to be permanently installed as princely rulers. We have no study of fiscal affairs for this period or for the early years of the new ducal government. The ascension of Cosimo I in 1537, however, ushered in an era of peace that was interrupted only by the war to conquer Siena in 1554–55. The ducal government occasionally levied a direct tax on wealth (*balzelli*), along with forced loans (*accatti*), but as already said, the decima remained the basis of the system of direct taxation, now partly applied on a graduated scale, with the rich paying a higher rate. Yet a glance at some private accounts books at the end of the century reveals that in fact they were paying very little in direct taxes. The sons of Giovanni di Iacopo Corsi record paying only *du.*806 from 1571 to 1587, when their total income amounted to *du.*144,600. The

---

[39] Matteo Palmieri, *Ricordi fiscali (1427–1474)*, ed. Elio Conti (Rome, 1983). Conti summarizes Palmieri's fiscal history in *L'imposta diretta*, 353–60.

[40] Conti, *L'imposta diretta*, 79, 82–83.

personal profit-and-loss account for the years 1582–87 of one of the Corsi brothers, Iacopo, shows a loss of *du*.128 for taxes and a credit balance of *du*.3,997. In his study of the income, expenditures, and growing patrimony of the Riccardi at the end of the century, Paolo Malanima did not consider it necessary to mention any tax burden at all.[41] In short, the Medici managed the state in such a way as to avoid imposing heavy direct taxes, notwithstanding their use of state funds to amass a large personal patrimony. Toward the end of the century the Venetian ambassadors reported that about half of the state revenues of just over a million scudi went to the dukes personally, and contemporary rumors had it that they built up a considerable hoard of cash.[42]

The chief source of the state's fixed income came from indirect taxes, or gabelles. These taxes, first imposed at the end of the thirteenth century, became the major source of steady revenue for the commune, especially given the size of the local market, and they increased as the territory expanded. They were imposed on goods passing in and out of the city gates, on notarial contracts, on the processing and sale of wine and other foods, and on retail sales. The state had other revenues from its salt monopoly, fines, penalties, rents, certain operations such as the mint and communal mills, and other miscellaneous sources, but gabelles provided the bulk of its fixed income, being even more important than direct taxes in normal times. They offered a certain flexibility, since they could be raised quickly, and they were collected continually, on a daily basis. Initially, in the early fourteenth century, they were difficult to collect, but since they were a marketable form of revenue, they could be farmed out to private contractors. Over the course of the century, however, the collection of many of them passed from the hands of private contractors to the commune itself—another development in the streamlining of fiscal administration. With the funding of the public debt in the fourteenth century, the state committed future revenues from gabelles to guarantee payment of interest. This fiscal device resulted in continuing pressure to raise them, especially on food products such as wine and meat, and to introduce new ones. Since gabelles hit all residents equally, regardless of economic status, they were regressive, subject to what society could tolerate, and during difficult times they could provoke popular outcry and even violence. Indirect taxation, however, did not find a place in the program of the Ciompi.

---

[41] For the Corsi, see Richard A. Goldthwaite, *Wealth and the Demand for Art in Italy, 1300–1600* (Baltimore, 1993), 57. R. Burr Litchfield, *Emergence of a Bureaucracy: The Florentine Patricians, 1530–1790* (Princeton, NJ, 1986), 99ff., surveys state finances during the entire period of the grand duchy. Reports of the Venetian ambassadors provide some statistics: *Relazioni degli ambasciatori veneti al senato*, ed. Arnaldo Segarizzi (Bari, 1916), 3, pt. 1:106–9 (1533), 212 (1576); pt. 2:46–47 (1588).

[42] Cipolla, *Money in Sixteenth-Century Florence*, 115.

The history of indirect taxes should include a discussion of how much of a burden the lower classes had to bear and what impact they had on market activity and thereby on the economy in general. Unfortunately, few materials survive for the documentation of indirect taxation, and the subject has hardly been studied. As it is, one can have it both ways in interpreting what few figures we have for the amount of revenue the city collected from gabelles. Increases have been regarded both as a sign of oppression and hard times and as a positive indicator of greater market activity and therefore of prosperity.[43]

Business Interests and Government

The historiography of the economic and political life of republican Florence gives little more than lip service to the fact that the elite who ran the city were largely business entrepreneurs. It is enough to look at the histories that have been written about specific businesses and businessmen, from the Bardi and the Peruzzi to the Medici, to see that economic historians have failed to consider that many of these men spent a good deal of time on the innumerable committees and legislative bodies that constituted the government of the republic, as well as in occasional service as magistrates in the provinces and as ambassadors abroad, not to mention their intense involvement in the factionalism so characteristic of the city's political life.[44] Likewise, political historians, while sounding economic themes in their obsession with class conflict, never ask themselves what these men did for a living, how they spent most of the day, and whether economic interests might have impinged on the often violent factional conflict within the ranks of the ruling elite.

In the early history of the city, going back to the thirteenth century, the politics leading to the foundation of a guild republic evolved around the effort of major guildsmen to curb the violence of the landed magnate class. But by the end of the century any class division between businessmen and a landed aristocracy, or between city and countryside, is difficult to find. In discussions of the rivalry between the Ghibillines and the Guelfs in the later thirteenth century and of the factionalism among the Guelfs at the turn of the next century, it is clear that

---

[43] The only detailed study of gabelles is that for the period leading up to the Ciompi revolt by Charles M. de La Roncière, "Indirect Taxes or 'Gabelles' at Florence in the Fourteenth Century: The Evolution of Tariffs and Problems of Collection," in *Florentine Studies: Politics and Society in Renaissance Florence*, ed. Nicolai Rubinstein (London, 1968), 140–92. See also Ginatempo, *Prima del debito*, 87–97, 158–61, 179–80. For the subsequent period, down to the 1420s, see Molho, *Florentine Public Finances*, 45–59.

[44] Notable exceptions are Michele Luzzati, *Giovanni Villani e la compagnia dei Buonaccorsi* (Rome, 1971), esp. 75–81; and Melissa Bullard, *Filippo Strozzi and the Medici: Favor and Finance in Sixteenth-Century Florence and Rome* (Cambridge, 1980).

merchant-bankers were to be found on both sides, but we are not told how, or if, party affiliation might have related to business interests. Gino Arias has suggested that the intense factionalism at the end of the thirteenth century arose partly from rivalry among bankers over ties to the papacy.[45] Yves Renouard has seen the subsequent disintegration of the Guelfs into the Blacks and Whites as reflecting, among other things, the extensive international business interests of the former in Naples, France, and the papacy as compared with the more confined regional interests of the latter in Pisa and Bologna.[46] Yet according to Giuseppe Petralia, merchants of both Guelf and Ghibelline factions were active in Sicily notwithstanding the Ghibelline sympathies of the monarchy, and the merchant community there had a stability that defied political changes.[47] Nor do we know how much of the factionalism dominated by the Ricci and the Alberti and by the Albizzi and the Medici in the later fourteenth and early fifteenth centuries arose out of, or impinged on, the business interests of these men and their allies. Later we hear about the rivalry between the Medici and the Pazzi over the specific contracts with the papacy each sought for their banks but not about competition over more basic economic issues facing their government at home. And how divided were the two "lobbies" for and against the French in 1494, at the time of the impending invasion by Charles VIII, by business interests at Lyons on the one hand and at Rome and Naples on the other?[48]

In short, the great divide between the political and the economic life of the city leaves each in almost surrealistic isolation. This book hardly escapes this fate; but now, in considering the role of government in the economy, the discussion has reached the point where a more comprehensive view of the political reality of these men's lives needs to be confronted.

In the historiography much is made of the exploitation of political power for personal interests—how government contracts opened up channels for making profits, how the tax system benefited members of the elite, how the funded debt favored the rich, how the floating debt gave rise to a financial oligarchy, and how central the emoluments of public office were to the republican organization of the state, how, even, some enriched themselves through fraud and corruption in their

---

[45] Gino Arias, *Studi e documenti di storia del diritto* (Florence, 1902), 123–30.

[46] Yves Renouard, *Le città italiane dal X al XIV secolo* (Milan, 1976), 2:264–69, 285–88. See also Gino Masi, "I banchieri fiorentini nella vita politica della città sulla fine del Dugento," *Archivio giuridico "Filippo Serafini"* 105 (1931): 57–89.

[47] Giuseppe Petralia, "Sui toscani in Sicilia tra Due e Trecento: La penetrazione sociale e il radicamento nei ceti urbani," in *Commercio, finanza, funzione pubblica: Stranieri in Sicilia e in Sardegna nei secoli XIII–XIV*, ed. Marco Tangheroni (Naples, 1989), 129–218.

[48] Alison Brown, "The Revolution of 1494 in Florence and Its Aftermath: A Reassessment," in *Italy in Crisis: 1494*, ed. Jane Everson and Diego Zancani (Oxford, 2000), 20ff.

administration of state finances.[49] A prime exhibit for the corruption of political power during the republic is Lorenzo de' Medici, who even in his own time was the subject of such accusations, but the fact that the hard evidence for the case against him still eludes modern researchers is a sign of the general historiographical situation with respect to this subject.[50] Historians of Florence tend to take it for granted that the rich and powerful used the state to pursue their own economic interests and to exploit the poor, but this is hardly surprising. The real questions left unanswered are, how did they do this and were they more or less successful than the rich and powerful in other places? Moreover, no one has ever raised the question whether there were economic issues that brought on disagreement among these men and even controversy over different sectorial interests. For on first glance, it does not seem that state economic policy ever generated any real debate between lanaioli and setaioli, between either of these and international merchant-bankers, or between entrepreneurs as a whole and landowners. The city's chroniclers and contemporary historians—so much more numerous for this precapitalist city than for any other, perhaps more than for all the other Italian cities taken together—have nothing at all to say about economic interests in the political life they document so richly.

Hardly any specific instances of conflict of interest have been documented. Legislation in 1393 directed to protecting local cloth producers by imposing high duty charges on cloths imported into the Florentine state ran against the interests of cloth importers (as the many exceptions allowed in the legislation indicate).[51] This legislation, however, was directed to protecting the textile industry in its local market and did not signal the formulation of a consistent and continuing policy. In any event, by the end of the fourteenth century the local market for foreign cloth was not a major interest of importer-exporters. A thesis has also been advanced for the distinct division of lanaioli and setaioli into two factional groups in the early fifteenth century (around, respectively, the Albizzi and the Medici), although the supporting material does not point to a difference over economic policy.[52] It has also been argued that the failure of the galley system

[49] In addition to the discussion above on the floating debt and the tax system, see, for the emoluments of public office, Alison Brown, "Uffici di onore e utile: La crisi del repubblicanesimo a Firenze," *ASI* 161 (2003): 285–321. David Herlihy, in "The Distribution of Wealth in a Renaissance Community: Florence, 1427," in *Towns in Societies: Essays in Economic History and Historical Sociology,* ed. Philip Abrams and E. A. Wrigley (Cambridge, 1978), 144, collects the references of the contemporary chronicler Giovanni Cavalcanti to men who enriched themselves through fraudulent administration.

[50] The most informed statement about the charges against Lorenzo is Alison Brown, "Lorenzo, the Monte and the Seventeen Reformers: Public and Private Interest," in *The Medici in Florence: The Exercise and Language of Power* (Florence, 1992), 151–211.

[51] Franceschi, "Intervento del potere centrale," 897–98.

[52] John F. Padgett and Paul D. McLean, "Economic Credit and Elite Transformation in Renais-

later in the century is at least partly attributable to those Florentines who were able to redirect the activity of the Sea Consuls to land reclamation in the Pisan countryside, where they were building up large estates.[53] On the whole, however, it is difficult to identify conflicting business interests among merchant-bankers, lanaioli, and setaioli, who drove the forward sectors of the economy. Lanaioli and setaioli did not compete for resources, markets, capital, or labor; both were dependent on the same importer-exporters, and men in each of the three kinds of business invested in the others. The almost complete lack of debate among these men about economic issues may in fact explain why none of them ever engaged in an intellectual exploration into what it was that they were doing and why this precapitalist society never generated any real economic theory.

These men must have shared a consensus about what their interests in the economic life of the city were. In studying the political elite that consolidated in reaction to the Ciompi revolt, historians have been preoccupied, on the one hand, with its internal cohesion around patronage networks, clientage systems, and ties binding "relatives, friends and neighbors" (a repeated theme in the literature) and, on the other hand, with the ongoing dialectic between the elite as a whole and the *popolo*—all problems regarded as strong affirmations of a sense of class. They have failed, however, to search for an economic component of social cohesion. Yet the consensus men at the time shared about economic matters extended beyond factional and class boundaries. However vigorously the elite used political power to promote private individual interests, these men were reasonably objective, as we have seen, in establishing the legal validity of contracts throughout the society and in opening their ranks as businessmen to outsiders. It is particularly striking that political infighting within the elite does not seem to have intruded into their business affairs. The city's most successful entrepreneurs in the fifteenth century included Francesco Datini and Filippo di Matteo Strozzi, who managed to avoid formal political involvement, and Giovanni Rucellai, who was regarded with some suspicion by the regime and, it is claimed, subjected to unfair taxation.

Not even exile, after execution the harshest penalty meted out in the often violent factional strife that characterized the political life of the republic, resulted in exclusion from the network. Over a period of fourteen years, from 1387 to 1401, all the Alberti were banished from the city to places where they could continue on in business—Padua, Venice, Rome, London, Bruges, Paris, Montpellier. Operating in

---

sance Florence," forthcoming in the *American Journal of Sociology;* also available on the Internet at http://home.uchicago.edu/~jpadgett/.

[53] Franco Angiolini, "L'arsenale di Pisa fra politica ed economia: Continuità e mutamenti (secoli XV–XVI)," in *Arsenali e città nell'Occidente europeo,* ed. Ennio Concina (Rome, 1987), 69–82.

exile abroad all over Europe, the family cluster of businesses reached even higher levels of prosperity. Likewise, the Ricci, banished in 1400 for their part in a conspiracy, continued in banking abroad, one of them soon becoming depositary of the Apostolic Chamber. In 1433 the Medici were sent off to Padua, Venice, Rome, and Naples, where they probably were able to run their bank just as efficiently as in Florence; when they returned to Florence the next year, they in turn sent their enemies of the Albizzi faction off to no fewer than forty-four places, most of which were important business centers. After the failure of the conspiracy involving the Neroni in 1466, Nerone's two sons were sent to places where the family already had business interests—Francesco to Naples, Dietisalvi to Sicily—while Agnolo Acciaiuoli and his sons were sent to Barletta, and Niccolò di Lorenzo Soderini and his son to Provence, both important commercial centers. Notwithstanding the disaster suffered by the Pazzi as a result of the 1478 conspiracy, several members of the family continued to operate a firm in Valencia. A tentative census made of all exiles during the Medici period, from 1433 to 1494, lists the places where some 150 of these men were sent: more than a third went to cities in central and southern Italy; more than a fourth to cities in the Po valley, including Venice; and yet others to Rome and Avignon—all places of some economic importance on international commercial routes.[54] Later, Cosimo I, for all his authoritarianism, showed a degree of flexibility in dealing with the great bankers in Rome and Lyons whose support of the militant action by exiled rebels continued down to the war against Siena.[55] He and his successors were careful not to go too far in penalizing those merchant-bankers who were declared enemies and even rebels of the state.

A merchant sent into exile found himself subjected to fines and loss of property, separated from friends and relatives, and uprooted from the cultural foundations of his native land, though not necessarily ostracized from the international business community of Florentines abroad. Most were ordered off to places where they could continue in business, which they could hardly have done without access to the network. Through their contacts in the network they could even operate surreptitiously back in Florence itself.[56] The impact of exile on their personal lives too was often tempered by ad hoc arrangements at home that allowed them to rely on friends for the protection of their property from punitive

[54] Alison Brown, "Insiders and Outsiders: The Changing Boundaries of Exile," in *Society and Individual in Renaissance Florence*, ed. William J. Connell (Berkeley and Los Angeles, 2002), 348 (fig. 14.2) and 363–83 (appendix).

[55] Paolo Simoncelli, "Florentine Fuorusciti at the Time of Bindo Altoviti," in *Raphael, Cellini, and a Renaissance Banker: The Patronage of Bindo Altoviti*, ed. Alan Chong, Donatella Pegazzano, and Dimitrios Zikos (Boston, 2003), 308.

[56] As did the Alberti. See Caferro, "L'attività bancaria papale," 722 and n.

taxation and confiscation and for taking legal action on their behalf. Moreover, the annals of Florentine business provide instances of prominent entrepreneurs who had a son or brother sent into exile while they themselves were able to remain at home managing their business, unaffected by the personal and political misfortune of even their closest relatives.

Maybe the historiographical tradition has it right after all—that for these men politics and business were not overlapping spheres.

The Region and the City

At the beginning of this book it was asserted that Florence, for all the orientation of its economy to foreign markets, was very much on the periphery in the geography of international commerce and banking. The city was not located on a major international trade route. To the north and east, the Apennines separated it from the major market area that included the many cities scattered throughout the Po valley and along the Adriatic coast; and central Italy, to the south, was not as highly urbanized and became much less so further south. Moreover, in its own region, perhaps the most urbanized in all of Europe before the Black Death, the links of many of the other Tuscan towns to international trade routes did not pass through Florence. The city lay alongside the mountains at the edge of the region and off the major routes linking the many urban areas to one another and to the sea. Nearby Prato and Pistoia had access to the Arno downstream from Florence, as well as their own routes over the Apennines to Bologna and the Po valley. The only major town that lay beyond Florence upstream along the Arno was Arezzo, and it had routes to the Adriatic as well as alternative routes to the Tyrrhenian Sea. Not only was Florence off the beaten path in the geography of regional and international commerce but it was located in a region that had limited agricultural potential and did not offer the basic raw materials—wool and silk—in sufficient quantity and quality to sustain the major textile industries on which the urban economy depended. In fact, the dynamics that drove Florentine merchants to venture beyond the region and into international markets were, first, the search for wheat to provide food for the city's continually growing population and, second, the need to sustain the wool industry, which employed many of these people, by supplying it with the basic raw materials and finding markets for its finished products. The Arno was the one natural feature that saved the city from relative isolation by linking it both to the sea and to central Italy, giving it a way out of the region to the resources and markets it needed.

In the light of these observations, one might consider Florence a city uprooted from its region, and indeed little enough has been said up to now about the links of the city's economy to the surrounding territory. The city, of course, was not isolated from its region. As a large and rich city, it lived off its countryside for foodstuffs, raw materials, and the products of a few rural industries. The city depended on its countryside for labor as well. The putting-out system of the textile industries did not extend any farther beyond the city's walls than the places nearby where women spun wool, but immigrants from all over Tuscany, and from abroad as far away as northern Europe, were always showing up to find work in a city that by contemporary standards was heavily industrialized. As late as the end of the sixteenth century we still find immigrants employed as silk weavers. The fluctuations in this flow, however, have never been tracked. There is no question that these resources of foodstuffs and labor—what most premodern cities took from their countryside—went a long way toward integrating Florence with its territory, rendering it largely self-sufficient except for the raw materials needed by its basic industries. In this sense the region counted for much in the success of the economy of the capital city. There were other ways, however, in which city and region fit together to create an economic structure.

Urban Geography

Tuscany was one of the most urbanized regions in medieval Europe. The rank-size distribution of its urban centers before the Black Death, in the early fourteenth century fits into the classic pyramid form, with, however, gaps between the upper levels.[57] Florence, with its population of some 100,000, far outnumbered Pisa and Siena, with about 50,000 each; and there was yet another gap between those towns and Lucca, which had between 20,000 and 30,000. Below this level the rankings are more gradual, five towns having between 10,000 and 20,000 (Arezzo, Prato, Pistoia, Volterra, and Cortona) and seven more between 5,000 and 10,000 (Massa Marittima, San Gimignano, Colle di Val d'Elsa, Montepulciano, Montalcino, San Miniato al Tedesco, and Grosseto).

Within just about any other arrangement one wants to impose on these places, however, the position of Florence in the region was eccentric in a way that cut into any economic advantage one might think it would have had. It was not at the geographic center of Tuscany; in fact, the region lacks clear geographic definition. The sea marks its boundary to the west and southward, and mountains separate it from other regions in the north and east, but to the southeast it has no clear demarcation. Within its boundaries the hilly countryside divides the area into

[57] For the population figures here and below, see the figures, tables, diagrams, and maps in Maria Ginatempo and Lucia Sandri, *L'Italia delle città: Il popolamento urbano tra Medioevo e Rinascimento (secoli XIII–XVI)* (Florence, 1990), 148, 224–41.

microregions—the upper Valdarno and the Valdichiana, the lower Valdarno and the Valdinievole, the Valdelsa, the maremme along the Tyrrhenian littoral at Pisa and Grosseto. Even the immediate vicinity of Florence, as Johan Plesner described it in his notable study of the road system in the thirteenth century, "is part of the most complicated group within the entire system of interpenetrating ranges, which come together precisely at this point in a labyrinth of large valleys—this chaos of mountainous bastions."[58] Moreover, the region was politically fragmented. That most of the towns scattered about this region were still autonomous city-states in 1300 goes without saying. Florence had not yet incorporated any one of them into its territory, and it faced serious competitors in the inevitable power struggle that characterized the political life of the times. Finally, the economic life of the region was not organized around a dominant market center. As we have already had occasion to remark, Florence did not serve its region as an international emporium: Lucca, Siena, the towns in the Valdinievole from Prato to Pescia, and the towns in the Valdelsa all had access to the sea and terrestrial routes leading out of the region that bypassed Florence. In short, notwithstanding the rank distribution of this Tuscan collection of towns and cities, these places were not integrated into a collectivity with a dominant central place and a neatly unifying trade network.

The expansion of Florence into a territorial state did not change the urban geography of the region, but that geography changed in the course of the formation of the state, primarily as a result of the Black Death. For this reason, it is convenient to divide that process of territorial expansion into two stages, before and after this event. In the earlier period, Florence had not taken possession of any of the major towns of the region. In the twelfth century it expanded into its immediate countryside, an area that extended upstream on the Arno to Incisa and Figline and downstream as far as Empoli, taking in also the Valdipesa. The city then proceeded slowly over the next century to push its borders northeastward into the Mugello, further upstream along the Arno to Montevarchi, and westward into the Valdelsa to take in Castelfiorentino, Certaldo, and, on the other side of the valley, Poggibonsi. By 1300 Florence had emerged as a major state in the region, fully involved in trying to suppress the feudal lords who remained in power around its borders, competing in power struggles with the other regional city-states, especially Siena, Lucca, and Pisa, and occasionally having to deal with foreign invaders. And it continued to expand, now also motivated by the need to secure provisioning in expectation that further growth of its population would fill the area within its vast new circle of walls. From the Mugello it

---

[58] Johan Plesner, *Una rivoluzione stradale del Dugento* (Copenhagen, 1938), 4.

pushed its borders across the Apennines over the Futa pass into the Romagna, an important source for grain, salt, and raw silk. And to the northwest it took over the rich agricultural flood plain of the Valdinievole, from Fucecchio to Pescia. The cost of this territorial expansion occasioned the fiscal innovations of the early fourteenth century that put the city's finances on a foundation of indirect taxes, forced loans, and, in the 1340s, the funding of the public debt in the Monte. All of the larger urban centers in Tuscany, however, remained for the moment outside this growing state.

Conquest of these towns came only after the Black Death. Florence first took over the valley of the Ombrone, with Prato (1350) and Pistoia (1352), as well as the area west of the Valdelsa, with Colle (1349), San Gimignano (1353), Volterra (1361), and San Miniato al Tedesco (1370). In the 1380s, it extended its territory over the Apennines in the Romagna to include Marradi and Modigliana, and the conquest of Arezzo in 1384 gave it a foothold in the Valdichiana. In the 1390s Florence had to deal with the threat posed by the invasion of northern Tuscany by Giangaleazzo Visconti, whose sudden death in 1402 released another spurt of expansionist activity—to the southeast into the Valdichiana as far as Montepulciano (1404) and Cortona (1411) and westward to Pisa (1406) and Sarzana (1409). The purchase of Livorno from Genoa in 1421 completed Florence's control over the coast at the Arno delta, and twenty years later it rounded out its territory to the southeast with the purchase of Borgo Sansepolcro and the occupation of the upper Valtiberina (1441), including another foothold over the Apennines at Sestino, in the Marche. The conquest of northern Tuscany was virtually complete by the mid-fifteenth century, and with the annexation of Siena a century later, in 1555, the new duchy of the Medici embraced all of modern Tuscany except the republic of Lucca, the lordship of the Cybo Malaspina over Massa and Carrara in Versilia, the lordship of the Appiani over Piombino and the island of Elba, several miniscule pockets at the edges, on the borders with Lazio and the Lunigiana, and the places along the Tyrrhenian coast where Spain had fortresses.[59]

The urban system under Florentine control by the mid-fifteenth century, however, was not what it had been a century earlier, before the Black Death (table 7.1). The plague had been especially severe for the cities and towns of Tuscany; besides radically reducing their populations, it had left their rank distribution even more askew. From its population of some 100,000 in the early fourteenth century, Florence dropped down to fluctuate between 40,000 and 70,000 through the rest of the period covered in this book. We have encountered many cities whose population grew by two and more times from the fourteenth to the sixteenth

---

[59] Specific details about these states can be found in Diaz, *Il Granducato di Toscana*, 165–66.

century; some of these were new or revitalized capital cities (Avignon, Rome, Naples), and some were rapidly growing emporia (Valencia, Geneva, Lyons, Marseilles, Antwerp). The comparatively modest growth of Florence is another sign of its provincial status as both capital and emporium. The large gap remained between Florence and the two next largest Tuscan cities, Lucca and Siena, whose populations hardly ever exceeded 20,000 in the same period, and yet another gap separated the five towns that had a population fluctuating between 5,000 and 10,000 (Pisa, followed by Pistoia, Prato, Arezzo, and Cortona). Moreover, by the criteria of the 1427 catasto, these five towns plus Volterra had a disproportionately small share of the wealth of the state, collectively only between one-fifth and one-sixth that of Florence.[60] Tuscany had fewer centers of this size than before the Black Death; furthermore, the urban system was all the weaker because two of its major centers, Pisa and Siena, had by that time lost their former international status: the maritime power of Pisa ended with the victory of Genoa at Meloria in 1284, by which time the Sienese were rapidly retiring from international banking after losing their grip on papal finances to the Florentines. The much smaller town of San Gimignano also went into economic decline as a result of the collapse of demand in international markets for the saffron from its area. Lucca alone maintained its international status through the sixteenth century, but it also maintained its independence.

In short, the Tuscany that Florence came to dominate after the Black Death was no longer one of Europe's most urbanized areas. The percentage of the total population that lived in towns with more then 5,000 inhabitants fell by almost one-half, from about 30 percent to close to 16 percent, never to rise much higher during the rest of the period covered by this book. In fact, Tuscany and Sicily were the only areas in Italy that saw a decline in urbanization during the two centuries following the Black Death. Even the Romagna had as many towns with a population of 5,000 to 10,000 as before, and both the Marche and the combined region of Umbria-Lazio had twice as many. In the sixteenth century the Po valley triangle defined by Milan, Venice, and Bologna was much more urbanized than Tuscany, with both Milan and Venice being much larger than Florence, five other cities being of about the same size, and some half-dozen more with populations of above 15,000—a contrast that puts into relief the much greater internal commercial potential of this region as compared with Tuscany, not to mention the easier transport throughout this area, spread out over a valley floor, than in the hilly "chaos" of Tuscany. Tuscany's place on the map of urbanization in Italy

---

[60] David Herlihy and Christiane Klapisch-Zuber, *Les toscans et leurs familles: Une étude du catasto florentin de 1427* (Paris, 1978), 243.

TABLE 7.1
Population of Tuscan Towns ca. 1300 and in the First Half of the Sixteenth Century

Approximate Population	Ca. 1300	First Half of the Sixteenth Century
100,000	Florence	
50,000–70,000		Florence
50,000	Siena	
	Pisa	
20,000–30,000	Lucca	
10,000–20,000	Arezzo	Lucca
	Prato	Siena
	Pistoia	
	Volterra	
	Cortona	
5,000–10,000	Massa Marittima	Pisa
	San Gimignano	Arezzo
	Colle	Prato
	Montepulciano	Pistoia
	Montalcino	Cortona
	San Miniato	
	Grosseto	

SOURCE: Maria Ginatempo and Lucia Sandri, *L'Italia delle città: Il popolamento urbano tra Medioevo e Rinascimento (secoli XIII–XVI)* (Florence, 1990), 148.

about 1600 appears much reduced, whether one looks at its urbanization compared with that of the relatively backward regions of the Romagna, the Marche, Umbria, and Lazio or at the population of its capital city (70,000) as compared with Venice (139,000), Milan (120,000), and Genoa (up to 100,000), three other cities with a glorious economic past, or the newly growing cities of Rome, Palermo (both just over 100,000), and Naples (281,000).[61]

Industrial Resources

The survey of Tuscany at the outset of this book emphasized the natural resources that gave rise to two industries that helped drive the economic development of the region—cloth and metalwork. By the time Florence was extending its control over northern Tuscany in the later fourteenth century, both these industries were in decline. The production of wool was of major importance during the early stage in the rise of local economies, but with the expansion of the commercial revolution and the widening geographic reach of international trade, the development of the industry in general throughout Mediterranean Europe eventually, by the fourteenth century, left Tuscany behind. The market for its mediocre cloths shrank to an area that hardly extended beyond the towns where the industry was located.

[61] Population figures are from Jan de Vries, *European Urbanization, 1500–1800* (London, 1984), app. 1.

The Florentine industry expanded, but only by shifting to imported raw materials; by the fourteenth century it had largely abandoned those produced locally that had given rise to the industry in the first place. Imports from beyond Tuscany included the secondary raw materials as well as the wool itself. Alum was now being supplied by the Genoese from their monopoly over its production at Phocaea in Anatolia; San Gimignano lost its importance as a major producer of saffron to the Abruzzi; and later, in the fifteenth century, the woad and madder produced in the area of Arezzo and in the upper Valtiberina, around Borgo Sansepolcro, seem to have lost their markets abroad to products coming out of Lombardy and southwestern France. In short, the Tuscany that Florence had brought under its dominion by the fifteenth century lacked much of the economic vitality in this industrial sector that it had had two centuries earlier. Moreover, with respect to raw materials, the industry in Florence was largely uprooted from its region.

The natural mineral resources of Tuscany, which had been an important foundation for economic expansion during the commercial revolution, also were drying up in the fourteenth century. Many of the mines, such as the silver mines at Montieri and others in the vicinity of Massa Marittima, simply gave out, and limited technology rendered further exploitation of others more difficult and therefore more costly.[62] The iron industry, by way of contrast, continued to prosper thanks to a plentiful supply of the raw material, the mines on Elba being the largest in the Mediterranean. The importance of the industry in Florence itself has already been noted. The major capital investment in the industry focused on the *magone*, the operations organized by entrepreneurs for the consignment of ore at one of the ports, where it was delivered under the auspices of the lords of Piombino. The magona saw to its distribution throughout the countryside for processing and to the further distribution of iron and iron products within the specific sales area specified by the contract. Not much is known about Florentine investors' interest in these magone except for the ones that the Medici had at Pisa and at Pietrasanta, documented by accounts for the years 1489–92, which supplied markets in Florence, Rome, and Naples.[63] As we shall see below, Cosimo I, in characteristic fashion, brought this traffic under more central control and ex-

---

[62] A. Mencione, "Studi antichi e recenti sulle miniere medievali in Toscana: Alcune considerazioni," *Ricerche storiche* 14 (1984): 203–26.

[63] Piero Ginori Conti, *Le magone della vena del ferro di Pisa e di Pietrasanta sotto la gestione di Piero dei Medici e comp. (1489–1492)* (Florence, 1939). For the magona contracted by a Pisan merchant earlier in the century, see Sergio Tognetti and Patrizia Meli, *Il principe e il mercante nella Toscana del Quattrocento: Il Magnifico Signore di Piombino Jacopo III Appiani e le aziende Maschiani di Pisa* (Florence, 2006), 89–104.

tended his initiatives to the processing of the ore in various places in the countryside.

Tuscany is also richly endowed with stone of all kinds, a natural resource that gave rise to a major industry within the local economy of Florence. Good building stone was found even within the city (where today the Boboli Gardens are located) and to the south, just outside the city walls, in the hills on the left bank of the Arno. The hills north and east of the city, from Fiesole to Settignano, were dotted with quarries of *pietra serena,* a gray stone that was used extensively in the fifteenth century for decorative architectural details, and Fiesole, the seat of a large diocese, derived much of its economic vitality from this activity. Probably no other city in Europe has as easy access to stone with this range of quality as Florence, and its use for building increased the labor component of the construction industry qualitatively as well as quantitatively. Florence has been called a city of stone, which is also to say that it was a city, as few others were, of stone carvers and architects.

Farther away were quarries of marble—green on Monte Ferrato, north of Prato; red at Monsummano, in the Valdinievole, the Chianti, and other places; and white in the Apuan Alps above Carrara. Green and red marble were used in relatively small quantities as decorative stonework, but the white marble at Carrara was a major resource for architecture and sculpture. These quarries had ceased to be worked after the demise of the Roman Empire, but beginning in the twelfth century quarrying again became a major activity in the region, with demand coming from the cathedrals going up in Pisa, Lucca, and Florence.

Florentines were by far the most prominent of the outsiders from these and other towns who went to Carrara looking for marble and working the quarries. For the few prestigious buildings erected in the early centuries of Florence's expansion, marble was taken from preexisting Roman buildings, but when work got under way for enlarging the cathedral at the end of the thirteenth century, a works operation was set up on a scale that permitted it to take initiatives to obtain marble directly from the quarries at Carrara. Construction at the cathedral went on until the completion of the cupola in 1436, and twice during this time the project was enlarged, resulting in the largest cathedral in Christendom. In order to get the enormous quantities of marble it took to face the building, the cathedral works put into place an efficient supply channel based on contracts with entrepreneurs who saw to the working of the quarries and the transport of cut stone by sea to Pisa, by river to Lastra a Signa, just outside Florence, and then overland to the city. The cathedral warehouse became in effect a source of supply for the entire city, both the public and the private market. Marble was thus available for the extensive sculptural programs at the cathedral and at Orsanmichele, and private clients could obtain it to furnish their homes and chapels with sculpture and other decorative work in marble. In this way delivery of the raw material to the city provided the foundation for one of the city's most distinctive artisan traditions. The reopening of the quarries around Carrara, in fact, has been called "as decisive an event in the history of western European art as the development of painting in an oil medium in the Netherlands"[64]—and in art history that "event" is best documented by what happened in Florence.

The widespread demand for marble sculpture throughout Italy and Europe during the Renaissance stimulated initiatives by the inhabitants of Carrara to work the quarry sites for themselves, and slowly over the later fifteenth and sixteenth centuries a local industry emerged that generated a tradition of quarrying and working stone. The town's population grew to about two thousand inhabitants during the second half of the sixteenth century. This development, however, fell outside the political and economic reach of Florence. Carrara belonged to the miniscule principality of the Cybo-Malaspina family, whose capital was at nearby Massa. In 1564 the marquis set up an organization to regulate production by the quarriers and to contract for the selling of cut stone with Genoese merchants, some of whom went on to buy quarries as capitalist investors. The orientation of the local quarrying industry to international markets was therefore through Genoa, outside the Florentine state. It was precisely at this time, during the 1560s, that Cosimo I, anxious to find a supply of marble in his own state, opened the quarries at Seravezza, in Versilia, just a short distance south of Carrara, but this operation was organized primarily to supply his own building and sculptural projects and those of the two sons who succeeded him. At the beginning of the seventeenth century these quarries were largely abandoned.[65]

Industrial activities based on other natural resources of the region attracted Florentine investment or grew in response to demand from the city. In economic importance these ranged from salt, a necessity for everyone, to mineral waters, enjoyed at spas by the privileged few, and they included the mining of copper and the production of paper, ceramics, and glass. Salt was to be had from the pans along the coast around Pisa and Grosseto, as well as from mines of rock salt and springs of brackish waters near Volterra. In 1265 Volterra granted privileges for the export of salt to Florence. As to mineral waters, the enthusiasm for their cura-

---

[64] Nicholas Penny, *The Materials of Sculpture* (New Haven, CT, 1993), 52.

[65] The most comprehensive survey of the development of the quarries at Carrara is Christiane Klapisch-Zuber, *Les maîtres du marbre: Carrare 1300–1600* (Paris, 1969). See also Marco Della Pina, "I Del Medico: L'ascesa di una famiglia nell'area economico-sociale della produzione marmifera carrarese," in *Ricerche di storia moderna* 2 (1979): 141–224; and Luigi Zangheri, "La breccia medicea detta di Seravezza," in *Le pietre delle città d'Italia: Atti della giornata di studi in onore di Francesco Rodolico*, ed. Daniela Lamberini (Florence, 1995), 59–71.

tive properties led to the opening of many spas throughout the peninsula in the fourteenth and fifteenth centuries; the Tuscan spas were by far the most numerous and the most frequented among those in central and northern Italy. Sixty sites have been identified as open during the period. Running a spa was a minor economic activity in the rural places where they were located. The business required the construction of facilities and arrangements for management, and it invited both taxation and legislation defining rights and laying down regulations. Most were concentrated in Sienese territory, but Florentines were the most numerous visitors. "Here there are many Florentines," a friend wrote to Francesco Datini from the spa at Petriolo in 1410, "and there are so many people that one can't live; but I am doing well and have a good place and am well served; however, there are some that God alone knows how they are doing."[66]

The particular quality of the water in the area of Colle di Val d'Elsa explains the location there of one of Italy's strongest paper industries in the late Middle Ages. The production of rag paper in Italy got under way at Fabriano, in the Marche, in the thirteenth century, and from there the industry spread elsewhere. Colle was one of the first places where immigrant artisans from Fabriano showed up. What attracted them must have been the water, which was of decisive importance, not so much as a source of power to run the stamping mills as for its qualities that minimized unwanted residues on the machinery and in the paper itself during the pulping process. A less important advantage of the region for this industry was the population density, which guaranteed the ready availability of the basic raw material—rags—and markets for the final product.

The industry at Colle was already well established and attracting Florentine investment by the time of its earliest documentation, in 1319. In that year Bandino de' Rossi owned buildings that were used for making paper, and later the heirs of Attaviano Brunelleschi owned five of the twelve shares in the operation of a paper mill, the other investors being from Siena and Colle. Surviving letters written about 1400 by manufacturers in Colle to Datini firms in Pisa and Florence document the export of paper throughout the western Mediterranean, from Genoa to Seville. In the mid-fifteenth century this connection opened up the possibility for at least one effort of local papermakers themselves to move into international commerce: the brothers Giovanni and Iacopo da Colle had a firm in Pisa in partnership with the Salviati that had a branch in Lisbon. In 1478 two printers had presses in Colle, just seven years after printing was introduced in Florence. A paper mill was opened in Pescia in 1481, and later one was opened in Prato, but at

---

[66] Fabrizio Borelli, *Le saline di Volterra nel Granducato di Toscana* (Florence, 2000); Didier Boisseuil, *Le thermalisme en Toscane à la fin du Moyen Âge* (Rome, 2002), quotation from 180n.

the beginning of the seventeenth century 90 percent of the paper produced in Tuscany came from Colle, which had seventeen mills, compared with two each in Pescia and Prato. In 1548 the manufacturers in Colle organized themselves into a protective guild, complete with statutes, officials, and a warehouse, in a common effort to secure the supply and distribution of raw materials, maintain standards, and prevent monopolization. Although papermakers owned their own mills and made arrangements with merchants for the marketing of their products, the presence of the guild discouraged outside investment; the new guild had to appeal to the ducal government for financing, which was arranged through the Monte di Pietà and the wool guild at Florence.[67]

Medieval archaeology, a relatively new discipline in Italy and one with a particularly sharp focus on Tuscany, has brought to light two other regional industries heretofore little known—ceramics and glassmaking. The growth of both in the later fourteenth and fifteenth centuries is evidence of increasing demand for consumer goods, and markets for the former extended beyond the region. Ceramics require the right kind of clays, and glass requires sand with silica content, and essential to both was the fuel readily available from the region's heavily wooded areas. Through Pisa, producers had access to what had to be imported—tin from England and elsewhere in northern Europe for majolica and soda ash from Syria and other places in the Levant for glass, although some soda ash of inferior quality was to be found in the vicinity of Piombino.

Ceramics were produced in numerous places throughout Tuscany from the thirteenth century on, and the industry underwent remarkable growth as the quality of its products evolved from the archaic kind to Renaissance tin-glazed majolica. It improved the technology of glazings and pigments, and it expanded the functional and decorative typology of its products in response to steadily growing demand. The area of Montelupo, downstream on the Arno with easy access to the Florentine market nearby, became one of the most important centers in Italy for the production of ceramics. Potters there developed a distinctive style of high artistic quality, and they showed considerable talent in responding to competition from elsewhere. Beginning in the late fourteenth century Floren-

---

[67] Renzo Sabbatini, "Una manifattura in cerca di protezione, capitali, capacità imprenditoriale: Le cartiere di Colle dalla riforma dei Capitoli alla fine dell'Appalto (1548–1749)," in *Colle di Val d'Elsa: Diocesi e città tra '500 e '600*, ed. Pietro Nencini (Castelfiorentino, 1994), 307–40; Marco Piccardi, *La cartiera de La Briglia e la manifattura della carta nel granducato di Toscana* (Prato, 1994). On the earlier period, before 1600, see Judith C. Brown, *In the Shadow of Florence: Provincial Society in Renaissance Pescia* (Oxford, 1982), 108–9, 113–14; Curzio Bastianoni, "Le cartiere di Colle Val d'Elsa e i loro segni nella prima metà del secolo XIV," in *Produzione e commercio della carta e del libro, secc. XIII–XVIII*, ed. Simonetta Cavaciocchi (Florence, 1992), 221–32; and Oretta Muzzi, "Attività artigianali e cambiamenti politici a Colle Val d'Elsa prima e dopo la conquista fiorentina," in *La società fiorentina nel Basso Medioevo per Elio Conti*, ed. Renzo Ninci (Rome, 1995), 221–53.

tines developed a taste for Hispano-Moresque ceramics with metallic glazes from Valencia, which they imported in large quantities, some made to order on specific commission, but during the fifteenth century potters at Montelupo succeeded in cutting into this market with imitations. Moreover, they eventually drove out the competition altogether by elaborating on the Hispano-Moresque style in their own distinctive way, advancing from import substitution to stylistic innovation. About 1500 production of majolica got under way at Cafaggiolo, in the Mugello, north of Florence, and it too is famed for its distinctive style. There is some evidence that Florentine entrepreneurs made investments for the marketing of the products of Montelupo. In 1490 Francesco Antinori made a collective contract with no fewer than twenty-three potters there committing them to provide him with all their output for three years; and three years later, in 1493, the company of Giuliano Salviati, at Pisa, shipped sixty-three hundred pieces of Montelupo ceramics to Constantinople.[68] Archaeological work has turned up products of Montelupo abroad, from North Africa to northern Europe. More ceramics from Montelupo were imported into England in the sixteenth century than from any other place, and Tuscan potters themselves turned up in Lyons and Antwerp. On several occasions in the second decade of the seventeenth century Cosimo II ordered tiles of Montelupo as gifts to Marie de' Medici for floors of the Luxembourg Palace in Paris.[69]

The area around Gambassi and Montaione, in the Valdarno, had one of the densest concentrations of glassworks in Italy. The industry can be documented back to the early thirteenth century, and by 1276 there were at least eight glassworks in operation. Production increased considerably in the later fourteenth and fifteenth centuries. Glassmakers from Gambassi emigrated throughout Italy: they are documented as having set up operations in the south, at Rome, Naples, and Palermo; in the Marche at Urbino; and in many of the major cities across the Po valley, from Bologna to Milan and Venice itself. They were the most numerous documented group of foreign workers at Murano, although their presence seems to have been fleeting, perhaps because they went to learn techniques, not to work permanently. Émigrés from the Valdelsa probably founded the industry in Florence, where we have already encountered them among the more prosperous artisans of the city, and they established another major center of production in the

[68] Marco Spallanzani, "Maioliche di Montelupo per Costantinopoli (1493)," *Faenza* 93 (2007): 36–42.

[69] Guido Vannini, "Produzione ceramica e mercato nel 'mediovaldarno fiorentino' fra tradizione medievale e innovazione rinascimentale," in *Le ceramiche di Roma e del Lazio in età medievale e moderna*, vol. 4, ed. Elisabetta De Minicis and Gabriella Maetzke (Rome, 2002), 18–32; Timothy Wilson, "Le maioliche," in *Commercio e cultura mercantile*, ed. Franco Franceschi, Richard A. Goldthwaite, and Reinhold C. Mueller, vol. 4 of *Il Rinascimento italiano e l'Europa*, ed. G. L. Fontana and L. Molà (Treviso, 2007), 227–45.

upper Valdarno. By the end of the fifteenth century Tuscany had more centers of production than any other region in Italy.

These glassworks could be large operations by artisan standards. Accommandita contracts survive for sizable investments by several makers of glassware, one of *fl.*450 for an operation in Figline Valdarno in 1546 and another of *sc.*800 in Pisa in 1573. A project to establish a glassworks in the Mugello in 1481 envisaged an operation with eleven workers and a production of sixty-six thousand glasses a month plus several thousand other objects. In 1605 an operation at Gambassi had twenty-one employees. These Tuscan manufactories produced glass for daily use, not artistic wares, and there is no evidence that their markets extended beyond the towns of Tuscany.[70]

From the mid-fourteenth to the mid-fifteenth century new efforts were made in the Sienese state—as throughout Europe—to locate and open new mines, driven by shortages in silver, by the demands of new military technology, and by problems in the supply of alum from the Levant. Much of the technical know-how and even some of the initiatives came from outside the region and outside Italy, and on the whole they met with only modest success.[71] One of these areas was the Val di Cecina, just west of Volterra, an area rich in mineral resources but not extensively worked until the mid-fifteenth century. The searches for new mines were directed especially to securing supplies of alum, since imports by the Genoese from the traditional sources in the Levant fell off with the rise of the Ottoman Empire. From 1441 to 1482 eight prospectors, three of them Florentine, are known to have made requests for searches with the assurance of enjoying mining privileges in the hope of finding gold, silver, copper, lead, tin, iron, and alum. One of these prospectors, a Sienese who in 1470 won special privileges from the commune of Volterra, worked in partnership with two men from Volterra and three from Florence—Gino di Neri Capponi, Antonio di Bernardo Giugni, and Bernardo di Cristoforo Buonagiusti. The concessions granted him after his discovery of a mine at Castelnuovo, south of Volterra, aroused factional tensions in the city that had repercussions in Florence, leading to the military intervention by Lorenzo de' Medici and the infamous sack of the subject city in 1472. Capponi

[70] Marja Mendera, *La produzione di vetro nella Toscana bassomedievale: Lo scavo della vetreria di Germagnana in Valdelsa* (Florence, 1989), chs. 2–3; idem, "Produrre vetro in Valdelsa: L'officina vetraria di Germagnana (Gambassi-Florence) (secc. XIII–XIV)," in *Archeologia e storia della produzione del vetro pre-industriale,* ed. Mendera (Florence, 1990), 15–50; Guido Taddei, *L'arte del vetro in Firenze e nel suo dominio* (Florence, 1954), 20–23 (for the accomandita contracts); Marco Spallanzani, "Un progetto per la lavorazione del vetro in Mugello nel secolo XV," *ASI* 140 (1982): 569–602.

[71] Gabriella Piccinni, "Le miniere del senese alla fine del Medioevo: Contributo alla messa a punto della cronologia dell'abbandono e della ripresa delle attività estrattive," in *La Toscane et les toscans,* 239–54.

had earlier entered into a partnership with Tommaso di Lorenzo Soderini, Luigi di Piero Guicciardini, Paolo di Domenico dal Pozzo Toscanelli, Michele di ser Piero Migliorelli, and the prospector Tommaso di ser Bonifazio Marinai, all Florentines, for a mining enterprise at Montecatini, to the west of Volterra. The profits of this venture in one five-year period, from 1479 to 1484, amounted to no less than *fl*.21,936. These new discoveries led to the increased mining of copper and other minerals needed for the production of alum and sulfates used in dyeing and for the preparation of medicines. The copper mines remained a major activity until the nineteenth century.[72]

Agriculture

Finally, there are the resources for agriculture, hardly the least important sector of the regional economy inasmuch as it provided the necessities for life itself but perhaps, as Giuliano Pinto has suggested, last in importance in any discussion of the relevance of the natural resources of the region to the economic growth of Florence.[73] Topography, soil, and climate limited agricultural development in the region; except for those crops cultivated for industrial purposes mentioned above, the sector was not oriented to interregional or international trade. Tuscany has an extremely varied countryside, ranging from mountains to flood plains and swamps, with a balance very much in favor of the former. About 20 percent of the area is mountainous, about two-thirds hilly, and only about 10 percent flatland; much of the latter, with its malaria swamps and sand dunes—along the coast from the Lunigiana to the maremma of Grosseto and inland in the lower Valdarno around Fucecchio and in the Valdichiana—was, before modern times, unhealthy. Moreover, most of the land is poor for farming, being arid and having topsoil with little depth. Yet the area is not without some positive features. The grazing lands of the maremma in the

---

[72] A. Lisini, "Notizie delle miniere della Maremma toscana e leggi per l'estrazione dei metalli nel Medioevo," *Bullettino senese di storia patria*, n.s., 6 (1935): 185–256; Gioacchino Volpe, "Montieri: Costituzione politica, struttura sociale e attività economica d'una terra mineraria toscana nel XIII secolo," *Maremma: Bollettino della Società Storica Maremmana* 1 (1924): 26–130; Guido Pampaloni, "La miniera del rame di Montecatini Val di Cecina: La legislazione mineraria di Firenze e i Marinai di Prato," *Archivio storico pratese* 51 (1975), fascicle 2, pp. 3–169; Enrico Fiumi, *L'impresa di Lorenzo de' Medici contro Volterra (1472)* (Florence, 1948). On Lorenzo's role in the events leading to the sack of 1472, see Riccardo Fubini, "Lorenzo de' Medici e Volterra," in *Quattrocento fiorentino: Politica diplomazia cultura* (Pisa, 1996), 123–39.

[73] Giuliano Pinto, "L'economia della Toscana nella seconda metà del Duecento," in *Toscana medievale: Paesaggi e realtà sociali* (Florence, 1993), 13. Pinto and Giovanni Cherubini have written extensively on all aspect of the agricultural sector—its foundation in the physical character of the region, the economic utilization of these resources, and the social and cultural world of the people who worked the land. For viticulture, see Charles de La Roncière, *Tra preghiera e rivolta: Le folle toscane nel XIV secolo* (Rome, 1993), 17–47.

southwest were, even before reclamation, extensive enough to permit trans-humance, and this increased the possibility of efficient utilization of much of the highlands all along the Apennines, from the Garfagnana to the Casentino and into Umbria, for raising sheep and cattle, an activity important for supplying food for human consumption as well as wool and hides for industry. The many weirs, most connected to mills, all along the Arno in the vicinity of Florence and the marshes downstream around Fucecchio provided a plentiful supply of freshwater fish.

The limitation of the land for the cultivation of grains, the staff of life, was the basic problem in the performance of the agricultural sector of an economy that by medieval standards was highly urbanized. The problem was particularly acute for Florence, whose territorial expansion, however much it was driven by political considerations, can be read as an effort to secure provisioning by bringing the relatively fertile valley floors of the Arno and its near tributaries under the city's direct control. Already in the thirteenth century Florence had extended its rule over the Valdipesa and downstream along the Arno as far as Empoli and into the Valdelsa, and upstream in the Valdarno it had built new market towns at San Giovanni Valdarno and Castelfranco di Sopra. The big push, however, came after 1300, by which time the city had reached a population estimated at more than 100,000, making it one of the very largest in Europe, and was building a new circle of walls eight and a half kilometers long enclosing more than six hundred hectares to increase the urban area (exclusive of the river) fivefold, presumably in anticipation of further growth of boom proportions. It took over the Mugello, laying out new market towns at Scarperia (1306) and, over the crest of the Apennines, at Firenzuola (1332), giving access to grain supplies from the Romagna. In the 1320s it moved into the Valdinievole, taking in much of the lower Valdarno, and then it moved further into the upper Valdarno, building a new market town at Terranuova (1337). Yet, notwithstanding this conquest of some of Tuscany's most fertile land in the Arno valley, the territory controlled by Florence produced only enough wheat to feed the city for five months out of a year, according to the estimate made by the grain dealer Domenico Lenzi in his chronicle of the grain market during the years from 1320 to 1335. Supplies from other places in Tuscany, above all from Siena, were hardly sufficient to make up the balance. The resulting search for grain in foreign markets was, as we have seen, one of the chief dynamics that gave rise, already in the thirteenth century, to foreign trade with places all around the western Mediterranean, including especially Sicily, Puglia, and North Africa.

Down to 1348 the steadily mounting pressure on the surrounding land to produce what was most needed—grain—led, as in so many places all over Europe at the time, to the less efficient use of land that already had limited potential for agriculture. The release of this pressure in 1348 virtually revolutionized the sector, since land was withdrawn from the cultivation of grain and put to use in ways more suitable to its nature. One result was the greater diffusion of viticulture and hence the increased production of the beverage that, with its caloric content, complemented wheat as an essential component of the basic diet for survival. Olive trees began to appear, slowly transforming the landscape into what we see today, as did fig trees, important for yielding a fruit that could be preserved for a long time. Furthermore, it was now possible to raise animals, so that meat too showed up much more often on the plates even of people of modest status. The reduction of population prompted Siena to promote increased transhumance in its maremma, and this opened up the possibility of herding more animals, both sheep and cattle, in the upland zones stretching along the Apennines from Lucca to the Casentino and the Valtiberina and extending into central Italy and even over the crest into Emilia, the Romagna, and the Marche. This more efficient utilization of these semimountainous areas increased the supply of animal products for human consumption as well as for the wool and leather industries. Finally, the diffusion of sericulture in the fifteenth century, which provided a raw material for the Florentine industry, also increased the efficiency of the agricultural sector.

The growth of the population across the fifteenth and sixteenth centuries, while never reaching its earlier height, renewed pressures to maintain adequate grain supplies. But conditions had changed in two fundamental ways, so that these renewed pressures were not disruptive of the promiscuous and more efficient agriculture that had developed in the meantime. First, the government, being larger and more powerful, was in a better position to take action. Over the half-century following the Black Death the further expansion of the state into the upper Valdarno to Arezzo (1384) and Cortona (1411) and downstream into the Pisan maremma (1406) brought two other fertile areas under direct control. The regional vicariates through which the republic ruled its territory had extensive powers to intervene in matters of food supply to the capital, overriding the traditional authority of subject towns in their immediate countryside. On occasion in the early fifteenth century the state was even in a position to grant concessions to Genoese and Catalan merchants for grain purchases in the Pisan maremma. Supply and demand in the grain market were often close to a precarious balance as a result of frequent severe shortages—at least one every decade over the fifteenth century—and a slowly growing population, but the pressures were never so great that the land freed from the inefficient cultivation of grain after the Black Death reverted to that use.

The second condition that rendered less critical the problem of provisioning a population slowly approaching its earlier height was the safety valve of a more efficient maritime commercial service that offered lower transportation costs and access to the granaries of northern Europe. The so-called transport revolution of the later fourteenth century cut the costs of importing bulky inexpensive goods, such as wheat, and created a more vigorous trading area in the western Mediterranean, facilitating access to supply, while the absorption of Pisa and Livorno into the state guaranteed permanent port faculties. And the government had the international network at its disposal to locate needed supplies, as it did during a severe shortage in 1411–12, when it sent out some 150 letters to places outside of Tuscany, including Naples, Palermo, Barcelona, Arles, Montpellier, and Avignon, as well as beyond the Mediterranean to Lisbon, Bruges, and London.[74]

Demographic pressures continued to grow in the sixteenth century, but the city's population never came close to what it had been two centuries earlier, and the region was much less urbanized. In any event, the government gained an ever more secure control over supply. Land reclamation in the areas of Pisa, Fucecchio, and the Valdichiana increased local production, and the conquest of the Sienese state in 1555 brought an important source of wheat under Florence's direct control. Finally, one of the objectives in building the port at Livorno was the possibility, in times of need, of plugging into the growing Mediterranean traffic of grain from the North Sea.

In the fifteenth and sixteenth centuries bread, meat, wine, and oil constituted the basic diet of Florentine working people. In the budget Guasparre Parigini drew up in 1481 for the operation of the aforementioned glassworks in the Mugello, the entry for the daily ration of food to be provided for the eight artisans included not only bread, salt, vinegar, oil, and vegetables but also fresh meat three times a day, red wine with the principal meal, and white wine in the morning while at work and again at night. The agricultural sector performed sufficiently well to provide most of these things in normal times for the reduced urban population after the Black Death. The provisioning mechanisms of the state functioned sufficiently well to assure that wheat, and not inferior grains, was available for the making of bread when the local supply gave out. In short, few food products other than exotic items were imported, the principal ones being special wines, above all from the Campania, and animals from Puglia (following the contemporaneous expansion of transhumance in the Neapolitan kingdom under the Aragonese).

---

[74] Giuliano Pinto, "Commercio del grano e politica annonaria nella Toscana del Quattrocento: La corrispondenza dell'ufficio fiorentino dell'Abbondanza negli anni 1411–1412," in *Città e spazi economici nell'Italia comunale* (Bologna, 1996), 97–122.

Economic Integration

STATE INITIATIVES   The only study of the market infrastructure within Florentine territory is Charles Marie de La Roncière's for the *contado,* the area within the immediate countryside over which the city had established its rule before the Black Death, in the fourteenth century.[75] By this time the government had long established its authority throughout this area, eliminating feudal and manorial jurisdictions and subjecting the population to taxation, and the redirection of traffic from the hills to the now secure and safe valley floors generated a strong market structure. The state had a general policy, at least in principle, to improve and maintain roads and bridges, to assure the navigability of the Arno, to regulate market standards, to police traffic, and, of course, to expand its tax base. It built new towns with privileges to host periodic fairs—at Castelfranco di Sopra (1299), San Giovanni (1302), and Terranova (1337) along the Arno, at Scarperia in the Mugello (1306), and at Firenzuola (1332) over the Apennines in the Romagna—to tighten the market network in the effort to better assure provisioning of food supplies at a time when its population was growing. In practice, the policy was halting and not altogether effective in establishing the capital city's complete domination, in part because of hesitancy to push too hard against local interests, and much of the supervision was left to local authorities. In the private sector, however, local and regional merchants built up an effective network facilitating trade between localities, between them and local market centers, and between these and the capital and places even beyond Tuscany. Some of these merchants operated out of Florence, trading chiefly in grain, wine, meat, and oil, the essential components of the diet of the time. De La Roncière has described the sophisticated business practices of these men: they worked through partnerships to gain greater flexibility; they had knowledge of accounting; they had ways to handle long-term credit for both themselves and their clients; and they could conduct trade over distances, some extending well beyond the immediate region.

As it expanded into other areas, the government of the republic eliminated what feudal authority remained and effectively established its dominance in military, judicial, and fiscal matters. It also left much local communal administration in place, hesitating to intrude too far on the interest of local elites. In the historiography of the city the trends of scholarly judgment about this contradictory policy have been conditioned by preoccupation with the question whether

[75] Charles Marie de La Roncière, *Firenze e le sue campagne nel Trecento: Mercanti, produzione, traffici* (Florence, 2005). The most intelligent assessment of the economic role of the new towns founded in this region is that of Giuliano Pinto, "Il comune di Firenze e le 'terre nuove': Aspetti della politica cittadina," in *Le terre nuove,* ed. David Friedman and Paolo Pirillo (Florence, 2004), 153–62.

something like the modern state was emerging, and this focus on political power has left problems of economic integration in the dark. In commercial matters, it is anachronistic to expect that the overriding interest of Florence was to establish a monopoly on indirect taxation and a degree of integration. Its regulations and direct controls were often unsystematic, varying from place to place according to what it could impose on subject towns with different traditions, so that in the end some local control of these places over their countryside was left in place. Still, the interest of the capital city clearly dominated. Thus, for instance, it affirmed the regional monopoly of the city's wool industry over production of high-quality woolens for export, it promoted sericulture to support its silk industry, it took measures to raise the water level in the swamps around Fucecchio in order to increase the supply of freshwater fish for its own market, and, above all, it did what was necessary to assure its population a supply of grain. The government, however, showed little interest in promoting local independent economic activities. Commercial traffic probably moved more smoothly, one result being the stabilization of prices throughout the region. Whether this resulted in a more rational market structure to the advantage of local industries or, on the contrary, the dominance of the capital suppressed local initiatives and blocked the further economic growth of Tuscany is an open question.[76]

By the mid-fifteenth century Florence had rounded out its territory to take in all of northern Tuscany except Lucca, Massa Carrara, and several miniscule pockets of territory at the extreme northwestern border. It had a port, and it possessed most of the natural resources mentioned above—the mineral deposits around Volterra, access to the iron ore on Elba, the mountainside woodlands with their ironworks, the entire valley of the Arno with all its tributaries. With the conquest of Siena in 1555, it annexed all of southern Tuscany, which included the resources of the metalliferous hills and the maremma of Grosseto. Expansion of the territorial state of Florence over the entire region brought with it a degree of economic as well as political integration, but it probably did not change the basic market structure that existed before political unification very much. Goods imported into the region through Pisa and then Livorno were not relayed to Flor-

---

[76] The theme of state formation in the political historiography of Florence is most intelligently assessed by Giorgio Chittolini in his conclusion to the collection of essays in *Florentine Tuscany: Structures and Practices of Power*, ed. William J. Connell and Andrea Zorzi (Cambridge, 2000). The only essay in this volume on economic matters, however, is by Stephan R. Epstein, "Market Structures," 90–121; it offers a comprehensive overview of the regional economy of the Florentine state and has references to the scarce literature on the subject, mostly interpretations rather than studies. Giuseppe Petralia, "Imposizione diretta e dominio territoriale nella repubblica fiorentina del Quattrocento," in *Società, istituzioni, spiritualità: Studi in onore di Cinzio Violante* (Spoleto, 1994), 639–52, emphasizes the diverse forms of the "soft subjugation" practiced by Florence in the fiscal administration of its territory.

ence for redistribution, nor did Florence function as a redistribution center for interregional trade. Moreover, because of the considerable decline in the urbanization of the region after the Black Death, any market advantage one might have expected to accrue to Florence itself as a consequence of political conquest is unlikely to have materialized. Not only were there fewer towns of intermediary size but a lower percentage of the total population lived in towns. In short, both the acentric geography of regional trade and the de-urbanization of the population worked against the growth of a strong central regional market in the capital city. Products from the specialized manufacturing centers in the region arrived in the Florentine market to satisfy local demand—metal products from the Pistoiesi mountains, minerals from the region of Volterra, paper from Colle, ceramics from Montelupo, woad from Borgo Sansepolcro, grain from the maremma— but this trade was limited to what the local market of the capital city could support. The flow in the other direction, from Florence to the subject towns, probably consisted mostly of the specialty products manufactured in the city, many in the luxury category, such as wool and silk cloth.[77] In fact, the market region directly served by the capital city—the area between the Valdipesa and the Valdelsa, the valley of the Ombrone to Pistoia, the Mugello, and the upper Valdarno—saw the least population growth in Tuscany over the following century, from 1552 to 1642.[78]

Duke Cosimo I de' Medici introduced a much more vigorous interventionist policy to establish the authority of the state, putting into place a stronger and more centralized political and judicial system. Just as he and his two sons stamped the urban scene in Florence with architectural and sculptural symbols of this new spirit of government, so, too, they imposed their presence throughout the subject territory with new fortifications in the towns and villas in the countryside. As Furio Diaz observed, on this road to absolutism the new Medici rulers got a head start over the better-established monarchs of the large states in northern Europe because they were not blocked by the privileges of corporate bodies and elites securely embedded in traditional medieval institutions.[79] Likewise, ducal economic policy throughout the state, as in the city, anticipated the vigorous mercantilism of a later generation of European rulers.

---

[77] The only study of Florence as a market center for its immediate countryside is that of Charles Marie de La Roncière, but it is limited to the fourteenth century and has little to say about trade out of the city to the countryside: *Firenze e le sue campagne*, 21–23. In his study of bankers in Siena, "'Fra li compagni palesi e li ladri occulti': Banchieri senesi del Quattrocento," *Nuova rivista storica* 88 (2004): 27–101, Sergio Tognetti found little evidence for trade with Florence.

[78] Lorenzo Del Panta, *Una traccia di storia demografica della Toscana nei secoli XVI–XVIII* (Florence, 1974), map 1.

[79] Diaz, *Il Granducato di Toscana*, 161–62, 179–82; Cosimo's economic policy is summarized on 127–48.

Cosimo's strong sense of the state resulted in a policy of provisioning and price control of basic foodstuffs—grain, meat, oil, and wine—that included the entire territorial population, not just his capital city.[80] Another primary concern was reform of the patchwork of indirect taxes to lift tax barriers and bring the towns together into a unified system for the facilitation of commercial traffic. To this end the road system received particular attention: in 1575 the first magistracy was set up for the periodical inspection of road conditions, and in the early 1580s the government conducted a descriptive and cartographic census of the road system throughout the entire state. New bridges were built across the Arno. The navigability of the Arno was also improved by regulating the practices of millers and beaters of linen and hemp that blocked waterways. Cosimo built canals between Pisa and Livorno and between Pisa and Lucca, and for a moment in 1558 he even considered reviving Leonardo da Vinci's project of linking Florence to the sea with a canal. What was actually achieved by these and other related projects left much to be desired, but they signaled a new spirit in the government of the Florentine state. In their attention to improvements in transportation, the Medici were concerned with defense, and they were not unmindful of their travel to their various properties throughout the territory and of visits by prominent foreigners. Nevertheless, benefits must also have accrued to internal commerce, since a uniform administrative fiscal and commercial system helped integrate the territorial state. Reforms like these presumably had the effect in the marketplace of reducing the costs of doing business—what are called transactions costs—but no one has yet taken the measure of how much more efficiently the economy functioned as a result.[81]

Cosimo and the two sons who succeeded him introduced land-reclamation projects in the Valdichiana, the Fucecchio marshes, and the maremme along the Tyrrhenian littoral from Pisa to Grosseto. They acquired a significant part of these areas for themselves and brought them under a more rational system of estate management. The waterworks system for drainage, irrigation, and flood control in the Pisan maremma was put under the supervision of a specific magistracy that had been founded earlier, during the republican period, but allowed to lapse. Settlement of the area was encouraged by offering tax privileges and by taking measures to promote the use of land for grain rather than for pasturage.

---

[80] Anna Maria Pult Quaglia, *"Per provvedere ai popoli": Il sistema annonario nella Toscana dei Medici* (Florence, 1990).

[81] Leonardo Rombai, "Prefazione: Strade e politica in Toscana tra Medioevo ed Età Moderna," in *Il libro vecchio di strade della Repubblica fiorentina*, ed. Gabriele Campi (Florence, 1987), 5–36; idem, "Le acque interne in Toscana tra Medioevo ed Età Moderna," in *Incolti, fiumi, paludi: Utilizzazione delle risorse naturali nella Toscana medievale e moderna*, ed. Alberto Malvolti and Giuliano Pinto (Florence, 2003), 17–42.

Cosimo also was notably successful in developing the iron industry.[82] In 1543 he obtained the contract for a single magona for the distribution of ore in all of Tuscany. Although it had no central management, the magona had monopoly control over all production, which it contracted out to some forty ironworks, some of them new establishments. Legislation assured rights of producers to surrounding woodlands for fuel against the interests of the local population, and the magona had jurisdiction over any resulting controversies. It built warehouses for iron products both at Livorno and near Pistoia, where the greatest inland concentrations of ironworks were to be found, and it improved access from Pistoia to the river port at Signa. A new type of furnace that required less fuel and produced a better, more malleable product was built in each of the major areas of production—Pracchia in the mountains above Pistoia, Caldana near Piombino and its maremma, and Ruosina in the Apuane Alps above Pietrasanta. This technological innovation has been seen as raising production from an artisan to an industrial level. The Medici were less successful in their vigorous searches throughout Tuscany for new sources of iron, copper, silver, alum, mercury, and marble, although some mines were opened and worked for awhile.

To protect the paper industry in Colle and Pescia, Cosimo took measures in 1544 to block the export of rags and animal materials used for glue, and he must have been instrumental in arranging the loans that the Monte di Pietà and the wool guild in Florence made to support the guild set up in 1548 by the manufacturers in Colle. Cosimo dedicated particular attention to Pisa, which had suffered much from the long period of rebellion early in the century and faced the possibility of complete eclipse by the plans for Livorno. To promote the city as a marketplace, an emporium, to complement the port at Livorno, he established semiannual fairs and offered privileges and certain immunities to people who settled in the city. Cosimo supported the traditional leather industry, permitted the manufacturing of silk, opened a sugar refinery, and invested in a venture to have coral sent to the city for processing. Moreover, the relaunching of the university in 1543 and the establishment of the headquarters of his new military order, the Knights of Santo Stefano, as well as the opening of a mint toward the end of the century, stimulated the local economy and also brought prestige to the city. These measures, along with the land reclamation in the surrounding maremma, revived Pisa's fortunes. The city's population almost doubled in the second half of the century—one of the highest rates of demographic growth in Tuscany, higher than that of Florence. Among the signs of revival were, on the one hand, the arrival

---

[82] Angela Quattrucci, *La magona del ferro: Gestione aziendale e "Provvidenze" sociali nell'evoluzione delle fabbriche del Granducato di Toscana (XVIII–XIX secolo)* (Naples, 1994); Ivan Tognarini, "La via del ferro: Un patrimonio dell'umanità?" *Ricerche storiche* 31 (2001): 5–39.

of foreign merchants who took up residence in the city and, on the other, the re-appearance of Pisan merchants in some of the great international emporia abroad, including Ancona, Seville, and Antwerp.[83]

The evidence of the initiatives taken above all by Cosimo I but also by his two sons points to as impressive an economic policy for the region as for the capital city. However, the evidence is scattered in the literature, and no one has brought it all together in a comprehensive overview, let alone subjected it to a thorough economic analysis with respect to objectives, results, and underlying assumptions about what an economy is. In some respects, ducal policy had antecedents in the republic and in what has been called the protomercantilism of the Italian communes in general, but the Medici princes introduced a vigor in the pursuit of policy that suggests a qualitative, and not just a quantitative, difference. Driving much of this vigor was a search for personal wealth to increase the family patrimony. The Medici built up large estates in the areas where they promoted reclamation projects, and the iron magona, the new ironworks, the coral industry at Pisa, and other projects were their private ventures. The Medici were, as Giorgio Spini observed, the largest landowners and the greatest capitalists in the state. Military concerns also drove policy, especially that directed to developing an iron industry. The problem is how to assess the balance between, on the one hand, this identity of family interests with the state and, on the other, the universal good much touted in the relevant legislation.

The ducal government established in the sixteenth century marked a point of arrival for the political development of Tuscany over the preceding centuries. A region that was a collection of city-states and rural seigniories in the thirteenth century had evolved, with the exception of Lucca and some small places at the edges, into two states, Florence and Siena, both now under a single ruler. The formation of the Medici state also marked a point of departure, for with it came, more so than under the republic, the process of political integration under a single government that slowly would erode the many surviving local privileges and institutions and go on to form a coherent whole out of what was still an aggregation, albeit one with a strong central authority. The historiography of the economy of the region is so lacking in studies that cover the entire region over a long period that it is difficult to say whether the new ducal government can serve as a benchmark in the economic history as well as it does in the political history of the region. In the early period Tuscany was a place of vibrant urban economies that had international dimensions, several of them being on a scale comparable

---

[83] Rita Mazzei, "Economia e società a Pisa nella seconda metà del Cinquecento," in *Quaderni stefaniani* 12 (1993): 45–60.

to that of Florence. By 1600 only Lucca and Florence remained in that league; all the other towns, now subject to Florentine rule, were of little more than regional economic importance, with the exception of Livorno, a creation of the ducal government.

In several ways, however, the regional economy was integrated into the urban economy of the capital city as it had never been before. First, there was the natural function of a market area created by a city with an increasingly disproportionate concentration of wealth and a much larger population than any other city in the region. Florence was a major market that attracted goods produced throughout the territory beyond its immediate countryside, from foodstuffs, ironwork, and other basic necessities to specialty products such as paper from Colle and ceramics from Montelupo; the balance of this trade with its territory was probably highly unfavorable inasmuch as the city produced relatively little that sold in regional markets. Territorial expansion resulted in a more efficient functioning of this market as a result of a statewide policy of administration, defense, provisioning, transport improvements, and regulations. Territorial expansion, however, also generated wealth in forms that flowed the other way, from the region into the city. Political unification resulted in a single fiscal system that brought revenues into the central treasury, and private investment in the countryside by Florentines (including the Medici) paid profits that ended up in their pockets. The balance of these flows was very much in Florence's favor and became more so in the course of the fifteenth and sixteenth centuries. Finally, the Medici dukes took both personal and state initiatives that had repercussions throughout the region: land reclamation, mining enterprises, the iron magona, the building of Livorno, sponsorship of activities at Pisa, support of the paper industry at Colle. In short, in giving impetus to the role of the capital city, the ducal government marked a point of departure for a new direction in the economic history of the region. But that history, with its themes of exploitation, decline, growth, development, and redistribution of initiatives and factors of production, has yet to be written.[84]

There were countervailing forces, however. In two basic ways the economies of city and region were not well integrated. First, the textile industries of Florence, the city's leading industrial sector by far, had few roots in the region except for immigrant labor, since it imported most of its raw materials from abroad and

---

[84] For two different views of the integration of the regional economy during the republican period, see Epstein, "Market Structures," and two articles by Paolo Malanima: "La formazione di una regione economica: La Toscana nei secoli XIII–XV," *Società e storia*, no. 20 (1983): 229–69, and "Politica ed economia nella formazione dello stato regionale: Il caso toscano," *Studi veneziani*, n.s., 11 (1986): 61–72. The theme of exploitation has been played by political, not economic, historians: see Judith C. Brown, *In the Shadow of Florence*, xvii–xxii. Mario Mirri, "Formazione di una regione economica: Ipotesi sulla Toscana, sul Veneto, sulla Lombardia," *Studi veneziani*, n.s., 11 (1986): 47–59, makes some useful observations about what course future studies should take.

sold most of its finished products in foreign markets. The government protected the urban wool industry by specifically forbidding the production of high-quality cloth outside the capital. The silk industry, however, had some impact on the territorial economy. It slowly forged backward links in the countryside through the spread of sericulture, and this provided significant additional income to some of the rural population, while the establishment of throwing mills at Pescia at the very end of the sixteenth century decentralized one phase in the manufacturing process in the industry. In addition, Pisa became a center of production thanks to the initiatives of the Medici dukes. The textile industries, however, remained almost exclusively confined to the capital city and had few repercussions in the economy of the region. A second limit on the economic integration of region and capital city was the eccentric market system of Tuscany, already described. However strong the pull of Florence had become by 1600 as the seat of government, as the source of investment capital, and as a market for goods from the region, it was not a central emporium for regional trade routes or the region's gateway to foreign markets, nor did it lie on the path to such a gateway for most of the region's larger towns.

PRIVATE INVESTMENT   Another dynamic integrating the urban economy with that of the region was acquisition of land by Florentines. Most city residents bought rural property if they could. A piece of land outside the city walls was a good investment: it yielded things that helped meet one's everyday needs, and in the long run it provided a minimum of security and possibly the only kind of support in old age. Before the rise of deposit institutions in the later fifteenth century, real estate was also about the only kind of investment working people could hope to make with the limited savings they could accumulate. For the better off, it was a way to diversify their portfolio of investments. The cultural values attached to landholding also counted for something. For many who had emigrated from the countryside, from magnates who came in the early period to those who were always moving into the city in search of their fortune, purchasing land (or more land, if they had held on to something in the countryside) was a way to reaffirm one's roots. Memory embodied in land could be a potent social force: it established the status of those great families who could trace their roots back to a castle in the outlying territory, and it provided a model for others who aspired to generate such a memory for their descendants by building a rural villa and patronizing a nearby church or chapel.

The area where Florentines concentrated their purchases was, of course, the immediate countryside, the city's contado, which extended from the flood plain immediately downstream to the Valdipesa and the Valdelsa and into the

Mugello and the upper Valdarno. The city directed its expansion into this area in the twelfth and thirteenth centuries largely against the feudal nobility, and conquest resulted in clearing the land of all feudal encumbrances and thereby opening it up to market forces. The demographic crises of the fourteenth century, and especially the severe blow of the plague in 1348, must have had an invigorating effect on the supply and demand forces in this land market. On the supply side, the population in the countryside fell; on the demand side, higher earnings in the city generated savings looking for an outlet. Data from the 1427 catasto reflect what happened in the land market: 67 percent of declarants in Florence owned real estate of some kind other than their residence either inside or outside the city, and collectively Florentines, who constituted only 14 percent of the total population, owned 51 percent of all property in the territorial state (the figure went up to 60 percent in the early sixteenth century).[85] The same dynamics were at work in the other urban centers in the state, with the result that rural residents owned only 17 percent of the land; in the immediate countryside of Florence, the percentage was even lower, about 10 percent. Moreover, a comparison of the 1427 and 1480 catasti shows a downward redistribution of real-estate holdings: those who had more than *fl.*1,500 invested in real estate held 49 percent of the total value of that kind of property in 1427 but only 35 percent in 1480 (table 7.2). Unfortunately, the sixteenth-century decima records have not been studied to find out something about the further redistribution of real-estate holdings. A sample survey of the decima assessments of fifteen families from 1534 to 1604 reveals an increase in holdings that averaged 58 percent, but just three of the largest of these landowning families account for almost two-thirds of the increase in the absolute value of the sample, while four of the families with relatively modest holdings in 1534 increased their holdings by between two and three times.[86] This sample confirms the general impression that some Florentines increased their landholdings in the sixteenth century, but there is no way to quantify this increase or to assess its social distribution.

Already toward the end of the thirteenth century absentee landownership led to the spread of sharecropping as a form of management by remote control. The reduction of the rural population after the Black Death resulted in the consolidation of plots into units, called in Italian *podere,* or farms, large enough to support a peasant family; this situation favored the organization of the working

---

[85] Herlihy and Klapisch-Zuber, *Les toscans et leurs familles,* 243; Giovanni Cherubini, "L'espropriazione contadina e la distribuzione della proprietà fondiaria al centro-nord," in *L'Italia rurale nel Basso Medioevo* (Rome, 1985), 70 (for the early sixteenth-century figure). The catasto printout makes no distinction between real estate inside and outside the city.

[86] Litchfield, *Emergence of a Bureaucracy,* table on 218–19; for a survey of landownership through the eighteenth century, see 215–32.

TABLE 7.2
Distribution of Landownership, 1427 and 1480

Value of holdings in florins	Number of households		% of total value	
	1427	1480	1427	1480
Above 1,500	679	477	49	35
500–1,500	1,542	1,968	32	42
100–500	2,693	3,122	17	21
20–100	1,338	926	2	1

SOURCES: *Online Catasto of 1427,* version 1.3, ed. David Herlihy, Christiane Klapisch-Zuber, R. Burr Litchfield, and Anthony Molho (machine-readable data file based on *Census and Property Survey of Florentine Domains in the Province of Tuscany, 1427–1480,* data file by David Herlihy and Christiane Klapisch-Zuber) (Providence, RI: Florentine Renaissance Resources/STG, Brown University, 2002), http://www.stg.brown.edu/projects/catasto/overview.html; Anthony Molho, "Investimenti nel Monte delle Doti di Firenze: un'analisi sociale e geografica," *Quaderni storici* 21 (1986): 147–70.

of the land around sharecropping. The absentee owner desired stability and autonomy with respect to the working of the land and had to assure the sharecropper of self-sufficiency. Hence, crops were mixed. Sharecropping has been seen as the stimulus for the planting of both vines and olive trees. It also entailed investment by owners in planting, livestock, and buildings, especially homes for the sharecroppers and possibly a mill, a kiln, or some other rural industrial structure, along with a residence for themselves *(casa da signore).* If the land was near the city, the owner might tend to the marketing of any surpluses, but since there was little long-distance commerce in basic foodstuffs within the region, sharecropping was not a strongly profit-driven system of agricultural management. The high degree of fragmentation of the land into units that the sharecropper could work for his own self-sufficiency limited technological and crop innovations. Inasmuch as sharecroppers also sold surplus produce in nearby markets, they were not unaware of market pressures resulting from the increase in population over the later fifteenth and sixteenth centuries. A recent study has shown how, in one local market, the reorganization of cultivated land into farms worked by sharecroppers increased productivity as measured by the caloric value of the food produced.[87] In fact, as Giuliano Pinto has argued, sharecropping was not an irrational form of agriculture, given the characteristics of the land in Tuscany. The social aspect of the system is another matter. Urban landowners imposed a rigid structure, controlled by them, on the agricultural sector and reaped the profits of rural labor, resulting in what has been called both the urban feudalization of the land and the proletarianiza-

[87] Cinzia Capalbo and Claudio Rotelli, "Il valore energetico delle trasformazioni agrarie nella Toscana del XV e XVI secolo: Le proprietà agricole dell'Ospedale della Misericordia di Prato," in *Economia e energia, secc. XIII–XVIII,* ed. Simonetta Cavaciocchi (Florence, 2003), 879–99.

tion of peasants. In this sense, the growth of the territorial state led to economic stagnation in the agricultural sector.[88]

In the fourteenth and fifteenth centuries there was little sense that such holdings collectively formed an estate with central management. Even though the rich who bought land in the countryside may have tended to concentrate their holdings in areas associated with their ancestral roots, the holdings themselves were usually scattered about in the vicinity and not contiguous, not necessarily even near the villas that many of them built or remodeled. For example, Palla di Nofri Strozzi's landholdings, by far the largest reported in the 1427 catasto (worth *fl*.53,000, three times the worth of the next highest landowner's), consisted of 211 itemized holdings plus innumerable other pieces of land, including 88 farms. They were located in eighty-four different parishes and within nine local markets zones, one at Empoli, in the upper Valdarno, another at Figline, in the lower Valdarno, and the others nearer to Florence, scattered about in the floodplain between Florence, Prato, and Poggio a Caiano. The richest of absentee landlords in the city might have a local factor to watch over his interests, but these men were likely to be as numerous as the localities where the landlord's farms were to be found, and they worked only part time.[89]

A landownership trend in the sixteenth century toward more compact estates would seem to support the hypothesis that the rich were increasing their landholdings at the time. The villa phenomenon, such a notable aspect of Florentine culture in the Quattrocento, may itself have been the stimulus for a more rational organization of landed possession around a prestige property, leading to the emergence, toward the end of the sixteenth century, of the great landed estate. At that time, toward the end of a period of steep price inflation, the more rational organization of rural properties and further acquisitions may have been economic decisions taken with the prospect of higher profits from the sale of agricultural products in local markets. Although individual farms with their sharecropping families remained intact, large property owners tended to concentrate them into contiguous geographic units managed as a single enterprise, or *fattoria,* with a full-time salaried and resident manager *(fattore)*. It would seem that,

[88] On the administration of rural properties in the early fourteenth century, see Charles Marie de La Roncière, *Un changeur florentin du Trecento: Lippo di Fede del Sega (1285 env.–1363 env.)* (Paris, 1973), ch. 6; Giuliano Pinto, "Ordinamento delle colture e proprietà fondiaria cittadina," in *La Toscana nel tardo Medioevo: ambiente, economia rurale, società* (Florence, 1982), 195–204; idem, "Ceti dominanti, proprietà fondiaria e gestione della terra a Firenze nel Trecento e nel primo Quattrocento," in *Città e spazi,* 125–37; Giovanni Cherubini, "Qualche considerazione sulle campagne dell'Italia centro-settentrionale tra l'XI e il XV secolo," in *Signori, contadini, borghesi: Ricerche sulla società italiana del Basso Medioevo* (Florence, 1974), 51–119; and Paolo Pirillo, *Costruzione di un contado: I fiorentini e il loro territorio nel Basso Medioevo* (Florence, 2001).

[89] Amanda Lillie, *Florentine Villas in the Fifteenth Century: An Architectural and Social History* (Cambridge, 2005), ch. 2.

as a result, estate owners in the city increased the profits they extracted from labor in the countryside, but this is to pursue the logic of a development whose reality has remained largely unstudied, notwithstanding the immense archival holdings of private estate records for the sixteenth century.[90]

Already during the fifteenth century there were signs that the profit motive was uppermost in the minds of at least some of these urban capitalist entrepreneurs who invested in the agricultural sector—and the evidence might be more substantial if someone were to look for it. After the conquest of Pisa and the launching of the galley system, some Florentines built up large holdings in the Pisan maremma. Given the nature of this land and its remoteness from Florence, they must have been motivated by commercial interests.[91] From 1464 to 1468 Amerigo di Giovanni Benci and his brothers had an investment in a company set up for trafficking in animals *(magona di bestiame)* that in 1466, when it assumed the name of Filippo Rinieri, Piero Neretti & Partners, had a capital of fl.13,000 di suggello.[92] Carlo di Antonio Serristori, who began accumulating land in the region in the 1460s, eventually organized a firm—Carlo Serristori & Partners—for managing a stock farm on land it owned and rented.[93] Lorenzo de' Medici, who built up extensive consolidated holdings in several areas around Pisa and at Fucecchio, also organized a magona di bestiame that rented oxen, buffalo, and horses to small landowners in the Pisan maremma.[94] We have already mentioned the interest of the Serristori in promoting sericulture on their lands in the upper Valdarno and in the Valdinievole and the thousands of mulberry trees Giovanni Rucellai planted on his land at Poggio a Caiano. Much more notable is what happened to this latter property after Rucellai sold it to Lorenzo de' Medici in 1474. Lorenzo went about building up a large dairy farm on the property. He made additional purchases to enlarge his pasturelands, he made improvements to protect this low-lying land from flooding, he imported special animals from Lombardy, and he erected an enormous building for stabling and storage that also incorporated facilities for making cheese and a large fishpond.[95] Florentines had interests, too, in the grain trade and animal hus-

---

[90] Malanima, *I Riccardi*, 76–85.

[91] Michael Mallett, "Pisa and Florence in the Fifteenth Century: Aspects of the Period of the First Florentine Domination," in Rubinstein, *Florentine Studies*, 435–41.

[92] ASF, Carte strozziane, ser. 2, 19 (*libro segreto* of Amerigo Benci), fols. 18, 21.

[93] Sergio Tognetti, *Da Figline a Firenze: Ascesa economica e politica della famiglia Serristori (secoli XIV–XVI)* (Florence, 2003), 133; see also Tognetti and Meli, *Il principe e il mercante*, 85–86.

[94] Amanda Lillie, "Lorenzo de' Medici's Rural Investments and Territorial Expansion," *Rinascimento* 44 (1993): 53–67; Philip E. Foster, *La villa di Lorenzo de' Medici a Poggio a Caiano* (Poggio a Caiano, 1992), 157–69. An overview of the growth of Medici estates in the fifteenth century is presented by Patrizia Salvadori, *Dominio e patronato: Lorenzo dei Medici e la Toscana nel Quattrocento* (Rome, 2000), ch. 6.

[95] F. W. Kent, *Lorenzo de' Medici and the Art of Magnificence* (Baltimore, 2004), 72–73.

bandry as well as mining in Sienese territory; and their hold on these sectors of the economy became so substantial that the political conquest of Siena in 1555 has been called "the logical epilogue of an economic subjugation long in process."[96] Outside the agricultural sector, however, there is little evidence for Florentine private investment in the resources of the territory except for the occasional mining venture, already mentioned. Only 7 percent of the investment capital registered in accomandite in 1602–4 went to ventures in Tuscany outside Florence and Livorno.[97] In Tuscany there was nothing like the "agrarian capitalism" that was such a prominent phenomenon in rural Lombardy at the end of the Middle Ages, arising from speculation, especially in the agricultural and metallurgical sectors, by merchants and others.

One of the themes in the recent political historiography of the Florentine territorial state during the republican period is the extension of the influence of the city's leading families into the territory through clientage and alliance systems they built up as local landowners and as local officials representing the central state. Political patronage by these families at local levels, in fact, has been considered more important as a dynamic that helped integrate the territory than the presumed instruments of a centralizing government associated with "the rise of the modern state." Here again, as in so many other aspects of the historiography of the city, the economic implications of political developments have not been explored. Subjugation of territorial towns and the local presence there of Florentines as landlords and as magistrates, however, did open at least one political outlet for private investment capital in the form of loans to local governments so that they could meet what they owed to the capital city from tax receipts. Florentine merchant-bankers made high-interest loans to some of these places in the early fifteenth century, and in at least one town—Volterra—they had a strong hand in local finances.[98] This kind of private investment, however, must have dried up in the sixteenth century, when the new ducal government incorporated the entire territorial state into its centralized fiscal apparatus.

---

[96] Giuliano Pinto, "Le strutture ambientali e le basi dell'economia rurale," in *La Toscana nel tardo Medio Evo* (Florence, 1982), 89.

[97] Litchfield, *Emergence of a Bureaucracy*, 208.

[98] For the political historiography, see the papers collected in Connell and Zorzi, *Florentine Tuscany,* esp. Giorgio Chitolini's concluding remarks. The reference to Volterra comes from Lorenzo Fabbri's contribution, "Patronage and Its Role in Government: The Florentine Patriciate and Volterra," 231–32; it is the only mention of private financial interests tied to political patronage. Private loans to local communes are mentioned in Molho, *Florentine Public Finances,* 40–42. Sergio Tognetti suggests that a credit of *fl.*3,200 with four men from Cortona that appears on the 1431 balance sheet of the bank of Antonio Serristori & Partners may have been a loan they negotiated for their town. *Da Figline a Firenze,* 85.

Private Wealth
Social Mobility

NEW MEN IN THE FOURTEENTH CENTURY   A reader of the early political history of Florence is likely to be most struck, if not baffled, by an extraordinary fluidity within the ruling classes. The transformation of the earlier consular regime into the guild republic that emerged toward the end of the thirteenth century and the evolution of a central government solidly based in a clearly defined set of institutions in the fourteenth century were accompanied by social conflict, much of which arose from efforts, on the one hand, to widen the political constituency and, on the other, to secure power in the hands of a relatively small oligarchy. Perhaps the most prominent recurring theme in political histories of these developments is the appearance of "new men," *gente nuova,* in the councils of government. The purpose of the electoral reforms of the guild government enacted in the Ordinances of Justice of 1293 was to break the hold of an elite by opening political office to new men. A half-century later the revolutionary reforms of 1343 following the expulsion of the Duke of Athens put into place a government broadly based in wider guild participation, opening the way to another influx of new men onto the political scene, and this flow continued after 1348, when the way was cleared for replacement of the victims of the Black Death. New men continued to arrive for the next quarter-century, down to the Ciompi revolt, and even the reactionary regime installed in 1382 left open plenty of opportunities for new men to enter into the political life of the city down to the end of the republic.

Political mobility does not signal anything like the evolution of democracy, only the expansion, or redefinition, of a political class. Riding the tide of all this fluidity, however, was a core group of older, more established families. Most historians agree that by 1400 this elite had managed to tighten its grip on government despite the opening of offices to an ever-larger segment of the male population. The republic, after all, was administered, not by a central bureaucracy, but by some forty citizen committees, each with its own sphere of authority and all subject to renewal every three, four, or six months. Thus, about a thousand different men passed through government service in the course of a year, along with an equal number that served in the legislative bodies. Moreover, from 1382 to 1484 the number of names that went into the electoral bags for the selection of men to fill these posts increased from 5,350 to 8,000. These are not insignificant numbers for a city with 10,000 households (in 1427) and a total population of about 45,000 to 50,000, figures whose arithmetical implications have not yet been addressed by political historians. In fact, within this politically active segment of the population, the ruling class in the fifteenth century, as defined by officeholding and tax status, has been estimated as comprising almost a third of all households—hardly an elite, in the usual sense of the term.[99]

In the historiography one finds this theme of "new men" played repeatedly but without any economic counterpoint; the new men who kept showing up lack much of an economic identity. What is most noticed, in accordance with the overriding interest in the evolution of the particular kind of government Florence had, is their guild affiliation, but in Florence guild membership did not necessarily define a man's economic activity, let alone his economic status. For the moment, given the literature, one can only assume that behind the political ambitions of these new men lay their success as entrepreneurs of one kind or another. The extraordinary growth of the city's population and the expansion of its economy abroad in the thirteenth century clearly opened many opportunities to make one's fortune in industry and commerce, and opportunities were all the greater for the absence of a ruling elite empowered by its hold on a strong central government. These opportunities attracted men from the older landed classes in the countryside as well as those out to make their fortune. Some of the prominent merchant-banking families—the Bardi, the Frescobaldi, the Mozzi—came from the feudal countryside. Others—the Alberti del Giudice, the Albizzi, the Peruzzi, the Scali—had more humble origins; some of these, like the Acciaiuoli, had come from outside Tuscany. But there were also great feudal families, like the Buondelmonti, the Guidi, the Ricasoli, and the Uberti, who rarely surfaced in the ranks of the city's business elite. All these people were mixed up in the city, however: they intermarried, entered into partnership arrangements with one another, and above all joined together in political factions, thereby dissolving any clearly defined class structure to this society. Moreover, in this early period the dominant chivalric culture of the traditional feudal elite precluded a challenge from a still ideologically inchoate business class. One can hardly call Florence at the time of Dante, for all its bustling economic activity and its population explosion, a melting pot, but there was much fluidity of wealth and mobility of status. "New men" is as important a theme in the early economic history of the city as it is in its political history, and the subject deserves more research.

The biggest inflow of new men came in 1348. The plague that struck the city in the late spring and summer of that year was the most severe blow the economy

---

[99] John M. Najemy, in *Corporatism and Consensus in Florentine Electoral Politics, 1280–1400* (Chapel Hill, NC, 1982), emphasizes "the continuous introduction of new men into the offices of communal government" in the 1290s (51), "the avalanche of *gente nuova* between 1343 and 1348" (200), "the real and considerable . . . advance of the gente nuova" between 1352 and 1377 (202), and "a high level of opportunity for new men and new families" after 1382 (274). The size of the ruling elite in the fifteenth century has been estimated by Molho in *Marriage Alliance in Late Medieval Florence*, 211 (table).

suffered during the entire four centuries surveyed in this book. It was a demographic disaster, reducing the population of the city and its countryside by two-thirds, according to the contemporary chronicler Matteo Villani, and the city alone by three-fourths, according to another observer, messer Pagolo di Bingeri Rucellai, or from 90,000–120,000 to 32,000–42,000, according to the best modern estimates. The plague arrived in the late spring, reached its height in June and July, and had subsided by September. With all allowance for artistic license, Boccaccio caught something of the horror the city went through during those months in the famous description with which he set the backdrop for the stories in the *Decameron*. The immediate effect on business must have been traumatic. The only surviving ledger of business accounts kept open during these months, that of Iacopo and Bartolomeo di Caroccio degli Alberti & Partners, Calimala merchants, records the gravity of the situation. The partners themselves escaped, Bartolomeo being at the time off in Flanders and Iacopo fleeing the city for the Chianti, but they lost their mother, the husband of a sister, an uncle and his wife, and a cousin of their father's and his wife. The firm fared badly: it lost six of its eighteen employees; the number of exchange transactions involving cash payments registered in its surviving ledger fell off, and wool sales came to a halt; and its branch abroad ceased shipping cloth from Flanders, the mainstay of its business. The wool firms of Antonio di Lando degli Albizzi and his sons must also have been hit hard inasmuch as in the months of June and July Antonio lost his wife, three sons, four daughters, and a grandson before he himself died of the plague on the last day of July, but we have only a son's personal record book documenting this family tragedy, not any business accounts.[100]

The plague subsided very quickly, leaving in its wake—for all the obvious reasons—the considerable wealth of the city very much redistributed. Not surprisingly, "many citizens have become poor and many poor have become rich," as one communal provision stated in October. "Complaints, questions, controversies, and litigation rose up among citizens everywhere concerning estates and inheritances," commented Matteo Villani, "and this filled up the courts of our city of Florence long thereafter, at great cost and unaccustomed trouble," and the commune had to intervene to bring some order to the chaotic situation. As a result of depletion of the ranks of heirs, money poured into the city's great charitable institutions. Villani estimated that bequests of all kinds to the confraternity of Orsanmichele amounted to *fl.*350,000, with another *fl.*60,000 going to the

---

[100] *Due libri mastri degli Alberti: Una grande compagnia di Calimala, 1348–1358*, ed. Richard A. Goldthwaite, Enzo Settesoldi, and Marco Spallanzani (Florence, 1995), 1:xxiv, xli, xlvii, li; Hidetoshi Hoshino, "Note sulla compagnia commerciale degli Albizzi del Trecento," *Annuario* of the Istituto Giapponese di Cultura in Roma 7 (1969–70): 8–13.

hospital of Santa Maria Nuova and the Misericordia, estimates that are not un-reasonable, for all their enormity. Heirs who survived, however, fared well. As Villani adds, "All poor women had such an abundance of things that they did not go begging." The consequences in the labor market were clear: everyone, even stable boys, wet nurses, and the least skilled workers, complained Villani, wanted higher wages. By January 1349 salaries had shot up. During the next few months, for which period we have more substantial documentation, the unskilled laborer was making twice as much as he had been a year earlier, and immigrants flowed into the city. Meanwhile, the cost of food also rose, but hardly as much, leaving the worker with much more disposable income than ever. In addition, rents fell: by October 1348, with much of the stock of housing empty, the commune was considering abandoning its policy of rent controls. Under these circumstances employment opportunities improved. In January 1349 the officials of the Con-dotta, in charge of defense and public order, reported difficulties in filling posts, and in the same month the mint complained that it was unable to find the skilled workers it needed. A contemporary, messer Pagolo di Bingeri Rucellai, summed it all up: "All those who survived remained rich from the inheritance they had, and after the plague one could not find artisans of any kind who wanted to work, because it seemed to them that they had enough left over; and it was necessary that new artisans come in from outside."[101] Villani was shocked that now men from the lower classes often refused work and wanted more expensive food and clothes. When a few years later, in 1353, shortages caused wheat prices to rise, it seemed to him that the lower classes did not care "because all were rich from their work, they earned greedily, they were ready to buy and enjoy the very best things notwithstanding the shortages, and they wanted them before the older and richer citizens got them—an unbecoming and astonishing thing to recount, but some-thing seen continually, as we can give clear witness to."[102]

What has been little noted in all this is how quickly, and how substantially, business had picked up by September 1348. The plague took a severe toll on the population, disastrous almost beyond belief at a personal level, but it halted eco-nomic activity only temporarily. The foundations of the economy in the textile industry and trade networks abroad were strong; foreign markets held despite the crisis, or perhaps because of it, considering the consequent increase in dis-posable wealth in the hands of the fewer people who survived; and as soon as the

---

[101] All these quotations but Rucellai's come from Alberto Benigno Falsini, "Firenze dopo il 1348: Le conseguenze della peste nera," *ASI* 129 (1971): 425–503. The Rucellai account is published in F. W. Kent, "The Black Death of 1348 in Florence: A New Contemporary Account," in *Renaissance Studies in Honor of Craig Hugh Smyth*, ed. A. Morrogh et al. (Florence, 1985), 1:117–28.

[102] Villani, *Cronica*, 1:iv; 3:lvi.

plague receded, production must have been back in full force. The Alberti company took on three new employees in September, one more in October, and yet two more in November. Shipments to the firm out of the Low Countries resumed over these months, many of them going to Avignon, and in November cloth was again arriving in Florence. The two Albizzi firms, incorporating three wool shops and a warehouse between them, showed only slightly lower profits at the end of the year than those of the previous year. Although profits continued to fall slightly in the subsequent two years, at 20 percent and 14.5 percent, respectively, they still represented a very good performance by any standards, notwithstanding the crisis. Business picked up quickly, in other words, and with it opportunities opened up for new men to move into the ranks of entrepreneurs working in the forward sectors of the economy—probably the same men who show up on the political scene, but that remains to be seen. Francesco di Marco Datini, the orphaned son of a hosteller struck down by the Black Death who rose to become the famed "merchant of Prato," is representative of an entire generation of these new men. In 1350, at the age of fifteen, he moved into the breech at Avignon, the new papal capital, and took full advantage of the commercial opportunities then opening up in the western Mediterranean.

The phenomenon of new men was not just another immediate effect of the demographic crisis. Other dynamics generated continuing mobility within the ranks of the upper classes throughout the later fourteenth century and into the fifteenth. Fluidity in the possession of wealth arose from the very structure of the Florentine economy. In part, it was a function of partible inheritance practiced by men who continued to have many male children without much thought about laying the foundation for an enduring dynastic patrimony. Within any cognate group, whatever the relationship between individuals, there was likely to be much diversity of wealth and much volatility of fortune over the generations. Fluidity was also a function of the looser organizational structure of business, the primary source of wealth in the second half of the century. Above all, fluidity in the ranks of the business classes resulted from continually changing economic conditions, all the more fluid for the elimination, after the banking crises of the 1340s, of the largest dominating players. The second half of the fourteenth century may in fact have been the most expansive period in the history of the Florentine economy. These years saw the move into papal finances, the intensification of trade in the western Mediterranean, the shift in the wool industry to the higher-quality San Martino cloths, and the rise of the silk industry at end of the century. These events were followed in the fifteenth century by the consolidation of the international exchange market around the great fairs of Geneva and then Lyons, another shift in the wool industry to the use of the cheaper matricina wool, and, finally, the opening of the new markets for luxury textiles at Rome, Naples, Constantinople, and, by the end of the century, in central Europe. Each of these shifts, especially those in markets abroad, opened up new opportunities for men seeking to make a fortune, if they did not also see the withdrawal of entrepreneurs from those places that fell behind.

UPWARD MOBILITY   For the fifteenth century some statistical measure of mobility can be taken in the appearance of the 392 lineages that presumably constituted the ruling class among the top 500 assessments (approximately the highest 5 percent) on the successive tax rosters of 1403, 1427, 1457, and 1480.[103] Of these lineages 55 percent appeared for the first time after 1403, 22 percent appear for the first time in 1427, 19 percent in 1457, and 14 percent in 1480. At first glance, and for lack of any comparative data, these figures suggest considerable mobility, and although the figures read in progression seem to hint at declining mobility, only 21 percent of these families appear on all four lists, and 35 percent appear on only one list. Assessments made in 1457 and 1480, as we shall see, were based on real-estate holdings alone, hardly a reliable index to total wealth in a city like Florence. But these statistics, which are all we have at the moment, provide substance for at least a hypothesis about economic fluidity.

The theme of upward mobility finds a contemporary resonance in the social analysis Piero di Iacopo Guicciardini (the historian's father) made of the men declared eligible for political office in 1484. The eight thousand nominations that were presented for the scrutiny required for election to public office in 1481 were a clear sign to him that "the most ignoble of the lowest artisans are forever rising in status, and in their place appear yet other new men to fill up the ranks of the ignoble; and thus new groups are continually moving up." He divided this political class into five groups: At the top were the magnates *(estremo nobile)*, followed by the nobles of popular but ancient origins *(popolani antichi nobili)*. The others he defined, significantly, according to stages upward from the lowest: the ignoble artisans of the meanest kind *(ignobili, artefici più infima)*; the more noble artisans *(artefici più nobili)*, who have only recently risen above the others but are still like them; and finally those just below the nobles, for whom Guicciardini can find no single term, describing them as not yet noble but not completely ignoble, recently

---

[103] This "ruling class" has been defined by Molho in *Marriage Alliance in Late Medieval Florence*, and Molho also uses officeholding as a criterion; the tax data are presented there in app. 3. Molho has 395 lineages and does not include the 1403 tax list, which I have taken from Lauro Martines, *The Social World of the Florentine Humanists, 1390–1460* (Princeton, NJ, 1963), app. 2. This mobility on the tax rosters is all the more striking in view of the fact that this ruling elite of lineages comprised about one-third of all households on the roster of 1480 (Molho, *Marriage Alliance in Late Medieval Florence*, 211).

arrived *(di fresco)* but having held all the offices of the state. And unrestrained by any sensitivity about judging the social status of his contemporaries, he clarified his classification by mentioning specific families that fell into each group.[104]

The hierarchical economic structure of Florentine society was not rigid, blocking the workingman from access to the road to greater wealth and, perhaps, into the ranks of the upper class, even if realistically the vast majority of these men did not have such a prospect. The guilds, for one, did not present an insuperable institutional barrier. The guild elites of merchant-bankers and wool and silk manufacturers did not block the move of outsiders into their ranks as entrepreneurs any more than they closed their rosters to outsiders who wanted to enroll for purely political purposes (and membership of this kind in more than one guild was hardly uncommon). Moreover, Florentine society was relatively open and fluid in the horizontal movement of men across social categories. The study of Florentine social history, however, has largely ignored the many occasions when workers and men of high status met outside the marketplace. Until the end of the fifteenth century boys of all classes attended the same schools to learn how to read, write, and do commercial arithmetic. As a brass worker wrote to Lorenzo de' Medici in 1473, "Your [father] Piero . . . liked me very much inasmuch as we were both at the abacus school to learn together."[105] Moreover, all the guilds had representation in the large complex of citizen committees, councils, and colleges that constituted the government, from petty magistracies to major administrative posts in the countryside and the Signoria of nine priors, and since all of these were renewed every two, three, four, or six months, the turnover increased the possibility of participation. Although not to a degree at all commensurate with their numbers, a few workingmen were always to be found sitting alongside the rich and powerful on these committees making decisions at all levels of government, notwithstanding the political realities behind the scenes. Their active participation has been documented at the level of the *gonfaloni,* the administrative units in which the city was subdivided. Men from different economic levels also came together in confraternities, the principal centers of the religious life of the laity, where they shared ritual observances and worked together in welfare activities, and even in those confraternities where patricians dominated the management workers were not altogether excluded. Outside these encounters within a formal institutional context and outside the workplace, workingmen and patricians often met on a variety of occasions, including even the baptism of a child of

---

[104] The document is published in Nicolai Rubinstein, *The Government of Florence under the Medici (1434 to 1494)* (Oxford, 1966), 319–25, with a comment on 213–16.

[105] Quoted in F. W. Kent, "Be Rather Loved Than Feared: Class Relations in Quattrocento Florence," in Connell, *Society and Individual in Renaissance Florence,* 37.

a patrician, when the very few invited witnesses usually included one or more men of humble status (whose presence many patricians themselves recorded in their memoranda about the event). In short, many artisans in the course of their daily lives—conducting business in the marketplace, participating in the activities of a confraternity, serving on a communal committee—found themselves alongside men from the upper class.[106]

Although most artisans or shopkeepers who achieved middling economic status, even those of the major guilds, had no reasonable expectation of improving their situation to the point where they could enter the upper ranks of the city's wealthiest class, some did. On these pages we have commented on the fluidity in the ranks of lanaioli, setaioli, and merchant-bankers, many of whom were sons or grandsons of shopkeepers and artisans. Some families with names taken for granted today as having patrician status emerged, especially at the end of the fourteenth century and in the early fifteenth century, from the ranks of men of modest occupations such as furriers (Spinelli), goldsmiths (Dei, Olivieri), and, from the minor guilds, linen drapers (Cambini), wine dealers (Torrigiani), woodworkers (Canacci, Pucci), brickmakers (Corsi), armorers (Parenti), and painters (Gaddi). It is highly unlikely that an artisan was able to do this within the confines of his craft, that is, without moving into one of the leading sectors of the economy. Nevertheless, one of the most impressive success stories that can be told of artisan upward mobility is that of the Giunti, already recounted, although their economic success was built on a new technology and a new international market that centered in Venice, not Florence. Within the silk industry one man who might have been able to make the transition from artisan to setaiolo within his own lifetime was Iacopo di Tedesco, the entrepreneurial silk weaver frequently encountered in these pages, and he would not have been the first.[107] Over his long career, in which he worked for more than a hundred silk firms and in all branches of the industry, he must have been a well-known figure among setaioli (his second wife, in fact, was a Neroni). And with his own battiloro firm and an investment in a setaiolo firm, he presumably had already surmounted any guild barriers standing in his way. He certainly had the capital to finance such a venture. Iacopo died, however, without sons, sons-in-law, or nephews to promote,

---

[106] Dale V. Kent and F. W. Kent, *Neighbours and Neighbourhood in Renaissance Florence: The District of the Red Lion in the Fifteenth Century* (Locust Valley, NY, 1982), 78–80, 86–91, 107–21; Ronald F. E. Weissman, *Ritual Brotherhood in Renaissance Florence* (New York, 1982), 67–80; F. W. Kent and Amanda Lillie, "The Piovano Arlotto: New Documents," in *Florence and Italy: Renaissance Studies in Honour of Nicolai Rubinstein,* ed. Peter Denley and Caroline Elam (London, 1988), 355–58; Nicholas A. Eckstein, *The District of the Green Dragon: Neighbourhood Life and Social Change in Renaissance Florence* (Florence, 1995), 77–87 and chs. 5–6.

[107] Florence Edler de Roover, *L'arte della seta a Firenze nei secoli XIV e XV,* ed. Sergio Tognetti (Florence, 1999), 80.

leaving instructions that he be buried alongside his fellow weavers in their chapel at San Marco.

The usual way of opening up a possible channel to greater wealth and status was for the artisan, even one without much capital, to place a son, still a boy, as a shop or office assistant in a merchant bank or textile firm in the hope that, once having found his way into a leading sector of the economy, he could somehow make his way upward through the ranks. The entrepreneurial brickmaker Benedetto da Terrarossa (encountered in chapter 5) has left traces of this normal path upward in his successive catasto declarations from 1427 to 1469. In his 1427 catasto return Benedetto, the grandson of a waller from the countryside, reported two defunct partnerships for operation of a kiln near the family's place of origin and the investment of £800 that he and his brother had in a one-third share of a partnership for the operation of a kiln in the city rented for *fl.*45 a year. The balance sheet of the firm lists credits with 104 parties worth a total of £2,219. The da Terrarossa brothers owned their own residence in the city, as well as part of another urban house and a substantial farm in their place of origin worth *fl.*357. Their business grew in the complex manner indicated above, and the parent firm was the top business of its kind on a list of the city's company partnerships drawn up for tax purposes in 1451 (but surviving only in part). At the time, Benedetto's brother Paolo had placed his sons in the wool business (Benedetto had no sons), having invested *fl.*725 for a one-fourth share in the firm of Lorenzo d'Ilarione Ilarioni, one of the most prominent figures in the city and a man with close ties to the Medici, whose firm was the top one in its category in the 1451 census of businesses. In his last catasto declaration, in 1469, Benedetto, then eighty years old, owned a kiln worth *fl.*410, a 35 percent share in his firm, and real estate valued at *fl.*1,857—enough to rank him well within the upper middling class.[108]

The two sons of the painter Neri di Bicci, the wealthiest painter in the 1480 catasto, followed the same path upward. In 1460 Neri placed one son, Antonio (b. 1446), with a firm of setaioli and the other, Lorenzo (b. 1447), who had entered a school of commercial arithmetic at the age of eight, with the prominent banker Antonio da Rabatta. The next year, Neri shifted Lorenzo to a firm of setaioli, where he stayed two years and then (at age sixteen) moved on to another firm of setaioli. By 1471 the two brothers had their own firm as setaioli. In 1473 Lorenzo married a woman whose father was a speziali and whose mother was the daughter of a linen draper, "all respectable [*da bene*] artisans of good quality," as Neri commented.[109]

---

[108] Richard A. Goldthwaite, *The Building of Renaissance Florence: An Economic and Social History* (Baltimore, 1980), 192–95.

[109] For Lorenzo's career, see the references in the index entry for him in Neri di Bicci, *Le ricordanze*.

The family of another painter, Sandro Botticelli, also illustrates the kind of professional mobility that led to at least the possibility of economic ascent. His father, Mariano di Vanni Filipepi, was one of three brothers who had a modest tanner's shop. They all lived together in the large household of a grand family, changing their rented residence every so often, and Mariano never accumulated any property of much value. Yet somehow he managed to put his four sons on different paths: one was the painter, one found employment as a broker for the communal dowry fund, one worked with a goldsmith and for a while had his own shop as a battiloro, and one made it into an international merchant-banking firm. This latter, Simone di Mariano Filipepi, was in Naples at the age of fourteen, in 1458, working for the firm of Paolo di Paolo di Bingeri Rucellai. Later he found employment with the Roman bank of Tommaso Spinelli, one of the most prominent bankers in the Holy City, and in 1472, on reorganization of the bank, he became a partner. At that time, since he had no money to invest (as the articles of association state), Spinelli and the other partner gave him an 11 percent share in the corpo of the firm, which represented the capitalization of the value of his service to the company as an accountant and scribe beyond his salary of *fl.*100. Subsequently Simone was occasionally in Naples on what could have been business matters, but he eventually returned to Florence, apparently no longer working for a bank, where he, like his famous brother, became an ardent Savonarolan, giving himself fully over to the cause.[110]

We do not know how things worked out for the sons of da Terrarossa, the sons of Neri di Bicci, or the Filipepi brothers, but they were all taking steps along the usual upward trajectory to greater wealth—assistant (probably as a minor) in a textile firm or a merchant bank, then manager, and finally partner with a share in the capital, often representing the capitalization of his *persona*. Another painter's son who definitely made it all the way was Zanobi di Taddeo Gaddi, although the path cannot be precisely charted. Zanobi made his fortune as a merchant in Venice, where he was associated with Francesco Datini. After his death in 1400 three of his sons returned to Florence to set up a firm, one son going on to rank among the richest men in the 1427 catasto; the fourth, Francesco, set up a company in Rome, where one of his sons became a cardinal and the others major papal bankers.[111]

---

[110] Alessandro Cecchi, *Botticelli* (Milan, 2005), 12–23, recounts the family history. The articles of association of the firm in Rome are found in Yale University, Beinecke Library, Spinelli Papers, box 85a, no. 1597.

[111] Reinhold Mueller, "Mercanti e imprenditori fiorentini a Venezia nel tardo Medioevo," *Società e storia*, no. 55 (1992): 44–46.

The complete ascent, culminating with entrance into the political and social elite, is best documented for the Romoli, thanks to the survival of account books of those in the family who made it to the top. At the beginning of the fifteenth century they were a prominent family of stoneworkers. Romolo and his son Nofri worked at Santa Maria Nuova; Nofri, identified as a stoneworker from Settignano, supplied much of the decorative stonework at the hospital of San Matteo. In the 1427 catasto Nofri's sons, Giuliano and Andrea, reported joint ownership of a stoneworker's shop that had an inventory valued at *fl.*200, and they appended a list of 220 debtors for a total of *fl.*545. Andrea appears as a supplier of decorative stone in the accounts of many of the city's prestigious buildings erected in the second quarter of the century, including the cathedral. In 1450 he was working in his own shop, and he owned a quarry. On the settlement of his estate in 1457, his real-estate holdings were assessed at *fl.*763. Andrea set his sons on a different professional path, however. In 1448 he placed Romolo as a partner in a firm of mercers, and extant ledgers show that by the time of his death in 1472 Romolo was calling himself a battiloro and was trading in silk, with business contacts in Lisbon and Lyons. He nevertheless served occasionally on the consulate of the guild of construction workers. In the 1480 catasto, Romolo's sons, now identifying themselves with the family surname of Romoli, declared real-estate holdings worth *fl.*1,273. One of these sons, Andrea, had a wool shop; another, Francesco, was treasurer of the Monte in 1486–87, one of the highest-paid positions in the government. In 1487 the canons of the cathedral of Fiesole bestowed on Francesco the patronage of their chapel dedicated to San Romolo, which he completely rebuilt. He also had the patronage of a chapel in the Santissima Annunziata in Florence. The ledgers of Romolo and his sons document expenditures, properties, and activities consonant with the economic status the family had gained in its upward trajectory from artisan to entrepreneur in two generations. Their social credentials, however, were only good enough to merit their being mentioned among "the more noble artisans" that Guicciardini consigned to the next to the lowest rank in his five-tiered hierarchy.[112]

Notaries, being members of a major guild and doing the kind of work that opened up personal contacts with the rich and powerful, had clear advantages over most workingmen in undertaking an upward ascent. In fact, many of the new men who appear in the upper ranks on the tax roles of 1403 and 1427 identified themselves as sons of notaries (to judge from the professional title *ser* before their father's name). The story of the upward mobility of the Serristori begins

---

[112] Goldthwaite, *Building of Renaissance Florence*, 277–78. The Romoli account books are located in ASF, Canigiani, 63–69.

with a notary from the provinces and ends with the entrance of his offspring into the ranks of the very rich. Ser Ristoro di ser Iacopo, son of a notary in Figline, upstream on the Arno, probably immigrated to Florence, as did so many others, in the immediate wake of the Black Death. He built up a large practice with prominent clients, achieved some visibility on the political scene, and married a woman with a solid patrimony, the daughter and only heir of another notary who had immigrated from Figline. He sent one of his sons, Giovanni, to the university in Bologna to study law, and the other two he set up in the wool business, he himself having matriculated in the wool guild in 1382. He must have supplied the capital that allowed his son Giovanni, just two years out of the university and a matriculated member of the guild of notaries and lawyers, to invest *fl*.4,000 in an international merchant-banking firm in 1399. Ser Ristoro died in 1400. On the tax rolls three years later, in 1403, the family household, inscribed in Giovanni's name but including also the offspring and heirs of his two deceased brothers, was the fourth wealthiest in the city. The final step in this ascent came with the habit, begun in the following years, of using the surname Serristori. And yet a full two generations later Guicciardini recognized them only in his middle rank, neither noble nor altogether not noble, having arrived on the scene too recently.[113]

Mobility, of course, goes both ways: if some men made it, others did not. Moreover, there were those who went bankrupt, probably several every year. In short, there was downward as well as upward mobility, and both contributed to the considerable fluidity of wealth. An impressionistic sense of this mobility comes from a reading of the city's famed Renaissance palaces. Some are monuments to the success of new men (Serristori, Spinelli, Torrigiani) or of men with ancient names but born into branches that had fallen onto hard times (Gianfigliazzi, Gondi, Rucellai, Strozzi, Tornabuoni-Ridolfi-Corsi); some did not reach completion because of economic problems (Alberti-Corsi, Barbadori, Ilarioni, Nasi-Del Nero-Torrigiani) or because of partible inheritance (Gondi, Rucellai); and others for one reason or another soon changed hands (Albizzi-Valori, Boni-Martelli-Antinori, Pazzi, Pitti).

Yet one of the principal intentions of a palace builder, as we know from their testaments, was to assure the stability of his family's wealth and status in the future. The appearance of so many palaces in the fifteenth century, therefore, represented

---

[113] Tognetti, *Da Figline a Firenze*, ch. 1. The emergence of the Dei from immigrant to goldsmiths and then to setaioli and lanaioli has been traced by Doris Carl in "Zur Goldschmiedefamilie Dei, mit neuen Dokumenten zu Antonio Pollaiuolo und Andrea Verrocchio," *Mitteilungen des kunsthistorischen Institutes in Florenz* 26 (1982): 129–66. The rise of the Cambini is documented in Sergio Tognetti, *Il banco Cambini: Affari e mercati di una compagnia mercantile-bancaria nella Firenze del XV secolo* (Florence, 1999), ch. 1, but that ascent is less problematic since they are first documented as already established as linaioli with their own firm.

a certain brake on social mobility. That brake took effect in part because of the ever-widening cultural gap, from the end of the fifteenth century on, between people at different economic levels, demarcating more sharply the social confines of a worker's daily life. As the rich became very much richer, their consumption habits set them off more conspicuously, while their increasing recourse to private tutors for education and the formation of academies in the sixteenth century for the social exchange of ideas generated cultural interests that defined a more closed elite status. Now more anxious to define their identity as nobles, and with no feudal behavioral models to appeal to in their own past, they also became more explicitly contemptuous of professional activities requiring working with one's hands, including retail dealing with the public, as a disqualification for noble status, though this did not bar them from their traditional upper-class activities as entrepreneurs. The structure of political society also hardened following the abolition of the institutions of the widely participatory government of the republic and the reorganization of the state around a princely court complete with bureaucracy and consultative bodies. In the sphere of religious practice too a process of social segregation set in. It manifested itself in the appearance of private chapels in the homes of the rich and in the transformation of confraternities into more exclusive social organizations. Whereas in the fifteenth century membership in these institutions was open to people from across the social spectrum, toward the end of the century they tended to become more socially homogeneous, taking in people only from the same neighborhood and from the same social background and occupations. Also manifesting a kind of segregation, this one at the lowest level of society, were the numerous brigades *(potenze)* of working-class men who joined together for festive activities. First appearing on the scene in the late fifteenth century, these groups were formed, very likely by men in the same trade, in neighborhoods throughout the city, and the considerable prominence they gained in the public life of the city in the course of the sixteenth century reflects something of a class consciousness (albeit with no political, let alone radical, agenda).[114] It is not without some irony that in this more consciously structured society the men at the top were at the same time demonstrating considerable appreciation of the artistic products created by men who made their living working with their hands.

Although these changes did not result in any institutional definition of nobility, upper-class families found it for themselves in the long historical record of their ancestors' political officeholding during the period of the republic, which

---

[114] For the transformation of one confraternity, see Lorenzo Polizzotto, *Children of the Promise: The Confraternity of the Purification and the Socialization of Youths in Florence, 1427–1785* (Oxford, 2004), 43, 155. The brigades are described in David Rosenthal, "The Genealogy of Empires: Ritual Politics and State Building in Early Modern Florence," *I Tatti Studies* 8 (1999): 197–234.

they compiled in family *prioriste,* a new kind of document conceived as an affirmation of their antiquity and hence their nobility. In the documentary record of Florentine social life, the prioriste replaced the *ricordanze,* private record books, one of the most characteristic types of private documents generated by Florentines in the later fourteenth and fifteenth centuries. The existence of these ricordanze in Florence as in no other Italian city has been explained as the expression of a mentality generated in a relatively fluid, open, and changing society in which men sought legitimization in the preservation of knowledge of practical family use and genealogical interest. Keeping such a record, a habit so well documented for the late fourteenth and fifteenth centuries, fell out of fashion in the course of the early sixteenth century, to be replaced by the compilation of a priorista, a list of all of one's ancestors who had held the priorate, the highest office in the state. A record book was a personal document resembling a diary, kept over the years and often taking the form of an appendage to a ledger of ongoing accounts; the priorista was an impersonal construction, a formal historical document drawn up with great care and usually illustrated with the family's coat of arms. If the former was a document born in the search for legitimization, the latter was the proof of status. The replacement of the record book of the late fourteenth and fifteenth centuries by the priorista of the sixteenth century as a record of family history can thus be read as yet another signal of a brake on social mobility.

Yet mobility, however attenuated, continued into the sixteenth century despite a changing social culture, the geographic contraction of merchant-banking activity abroad, and the transformation of the state from a republic into a principality. The story of Benvenuto Olivieri's success early in the century has already been recounted, and the rise of the Riccardi in the course of the century to become perhaps the wealthiest family after the Medici has been well documented.[115] The roster of entrepreneurs who went off to Germany and Poland includes many names unfamiliar to historians of the city's republican past. When Cosimo de' Medici went about consolidating his power as duke, he brought yet other new men onto the scene. Some came from abroad, some came in from the subject provincial towns, and some came up from the lower ranks of Florentine society. They were present in significant numbers at court, in the bureaucracy, in the military Order of Santo Stefano, and in the two principal consultative bodies of government, the Senate and the Council of 200. Of the appointments the Medici made to these bodies down to 1600, only 10 percent of those named to the Senate but 43 percent of those named to the Council of 200 were men whose families fell outside the

---

[115] Malanima, *I Riccardi.*

priorate elite of the republic.[116] So yet once again in the historiography we find the theme "new men." Later Florentine writers looking back over the history of the noble class commented on the rise of new families precisely at this time. Of course many of these men arrived, not through the ranks of entrepreneurs, but by way of the new channels to wealth and status opened up by the Medici regime. In any event, the newness of wealth was not yet a barrier to status. "He who is born rich, however much he may be of ignoble descent and a sheep with a golden fleece, is held to be noble and equal to one who is born noble," wrote Aurelio Grifoni, a man of high status whose family had recently moved from the provinces into the capital, in 1629.[117] One wonders what the descendants of Piero Guicciardini felt about the matter a century and a half after their ancestor's more contemptuously nuanced reading of the social scene.

In the final analysis, the degree of upward mobility in one place can be judged only by comparison with that in other places. It remains to be seen how Florence compared with other cities in Europe—to what extent it appears unique only because it is so much better documented than any other city and to what degree mobility slackened in the sixteenth century. In the meantime, we can take Michelangelo, for all the overpowering genius of his unique personality, as representative of his native city in at least this one respect. He initiated his career as an artisan in the workshop of a painter and spent most of his life in Rome working for the popes, but nothing obsessed him more, with all the passion consonant with his artistic personality, than the desire to establish his family with sound social credentials back in Florence, an ambition that had its roots in the realities of his native city. He knew that in the end what really counted was wealth. And he succeeded.

A Profile of Wealth Distribution in 1427

The famed 1427 catasto marks a moment of stasis in the fluidity of Florentine society, for it caught the distribution of wealth, at least for a moment, through a virtually complete and very detailed survey of the state's tax base in the city and its territory. It is generally regarded as a reasonably accurate survey of private wealth. A number of individual returns can be checked against surviving accounts of the people who submitted them. Fortunately, thanks to the Herculean efforts of David Herlihy and Christiane Klapisch-Zuber, we have a computerized version of some of it, which is now on the Internet and therefore available

[116] Litchfield, *Emergence of a Bureaucracy*, 25.

[117] Franco Angiolini, "Accumulazione della ricchezza e affermazione sociale nella Toscana medicea," in *Gerarchie economiche e gerarchie sociali, secoli XII–XVIII* (Florence, 1990), 633–47, quotation on 636.

to everyone.[118] Their objective, however, was to collect data primarily for the construction of a demographic profile of the population; given the limitations of computer technology when they were doing their work, in the late 1960s, they could not have handled the vast economic data in the document as well. Their computer version provides only total values for four categories of the private wealth of each household: real estate, credits in the Monte, other assets, and liabilities. These totals, however, hardly lend themselves to much economic analysis. Only that for real-estate holdings is fairly solid, although it cannot be broken down into urban and rural property or into residential and business property. The others disguise so many variables—for example, the difference between a shop inventory, outstanding credits, and a share in an international merchant-banking firm or the difference between money owed as a debt and liens on current income, such as rent—that generalizations based on them are precarious. It is surely only a matter of time before further research exploits the much greater potential computer technology has today in order to mine these documents for the enormous quantity and variety of economic data they contain. Once that is accomplished, we can proceed to construct a much more precise profile of the social structure of the economy. Still, we already have significantly more data for Florentine society than for any other society at the time, and the following analysis is an attempt to make some use of the data currently available, however subject they are to reservations relative to these highly generalized economic categories.

Taken for what it is, the survey of the 1427 catasto reveals a highly skewed distribution of total wealth: the top 1 percent of the population—just under a hundred households—owned 27 percent of the entire wealth of the city; for 16 percent of heads of households the value of their liabilities was higher than the value of their assets, leaving them with no net worth for taxable purposes; and an additional 15 percent had no assets whatsoever to report. Put in the perspective of the entire territorial state, the upper 1 percent of the city's population possessed only 18 percent of the total net wealth of the state, whereas the number of city residents equal to 1 percent of the total population of the state possessed 38 percent of that total wealth. Florentine historians have tended to take these data at face value to emphasize the concentration of wealth in the hands of the rich on the one hand and the extent of poverty on the other; unfortunately, they have not compared these data with data for any other places. For example, a comparison

[118] *Online Catasto of 1427*, version 1.3, ed. David Herlihy, Christiane Klapisch-Zuber, R. Burr Litchfield, and Anthony Molho (machine-readable data file based on *Census and Property Survey of Florentine Domains in the Province of Tuscany, 1427–1480*, data file by David Herlihy and Christiane Klapisch-Zuber) (Providence, RI: Florentine Renaissance Resources/STG, Brown University, 2002), http://www.stg.brown.edu/projects/catasto/overview.html.

TABLE 7.3
*Wealth Distribution by Household in Florence in
1427 and in the United States in 1995*

Wealth bracket	% of total wealth possessed	
	Florence	US
Top 1%	27.0	38.5
Top 5%	54.1	60.3
Top 10%	68.9	71.8
Top 20%	84.2	83.9
Top 40%	99.7	95.3

SOURCES: For Florence, *Online Catasto of* 1427 (see table 7.2);
for the United States, Lisa A. Keister, *Wealth in America:
Trends in Wealth Inequality* (Cambridge, 2000), 64.

of the ownership of wealth in Florence in 1427 with the ownership of wealth in
the United States in 1995, laid out in table 7.3, shows very similar distribution patterns at both the highest and the lowest levels. Such a comparison of two very
different economies presents many problems, especially relative to the difference
in the distribution of total net worth as compared with total income in a modern
economy, and in the end is completely deceptive, but the similarity at first sight
ought to be a warning to historians about judging the social quality of this economy without first looking at other places.

On the basis of the data we have, we can break the population down into
classes of wealth ownership, the term *class* being used here only in this strictly
quantitative sense, without any ideological overtones. Table 7.4 does this in a way
that allows us to talk about three basic economic classes—the rich, a middling
class, and the poor. The table represents an arbitrary ranking order in the
household distribution of both gross and net (taxable) wealth, and it further indicates the percentage of the total population that falls into each rank. The rich
as defined here are those 267 households, or 2.73 percent of all households, that had
more than *fl.*5,000 in net taxable assets. Below them are the "middling classes,"
comprising 60 percent of all households, whose net taxable wealth ranged between *fl.*36 and *fl.*5,000. The lower echelons of this middling class—the lower
middle class—are here considered to be those with net taxable assets ranging
from *fl.*100 down to *fl.*36; below are the poor, who had no more than *fl.*35 in net
assets.

The division separating the lower middling class from the poor has been set at
*fl.*35, which was approximately what an unskilled workingman in the construction industry could hope to earn in a year if he worked full time (250 days at 10
soldi a day, with the price of the florin being 80 soldi). Presumably, any worker
who could build up a patrimony equal to what he earned in a year was marginally

TABLE 7.4
Classes of Wealth as Reported in the 1427 Catasto

Class	Range of wealth (fl.)	Gross wealth (before deductions)			Net (taxable) wealth		
		% of total wealth	Households		% of total wealth	Households	
			Number	%		Number	%
Upper, rich	5,001+	45.93	372	3.80	42.59	267	2.73
Upper middling	1,001–5,000	37.24	1,747	17.86	37.87	1,376	14.07
Middling	101–1,000	15.91	4,027	41.18	18.60	3,573	36.53
Lower middling	36–100	0.75	1,172	11.98	0.78	908	9.28
Poor	1–35	0.18	1,031	10.54	0.15	630	6.44
Propertyless poor	0		1,431	14.63		3,026	30.94
Total		100.01	9,780	99.99	99.99	9,780	99.99

above the poverty line. If one defines poverty as propertylessness, then only about 15 percent of households were poor. But by the definition of poverty used here—a cutoff value of *fl.*35 in gross assets—25 percent of households were poor. This figure rises to 37 percent if we use net taxable wealth after deductions as the criterion.

The distribution of wealth based on Herlihy and Klapisch-Zuber's survey of the 1427 catasto is especially deceptive at the low end. The data defining the lowest two categories of wealth as reported in table 7.4 are ambiguous because many of these households had liabilities that more than cancelled out relatively substantial assets. The extent of this kind of indebtedness was, in fact, much greater than what a poor person as ordinarily conceived could expect to incur, especially in a society not yet characterized by consumerism and easy credit. Some of this indebtedness allowed for deductions consisted in capitalization of rents paid for homes and shops and therefore represented a lien on income, not a debt in a strict sense. In other words, the poverty of many of the people in these lowest categories was relative. Even among the 1,431 people who had no assets to report, 456, or about one-third, had liabilities of more than *fl.*70 (the amount of liability that would represent the capitalization, at 7 percent, of the normal rent of up to *fl.*5 that a poor person paid for his residence). Some of these people, in fact, reported liabilities of up to several hundred florins (with one at *fl.*1,500). In a society in which the most skilled construction worker could expect to earn only about *fl.*60–70 annually, anyone who could run up such debts does not fit our definition of a poor person. Additional research into these individual returns would probably help clarify the situation.

A second problem of trying to measure the extent of poverty in the city on the basis of the catasto data is that too many people—residents of religious houses, servants, day laborers, the homeless, the desperately poor—were left out of the survey. The most numerous of these unknowns are servants and the structural poor, those who found what work they could, living from hand to mouth with no possibility of accumulating wealth of any kind. Inasmuch as a mid-sixteenth-century census of households documents the presence of at least one servant in 45 percent of the households at that time, it is not unreasonable to estimate that in 1427 servants were to be found in at least 15 percent of households.[119] As to the structural poor omitted from the 1427 catasto, they may have constituted about 15 percent of the population. For other preindustrial cities, estimates of the population too poor to be considered taxable range from 15 percent to as high as 40 percent.[120] Florentine authorities estimated in 1630, when the city faced serious plague, that 15 percent of the population (12,000 out of a population of around 80,000) needed some kind of charitable assistance in normal times.[121] Taken together, these two categories of people missed by the 1427 catasto would alone raise the total population of the city, even by conservative estimates, from the 38,144 living in the households registered in the catasto to between 45,000 and 50,000 (1,500 servants and about 6,000 to 7,000 adults, along with their families, who were too poor even to be considered for taxation). If we factor into our calculations the many people mentioned above who were not captured in the catasto, the number of poor might rise by another 15–20 percent, to 30–40 percent of the total population, depending on how many at the lowest level in the catasto records were really "poor." How much more or less extensive poverty was in Florence, a relatively highly industrial city, as compared with other cities at the time depends on, first, how one defines poverty; second, whether one thinks the catasto officials reached farther down the economic scale of the city's population than did their counterparts in other cities; and third, what estimates are made about the number of people the officials did not include. Speculation on such nebulous variables would require a complex discussion that is hardly appropriate in this context, and the subject remains open to future research. The objective of the preliminary exercise engaged in here is to caution against abuse in interpreting the data currently available.

The consideration of all those omitted from the 1427 survey changes another way the statistics derived from the computer printout are to be read. The sex ratio

[119] Pietro Battara, *La popolazione di Firenze alla metà del '500* (Florence, 1935), 70.

[120] Stefano D'Amico, *Le contrade e la città: Sistema produttivo e spazio urbano a Milano fra Cinque e Seicento* (Milan, 1994), 124 and ch. 7, estimates 15 percent for Milan; Marino Berengo, *L'Europa delle città: Il volto della società urbana europea tra Medioevo ed Età Moderna* (Turin, 1999), 790–92, estimates about 20 percent for German cities. In seventeenth-century England it has been estimated that about 40 percent of households were exempt from taxation because of poverty, but many of these were headed by workingmen "managing to keep their heads above water." Keith Wrightson, *Earthly Necessities: Economic Lives in Early Modern Britain* (New Haven, CT, 2000), 319.

[121] Carlo M. Cipolla, *Fighting the Plague in Seventeenth-Century Italy* (Madison, WI, 1981), 17.

that Herlihy and Klapisch-Zuber's analysis derived from the smaller population figure would be quite different, since many of these additional people, especially servants, were women. And this in turn would change some of the demographic and sociological analysis of Florentine society based on this ratio.

At the high end of the wealth distribution curve, more than three-fourths of the 164 men in the upper class, as defined by gross wealth, who identified their occupation (only about 45 percent of the total number in this class) were merchants, bankers, lanaioli, or setaioli. These entrepreneurs commanded the leading sectors of the economy and, accordingly, reaped the profits made therein. More than three-fourths of all the men in these occupations fall into the upper-middling and upper classes. The one other principal identifying category that appears alongside the entrepreneurs in these upper two classes of wealth is that of men with the title *messer,* a title used in Florence for judges, relatively high-ranking churchmen, and knights. Most of these men belonged to the upper-middling class and had probably been knighted while in state service of one kind or another, including that of ambassador to a foreign court. Many were most likely in business at a high level. In any event, men in the categories of bankers, merchants, industrialists, and messeri enjoyed substantial wealth, as table 7.5 shows. Within this group, a very large gap separates the merchants and bankers from the textile manufacturers and messeri; and another large gap separates all of these from everyone else, with the doctors and speziali alone (lumped together because they belonged to the same guild) falling in an intermediate range. The aforementioned survey made in 1451 to tax businesses has the same rank order and comparable gaps: merchant-banking firms were assessed an average of *fl.*53, textile firms *fl.*27–28, and all the others below *fl.*19.

The average wealth of almost all the principal occupational categories of artisans, shopkeepers, and others in the service sector as represented in table 7.5 puts them solidly in the middling class. If we look at real-estate holdings alone—the most secure kind of investment—37 percent of those who had assets, some 3,124 households, had property worth 70–500 florins, exclusive of the house they used as a residence, which was exempt from assessment. Some benchmarks can be used to relate the levels of wealth defining this middling class to the economic realities of the time: *fl.*40–60 was the top salary range of employees of an international merchant-banking firm, such as that of the Medici, below the level of the manager; *fl.*70 was what the most skilled construction worker could hope to earn in a year; *fl.*100 was what a bank manager might be paid, and it was what Brunelleschi earned as head of the staff of the cathedral works, the highest salary an artisan could have hoped to earn; *fl.*60–190 was the range of salaries in the city's chancellery, its bureaucratic center. Another benchmark is the investment it took to generate an income: *fl.*500 invested in real estate would have yielded a

TABLE 7.5
*Average Wealth of the Top Occupational Categories as
Reported in the 1427 Catasto*

Category	Number	Average wealth in florins	
		Net	Gross
Merchants, bankers	69	9,234	12,278
Messeri	47	4,862	7,041
Lanaioli, setaioli	319	3,404	4,209
Doctors, speziali	89	1,009	1,327
Notaries, judges	284	722	949
All other occupations		80–598	—

NOTE: Only 55 percent of heads of households reported an occupation. The figures for the different groups in the last category, only two of which were below *fl.*100, can be found in David Herlihy and Christiane Klapisch-Zuber, *Les toscans et leurs families: Une étude du catasto florentin de 1427* (Paris, 1978), 299.

passive income from rents equal to the maximum annual earnings of an un-skilled workingman (a calculation using the catasto formula of 7 percent as a basis for capitalizing income); *fl.*1,000 invested in real estate would have assured one a fairly comfortable life as a *rentier*. Of households with assets to report, 13 percent had real-estate holdings valued above *fl.*1,000; 26 percent, above *fl.*500; and 63 percent, above *fl.*70—all excluding residences.

Referring to all these people in the middling classes in terms of averages, we lose sight of the exceptional performers. Men who fall outside the top occupa-tional categories—that is, those of merchants, bankers, lanaioli, and setaioli, along with judges, doctors, and messeri—constituted no fewer than about one-third of those in the upper-middling class and above. Most of these came from the major guilds or worked in textiles (dyers, cloth retailers, linen drapers) or were upscale retailers (mercers, speziali, secondhand dealers), goldsmiths, or no-taries. Men from other, more modest occupations, however, can also be found in this upper-middling class. The 719 men who declared more than *fl.*1,000 in liquid investments alone, as distinct from land and government obligations, include 7 shoemakers, 7 wine dealers, 4 tanners, a carpenter, and a weaver of wool. Whether in so identifying themselves these men were indicating their occupation or their guild membership will require a closer reading of the catasto materials, but these documents have already revealed goldsmiths, mercers, linen drapers, and sec-ondhand dealers who participated in partnerships with a corpo of more than *fl.*1,000.

Unfortunately, no one has yet undertaken the task of dividing wealth reported in the catasto into other than three categories—government obligations, real es-tate, and everything else. Real estate is therefore the only form of private invest-ment for which we have valid statistics, and they are all the more valid because the authorities could verify them. About 73 percent of heads of households owned their own residence, and two-thirds possessed real estate of some kind or another, inside or outside the city, other than their residence. Of course, ownership was concentrated in the hands of the better off, but as we have seen, land did not have an overriding dominance in their investment portfolios. Of the rich as defined here, fewer than half—116, or 43 percent—had more wealth in land than in other kinds of investments (excluding government obligations); 51 had more than *fl.*5,000 invested in real estate, and 9 had more than *fl.*10,000, the largest land-owner being Palla Strozzi, whose holdings were worth *fl.*53,040. Of the top 1 percent of the wealthiest households, only one-seventh had more then 50 percent of their total wealth in real estate, while two-thirds had less than 25 percent of their wealth in this kind of investment, and fewer than half ranked among the top 1 percent of owners of real estate.

After 1427 no document captured the city's wealth in a moment of stasis. Subsequent tax records are useful for obtaining a global view only of real-estate holdings. Real estate, however, is hardly a valid measure of private wealth in a city like Florence, where the rich invested heavily in business enterprises.

Redistribution of Wealth in the Fifteenth and Sixteenth Centuries

The evidence presented throughout this book for the generation and circulation of wealth in its various forms, if brought together, justifies the hypothesis that the flow of wealth into the city increased during the fifteenth and sixteenth centuries. The phenomenon was in part the result of the strong performance of the traditional leading sectors of the economy. In the fifteenth century, international banking drew strength from the organization and growth of permanent exchange fairs and from new levels of government finances, especially in the Papal States, and the textile industries found strong new markets in the growing capitals of Rome, Naples, and Constantinople. In the sixteenth century, both the lanaioli and the setaioli were producing high-quality textiles that sold well in the expanding markets of northern Europe, with per capita output, as we have suggested, being perhaps as high as at any time in the history of the city. Profits from international merchant banking also remained high despite geographic contraction.

And the territorial state increasingly enriched the capital. Florentines' continually buying up land in the countryside meant that the city siphoned off that much more in profits from the agricultural sector. For lack of relevant studies, we do not know how much those profits might have increased as a result of the greater concentration of landholdings and hence a more productive management of estates, but the return from sales of agricultural products certainly grew, thanks to the "revolutionary" inflation of food prices that occurred over the course of the sixteenth century. The new ducal government also brought more wealth into the capital. Its more efficient fiscal administration raised tax revenues from the territorial state, while the immense private patrimony that Cosimo I and his sons built up by investing in rural properties and enterprises such as the iron magona paid profits that they used to support one of the grandest courts in Italy. The wealth that the Medici and their government brought to the city flowed into the private sector by way of the state bureaucracy and court expenditures, but it also permitted them to run both government and court in a way that paid dividends to Florentines in the form of lower taxes. The state Monte and the Monte di Pietà gave men of even modest means their first institutional outlet for savings that paid dividends. For all these reasons, in the fifteenth and sixteenth centuries more wealth was flowing into the hands of Florentines. And during much of this period, especially after the advent of Cosimo I in 1534, decreasing military expenditures enabled the government to reduce the burden of direct taxes on those who had property, leaving them with more disposable income.

THE RICH BECOME RICHER   It is hardly surprising that a disproportionate share of this increased wealth pouring into the city ended up in the pockets of the rich; indeed, there was a marked trend of the rich becoming much richer during the later fifteenth and sixteenth centuries. On his death in 1491 Filippo Strozzi left an estate worth *fl.*100,000, 75 percent more than the net worth of Palla Strozzi, the richest man on the catasto roster of 1427; and only five men on that roster had a total net worth higher than the *fl.*30,000 that Filippo paid out for his palace alone. A generation later, in 1528, the Venetian ambassador estimated that eighty Florentines had estates worth more than *fl.*50,000. In 1532 the estate of Iacopo Salviati in Rome amounted to *fl.*350,000. At the end of the century, as we have seen, the very rich, such as the Corsi and the Riccardi, were investing more in business enterprises than the rich had invested anytime earlier. The annual income of *sc.*24,040 that the Riccardi had from their business activities in the 1590s was, in real value, equivalent to half the capital the Medici had invested in the parent company of their agglomerate in 1451.[122] How much more the rich at the end of the century were spending for everything from household furnishings to chapels, described in chapter 5, is another index to how much richer they were. Dowries too were very much higher. Whereas the

[122] Malanima, *I Riccardi*, 74–75.

dowry of *fl*.3,500 that Filippo Strozzi provided one of his daughters was exceptionally high at the time, a century later, between 1585 and 1617, top dowries, at *fl*.15,000–20,000, were two to three times that in real value, equivalent to what would have been a major fortune in 1427.[123]

As noted above, many men also acquired more land and concentrated their holdings in large estates. The sixteenth century, however, did not see a major "move to the land" if by that one means the converse—that men abandoned the city as their principal residence and withdrew investments from the commercial, banking, and industrial sectors. At the end of the century, although many of the city's wealthiest residents increased their landholdings, they still had significant business interests; and we have encountered men who made great business fortunes in the sixteenth century. For instance, the Riccardi in 1600, not yet quite as rich as Filippo Strozzi a century earlier but well on their way to accumulating what was probably the biggest private fortune in the seventeenth century, had less than a third of their patrimony invested in land; the rest was in banking, commerce, and industry.[124] The much greater wealth of the rich, and the transformation of the state into a principality, did not generate a new sense of nobility that compromised their business interests. Many merchant-bankers were members of the Senate, the inner circle of advisers closest to the grand duke. As a correspondent in Florence wrote to the Spanish merchant Simón Ruiz in 1572, "In this town there is a very ancient tradition of high esteem for merchants: prince and nobles are themselves businessmen . . . they are all merchants."[125] In an appeal entrepreneurs made to the grand duke in 1605 responding to his proposal to regulate their account books, they claimed to be "noble and well born"; a sign of changing times is their further comment that support of business would help counter the tendency of the young to follow "the vocation of knight" (*la professione cavalleresca*).[126] Yet as late as 1654 an English visitor to the city, Richard Lassels, commented that

> the gentry here hold it no disgrace to have a ship at Sea, and a back warehouse, with a faithful servant and a countbooke at home, whiles they vapor it at Court, and in their Coaches. This makes them hold up their noble familiyes by the chinn, and not onely preserves them from sincking, but allso makes them Swimm in a full Sea of honour by being able to buy offices for their children in Princes Courts, whereby they come to greatest preferrements: whither when they are come, no man questioneth

[123] Richard A. Goldthwaite, *Wealth and the Demand for Art in Italy, 1300–1600* (Baltimore, 1993), 57–59. The information on dowries comes from Malanima, *I Riccardi*, 92.

[124] Malanima, *I Riccardi*, 74, 79.

[125] Felipe Ruiz Martín, *Lettres marchandes échangées entre Florence et Medina del Campo* (Paris, 1965), lxxv.

[126] Armando Sapori, "La registrazione dei libri di commercio in Toscana nell'anno 1605," *Studi*, 1:48.

the way they came thither: whether by water, or by Land: by traffic or by sword: by the Count-book or the army.[127]

Greater concentration of wealth in land, however, may account for the increasing attention the rich directed to the preservation of their patrimonies, thereby introducing a dynamic of accumulation into the history of private wealth that worked against the generational division of patrimonies effected by the earlier practice of partible inheritance. Although large estates were not bound by legal primogeniture, they tended to stay intact as a result of practices that had the same effect. The rich generally had fewer sons, and younger sons tended not to marry, with the result that patrimonies were less subject to generational fragmentation. In addition, the earlier practice of partible inheritance among male offspring came to be compromised by encumbering real-estate holdings, especially those that enjoyed a certain prestige, with fedecommessi to block any eventual alienation from family ownership.[128] The consequent accumulation of property within a single estate was yet another dynamic driving the greater concentration of wealth in the hands of the rich. This was not a phenomenon of "refeudalization," however, since the land, except in Sienese territory, had long been cleared of traditional feudal and manorial encumbrances. As Machiavelli observed, there were no real "gentiluomini" in Florence.

THE VICISSITUDES OF THE POOR   The poor are always present, in any society at any time, but their absence in the documents makes it difficult to learn anything about them. We have already attempted to define them and to estimate their numbers, using the criterion of assets as declared in the 1427 catasto. It is more difficult to get some sense of how poor they were and how the extent of poverty changed over time. One standard used to get a grip on this subject is the daily wage of the unskilled worker in the construction industry, which plausibly is an index to the level of the minimum wage in the economy. Relatively few men in the Florentine economy worked for a daily wage, however, and it is not a foregone conclusion that this index functions also for evaluating the level of earnings of the poor who worked on other terms. In some ways construction work is not typical: the work is hard and notoriously irregular, subject to seasonal variations, problems of financing, the usual fluctuations in the work on any building project,

---

[127] Edward Cheney, *The Grand Tour and the Great Rebellion: Richard Lassels and "The Voyage of Italy" in the Seventeenth Century* (Geneva, 1985), 170.

[128] Calonaci, *Dietro lo scudo incantato*. Calonaci sees the fedecommesso, which arose in the fifteenth century and was used increasingly in the sixteenth century, not as a symptom of economic stagnation and crisis but as an instrument "per perfezionare la traiettoria dei guadagni fatti durante il boom economico tardo medievale" (216).

and, more generally, building cycles. The poor, in any event, included more than just the lowest-paid workers. Besides these working poor, there were orphans, widows, the elderly, and other economically helpless people, not to mention beggars and those voluntary poor who joined together in religious communities or attached themselves to convents and monasteries—all the thousands of people, in short, who were not included in the 1427 catasto survey.

If the purchasing power of the construction worker's wage as traced in chapter 5 can be taken as an index, the level of poverty was at its highest in the years immediately before the Black Death (the data base thins out if one goes back much further), it fell after 1348 to remain relatively low for the next century and a quarter, and then it slowly began to rise, reaching the earlier level in the second half of the sixteenth century. Unfortunately, we cannot measure this change with any more precision. For the fourteenth and early fifteenth centuries we have reasonably good studies of the cost of a family food basket, but for the sixteenth century there is only one series of wheat prices and Giuseppe Parenti's classic but limited study of other components of the food basket.[129] Nor is there anything like the 1427 catasto records to provide the material for a survey of the distribution of wealth. Hence, comparisons across time are only suggestive at best. Nor are there any comparisons across space, so we have no sense of whether the situation in Florence was different from that in other cities at the time. Historians have not hesitated to bemoan the existence of poverty in the city, but they have not gone on to show whether this specific economy was more susceptible to poverty than others or that it was particularly successful in reducing it in comparison with other places. Florence had a more industrialized economy than most other cities, and its population reached a level toward the end of the sixteenth century, as it had in the first half of the fourteenth century, where it outgrew the capacity of its region to supply sufficient wheat, but it remains to be seen whether poverty was more severe there than in other places as a result.

There is also the problem of the reality that lies behind the statistics used to construct trends in laborers' wages. Both upward and downward movements were subject to much instability occasioned by ever-recurring bouts with the plague, bad harvests, sudden work stoppages, political unrest, and sometimes war. Even in the best of times life was precarious for those living on the edge of

---

[129] The most thorough study of all is that of Charles Marie de La Roncière, "Poveri e povertà a Firenze nel XIV secolo," in *Tra preghiera e rivolta*, 197–281. The subsequent period, to the end of the fifteenth century, is documented in Sergio Tognetti, "Prezzi e salari nella Firenze tardomedievale: Un profilo," *ASI* 153 (1995): 263–333. Wheat prices and wages over the entire period, to the end of the sixteenth century, are published in Goldthwaite, *Building of Renaissance Florence*, 317–50. The pioneering study by Giuseppe Parenti, *Prime ricerche sulla rivoluzione dei prezzi a Firenze* (Florence, 1939), is based on one small sample.

poverty. In normal times relief from hard work, and from the monotony of their lives in general, came in the form of the numerous civic and religious celebrations, which averaged about one a week, besides Sundays, over a year; and in hard times substantial assistance came from the city's numerous charitable institutions. These people remained on the margins of the market, however; they were powerless to do anything collectively about their situation for lack of any common institutional base or any energizing "class consciousness."

The Ciompi revolt, so famous in the European history of popular revolts, was a matter less of economic distress than of extreme dissatisfaction with the harsh system of justice imposed on wool workers by the guild. Driving it were the political ambitions of certain groups of low-skilled laborers who had been left out of the guild constitution of the state and were determined to set up their own guild. Nor, as we have seen, were they against taxes so much as they were against a tax system based on forced loans. Their program said nothing about indirect taxes, which, as a regressive form of taxation, hit the poor the hardest. The Ciompi revolt, in other words, manifested few signs of economic distress. Real wages had fallen slightly in the 1370s, but they were still much higher than they had been before 1348. If anything, one might argue, this dip in real wages may have dampened expectations aroused by the favorable conditions workers had become accustomed to during the preceding two decades, in the aftermath of the Black Death.

In any event, things got much better again in the 1380s. After the Ciompi episode, Florence seems to have been a place of relative political tranquility, to judge, as more than one historian has observed, from the almost total absence of mass lower-class insurrection, even if it is not clear whether this was due to domination by the ruling elite or, rather, to a relative stability in the economic lives of the poor. The city had its share of criminality and personal violence, much no doubt instigated by economic desperation, and workers were subject to a harsh, even cruel, system of justice for any violation of the laws, but on the few occasions when masses of people took to the street, they had more often than not been rallied by factionalism among the ruling class. In any event, Florence avoided the violent popular political unrest that frequently broke out in the industrialized areas of the Low Countries at the time, including Bruges, a city of about the same size as Florence. And poverty did not surface as a threat to the stability of the internal political order in the sixteenth century, when the "price revolution" reduced the purchasing power of day laborers' wages to the level where they had been before 1348.[130]

---

[130] For the most recent analysis of the Ciompi revolt, with full bibliographical references, see Franco Franceschi, "I Ciompi a Firenze, Siena e Perugia," in *Rivolte urbane e rivolte contadine nell'Europa del Trecento: Un confronto* (forthcoming). Charles Marie de La Roncière, in "La condition des salariés à Florence au XIVe siècles," in *Il "Tumulto" dei Ciompi: Un momento di storia fioren-*

Institutional structures for dealing with the poor have been studied for the period of the republic (although not for the sixteenth century), but it is difficult to relate that history to changes in the extent or depth of poverty.[131] Guild statutes, most of which date from the early fourteenth century, provide assistance to members for dowries and burials but reveal little concern for more comprehensive social-welfare programs. Around 1300, institutions called hospitals or hospices *(ospedali)* emerged to take care of specific kinds of problems. Widows, prostitutes, and victims of plague and venereal disease found refuge in these places. In 1419 the silk guild decided to build the city's great orphanage, the Ospedale degli Innocenti. Another category of public welfare institutions was the confraternity, or confraternal-like organization, which distributed alms directly to the poor. The confraternity of Orsanmichele, founded in 1294, gradually took on this public function and emerged as one of the city's most prominent institutions in the second quarter of the fourteenth century, a time when the extent of poverty as defined above was at its highest. The confraternity's annual income from donations and bequest was greater than that of the two other large welfare institutions, the hospitals of Santa Maria Nuova and San Paolo, together, and this status found a manifestation in the great public grain market that carried its name. As a charitable institution, however, Orsanmichele went into rapid decline after the Black Death, partly because it had a less pressing functional role to play in the improved economic situation. Other important conduits of assistance were the confraternities organized by discrete groups of artisans, such as painters, cobblers, farriers, tailors, construction workers, and the various workers within the textile industries. Although after the Ciompi revolt these institutions were regarded with some suspicion as providing people the opportunity to meet to organize political opposition rather than to share religious devotion, they became more numerous in the course of the later fifteenth and sixteenth centuries.

To whatever extent the level of poverty changed over the course of the fifteenth and sixteenth centuries, the poor came to be conceived in a different manner. The notion of the blessed poor as objects of charity gave way to a suspicion about their

---

tina ed europea (Florence, 1981), 31, recognizes that fiscal pressure even at this point was not disastrous; but in *Prix et salaires à Florence au XIVe siècle, 1280–1390* (Rome, 1982), 71–72, he puts considerable emphasis on the problem of indebtedness of the Ciompi, without, however, providing much evidence. Samuel K. Cohn Jr., "The Character of Protest in Mid-Quattrocento," in the same volume, remarks the political quiescence of the poor in the subsequent period. See also F. W. Kent, "Be Rather Loved Than Feared," 15, 24–29.

[131] Amleto Spicciani, "Solidarietà, previdenza e assistenza per gli artigiani nell'Italia medioevale (secoli XII–XV)," in *Artigiani e salariati: Il mondo del lavoro nell'Italia dei secoli XII–XV* (Pistoia, 1984); John Henderson, *Piety and Charity in Late Medieval Florence* (Cambridge, 1994). Still useful is Luigi Passerini, *Storia degli stabilimenti di beneficenza e d'istruzione elementare gratuita della città di Firenze* (Florence, 1853). For the sixteenth century, see Arnaldo d'Addario, "La continuità dell'impegno caritativo," in *Aspetti della contrariforma a Firenze* (Rome, 1972), 57–105.

moral status. Those humanists who found merit in poverty by no means went on to praise the poor as a class. With their emerging class consciousness, the ruling elite came to regard the poor with fear, for their potential rebelliousness and tendency to criminality, and also with contempt, for their lack of taste, refinement, and stability. And poverty came to be associated with sin. The new ducal government saw the poor as a social problem. It took action, in characteristic fashion, to impose some order on the welter of welfare institutions it had inherited, although policy was directed more to overall supervision than to elimination, amalgamation, or centralization. The city's major hospitals, for instance, were brought under a single system but left intact. In 1542 Cosimo also set up a commission to oversee the numerous welfare institutions throughout his territory that were engaged in caring for abandoned children, beggars, and the poor generally. To do this he appropriated the ancient confraternity of the Bigallo but completely transformed it into a state operation, while retaining its prestigious name. In dealing with poverty, the government's primary concern was with emergencies, and it did not replace the basic structure of ongoing charity built up over the centuries by the city's many lay and religious institutions. Judging from a survey taken to deal with the disastrous famine and plague that hit the city in the 1620s, the state still did not have a comprehensive public-welfare program: addressing itself to the resources the poor had recourse to, the report could not go much beyond listing the numerous institutions of the city that, along with begging and alms boxes in churches, provided alms to the poor.[132]

THE MIDDLING CLASSES   If the rich became richer and the working poor probably became much poorer in the sixteenth century, what about the people in between? The minimum-wage index to poverty, such as it is, has limited usefulness in judging the situation for all of the working population. It has some validity within the construction industry for those skilled construction workers who were paid a daily wage rather than a piece rate—wallers, masons, stonecutters, woodworkers. Given the lack of technological development in the building trades, skilled workers could hardly improve their bargaining position in the market based on improved productivity or innovative skills, and their wages remained within the range where they had always been (in Florence as throughout all of Europe), with a ceiling that rarely exceeded twice that of unskilled laborers, although there was considerable variation within that range. Hence, their wages too were resistant to change, and in the period of slow but steady inflation of prices during the sixteenth century the purchasing power of their wages declined, although

---

[132] Daniela Lombardi, "Poveri a Firenze: Programmi e realizzazioni della politica assistenziale dei Medici tra Cinque e Seicento," in *Timore e carità: I poveri nell'Italia moderna* (Cremona, 1982), 165–84; Litchfield, *Emergence of a Bureaucracy,* 245.

these workers had more of a margin to absorb higher prices. That decline cannot be easily assessed, since, in the absence of studies of the purchasing power of wages in the later sixteenth century like those for the later fourteenth century, we do not know at what point the marginal advantage of these skilled construction workers approached the poverty line, however that might be defined.

But can it be taken for granted, as it often is in the history of wages generally throughout Europe in this period, that the earnings of skilled construction workers are an index to the level of well-being of other categories of workers? We have few data about the annual earning of the artisans, shopkeepers, and others who constituted the bulk of the middling classes. They were paid for finished work or for specific services or took their earnings as a percentage of sales, and it is difficult to make comparisons with salaries paid on a per diem or annual basis in the construction industry. Men who identified themselves as artisans and shopkeepers in the 1427 catasto constituted a significant part of the substantial middling class at that time. Those artisans who perfected the skills needed to make highly complex luxury products, and who may also have been tastemakers, presumably had opportunities for increasing their earnings accordingly. We can imagine that the increased productivity resulting from entrepreneurial efforts, along with the prestige they enjoyed for the high level of their skills and the luxury of their products, somehow paid off in the market, at least for some of these men. The aforementioned proposal of 1481 to establish a glassworks in the Mugello projected an annual salary of £561 (*fl.*93½) for the supervisor and £351 (*fl.*58½) each for seven other craftsmen—this at a time when the most skilled masons could hardly hope to earn much more than £250. These wages were probably higher than normal in order to attract men to the countryside, but those who went were also to get housing and three meals a day, complete with an abundance of meat and different qualities of wine. Most men in the category of notaries, administrators, clerks, and other bureaucrats employed by the republican government earned £360 or above annually, which was much higher than the maximum earnings of a skilled construction worker.[133]

There is no reason to believe that the earnings of many of these men followed the downward trend of the real wages of the construction industry in the course of the sixteenth century. Table 7.6 presents a schedule of salaries paid to various workers—artisans employed in the Medici workshops, construction workers, and employees of the Monte di Pietà, a bank, and a silk firm—compared with what workers in some of the same categories had earned at the beginning of the preceding century. Most in the later period were earning much more than the

[133] Alison Brown, "Uffici di onore e utile," 319–21.

*fl.*100 paid in the 1420s to the head of the cathedral workshop, by far the highest salary an artisan could have hoped to earn at the time of Brunelleschi and equal to that of an office manager of a major international business. Whether the salaries paid at the ducal workshops were more or less in line with what the market offered remains to be seen. The table shows that the higher-ranking administrators at firms in the private sector as well as at the Monte di Pietà were earning more than their counterparts had a century and a half earlier. The table, however, was constructed on the basis of the index to the cost of labor alone—that is, the nominal wage of an unskilled construction worker—to establish a scale for judging the relative size of the earnings of various kinds of workers. It does not factor in the increase in the cost of living during the sixteenth century, which would cut into the apparent advantage of these later salaries, especially those at the lower levels.

Yet in the wool industry many workers at the end of the century were being paid wages that represented much higher rate increases than did the wages of construction workers. The most skilled of these, the weavers, were earning up to *fl.*100 a year, much more than the best-paid construction workers and much more than what weavers had earned two centuries earlier.[134] The presence among weavers of so many immigrants confirms the impression of favorable employment opportunities in the city. Immigrants were always showing up among the city's weavers, but it was only toward the mid-fifteenth century that special efforts were made to attract them. At the end of the following century we find them in large numbers, both in the accounts of wool companies and in the matriculation records of the guild (where 60 percent of apprenticeship contracts were made by people from outside Florence and its immediate countryside, 79 percent of these with weavers).[135] Of the 71 weavers the wool firm of Cristofano di Tommaso Brandolini & Partners employed in four years, from 1580 to 1584, 40 came from the more remote areas of Tuscany and 13 came from outside Tuscany.[136] Moreover, women had a greater presence in many of the lower-skilled jobs in the textile industries, a consequence of the greater attraction of male labor to the crafts producing higher-quality consumer goods.

---

[134] This is what a weaver of rascia working for the Brandolini firm in the 1580s would have earned if he wove one bolt a month, and out of this he would have had only the minimum expenses of ongoing repairs on his loom and a low-paid assistant (if he did not have a family member to help him). Richard A. Goldthwaite, "The Florentine Wool Industry in the Late Sixteenth Century: A Case Study," *Journal of European Economic History* 32 (2003): 553.

[135] Luciano Marcello, "Andare a bottega: Adolescenza e apprendistato nelle arti (secc. XVI–XVII)," in *Infanzie: Funzioni di un gruppo liminale dal mondo classico all'Età Moderna*, ed. Ottavia Niccoli (Florence, 1993), 240.

[136] Goldthwaite, "Florentine Wool Industry," 538, 543–46.

TABLE 7.6
Annual Salaries of Selected Workers in the 1580s
(with Comparison of Salaries from an Earlier Period)

1580s	Salary in scudi
The court: sculptor (Giambologna)	300
The court: cameo cutter	300
The court: 4 jewelers, 2 workers in *pietre dure*	240
The court: 1 painter	204
The court: worker in *pietre dure*	192
The court: 2 goldsmiths, 1 sculptor, and 1 clocksmith	180
The court: stucco artist	144
Monte di pietà: the central treasurer	144
The court: gardener, stucco artist, goldsmith	120
Monte di pietà: 3 branch managers	120
The court: painter, jeweller, distiller, miniaturist	96
Monte di pietà: 3 branch cashiers	96
Corsi bank: clerks (*du.* 70–150)	65–140
Martelli silk firm: shop staff (*fl.*30–72)	28–67
Annual earnings of highly skilled construction worker	67
Annual earnings of unskilled construction worker	33
Earlier period	*Equivalent value in scudi*
Cathedral works, 1420s: supervisor and architect (*fl.*100)	93
Medici bank, 1414: manager (*fl.*100)	93
Medici bank, 1414: staff (*fl.*15–50)	14–47
Cambini firm, 1451–81: staff (*fl.*12–65 di suggello)	9–43
Wool shop, 1387–93: supervisors (*fl.*43–45)	44–47

SOURCES: For court employees, Suzanne B. Butters, *The Triumph of Vulcan: Sculptors' Tools, Porphyry, and the Prince in Ducal Florence* (Florence, 1996), 2:407–8; and idem, "'Una pietra eppure non una pietra': Pietre dure e botteghe medicee nella Firenze del Cinquecento," in *La grande storia dell'artigianato*, vol. 3, *Il Cinquecento*, ed. Franco Franceschi and Gloria Fossi (Florence, 2000). For the Monte de pietà and the Corsi bank, Richard A. Goldthwaite, "Banking in Florence at the End of the Sixteenth Century," *Journal of European Economic History* 27 (1998): 483, 518. For the Medici bank, Raymond de Roover, *The Rise and Decline of the Medici Bank, 1397–1494* (Cambridge, MA, 1963), 232. For the Cambini firm, Sergio Tognetti, *Il banco Cambini: Affari e mercati di una compagnia mercantile-bancaria nella Firenze del XV secolo* (Florence, 1999), app. 2. For the wool shop, Franco Franceschi, *Oltre il "Tumulto": I lavoratori fiorentini dell'arte della lana fra Tre e Quattrocento* (Florence, 1993), 258–59.
NOTE: Equivalencies for earlier period are for the value of the florin in the labor market alone (see table A.1).

From the discussion in the second part of this book, dealing with the urban economy, other evidence has emerged for the accumulation of wealth among the middling classes over the course of the fifteenth and sixteenth centuries: the high percentage of home- and landownership, the rise of deposit institutions as outlets for savings, the large number of households with servants, and the increased consumption of durable goods. Another indicator of the affluence of a preindustrial economy is the consumption of meat. Although we have no statistics to document sales, activity in the market manifested itself both in the considerable entrepreneurial energy for the organization of the importation of animals, some from faraway places, and in the greater visibility of the butchers' guild. Most of the meat consumed in the city came from outside the immediate countryside, some from Pistoia and Siena and some from outside Tuscany altogether, from

Umbria, Lazio, and even as distant a place as Puglia. Often butchers themselves made the arrangements, dealing with middlemen, many of them in the countryside; these arrangements involved partnerships and extension of credit amounting to hundreds of florins for an operation to import thousands of animals, which might take months. In 1329, for example, a taverner in Florence worked through a partner in Incisa to buy 914 sheep and 100 hogs from Perugia. Unfortunately, we have only scattered evidence of this kind of activity of butchers and none of their personal records to give us precise information about how they organized their business. The 1427 catasto, however, attests to the success of some of them: 9 of the 72 men who identified themselves as butchers or poulterers (about 1 for every 136 households) had a net worth of more than *fl.*500, and the average was *fl.*258. And their guild attests to their collective success. It owned more real estate than any other after the top four, that is, the Calimala, the Cambio, the Lana, and the Seta; it was the only minor guild to build a new palace in the Renaissance style, which is notable also for its size and its prominence opposite Orsanmichele; and in 1410 it commissioned the yet unknown Brunelleschi to carve the statue of St. Peter for its niche on the exterior of Orsanmichele. The interior of the butchers' guildhall was also richly furnished, to judge from the request by the grand ducal court in 1605 to borrow the guild's rugs, tableware, and other objects for use in the festivities for a family marriage.[137]

A more solid index to the greater volume of wealth that stimulated greater consumer spending among people in the middling range—whether they had more money or there were more of them—is the increase in both the number and variety of coins. The increased activity in the local market that came with economic growth generated the need for a coinage system with a more refined calibration of denominations, apart from any intrinsic silver content, for use in the marketplace. By the end of the sixteenth century Florentines were handling nine coins, from the ducat on down, most of these of recent invention. In 1300, in contrast, there had been only three, the florin being separated from the two silver-based coins by an enormous gap. At the end of the fifteenth century coins were calibrated in units of 1 (the denaro), 4, 12 , 40, 80, and 1,680 (the florin); by the end of the sixteenth century, after a period of inflation, the units were 1, 2, 20, 80, 160, 240, 480, 840, and 1,680 (as fractions of the lira, following the arithmetical logic of the £/s/d system, these values of the first five coins were, respectively, 1/240, 1/120, 1/12, 1/3, and 2/3). Moreover, in the second half of the century the mint used 50 percent more bullion to create money than it had in the first half, not counting the increased output of billon coins of lower denominations. In short, the monetary policies of the first

---

[137] For butchers we have little more than the scattered references from the fourteenth century in de La Roncière, *Firenze e le sue campagne*, 209, 220, 223, 245, 272–74, 292–93, 338. See also G. Carocci, "Le arti fiorentine e le loro residenze," *Arte e storia*, n.s., 10 (1891): 153–55.

Medici dukes facilitated liquidity and hence can be read as an indicator of more activity in the local market, a theme that runs throughout the history of European monetary systems in the early modern period.

This relatively rapid expansion of the range of coins upwards in the sixteenth century was only in part a response to the inflation of the so-called price revolution, inasmuch as the higher prices of the new coins much outpaced the rate of inflation and the lower denominations were not abandoned. In fact, the Florentine had more small change at his disposal, as well as larger coins for higher-priced goods. The number of different coins in which an unskilled laborer could be paid for a day's wage doubled from three in the fourteenth century to six at the end of the sixteenth century. Whereas in the fourteenth and fifteenth centuries there was no single silver-based coin worth as much as his daily wage, by the end of the sixteenth century there were four worth his daily wage and above. Given the ingrained habit of Florentines to think in terms of moneys of account, the finer calibration of coins may have gone some way toward solving what Carlo Cipolla called "the big problem of small change,"[138] that is, the detachment of the monetary value of small coins from their commodity, or intrinsic, value. In any event, the increase in the denominations of coins at both the lower and higher levels, especially in the second half of the century, responded to greater consumer demand.

Taken all together, the evidence for wages and earnings outside the construction industry and for greater wealth circulating among the middling classes is hardly conclusive, and the current state of research does not allow us to speculate about the extent of poverty in the ranks of working people in the later sixteenth century or, conversely, how much better off these people were. Instances have already been noted of artisans who accumulated considerable wealth from the practice of their craft—the brickmaker Benedetto da Terrarossa, the painter Neri di Bicci, the Romoli family of stonecutters. The only artisan whose economic career is well documented—the by now oft-cited silk weaver Iacopo di Tedesco—made a small fortune for himself in the early sixteenth century operating entirely within the parameters of his skill. But it is likely that for every one of these success stories that can be turned up in the archives, one can find someone else who did not improve his position in the market very much.

This is true even among those who might have been expected to profit the most from the changing situation—above all, painters. No artisan activity anywhere in Europe gained so much cultural status across the fourteenth, fifteenth, and sixteenth centuries as did painters in Florence. With the fame

---

[138] Carlo M. Cipolla, *Money, Prices, and Civilization in the Mediterranean World, Fifth to Seventeenth Century* (New York, 1956), 31. The problem is fully explored in Thomas J. Sargent and François R. Velde, *The Big Problem of Small Change* (Princeton, NJ, 2002).

Giotto enjoyed even during his lifetime arose a tradition of praise for artists that became an essential element in that sense Florentines had of the greatness of their city, celebrated by writers within a generation after his death and recognized by men across the entire spectrum of society, from ordinary men to the humanist intellectuals. So strong had this tradition become by the sixteenth century that Cosimo I was able to incorporate the concept of Florence as a city of art, along with the history of the patronage of his family, into the rationale for the new role of Medici now as princes. By the end of the sixteenth century some men were consciously collecting these products. A few deceased producers whose products were still sought in the market acquired the new status of "old master"; and in reaction to the growing traffic in these products, the ducal government of Florence issued legislation in 1602—the first of its kind—to limit the exportation of the products of no fewer than sixteen producers, some of whom were not Florentine, and to lay down the procedures for adding new names to the list in the future. Nothing like this happened in any other manufacturing sector in the economy.

Meanwhile, artists themselves sought to promote their image as a class of men with a distinct identity: they claimed intellectual interests, established an academy, wrote about art. A clear image of the artist first emerges in the *Vite* of Vasari. Beginning with the idea of a rebirth of painting with Giotto, Vasari constructed a historical sequence of artists that demonstrated the continual improvement of artistic practice; Masaccio marked a step forward with respect to Giotto, as did Michelangelo with respect to Masaccio. Thus, in Vasari's book we have, perhaps for the first time, the concept of progress, and for Vasari this progress, evolving over two centuries following Giotto's death, culminated in his own time, a development concentrated in Florence but by now diffused throughout all of Italy. In short, an artisan—the painter—and his product—the painting—acquired considerable cultural prestige. Patricians became conscious of the possibility of self-fashioning through the patronage of art and the development of a kind of connoisseurship by collecting paintings and even drawings, including now for the first time both copies and prints of the work of deceased artists. A few took up painting as an amateur pastime, and at least one, Niccolò Gaddi, like the first grand dukes, dabbled in various other crafts and set up a workshop in his own home. We are still a long way from our contemporary notion of art and the artist, but people at the time—painters themselves, their clients, and intellectuals—recognized a new cultural status for an artisan producer and his products.[139]

---

[139] The prominence of Florence in the history of the rise in the status of the artist is emphasized by Edouard Pommier, *Comment l'art devient l'art dans l'Italie de la Renaissance* (Paris, 2007).

But this did not necessarily play out in the market to the painter's advantage. Take, for instance, the painter Alessandro Allori (1535–1607). Allori falls solidly in this tradition: as heir to Bronzino's shop, he enjoyed status in his craft, he worked for the Medici, at the age of twenty he had a poem dedicated to him by one of the city's prominent intellectuals, he taught painting to patricians, he wrote a treatise to explain the art of drawing to people outside his craft, he dedicated much time in the 1560s to the foundation of the artists' academy, the Accademia del Disegno, and his shop turned out copies of the work of the deceased artists Raphael and Andrea del Sarto, both of whom were rapidly becoming known as old masters. A portrait of Allori at midlife shows him surrounded by pretentious objects: a cushion bordered with a conspicuous Latin inscription from Catullus, an armillary sphere (which he certainly did not know how to use), books revealing a little too clearly the names of their Greek, not Roman, authors (which he certainly could not read), and a splendid villa in the background, which was far grander than anything he himself ever owned.

Allori's record book, one of the very few that survive from the period, gives some economic substance to the artist's pretentiousness. During the five years for which it documents his receipts, 1579–83, about 60 percent of his income came from thirty-eight clients in the private sector, for whom he did frescoes in their palaces, major altar pictures, portraits, and copies of the city's most popular religious image at the Santissima Annunziata. Allori's remarkable production certainly exceeded that of earlier artists, but his record book reveals few hints about the internal organization of his shop that might explain how he increased output. Like other painters of the period, he probably introduced certain efficiencies in production, such as the specialized labor of assistants, standardization, and technical innovations. A modern scholar has in fact called him "a most efficient manager" of an "almost industrialized" production process, organized around a veritable *équipe* of painters specialized in certain kinds of details, such as animals and landscapes.[140] That Allori's studio produced so many portraits, many costing only a few florins each, suggests that a degree of standardization may also have characterized his output.

Allori's total gross annual earnings as recorded in his account book and evaluated in terms of their purchasing power in the labor market at the time were enough to pay all together about six skilled construction workers; after defraying shop expenses and whatever had to be paid out to an associate and their assistants, he probably took home for himself somewhat more than a construction worker earned. Yet this could not have been enough to boost him out of his artisan

---

[140] Simona Lecchini Giovannoni, *Alessandro Allori* (Turin, 1991), 51–52.

status. At the time of his death, his estate and that of his brother (also a painter) together consisted of the family residence, 4½ small houses, 3 small shops, and 7 miscellaneous parcels of land in the countryside, not an insignificant patrimony for the two men but one entirely in line with that of any number of prosperous fifteenth-century artisans. Allori, the son of a sword maker, obviously did not build up enough of an estate to improve the social status of his family by much; and, in fact, his one son who did not enter the church became a painter.

Cultural prestige of the kind enjoyed by Allori did not necessarily count for very much in the marketplace of Renaissance Florence. As Vasari observed in the introduction to his life of Perugino, "If one wants to live other than as an animal day by day, and wants to become rich, he must go away from here and sell the quality of his work, and the reputation of this city . . . because Florence does with its artisans what time does with its things—once made, it unmakes them and consumes them little by little."

Conclusion

Economic Culture: *Attitudes and Behavior, Notions about the Economy.*
Performance: *The Economy in the Short Run, A Final Judgment.*

In the previous chapters we have examined the economy of Florence more or less sector by sector—international commerce, international banking and finance, the textile industries, artisan enterprises, local banking and credit—and then widened the perspective to see to what extent economic activity was conditioned by government intervention, how it interacted with regional markets, and how it functioned in the distribution of wealth throughout the society. Now it is time to step back, put everything in a yet larger perspective, and look at the economy as a whole. There are two questions to be asked that can lead to a final, global view of the economic history of this city: To what extent did all this economic activity impress itself on the attitudes and ideas of Florentines to condition their behavior in the marketplace and to heighten their awareness of what an economy is all about? and What is the final evaluation of the performance of this economy over the four centuries covered by this book?

Economic Culture
Attitudes and Behavior

By the standard definition of the term, the economy of Florence qualifies as a capitalist economy. The entrepreneur conducted his affairs relatively free from some of the strongest cultural restraints of medieval Europe. Merchant-bankers and wool and silk producers could gain full upper-class status, unhampered by any social prejudice against their activities. The market had penetrated into the countryside to uproot feudalism, thereby weakening a medieval prejudice against the entrepreneur for his social inferiority. In northern Europe, still dominated by the feudal aristocracy, it was virtually a law of social behavior that the focus of social ambitions was fixed on the nobility, so that a rich entrepreneur's greatest aspiration was to buy land, leave the counting house, and move into the rural gentry. Some scholars have taken up the sociologist Alfred von Martin's notion that this mentality was also at work in Renaissance Italy: for them, the increased luxury spending and the preoccupation with culture on the part of the business class thus signal the withdrawal from enterprise and the beginning of social climbing toward noble status. The three-generation cycle from business to land, however, does not obtain in the social history of this city. Guicciardini, commenting in one of his maxims on the proverb that a fortune gained dishonestly does not last to be enjoyed by the third generation, stated that the dissipation of any patrimony, however it was accumulated, was in the nature of things, resulting from the tendency of heirs to administer it badly or to consume it through spending. Florentines, in any event, never developed a prejudice against business, not even in the later sixteenth century, when ideas about nobility were much discussed throughout Italy. Prominent among these ideas was a notion about the indignity of working with one's hands and engaging in retail trade, a notion that separated entrepreneurs in commerce, banking, and the textile industries from the lower class by defining them for what they were not, not for what they were. But if they thus erected a barrier excluding everyone below them, there were no barriers above them qualifying their social status. An official definition of nobility, complete with an institutional structure, came only in the eighteenth century with the new Hapsburg-Lorraine regime. Meanwhile, many men from the city's "noble" families continued to be active in business.

Much more of an issue in the lives of these people who made their way in the marketplace were the moral problems arising from medieval churchmen's suspicion about the avarice and materialism inherent in the mentality of the entrepreneur and their condemnation of usury in any form. It is hardly surprising, considering the prominence of Florence as a center of a nascent capitalism, that two of the church's most outstanding spokesmen on the subject had a notable presence on the local scene in the second quarter of the fifteenth century—the popular preacher from Siena St. Bernardino (1380–1444) and the local bishop, St. Antonino (1389–1459). Churchmen, however, did not doubt the importance of commerce and industry in their society. The church went a long way toward placating the entrepreneur's anxiety about the morality of these activities through the sacrament of confession and the institution of purgatory; it put at the entrepreneur's disposal the instruments with which he could contract for divine favor with commemorative masses, private chapels, and donations to welfare and religious institutions. Florentines were especially energetic in transforming this religious patronage into a kind of self-glorification through art and architecture, and in this sense much of the splendor of Renaissance Florence is surely the measure of their effort to free themselves from anxiety about certain of their professional activities.

With respect to avarice, the entrepreneur's anxiety was softened by a countervailing current that arose from the circle of the so-called civic humanists. It is hardly surprising that these thinkers, with close personal and professional ties to the entrepreneurs of the city, turned some of their attention to the problem of the morality of private wealth at precisely the time when SS. Bernardino and Antonino were making the church's case. Avarice was the central problem. In the Middle Ages pride came before all as a major sin, but with the growth of a market economy avarice moved ever closer to the top. Churchmen recognized that wealth brought certain advantages, but this did not lessen their suspicion of the materialism inherent in the mentality of the entrepreneur, with its attendant social evils. The condemnation of avarice found one of its most eloquent expressions in Dante, who carved out separate places in Hell for its several manifestations—plunder, squandering, usury, fraud, theft, and counterfeiting. A century later, however, the Florentine humanists shifted the emphasis to the positive aspects of wealth, resorting to the classical concept of magnificence. Wealth is good for the individual because it provides the wherewithal to make one happy and therefore helps one to be virtuous and to participate in civic life. Hence, private wealth is also good for the state and for the social order in general. There was thus a reassessment of avarice as a motive for economic activity, or rather, a new positive view of the desire to obtain wealth that relegated avarice to a lower form of behavior where gain is sought for its sake alone. In other words, an important social distinction compromised the traditional condemnation. And Florentines could be unabashedly explicit about the desire to make money and the pleasures it provided: "I believe," Giovanni Rucellai famously observed about the fortune he had accumulated, "that the proper spending of it has brought me more honor, and more satisfaction in my soul, than the earning of it," for, as Guicciardini recognized in his *Ricordi*, "men always praise others for lavish spending and for conducting their affairs with generosity and magnificence." He added, however, a characteristic note of caution, saying that one should "measure these things against one's capabilities and against their honest and reasonable usefulness."

The church's condemnation of usury was a more serious problem. Unlike avarice, which could be dealt with only in the confessional, usury could be prosecuted in the real world of the courtroom. Yet an accommodation of theology to practice was made. On the one hand, Florentines, at whatever cost to their conscience, found ways to handily circumvent these restrictions—accounting devices, the bill of exchange, the discretionary deposit, official pawnbrokers—that they eventually did not even bother to disguise, and if any doubts remained, they made gestures toward atonement in their final testaments. On the other hand, churchmen, both intellectuals and preachers, were increasingly cognizant of the place of credit in a commercial economy and tried to adjust doctrine to a reality they could not deny. When notions began to circulate about organizing a Monte di Pietà in the city, the archiepiscopal court accepted the proposed low rates of interest, and subsequently it generally did not prosecute moneylenders so long as rates were not excessive. Problems of conscience remained, but by this time the threat of excommunication for usurious practices was considered little more than a "petty nuisance."[1] It is difficult to show that by the fifteenth century the usury doctrine had dampened entrepreneurial zeal.

It was in the course of their entrepreneurial adventures that Florentines gradually eroded these traditional religious and social prejudices against their activities, while at the same time laying the foundation of a different, capitalist culture. Those in the vanguard built up an international commerce, banking, and finance network that extended throughout much of Europe. These men, who made the large investment and took the big risks, meet Joseph Schumpeter's test for boldness, initiative, and creativity. They drove the economy: they found the raw materials that kept the local textile industries going and the markets where the finished cloth could be sold, and along the way they traded in any other product that might turn a profit, from dried fruit to expensive spices, from ostrich feathers to money itself. Their success or failure in these ventures conditioned the performance of the home industries and therefore of the local economy as a whole. Large profits were to be made in these markets abroad, but the risks were great. Investment in both the importation of raw materials and the export of finished cloth was exposed to the dangers of transport and the vagaries of time involved in these operations. Those men who also entered into international banking and government finance took even greater risks, but they operated outside the orbit of the home economy. If their success in these ventures brought enormous wealth back to the city, their failures had few repercussions there.

The boldness of these entrepreneurs was underpinned by the rational procedures they used in the conduct of their affairs. They set up their businesses as formal organizations that allowed long-term planning; they had devices for raising outside working capital; their development of accounting techniques gave

---

[1] Gene Brucker, "Ecclesiastical Courts in Fifteenth-Century Florence and Fiesole," *Medieval Studies* 53 (1991): 248.

them control over what they were doing, including knowledge of details and the possibility of striking a balance at any time and of conducting a cost analysis; they had a system for gathering information about faraway markets; they protected shipments of goods with insurance; they developed credit and transfer instruments that gave them considerable flexibility in meeting liquidity problems and in moving funds from one place to another. In these respects, entrepreneurial activity meets the criterion of "rationality" that is often invoked in the effort to define capitalism. Emblematic of this rationality is the sophisticated development of accounting, including double entry. As a device by which an arithmetical order could be imposed on market activity, accounting has been considered, along with artists' use of perspective to represent space, a characteristic feature of the mentality of Renaissance Florentines.[2] And nowhere else in all of Italy is there a richer documentary record for the widespread practice of accounting throughout the society, from the thirteenth century on.

At home in Florence these entrepreneurs had at the base of their operations a local economy in which they could conduct their affairs in a free and all-pervasive marketplace that functioned entirely on the cash nexus. The market was protected by a government that was careful not to assume an oppressive presence in it: mint policy assured operators of a sound monetary system that was not subject to careless debasements, and institutions were in place to guarantee the sanctity of contracts made in the marketplace. Moreover, the government was willing to pursue their common interests, it did not favor one economic elite over another, it avoided class conflict, and finally, it minimized the tax burden on the system. In this relative freedom from institutional restrictions, the market generated the extensive development of instruments and institutions that initiated most Florentines, even ordinary working people, into the sophisticated world of credit: they kept accounts, they shifted debits and credits on current account, and they handled written orders of payment and transfer. The universal use of moneys of account for most calculations in fact took Florentines a long way toward thinking about money as an abstraction.

A market of this kind, finally, transformed society. It dissolved traditional corporate structures: the elite urban consorteria yielded its economic cohesiveness to partible inheritance and individual business enterprise, and the absence of guild exclusiveness opened up the possibility of free movement upward in social ranking or laterally from one profession into another. The success of this market econ-

---

[2] For two recent references to this thesis by economic historians, see Ugo Tucci, "Tra Venezia e Firenze: Le scritture contabili," *Studi veneziani*, n.s., 27 (1994): 33–34; and Mario Del Treppo, "Le avventure storiografiche della tavola Strozzi," in *Fra storia e storiografia: Scritti in onore di Pasquale Villani*, ed. P. Macry and A. Massafra (Bologna, 1994), 503.

omy manifested itself in a high degree of specialization of labor and entrepreneurial energy at all levels of society. Alongside the men who set up businesses in the forward sectors of the economy—merchant-bankers, lanaioli, setaioli—many artisans also demonstrated considerable vitality in trying to adjust their production to market conditions. Among the most visible of these in the scholarly literature are the sculptors who introduced new and cheaper materials and the painters who devised ways to facilitate production in series and developed stylistic innovations to keep ahead of the market. But there were others, such as the brickmakers who used organizational techniques to increase production and the silk weavers who took on more workers in order to widen the range of their production. Even within the highly controlled wool industry, the putting-out system left some room for modest craftsmen to join forces in partnership ventures to improve their lot; they were not massed into a proletariat. None of these activities, however, required a large capital investment, and none resulted in technological innovations that led to a major increase in productivity.

In short, this was an economy notable not just for the presence of capitalists in it; it was an economy organized around some of the basic principles of the capitalist system. In the earliest accounting record to survive for this city, the fragment of a banker's accounts dated 1211, "capital" appears repeatedly with reference to the money he put to work as loans that earned him "interest" *(prode e kapitale);*[3] and over the following centuries interest would be frequently referred to as the "cost of money."

In other respects, however, these men were somewhat lacking in their "spirit of capitalism," as this phenomenon is often known. They seem not to have been driven by a strong competitive instinct, except for the rivalry of some of the biggest bankers for certain large government contracts abroad, such as the Tolfa alum monopoly. The market process by its very nature consists in competing in the search for gain through exchange, but in Florence this process can be understood as operating only at the general level of the collectivity, for example, to explain the rivalry between Florence and Venice or the successive shifts in the textile industries to new kinds of products. At the level of the individual entrepreneur, so well documented for this city, it is difficult to detect much of a competitive instinct, certainly nothing like the kind of competition that is an ongoing process of discovery, searching for opportunities for gain or for furthering other

[3] *Testi fiorentini del Dugento e dei primi del Trecento,* ed. Alfredo Schiaffini (Florence, 1926), 3–15. The first treatise in which the term *capital* appears is that by the Franciscan Peter Olivi (1248–98), where capital is considered not just money but money or property put to work for a certain gain. Julius Kirshner, ed., *Business, Banking, and Economic Thought in Late Medieval and Early Modern Europe: Selected Studies of Raymond de Roover* (Chicago, 1974), 28–29.

economic goals. Merchants' letters reveal the urge to be ahead of the others in taking advantage of changing market conditions and new opportunities but nothing about cost-cutting, underselling, or calculated stockpiling. Nor does the theme of competition appear in their business papers, their professional manuals, or their personal memoranda.[4] The cutthroat competition practiced by the new generation of merchants coming out of Antwerp must have been as foreign to these Florentines as it was to their Venetian colleagues.[5]

Moreover, these men made no effort to gain control over supply in order to strengthen their power in the markets where they operated. At home in Florence, where merchants supplied the textile industry with its raw materials and bought its finished products, they did not bind local manufacturers to them in a cohesive business structure that might have strengthened their position in the market. Abroad, none of them, not even the Medici, attempted to dominate the markets where they did business. In this respect, it is highly indicative that the biggest operators, such as Datini and the Medici, for all their accounting control over their separate enterprises, had no interest in keeping central accounts over the totality of them all (as Federigo Melis and Raymond de Roover, respectively, learned in trying to get an overall view of these businesses at any one time). Not even in the mass of materials that survive for Datini's activities is there a ledger that would have given him an overall, synthetic view of the performance of his various firms, nor is there any indication that there ever was such a ledger.

In the industrial sector at home, textile manufacturers took little risk. They seem to have deferred to the guild for decisions made collectively about industrial policy. They limited the capital invested in their firms to what was needed to get operations to the point where sales financed ongoing operations, they devised the means to meet short-term liquidity problems, and they had the flexibility to reduce or shut down operations at any time at little cost. They invested hardly anything in plant and equipment, and they limited their purchase of raw materials to a short-term production cycle. They held workers at a distance through the putting-out system, limiting their commitment as employers and avoiding direct management of labor. They made no attempt to enlarge the scale of their operations through organizational or technological innovation. Lanaioli and setaioli

[4] For example, the subject is completely absent from the recent survey of these writings by Gunnar Dahl, *Trade, Trust, and Networks: Commercial Culture in Late Medieval Italy* (Lund, Sweden, 1998). See also Kurt Weissen, "*Dove il Papa va sempre è caro di danari:* The Commercial Site Analysis of Italian Merchant Handbooks and Notebooks for the 14th and 15th Centuries," in *Kaufmannsbücher und Handelspraktiken vom Spätmittelalter bis zum beginnenden 20. Jahrhundert*, ed. M. A. Denzel, J. C. Hocquet, and H. Witthöft (Stuttgart, 2002), 72.

[5] See the comments of Ugo Tucci in "The Psychology of the Venetian Merchant in the Sixteenth Century," in *Renaissance Venice*, ed. J. R. Hale (Totowa, NJ, 1973), 357–58, where he addresses more than any other scholar before him the problem of competition.

took risks only when they ventured abroad as merchants to sell their products; the setaioli were more compelled to do this since import-export merchants were less likely to be interested in handling products that were not standardized and were very costly.

These men appear strikingly independent in contrast to the merchants of the English regulated companies, the Hanseatic towns, and the southern German cartels. In running their government they followed an economic policy of laissez faire, and privately they ran their businesses as highly individual enterprises. Yet their behavior at home and abroad often reveals an underlying spirit of corporatism that was no less strong for all its lack of institutional structure. The iter many of them followed through their apprenticeship years, passing from one firm to another, fostered lasting personal bonds with many of their future colleagues, and the very foundation of their network lay in cooperative interaction among them all.[6] This corporatism held firm despite their often violent factional divisions in the political arena at home; not even political exile excluded them from the network abroad. One might even go on to say that in a sense these men, however much their business practices anticipate modern capitalism, were still strongly tied into the medieval tradition of guild corporatism, a state of mind that may not have been altogether irrelevant to the dense networks that so characterized their social and political life as well. The persistence of this mentality appears all the more remarkable in view of the erosion of much of the anxiety the medieval entrepreneur traditionally felt about his moral position and his social status. The corporate spirit that bound these men together may not have been so very different from the spirit that united Venetians in Europe's most highly developed—and most lasting—political and economic institutional structure. This stage in the history of capitalism, as exemplified by the Florentine experience, was still too early for us to talk about a natural link to the kind of individualism exemplified by *homo oeconomicus,* so important to later economic thinkers, not to mention today's economic historians.

Notions about the Economy

Florentines were hardly unaware of the benefits of entrepreneurial activity. Medieval thinkers recognized these, begrudgingly and for all their condemnation of the entrepreneur's motives and practices. Men like Dante and his contemporary Remigio de' Girolami fall into this tradition, although, living at a

---

[6] One of the few scholars who comments on this corporate sense (although she does not use the term) is Rita Mazzei, in *Itinera mercatorum: Circolazione di uomini e beni nell'Europa centro-orientale, 1550–1650* (Lucca, 1999), 284, 285, 301, 303, 319.

time when the economy of the city was in full swing, they tended to come down rather hard on the negative aspects of what they saw happening all around them in the world of "il maladetto fiore." Subsequently, however, the emphasis shifts to the side of a more positive view. A half-century later, Giovanni Villani praised the commerce and industry of the city; he had in mind the common good, unclouded by moral prejudices. Yet another half-century later, the humanists, in their effort to justify private wealth, departed from their classical models to praise the activities that generated that wealth. Alberti considered the textile industries important for giving work to so many people. It is almost a commonplace in the writings of his contemporaries and in the discussions of the councils of government that merchants brought wealth and fame to the city. A commission of 1458 declared that Florence "became powerful and great through her industries and businesses, and thanks to these it defended itself from all oppression."[7] All this was in the tradition of the protomercantilist policies of the medieval commune, driven by what has been called an economic nationalism, a sense that the wealth generated by productive activities and commerce benefited the state, conceived both as the government, whatever its form, and the population. Policy went beyond protectionism to promote change. It was in this spirit that the commune in the early fifteenth century purchased the ports of Pisa, inaugurated a galley system, changed the dimensions of its prestigious florin, and issued a great deal of legislation in support of the silk industry, and it was also in this spirit that the ducal government more than a century later embarked on one of the period's most vigorous and most comprehensive programs of economic development, directed not just to emancipating the city from dependence on imports but to increasing employment and bringing more wealth into the state.

Whatever reasoning lay behind these policies and whatever thoughts Florentines had about their economy, none of these men ever crossed the intellectual barrier to analysis. No one ventured to devise a scheme for the justification of business, let alone to develop a theoretical understanding of economic activity. Economic theory never went beyond the normative thought of the scholastics. And the only classical texts on the subject available as an alternative model—the pseudo-Aristotelian *Economics* and Xenophon's *Oeconomicus,* both known in Latin translation—praise the rural world of work and are hostile to urban economic activities. A new Latin translation of the former (which is in part based on Xenophon's text) by the Florentine humanist Leonardo Bruni circulated in many copies

---

[7] Quoted in Franco Franceschi, "Intervento del potere centrale e ruolo delle Arti nel governo dell'economia fiorentina del Trecento e del primo Quattrocento: Linee generali," *Archivio storico italiano* (hereafter *ASI*): 151 (1993): 864.

during the fifteenth century, probably because of its emphasis on the social and moral justification of private wealth. It did not stimulate further writing about economic matters in any wider sense. The so-called civic humanists, including Bruni, instead dedicated some of their attention to constructing a system of secular values for the Florentine political world, but their observations on the economic activity of the men they were addressing were limited to the problem of the morality of private wealth. They went beyond the classical writers in recognizing what most Florentine writers recognized, namely, that commerce and industry benefit the state and society in general, but they took no interest in describing or analyzing those economic activities. Indeed, the emphasis of this economic humanism was on how wealth benefited the man who had it, to the exclusion of any interest in how he used it in productive economic activity; on how he spent rather than on how he invested; on morality rather than on the economy. The civic humanists' distinction between the just pursuit of wealth and avarice was one of social class, not economic consequences. They justified wealth without, however, introducing any new cultural values that informed and reshaped economic behavior.

If Florentines never engaged in closer analysis of the economy as a distinct sphere of human activity, perhaps it was because they never had to. The city's entrepreneurs were never compelled to justify what it was they were doing. Apparently, the various leading sectors never came into conflict with one another over government policy. So far as is known—for the political documents have never been explored for this kind of material—men did not argue among themselves in the councils of government about their specific interests as setaioli, lanaioli, merchants, bankers, and landowners. These were all the same men, after all, since the affluent tended to distribute their investments among these different sectors. Nor outside of government did they collectively have to defend their economic activities against the social prejudices of an established aristocratic class. If these men had ever been put on the defensive about why they pursued one specific economic activity rather than another, or if they had ever been compelled to promote one activity over another, they might have begun to separate out specific economic problems from their shared interests and from their concern about the morality of wealth in general.

Indeed, Florentines had little to say about their economy. The subject hardly ever surfaces in their writings. For all the praise heaped on Villani for the statistical content of his chronicle, no one can argue that he, though himself a partner in an international firm, had any serious ideas about the economy he describes, let alone anything like a "spirit of capitalism."[8] The numerous contemporary histo-

---

[8] The best analysis is that of Michele Luzzati, *Giovanni Villani e la compagnia dei Buonaccorsi* (Rome, 1971), 82–110.

ries and chronicles that so richly document the political life of the city, most written by entrepreneurs of one kind or another, rarely comment on the economy. These sources record natural disasters and, more frequently, the price of grain, but little else. At the most, we have the occasional snapshot descriptions of the city—above all, Villani's for the second quarter of the fourteenth century but also Benedetto Dei's for the third quarter of the fifteenth century and Benedetto Varchi's for the second quarter of the sixteenth century—which include observations and statistics about the economy. For Florence there is nothing comparable to the diaries of Marino Sanudo (1466–1533), which are a mine of information about many aspects of economic life in Venice.

Moreover, literary works do not mirror the economic life of the city. Dante, whose readers included the entrepreneurs of his native city, used a vocabulary generated by a market economy—*profit, loss, indebtedness, trade*—but not in a way that reflected anything of the vitality of the economy of his time. As Giovanni Cherubini has observed, anyone who looks for Dante's understanding of that economy will be struck by his deafness to what made Florence what it was.[9] Not even the *novelle*, the most relevant genre, reflect much of the reality of the city's life. Vittore Branca has called Boccaccio's *Decameron* a "merchant epic" and "the *chanson de geste* of merchant paladins," but one would have no idea from reading it or Sacchetti's *Il trecentonovelle* that Florence had a major wool industry or, indeed, that it had much of a population of entrepreneurs and artisans of any kind or even a highly developed market economy.

Not even the changes the Florentine economy underwent in the sixteenth century challenged these men to look at economic activity in a different light. Perhaps it was because the many generations of experience in a market economy had lulled them into "a static conception" not only "of operative strategy and business ethics"[10] but of economic activity in general. In this respect the humanist and vernacular historians had given them no sense of historical change nor even a sense that anything could be learned from history. So they took economic matters for granted. The contrast with contemporary England is highly instructive. There, in the late sixteenth century the economy began to change in a way that has been described as uncertain, uneven, and problematic, generating vigorous debate about new, as opposed to traditional, economic values, relations, and activities. This economic culture manifested itself in discussions of usury and exchange

---

[9] Joan M. Ferrante, *The Political Vision of the "Divine Comedy"* (Princeton, NJ, 1984), ch. 6, discusses "commerce and language" in the *Commedia* (which includes a good overview of contemporary thought on economic matters). Cherubini takes a very different view in his *Scritti toscani: L'urbanesimo medievale e la mezzadria* (Florence, 1991), 315–25.

[10] The phrase is Tucci's, with reference to Venice. "Psychology of the Venetian Merchant," 357.

operations, in hundreds of publications about bookkeeping and various commercial subjects, in advertisements for the opening of new schools of practical arithmetic, and even in literary work, especially that written for the stage, where all kinds of new subjects inherent in market activity, such as credit, risks, usury, money, and accounting, surface in literal and metaphorical references—all of which created a public image of the merchant and his world. In Florence, in contrast, notwithstanding its advances along the road to modern capitalism, little of the culture of a market economy manifests itself in writings of any kind outside the sphere of private business papers. Whatever their "spirit of capitalism," it did not surface in the intellectual and artistic culture for which this Renaissance city is so famous. And when in the eighteenth century Tuscan thinkers began to take an interest in the economy, elaborating a body of literature on their economic ideas, they focused exclusively—perhaps not surprisingly at this late date—on the agricultural sector, not on the commercial, banking, and artisan traditions of their capital city.[11]

Performance

The Economy in the Short Run

As in any medieval city, the economic life of Florence was repeatedly interrupted, often dramatically so, by disasters of various kinds. For the most part the area was spared severe natural disasters except for major flooding of the Arno about once a century, but the exogenous forces of plague and famine struck hard about every decade on the average, sometimes at the same time. Internal political crises sporadically disrupted the local scene with varying intensity, from the violent factional strife during the emergence of the guild republic at the end of the thirteenth century to the Ciompi revolt in 1378. Thereafter the streets of the city were relatively free from political and social unrest—as distinct from criminal

---

[11] The most intelligent remarks about the economic ideas of Florentines in the Renaissance, from the perspective of a scholar who knows later English economic thought, appear in two articles by Maria Luisa Pesante: "Il commercio nella repubblica," *Quaderni storici* 35 (2000): 655–95; and "Un pensiero economico laico?" in *Commercio e cultura mercantile*, ed. Franco Franceschi, Richard A. Goldthwaite, and Reinhold C. Mueller, vol. 4 of *Il Rinascimento italiano e l'Europa*, ed. G. L. Fontana and L. Molà (Treviso, 2007), 71–102. For the eighteenth century, see Till Wahnbaeck, *Luxury and Public Happiness: Political Economy in the Italian Enlightenment* (Oxford, 2004). An excellent survey of the economic culture that began to emerge in England in the sixteenth century is Keith Wrightson, *Earthly Necessities: Economic Lives in Early Modern Britain* (New Haven, CT, 2000), esp. chs. 6, sec. vi, and 9, sec. i, and the conclusion. Of considerable interest also for the English scene is the literary scholarship of the so-called New Economic Criticism, for example, Ceri Sullivan, *Merchants in Early Modern Writing* (London, 2002); and Linda Woodbridge, ed., *Money and the Age of Shakespeare: Essays in New Economic Criticism* (New York, 2003). The editor's introduction in the latter volume includes a bibliography of books published in the period on arithmetical and commercial subjects.

violence—except in the second half of the 1490s, when the city was thrown into considerable turmoil by the French invasion, the expulsion of the Medici, and the Savonarolan reform effort.

From abroad, however, came the occasional threat of war. Once the city emerged as a major regional state in the later thirteenth and early fourteenth centuries and then went on to become one of the principal players in the Italian state system, it found itself increasingly involved in wars in its immediate vicinity, if not on its home turf. Military operations were particularly intense and close to home in the period from 1390 to the 1430s. The Tuscan campaigns of Gian Galeazzo Visconti in the 1390s seemed to be headed toward conquest of the city itself when he was cut down by sudden death in 1402. Florentines then took the initiative to conquer Pisa (1405–6), which subsequently involved them in war with Genoa from 1409 to 1411 and against Ladislao di Durazzo in 1413–14. From 1424 to 1433 the city was almost continually at war against Lucca and Filippo Maria Visconti. Alfonso of Aragon conducted two wars against the city from 1447 to 1454, which were fought on both military and economic grounds. Then came the invasion of Charles VIII in 1494, which did not involve the city in outright war but led instead to the rebellion of Pisa, not to be put down until its conquest in 1509. None of these wars, however, were fought close to the walls of the city, subjecting its residents to anything like what they suffered following the expulsion of the Medici in 1527, when the restored republic found itself in a war against the emperor that culminated in the disastrous siege of 1529–30, the demise of the republic, and the restoration of the Medici.

Such disasters, whether natural or political, were disruptive of economic activity in the local marketplace and took their toll, sometimes causing severe distress, which was all the harsher at the lower levels of the economic and social order. But we must be cautious about judging the performance of the economy on the basis of such moments of economic distress, however much people suffered, first, because often the causes of these disasters were extraneous to the functioning of the specific economy of Florence and, second, because these disasters rarely had more than a temporary impact on the economy. In addition, there is the question whether the economy of this city responded better or worse than the economies of other cities faced with disasters of the same magnitude. In the historiography we seldom encounter serious efforts to look to the economic context for some of the troubles Florence faced during the period covered in this book. Probably no disaster in the entire history of the West was so destructive of life as the Black Death, but in Florence it receded after just a few months, about as quickly as it had arrived, leaving those who survived, even ordinary working people, much better off in strictly economic terms: real wages almost doubled, employment opportunities increased, and upward economic and social mobility took off.

Nor was war always as disruptive of normal economic activity as we are often led to believe.[12] At times it took its toll, of course, but usually these were only momentary disruptions, and however difficult, they rarely caused any structural damage to the economy. Bartolomeo di Caroccio degli Alberti & Partners suffered not one loss in its many shipments of Flemish and Brabantine cloth in the 1350s all the way across central France, from Bruges to Avignon, then in the throes of the Hundred Years' War. Closer to home, the War of the Eight Saints, directed against the city by the pope, lasting from 1375 to 1378, hardly led to a shutdown of the wool industry, notwithstanding a papal interdict. We have encountered two dealers in woad, Giovacchino Pinciardi, working out of Borgo Sansepolcro, and Simo d'Ubertino, working out of Arezzo, who made large profits on exports to Florence precisely in these years. And in 1377 the wool guild set up an enterprise for trade in woad, amassing capital of no less than *fl*.25,000 for this purpose, half of it from private investors. Moreover, in the program the Ciompi drew up in the summer of 1378, at the very moment when peace was made with the pope, there is not the slightest reference to a crisis in the industry.[13] Merchants abroad in some places faced expulsion, especially in the papal capital at Avignon, but most governments stopped far short of enforcing the interdict.[14] From the 1390s to the early 1430s the city was frequently at war, and historians have made much of the extraordinary—and for some, oppressive—fiscal burden Florentines had to bear as a result. Yet somehow during these years the city found enormous sums for nonmilitary projects: in 1411 it paid *fl*.60,000 for Cortona, in 1421 it purchased Livorno and Porto Pisano for *fl*.100,000, and the next year it launched its first galleys. And all the while public spaces were being embellished with major sculptural programs at both the cathedral and Orsanmichele, including the expensive casting of larger than life-size statues in bronze, the first since antiquity; and major construction was under way on a substantial addition to the palace of the Parte Guelfa, on the loggia announcing the new Ospedale degli Innocenti, and on

---

[12] The most insistent and recent argument for the negative consequences of war on the European economy at the end of the Middle Ages is John Munro, "The 'New Institutional Economics' and the Changing Fortunes of Fairs in Medieval and Early Modern Europe: The Textile Trades, Warfare, and Transaction Costs," *Vierteljahrschrift für Sozial- und Wirtschaftsgeschichte* 88 (2001): 1–47.

[13] ASF, Conv sopp. (San Bartolomeo), 168 (Pinciardi's ledger), fol. 133; Bruno Dini, *Arezzo intorno al 1400: Produzioni e mercato* (Arezzo, 1984), 33; Franco Franceschi, "Istituzioni e attività economica a Firenze: Considerazioni sul governo del settore industriale (1350–1450)," in *Istituzioni e società in Toscana nell'Età Moderna* (Rome, 1994), 91.

[14] Richard C. Trexler, *The Spiritual Power: Republican Florence under Interdict* (Leiden, 1974), offers the most comprehensive survey of the economic consequences of the interdict.

Brunelleschi's great cupola, the largest groin vault ever built in the West up to that time, thus completing the city's cathedral (dedicated in 1436).

In any event, much of the money the city spent on war during this period, far from being a loss to the economy, ended up being recycled through the economy, since it conducted most of its military operations within the region. During the Visconti wars, Goro Dati observed that some of the gold put out for military operations got spent by soldiers in the region for their livelihood and hence re- turned to the city "as the water that evaporates from the sea into the clouds over the earth returns by way of rain in ditches, streams and rivers to the sea."[15] In a speech in 1426, haranguing the magnates to take a harder line against the minor guilds (as reported by Cavalcanti), Rinaldo degli Albizzi made the point that the lower classes profited from war: it cost them nothing, since they did not bear the tax burden; their shops continued to do business; and besides, when the troops were in the city, they spent the money they were paid, so that "artisans become fat and stuffed with money [*stanno grassi e bene indanaiati*]. . . . War makes them feel grand and brings them wealth. . . . Your ruin [resulting from wartime taxes] is their glory and exaltation."[16] Five years later in the councils of government it was observed how well artisans and shopkeepers had done during wartime.[17] In fact, in the 1420s the index of the purchasing power of workingmen's wages reached its historical high for the entire period covered by this book.

At the end of the century came the period of the Italian wars, when the major crowns of Europe converged on Italy in competition for the spoils. One good index of what this meant to Florentine industry is the production record of the silk weaver Iacopo di Tedesco, whose fully documented career spanned the entire period, from 1490 to 1538. Iacopo worked entirely on commission from setaioli, who ordered only what they planned to sell immediately. Setaioli and export merchants did not stockpile; Iacopo had work only so long as they were sending his silks to markets abroad. Iacopo reduced production in 1494, when Charles VIII passed through Florence on his way to Naples, but the next year his looms were back in operation. For the next thirty years he worked steadily, taking on more workers, adding more looms, and increasing production, despite the agita- tion of the Savonarolans in the streets outside his shop, the rebellion of Pisa, which was not finally squashed until 1509, and even the sack of Prato in 1512 and the restoration of the Medici, not to mention the turbulence in the rest of Italy

---

[15] *Istoria di Firenze di Goro Dati dall'anno MCCCLXXX all'anno MCCCCV con annotazioni* (Flor- ence, 1735), 129.

[16] Giovanni Cavalcanti, *Istorie fiorentine,* ed. Guido di Pino (Milan, 1944), 48 (bk. 3, ch. 1).

[17] Anthony Molho, *Florentine Public Finances in the Early Renaissance, 1400–1433* (Cambridge, MA, 1971), 156.

occasioned, first, by Louis XII's invasion of Lombardy in 1499 and his war against the Spanish king following his move to Rome and Naples and then by Francis I's invasion in 1515 and the consequent Hapsburg-Valois wars. These were the very years when setaioli were opening new markets in southern Germany and lanaioli were busy supplying the market in Constantinople through the booming port of Ancona. Only when war threatened the very walls of the city did Iacopo cease production again. And that came in 1526, with the formation of the League of Cognac pitting emperor against pope and leading to the move of imperial forces to Rome and revolution against the Medici in Florence. Iacopo di Tedesco closed down his shop that year, and he did not reopen it until 1531, after the Medici had successfully reestablished their rule following the tragic siege of the city and the collapse of the last republic. And many setaioli were back in business ready to send commissions to him.[18]

Disasters, whether natural or man-made, are not difficult to find in the diaries, chronicles, and histories that so richly document the history of Florence, more so than any other Italian city, and modern historians who have duly noted them have perhaps been a little too ready to jump to conclusions about their economic consequences. Crises arising from problems within the economy, however, are difficult to identify. We have seen that bankruptcies in the banking sector had hardly any repercussions on the local scene after the crises of the 1340s. There was never a significant cluster of them among local firms at any one time. In any event, deposits in local banks even collectively did not represent a large share of the disposable wealth in the city. And since the great international banks for the most part operated outside the sphere of the local economy, a bankruptcy in that sector affected relatively few creditors back home in Florence. Moreover, the wool industry, thanks to its business structure, was virtually immune to the phenomenon. Unfortunately, we have too little material to measure fluctuations of performance in the textiles industries. Global production statistics—used to construct tables 4.1 and 4.2—are skimpy at best, and no customs records survive to document imports of raw materials or exports of finished products. There must have been momentary problems both in the markets where merchants bought raw wool and silk and in the markets where they sold textiles, and there must have been problems arising from the adjustments in the wool industry as it shifted from one kind of wool to another and also in the silk industry as it shifted to products at the lower end. It is difficult, however, to correlate these external conditions with industrial performance at home. The only long downturn in the

---

[18] Richard A. Goldthwaite, "An Entrepreneurial Silk Weaver in Renaissance Florence," *I Tatti Studies* 10 (2005): 113–15.

wool industry that has been documented (by Franco Franceschi) extended through the last two decades of the fourteenth century and into the fifteenth century, which was also a time when the city was involved in almost continual warfare. Yet the government's vigorous and expensive program to help the industry—the conquest of Pisa, the purchase of ports, the launching of a galley system, the redesigning of its prestigious florin—can be read as an optimistic and creative response to this crisis in the industry. Moreover, the contemporaneous growth of the silk industry, also encouraged by the government through legislation, was a countervailing boon to the economy, although the setaioli could not offer work for most of the workers who might have been left unemployed by a slack in the wool industry.

So how are we to track the ups and downs of the economy? Historians have not hesitated to talk about the latter almost to the exclusion of the former, so that the overall performance gets flattened out at the lowest level. Hence putting together these pieces of scholarship in the jigsaw puzzle of where the Florentine economy was going during the Renaissance results in a view of steady, irreversible decline over two centuries, beginning with the great banking crisis of the 1330s and 1340s. "The Florentine economy," writes Charles de La Roncière, ". . . shows signs of distress from 1339 [and] by 1343–44 was in a state of collapse"; if things thereafter improved somewhat, nevertheless "after 1360 [there was] a general malaise." He concludes that "Florence did not escape the economic slump which hit the West after 1350." And the economy "continued to stagnate" into the beginning of the next century, according to Gene Brucker, who goes on to call the years from 1414 to 1426 a period of "peace without prosperity" for a city with its "middle echelons depleted and impoverished, and its huge concentrations of the poor and the marginally poor." Anthony Molho thinks that this "difficult period" of the economy extended through the entire second quarter of the century and that things got worse, for "it would seem clear that in those decades Florence went through a time of economic crisis." At midcentury the economy was still in "recession," according to Samuel Cohn, who, however, saw some "recovery commencing by the latter part of 1458." Yet this did not last long, if we are to believe Brucker, who argues that "the Laurentian era was a time of deep and pervasive economic crisis"; and the 1470s especially, according to Sergio Tognetti, was a decade of "general stagnation . . . in every sector." John Najemy too insists that in the course of the century the "economy underwent a major shift" toward "the severely unbalanced distribution of wealth" with "stagnating wages" and "endemic poverty within the working class." "The direction of economic change," adds Lauro Martines, sounding another theme in this sorry story of decline, "was thus towards agriculture, and the 'return to the land.'" "By the last decades of the fifteenth century," according to Cohn, "and perhaps as early as mid-century, Florence was no longer prospering. . . . The Florentine economy of the second half of the fifteenth century was hardly dynamic; indeed, it was wedged in old late-medieval guild and household structures," and it "began to decline in the late fifteenth and early sixteenth centuries." Then came the Italian wars. Melissa Bullard concludes that by 1530, on the final return of the Medici, "the cumulative effect of years of heavy taxation and the disruption of business and agriculture brought by the constant wars in Italy [had] forced most Florentines other than the super-rich to their knees. . . . Unfortunately Florence never recovered from the financial consequences of the early sixteenth-century wars." In contrast to all this, Eric Cochrane would "wipe out the nineteenth-century myth [and that of the later twentieth century] about the economic collapse in the sixteenth. Florence was still, in 1551, an industrial and commercial city . . . still the center of many international commercial companies." So Florence somehow shifted gears to arrest its two-century descent downhill to move into the higher clime of an Indian summer precisely at a time when all around it the economies throughout the rest of Italy, according to a venerable historiographical tradition, were in decline.[19]

Clearly, there is a discrepancy between the solution to the puzzle that results from putting together these pieces of scholarship and the one that emerges from putting together the pieces presented in this book. What both lack is the in-depth study of any one of these moments of presumed economic downturn that penetrates into all sectors of the economy to uncover what malaise they suffered in common, expose the underlying causes, and so evaluate each situation, one by one, as they occurred and in comparison with one another. And fundamental to that enterprise will be what is lacking in the above assessments: first, a sense of what an economy is, and second, a clear definition of the criteria by which the ups

---

[19] Charles Marie de La Roncière, "Indirect Taxes or 'Gabelles' at Florence in the Fourteenth Century: The Evolution of Tariffs and Problems of Collection," in *Florentine Studies: Politics and Society in Renaissance Florence,* ed. Nicolai Rubinstein (London, 1968), 171; Gene Brucker, *The Civic World of Early Renaissance Florence* (Princeton, NJ, 1977), 191, 406, and "The Economic Foundations of Laurentian Florence," in *Lorenzo il Magnifico e il suo mondo,* ed. Gian Carlo Garfagnini (Florence, 1994), 5; Anthony Molho, "Fisco ed economia a Firenze alla vigilia del Concilio," *ASI* 148 (1990): 834, 841; Sergio Tognetti, "Attività industriali e commercio di manufatti nelle città toscane del tardo Medioevo (1250 ca.–1530 ca.)," ibid. 159 (2001): 471; Samuel K. Cohn Jr., "The Character of Protest in Mid-Quattrocento," in *Il tumulto dei Ciompi: Un momento di storia fiorentina ed europea* (Florence, 1981), 204, and "The Political Economy of Urban Decline in the Renaissance," in *Towns in Decline AD 100–1600,* ed. T. R. Slater (Aldershot, 2000), 298; John M. Najemy, *A History of Florence, 1200–1575* (Oxford, 2006), 309–10; Lauro Martines, *The Social World of the Florentine Humanists, 1390–1460* (Princeton, NJ, 1963), 291; Melissa Bullard, *Filippo Strozzi and the Medici: Favor and Finance in Sixteenth-Century Florence and Rome* (Cambridge, 1980), 18–19; Eric Cochrane, *Florence in the Forgotten Centuries, 1527–1800: A History of Florence and the Florentines in the Age of the Grand Dukes* (Chicago, 1973), 56.

and downs of this economy, both in depth and in duration, are to be measured. In short, much work remains to be done.

A Final Judgment

In the first chapter of this book a four-part periodization was proposed for the history of the Florentine commercial and banking network abroad: (1) through the commercial revolution to the point where a solid documentary record emerges; (2) to the mid-fourteenth century; (3) from the second half of the fourteenth century to the early sixteenth century; and (4) the later sixteenth century. Given the importance of this sector, it is hardly surprising that the same scheme works for organizing the history of the economy as a whole. The passage from the second period to the third is as clearly demarcated as any such periodization permits. Where the third ends and the fourth begins, however, is hardly perceptible, but that something fundamentally changed somewhere along the line is apparent when we get to 1600 and look back over the preceding two and a half centuries.

The second period in the growth and development of the economy ends dramatically in the bankruptcies of the 1340s and the Black Death. Given the limited documentation, it is impossible to detect fluctuations within this period, and it is easy to see it as one of vigorous expansion at home and abroad, manifest in the extraordinary demographic growth of the city. The two dramatic events in the 1340s, however, mark a certain closure. The bankruptcies reduced, at least momentarily, major ventures abroad by merchant-bankers into government finance on a large scale, and the population loss in 1348 cut deeply into their traffic in the grain trade. Nevertheless, painful as these events were for the people who lived through them, the "crisis" of the 1340s is more useful as a dramatic end to a story than symptomatic of structural problems in the economy. At home, one can talk about a notable change in the industrial sector that reached a point of closure at about the same time: the withdrawal of the Calimala merchants from finishing operations in the wool industry, which was complete not long after the mid-fourteenth century. This decline was gradual, however, not tied to either of the dramatic events of midcentury. Moreover, it did not mark a major shift within the wool industry, inasmuch as the full-scale production of quality cloth was already well under way by this time. The vitality of the wool industry, in fact, was not to be suppressed by either the bankruptcies or the Black Death. Production declined only because the working population declined, but demand for its products was, if anything, relatively higher after the recession of the plague, to judge from the behavior of wages. The industry had its own upward trajectory through most of the fourteenth century, and its continuing strong performance, especially in the third quarter of the century, is an argument against the thesis that the dramatic midcentury crises marked a sharp break, let alone a structural one, between two distinct periods in the economic history of the city.

The third period, from the crises of the 1340s to the early sixteenth century, is the most studied in particular aspects but the least coherent as a period in the historiography. The economic historians who have studied these two centuries have seldom moved from detailed description to broad interpretive overviews, while other historians, often conditioned by the older historiographical tradition of the general economic decline of Europe at the end of the Middle Ages, tend to apply notions of decline or prosperity to economic performance according to whether these notions fit into their own, noneconomic scheme of things. Out of the description of the economy presented in the previous chapters, however, emerges the theme of substantial and sustained growth resulting from a series of new initiatives. These were, in rough chronological order, the intensification and expansion of trade throughout the western Mediterranean; the move into papal finance, especially after the popes returned to Rome; the growth of the silk industry; the organization of the international exchange market around the fairs, first at Geneva and then at Lyons; and the opening of major markets for Florentine textiles, both wool and silk, in the growing capital cities of Rome, Naples, and Constantinople, as well as, first for silk and then also for wool, in northern Europe. Business in each one of these activities must have had its ups and downs over the years, but except for the recession in the wool industry at the end of the fourteenth century, these fluctuations have not been clearly identified, let alone seen in any configuration revealing overlaps among them and indicating overall trends.

In the course of the sixteenth century other signs of considerable vitality manifested themselves: the flexibility of the cloth industry in adapting its products to changing market conditions; the initiative to push silks in the markets of southern Germany and eastern Europe; the organization of the Gran Parti; the development of the free port of Livorno; the appearance of a new breed of economic entrepreneurs in the guise of inventors anxious to take advantage of economic opportunities; the opening of the ducal artisan workshops. By 1600, however, the economy had undergone significant changes that mark, in retrospect, a fourth stage in its historical evolution. Abroad the international commercial and banking network was much less geographically extensive than it had been in 1500, being largely confined to Italy itself and to southern Germany, with some hangers-on still at Lyons but insignificant representation in Antwerp and Amsterdam. In the realm of government finance abroad, Florentine bankers were to be found in force only in Rome, where they had to share the spoils with the Genoese, and those spoils must have been less lucrative, since the papacy was losing so much of its revenues from northern Europe. Furthermore, in foreign markets Florentines were now up against stiff competition—from northern Europeans in the market for wool cloth and, within Italy itself, from the Genoese in international banking and exchange, from the Venetians in the market for wool cloth, and from these and yet other cities in the market for silks. Finally, the government under the dukes assumed a much stronger role in the economy than its communal and republican predecessors, including the vigorous extension of its economic interests and fiscal authority throughout the territorial state, which had been considerably enlarged by the acquisition of Siena. Not to be underestimated—although this was exogenous to the economy—is the general peace that settled over Italy in the second half of the sixteenth century, which meant that for the first time in its history the economy was not burdened with heavy military expenditures. By 1600, in short, the economy looked somewhat different from what it had been a century earlier.

Yet in 1600 much wealth was still coming into the city in the form of profits from the textile industries, and despite the shrinking of the network abroad, large profits were still being made in international commerce and exchange banking. The rich were still investing in the forward sectors of the economy, and however much that investment may have begun to fall off—a phenomenon yet to be documented—they certainly were not held back by social and cultural norms of the kind that asserted themselves in so many other places at the time. The much greater disposable wealth in the local market manifested itself conspicuously in consumption and in the vitality of the artisans who satisfied this demand. It also manifested itself in the growth and development of the banking sector: the institutional structure was more refined as a consequence of the greater demand both for credit and for outlets for disposable wealth. Exchange banking was organized more efficiently around the Besançon fairs and refinements in the bill of exchange, and increasingly it was oriented to the local credit market. There were now both a public deposit-and-loan bank and something like central clearance banks. Even people of modest economic means had profitable outlets for savings in the Monte di Pietà, the several state Monti, and private exchange banks. And they had easy access to affordable credit from these same institutions, not to mention all the traditional ways used in the private sector to borrow and lend money. They also had an investment outlet through the limited-liability accomandita contract. Indices of market activity are the higher scale of local operations of private banks and the more active current accounts businesses had in banks. At the most basic level of market activity, finally, monetary exchange was better served by a more refined calibration in the denomination of coins.

The distribution of this greater wealth was probably as inequitable as that in any other European city at the time. On the whole, the rich may have been much richer than the rich in most other cities because some of them were still making large profits in businesses oriented to international markets. There was also a sizable population at what in this book has been defined as a middling level of wealth. These were the people whose success in satisfying demand in the growing consumer market precluded the recourse to imports for most quality products, thereby generating the internal circulation of profits coming in from abroad that might otherwise have been reexported. These were also the people whom the banking institutions had come into existence to serve. One corollary to the growth in their ranks was the increased number of female and immigrant weavers—skilled workers—in the textile industries.

Finally, there were the poor. They were numerous, and the situation of working people at the bottom of the wage scale worsened in the sixteenth century, to judge from the declining index of the real wages of day laborers in the construction industry. Historians of Florence have been only too ready to make this point about the city in the fifteenth century, often to the exclusion of any other criteria in judging the performance of the economy. All the indicators we have, however, point to a situation that obtained everywhere throughout Europe, and on the basis of the current bibliography, there is no reason to think that things were worse in Florence than elsewhere. In how many other places in Europe, for instance, did the real wages of workingmen in the construction industry—the only comparative wage data we have—jump so quickly and so high as in Florence in the months immediately after the Black Death, to remain at a very high level for the next three-quarters of a century? And if those wages fell in the later fifteenth and sixteenth centuries, they did so elsewhere as well. In Bruges the worth of bricklayers' wages expressed in the amount of wheat they could buy fell by one-half from the later fifteenth to the mid-sixteenth century, and everywhere in Europe wages of construction workers fell through the first three-quarters of the sixteenth century. Even in Antwerp, then a booming city, and in England and Holland, then beginning their extraordinary economic growth, real wages fell by about one-third, to a level much below where they had been a century earlier. The "Golden Age" of Antwerp has also been called its "Iron Age" for many of the city's inhabitants, and English historians do not fail to observe the extreme social polarization that accompanied the great economic expansion at the end of the sixteenth century. Only in Holland, and only beginning in the last quarter of the sixteenth century, did the real wages of the unskilled laborer begin to rise. Certainly, poverty is an essential criterion for judging the performance of an economy, but the historian of a preindustrial city should also be sensitive to the context of Europe generally at the time rather than limiting him- or herself to an absolute standard in isolation. Poverty as something that could be, and should be, eliminated and not just tended to as a natural and unavoidable state was, after all, an idea arising from the sensibilities of a later time. The situation during the period covered in this book was structural, in both an economic and a cultural sense, at a European level, not particular to any one place. The problem remaining for Florentine historians is to find out whether the local economy—so much better documented for this city than for most others, especially for the sixteenth century—performed better or worse with respect to the workingman.[20]

One can hardly draw up a balance sheet for the state of the economy in 1600 without an eye to the difficult times that lay just around the corner. The export branch of the wool industry began its rapid decline in the second decade of the seventeenth century; the outbreak of the Thirty Years' War in 1618 led eventually to the abandonment of Germany by silk merchants; in 1630 the city was struck by a devastating plague; and in 1638 the city's bankers ended their short-lived secession from the Genoese fairs, thereby finally relinquishing any claim to be the leading international exchange bankers even in Italy. No one has yet studied how these events collectively impacted on the economy. When that is done, we shall have a new perspective on this fourth phase—the sixteenth century—in the economic history of the city. The view from that perspective, moreover, will need to be expanded to take in the larger context of the Italian economy in general in the early modern period, another subject long neglected by scholarship.[21]

In the meantime, developments during that century in the European economy as a whole exposed a fatal weakness in the very structure of this local economy: isolation, as ironic as that may seem for a city whose merchants had created the largest international commercial and banking network in Europe. Not being a major emporium, not even much of one within its own region, Florence remained isolated on the fringes of its own network. Its merchants lacked, first, the underpinnings of a shipping service and, second, a central emporium out of which to

[20] Wim Blockmans, "*Fondans en melencolie de povreté:* Living and Working in Bruges, 1482–1584," in *Bruges and the Renaissance: Memling to Pourbus,* ed. M. P. S. Martens (Bruges, 1998), 26–32; Hugo Soly, "Social Relations in Antwerp in the Sixteenth and Seventeenth Centuries," in *Antwerp, Story of a Metropolis, 16th–17th Century,* ed. Jan Van der Stock (Ghent, 1993), 37–47; Jan de Vries and Ad van der Woude, *The First Modern Economy: Success, Failure, and Perseverance of the Dutch Economy, 1500–1815* (Cambridge, 1997), 630–32; Wrightson, *Earthly Necessities,* 200.

[21] The *Revue d'histoire moderne et contemporaine* 45 (1998), no. 1, dedicated to the historiography of Italy from the sixteenth century on, has no contribution on economic history. Paolo Malanima, in his recent survey, *La fine del primato: Crisi e riconversione nell'Italia del Seicento* (Milan, 1998), has a positive view of the performance of the economy at the end of the sixteenth century, when the per capita GNP was still one of the highest in Europe, the balance of trade was favorable, and entrepreneurial profits were high, but he accepts the traditional notion of a crisis in the seventeenth century.

operate. They could plug into trade and international exchange at Venice, Barcelona, Bruges, Lyons, Antwerp, and any number of other emporia, but they could by no means propel their city—or Pisa, for that matter—into the ranks of such places. Florence became even more isolated as the network contracted and the economy of northwestern Europe took off on its transatlantic adventures, leaving the Mediterranean area behind as a secondary region. In its own region too the urban economy was relatively isolated, there being little integration between it and the rural and regional economies except for the basic needs that any city takes from its countryside. On the one hand, the textile industries, except for the limited growth of sericulture, had long outgrown their original foundation in the regional economy, having become completely dependent on an international commercial network, with few factor inputs from outside the city except immigrant labor. On the other hand, in the countryside the agricultural sector had evolved into a system that precluded self-generated change from within and resisted change from without, thus minimizing any creative interaction with the economy of the capital city. The natural resources of the region had been a solid foundation from which Florence—and the other Tuscan towns—took off during the commercial revolution, but those resources counted for less and less as the European economy grew. The traditional leading sectors of the Florentine economy gained little from the city's eventual absorption of the region, no longer the most urbanized in Europe, into its own territorial state. Finally, the economy's isolation was buttressed from within by the internal productive forces that succeeded in meeting almost all the consumer demand arising from the wealth flowing into the city, without, however, extending production to supply consumer markets abroad. In other words, the sector successfully reduced imports but contributed little to exports, leaving the city self-sufficient but isolated and with little potential for growth within this sector. From this perspective it is hard for us to see where the economy in 1600 could have gone, and we are not yet informed about any notions Florentines themselves had at the time about where they thought it might go.

Yet in its isolation this economy performed quite well, perhaps as well as any urban economy in Europe. The commercial, banking, and industrial sectors generated considerable wealth, and if the former two sectors fell off somewhat in the course of the sixteenth century, the textile industries remained strong. As Giuliano Pinto has observed, through this entire period the economy did not meet with any "harsh traumas or sudden standstills."[22] For four centuries, from the thirteenth through the sixteenth, it showed considerable vitality in responding to the changing markets abroad on which its home industry depended for

[22] Giuliano Pinto, *Toscana medievale: Paesaggi e realtà sociali* (Florence, 1993), 18.

both raw materials and outlets for finished products. The network, besides its essential function of supporting the home industry, served other commercial, financial, and governmental functions abroad that brought home huge profits. The economy was remarkably resilient in reacting to all the external shocks that arose from natural disasters, such as plague and climatic calamities, including the so-called Malthusian trap, as well as to the impact of other exogenous forces, such as war and international bullion flows, that figure so prominently in the historiography of the late medieval economy of Europe. It was just as resilient against the occasional threats to the internal stability of urban life, ranging from the violence of factional politics to the revolt of the Ciompi and the Savonarolan episode, and it continued to function smoothly after the transformation of the government from a guild republic to a princely despotism.

It cannot be claimed that this was a modernizing economy, for it did not generate a sustained growth riding on constant technological progress, let along break through the technological barrier that opened the way to an industrial revolution. Through the fifteenth and sixteenth centuries production for the internal market rose to the point of generating some new consumption, but without setting off an upward spiral leading to anything like the "consumer revolution" of the eighteenth century. Nevertheless, the economy enjoyed, if not sustained growth, at least a long-term stability in the statistical sense of the per capita wealth it generated. There was also a degree of economic development, ranging from the improvement of business techniques and the wide diffusion of efficient credit instruments to the proliferation of crafts and the refinement of skills. The commercial, banking, and industrial sectors performed extraordinarily well in bringing the city out of its isolation. If their eventual failure did not see the return of the city to isolation, it was thanks to the artisan sector, which in the meantime, fed by the wealth these other activities brought into the city, grew and prospered. For in the long run the greatest success of the Florentine economy was the development of this sector through which the wealth generated by its forward sectors was recycled and thereby invested in human capital and transformed into the patrimony of urban architecture, artwork, and a tradition of craftsmanship unequaled in any other city. Whereas the other sectors gained a certain momentary fame for the city in the economic historiography of the West, the splendor achieved by the city's artisans radiates well beyond the scholarly confines of that historiography to assure, once and for all, that Florence would never fall into isolation.

Changing Values of the Florin

This appendix is designed to help the reader understand certain problems about the Florentine monetary system that emerge in the course of the economic history of the city as presented in the text of this book, namely, what is meant by the "price" of the florin, how to compare values in florins across time, how the monetary system helped shape the economic culture of Florentines, and the importance of the monetary system as an indicator of the government's economic policy.

The Price of the Florin

Florence had a bimetallic monetary system, with various silver-based and billon coins, on the one hand, and a single gold coin, the florin, on the other. The silver coins derived from the silver *denarius,* or denaro, created by the Carolingian reforms, which became the principal coin in early medieval Europe. Since 240 denari were coined from one pound (*libbra,* or lira) of silver, the term *lira* came to be used as a money of account to express that multiple of denari, and a submultiple, the soldo, was used to express 12 denari, or one-twentieth of the lira; the soldo and the lira did not exist as coins. Thus emerged what is called the £/*s*/*d* system, with 12 denari equal to 1 soldo and 20 soldi, or 240 denari, equal to a lira. The lira with its subdivision into soldi and these into denari was a money of account that remained the basis of the monetary system for most of Europe, including Florence, throughout the entire period covered in this volume and on into the eighteenth century. This practice of dividing units into twentieths and then dividing those into twelfths, along with the use of the terms *soldo* and *denaro* for these fractions, became the basis for the mensural system used by Florentines for other things besides moneys (see chapter 7).

After the demise of the Carolingian empire, governments minted their own denaro according to different standards of purity, and over the following centuries a slow and steady debasement varying from place to place meant that 240 denari no longer equaled a pound of silver, thus uprooting the lira from any fixed value in silver. In the twelfth century the denaro minted by the two cities in Tuscany in the forefront of the economic expansion of Italy—Lucca and Pisa—had a silver content of about 0.7 grams, down from the 1.7 grams of the original Carolingian *denarius.* Accompanying this debasement was a

---

For a more thorough description of all aspects of the Florentine monetary system, see Richard A. Goldthwaite and Giulio Mandich, *Studi sulla moneta fiorentina (secoli XIII–XVI)* (Florence, 1994).

need for coins of higher value to meet the exigencies of a rapidly growing international commercial economy. In the early thirteenth century both Lucca and Pisa, following the example of Venice and Genoa, coined a silver grosso worth 12 denari, or a soldo; and the Lucchese and Pisan denaro and grosso were the principal coins in circulation in Florence well into the thirteenth century. It was not until the middle years of that century that Florence began minting its own coins: a silver grosso in 1237, the gold florin in 1252, and a silver denaro a few years later, before 1260. Following the logic of the mensural system, the grosso contained 12 times the amount of silver in a denaro, and the florin contained the quantity of gold worth an amount in silver that was twenty times the amount of silver in a grosso, or 240 times the amount of silver in a denaro. Hence for a brief moment in the 1250s Florentine coins had a direct correspondence to the denominations of the £/s/d system: the florin was worth one lira and the grosso one soldo, and the denaro was the base coin. We call these values expressed in lire the coin's *price,* as distinct from both its *commodity value,* or the quantity of gold or silver it contained, and its *real value,* or its purchasing power in the local market. The price in lire served as a single standard of measurement for bringing coins of different commodity content—in this instance gold and silver—into line with one another. The price of a coin is a way of relating its value to all other coins in the system; it in itself tells us nothing about either the coin's commodity value or real value. (To distinguish between the soldo as one-twentieth of the florin and the soldo as one-twentieth of the lira, the price of the florin was stated as so many soldi *di piccioli,* piccioli being the generic name for silver-based coins that were the basis of the £/s/d system.)

The correspondence of the lira, the soldo, and the denaro to, respectively, the gold florin, the silver grosso, and the silver denaro did not last for long, however. Two dynamics worked against the maintenance of the same ratio between the commodity value and the price of these coins: debasement and the need to price coins to maintain the fluctuating gold-silver ratio (over which the government had no control, since this was determined in international bullion markets). The silver-based currency was subject to defensive debasement (see chapter 7). And as it was debased, the price of the florin, which was never debased, rose to more than 240 denari di piccioli, or one lira; that is, the more the denaro was debased, the more denari it took to equal a gold florin. The debasement of the denaro continued to the point where it lost all of its silver content and became a billon coin. The process of change in the denaro subjected the grosso to two pressures. On the one hand, it too was subject to debasement to maintain its 12:1 ratio to the denaro, that is, its price of 1 soldo. And after the denaro's reduction to a billon coin, when the grosso replaced the denaro as the base silver coin, it continued to be subject to defensive debasement. This dynamic, if operating alone, would have meant that the grosso ceased to be equal to one-twentieth of a florin. On the other hand, instead of debasement, its price could be increased to maintain that 1:20 ratio to the florin, or its silver content could be augmented to counter earlier debasements. Both these dynamics—change in its silver content and change in its price—entered into the history of the grosso, which in its successive reissues over time underwent changes in both price and commodity value. From the mid-thirteenth to the mid-fifteenth century the price of the grosso went from 1 soldo to 5½ soldi, but its ratio to the gold florin remained more or less 1:20 (the price of the florin during the same period going from 20 soldi to 110 soldi di piccioli), a ratio that reflected the ratio of the commodity values of the two coins, that is, the ratio of the silver content of the grosso to the gold content of the gold florin (which depended on the current gold-silver ratio). One consequence of these changes was that the basic denominations of the £/s/d system were no longer manifest in silver coins: the denaro eventually had no silver content, and the grosso came to have a price higher than 1 soldo. Another consequence was that over the course of the fourteenth and fifteenth centuries the value of the lira in silver—the commodity value of the silver-based coins, whose total price was equal to 20 soldi di piccioli—declined from 17–18 grams to about 5 grams, or by more than 70 percent.

Given the debasement of the silver coinage and hence the lowering of the lira's value in silver, the price of the florin was bound to rise. That price reached £2 (or 40 soldi di piccioli) by the end of the thirteenth century, £4 (80 soldi di piccioli) by the early fifteenth century, and £7 (140 soldi di piccioli) by the early sixteenth century–a 700 percent increase. (The price of the florin was usually expressed in soldi di piccioli, not lire; since the price at any one moment was rarely equivalent to an exact number of lire, fractions thereof, that is the soldo and denaro, had to be used.)

The reader probably feels lost in this complex history of debasement and price fluctuation of coins (and two other dynamics further complicate the situation as presented here: the ever-fluctuating gold-silver ratio, which was beyond the control of any local government, and the slow proliferation of silver coins with different commodity values and different prices), but this history helps explain the function of money in the lives of Florentines. They thought about the value of coins, despite debasement, as their price in so many denari and soldi even though these values had no equivalent in specific coins (and no coin ever had the name *lira* or *soldo*). In fact documents, even accounts, very rarely mention actual coins; for this reason most Florentine historians are not even aware of the coins in circulation (nor, for the most part, do they need to be). Some of the implications of this mentality of Florentines are remarked in chapter 6.

Florins of Account

The florin generated several moneys of account that came into existence successively, one replacing the other, each with its subdivisions of soldi and denari. These florins of account lost their equivalence to the gold coin; they were tied into the monetary system by being given, not an equivalent value in gold florins, but a price in lire, or rather in soldi di piccioli. Down to the end of the fourteenth century these florins of account were primarily two—the *fiorino a fiorini*, or *affiorini* (and its derivative, the *lira a fiorini*), and the *fiorino di suggello*. In the fifteenth century the fiorino a fiorini was replaced by the *fiorino largo d'oro*, which, in turn, was replaced by the *fiorino largo d'oro in oro*. In the sixteenth century accounts were kept in the ducat, the scudo, and the florin. Each of these florins of account also had three values: its price, its real value, and (rather than a commodity value, since it was not a commodity) its value in relation to the gold coin (i.e., its value in gold). This latter value is usually expressed as the percentage premium, or *aggio*, of the gold coin over the florin of account. For instance, the fiorino di suggello, as explained in the text, was defined by the aggio of the gold florin over it, which had reached 42 percent by the beginning of the sixteenth century.

Readers of this book have no need for a technical explanation of these various florins of account, which came and went over the years. In the context of the general economic history of Florence, however, the subject is important for two reasons. First, these ghost moneys, as Carlo Cipolla called them, were created by the government and therefore were an aspect of economic policy. That policy with respect to the fiorino di suggello has been adumbrated in the text (see chapter 6). The policy behind the creation of the other florins of account, however, is not so clear. Historians studying the government and politics of fifteenth-century Florence have completely overlooked this phenomenon, notwithstanding its obvious importance for the issues of taxation and the public debt so fundamental to the political life of the city, just as economic historians have not wondered how monetary policy impinged on the activities of capitalist entrepreneurs, who, after all, constituted a major group within the political elite that made monetary policy. For the moment there is no recognition of the problem, let alone a study of the history of monetary policy. The underlying assumption of such a history has to be a general definition of money that goes beyond the three functions traditionally attributed to money—a medium of exchange, a unit of measure, and a store of value. Money also served as a state mechanism for payment, a function that rarely enters into the monetary histories of the period. If the reader remains confused by this complex replication of moneys of account, it is because we do not yet understand the logic behind state monetary policy; and perhaps confusion will alert him or her to how little we know about a fundamental aspect of the Florentine economy.

The second, more pressing reason the reader of this book should be at least aware of the problem, if not the details, of florins of account is the need to make comparisons across time–of investments, capital, profits, and so on. What is fundamental to such a comparison is the *real* value of the florins being compared, that is, their purchasing power in the marketplace. Such comparisons require knowing (1) which florin of account is used in the documents being cited, (2) its price at the time in lire or soldi di piccioli, and (3) a series of commodity prices to show the changing purchasing power of the lira, for the price of most goods and labor in the local market was quoted in piccioli. These prices also changed over time. In 1400 and again in 1500 it cost 10 soldi di piccioli to pay an unskilled construction worker for a day's work, but in 1600 it cost 1 lira, or 20 soldi—a 100 percent increase in its nominal value. Yet the price of the current florin of account went from about 75 soldi in 1400 to 140 soldi in 1500 and remained at that level for the next century. In other words, a florin bought 7½ days of work in 1400, 14 days of work in 1500, and 7 days of work in 1600. Obviously, this change has to be considered in comparing values quoted in florins across time.

Table A.1 is a general guide to help the reader in making such comparisons. It indicates the changing real value of the current florin of account, that is, the florin of account that was being used at the time for keeping most business accounts, over the period from 1300 to 1600. The criterion for real value is the power of the florin to purchase unskilled labor, which, as a factor of production, is a better economic indicator than a cost-of-living index. Calculations are based on (1) the price of the florin in soldi di piccioli and (2) the nominal daily wage of a laborer in soldi di piccioli. The reader should be alerted to some slippage in these data. The data base for the daily wage during the early fourteenth century is very weak. It is solid for the long period of stability from 1348 down to the early sixteenth century, and although thereafter it is weak for specific years, the trend across the century is clear. The florin of account was also subject to variations

TABLE A.1
Index of the Real Value of the Current Florin of Account, 1300–1600
(for Shifting Base Years)

Number of florins needed to purchase given amount of labor: *read down*

	Real value of one florin in the labor market: *read across*												
	1300	1325	1350	1375	1400	1425	1450	1475	1500	1525	1550	1575	1600
1300	**1.00**	0.98	0.39	0.42	0.45	0.48	0.51	0.66	0.84	0.84	0.70	0.47	0.42
1325	1.03	**1.00**	0.40	0.43	0.46	0.49	0.52	0.68	0.86	0.86	0.72	0.48	0.43
1350	2.56	2.50	**1.00**	1.08	1.15	1.23	1.31	1.69	2.15	2.15	1.79	1.20	1.08
1375	2.38	2.32	0.93	**1.00**	1.07	1.14	1.21	1.57	2.00	2.00	1.67	1.11	1.00
1400	2.22	2.17	0.87	0.93	**1.00**	1.07	1.13	1.47	1.87	1.87	1.56	1.04	0.93
1425	2.08	2.03	0.81	0.88	0.94	**1.00**	1.06	1.38	1.75	1.75	1.46	0.97	0.88
1450	1.96	1.91	0.76	0.82	0.88	0.94	**1.00**	1.29	1.65	1.65	1.37	0.92	0.82
1475	1.52	1.48	0.59	0.64	0.68	0.73	0.77	**1.00**	1.27	1.27	1.06	0.71	0.64
1500	1.19	1.16	0.46	0.50	0.54	0.57	0.61	0.79	**1.00**	1.00	0.83	0.56	0.50
1525	1.19	1.16	0.46	0.50	0.54	0.57	0.61	0.79	1.00	**1.00**	0.83	0.56	0.50
1550	1.43	1.39	0.56	0.60	0.64	0.69	0.73	0.94	1.20	1.20	**1.00**	0.67	0.60
1575	2.14	2.09	0.84	0.90	0.96	1.03	1.09	1.41	1.80	1.80	1.50	**1.00**	0.90
1600	2.38	2.32	0.93	1.00	1.07	1.14	1.21	1.57	2.00	2.00	1.67	1.11	**1.00**
Price of the florin in soldi	50	65	65	70	75	80	85	110	140	140	140	140	140
Daily wage (soldi)	3	4	10	10	10	10	10	10	10	10	12	18	20

SOURCE: Wage data are from Richard A. Goldthwaite, *The Building of Renaissance Florence: An Economic and Social History* (Baltimore, 1980), 436–37.

NOTE: Selecting 1325 as the base year, for example, and reading across, $fl.1$ in 1600 could buy 43 percent of what $fl.1$ could buy in 1325; reading down, what cost $fl.1$ in 1325 cost $fl.2.32$ in 1600. Calculations of the real value of the florin are based on the price of the florin and an unskilled construction worker's daily wage, both in soldi di piccioli, for the respective years.

in value, especially from 1425 to 1500, depending on the florin used in specific documents (and at some moments more than one florin of account might be in use). In 1600 the scudo was worth 150 soldi di piccioli, or approximately 7 percent more than the florin (and the ducat).

Unless otherwise indicated, most entries refer to Florence or Florentine economic interests. Entries for Florentines refer to firms that carry their names or to their economic activities; firms are not entered as such. For the most part, only places, products, and natural resources related to Florentine interests are included. Entries for European states, regions, and towns (for example, Low Countries, Flanders, Bruges) are mutually exclusive and not cross-referenced.